Advanced Praise for *Circuits, Packets, and Protocols*

"The key technologies that brought us our modern networked society—routers, packet switching, multiplexers, Internet protocols—were all invented by people in the short period between 1968 and 1988. James L. Pelkey interviewed these people at that time and recorded their stories. This book is the result: a detailed and up-close personal history of a world being born. Fascinating."

- W. Brian Arthur, Author of *The Nature of Technology: What It Is and How It Evolves*

"Data communications is a complex ecosystem with a host of interrelated components: technology, markets, government and commercial entities, individual contributors, etc. Add the external influence of semi-conductors, personal computers, and venture capital starting in the late 60s, and its intricacy discourages comprehensive commentary. *Circuits, Packets, and Protocols* delves into this milieu and creates a coherent narrative which brings order and reasoning to its complexity. As personal, institutional, and technical relationships are put in context, a revolutionary period of advancement resulting in pervasive influence of 21st Century society can be appreciated and understood from a logical, evolutionary perspective."

- Charles Bass, Co-founder, Ungermann-Bass

"A carefully researched work that significantly benefits from the many interviews that enlighten the complexity of the crosscurrents and decisions made by entrepreneurs, technologists, and regulatory, legal, and legislative participants at the time. A window on what was the beginning of the foundation for all of the myriad apps and resources made available by todays networks."

- Art Carr, Retired CEO, Codex Corporation

"A marvelous and personal exploration of a poorly documented period in the history of data communication! I lived through it and re-lived it in these interviews and narrative."

- Vint Cerf, Internet Pioneer

"Our ability to communicate with a computer, later the existence of the Internet, was not inevitable. This book provides the best and most detailed history of how computers were given the ability to talk to each other, about how we—billions of us—were given the possibility of doing the same. These authors have written one of the most important histories of information technology that will remain an essential source for decades."

- James Cortada, Senior Research Fellow, Charles Babbage Institute

"As the three bricklayers working side by side varyingly reported 'I am laying bricks,' 'I am building a wall,' and 'I am helping to build the world's greatest cathedral,' so might the tech laborers revealed in the successive pages of this book have progressively answered 'We are making these two computers talk to one another,' 'We are making a network of computers that can span the world,' and 'We are helping to improve human communications.' This book does a remarkable job of describing our attempts to harness computers for purposes of communication. Thank you for telling our story."

- Dr. John Davidson, Successively an ALOHANET and ARPANET technologist, a LAN and Internet entrepreneur, and now an investor in communication startups

"In 1968, an FCC decision to open telecom networks unleashed technology entrepreneurs and by 1988 the underpinnings were set for digital pervasiveness. Mr. Pelkey chronicles this critical 20-year period and the people, companies, and technologies that formed the foundation for today's information ubiquity."

- Charles DiSanza, retired security analyst and former Institutional Investor magazine "All Star Analyst"

"This book is an impressive *tour de force* on the co-evolutionary stories of the computer and telecommunication industries and their convergence. It is a must-read for all scholars interested in the roots of the contemporary information-based techno-economic system. It is not only a story of industrial evolution but also of its embedding into institutional and policy dynamics. It is written by a practitioner of the industry, but without self-serving aims or mythology about the legend of the 'heroic entrepreneurs' in their garages. Indeed, it is a much more rigorous contribution to industrial history and economic theory than those of most academics."

- Professor Giovanni Dosi, Institute of Economics, Scuola Superiore Sant'Anna, Pisa

"This book reveals both the intricacies of the emerging networking market and the complexities of the brilliant individuals who created it."

- Esther Dyson, Investor

"*Circuits, Packets, and Protocols* is historical, technical, and a good read for anyone wishing to understand how the Silicon Valley/Internet/Information Age came about. Most sources come at this history from one point of view. Here the authors have investigated several phenomena and have looked at how they intersected. Although they have emphasized the infrastructure and entrepreneurship leading to the Digital Age, they have also investigated the impact of such things as government funding, regulations, academic participation, protocol development, venture capitalism, market acceptance, cost reduction, miniaturization, and information digitization. They have then given a comprehensive overview of how all of these worked together to create the information infrastructure we all use today. The book is not all about 'winners' either but includes the story of 'losers' as well, and what can be learned from failures as well as successes. Both the references and many associated oral histories give the book credence and make this a seminal work of history. If you wonder whether there was a one-time confluence of events that brought us to the Digital Age, or a pattern we can learn from and pursue, this book will help you decide."

- Elizabeth (Jake) Feinler, Director of Network Information Systems Center, Stanford Research Institute, 1972–1989

"At the core of a technological revolution is the self-winding process of innovation, in which an answer to a challenge raised by practical need is accepted by virtue of becoming the foundation for new need and associated markets. Yet, what in hindsight appears unstoppable was at the time far from foregone conclusion. Thus, on another, perhaps more fundamental level, the book is a vivid tribute to the enigmatic figure of the entrepreneur, the soul of innovation. Whether in the realm of venture capital, commerce, government, or education, the entrepreneur shows up as the ultimate interdisciplinary pragmatist, the alchemist who marshals human and economic capital bound together by technical vision in pursuit of the ultimate goal: the creation of reality."

- Walter Fontana, Harvard University

“A remarkable history of the first two decades of the data communications industry, based on a unique set of insider interviews.”

- Dave Forney, Modem Pioneer

“The authors take you on an astounding journey into the origins of the Digital Revolution. They help you understand how the entrepreneurs, technicians, bureaucrats, and the military cooperated, competed, and finally succeeded in creating some of the most interesting electronic dimensions of our modern society.”

- Louis Galambos, Research Professor, The Johns Hopkins University

“Pelkey, Russell, and Robbins have produced a monumental treatise on the origins of human and computer communication during the two-decade period from 1968 to 1988. For any professional who wants to understand the computer and human communication world prior to the Internet, this book is required reading.”

- Burton Grad, Software History Center, Computer History Museum

“By the late 1960s computers had improved immensely. However, transmitting data from one digital device to another was very awkward. Communicating between remote locations was even worse. It was not uncommon to send data to a remote location with a courier carrying a box of tape reels on a plane. It was clearly desirable to connect everything to everything, and this was a task of immense complexity. *Circuits, Packets, and Protocols* is a magnificent account of the myriad of independent developments it took to create the digital age. The book is based on interviews with most of the key people who made it happen. I helped fund a number of the computer communications ventures that contributed to the achievement, but until I read this book I appreciated only a small part of this world-changing accomplishment.”

- Stewart Greenfield, Co-founder, Oak Investment Partners

“*Circuits, Packets, and Protocols* is a masterpiece of scholarship—of a rare and beautiful kind. The co-author, James L. Pelkey, was a practiced entrepreneur at a time when his investment needs led to meeting a panoply of inventors and entrepreneurs busily engaged in a game that many sensed, but too few recognized the true outlines. The astonishing and fortuitous fact for us is that Pelkey had the rare instinct to record oral interviews with 88 ‘significant people’ from 31 companies and organizations who were vying to ‘win the game.’ The game turned out to be *networking connectivity*—essentially the communications pivot upon which our entire global society operates today. Economics, politics, health, entertainment, education—all have been transformed by this networking fabric—and the reader will get to see 'behind the curtain' for how difficult this evolution was, how it came about, and who were the kingpin figures in it all.

Historians long eschewed the value of the oral interview of protagonists, noting that the approach all too easily devolves into self-aggrandizement and braggadocio, or worse, into self-denigration by key principals. But Pelkey's immersive effort allows contrast and comparison, and importantly, gives glimpses of the doubts and frustrations of the protagonists during a tumultuous and conflicted evolution for which they themselves had yet to know the answers. The consequence is of especial historical note—this is not a work of hagiography, no pure view of the omniscient bold leader who 'saw all,' no after-the-fact glossing of failure and celebration of success. No Edison, Watson, Jobs, or Gates emerges here, thankfully.

Pelkey, Robbins, and Russell have given the historical world a treasure, one that is unexpected and vital for a fundamental pivot-point in technology and its impact on world history."

- Chuck House, Founder and CEO, InnovaScapes Institute

"Grounded by extensive primary research, *Circuits, Packets, and Protocols* documents the origin of an information revolution that began with the confluence of computers and communications in the late 1960s. This book details the struggle between entrepreneurial creativity and institutional resistance, a conflict that continues to this day. The authors have given us a noteworthy, timeless, classic comparable to *The Federalist Papers* of James Madison."

- Manley R. Irwin, Former FCC Staff Economist, and Professor Emeritus of Economics at the University of New Hampshire Whittemore School of Business and Economics

"*Circuits, Packets, and Protocols* was a great read on both a personal and professional level. From a personal standpoint it was fun to reacquaint myself with the industry legends and companies that I knew well back then. On a professional level, this is the definitive book covering a transformational 20-year period in the communications industry revolution."

- Rick Kimball, Founding General Partner, TCV

"This book tracks all the players in the data revolution that has swept our world by now. Not many survived. Find out who and why."

- Dan Lynch, Founder, Interop

"*Circuits, Packets, and Protocols* is one of the most detailed accounts of the 1980s that I have seen. The authors have managed to document the technical history accurately while capturing the entrepreneurial color of one of the most interesting and prolific eras in Silicon Valley history."

- Audrey MacLean, Co-founder, Network Equipment Technologies.

"This is an important historical document, an interesting and compelling story of the first two decades of computer communications, accurately reviewing executives, companies, entrepreneurs, products, markets, venture capitalists, and governments which changed the world, but may be forgotten because few of the firms survived without consolidation, merger, or failure."

- James I. Magid, Co-founder, Capital Counsel LLC

"The history of data communications has been the least-told story of the electronics revolution—and yet, it is one of the most important. Finally, that tale has been told by Pelkey, Russell, and Robbins. In the process, they have performed an enormous service to technology history. Their book is insightful, detailed, and definitive. *Circuits, Packets, and Protocols* is destined to become the ultimate reference volume for students and historians for generations to come."

- Michael S. Malone, Author *Bill & Dave* and *The Intel Trinity*

"The Internet didn't happen overnight. It was the product of a set of quiet and diverse engineering efforts that took place over two decades long before the Internet became America's digital Main St. *Circuits, Packets, and Protocols* tells that story."

- John Markoff, Stanford Institute for Human-Centered Artificial Intelligence

"This book uniquely includes the perspectives of the entrepreneurs, using dozens of interviews made in the midst of the rapid market changes. It will be an important resource for historians, economists, and entrepreneurs who want to acquire a deep understanding of the complex processes that drive massive innovation in the information industry."

- Bob Maxfield, Co-founder, ROLM Corp.

"This eminently lucid history of telecommunications from the late 1960s to the late 1980s is a lesson about the intertwining forces of technology, vision, entrepreneurship, and luck. All of us have been enriched by the breakthroughs of this period, and this lively book maps the adventure beautifully."

- Pamela McCorduck, Author of *Machines Who Think*, *The Fifth Generation*, and *This Could be Important: My Life and Times with the Artificial Intelligentsia*

"The technology platform underlying today's Internet was developed over a 20-year period from 1968 to 1988. Jim Pelkey and his co-authors comprehensively recount this historic period of industry, government, and university activity in a compelling narrative style that becomes an extended business case. This is a deep dive, not a superficial treatment. The narrative provides a compelling and educational read for technologists, investors, entrepreneurs, and other business operators."

- James McGill, Morgan Stanley Asia Chief Information Officer and Managing Director, 1996–2016

"Pelkey's Internet histories are full of revelations for me even though I was there. Never had it explained so clearly how my distributed computing strategy was the wrong one for 3Com in the 1980s."

- Bob Metcalfe, Internet pioneer, Ethernet inventor, 3Com founder, UT Austin Professor of Innovation

"I spent 18 years on the Board of Visitors of the National Defense University, Ft. McNair WDC, the Think Tank of the Pentagon, all pro bono but an honor to serve. I was frequently asked questions by both the faculty and students about the history of technology and Silicon Valley, often questions I had trouble answering, I wish this magnum opus on technology had been available."

- Stephen Millard, former CFO of several data communications start-ups and venture capitalist.

"This book is a fantastic contribution to the history of Silicon Valley. Based on Pelkey's interviews conducted at the time, this book presents an on-the-ground and live-action portrait of the development of the technological 'connective tissue' (modems, routers, local area networks) of the Internet in the period 1968–1988. Readers with simplistic teleological preconceptions about the inevitability of progress will be disabused by this rich mosaic account of 'history as it is experienced.' The authors present the 85 interviewed entrepreneurs in their story as courageous, even if not always successful, but the facts back up their admiring portrait. They did indeed accomplish a breakthrough."

- John Padgett, Professor in Political Sciences, University of Chicago

"In 1968, a new networked future of the world was born. Over the next two decades as computers and communications merged the foundations were being laid for the world in which we are now living. In *Circuits, Packets, and Protocols* Jim Pelkey and his co-authors give us a view from the inside of that revolution from their own experience and those of the other entrepreneurs who shared their stories, often for the first time. The networked world of today was the result of highly educated leaders and workers, entrepreneurs willing to be part of the cycles of creative destruction that built that world at the interface of the government and businesses. Navigating the currents of the future requires a deep understanding of what has brought us here. No one has articulated those currents better than Pelkey, Robbins, and Russell."

- Peter Schwartz, Senior Vice President Strategic Planning, Salesforce

"Enlivened by extensive interviews with many of the major players and grounded in remarkably thorough research, this book offers a comprehensive history of the most transformative technical development of our times: the global computer network. The authors break new ground in demonstrating how the network emerged in the United States from a rich mix of creative entrepreneurial activities conducted by private firms *and* public servants. Lively yet analytical, their richly textured portrait offers invaluable insights to anyone interested in the dynamics of innovation in modern America."

- Steven W. Usselman, Georgia Institute of Technology

"This is the only history that sees the early evolution of computer networking whole. It tells not just the familiar Internet story but the equally important hardware and telecommunications stories too. It is not just a history of technical invention but of the business innovations and standards wars that shaped how we live online. The underlying interviews and research materials are permanently preserved at the Computer History Museum; this is an example of 'open source' history that I hope others will follow."

- Marc Weber, Curatorial Director, Internet History Program, Computer History Museum

Circuits, Packets, and Protocols

ACM Books

ACM Books is a new series of high-quality books for the computer science community, published by ACM in collaboration with Morgan & Claypool Publishers. ACM Books publications are widely distributed in both print and digital formats through booksellers and to libraries (and library consortia) and individual ACM members via the ACM Digital Library platform.

Theories of Programming: The Life and Works of Tony Hoare
Editors: Cliff B. Jones, *Newcastle University, UK*
Jayadev Misra, *The University of Texas at Austin, US*
2021

Software: A Technical History
Kim W. Tracy, *Rose-Hulman Institute of Technology, IN, USA*
2021

The Handbook on Socially Interactive Agents: 20 years of Research on Embodied Conversational Agents, Intelligent Virtual Agents, and Social Robotics
Volume 1: Methods, Behavior, Cognition
Editors: Birgit Lugrin, *Julius-Maximilians-Universität of Würzburg*
Catherine Pelachaud, *CNRS-ISIR, Sorbonne Université*
David Traum, *University of Southern California*
2021

Probabilistic and Causal Inference: The Works of Judea Pearl
Editors: Hector Geffner, *ICREA and Universitat Pompeu Fabra*
Rina Dechter, *University of California, Irvine*
Joseph Y. Halpern, *Cornell University*
2022

Event Mining for Explanatory Modeling
Laleh Jalali, *University of California, Irvine (UCI), Hitachi America Ltd.*
Ramesh Jain, *University of California, Irvine (UCI)*
2021

Intelligent Computing for Interactive System Design: Statistics, Digital Signal Processing, and Machine Learning in Practice
Editors: Parisa Eslambolchilar, *Cardiff University, Wales, UK*
Andreas Komninos, *University of Patras, Greece*

Mark Dunlop, *Strathclyde University, Scotland, UK*
2021

Semantic Web for the Working Ontologist: Effective Modeling for Linked Data, RDFS, and OWL, Third Edition
Dean Allemang, *Working Ontologist LLC*
Jim Hendler, *Rensselaer Polytechnic Institute*
Fabien Gandon, *INRIA*
2020

Code Nation: Personal Computing and the Learn to Program Movement in America
Michael J. Halvorson, *Pacific Lutheran University*
2020

Computing and the National Science Foundation, 1950–2016: Building a Foundation for Modern Computing
Peter A. Freeman, *Georgia Institute of Technology*
W. Richards Adrion, *University of Massachusetts Amherst*
William Aspray, *University of Colorado Boulder*
2019

Providing Sound Foundations for Cryptography: On the work of Shafi Goldwasser and Silvio Micali
Oded Goldreich, *Weizmann Institute of Science*
2019

Concurrency: The Works of Leslie Lamport
Dahlia Malkhi, *VMware Research* and *Calibra*
2019

The Essentials of Modern Software Engineering: Free the Practices from the Method Prisons!
Ivar Jacobson, *Ivar Jacobson International*
Harold "Bud" Lawson, *Lawson Konsult AB (deceased)*
Pan-Wei Ng, *DBS Singapore*
Paul E. McMahon, *PEM Systems*
Michael Goedicke, *Universität Duisburg-Essen*
2019

Data Cleaning
Ihab F. Ilyas, *University of Waterloo*
Xu Chu, *Georgia Institute of Technology*
2019

Conversational UX Design: A Practitioner's Guide to the Natural Conversation Framework
Robert J. Moore, *IBM Research–Almaden*
Raphael Arar, *IBM Research–Almaden*
2019

Heterogeneous Computing: Hardware and Software Perspectives
Mohamed Zahran, *New York University*
2019

Hardness of Approximation Between P and NP
Aviad Rubinstein, *Stanford University*
2019

The Handbook of Multimodal-Multisensor Interfaces, Volume 3: Language Processing, Software, Commercialization, and Emerging Directions
Editors: Sharon Oviatt, *Monash University*
Björn Schuller, *Imperial College London and University of Augsburg*
Philip R. Cohen, *Monash University*
Daniel Sonntag, *German Research Center for Artificial Intelligence (DFKI)*
Gerasimos Potamianos, *University of Thessaly*
Antonio Krüger, *Saarland University and German Research Center for Artificial Intelligence (DFKI)*
2019

Making Databases Work: The Pragmatic Wisdom of Michael Stonebraker
Editor: Michael L. Brodie, *Massachusetts Institute of Technology*
2018

The Handbook of Multimodal-Multisensor Interfaces, Volume 2: Signal Processing, Architectures, and Detection of Emotion and Cognition
Editors: Sharon Oviatt, *Monash University*
Björn Schuller, *University of Augsburg and Imperial College London*
Philip R. Cohen, *Monash University*
Daniel Sonntag, *German Research Center for Artificial Intelligence (DFKI)*
Gerasimos Potamianos, *University of Thessaly*
Antonio Krüger, *Saarland University and German Research Center for Artificial Intelligence (DFKI)*
2018

Declarative Logic Programming: Theory, Systems, and Applications
Editors: Michael Kifer, *Stony Brook University*
Yanhong Annie Liu, *Stony Brook University*
2018

The Sparse Fourier Transform: Theory and Practice
Haitham Hassanieh, *University of Illinois at Urbana-Champaign*
2018

The Continuing Arms Race: Code-Reuse Attacks and Defenses
Editors: Per Larsen, *Immunant, Inc.*
Ahmad-Reza Sadeghi, *Technische Universität Darmstadt*
2018

Frontiers of Multimedia Research
Editor: Shih-Fu Chang, *Columbia University*
2018

Shared-Memory Parallelism Can Be Simple, Fast, and Scalable
Julian Shun, *University of California, Berkeley*
2017

Computational Prediction of Protein Complexes from Protein Interaction Networks
Sriganesh Srihari, *The University of Queensland Institute for Molecular Bioscience*
Chern Han Yong, *Duke-National University of Singapore Medical School*
Limsoon Wong, *National University of Singapore*
2017

The Handbook of Multimodal-Multisensor Interfaces, Volume 1: Foundations, User Modeling, and Common Modality Combinations
Editors: Sharon Oviatt, *Incaa Designs*
Björn Schuller, *University of Passau and Imperial College London*
Philip R. Cohen, *Voicebox Technologies*
Daniel Sonntag, *German Research Center for Artificial Intelligence (DFKI)*
Gerasimos Potamianos, *University of Thessaly*
Antonio Krüger, *Saarland University and German Research Center for Artificial Intelligence (DFKI)*
2017

Communities of Computing: Computer Science and Society in the ACM
Thomas J. Misa, Editor, *University of Minnesota*
2017

Text Data Management and Analysis: A Practical Introduction to Information Retrieval and Text Mining
ChengXiang Zhai, *University of Illinois at Urbana–Champaign*
Sean Massung, *University of Illinois at Urbana–Champaign*
2016

An Architecture for Fast and General Data Processing on Large Clusters
Matei Zaharia, *Stanford University*
2016

Reactive Internet Programming: State Chart XML in Action
Franck Barbier, *University of Pau, France*
2016

Verified Functional Programming in Agda
Aaron Stump, *The University of Iowa*
2016

The VR Book: Human-Centered Design for Virtual Reality
Jason Jerald, *NextGen Interactions*
2016

Ada's Legacy: Cultures of Computing from the Victorian to the Digital Age
Robin Hammerman, *Stevens Institute of Technology*
Andrew L. Russell, *Stevens Institute of Technology*
2016

Edmund Berkeley and the Social Responsibility of Computer Professionals
Bernadette Longo, *New Jersey Institute of Technology*
2015

Candidate Multilinear Maps
Sanjam Garg, *University of California, Berkeley*
2015

Smarter Than Their Machines: Oral Histories of Pioneers in Interactive Computing
John Cullinane, *Northeastern University; Mossavar-Rahmani Center for Business and Government, John F. Kennedy School of Government, Harvard University*
2015

A Framework for Scientific Discovery through Video Games
Seth Cooper, *University of Washington*
2014

Trust Extension as a Mechanism for Secure Code Execution on Commodity Computers
Bryan Jeffrey Parno, *Microsoft Research*
2014

Embracing Interference in Wireless Systems
Shyamnath Gollakota, *University of Washington*
2014

Circuits, Packets, and Protocols

Entrepreneurs and Computer Communications, 1968–1988

James L. Pelkey

Andrew L. Russell
SUNY Polytechnic Institute, New York

Loring G. Robbins

ACM Books #40

Circuits, Packets, and Protocols: Entrepreneurs and Computer Communications, 1968–1988
James L. Pelkey, Andrew L. Russell, Loring G. Robbins

books.acm.org
http://books.acm.org

ISBN: 978-1-4503-9726-1 hardcover
ISBN: 978-1-4503-9727-8 paperback
ISBN: 978-1-4503-9728-5 EPUB
ISBN: 978-1-4503-9729-2 eBook

Series ISSN: 2374-6769 print 2374-6777 electronic

DOIs:

10.1145/3502372 Book
10.1145/3502372.3502373 Preface and Acknowledgments
10.1145/3502372.3502374 Introduction
10.1145/3502372.3502375 Chapter 1
10.1145/3502372.3502376 Chapter 2
10.1145/3502372.3502377 Chapter 3
10.1145/3502372.3502378 Chapter 4
10.1145/3502372.3502379 Chapter 5
10.1145/3502372.3502380 Chapter 6
10.1145/3502372.3502381 Chapter 7
10.1145/3502372.3502382 Chapter 8
10.1145/3502372.3502383 Chapter 9
10.1145/3502372.3502384 Chapter 10
10.1145/3502372.3502385 Chapter 11
10.1145/3502372.3502386 Chapter 12
10.1145/3502372.3502387 Chapter 13
10.1145/3502372.3502388 Chapter 14
10.1145/3502372.3502389 Appendix A
10.1145/3502372.3502390 Appendix B
10.1145/3502372.3502391 Appendix C
10.1145/3502372.3502392 Bios/Index

A publication in the ACM Books series, #40

This book was typeset in Arnhem Pro 10/14 and Flama using pdfTEX.

First Edition

10 9 8 7 6 5 4 3 2 1

Contents

List of Figures

List of Tables

List of Acronyms

ACM	Association for Computing Machinery
ACS	AT&T Advanced Communications Service
ADPCM	Adaptive differential pulse-code modulation
ADS	American Data Systems
AFIPS	The American Federation of Information Processing Societies
AMD	Advanced Microchip Devices
AMEX	American Stock Exchange
AMI	American Microsystems, Inc
ANSI	American National Standards Institute
ARCNET	Datapoint LAN product
ARD	American Research and Development
ARPA	Advanced Research Projects Agency
AT&T	American Telephone & Telegraph
ATTIS	AT&T Information Systems
BPO	British Post Office
BSD	Berkeley Software Distribution
CAD	Computer automated design
CAE	Computer-aided engineering
CATV	cable television
CBX	computerized branch exchange
CCB	Common Carrier Bureau
CCI	Concord Communications, Inc.
CCIA	Computer & Communication Industry Association
CCITT	International Telegraph and Telephone Consultative Committee
CDS	Concord Data Systems

CEO	Chief Executive Officer
CHM	Computer History Museum
CIO	Chief Information Officer
CLNS	Connectionless Network Service
CMC	Computer Machinery Corporation
CMU	Carnegie Mellon University
COO	Chief Operating Officer
COS	Corporation for Open Systems
CPE	Customer Provide Equipment
CPU	Central Processing Unit
CRT	Cathode-Ray Tube
CSC	Computer Science Corporation
CSMA/CD	carrier sense multiple access/collision detection
CTOS	Convergent Technologies Operating System
CVSD	continuously variable slope delta modulation
CXC	CXC Corporation
DAA	digital access arrangements
DARPA	Defense Advanced Research Projects Agency
DBMS	data base management system
DCA	Digital Communication Associates
DCE	data communications equipment
DDCMP	Digital Data Communications Message Protocol
DDN	Defense Data Network
DDP	digital data processing
DDS	Digital Data Service
DEC	Digital Equipment Corporation
DIS	Draft International Standard
DISOSS	Distributed Office Support System
DIX	DEC-Intel-Xerox
DOD	Department of Defense
DOS	Disk Operating System
DP	Draft Proposal
DSP	digital signal processor
DTE	data terninsal equipment
ECMA	European Computer Manufacturers Association
EDP	electronic data processing
EIN	European Informatics Network

ENE Enterprise Network Event
ERISA Employee Retirement Income Security Act
EVP executive vice president
FCC Federal Communications Commission
FDM frequency division multiplcxcr
FDMA frequency division multiple access
FIPS Federal Information Processing Standards
FTAM File Transfer Access Method
GDC General DataComm Industries, Inc.
GE General Electric
GI General Instruments, Inc.
GM General Motors
GOSIP Government Open Systems Interconnection Profile
GTE General Telephone Electronics
HAPC Hush-A-Phone Corporation
HDLC High-Level Data Link Control
HP Hewlett-Packard
IAB Internet Activities Board
IBM International Business Machines
ICA International Communications Association
ICBM Intercontinental Ballistic Missile
ICC Interstate Commerce Commission
ICCB Internet Configuration Control Board
ICCC International Conference on Computer Communications
ICST Institute for Computer Sciences and Technology
IDCMA Independent Data Communications and Manufacturers Association
IEEE Institute of Electrical and Electronics Engineers
IETF Internet Engineering Task Force
IFIP International Federation of Information Processing
IMP Interface Message Processor
INI Industrial Networking Inc.
INWG International Network Working Group
IP Internet Protocol
IPO Initial Public Offering
IPTO Information Processing Techniques Office
ISO International Organization for Standardization
ITT International Telephone & Telegraph, Inc.

LACN	Local Area Communications Network Symposium
LAN	Local Area Networks
LANCE	Local Area Network Controller Ethernet
LATA	Local access and transport area
LCS	Laboratory of Computer Science
LISP	LISt Processor
LNI	Local Area Network Interface
LSI	Large-scale integration
MAC	media access control
MAP	manufacturing automation protocols
MBA	Master in Business Administration
MIS	management information systems
MIT	Massachusetts Institute of Technology
NARUC	National Assoc of Regulatory Utility Commissioners
NAS	National Academy of Sciences
NBS	National Bureau of Standards
NCC	National Computer Conference
NCP	Network Control Protocol
NCR	National Cash Register
NMC	Network Measurement Center
NPL	National Physical Laboratory
NRC	National Research Council
NSF	National Science Foundation
NWG	Network Working Group
NYSE	New York Stock Exchange
OEM	Original Equipment Manufacturer
OSI	Open Systems Interconnection
PARC	Palo Alto Research Center
PBX	Private Branch Exchange
PC	Personal Computer
PCA	Protective Connecting Arrangement
PCM	pulse-code modulation
PSTN	Public Switched Telephone Network
PTT	Postal, Telegraph & Telephone
PUC	Public Utility Commission
PUP	PARC Universal Packet
QAM	Quadrature Amplitude Modulation

RBOC	Regional Bell Operating Company
RCA	Radio Company of America
RFC	Request for Comments
RFNM	Request for Next Message
RFQ	request for quotation
RTL	register-transfer level
SAGE	Semi-Automatic Ground Environment
SBIC	a small business investment company
SBS	Satellite Business Systems
SC	Subcommittee
SDC	Systems Development Corporation
SDD	Systems Development Division
SDLC	Synchronous Data Link Control
SDS	Scientific Data Systems
SEC	Securities Exchange Commission
SNA	System Network Architecture
SNMP	simple network management protocol
SRI	Stanford Research Institute
SUN	Stanford University Network
TC	Technical Committee (ISO)
TCCC	Technical Committee on Computer Communications (IEEE)
TCP	Transmission Control Program
TCP/IP	Transmission Control Protocol/Internet Protocol
TDM	Time Division Multiplexer
TIP	Terminal Interface Processor
TOP	Technical Office Protocol
TP	Transfer Protocol
UART	Universal Asynchronous Receiver and Transceiver
UB	Ungermann-Bass
UCI	University of California Irvine
UCLA	University of California Los Angeles
UCSB	University of California Santa Barbara
UDS	Universal Data Systems
USAF	United States Air Force
USART	Universal Synchronous Asynchronous Receiver Transmitter
VAR	Value Added Reseller
VC	Venture Capital

VLSI	Very Large Scale Integration
WAN	Wide Area Network
WD	Working Draft
WE	Western Electric
WG	Working Group
XNS	Xerox Network System

Preface and Acknowledgments

It was the summer of 1987, and James L. Pelkey, a partner at the San Francisco investment bank Montgomery Securities, was perplexed. Three years earlier, Pelkey had joined Montgomery to take charge of its venture capital investments. He had a special interest in data communications and networking markets. The core enabling products of those markets—such as modems and local area networks—were relatively new innovations. The personal computer boom was under way, and internetworking hardware was available to purchase. Yet almost no one at this time saw the earth-shrinking changes that lay only a few years away, fueled by the commercialization of the Internet and the rapid adoption of the World Wide Web.

The internetworking products of the late 1980s worked well enough to demonstrate the vast potential for sharing information between computers and their applications. Pelkey and his peers knew that there was money to be made, especially if the futurists were correct in predicting that the global economy was moving from the Industrial Age to the Information Age. But it was increasingly difficult to see through the thicket of competing technologies, companies, and standards. Nobody had convincing answers to deceptively simple questions. For example, why were some entrepreneurs successful when most others failed? Which standards would get the fastest market acceptance? And how was it possible that established companies—including the American titans of computing and communications, IBM and AT&T—were failing to dominate this promising market?

Pelkey was well positioned to guide Montgomery's strategy in computer communications.[1] Before arriving at Montgomery, he spent 18 months as the chief

1. Pelkey first moved to San Francisco after earning a degree in engineering from Rensselaer Polytechnic Institute (1968) and an MBA from Harvard (1970). He initially worked in leasing and finance, and gained experience in management with several companies. In 1980, he moved to Santa Barbara to become president of the technology start-up Digital Sound. He then consulted for companies with a focus on communications, software, and graphics. Pelkey recalls, "One client, Communications Machinery Corporation (CMC), was a small engineering shop headed by Larry Green. They believed one of their projects could lead to real products. I had a hard time

executive of Sorcim, a company that sold SuperCalc, an early spreadsheet program that helped popularize desktop computing. When he arrived at Montgomery in 1984, Pelkey had established a strong record of success managing early-stage start-ups. Montgomery wanted his expertise to help turn around underperforming companies in its portfolio, and to find new companies to invest in. Paths to success in venture capital traveled through social networks, so Pelkey decided—some time in the summer of 1987—to make contacts with executives of leading companies in computer communications. Seeking introductions to some experts in the field, Pelkey called on Paul Baran, whom Pelkey had met after joining the board of Baran's start-up, Telebit. Baran was the co-inventor of packet switching, a highly respected figure in government and technical circles, an advisor to several start-ups, and an entrepreneur himself. Baran and Pelkey discussed various people that Pelkey should meet—scientists, engineers, regulators, and entrepreneurs who were widely considered to be key figures in computer communications. Baran generously made introductions to a handful of people, and Pelkey found they were willing to speak candidly.[2]

Pelkey interviewed these experts throughout 1988, part of an exhausting year when he traveled frequently from San Francisco to cities around the world. In Boston, London, Paris, Singapore, Tokyo, Melbourne, and many places in between, Pelkey met investors, served on corporate boards, and squeezed in time to interview experts. His purpose was to build relationships and look for opportunities that would benefit Montgomery—perhaps young companies with potential for a strong IPO, or others that needed a merger to realize their potential. Once he started interviewing people from the list that Baran had shared with him, some interviews led to others—an incremental approach that social scientists refer to as the "snowball method."

Pelkey's vision for these interviews was much broader than a typical process of market research and discovery. He decided to record these interviews—but only the parts about history, not industry gossip or investment strategies. His goal was to understand the industry better, to identify how populations of companies emerged, and to answer some big questions of broad interest: how do ideas become products, companies, and industries? How does this process generate economic growth and prosperity? Prevailing economic theories, presuming

understanding why or how. The project was an emulator for a new Ethernet semiconductor chip named LANCE. It took nearly a year of Saturdays for me to finally grasp its importance and, really, the importance of computer networking." James L. Pelkey, "About James L. Pelkey," http://www.historyofcomputercommunications.info/About/JimPelkey.html.

2. The initial list included Bernard Strassburg, Vint Cerf, Robert Kahn, Lawrence Roberts, Donald Davies, John Heafner, Leonard Klienrock, Johnny Johnson, Gordon Bell, Frank Heart, and David Farber.

a general tendency toward equilibrium, poorly described the dynamic conditions he observed in computer communications. Pelkey sensed that the experts he was meeting could provide some raw material to understand these old questions in new ways.

Pelkey decided that his interviews could be the basis for writing a history of computer communications for the years 1968 to 1988. In the end, he recorded 85 interviews that altogether fill 1,887 pages of printed transcripts.[3] Along the way, Pelkey concluded that a traditional, linear history could not do justice to the stories he heard. He wanted to present them in a format that could capture the uncertainty, stress, and rewards of the time. A hypertext format could give readers the opportunity to explore this history in the order they chose; it also could support links to the substantial source material that informed his analysis, such as the transcripts from his interviews as well as data on revenues, sales, market projections, and more.

The hypertext book took time to emerge. Pelkey decided to leave Montgomery Securities at the end of 1988 to form his own investment company. He moved to Santa Fe, NM, in 1989, and, among other things, found a new home amongst the economic theorists at the Santa Fe Institute. He became a Trustee in 1989, and served as Chairman of the Board of Trustees from 1992 to 1994. Through attending workshops and engaging in discussions with scientists from many disciplines such as Brian Arthur, Chris Langton, David Lane, Walter Fontana, and John Padgett, he learned about complex adaptive systems and the notions of emergence, self-organization, and punctuated equilibriums. These ideas helped Pelkey understand his experiences and interview data in a new light, and provided some theoretical underpinnings for his hypertext book, *Entrepreneurial Capitalism & Innovation: A History of Computer Communications, 1968–1988*.[4]

Published on-line as a series of linked webpages, *Entrepreneurial Capitalism & Innovation* fulfilled Pelkey's vision of providing fertile ground for reader exploration. But visitors to Pelkey's website regularly contacted him to request a version of the material as a traditional book. The first collaborative steps toward this book occurred in 2007, when the computer scientist John Day introduced Pelkey to Andrew L. Russell. At the time, Russell was a Ph.D. student at Johns Hopkins University, finishing a dissertation on the historical aspects of technical standards for communication networks. They struck up a friendship and shared ideas. Russell agreed to help finish the final chapter of *Entrepreneurial Capitalism & Innovation*,

3. These transcripts and recordings are now deposited at the Computer History Museum in Mountain View, CA.

4. James L. Pelkey, "*Entrepreneurial Capitalism & Innovation: A History of Computer Communications, 1968–1988*," http://www.historyofcomputercommunications.info.

an assignment that brought him to visit Pelkey on Maui for a week in March 2013. The pair agreed to work together toward the publication of a book, but progress was slow until Pelkey began to work with Loring G. Robbins in November 2017. Robbins quickly and enthusiastically threw himself into the research, revision, and writing necessary to complete the book—and utilized his skills in graphic design to create and update illustrations that provide visual depictions of some complex technologies described in several chapters.

As we bring this unusual project to completion, we believe it will be helpful to be explicit about the different types of readers we have imagined as we have crafted *Circuits, Packets, and Protocols*. One group is historians, professional and amateur alike, who are already familiar with the rise of Silicon Valley and the emergence of the ARPANET and Internet. We know that much of the material we present here cannot be found in existing published books, and we hope that these readers will discover our book to be a different take on a familiar story. In the Introduction, we go into some depth about how *Circuits, Packets, and Protocols* both overlaps with and departs from the existing literature.[5]

In addition, professionals who are not historians will find something of value in these pages. Those who are active in business and technology may find some lessons applicable to their own circumstances. For example, how do entrepreneurial ventures coalesce into populations of firms and products? How do these new collectives challenge—or become challenged by—incumbent firms? In contrast to the conventional business school case study, focused on a single firm, *Circuits, Packets, and Protocols* captures the experience of dozens of firms, interacting with one another, that eventually became more than the sum of their parts.

We also hope that general readers—such as ACM members—will appreciate our effort to illuminate the respective roles of individuals and collectives in history. We believe that the episodes detailed in the following pages illustrate the power, and at times decisive role, of individuals. And even more generally, we believe that our historical account of computer communications has captured the nascent stages of technologies that are widely regarded as transformational. In business, politics, and our personal lives, it seems that no aspect of modern life is untouched by networked digital communications—for better or worse. Digital data networks in general, and the Internet in particular, are remarkable (if imperfect) developments

5. For a condensed version of our arguments, with particular attention to standards in international business, see Russell, A., Pelkey, J., & Robbins, L. (2022). The Business of Internetworking: Standards, Start-Ups, and Network Effects. *Business History Review*, 1–36. doi:https://doi.org/10.1017/S000768052100074X.

in human history. The interviews that Pelkey recorded capture some inspiring stories about the origins of the information infrastructure that keeps the world connected, even as we all endure the terrible COVID-19 pandemic. Indeed, the ease with which the Internet has absorbed so much traffic—thereby sustaining unprecedented amounts of the world's economic and social life—should inspire readers to learn about the origins of the technologies that move data around the world.

Acknowledgments

Loring G. Robbins would like to thank both Jim and Andy for the opportunity to work on this project. The collaboration has been a great experience, not only for the understanding I have gained about this important period in history but also for the friendship I share with these two authors. Jim's patience and willingness to pass on his personal stories and knowledge of the business world has given me a deep appreciation for the challenges and the allure of the entrepreneur's journey. Andy's encouragement, sense of humor, and his deep knowledge of business and technology history have been invaluable throughout this process. I would also like to thank Rick and Kathy Kimball, Stu Greenfield, and Bob and Kathie Maxfield, whose generous gifts in support of this project made my work possible. A big thanks also to Manley Irwin, who generously gave me his time to answer questions in person at his home in New Hampshire as well as via phone and email. I would also like to thank my wife Gena and daughter Sophia for their support during my work on this project.

Andy Russell would like to thank John Day, the computer scientist who introduced Andy to Jim Pelkey. Day's passion for history—and for understanding the mix of contextual factors, technical details, and long-term consequences—has been a source of motivation over the past 15 years. I am likewise grateful to acknowledge encouragement and insight from Bradley Fidler, Louis Galambos, Massimo Petrozzi, Valérie Schafer, Marc Weber, and Joanne Yates. It's difficult to imagine where this project would be without Tom Misa's extraordinary advocacy and enthusiasm, as well as the diligence and intelligence of Loring G. Robbins. My wife and kids—Lesley, Reese, and Calvin Russell—have been the best writing partners and supporters anyone could ask for. Finally, I am profoundly grateful that Jim Pelkey welcomed me into his vast intellectual universe and allowed me the privilege of working with him to bring this project to completion.

James L. Pelkey would like to acknowledge the following people.

Paul Baran

I met Paul Baran shortly after I joined Montgomery Securities, in September 1984. I soon made a client solicitation call on Packet Technologies, also known as Packet Cable. Little did I know at the time that lifelong friendships would be formed with Paul Baran, William Houser, and Steve Millard, Packet Technologies' founder and Chief Scientist, CEO, and CFO, respectively. Paul Baran's creative mind soon conceived an innovative technology for high-speed modems that became the basis for another start-up—Telebit. Montgomery Securities' Venture Fund soon led the investment round and I joined the Board of Directors. My relationship with Paul blossomed and when, years later, I shared with him my desire to write a history book that would reconstruct computer communications for the years between 1968 to 1988, he could not have been more encouraging. In addition to a very frank interview, he willingly introduced me to many of the key people I interviewed, read early drafts of my text, and was always available to answer any questions or be of help.

Paul Baran was as fine a gentleman as it has been my honor to know. He essentially became my surrogate father. He was brilliant, gracious, humble, compassionate, always willing to lend a helping hand, and believed that the act of innovation was a team effort. I never heard him voice a critical word of anyone. In addition to co-inventing the seminal technology of "packet switching," by 1988 he had founded seven successful start-ups.[6] Paul passed away on March 26, 2011, from complications of lung cancer. The last meal I had before moving to Maui in 2004 was with Paul. Often called "the father of the Internet," the Computer History Museum (CHM) honored him "for fundamental contributions to the architecture of the Internet and for a lifetime of entrepreneurial activity." He was the most important person in helping me finish the on-line version of this book and it saddens me that he will not be able to read this version as well.

I can vividly recall the second meeting we had after I had further refined my thoughts. We were sitting at his desk at yet another start-up—Metricom—when he said I absolutely had to interview Vint Cerf and Robert Kahn who were engaged in starting a new firm themselves. I asked him how I could arrange interviews, when he picked up his phone and called Vint, who took the call and they began talking as if friends, which it turns out they were. Paul soon told Vint what I was up to and passed the phone to me; Vint introduced himself and said when I knew I was coming to Washington, DC, to call and they would meet me.

Montgomery Securities

Next must come Montgomery Securities, for without their support the 85 interviews would undoubtedly been just a dream. I joined Montgomery Securities

6. These companies were Packet Cable, StrataCom, Telebit, Institute for the Future, Metricom, Interfax, and Com21.

in 1984, reporting to Thom Wiesel, to assume responsibility for their struggling venture-capital operations. In 1985, I was promoted to general partner and had an office next to Thom's. I couldn't have been more fortunate for Thom took a keen interest in introducing me to many of the venture capitalists with whom I would work with over the next four years. Working for Thom was a gift, and I would not have resigned were it not for personal reasons.

Thom was the best manager I ever had, and he gave me the freedom to conduct the interviews essential to writing these histories. I am deeply indebted to Thom and his firm and partners for trusting me and seldom questioning my priorities.

In addition to Thom, one partner and his wife are due special mention. Rick Kimball joined Montgomery at the same time as I did and reported to me. He had just graduated with an MBA and proved to be an exceptional research analyst. He later went on to start his own successful venture capital firm. We stayed in touch over the years as his career took off and when, in 2015, I had exhausted my means to fund the book project, I called Rick, and without any hesitation he said Kathy and he would give me the money I needed. It was a very special moment in my life and was essential to completing the book project. I was deeply honored.

Early Book Reviewers

Six individuals deserve special mention for having taken an early and meaningful interest in this book project: Stu Greenfield, Harold Shattuck, Douglass North, Manley Irwin, Robert Maxfield, and Kathie Maxfield.

Stu Greenfield

Stu has been with me throughout the long history of first reconstructing the 20-year history of computer communications in the form of a hypertext on-line version capturing many lengthy excerpts from the 85 interviews. Then, after that had been accomplished, to more selectively answer questions that I had, he blocked out time for lengthy conversations, and finally continued in the role of one of my most trusted reviewers of drafts of the book. Stu worked for IBM for many years as a senior software engineer before assuming important staff roles as his career advanced. With Ed Glassmeyer he formed one of the most highly regarded East Coast venture capital firms, and as one of the firm's senior partners, Stu served on many boards of directors, including those of Ungermann-Bass, Micom, NET, and Equinox, and others important to this history, which clearly gave him a unique perspective to understand and critique my work. Stu and his wife Connie steadfastly encouraged and supported me throughout these many years. While I had never written a book, Stu assured me that was less important than what I knew, all the data that I had collected, and what I had experienced. Finally, Stu helped convince Gardner Hendrie, a CHM board member, to accept the gift I was proposing. He is a wonderful friend.

Harold Shattuck

Harold and I worked together at Montgomery Securities and his competence was as a talented computer scientist and engineer as well as having been president of a public and substantial company. Over the four years that we worked together we always traveled together when we held limited partner meetings, when we attempted to raise more capital, or when we were doing due diligence on potentially new investments, or to justify investing more in existing investments. We often discussed my idea to write a history book, so when I finally began to do so, I always passed drafts by him to make sure I had my technology descriptions correct. Frequently, he would come to my home with a bottle of wine and we talked outside for hours before going to a favorite restaurant. I totally trusted his contributions that unfortunately got fewer over time. He even came to Maui to continue our conversations. He will always be a friend for life.

Douglass North

I met Professor Douglass North at one of the frequent talks he gave on the Stanford campus in the late 1990s, after he had already won his Nobel Prize in 1993. Upon first meeting him I briefly told him a little about myself and invited him to have lunch. Unfortunately, I was so busy, and living alone, that I never studied up on Professor North even though I knew he had won the Nobel Prize in economic history. We had as I remember four lunches at the Il Fornaio restaurant in downtown Palo Alto. I was honored to be sitting and talking about institutions as if friends and for a few minutes as if equals and economic researchers helping each other, even if only a fantasy running in my mind. Most of what we said is lost with time, but I clearly recall his emphasizing the importance of population growth, a fact that I had overlooked in my work. He encouraged me to continue to send him my writings and he always edited them and returned them promptly. He might have gained little from our interchanges, but I always felt honored.

Professor Manley Irwin

I first heard about Manley when I interviewed Bernard Strassburg. Realizing how important his many contributions were, I initiated conversations that led to him providing a treasure trove of documents to our historical project. Unfortunately, I never interviewed Professor Irwin, but he met and talked at length with one of my co-authors, Loring G. Robbins. He has continued to provide critical insights into the history we are reconstructing, especially the early years. I am so very glad we have become friends, and thank him for so many important documents that he is trusting us to make public.

Robert (Bob) and Kathie Maxfield

In one of our final drafts, we realized we had overlooked the history of ROLM, so we did some additional research. In doing so we discovered a treasure of a book written by Kathie Maxfield, the wife of one of the founders of ROLM—the M in fact. Her book is a wonderful account of the evolution and culture of Silicon Valley. After learning that the Maxfield's have a home on Maui, I arranged to have them visit me in my home. We discussed Kathie's book and then asked Bob questions that he patiently answered.[7] Afterwards he sent us a diagram he had drawn of the ROLM CBX, which we used as the basis for the one in the book. When we needed some additional financial support, even though we had just met, they responded graciously. We are forever grateful.

Computer History Museum

John Toole and John Hollar

Both recent Presidents deserve thanks in supporting my efforts to gift my website and 85 interviews to the museum. Before I moved to Maui in 2004, I met with John Toole twice to hammer out the agreement that was then finalized soon after John Hollar became president in 2008. Both presidents committed the CHM to host both my website: (historyofcomputercommunications.info) and all my interviews in perpetuity.

I finally met John Hollar in July 2015 and had the opportunity to thank him personally. Then in 2017, I raised the issue that I was hoping that the Museum would make more of an effort marketing my completed website. Their response was that I needed to convert the website into a book that could more easily be marketed. I said I could not do it by myself and they said that did not matter as long as it became a book. The result was I asked the most ideal person I knew, Andy Russell, who agreed to partner the project with me. As time passes, I am ever more certain that the CHM is the best permanent home for my works.

Chuck House

Chuck was one of two longstanding CHM board members who facilitated my desire to gift my oral interviews and my on-line book to the museum. Chuck soon contacted me and explained that he was reconstructing the history of Cisco and wanted to come to Maui to get to know me and review the materials I had collected. I thought it was a great idea and invited him to stay with me. He did and we had a great time together. In addition to familiarizing himself with all of my materials,

7. Katherine Maxfield. *Starting Up Silicon Valley: How ROLM Became a Cultural Icon and Fortune 500 Company*. Greenleaf Book Group, 2014.

he left with a small suitcase of duplicated documents. I thought that was the last of our interchange until I received a letter from the NOVIM non-profit organization for science and global change on April 19, 2019, announcing that I had received the Science Inspiration Award for Historical Preservation for my computer communications project. As I cannot travel, a week later I received a sculptured glass award trophy. I was and will always be truly honored.

Gardner Hendrie

I have never met Gardner but have talked to him at length on the phone. I do know Stu introduced my project to Gardner, who, as a CHM board member, along with Chuck House, helped convince the two presidents of the value of the project, especially given the early date of the interviews.

Marc Weber

Once my gift had been given an initial approval, it was turned over to Marc Weber, the Founding Curator of the Internet History Program, to negotiate the final details. Marc and I began an exchange of letters in early April 2010 that quickly led to a satisfactory mutual exchange. Marc and I have enjoyed a productive and constructive relationship ever since.

Interviewees

My 85 oral interviews have resulted in 1,185 pages of transcriptions. It is an unenviable task to indicate that any interviews were better than any others. I would prefer the reader to conclude that I was blessed to have every one of the interviewees sit with me and record their thoughts for posterity. If you read any of them, I believe you too will conclude I was indeed very lucky. I will identify a few interviewees whose time with me was exceptionally noteworthy. But to everyone I say thank you and I hope the transcription captures both the content and spirit of our conversation.

Vint Cerf

Our time together was rescheduled a number of times, and a serious snowstorm cut our time together even shorter. But a very valued friend, Bill Houser, gave me a ride from the city out to Reston where Vint's office was. The last thing I wanted was for us to have an accident, so while my conversation with Vint was brief we had a great connection, and over the years we had many conversations that all proved valuable. After meeting Robert Kahn two weeks later, I could sense how they became lifetime friends.

Robert Kahn

Dr. Robert (Bob) Kahn is one of the smartest men I have ever met. I called on him right after lunch, and as I began questioning him, he could sense how little I knew about what I was hoping to learn from him. So he gently interrupted me and asked me why I was in a rush. He said he had set aside the afternoon for us, and thought it might be best if he started. He was so right. I knew so little of his history and experiences. Dr. Kahn was so patient, clear, and thorough with his descriptions. Hours later he said he needed an hour to finish up some work, but then how would I like to have dinner together? Knowing I had some time before I was to meet Dr. Kahn before dinner, I drove past the restaurant so I was sure not to get lost, and found a place where I could pull over and park and I began to reflect on all that I had just heard and reviewed what was written down. Before the interview I had felt overwhelmed and lost. But in listening to Dr. Kahn's explanations, I began to sense a glimmer of hope that there might be a way that I could organize my thoughts and communicate them so that others might see and understand the evolution and importance of computer communications. Later, we met at the restaurant and continued our conversation. We enjoyed a great French dinner together and ended up closing the restaurant many hours later. Indeed, Bob Kahn was a great person to interview.

Robert Metcalfe

When I called Bob to ask him if he was willing to be interviewed, without any hesitation he said yes and invited me to come by after dinner some agreed upon night. He was alone that night and we proceeded directly to his home office in his attic. I eyed a convenient couch with glass-topped table where I could set up my recording system and microphone. Bob sat across from me and waited for me to begin. Having learned the benefits of being prepared, I didn't act rushed, and we took a few minutes getting to know each other. I then turned my system on and, nevertheless, asked him an awkward question to begin. He seemed not to mind and thus began a lengthy and very enjoyable interview that could have gone on for much longer, but it was getting late and I felt I had overstayed his gracious offer. I highly recommend reading the interview and the great story of how Ethernet was birthed. I left having absolutely no doubt that Bob was a heroic entrepreneur in Schumpeter's best sense of the word.

Jay Hill

I first met Jay at Doelz Networks Inc. board meetings. I was attending as an observer and potential investor in my role with and for Montgomery Securities. At the time

Doelz was considered a "hot" investment and I was not the only observer attending. One member of the board was Stu Greenfield's partner, Ed Glassmeyer. When it came time for the vice president's report, in came Jay Hill, who was the best dressed executive I had ever seen in business. His report also bore the signs of his time working for IBM. Afterwards, I asked Jay if I could buy him dinner. He said yes and it soon became a standing practice with others often joining us, including Frank Conners, the company president.

I learned a lot during our meals together, not only about Doelz but the industry in general and even the practices of marketing and sales. Jay became a friend and often visited me. It was during these times together that we were inexorably drawn to sharing our personal lives. It was then that I learned Jay's wife was a minister in their faith, and the incredible commitment they made, and the extended time spent with Alaska Natives in outer Alaska. During this period, Jay was no longer with Paradyne and was a consultant and our conversations became more spiritual than business, and frankly more meaningful, and Jay became a close friend.

Louis Pouzin

Unfortunately, Louis Pouzin's schedule and mine never overlapped when I was in Paris; as mine had with Hubert Zimmerman's. But we were persistent, and finally on November 28th, when I had only two more scheduled interviews left to complete the list of interviewees, Louis and I finally arranged to meet in Florida, for dinner. We both had had busy days; I had two interviews in Huntsville, Alabama, before flying into Atlanta on my way to our dinner in Tampa Bay. Louis had had a similar busy day, so we were glad to finally have met so that he could share his unique and important story in the history of global packet switching. He was a gracious, open, and forthright interviewee.

Bernard (Bernie) Strassburg

Bernard Strassburg had retired from the Common Carrier Bureau (CCB) years earlier. But he arranged for our interview to be conducted in his old office in the CCB's department. As I walked down the large hallways, I could almost sense the history that had been made therein. When I reached the CCB's offices, I pushed on the large oak paneled doors, and entered the magisterial chambers. Before me were a series of wood railings and gates and I could see Mr. Strassburg beckoning me forward. We shook hands and before I could say anything, he said to call him Bernie. We began the process of introducing ourselves as I set up my recorder and he finished by telling me that his office, together with the adjacent conference room was where the future of the telecommunications industry had been negotiated. I said I was hoping to hear his views and feelings of those times, and I believe I did.

One important fact coming from the interview was Bernie mentioning the name of Dr. Manley Irwin, who has proved to be a remarkable source of documentation and very willing contributor to our historical reconstruction. I consider Bernard Strassburg to be one of the unsung heroes of the *information economy* and he was acting as a social entrepreneur. It was a huge honor to spend an hour and a half with him.

Dan Lynch

I will never forget the day I called on Dan Lynch for an interview. I found his street address in Cupertino and pulled up a steep driveway and stopped before the garage. I could see a covered picnic table in the backyard with people milling about. Dan was in the kitchen, which was anything but a kitchen. It looked more like a crowded office with computers, fax machines, and copiers and stacks of Connexions magazines.

Dan began by explaining how he became responsible for the computer facilities at a number of important institutions that led to his being responsible for the important task of the conversion of the ARPANET from NCP to TCP/IP. Although our conversation was very interesting, it ended with a brief discussion of OSI versus TCP/IP when I had to unfortunately end the interview as I had another engagement I had to attend.

We agreed to meet again, but the year slipped away. Then one day I got a call from Dan and he wanted to come visit. On arriving, we began talking aside my backyard pool when he suddenly pulled at a gift and proceeded to inflate a three-foot long dirigible that once inflated could be steered since it was powered by a small fan at one end of the football-like balloon. We then began taking turns racing it around a course we set up around the pool. We soon discovered we were enjoying being competitive and couldn't stop laughing. It was a moment of sheer joy and I'll never forget it, knowing we would always be friends.

There would be other days of racing and discussing his history and the success of the tradeshow Interop, an organization dedicated to the importance of TCP/IP. Months later in 1990, Dan even sought advice on his decision of whether to sell Interop or not. Years later he remains a dear friend through our time together on the board of Santa Fe Institute and this book project. Finally, we owe Dan many thanks for the photo that is on the cover of this book.

Joseph Carl Robnett (J.C.R., or "Lick") Licklider

It was a rainy afternoon in June 1988, when I pulled up in front of Dr. Licklider's home in Arlington, MA. I sat hoping the rain would let up, but not wanting to be late, I finally decided to get wet and walk up his pathway to his front door. When the door opened, I said "Dr. Licklider?" And he replied: "Just call me Lick." He took my raincoat, then guided me to his living room. As I began to set my recorder up, he pulled a well-worn chair up to the table between us, and his wife, Louise, came in and asked if we want anything, to which we replied: "no, thank you." Lick then began by saying he was not sure he could help me, but what questions did I have? If I was nervous before, and I should have been, I was now dumbstruck. He broke the silence and asked where he should begin. For anyone who knows who Lick is, my being a bit nervous is understandable. But as I would soon learn, it was totally inappropriate, for Lick was warm-hearted, gracious, and as interested in me and my project as I was in him and his indelible imprint on the history of computing and computer communications. This interview is a casual walk through Lick's career and accomplishments. He was open and humble, and an absolute joy to be with.

Art Carr

Art Carr resisted the idea of sitting for an interview. When I told him who else had already agreed to be interviewed, he said that was even more reason that he did not need to be interviewed. But it was essential that I interview Art, so he finally agreed if I kept it short. I arrived on time and sat outside his office until his door opened. He was polite but not particularly friendly. The process went reasonably well until he realized that very day, April 6, was the day 18 years ago when he had learned that Jim Cryer, the president of Codex, had died, setting in motion events that would forever change Carr's fortunes at Codex. On realizing the serendipity of the moment, he asked that I turn the recorder off, then leaned back, remembering that time in his career. He then dialed his secretary, asked her to clear his schedule, asked if I wanted a coffee, then turned to me and said: "where were we? There is no need to rush, for I have all the time we need." From that moment on, I could not have asked for a more patient and thorough interviewee. It had felt like a seminal moment and I never second guessed any question I had, I just asked them. It was the most enjoyable interview I conducted. Equally important, when I reflected on the experience afterwards, I realized I had had a profound shift, from questioning the value of what I was doing to feeling excited about meeting others on my list.

G. David Forney

I interviewed Dave in July, well after my time with Art Carr, who was president of Codex while Dave was vice president of research. I will never forget meeting Dave Forney for he was such a gentleman who never asserted his obviously superior intelligence. When I reached his office, which was in the engineering section but a few steps up from the floor level, he greeted me graciously. As I followed him into his office, I could see most of the four walls had floor to ceiling shelves stuffed with technical books. The floor behind his desk was stacked high with magazines and papers, creating the impression of a very busy man engaged in many projects and managing many engineers and scientists. This proved to be true. I was concerned as I set up my recorder because I was intimidated about how to interview such an accomplished individual. But when it was transcribed, the interview turned out to be only five pages shorter than the one with Art Carr. This wasn't because I was a skilled interviewer, it was indicative of how easy he was to be interviewed.

By the end of our time together, it was crystal clear that the history of Codex owes much to the engineer from MIT with a doctoral degree who took a job with a 12 person company in a second-story office above a tailor shop on Mass Ave. to gain some practical experience.

I and another co-author, Loring G. Robbins, reached out to Dave on many occasions when writing *Circuits, Packets, and Protocols* for help for many reasons, and Dave was always of expert assistance. As with Art, it seemed as if I had made two new wonderful friends.

John Day

John was a very unexpected surprise on many accounts. First of all, he was not on my initial list of people I felt I needed to interview but was added because others strongly encouraged me to talk to him. John proved to be an essential read if one wants to understand the early days/years of the Open Systems Interconnection (OSI) history. In addition, John as a graduate student began participating in the ARPANET Network Working Group, and after receiving his M.Sc. in computer science in 1976, went to work for a local company in Illinois and participated in the International Network Working Group, or INWG. Furthermore, John became a leader in the evolution of the OSI standards. If that wasn't enough, John was an avid and accomplished collector of ancient maps, a habit I have indulged in since meeting John.

When John and I discussed why I wanted to interview him, it devolved into both the longer story of my project and his excitement of how he wanted to affect my conclusions, as well as the fact that I was a venture capitalist and that he had hopes to start a company. For various reasons his schedule brought him to the Bay Area roughly once a month, and when it did, he always looked me up. For years before I moved to Santa Fe, we were developing an intense relationship around his arguments that the ARPANET and therefore the Internet were fundamentally flawed and his intellectual aim to prove that fact. He hoped I would be persuaded by him and would document it in my project. I wanted to understand him, but it went against what I was learning from others I had interviewed and that created problems. John was dogmatic and enjoyed the give and take, however. When I had to go to Boston, we always had dinner and continued our conversations. I always believed his "educating" me helped me write a better history.

My Co-authors:

Andy Russell

I first learned of Andy Russell shortly after I moved to Kula, Hawaii, in early 2007. One night I decided to go out to dinner and, as was my habit, took a stack of reading material with me. On this occasion in my stack of material was an article by Andy Russell titled: "'Rough Consensus and Running Code' and the Internet–OSI Standards War," *IEEE Annals of the History of Computing* 28 (2006): 48–61. I loved the article and couldn't wait to call Andy and introduce myself and hopefully engage him in a conversation. It would be a couple of days before I called only to learn that one of the scientists I had interviewed, John Day, had called Andy on February 4th, a week earlier, recommending that the two of us talk. We did and I shared the historical reconstruction project I was engaged in, and we decided we wanted to collaborate if and when possible.

An opportunity came up in early 2013 when I was in a fix writing one of the last sections of a final chapter, so I called Andy and he was willing to come help me. He proved more than capable and as the week passed, we had time to get to know each other. One of the ideas we discussed was turning my on-line book into a real book, but I didn't think I had the energy or focus. Then in 2017 the CHM requested that to market my website required that I produce a book, I said I could not do it by myself. The president wanted to know whom I would choose, and I said Andy if he could make the time. He wholeheartedly approved, and Andy did as well. Andy then took on the task of finding a publisher and connected us to Tom Misa and ACM. I can't imagine anyone being a better partner, unless if we lived near each other so that we could find the time to work together in person as opposed to using telecommunications. We have not had one argument or rough spot, all the while becoming closer friends. Thank you, Andy, for I am one lucky co-author.

Loring G. Robbins

Not long after I moved to Kula, I concluded I needed to retain a personal trainer to work with me two or three days a week. It wasn't long before I found Loring, and we settled into a wonderful working friendship. Then in 2017 when I took on the project of writing a book with Andy Russell, and I reluctantly concluded that I could no longer hold up my end of our agreement and I needed to find someone to help me, I naturally asked Loring. After a few days of asking questions and reflection, he agreed. The truth is it is a partnership that has turned out better than I think either of us ever imagined, and I can assert has turned out better than I could have ever hoped. Loring has, without doubt, earned his way from helping me to being a co-author with Andy and me. It has been a profoundly wonderful journey, and I know I speak for Andy when I say Loring has contributed his full share in getting this book birthed! It has been fun, with a little stress thrown in, and it is going to be a book we will be very proud of. Thank you my and our friend.

Introduction

Your presence in a global, digitized society depends on modems and routers. These are devices—in every home and business—that, at first glance, may come across as modest and unremarkable. Typically, they are black plastic boxes with a few blinking lights, no larger than a book or small box of chocolates. These unassuming devices sustain and enable the global economy of the 21st century—but you won't find them heralded in most accounts of the digital age.

The purpose of *Circuits, Packets, and Protocols* is to shed some light on the historical origins of today's modems and routers, and the multiplexers and local area networks (LANs) they connect. Although there are many books about the creation of the Internet, the World Wide Web, and digital culture in an age of ubiquitous search and social media, the story of the devices and systems that make it all possible—networking, specifically internetworking—has not yet been told.

The background of our story begins just after World War II, with events that catalyzed the convergence of telecommunications and computing. Our story takes off in 1968 with the Carterfone decision, ARPA's funding of the ARPANET, the first 9,600 bps modem and time division multiplexer, and a rush of minicomputer start-ups.

Our story ends in 1988, for several reasons. First, in 1988 two trade shows—the Enterprise Networking Event and Interop—successfully demonstrated internetworking hardware and software. Computers from different vendors running different operating systems could now share data over diverse communication networks. This had been the goal of networking specialists for nearly two decades. It was accomplished in 1988. Second, 1988 was when one of the authors of this book, James L. Pelkey, began to interview industry and technical leaders in the field. He was interested in understanding this recent history, not predicting the murky future. And he wanted those interviewed to know that he was only interested in the past—a condition readily agreed to by the interview subjects.

Later in this introduction, we further expand on our decision to end our story in 1988—when internetworking had been demonstrated publicly and when the global market for computer communications equipment reached $5 billion, setting the stage for the commercialization of the Internet and the emergence of the World Wide Web. But first, let's preview the most important themes in the extraordinarily dynamic field of computer communications.

Three Themes

The theme of entrepreneurship is front and center. Entrepreneurs, as the economist Joseph Schumpeter described, were the people who were able to transform a new idea into a successful innovation—whether a new product, a new method of production or distribution, a new market, or, in the widest sense, a new industry structure. Schumpeter observed that entrepreneurs had three types of motivations:

> First of all, there is the dream and the will to found a private kingdom... Then there is the will to conquer: the impulse to fight, to prove oneself superior to others, to succeed for the sake, not of the fruits of success, but of success itself... Finally, there is the joy of creating, of getting things done, or simply of exercising one's energy and ingenuity.[1]

Throughout this book, we emphasize two aspects of entrepreneurship. *Vision* involves seeing latent opportunity within a new technology or new way of doing things. *Leadership* is the ability to establish a shared vision and persuade others to work in pursuit of it. When entrepreneurs are effective, it is because they are able to harness the spirit of creativity—that is, to bring a fresh approach to established problems. But as the historian Louis Galambos has pointed out, not all entrepreneurs embody Schumpeter's grandiose, heroic role. Entrepreneurs face confusing, frustrating, and often unresolvable obstacles. Entrepreneurs can work on modest, small-scale problems. And, crucially, not all entrepreneurship is synonymous with starting a business from scratch. Entrepreneurship occurs within existing institutions and it can also take root within non-profit settings, such as in government agencies, academic institutions, professional societies, and technical organizations.[2]

1. Joseph A. Schumpeter. 1983 [1934]. *The Theory of Economic Development: An Inquiry into Profits, Capital, Credit, Interest, and the Business Cycle.* Transaction Publishers, 93.

2. Louis Galambos. 2018. The entrepreneurial culture and the mysteries of economic development. *Essays in Economic & Business History* 36, 290–320; Louis Galambos. 2020. The entrepreneurial culture and bureaucracy in twentieth-century America. *Enterprise & Society* May 12, 2020, https://doi.org/10.1017/eso.2020.15; Louis Galambos. 2020a. The entrepreneurial culture: Mythologies, realities, and networks in nineteenth-century America. *Academy of Management Perspectives* 7 February 2020, https://doi.org/10.5465/amp.2019.0132.

Entrepreneurship tends to refer to individuals, but, paradoxically, entrepreneurship in computer networking required the collaboration of many people working together as teams and in loosely coupled networks. In many cases, acts of entrepreneurship also inspired imitators, which in turn created a critical mass of activity that generated swarms, flurries, and communities of individuals all working on varied aspects and approaches to one big overarching challenge—like the challenge of connecting computers into networks. Our focus on entrepreneurs should not be read as an attempt to diminish the contributions of all kinds of other people—such as managers, executives, administrators, scientists, and engineers. Rather, by featuring entrepreneurs we are highlighting the challenging nature of bringing new technologies to profitable use, and some obstacles that may await those who try to transform existing institutions.

Another of Schumpeter's foundational contributions to the study of business is his memorable insight that entrepreneurship and innovation fuel the "perennial gale of creative destruction." Entrepreneurs trigger these gales through their ability to attract support (in the form of capital) for their ideas. Many chapters in *Circuits, Packets, and Protocols* detail these abilities, typically in the form of venture capital, initial public offerings, and mergers, acquisitions, and divestments. The entrepreneurs in our story worked in a different era than Schumpeter's, and, accordingly, gathered capital in ways that he did not fully anticipate. An important phase of growth and expansion in the availability of venture capital occurred at the same time as the technological developments in our story. Indeed, these developments were connected—evident in the accumulation of wealth among those who led and financed successful corporations in California's Silicon Valley. In addition, regulatory changes in the late 1970s and early 1980s—such as reductions in the capital gains tax and the 1980 Small Business Investment Act—provided further impetus for investment at a crucial phase of transition in the networking industry. Our history shows the many ways that success in business and technology depended upon success in attracting capital, and how increasing returns accrued to successful firms.

Like Schumpeter, our central focus is not the wreckage that is the inevitable consequence of "creative destruction"—although readers will notice how many companies and individuals fall by the wayside in the chapters that follow. The most notable examples of these are the titans of telecommunications and computing at the beginning of our book, IBM and AT&T, which were pale shadows of their former selves by the late 1980s.[3] Rather, our chapters document the "creative" side

3. The literature on these two companies is vast. Two useful starting points are Richard H. K. Vietor. 1994. *Contrived Competition: Regulation and Deregulation in America*. Harvard University Press; James W. Cortada. 2019. *IBM: The Rise and Fall and Reinvention of a Global Icon*. MIT Press.

of the equation—a progression in business development that demonstrates how entrepreneurship can catalyze the growth of individual companies, then multiple companies interacting within a dynamic market-structure that, in turn, generates economic growth and therefore prosperity.

In anticipation of the dozens of entrepreneurs you will meet in the pages that follow, we want to highlight three individuals who played outsized roles in the convergence of telecommunications and computing.

The first is a lawyer, Bernard Strassburg, who spent three decades with the Common Carrier Bureau (CCB) of the Federal Communications Commission. He was named bureau chief on November 22, 1963. At that time, the responsibility of the CCB was largely the regulation of the circuit-switched telephone industry, which meant the regulation of AT&T. Working with a staff economist, Dr. Manley Irwin, Strassburg took aggressive steps to steer the convergence of telecommunications and computing in a way that would serve the public interest—and that ultimately led to the breakup of AT&T.

Second is Paul Baran, an engineer celebrated as the co-inventor (along with Donald Davies) of the packet switching technology that is the foundation of digital networks. While working at RAND, Baran conceived of packet switching as part of a design for a communications system that could survive an attack by nuclear weapons. Throughout his subsequent career, Baran was widely respected as an expert on packet switching and computer communications more generally. He also was an energetic figure in the business world: he was comfortable in social networks and founded seven companies that applied packet-switching technologies to wired and wireless communications and home networking. Baran's career accomplishments were recognized with prestigious awards such as the IEEE Alexander Graham Bell Medal, the Marconi Prize, and the National Medal of Technology and Innovation.

Robert Metcalfe is the third entrepreneur you'll encounter in this book. In 1969, as a graduate student in applied mathematics, he connected MIT's minicomputers to the ARPANET. He quickly became an important member of the ARPANET community. Upon graduating, he worked as a research scientist for Xerox PARC and co-invented Ethernet, a design that enabled local area networking. Metcalfe spent years proselytizing the superiority of Ethernet including the formation of the DEC–Intel–Xerox consortium known as DIX. Afterwards he co-founded 3Com, a computer networking equipment manufacturer that would grow to $251 million in revenue by 1988.

Strassburg, Baran, and Metcalfe illustrate the rich and multifaceted meanings of entrepreneurship that we highlight throughout the book. While Baran and Metcalfe are more in the Schumpeterian heroic mold, Strassburg was a public servant who did not form companies but who was nevertheless profoundly influential.

After entrepreneurship, a second major theme of this book surrounds the tensions that arisc at thc *boundaries of markets and governments*. In somc cascs, governments seek to constrain market actors—such as the antitrust suits that the US federal government pursued against AT&T and IBM over several decades. In other cases, government agencies often subsidize or even coordinate market activity, as with Department of Defense funding for the development of the ARPANET and standards setting activities overseen by the National Bureau of Standards. And in still other cases, governments establish and enforce rules that market participants must follow, such as protection for intellectual property, conditions for market entry, immigration and labor policies, tariffs for international trade, and rules for corporate governance and taxation. The boundaries of markets and governments change over time and across state, national, and international jurisdictions.[4]

A third theme that recurs throughout this book is *learning*. Formal educational institutions played crucial roles, and this era was an important phase of growth for some important computer science programs such as at MIT, Stanford, UCLA, and University of Utah, among many others. Equally important are informal processes such as learning by doing, market research and discovery, and the retraining of engineers and technical staff. Membership on corporate boards sometimes permitted cross-fertilization of ideas, expertise, and tacit knowledge. Successful high-tech firms have access to teams of expert researchers—typically postdocs or graduates of elite universities—who keep abreast of changes in computer science and technology. Additionally, researchers, managers, and investors need their own continuing education. As we will see, learning occurs within *communities* that form, sometimes organically, when students and employees socialized or attended parties together. Experts form insights and knowledge about technology and markets in these venues, outside the typical domains studied by economists, such as market exchanges governed by price mechanisms.[5]

4. Stuart W. Leslie. 2000. The biggest 'angel' of them all: The military and the making of Silicon Valley. In Martin Kenney, ed., *Understanding Silicon Valley: The Anatomy of an Entrepreneurial Region*. Stanford University Press; Mariana Mazzucato. 2013. *The Entrepreneurial State: Debunking Public vs. Private Sector Myths*. Anthem Press, London; Lee Vinsel. 2019. *Moving Violations: Automobiles, Experts, and Regulations in the United States*. Johns Hopkins University Press; Margaret Pugh O'Mara. 2019. *The Code: Silicon Valley and the Remaking of America*. Penguin Press.

5. There is a vast literature on organizational learning and communities of practice. Some good starting points are Naomi R. Lamoreaux, Daniel M. G. Raff, and Peter Temin, eds. 1999. *Learning by Doing in Markets, Firms, and Countries*. University of Chicago Press, Chicago; Urs von Burg. 2001.

Trade shows, demonstrations, professional conferences, and public expositions arguably were the most important sites for learning. These meetings provided opportunities for the public to learn about new technologies and products—and for companies to learn about their competitors. The outsized import of these kinds of meetings is clear at almost every step of our story—from the ARPANET demo in 1971, to the National Computer Conference of 1980, to the Interop expo founded by Dan Lynch starting in the mid-1980s. Our cover image was taken at Interop '88, a meeting that, as we describe in Chapter 13, was a tipping point for the victory of TCP/IP in the international competition to establish internetworking protocols.

These different forms of learning provide the best insurance against the pervasive uncertainty and the chance of failure that are permanent fixtures of high-tech industries. Uncertainty reigns in the early phases of market development, when knowledge and technologies are changing fast, firms have yet to establish organizational capabilities, and customer wants and needs are unknown. The experience gained with diverse combinations of technologies, financial structures, market strategies, and customer feedback is essential for a new field to grow. The failure of specific firms and products can be dramatic and traumatic, but such failures are normal and healthy aspects of the emergence of new market-structures. Most entrepreneurial ventures fail. The reasons are endless: mismanagement, bad luck, poor decisions, bad timing, betting on the wrong technology, inability to adapt to market trends and customer demands. But entrepreneurs, venture capitalists, and larger firms can learn from failures—a process that works best when individuals and organizations learn to see failure as only one stage in a complex and unfolding process of market development.

These three themes—entrepreneurs, market–government boundaries, and learning—are conceptual touchstones for the vast amount of material we present in *Circuits, Packets, and Protocols*. Our emphasis, in a conscious departure from other existing histories of internetworking, is to devote particular attention to the forces that constrained and directed entrepreneurship in the products that enabled computer communication—as well as the consequences of entrepreneurial initiatives.

Sources and Methods

All histories are defined by their starting points and end points. Ours is not the first history of internetworking to start in the late 1960s, but we may be alone in

The Triumph of Ethernet: Technological Communities and the Battle for the LAN Standard. Stanford University Press; Paul Miranti. 2008. Chandler's paths of learning. *The Business History Review* 82, 2, 293–300; Linda Argote. 2013. *Organizational Learning: Creating, Retaining and Transferring Knowledge*. Springer, New York; Mantzavinos, C., Douglass C. North, and Syed Shariq. 2004. Learning, institutions, and economic performance. *Perspectives on Politics* 2, 1, 75–84.

choosing to end our story in 1988—well before the dot-com boom, and even before the invention of the World Wide Web or the commercialization of the Internet.

As noted above, we chose 1988 purposefully. This decision was shaped by Pelkey's interviews of 85 industry and technical leaders during that year. His interviews are an invaluable resource, now available through the Computer History Museum, and this is the first book to use them extensively to understand computer communications. His interviewees include such leaders as Paul Baran, J.C.R. Licklider, Vint Cerf, Robert Kahn, Larry Roberts, Louis Pouzin, Robert Metcalfe, and dozens of others—many of whom are unfortunately unknown in existing histories of the Internet. These interviews, together over 1,887 transcript pages, are a singular resource for historians of computing and business. We encourage you to take a few minutes to read the Preface and Acknowledgments, which convey a sense of the richness of Pelkey's encounters with these dozens of industry leaders. Unless otherwise noted, all quotations in this book are drawn from these interviews. A full list of interviews appears in Appendix A.[6]

To complement these interviews, Pelkey collected data during the late 1980s about three distinct markets—data communication, networking, and internetworking. This data includes detailed firm-level sales and income statements, as well as data published by a variety of sources, including two leading market research firms, Dataquest and Datapro, and two leading investment banks, Alex. Brown & Sons and Montgomery Securities. A summary of these sources appears in Appendix B, Bibliography. These data, in combination with the original interviews, constitute an extraordinarily rich body of source material. They were the foundations of Pelkey's hypertext book, *Entrepreneurial Capitalism & Innovation.*

We co-authors have reflected at length on our interpretations of our source material, as well as our decision to end the narrative in 1988. We have tried, to the best of our abilities, to write these chapters to capture the points of view of our protagonists. That is, we're telling history moving forward. In doing so, we capture the contingency that typically is lacking, especially in histories that seek to explain how the heroes of the digital age came to occupy their places of glory. The messiness, complexity, and uncertainty that we present will feel familiar to all managers and engineers who have stumbled through the confusion of new markets and emerging technologies. Our goal is to show how individual struggles combined, over time, into collective actions of deep significance—Schumpeter's "gale of creative destruction."

In writing this book, we sought to avoid the myopia that results from oversimplified accounts where the "winners write history" and the "losers" are cast

6. In several cases, selections from interviews that appear in this book have been edited for clarity.

aside. These tendencies toward myopia and hagiography are especially prevalent in books about the pioneers of business and technology histories, which are often dominated by successful men such as Edison, Rockefeller, Watson, Gates, or Jobs. Unfortunately, such hero-worship obscures the real challenges that people faced, and the broader and more systemic factors that shaped the emergence of some technologies over rival alternatives.[7] To put the point another way, the biggest difference between our book and every other history of the Internet lies in this simple fact: in our book, standards for Ethernet local area networking and TCP/IP internetworking were not the preordained winners. In fact, when our account ends in 1988, tremendous uncertainty remained about which competing approach to networking and internetworking—Ethernet or Token Ring, TCP/IP or OSI—would emerge as global standards.

The fact that Pelkey's interviews were conducted during this phase of technological and commercial churn—and *before* the final outcome was known—gives them some special characteristics that are now impossible to replicate. In most cases, the people Pelkey interviewed were only dimly aware, if at all, that they might have any "legacy" to defend. Instead, the interviews contain candid reflections from leaders of business, government, and engineering who were, along with their interviewer, trying to piece together the various events that defined the growth of computer communications.

With our approach to historical writing—where the "winners" are not preordained—the technologies we describe can seem bizarre, and the cast of characters can be Tolstoy-esque. If we have been successful, our readers will perceive a viable balance between including enough detail to capture the complexity of the era while also keeping the narrative adequately paced and reasonably bounded. The scale of our analysis evolves; the earlier chapters are broad and engage some sweeping themes of political economy and technology. By the later chapters we're deep in the details of significant conferences, product demos, customer deals, and meetings of standards committees. Whenever possible, we rely primarily on the primary source material that Pelkey created and collected during the 1980s. We have sought to preserve the inherent complexity of the material, without making the narrative unduly complex. To help them get oriented, we encourage readers to consult both the list of acronyms at the beginning of the book and the Appendices and Index at the end.

This book is more a work of historical narrative than it is economic theory, but there is a body of scholarship that has informed and structured our understanding

7. Andrew L. Russell. 2017. Hagiography, revisionism & blasphemy in Internet histories, *Internet Histories: Digital Technology, Culture and Society* 1, 15–25.

of economic change. In particular, we have been guided by work in the fields of complexity theory, industrial change, and evolutionary economics. We have been inspired and influenced especially by scholars such as Brian Arthur, Giovanni Dosi, Louis Galambos, David Lane, David Mowery, Richard Nelson, Douglass North, John Padgett, Carlota Perez, Nathan Rosenberg, and Sidney Winter. It is pleasing to note that this influential literature, sometimes labeled "neo-Schumpeterian," was emerging at the same time as internetworking was evolving.

We believe readers will find it useful for us to describe how *Circuits, Packets, and Protocols* fits alongside existing historical accounts of the convergence of telecommunications and computing. A vast majority of this literature, published since the mid-1990s, documents and explains the sudden rise of the Internet—arguably one of the most consequential technological systems of the 20th century. Scholars writing in this vein track the invention of packet-switching, ARPA's investments in computing, the growth of the ARPANET, Vint Cerf and Robert Kahn's leadership in the creation of the TCP/IP standards, and some of the international collaboration and competition that set the stage for the Internet's global spread.[8] Many of these events took place during the time period that we examine in the pages that follow—and, indeed, we also describe these and related events, primarily through the lens of the interviews Pelkey conducted in the late 1980s. More recently, historians and scholars in related fields have explored the explosive growth of the commercial Internet in the 1990s, driven in large part by its "killer app," the World Wide Web.[9] By and large, the primary goal of historians of the Internet and Web

8. See, for example, Hans Dieter Hellige. 1994. From Sage via Arpanet to Ethernet: Stages in computer communications concepts between 1950 and 1980. *History and Technology* 11, 1, 49–76; Andrew S. Tanenbaum. 1996. *Computer Networks*. Prentice Hall; Arthur L. Norberg and Judy E. O'Neill. 1996. *Transforming Computer Technology: Information Processing for the Pentagon, 1962–1986.* Johns Hopkins University Press, Baltimore; Roy Rosenzweig. 1998. Wizards, bureaucrats, warriors & hackers: Writing the history of the Internet. *American Historical Review* 103, 5 (December 1998); Janet Abbate. 1999. *Inventing the Internet*. MIT Press; Katie Hafner and Matthew Lyon. 1996. *Where Wizards Stay Up Late*; M. Mitchell Waldrop. 2002. *The Dream Machine: J.C.R. Licklider and the Revolution That Made Computing Personal.* Penguin; Urs von Burg. 2001. *The Triumph of Ethernet: Technological Communities and the Battle for the LAN Standard*. Stanford University Press; Andrew L. Russell. 2014. *Open Standards and the Digital Age: History, Ideology, and Networks*. Cambridge University Press; Bradley Fider and Morgan Currie. 2016. Infrastructure, representation, and historiography in BBN's Arpanet maps. *IEEE Annals of the History of Computing* 38, 3, 44–57.

9. See, for example, Tim Berners-Lee and Mark Fischetti. 1999. *Weaving the Web: The Original Design and Ultimate Destiny of the World Wide Web by its Inventor.* Harper, San Francisco; James Gillies and Robert Cailliau. 2000. *How the Web Was Born: The Story of the World Wide Web*. Oxford: Oxford University Press; Shane Greenstein. 2015. *How the Internet Became Commercial: Innovation, Privatization, and the Birth of a New Network.* Princeton University Press; David Kirsch and Brent Goldfarb. 2019. *Bubbles and Crashes*; Shane Greenstein. 2008. Innovation and the evolution of

has been to explain how the Internet came to be. We would draw your attention to the differences between their approach and chronology vis-à-vis ours—particularly since our account ends in 1988, before the commercial Internet traffic was permitted and before the public release of Tim Berners-Lee's World Wide Web browser in 1989.

Over the past decade, and in recognition of the Internet's global importance, the scholarship on Internet and computer networking developments and adoption outside the US has grown considerably.[10] Some of this work has demonstrated the importance of international contributions to the growth of the Internet itself, which is often perceived as a strictly US-based phenomenon. Other accounts have emphasized instead the fact that global adoption of Internet technologies took place against the backdrop of varied national and regional strategies to build networks for data and computer communication. Our story in *Circuits, Packets, and Protocols* complements these histories insofar as we identify and wrestle with the inescapable power of regulation and government power—including the shifting landscape of competition, antitrust, privatization, and intellectual property laws that set conditions for entrepreneurship and corporate change.[11]

market structure for Internet access in the United States. In William Aspray and Paul E. Ceruzzi, eds., *The Internet and American Business*. MIT Press; Janet Abbate. 2010. Privatizing the Internet: Competing visions and chaotic events, 1987–1995. *IEEE Annals of the History of Computing* 32, 1 (January 2010), 10–22; Martin Campbell-Kelly. 2003. *From Airline Reservations to Sonic the Hedgehog*; Tom Nicholas. 2019. *VC An American History*; Niels Brugger and Ian Milligan (Eds.). 2018. *The SAGE Handbook of Web History*. SAGE Publishing.

10. See, for example, Martin Campbell-Kelly. 1987. Data communications at the National Physical Laboratory (1965–1975). *IEEE Annals of the History of Computing*, 9, 3–4 (July–Sept 1987), 221–247; Andrew L. Russell and Valérie Schafer. 2014. In the shadow of ARPANET and Internet: Louis Pouzin and the CYCLADES Network in the 1970s. *Technology and Culture* 55, 4, 880–907; Ben Peters. 2016. *How Not to Network a Nation*. MIT Press; Eden Medina. 2011. *Cybernetic Revolutionaries*. MIT Press; Ignacio Siles. 2020. *A Transnational History of the Internet in Central America (1985–2000): Networks, Integration and Development*. Palgrave Macmillan; Susanne K. Schmidt and Raymund Werle. 1998. *Coordinating Technology*. MIT Press; Thomas Haigh, Andrew L. Russell, and William Dutton. 2015. Histories of the Internet: Introducing a special issue of information & culture. *Information & Culture* 50, 2; Valerie Schafer. 2012. *La France en Reseaux*. Nuvis, Paris; Ignacio Siles. 2012. Establishing the Internet in Costa Rica: Co-optation and the closure of technological controversies. *The Information Society* 28, 13–23; and Martin Campbell-Kelly and Daniel D. Swartz-Garcia. 2013. The history of the Internet: The missing narratives. *Journal of Information Technology* 28, 18–33.

11. See, for example, Jasper L. Tran. 2019. The myth of Hush-A-Phone v. United States. *IEEE Annals of the History of Computing* 41, 4, 6–19; Steven W. Usselman. 2004. Public policies, private platforms: antitrust and American computing. In Richard Coopey, ed., *Information Technology Policy: An International History*. Oxford University Press, Oxford; Steven W. Usselman. 1996. Fostering a capacity for compromise: Business, government, and the stages of innovation in American computing.

Scholars writing about Internet history (and related topics) have been preoccupied with innovation and growth. Such a preoccupation is not unusual for histories of technology, which tend to skew toward novelty—and ours is no exception. With that said, there has been a noticeable uptick in scholarly interest in infrastructure, maintenance, and the underlying material conditions—from rare earth minerals to fiberoptic cables—that sustain access to the Internet.[12] And, general histories of computing have long documented the steady trend of miniaturization (mainframes to PCs to handheld), albeit with a focus mostly on consumer devices instead of middleboxes like modems, gateways, and routers. There are very few books or essays that attend to the individuals and companies who built the modems, multiplexers, and routers that fascinate us and that fill the pages of this book.[13]

As we combed through the substantial published literature, and reflected on the interviews and data that Pelkey collected, we found some structural aspects of computer communication that were not adequately recognized. We concluded that a new concept, a *market-structure*, could best capture some of the nuances that we wish to highlight.

Market-Structures

The basic terms of economic interactions are well known—firms, markets, industries—and thousands of books and articles by historians and economists document their workings.

Firms combine a number of business functions within a single organization. Firms can come into being through the actions of entrepreneurs, whose roles we

IEEE Annals of the History of Computing 18, 30–39; Steven W. Usselman. 2009. Unbundling IBM: Antitrust and incentives to innovation in American computing. In Sally H. Clarke, Naomi R. Lamoreaux, and Steven W. Usselman, eds., *The Challenge of Remaining Innovative: Insights from Twentieth-Century American Business*. Stanford University Press, Stanford, 249–280; Gerardo Con Diaz. 2019. *Software Rights*. Yale University Press.

12. See, for example, Andrew Blum. 2012. *Tubes: A Journey to the Center of the Internet*; Andrew L. Russell and Lee Vinsel. 2018. After innovation, turn to maintenance. *Technology & Culture* 29 (January 2018), 1–25; Brad Fidler and Andrew L. Russell. 2018. Financial and administrative infrastructure for the early Internet: Network maintenance at the Defense Information Systems Agency. *Technology & Culture* 59 (October 2018), 899–924; Brad Fidler and Amelia Acker. 2016. Metadata, infrastructure, and computer mediated communication in historical perspective. *Journal of the Association Information Science and Technology* 68, 2, 412–422; Nicole Starosielski. 2015. *The Undersea Network*. Duke University Press.

13. Ronald R. Kline. 2019. The modem that still connects us. In William Aspray, ed, *Historical Studies in Computing, Information, and Society*. Springer; Jeff Chase with Jon Zilber. 2019. *3Com: The unsung saga of the Silicon Valley startup that helped give birth to the Internet—and then fumbled the ball*. Pseudepigrapha; David Bunnell and Adam Brate. 2000. *Making the Cisco Connection: The Story Behind the Real Internet Superpower*. Wiley.

emphasized above and who are the major subjects of this book. Firms become successful if they can supply products through distribution channels that satisfy the buying demand of a sufficient number of customers. Such firms are vendors of these products. As time passes, firms develop organizational capabilities and often move through different phases, where they test their abilities to compete, persist, and adapt to change. Firms take diverse forms, such as proprietorships, corporations, and multinationals.

Markets are abstract and practical mechanisms that enable buyers and sellers to exchange artifacts, goods, or services. They include vendors in competition and cooperation with each other; they also include customers. Successful markets evolve over time, typically, from a few corporations to a population of many corporations. In many cases, markets can tend toward oligopoly or monopoly, where a single vendor presides over a dominant design for a technology (or service) and has eliminated practically all competitors.

Industries refer to a group of vendors that produce similar products or services. Industries typically are defined by principal product categories or activities, such as automobiles, computers, or mining. Industries can be understood as aggregates of firms that produce for the markets.

These three elements of an economic system—firms, markets, and industries—all fit together within the emergent process that we define as a *market-structure*. This concept points to the dynamic system in which firms, markets, and industries act upon each other and shape one another's trajectories. These dynamic interactions also are shaped by the factors we discussed above, namely, formal and informal institutions for education as well as a variety of government and legal institutions—regulation, investments in research, financial markets, and so on. By using the concept of a market-structure we demonstrate how markets act on an industry; how an industry, in turn, conditions the dynamics of markets; and how individual firms both shape and are shaped by the broader dynamics of markets and industries.

Market-structures are complex, adaptive systems. The economic historian W. Brian Arthur observed, "To look at the economy, or areas within the economy, from a complexity viewpoint then would mean asking how it evolves, and this means examining in detail how individual agents' behaviors together form some outcome and how this might in turn alter their behavior as a result."[14] Clearly, when a

14. W. Brian Arthur. 2013. Complexity economics: A different framework for economic thought. Santa Fe Institute Working Paper 2013-04-012. Retrieved February 7, 2021, from https://www.santafe.edu/research/results/working-papers/complexity-economics-a-different-framework-for-eco.

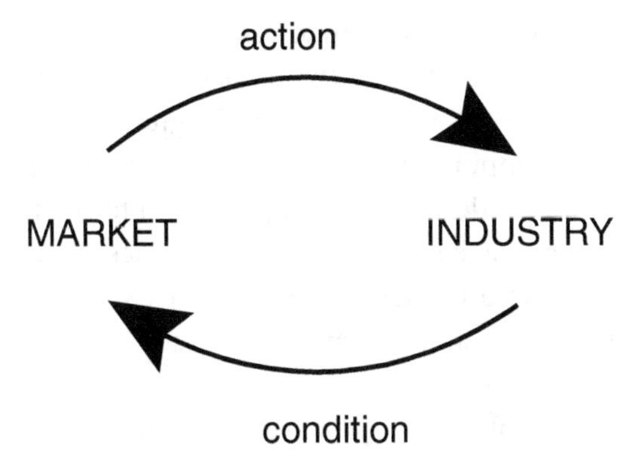

Figure 1 Market-structures. Illustration by James L. Pelkey and Loring G. Robbins.

complex system takes shape, it influences behaviors of the individual agents and actors. These elements are mutually constitutive and ever-changing (see Figure 1). At the same time, there are elements of stability present: the very existence of a market-structure—a firm, market, or industry—indicates that order has been achieved at one scale, even though there can be elements of chaos or disorder at other scales.

Market-structures embody both micro- and macro-economic features, such as: intra- and inter-firm decision-making, interactions between firms, prices, and interactions within markets (all the realm of microeconomics); and government actions such as antitrust enforcement and investments in research, monetary policy, the availability of investment capital, and the fluctuations of business cycles (all in the realm of macroeconomics). There are other institutions and other market-structures that form the environment of any given market-structure. It is this dynamism, complexity, and accounting for change over time that makes the concept useful for us. It is important to distinguish our term "market-structure" from the common term "market structure," as the latter refers to a static picture of actors in a given market. For us, the hyphen is essential because it indicates dynamic interaction. Since our book is a work of history, we ask how market-structures come into being, how they change over time, and how they decline.

One ready example of a market-structure is mainframe computing. IBM introduced the System/360 in 1964, which quickly became a commercial success and prompted other firms to change their behaviors in the market. System/360 became the "dominant design" because IBM was able to anticipate and learn how its customers—especially large manufacturers, government agencies, and universities—could adopt and use computers.[15]

15. Steven W. Usselman. 1993. IBM and its imitators: Organizational capabilities and the emergence of the international computer industry. *Business and Economic History* 22, 1–35; JoAnne

Some firms, such as GE and RCA, lacked the capabilities to keep up, and subsequently exited the market. Their decision allowed IBM to become more dominant. Over time, the cumulative actions of IBM, other firms, and legions of diverse customers changed the nature of the computer market-structure writ large. The same pattern recurred over the next several decades as computer and telecommunication technologies converged around packet-switching technologies. Technologies such as modems, LANs, and routers all emerged from a great variety of experiments and prototypes. Markets grew significantly once variation gave way to standardization, and dominant designs emerged.[16]

Clearly, the behavior of individual firms can have enormous consequences for markets, industries, and market-structures. Firms often struggle to adapt to change, and many firms fail. Firm-level behavior can be likened to the process of niche construction in evolutionary biology: the activities and choices of firms influence other firms, which modify their own behaviors in order to respond to competitors and customers and flourish in the environment (markets). These behaviors generate feedback that informs the overall direction of the process of change. As Schumpeter pointed out, competition takes place on at least two scales: between individual firms within an existing market and in the creation of an entirely new market. These acts of creation proceed from five forms of innovation: products, processes, business models, sources of supply, and mergers & divestments. In other words, it is a mistake to reduce innovation simply to changes in technology. Innovation can and does come from other sources—and, according to Schumpeter, innovation is the lifeline for firms that seek to maintain profitability over the long term.[17]

The developmental dynamics of firms occur within an ecology of social organizations and networks. There are competitive corporations, customers, vendors, law firms, accounting firms, venture capital partnerships, commercial banks, investment banks, governments, standards-making bodies, universities, and more. The

---

Yates. 2005. *Structuring the Information Age: Life Insurance and Technology in the Twentieth Century*. Johns Hopkins University Press.

16. Philip Anderson and Michael L. Tushman. 1990. Technological discontinuities and dominant designs: A cyclical model of technological change. *Administrative Science Quarterly* 35, 4 (Dec. 1990), 604–633. See, especially, page 613 ff, "A dominant design is a single architecture that establishes dominance in a product class. Once a dominant design emerges, future technological progress consists of incremental improvements elaborating the standard and the technological regime becomes more orderly as one design becomes its standard expression." There is a substantial literature on dominant designs, organizational capabilities, and the evolution of technological systems such as electric power, bicycles, automobiles, and computers.

17. Schumpeter, *Theory of Economic Development*.

most important organizations or individuals to a firm are customers, customers which in this history are large corporations. Second in importance are competitors. There are direct competitors, those selling essentially the same product, and indirect competitors selling products that can be used for the same purpose but achieve the functionality through different means. If start-ups and existing firms seeking to capitalize on new technologies introduce similar products within a short period of time, the firm interactions may coalesce into the formation of a new market.

Market-structures proceed through three phases: *emergence*, *competition*, and *order*. (Note that these three phases map to the varying slopes on the S curve that all business students learn.) Emergence can last for many years and will consist of firms ranging from entrepreneurs attempting to form corporations to existing firms attempting to adapt into the new product category. What remains uncertain in the emergence phase is whether the products being commercialized hold enough economic potential to generate the sales to support successful firms. In the competitive phase of market formation, the product category has traction but it remains unclear how large the market will be or how long it will last. It is during this phase that weaker or less successful firms begin being acquired or merge or fail completely. The last phase of market formation, *order*, is when the often hundreds of firms that introduced products have shrunk to an oligopoly of as few as a half a dozen firms controlling two-thirds of the market.

These phases look different in different market-structures, as we'll observe through our study of three distinct market-structures that arose between computer and communications technologies, all in an astonishingly brief period of time, between 1968 and 1988: data communications, networking, and internetworking. Owing to Pelkey's extensive interviews and insider market data, we believe we have the most powerful and compelling set of data and analysis about computer communications available anywhere thus far.

To guide readers through the rich material collected here, we have provided a visual aid in the form of a "Roadmap" that appears in Appendix C. This Roadmap is a guide to the overall narrative and argument so that readers will know how any specific chapter fits into the book's overarching narrative. Finally, before we move on, we would like to highlight and reflect upon the three key terms in our title, *Circuits, Packets, and Protocols*. We purposefully chose these three words to correspond to the dominant technologies of the three market-structures we examine. *Circuits* refers to the circuit-switched telephone network, which was the established infrastructure for communications that became the backbone for modem technologies in the data communication market-structure. *Packets* refers to packet-switching, co-invented by Paul Baran, that created new possibilities for computer networking, manifest in the ARPANET and local area networking.

Protocols refers to the software code necessary to bring intelligence to packet switching, and build networks of networks—that is, internetworks—that blossomed in the 1980s and beyond.

Three Market-Structures at the Intersections of Communications and Computing, 1968–1988

In the late 1950s, corporate America began using computers in earnest. Executives began to take notice of the cost savings and productivity gains promised by Remington Rand, NCR, Burroughs, and the industry leader, IBM, and soon enough GE. Corporate computing began to spread widely in 1960 with IBM's introduction of the 1401, which sold an astounding 2,000 units. With IBM's introduction of the System/360 in 1965, corporate computing changed forever. Soon enough, two additional revolutions in computing reshaped American business: first minicomputers and then personal computers.

Mainframes suited centralized corporate cultures of the 1960s. One big computer, the Host computer, sat in a raised-floor, air-conditioned, often high-security room, with terminals and printers and other peripherals directly wired to it. Over time, however, corporate users wanted to locate terminals and printers at remote locations. To do so required sending the bits over the analog circuits of the telephone system. The devices that facilitated this arrangement were modems—products that converted the digital bits to analog sounds and then back to bits.

Data communications emerged between 1967 and 1971 in response to several factors. The environment for entrepreneurship became more favorable, thanks to regulatory changes in favor of competition and the availability of venture capital. There was also the increasing demand from mainframe users to connect to remote peripherals. As we describe in Chapters 1 and 2, over one hundred firms announced modem or multiplexer products. In 1968, Codex Corporation introduced the world's first 9,600 bit per second modem, and American Data Systems (soon Micom) the first time division multiplexer. Other competitors included Milgo, Infotron, General DataComm, Timeplex, Paradyne, Vadic, and Universal Data Systems. The data communication firms were shielded from new competition through most of the 1970s when market researchers predicted sales to peak at an uninteresting $150 million. In Chapter 4, we'll describe the market order that emerged in the late 1970s; by 1980, worldwide sales of data communication products exceeded $1 billion.

The second market-structure we examine, networking, emerged with the boom in minicomputing. The minicomputer revolution arrived in 1965 when Digital Equipment Corporation, a company financed by American Research and

Development, the first venture capital firm, announced its PDP-8. By 1968, entrepreneurs were flooding into the field of minicomputers; within four years, 92 competitors had announced products. Corporations, governments, and universities bought minicomputers because they were significantly less expensive than mainframes, and application software was readily available. With software readily available and the number of applications growing, corporate and government employees had newfound needs to access multiple computers and peripherals.[18] This need drove market demand for a new kind of product, the second wave in computer communications: networking. This market-structure was engulfed quickly in competitive chaos, with over a hundred firms offering competitive products.

In Chapter 3, we describe some of the origins of networking technologies—particularly packet-switching experiments funded by the US Department of Defense's Advanced Projects Research Agency. In Chapters 5, 6, and 7, we'll focus on the emergence of networking technologies as well as the strong currents of competition in the market-structure, which operated alongside cooperative movements to establish industry-wide standards. Our analysis features both established data communications companies and start-ups that entered markets for LANs.

During the 1970s, the proof that packet switching worked also inspired the creation of many kinds of networks. Three types of local networks evolved from packet switching and were designed for the offices and factories: Ethernet, token ring, and token bus. At first, these LANs did not use the telephone network but rather coaxial cable to interconnect the computers in a building or campus. This distinction would cause the data communication firms to ignore LANs until, often, it was too late.

As the 1970s came to a close, corporate managers purchased minicomputers, and looked for products to help them connect single terminals to multiple computers. In 1979, eager entrepreneurs launched three important LAN start-ups: 3Com, Ungermann-Bass, and Sytek. Along with two leading data communication firms, Codex and Micom, and a variety of other start-ups, companies experimented with different technologies to meet customer demands. Some firms offered products that were incremental improvements on circuit-switching equipment; others embraced the greater speed that packet-switching technologies enabled. The competitive phase of networking was particularly intense as over one hundred firms announced products. Other prominent firms include

18. Nathan Ensemenger. 2010. *The Computer Boys Take Over*. MIT Press; Campbell-Kelly, *From Airline Reservations to Sonic the Hedgehog*.

Interlan, Bridge Communications, Concord Data Systems, Proteon, Excelan, and Communication Machinery Corporation.

When personal computers were introduced in the early 1980s, they illustrated the impact of microprocessors, which were getting smaller and cheaper at the relentless rate described by Moore's Law.[19] Personal computers raised the stakes for networking. When networking first emerged, the need was to interconnect "dumb" computer terminals to multiple computers. The communication speeds were slow and the amount of data sent back and forth was modest. Personal computers would change those dynamics for they could transfer data at significantly higher interconnection speeds and the application software drove the needs for vast amounts of data. When IBM introduced its personal computer in August 1981, corporations went on a buying spree and within two years, more than twice as many personal computers were being bought as terminals. While it would take a few years for the profoundly different bandwidth requirements of personal computing to become evident in consumer demand, eventually packet-based LAN sales soared and circuit-switched data PBX sales collapsed. Not all LAN firms saw the changes being wrought by the personal computer, or reacted quickly enough. Corporations went on a tear installing networks, increasingly personal computer networks, and by 1985, networking sales totaled $1 billion, up from a mere $62 million in 1982. By 1988, it had become clear that the personal computer was giving rise to a new model of corporate computing, client server computing, with the mainframes and minicomputers functioning as data servers for the desktop personal computers. How the networking firms focused on terminal interconnection adapted, or not, to the needs of personal computers will be another focus of this history—and in Chapter 9 we'll see how market order for LANs was established.

The third market-structure of computer communications, internetworking, emerged from the conditions newly created by networking. Corporations soon discovered they had proliferating numbers of diverse networks that created isolated islands of computers. Interconnecting their network islands into larger enterprise-wide networks became the next focus. Fortuitously, many Fortune 500 companies were in the midst of building their own voice communication networks, appropriating the switching and circuits they historically had acquired from the telephone companies. Adding data to these wide area networks (WANs) was relatively easy because the technology was digital. But controlling WANs using circuit switching was still not optimal and again the advantages of packet switching prevailed when

19. Moore's Law refers to the 1965 observation from Gordon Moore, Intel founder, that the number of transistors on an integrated circuit doubles every 18–24 months. David C. Brock, ed. 2006. *Understanding Moore's Law: Four Decades of Innovation*. Chemical Heritage Foundation.

bridges, hubs, gateways, and routers were introduced to interconnect LANs over WANs. A new breed of internetworking firms emerged, including Retix, Cabeltron, Chipcom, StrataCom, Wellfleet, and Cisco Systems.[20] Their products introduced a new architecture and new operating systems designed for packet switching. Data communication firms, and most of the networking firms, were caught flat-footed or were so consumed with other opportunities, or problems, they lost out on what would in time be the largest computer communication market: internetworking.

The emergence of internetworking reflected the growing use of computers and, even more directly, the growing number of diverse networks. With ever-growing numbers of computers and networks, industry standards likewise became an ever-increasing bottleneck for suppliers and users. In Chapter 8 we'll see competition over standards for networking and internetworking. Standards committees, for decades, were widely perceived as the realm of backward-looking engineers who argued over the common denominator for established technologies. But the culture and practices of standards-setting changed with computer communications, where standards committees became forums for engineers to negotiate the parameters of industry for decades to come. In networking and internetworking alike, standards committees were meeting grounds where alliances of individuals and companies could seek to impose their will. In the late 1970s, a number of standards-making efforts were launched. The two that will be observed most closely are IEEE 802, to determine LAN standards, and ISO/OSI, to determine networking and internetworking protocols as well as LAN standards. IEEE 802 issued its Ethernet standard in 1983, and, in subsequent years, token bus and token ring standards. In Chapters 11, 12, and 13, we'll see how these alliances played out for internetworking—a fascinating case where market demand ran well ahead of supply. The OSI standards, especially those embracing LANs, took longer to negotiate. Vendors and customers gravitated to the only standard that was fully public, TCP/IP.

Our story concludes in Chapter 13, with descriptions of two public demonstrations in 1988. Both proved that internetworking could work—that is, computers from many vendors could function together seamlessly. At the Enterprise Networking Event, held in June in Baltimore, the OSI networking protocols were demonstrated in an installation connecting networks on site, in London and by satellite; plus, presentations from 50 vendors with OSI-compliant products and attended

20. In its early years, Cisco employees insisted that the company's name should start with a lowercase c, as homage to their hometown of San Francisco. Eventually, the company adopted the capitalized version of its name, although traces of the original spelling persisted in technical literature and software manuals for many years.

by an estimated 10,000 to 11,000 people. The focus was on large-scale connectivity across nations, government networks, and large industries like manufacturing. Interop was the third workshop organized by one individual entrepreneur, Dan Lynch, who had been instrumental in the transition of the ARPANET NCP to TCP/IP. The Interop Exhibition held in Santa Clara focused on the application of TCP/IP in internetworking products. In contrast to ENE, which was sponsored by government agencies and large corporations, Interop began with the continued leadership of Dan Lynch and a group of 54 vendors who were eager to present products and solutions to the specific challenges of interconnecting a wide variety of networks. Indicative of the interest in TCP/IP, Interop was attended by over 5,000 people.

In sum, the chapters in provide a new view of some deeply significant developments in computer history—and, arguably, world history. As we discuss in the next section, we're all still grappling with the consequences—good and bad—that follow from widespread adoption of internetworking. The fine-grained details of the entrepreneurs and researchers we present here shed light on the underlying and systemic relationships—the market-structures—that help us frame generalizations about technological and economic change. In the Conclusions, we'll apply some of our own lessons to analyze the internetworking market-structure in the decades after 1988. There, we will only gesture at some of the significant companies and issues since we do not have the same documentary basis of interviews and market data that inform our analysis of the earlier period. Accordingly, we end the book with an invitation to readers to apply the concepts and ideas that we use throughout the book, and let us know if you, too, find them helpful.

Why Do These Stories Matter?

The shift we document in this book—from centralized mainframe computers to internetworked personal computers—introduced changes in everyday life that were already obvious by 1988. Three decades later, and we now confront the ubiquity of smartphones, social media, and the "Internet of Things" that connects watches, cars, toilets, toasters, and so much more.

The economic value of internetworking is indisputable—just think about the stock market valuation of companies such as Google, Amazon, Facebook, and thousands of others around the world whose existence depends on internetworking technologies. The 20 years that we scrutinize in *Circuits, Packets, and Protocols* laid the foundations not only for the explosive business growth of the web and social media but for the economic and technological foundations of the global economy more generally. The products described in this book—modems, local area networks, and routers—should be considered as the essential "black boxes" of the global digital economy.

The changes that took place between the late 1960s and the late 1980s need to be understood in much finer detail. Through the Schumpeterian processes of innovation and creative destruction, a new global information infrastructure was established. There is a compelling analogy between digital data networks and the development of railroads in the mid-19th century. In both cases, technologies were at the heart of new, lucrative market-structures: the production of locomotives, steel rails, and freight and passenger operations; and the production of modems, LANs, and routers. These technologies also served as platforms or infrastructure for a vast range of social and economic activity, a function that economists and economic historians characterize as general-purpose technologies.[21] Scholars often pay attention to the linear aspects of infrastructure – railroad tracks, submarine cables, overhead telephone and telegraph wires, and today's globe-spanning optical fibers. But equally important are the connections between these lines: railroad switches and stations, telephone switchboards and central offices, and modems and routers. These points of connection are essential since they ensure that the entire infrastructure can be utilized efficiently.[22]

The two decades between 1968 and 1988 were remarkable times in American life, and we believe that some of the personalities and social dynamics we describe will contribute to the rich, textured understanding of American society. In the realm of political economy, the broader trends of deregulation and Reaganism are evident as the broader context behind rapid changes in technology and the growth of entrepreneurial capitalism that we document. These decades saw an alignment of regulation, technology, learning, and the availability of capital that was quite unlike other decades in the 20th century—and we see our story as a contribution to the effort to explain why change appears to happen with different intensities at different times. The self-evident international and global impact of digital, internetworked technologies also should be understood in large part as a product of distinctively American forms of political economy that prevailed between 1968 and 1988.

Pelkey started this project in the late 1980s because he wanted to make history meaningful and understandable to people who experienced it and lived through

21. Timothy Bresnahan and Manuel Trachtenberg. 1995. General purpose technologies: 'Engines of Growth'? *Journal of Econometrics*, Special Issue 65 (January 1995), 83–108.

22. Thomas Parke Hughes. 1993. *Networks of Power: Electrification in Western Society, 1880–1930.* Johns Hopkins University Press; Steven W. Usselman. 2002. *Regulating Railroad Innovation: Business, Technology, and Politics in America, 1840–1920.* Cambridge University Press.

that time, even though they might not have grasped the momentous technological changes happening around them. Like most people, Pelkey did not anticipate that the subject that captivated him would turn out to be such a crucial—and understudied—chapter in modern history. Rather, as an investor in computer communications, he felt that it was important to try to make sense of developments in the field for others who didn't have access to industry experts, and who might not have a passion for understanding the details of circuits, packets, and protocols. In a general sense, then, we hope readers appreciate that our book is simply an effort to explain the origins of the digital networks that surround, sustain, entertain, and bedevil us.

From our present vantage point, it's not at all clear how the long-term effects will shake out. We're currently in the midst of a "techlash"—a backlash against Silicon Valley companies and their products, which once promised to liberate users, but now appear equally likely to be tools of surveillance and oppression. Depending on who you ask, or how you're feeling, you may find different answers to some fundamental questions: Have these technologies led to widespread progress—or to inflated stock markets and deflated wages and sagging incomes? Has the unleashing of entrepreneurial energies been a good thing—and how widely shared have been the economic gains? As readers contemplate some hot-button issues of the day—net neutrality, the power of social media companies, the fates of privacy and security in a digital environment devoted to surveillance—they stand to benefit by learning more about how our digital, internetworked world came into existence. We hope that readers will gain a richer understanding of the dynamism, fragility, and complexity of socio-technical systems—as well as appreciation for the individuals who brought these systems to life.

Prelude to Change: Data Communications, 1949–1968

1.1 Overview

Some of the most iconic moments of the 1960s involved the blending of technology and ideas in new ways. Whether it was Neil Armstrong's walk on the surface of the moon or Jimi Hendrix's burning guitar in Monterey, the foundations of an astonishing era of technology-based change were being forged. And as with all iconic moments, hundreds of people and decades of effort went into the changes that crystallized in public perceptions as a history-altering spectacle. The 1960s were likewise a pivotal decade for the data communications industry, even if there was little public fanfare to accompany the key developments. Throughout this book we describe *market-structures*—dynamic relationships between markets and populations of firms that pursue similar product opportunities. During the 1960s, the market-structure for data communications slowly began to emerge, in spite of the dominance of two giant firms AT&T and IBM. The principal obstacle to the emergence of the data communications market-structure was AT&T's contesting the attachment of any devices not of its own, as well as the interconnection of other networks, to 'its' telephone network. But as we will see in this chapter, the FCC reversed its long-standing support of AT&T in 1968 and allowed independent companies to sell equipment that connected to the public telephone network. The FCC's decisions transformed telecommunications—clearing a path for a rush of new businesses forming around new technologies and the growing adoption of business computing. But before we get to the fateful events of 1968, and the extraordinary events of the next two decades that are the main subject of this book, we need to begin with a brief review of some of the important decisions and events that occurred between the end of World War II and 1968. We have organized this history into five sections: the federal government and its interactions with AT&T,

the emergence of the dominant computing firm IBM, technological innovation, new sources of capital, and entrepreneurial individuals who contributed to the emergence of the data communications market-structure.

1.2 AT&T, The Regulated Monopoly

Alexander Graham Bell invented telephony in 1876 and created the American Telephone & Telegraph Company in 1885. After a phase of competition with other telephone companies, AT&T became the most powerful telephone company in the United States. Its status as a regulated monopoly was established with the Kingsbury Commitment of 1913, a truce between AT&T and the Department of Justice. As a consequence, AT&T became the largest corporation in America by 1949, with revenue of $2.893 billion and net income of $233 million.[1] Enjoying the privileges of a monopoly, however, also invited the constant scrutiny of state and federal regulatory agencies.

When Harry S. Truman won the presidential election in 1948, he moved quickly to create an Administration with people who believed, as he did, in the aggressive use of antitrust to save the economy for competition. Monopolies were the enemy. And AT&T, the biggest of them all, had escaped the leveling cleaver of antitrust. Or so they believed. Holmes Baldridge, who became the new chief of the Antitrust Division's General Litigation Section, had for years harbored frustrations that AT&T had not been punished after an investigation during the 1930s—an investigation of which he had served as chief counsel.[2]

1.2.1 Hush-a-Phone

Baldridge had fresh justification handed to him on December 22, 1948, when the Hush-A-Phone Corporation filed a complaint with the FCC against AT&T. The complaint charged that AT&T's Foreign Attachment Tariff Restrictions prohibited telephone subscribers from using the Hush-A-Phone, a product that had been available since 1929. It was simply a plastic cup that fit over the telephone microphone to increase the privacy of telephone conversations and reduce extraneous noise. As innocent as it would seem, AT&T and the Bell operating companies interpreted the Foreign Attachment Tariff Restrictions as a very clear prohibition against any type of physical attachment to any AT&T equipment or facility, period—including a plastic cover on a telephone book in a public phone kiosk. AT&T's formidable legal

1. $2.893 billion in 1949 is equivalent to $31.6 billion in 2020.

2. "Baldridge later made it clear, at congressional hearings long after he left the government and after the case ended with a consent decree, that the complaint had been largely his personal project." Fred W. Henck and Bernard Strassburg. 1988. *A Slippery Slope: The Long Road to the Breakup of AT&T*. Greenwood Press, 57.

department argued, quite forcefully, that federal regulations were on their side. In place since 1911, the Tariff read:

> Equipment, apparatus and lines furnished by the Telephone Company shall be carefully used and no equipment, apparatus or lines not furnished by the Telephone Company shall be attached to, or used in connection therewith, unless specifically authorized in this tariff.[3]

Inspired by the growing number of complaints, on January 14, 1949, the Justice Department filed a civil antitrust suit against AT&T and its manufacturing subsidiary, Western Electric (WE). The Justice Department charged that the two companies had established a monopoly in the manufacture, distribution, and sale of telephone equipment. It asked the court to force WE to sell its 50% interest in Bell Labs to AT&T; divest AT&T of WE and split WE into three separate companies; require AT&T to bid all purchases competitively; and to license its patents to all applicants. Baldridge was not deterred by the conclusion from a recent investigation by California regulators that WE prices were 45% below an average of *independent* manufacturers' prices.[4] Under Baldridge, the Justice Department had clarity of purpose: AT&T was a monopoly. It needed to be broken up.

To defend itself, AT&T relied on a decades-old strategy: any chips in its technical foundation would undermine its exceptional technological service for the American public. Mike Slomin, who served as an FCC staff attorney in the 1970s, summarized AT&T's strategy in a 1988 interview: "Well, you know, the Hush-A-Phone distorts speech, and any one of 200 million people in this country might be called by, or might call, someone using a Hush-A-Phone. They're going to get a lousy telephone call. That's harm. They're not getting what they paid for."[5] The power in this defense was that it appealed both to the technological complexity of the telephone system as well as to AT&T's carefully crafted image as a civic-minded monopoly, one that had the unique and sacred responsibility of ensuring quality service for all Americans. The small office caught in the middle of this debate—AT&T on one side and antitrust regulators on the others—was the FCC's Common Carrier Bureau (CCB or bureau). The CCB eventually responded to its difficult position by acting creatively, and, ultimately, paving the ground for the emergence of a new market-structure.

3. Jordaphone Corp. of America and Mohawk Business Machines v AT&T, Decision, 18 FCC 644 (1954).

4. Alan Stone and William L. Stone. 1989. *Wrong Number—The Breakup of AT&T*. Basic Books.

5. Mike Slomin, oral history interview by James L. Pelkey, March 10, 1988, Allentown, NJ. Computer History Museum, Mountain View, CA. Available from https://archive.computerhistory.org/resources/access/text/2017/09/102740208-05-01-acc.pdf.

On February 16, 1951, the FCC released its initial decision and dismissed the Hush-a-Phone complaint in favor of AT&T. Hush-a-Phone petitioned for review, which sent the case into another phase of oral arguments and expert testimonies. As the months passed, AT&T successfully marshaled Department of Defense (DOD) support for their cause. DOD personnel began lobbying for case dismissal. AT&T had become indispensable to the DOD. It had recently taken on management of Sandia National Laboratories (responsible for the US nuclear stockpile). Moreover, in 1952 AT&T responded to the Defense Department's request for help in constructing a strategic air defense system. AT&T's role was to design an instrument capable of transmitting digital data over the analog telephone lines, and to design and build a telephone network connecting radar sites in Northern Canada to computers in the States and then onto aircraft and missile sites. This initiative would have lasting consequences for the Data Communication market-structure, as well as for the convergence between communication and computer technologies and market-structures.

The antitrust negotiations between the Justice Department and AT&T that began in the spring of 1953 had now dragged on for over two years. In the fall of 1955, the Justice Department once again solicited FCC advice on the issues of the antitrust suit. The chief of the CCB prepared the first response. The Commissioners thought it too weak in representing FCC powers and sent it back for redrafting. The job was assigned to CCB staff lawyer Bernard Strassburg—an individual who would go on to play a pivotal role over the next decades. Strassburg's response emphasized the Commission's powers to examine rate bases and to take appropriate actions, pointing out rate reductions that had been negotiated.

Independently, on December 21, 1955, Judge David Bazelon handed down the Court decision on the Hush-A-Phone case. Judge Bazelon reasoned that since the same effect of the Hush-A-Phone plastic cup could be created by cupping one's hands around the microphone, such a tariff was an:

> Unwarranted interference with the telephone subscriber's right reasonably to use his telephone in ways which are privately beneficial without being publicly detrimental. Prescribing what changes should be made in the tariffs to render them "just, fair, and reasonable" and determining what orders may be required to prohibit violation of subscribers' rights thereunder are functions entrusted to the Commission.[6]

Henceforth, independent equipment suppliers would be able to sell equipment that attached to the PSTN without requiring AT&T permission beforehand. What

6. Hush-A-Phone v. United States, 238 F.2d 266 (D.C. Cir. 1956).

mattered was that the conditions of being "privately beneficial without being publicly detrimental" were met. Hush-a-Phone's plastic cups, in the end, were proverbial stones in the hand of David that created the first chips in the foundations of AT&T's monopoly. AT&T responded by changing their tariff restrictions to allow foreign attachments, but only if they did not "endanger telephone employees, property or service." AT&T continued to restrict foreign attachments, thus ensuring that the debate over the boundaries of its monopoly power would continue.

Accordingly, the career staff in the Justice Department continued to keep a close watch on AT&T and other large firms, guided by prevailing economic theories that monopolies would inhibit innovation. Even so, the political winds above them had shifted. The election of Dwight D. Eisenhower as President in 1952 resulted in a more conservative, pro-business philosophy of antitrust enforcement. The Justice Department sought to resolve as many of the 144 active antitrust cases as quickly as possible.

This left a major impact on AT&T and the communications industry, namely when the Justice Department and AT&T announced on January 24, 1956, that an out-of-court settlement of US v. Western Electric had been reached. In some of the key terms of the agreement, AT&T:

1. Did not have to divest Western Electric, although Western Electric could not manufacture equipment other than that used by the Bell System, or the Government.
2. Was enjoined and restrained from engaging in any business other than the furnishing of common carrier communications services.
3. Was required to license Bell patents to any applicant that agreed to pay a reasonable royalty and agreed to make available their patents to Bell.

The significance of these latter two aspects of the Consent Decree—preventing AT&T from competing in the computer industry and licensing the Bell System's patents—can hardly be overstated. As we will see, the long-term dynamism of the data communications and internetworking market-structures flowed from these restraints on AT&T. But in the near and medium term, AT&T's continued ownership of Western Electric and continued monopolistic control over telephone service generated tremendous profits: from 1949 to 1968 the revenues of AT&T grew from $2.893 billion to $14.0 billion, or by 380%.

Again, AT&T had foiled the Federal Government's efforts to introduce competition into telecommunications. In essence, no one was willing to risk the uncertainty of what might happen if AT&T were forced to do what it steadfastly resisted; and not without reason, for not only had AT&T created the world's finest telephone system but as the world's largest corporation any negative impact on its hundreds of thousands of employees and shareholders would certainly have political consequences. So, the Justice Department did what it could to prevent the monopolist from interfering with other competitive markets, and constrained AT&T, and WE, to common carrier communications.

AT&T had equally fought off the efforts of other companies to connect non-AT&T devices to their network. Granted, their tariffs had to be "just, fair, and reasonable," but who was to say what those words meant other than AT&T; and challenging AT&T's interpretations had proven lengthy, and expensive, with little hope the FCC would rule against AT&T. The tradition of fighting any changes at the periphery of the network, a tradition dating to the 19th century, had again proven successful: AT&T's monopoly remained intact.

So, the world of telecommunications, as in AT&T, had walled itself away, steeling itself against change, seemingly harmonious with the pace of the 1950s, but soon to be at odds with the great changes to be introduced by computers. They were already facing the massive investment and challenging task of managing the conversion of their network from analog to digital. One of the reasons Bell Labs was innovating computers was to use them as digital switches. As a result, it made sense for AT&T to get into the computer business, both because they were one of the largest customers of IBM and Digital Equipment Corporation (DEC), and because Bell Labs was already designing and building computers. But the 1956 Consent Decree they had just signed prohibited their entering competitive markets.

1.2.2 Challenges to AT&T: MCI and Carterfone

Another set of business and legal challenges to AT&T came from aspiring competitors who petitioned the FCC to allow access to wireless frequencies for private communications. In 1956, a number of trade associations and manufacturers of microwave equipment lobbied the FCC for more relaxed regulation of the use of radio frequencies for private installations. This prompted the FCC to review its policies for allocating radio frequencies. A few years later, in 1959, the FCC ruled, in what would be known as the "Above 890" decision, that private companies could use radio frequencies above 890 megacycles (microwave frequencies) for use to meet private transmission needs.

In 1963, a company was launched that few at the time had any idea would become a serious competitor to AT&T. The original idea for the business came from a motivated entrepreneur who saw the opportunity in microwave technology to increase the sales of his short-wave radio equipment and service business. John D. "Jack" Goeken along with Donald and Nicholas Phillips, Leonard Barrett, and Kenneth Garthe founded Microwave Communications Inc. (MCI) on

October 3, 1963. Goeken's vision was to offer shipping companies in the Midwest affordable microwave communication lines, between truckers along Route 66 between Chicago and St. Louis, and between barges on the Illinois Waterway. Customers would share the same line so that their rates would be far less than was offered by the telephone company. Goeken planned to connect two-way radios with microwave relay stations—in short, a service for mobile business communications. Goeken filed an application for a license to the FCC in December 1963. In addition to the always pressing need to raise money, Goeken and the other founders knew they needed legal help. In January they hired Haley, Bader and Potts. Attorney Michael Bader, having recently fought a successful case against AT&T over a television microwave relay system in Texas, thought that if MCI were successful, this new area of communications law would be a promising source of business for his firm. Goeken and Bader began the lengthy process of making presentations to FCC commissioners and staff. Eventually, a hearing before Herbert Sharfman, the examiner appointed by the FCC, was scheduled for February 1966.[7]

As Bernard Strassburg, who had become chairman of the CCB in November of 1963, prepared to make the bureau's recommendations on the MCI application, he wasn't convinced Goeken and his company could deliver on their goal of a private microwave communication service. However, after consulting with two economists, Manley Irwin and William Melody, Strassburg decided that approving the MCI application would be a good way to test the waters of competition in the communications market. Convinced that the growing demands for new communications technologies would add to the market and stimulate additional communication services, he urged the FCC to grant the application. On July 1967, the CCB sent Sharfman their "Proposed Findings of Fact and Proposed Conclusions" recommending approval of the MCI application. Sharfman released the preliminary response in favor of MCI in October of 1967.

In the meantime, another wireless entrepreneur had made himself a thorn in AT&T's side and asked the federal government to stop the monopolist from crushing him. Thomas Carter was an easy-going entrepreneur from Texas—a practical man who invented a clever device named the Carterfone. His invention was motivated by the simple desire to solve the communication problem of oil field workers, far from phones, maybe aboard an offshore oil rig, trying to reach home.

It's important to note that Carter, like MCI's Goeken, was seeking to meet the communication needs of business users. Neither was looking to create a mass-market gadget; and neither was using output from a research lab to create new

7. Philip Louis Cantelon. 1993. *The History of MCI 1968–1988: The Early Years*. Heritage Press, 31–47.

technologies. Rather, these were practical men who saw opportunities for devices that could solve practical problems that arose in the course of ordinary business.

The Carterfone was a device that connected a two-way radio to the telephone network (see Figures 1.1 and 1.2). It would allow calls between users on a two-way radio and users on the telephone network. Once an operator made the connection between the two callers by placing the phone handset on the acoustic cradle, the Carterfone automatically transmitted the signal from the telephone handset to the radio and then stood by to receive the voice signal from the radio. The operator of the Carterfone could then monitor the call and adjust levels manually if needed.

When Carter first introduced the Carterfone in 1959, he had been surprised to learn the reasons why the telephone company objected to its use: it interfered with their end-to-end service responsibility and could be harmful to telephone service. As a result, it violated the tariffs banning foreign attachments to the telephone network. Carter was not so easily discouraged and sold Carterfones anyway—

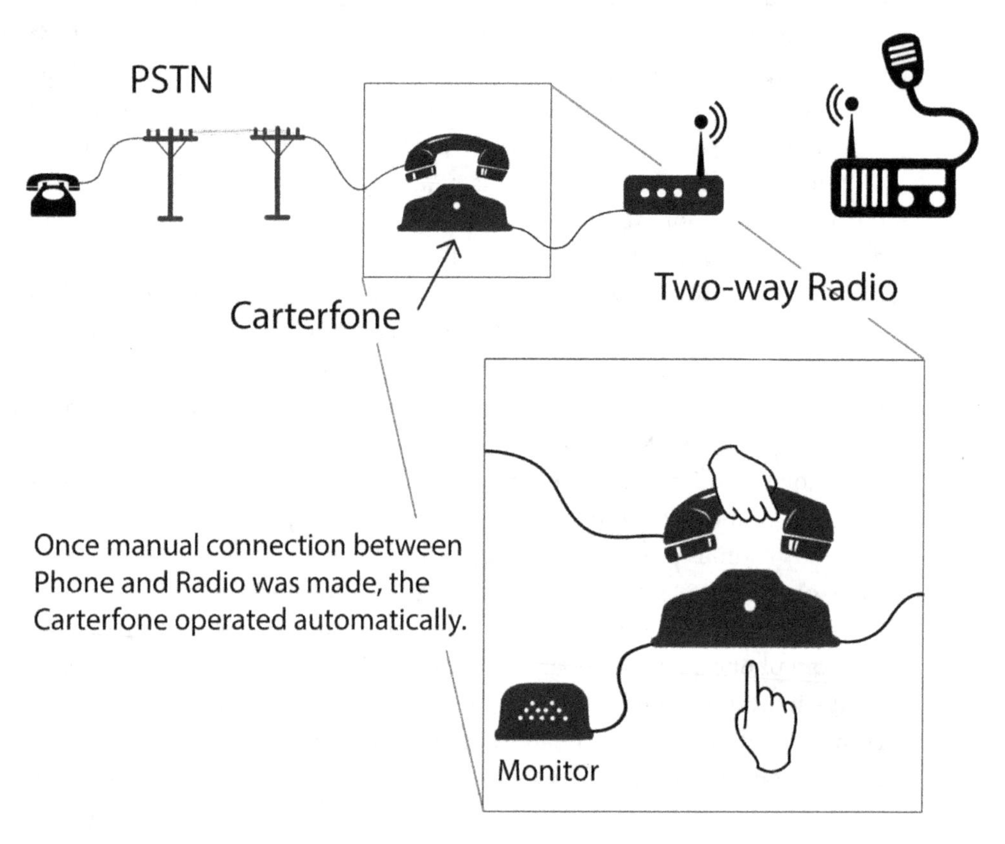

Figure 1.1 Carterfone connections with telephone and radio networks. Source: Illustration by Loring G. Robbins.

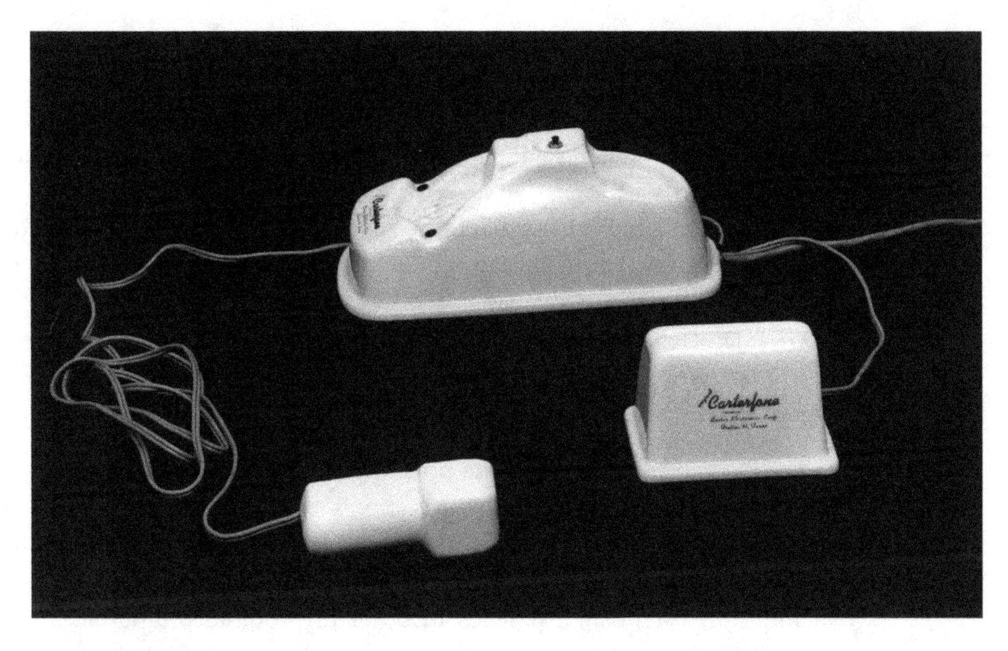

Figure 1.2 The Carterfone. Source: Image courtesy AT&T Archives and History Center.

approximately 3,500 units in the United States and overseas by 1966. But threats that the telephone company would terminate customers' telephone service posed a real obstacle to sales, so in 1966 Carter brought an antitrust suit against the Bell System and the General Telephone Company of the Southwest. The United States District Court, Northern District of Texas, referred Carter's case to the FCC under the doctrine of primary jurisdiction to resolve questions of whether the tariff permitting telephone companies to suspend, or terminate, service if non-AT&T devices were connected to telephone company facilities was valid. The key issue was one of "foreign attachments."

Once at the FCC, the Carterfone case was referred to the CCB, the same office that had dealt with the Hush-A-Phone controversy in the 1950s. The CCB scheduled hearings to collect information for both cases—MCI and Carterfone—for 1967. At the same time, bureau staff members were mobilizing to have an unprecedented public discussion about the future of communication services in the United States, with an eye toward anticipating technological changes that could alter long-established regulations and market-structures.

Strassburg, who had written the Bureau's opinion for the Hush-a-Phone matter, was beginning to speak publicly about the profound technological, political, and economic challenges that he saw on the horizon. In 1965, Strassburg assembled a task force to examine data communications, and spoke regularly—and publicly—

with industry professionals on subjects such as market entry, information privacy, and the coming convergence of computers and common carrier communications. He remarked in a 1966 speech: "Few products of modern technology have as much potential for social, economic and cultural benefit as does the multiple access computer."[8]

The far-reaching consequences that he discerned prompted him to view the FCC's role, and his bureau's role, in a broader way than one might expect from a career government lawyer steeped in the philosophy of supporting the monopolistic AT&T. On October 20, 1966, he gave a speech to an audience of computer and data processing professionals in which he articulated his understanding of the responsibilities and roles of the FCC:

> The Commission is obliged by the policies and the objectives of the Communications Act to ensure that the nation's communication network is responsive to the requirements of an advancing technology. The Commission has the obligation, the authority, and the means to reappraise and refashion any established policies in order to promote the public interest through an effective realization of the social and economic benefits of current technology.[9]

In early 1967, Haakon Ingolf (H.I.) Romnes, who had previously been President of Western Electric, became AT&T's new Chairman and Chief Executive Officer. Romnes did not fully subscribe to AT&T's long-standing policy of opposing foreign attachments. Shortly after taking office, he expressed the opinion that Bell's responsibility for the network could be maintained if there were "suitable interfaces or buffer devices to keep the attached equipment from affecting other users of the network."[10]

The MCI hearings began in February and lasted nine weeks. The Carterfone hearings were scheduled next, for April. Fred Henck, Editor of the respected trade publication *Telecommunications Reports*, would comment later that it was hard to find someone to report on these two insignificant cases, referred to around the office as the "cats and dogs."[11] Strassburg, on the other hand, began to see the

8. Bernard Strassburg. 1968. The marriage of computers and communications—Some regulatory implications. *Jurimetrics Journal* 9, 1, 12–18.

9. Strassburg, "The marriage of computers and communications."

10. Peter Temin and Louis Galambos. 1987. *The Fall of the Bell System: A Study in Prices and Politics*. Cambridge University Press, 44.

11. "At *Telecommunications Reports*, we reflected the view of our news sources that neither case was very important. Our main problem was finding someone on our small staff with enough time to cover what we considered rather insignificant hearings. Along with a few other minor cases going

Carterfone hearings as a way to revisit the foreign attachments tariff, which, as he was increasingly learning, was a real impediment to the use of the telephone system for data processing and to innovation of communication devices. He reflected on this period in a 1988 interview:

> We used the Carterfone issue and the Carterfone proceeding as a vehicle for revisiting the policy, which was basically a Bell System policy, which had been embraced by the FCC and the regulatory commissions for many generations, against customers, willy-nilly, interconnecting anything they chose to the telephone network, no matter how innocuous it might be unless the item was specifically authorized by the telephone company's tariffs. Well, the telephone company wasn't likely to tariff anything of consequence, so as a result, anytime anybody wanted to promote a piece of equipment and to have it work with the telephone network, they either had to sell it to the Bell System, if they could convince Western Electric and Bell that they had something sellable, or if they couldn't succeed in that channel, then attacking the tariff insofar as the claim was unlawful – and that the Commission should order it amended in order to accommodate their device. But that was a very cumbersome process to go through; the administrative hearing and the time and the cost involved that, to a small entrepreneur with a piece of equipment – it discouraged people. It discouraged the market from developing, and that's why, I think, the United States was so far behind other countries, because, in terms of customer-premise equipment, simply because there was no entrepreneurship, the entrepreneurship was blunted and discouraged by this institutionalized practice of saying: "You can't connect with us." In other words, everything that went on had to go on within the Bell System, Bell Laboratories. That was where innovation began and ended.[12]

When it came time to argue the Carterfone case before the Hearing Examiner, Chester F. Naumowicz, Jr., the CCB took the position that the tariff provisions limiting use of customer-provided equipment be canceled. It should be replaced, instead, by a clear and affirmative statement that "customer-provided equipment, apparatus, circuits, or devices may be attached or connected to the telephones furnished by the telephone company... for any purpose that is privately beneficial to

on at the time, the Carterfone and MCI hearings were referred to generically in the office as 'cats and dogs.'" Henck and Strassburg, *A Slippery Slope*, 102.

12. Bernard Strassburg, oral history interview by James L. Pelkey, May 3, 1988, Washington, DC. Computer History Museum, Mountain View, CA. Available from https://archive.computerhistory.org/resources/access/text/2015/11/102738016-05-01-acc.pdf.

the customer and not publicly detrimental."[13] In other words, the CCB was not arguing that users could substitute customer-provided equipment for that provided by the telephone company—only that it should be permissible to connect or attach devices to telephones furnished by the telephone company.[14]

The Carterfone hearings took but seven days. Maybe sensing a fundamental change in progress, Romnes assembled a high-level Tariff Review Committee to conceive alternative interconnection tariffs that would protect the network. The facts that AT&T permitted connection of foreign attachments by the military and government, as well as equipment of TV networks, all suggested there had to be a solution other than total prohibition.

In August 1967, Examiner Naumowicz issued his initial decision. Ignoring the argument for a broad policy change, he ruled narrowly that harm from use of the Carterfone had not been proven. Left unsettled were the overarching questions about how AT&T could defend the boundaries of its monopoly, and how the FCC and courts would define that monopoly in the face of technological change and entrepreneurial incursions.

1.3 IBM

Now to the story of the emergence of the computer industry, the features that made it so attractive to AT&T, and the potential that made it so concerning to Bernard Strassburg in his new role as chief of the bureau.

At the end of World War II, when AT&T dominated telecommunications as a regulated monopoly, IBM was a large corporation that dominated the office equipment market. It did not even enter the computer market until 1952. Yet within a few decades, IBM was ascendant—the largest computer firm within an oligopoly of a few firms. How that happened is critical to our history.[15]

13. Henck and Strassburg, *A Slippery Slope*, 104–105.

14. "We were also being very cautious in how far we thought the tariffs ought to be amended and how far we ought to go. We didn't view the issues in Carterfone as having to do with any replacements or substitutions for the equipment provided by the telephone company. It was how the telephone service provided by the telephone company, including the instrument, the terminal, should interface with other equipment and under what circumstances it should permit connection to other equipment which it didn't provide. We were not talking about eliminating or abandoning this whole concept of end to end responsibility by the telephone company. We were talking about what can be done at each end by the customer with the service that he buys from the telephone company." Strassburg interview, Computer History Museum.

15. See, generally, James W. Cortada. 2019. *IBM: The Rise and Fall and Reinvention of a Global Icon.* MIT Press.

IBM was already a substantial and successful company before the idea of selling computers ever crossed the minds of any IBM executive, in particular, Thomas Watson, Jr., the son of the president and CEO. In 1949, the revenues of IBM were $183 million, every dollar of which came from the office equipment market, which had been their primary source of revenue ever since their inception. None came from computers.

The initial genius and entrepreneur of IBM was Herman Hollerith who was the inventor of punch card tabulation machines in the mid-1880s. In 1911, he sold his company, Tabulating Machine Company, to Charles Flint, who merged it with two other firms he had recently acquired to form the Computing-Tabulating-Recording Corporation (C-T-R), the recognized starting point of IBM, although it was not until 1924 that they changed the name to International Business Machines. Thomas J. Watson, Sr., was hired as the general manager in 1914 after a successful career with the National Cash Register Company (NCR) and became president of IBM in 1915. By the 1950s, IBM's major competitors were Remington Rand, NCR, and Burroughs. When IBM chose to invest in expansion during the Depression, whereas the other three elected to retrench, IBM became the leading firm. In 1950, IBM controlled 90% of the punch card market.

When the Korean War broke out in 1950, Watson Sr. offered IBM's help. IBM undertook a study to determine how it could best aid in the war effort. James Birkenstock, manager of the IBM Future Demands department, and mathematician Cuthbert Hurd recommended IBM build a "general-purpose scientific" computer. Code-named the Defense Calculator, it became the most expensive investment in the company's history to that point.[16] Watson Jr. remembers the subsequent confusion: "Our engineers and production mangers weren't sure how to proceed."[17]

The year 1952 proved to be very busy for IBM. On January 21, the Justice Department filed an antitrust lawsuit against IBM alleging they had acted illegally to preserve their 90% share of the highly visible punch card business. (As with AT&T in the communications industry, the government wanted to restructure the leading firm in the office equipment industry. These would not be the last antitrust suits the Justice Department would file against AT&T and IBM.) Watson Sr. added fighting the lawsuit to running the company, while Watson Jr. focused on his passion—getting IBM into the computer business. On April 29, Watson Jr. announced at the annual meeting that IBM was building "the most advanced, most flexible

16. Thomas J. Watson and Peter Petre. 1991. *Father, Son & Co: My Life at IBM and Beyond*. Bantam Books, 216–217.

17. Watson and Petre, *Father, Son & Co*, 259.

high-speed computer in the world."[18] The new machine was introduced a year later on April 21, 1953, as the IBM 701 Electronic Data Processing Machine.

IBM was not the first company to sell an electronic digital computer; that distinction belongs to the Eckert–Mauchly Computer Corporation and Engineering Research Associates. It took little time for IBM to assert market dominance in the computer market behind the skillful leadership of Thomas Watson, Jr., who became president in 1952. Watson Jr. remembers his father believing: "the electronic computer would have no impact on the way IBM did business, because to him punch-card machines and giant computers belonged in totally separate realms."[19] Once IBM entered the commercial computer business with its IBM 701 in 1953 and their scientific computer the IBM 650 two years later, they lost no time in making sizeable capital and research investments to accompany their extensive organizational capabilities. Despite his father's cautionary advice, his son had seen a very different future for the company.

Understanding IBM's deficiencies in computing, Watson Jr. made it a priority to win the contract being let by MIT and the Air Force to develop a computer for the Semi-Automatic Ground Environment (SAGE) air defense system. Jay Forrester, the MIT engineer responsible for procurement, held serious discussions with Remington Rand, RCA, Raytheon, Sylvania, and IBM. In October 1952, he selected IBM to be the subcontractor assisting MIT's Lincoln Laboratories to finalize the SAGE computer design. For IBM, SAGE represented the opportunity to learn state-of-the-art computer technologies from the most advanced computer development laboratory in the world. But while IBM learned, staff at Lincoln Labs felt burdened. Norman Taylor, one of Forrester's most trusted managers, remembered: "IBM seemed awful stupid to us. They were still designing circuits like radio and TV circuits."[20]

The SAGE project was a prime example of a massive government-sponsored project with an explicit goal of innovating existing and new technologies. The scale of the project itself required a level of organizational complexity that few if any firms had ever considered. SAGE impacted the fortunes of IBM and other firms involved almost immediately. The technology trajectory of computers had accelerated significantly. SAGE innovations such as core memory, real-time response to multiple users, keyboard terminals, computer-to-computer communications, printed circuit board construction, and diagnostic and maintenance systems became standard features in all future computers. At the time, it catapulted IBM from a "stodgy company" (as Watson Jr. characterized it) to a technological leader.

---

18. "A Notable First: IBM 701," https://www.ibm.com/ibm/history/exhibits/701/701_intro.html.

19. Watson and Petre, *Father, Son & Co*, 200.

20. Glenn Rifkin and George Harrar. 1988. *The Ultimate Entrepreneur*. Contemporary Books, 22–23.

Watson Jr.'s first significant act after taking over the reins from his father was to sign a consent decree ending the 1952 antitrust lawsuit. In the 1956 decree, IBM agreed, among other restrictions, to separate itself from its Service Bureau Corporation. The restrictions placed on the punch card business were not severe and with each passing year would prove insignificant, for punch cards were becoming less and less important to the company as a whole.

By the mid-1950s, IBM management fully understood the benefits of designing and building advanced computers for the government—the company could generate invaluable goodwill while maintaining access to cutting-edge knowledge it could apply in its next generation of computer designs. After IBM lost a bid in 1955 to build a super-fast computer for the University of California Radiation Laboratory, they sold a more aggressive design, to become known as STRETCH, to the Los Alamos National Laboratory as well as to the Atomic Energy Commission and the National Security Agency (NSA).

The STRETCH computer was sold commercially as the IBM 7030, announced in April 1961, and like the earlier 7070 introduced in 1959, used transistors instead of vacuum tubes. Early transistor computers also included the IBM 7090, a mainframe designed for large-scale scientific and data calculations. An early application of the 7090 was for the massive airline reservation system for American Airlines (AA). The name of the project—as well as much of the underlying technology—was drawn from the SAGE project, and titled Sabre for "Semi-Automatic Business Research Environment."

The inspiration for Sabre came from a fortuitous airplane conversation in 1953 between senior IBM sales representative R. Blaire Smith and C.R. Smith, then president of AA. The two connected the concept of the SAGE network with the need for an automated flight reservation system in which flight reservations could be created and recorded and the data made available to agents in any location. Before the two organizations began discussions on how to implement the project, president C.R. Smith of AA was quoted as saying: "You'd better make those black boxes do the job, because I could buy five or six Boeing 707s for the same capital expenditure."[21] In 1959, IBM and AA signed a development agreement that eventually led to a $30 million project.

IBM failed to foresee the massive amount of software development involved in implementing the Sabre system and consequently the project experienced many cost and schedule overruns. Initially, IBM terminals were located in travel agencies

21. James L. McKenney. 1994. *Waves of Change: Business Evolution Through Information Technology*. Harvard Business School Press, 111.

and connected by telephone lines using modems to IBM computers in AA's headquarters. When it was finally operational in 1964, Sabre revolutionized the airline reservation industry and was quickly duplicated by other airlines.

In October 1959, IBM announced the 1401, targeted for small business customers. After deliveries began in 1960, more 1401s would be installed than any other computer at that time—by the mid-1960s more than 10,000 had been installed.[22] Business customers were clearly embracing the use of computers, and IBM was successfully positioned to benefit the most from this trend.

At the same time, IBM faced a major challenge in maintaining order across its two computer divisions: the General Products Division, which sold lower priced computers, and the Data Systems Division, which sold general-purpose scientific and business computers. These divisions were making and selling a variety of different computer models, effectively competing against each other. But the main issue was the massive cost in software development for each project. Of the main transistorized models in production in 1960, none ran compatible operating systems. In the early 1960s, senior executives sought a drastic simplification of IBM's products, reducing its several product lines to one computer architecture that could meet the full spectrum of customer requirements, all using the same peripherals and software.

In January 1961, Frederick P. Brooks, Jr., lead designer for a recently cancelled 8000 series of business computers, was assigned to head development of a new line of compatible products that could serve all the requirements of IBM customers. As product manager, Brooks oversaw the massive hardware and software development effort involved in developing this revolutionary new "computer architecture," a term he first coined. The new system would be called the System/360. Gene Amdahl, who had previously worked on the 704, 709, and STRETCH computers, was engineering manager and chief architect.

The production of the System/360 was a massive gamble, but based on the difficulties in developing software to operate the new family of processors, as well as previous experiences with Sabre, it is worth noting that the efforts IBM undertook to develop advanced understanding in software development foreshadowed the future importance of software in computer history. The challenges, delays, and huge time and cost demands on IBM resources were especially evident to Brooks. In his chronicles of the project, *The Mythical Man-Month*, he coined what became known as "Brooks' Law," which states that "adding manpower to a late software project makes it later."[23]

22. Pugh, *Building IBM*, 266.

23. Pugh, *Building IBM*, 295.

On April 7, 1964, Thomas Watson, Jr., and the management of IBM made the most important product announcement in their company's history. IBM would begin shipping six models of the revolutionary new System/360 in April 1965. In the first 30 days IBM sold an unbelievable 1,000 System/360s. At a cost to IBM of an estimated $5 billion, the System/360, the innovative new series of mainframe computers, sent IBM's competitors scrambling for survival.

By investing in large-scale production, distribution channels, and management structures, IBM had secured first-mover advantages and created a dominant design for the mainframe computer industry. The scale and scope of attention IBM was able to bring to an average sale would dwarf whatever any competitor could do. As evidence of IBM's dominant market-structure position, IBM was shipping "over 1,000 model 360 systems a month" by 1969.[24]

The competition could do little at first other than wage a war of words. They argued that IBM could never deliver, it was too expensive, and it was not even state-of-the-art—it didn't use integrated circuits, for example. But all were forced to develop new product lines to stay competitive. One way competitors tried to differentiate their products from System/360 was time-sharing—largely because IBM did not support time-sharing in the announced System/360s.

The explosion in growth of computer service bureaus seemed to validate the notion that computers were analogous to utility service in electricity or water.[25] Service bureaus sold computer time and services to other companies as independent organizations or operations of computer manufacturers.[26] Existing since the earliest days of commercial computing, it was not until time-sharing that service bureaus could support real-time access to many users at the same time. By 1966, an estimated 800 service bureaus generated $650 million in revenues—thought to be

24. "Since it entered the computer business 15 years ago, IBM's volume has increased 17 times (to $5.3 billion last year [1967]) and its net income has gone up 20 times (to $651.5-million). Last year, IBM zoomed past Texaco and U.S. Steel to become the nation's eighth largest industrial company when it added $1.1-billion in revenues. That is like creating another Coca-Cola or another Celanese in just one year. In Wall Street's assessment, IBM is now the most valuable corporation around. Early this week, IBM's common shares were worth $41.5-billion. The common shares of AT&T, with assets eight times larger, were worth $26.3-billion. The stock market appraises IBM stock as worth at least as much as the combined shares of 21 of the 30 companies that go to make up the Dow-Jones industrial average." "Where IBM looks for new growth," *Business Week*, June 15, 1968, 88.

25. Manley R. Irwin. 1967. The computer utility: Competition or regulation? *The Yale Law Journal* 76, 7, 1299–320; Robert M. Fano. 1967. The computer utility and the community. *IEEE, Int'l Conv Record* Part 12, 30–34; Paul Baran. 1967. The future computer utility. *The Public Interest*, Summer 1967, 75–87.

26. John L. Roy. 1970. The changing role of the service bureau. *Datamation*, March 1970, 52.

growing at 40% per year.[27] IBM, even though restricted as to how they could compete in the service bureau business by their 1956 Consent Decree with the Justice Department, ran two nationwide service bureaus.[28]

By the end of the 1960s, IBM dominated the mainframe industry, thanks to Watson Jr's entrepreneurialism, technologies fueled by defense funding, the flexible and modular architecture of the 360 line of computers, and an expert sales and marketing operation. But the increasing demand for time-sharing soon would create opportunities for competitors.

1.4 New Technologies for Computing

The shifting fortunes of the two dominant firms in the converging fields of communications and computing, AT&T and IBM, depended upon several factors, including the changing regulatory environment and the decisions of key executives to risk pursuing new opportunities. At the same time, the story of data communications in the decades between World War II and the late 1960s is in large part the story of technological innovation. During this period, new developments in computer technology, and the resulting decrease in the cost of computing, changed the landscape of possibilities for a growing number of institutional and commercial customers and the existing companies and many entrepreneurial start-ups that served them.

1.4.1 Transistors

The transistor was the first of three technological discontinuities to radically alter the computer market-structure, the other two being the integrated circuit and the microprocessor. Transistors became an alternative to vacuum tubes, which were large, costly, unreliable, and consumed large amounts of energy. Although functionally equivalent to vacuum tubes, transistors had profound technological differences from vacuum tubes: where tubes worked by electrons flowing through voltage gradient, transistors channeled electrons through semiconductor materials.

27. Gilbert Burck. 1968. The computer industry 's great expectations. *Fortune*, August 1968, 142

28. Irwin noted: "These new developments in technology and services raise the question, once again, of the status of IBM's consent decree. Does time sharing merely permit IBM to sell computer time over telephone lines, or is IBM processing customer data for a fee? What is legitimate activity for IBM as a manufacturer and IBM as a service bureau? The answers to these questions are not clear, but as if to hedge its short term anti-trust bet, both the Service Bureau Corporation and IBM, the parent corporation, have recently introduced nationwide systems of time-shared computer centers. In the long run, however, IBM many find it necessary to convince the Justice Department that new technology has invalidated major premises of its 1956 judgment." Irwin. The computer utility: Competition or regulation. *Yale Law Journal*, 1299.

Table 1.1 **Government purchases of semiconductor devices 1955–1960**

	Total Semiconductor Shipments ($ millions)	Shipments to Federal Government ($ millions)	Government Share of Total Shipments (percent)
1955	40	15	38
1956	90	32	36
1957	151	54	36
1958	210	81	39
1959	396	180	45
1960	542	258	48

Source: Richard R. Nelson, Government and Technical Progress: A Cross-Industry Analysis (Pergamon Press, 1982), 60. Used with Permission.

During World War II, the US government significantly increased funding of semiconductor research at Bell Laboratories, universities, and industrial companies, and created the MIT Radiation Laboratory to coordinate the research. These investments bore fruit on December 23, 1947, when the first transistor was demonstrated at Bell Labs. Walter H. Brattain and John Bardeen demonstrated a crude, but working, amplifying transistor made from germanium and wires. Their demonstration motivated William B. Shockley to work out the seminal principle of a solid-state transistor over the following five weeks, which was announced publicly in early 1948. AT&T subsequently sought to disseminate knowledge of transistors widely through seminars and licensing agreements. Managers at AT&T and Bell Labs understood that they would not be able to keep the technology to themselves. Had they kept the transistor proprietary, then the subsequent growth in the semiconductor, and all related industries, would certainly have been very different.[29]

By 1952, Western Electric (and a few other firms) manufactured approximately 90,000 point-contact transistors, which were sold primarily to the military. Data from 1955 to 1960 clearly shows the importance of government purchases (see Table 1.1). Two important sources of demand were the early commitment of the Air Force to use semiconductors in the Minuteman Missile in 1958 and the growth of IBM. IBM was the largest customer of every semiconductor company due to their transition to transistorized computers such as STRETCH in the mid-1950s.

29. On Bell Labs, see, generally, John Gertner. 2013. *The Idea Factory: Bell Labs and the Great Age of American Innovation*. Penguin.

One of the first transistor computers, the Burroughs Atlas Mod 1-J1 Guidance Computer built for the Air Force, was operational in September 1957. IBM announced its 7070 transistorized computer in September 1958; RCA, the 501, in December 1958. The first available commercial transistor computer was the General Electric 210, delivered in June 1959.

The transistor, as a technological discontinuity, as the economist Joseph Schumpeter might describe it, would strike "not at the margins of the profits and the outputs of the existing firms, but at their foundations and their very lives."[30] Transistors made computers more reliable, faster, smaller, and consume less power and generate less heat. Once firms started making computers with transistors, they never again used vacuum tubes.

1.4.2 Integrated Circuits

Transistors represented a major improvement over vacuum tubes but were not without problems of their own. Transistors came packaged as one transistor per each small "pot." The pots were much smaller than vacuum tubes, hence more devices could be squeezed into the same space. But as the desired complexity of device interconnections kept growing, wiring all these small devices became an interconnection nightmare, and very costly. From the years 1952–1959, firms and governments around the world searched for an answer to the problem of interconnections. Two companies—Texas Instruments (TI) and Fairchild Semiconductor—played the most significant roles in solving this problem.

In 1958, TI made the propitious decision to hire Jack Kilby. Within two months, he conceived of the solution to the problem of interconnecting large numbers of transistors and other components. Kilby's idea would come to be known as the "Monolithic Idea," where a single *monolithic* block of semiconductor material would contain all components and interconnections. Kilby hand-fabricated a monolithic, *integrated* circuit in September 1958, and TI filed for a patent in February 1959. But Kilby was not alone: another team of scientists, also with roots at Bell Labs, was likewise achieving impressive results with silicon.

In early 1956, William Shockley left Bell Labs to start Shockley Transistor Laboratories in Palo Alto, CA—located in the future Silicon Valley. Shockley recruited people who would become legends in the history of semiconductors, including Robert Noyce, Gordon Moore, and Jean Hoerni, to join his firm. But Shockley was no executive. Eight of his recruits were terribly dissatisfied, and made it known they would

30. Joseph A. Schumpeter. 1942. *Capitalism, Socialism and Democracy*. Harper & Brothers, 84.

prefer a new home. Instead of moving to an established firm, the "traitorous eight" raised venture capital and founded Fairchild Semiconductor Corporation in early 1957. Noyce is considered the father of the integrated circuit because he not only conceived of the Monolithic Idea, as had Kilby, but also its means of manufacture—the planar process. Fairchild's patent was filed in July 1959. The problem of interconnecting transistors had been solved. Ever since, the path of innovation has been to make device and interconnection features smaller, and the resultant integrated circuit, or chip, bigger.

The integrated circuit was not an overnight success for one simple reason: they cost too much to make. Development of the integrated circuit soon received a boost in May 1961, when President John F. Kennedy challenged the imagination of the American public to put a man on the moon. To do so would require the use of integrated circuits. Through 1964, purchases of integrated circuits for the Apollo Guidance Computer, used in the Apollo spacecraft modules, and the Air Force Minuteman guidance computer drove the market for integrated circuits (see Table 1.2). Once again, government support proved essential to market lift-off.

Even though the government had committed two critical programs to integrated circuits, into 1963 there remained sharp debate as to whether integrated circuits were the ultimate solution. But by then the costs of manufacturing integrated circuits were in steep decline due to the volume purchases by the government, and any doubt as to their reliability was dispelled.

A new computer start-up, Scientific Data Systems, founded in 1961 by Max Palevsky, was the first to introduce a computer using integrated circuits. The SDS

Table 1.2 **Government purchase of integrated circuits, 1962–1968**

	Total Integrated Circuit Shipments ($ millions)	Shipments to Federal Government ($ millions)	Government Share of Total Shipments (percent)
1962	4	4	100
1963	16	15	94
1964	41	35	85
1965	79	57	72
1966	148	78	53
1967	228	98	43
1968	312	115	37

Source: Richard R. Nelson. *Government and Technical Progress: A Cross-Industry Analysis*, 63. Used with permission.

92 shipped in 1964; IBM did not ship a computer using integrated circuits until 1969.

1.4.3 Modems

The SAGE system described above was the source of several landmark innovations in the history of computing, including advancements in memory; novel input/output devices such as cathode ray terminals and light pens; and a systems approach to the coordination of thousands of engineers, programmers, and managers. But for the purposes of our focus on data communications, the innovations that supported its data communication capabilities stand out above the rest—specifically, the invention of the modem.

By 1955, SAGE consisted of two Q7 computers residing at each of 23 direction centers across the United States. These direction centers were in turn connected to radar sites across northern Canada and to the airfields and missile sites in the US. AT&T was contracted to design and build the telephone line network as well as the instrument to convert the digital signals to analog for transmission and then back to digital for the computers. AT&T Bell Labs worked with the Cambridge Research Laboratory of the Air Force to create the radar data processing and transmission equipment for the SAGE system. The first modems emerged from this collaboration. These modems transmitted data from remote radar sites in Canada to IBM 790 computers in the United States. A paper, "Transmission of digital information over telephone circuits," describing this first modem implementation was published in the *Bell System Technical Journal* in 1955. The name modem comes from its function: *mod*ulating, or suppressing, information onto a telephone line, and then *dem*odulating, or recovering, the modulated information from the line. The design objective is to accurately transmit as many 0's and 1's as possible in a fixed period of time. Since each 0 or 1 is a bit, the convention is to rate modems by how many bits per second (bps) they transmit. The faster the modem, the more challenging it is to engineer.

By the time the SAGE system was completed, AT&T built and installed well over two hundred SAGE modems. In addition, AT&T then redesigned the modem and began selling commercial modems in 1958, beginning with the Bell Data Set 101 that transmitted at the "blazing" speed of 110bps. This formally marked the beginning of the Data Communication market-structure (see Figure 1.3).

1.4.4 Mainframes and Modems

The mainframe era of computing refers to the 1950s, when IBM and its competitors produced systems like the IBM 700/7000 series that suited the highly centralized

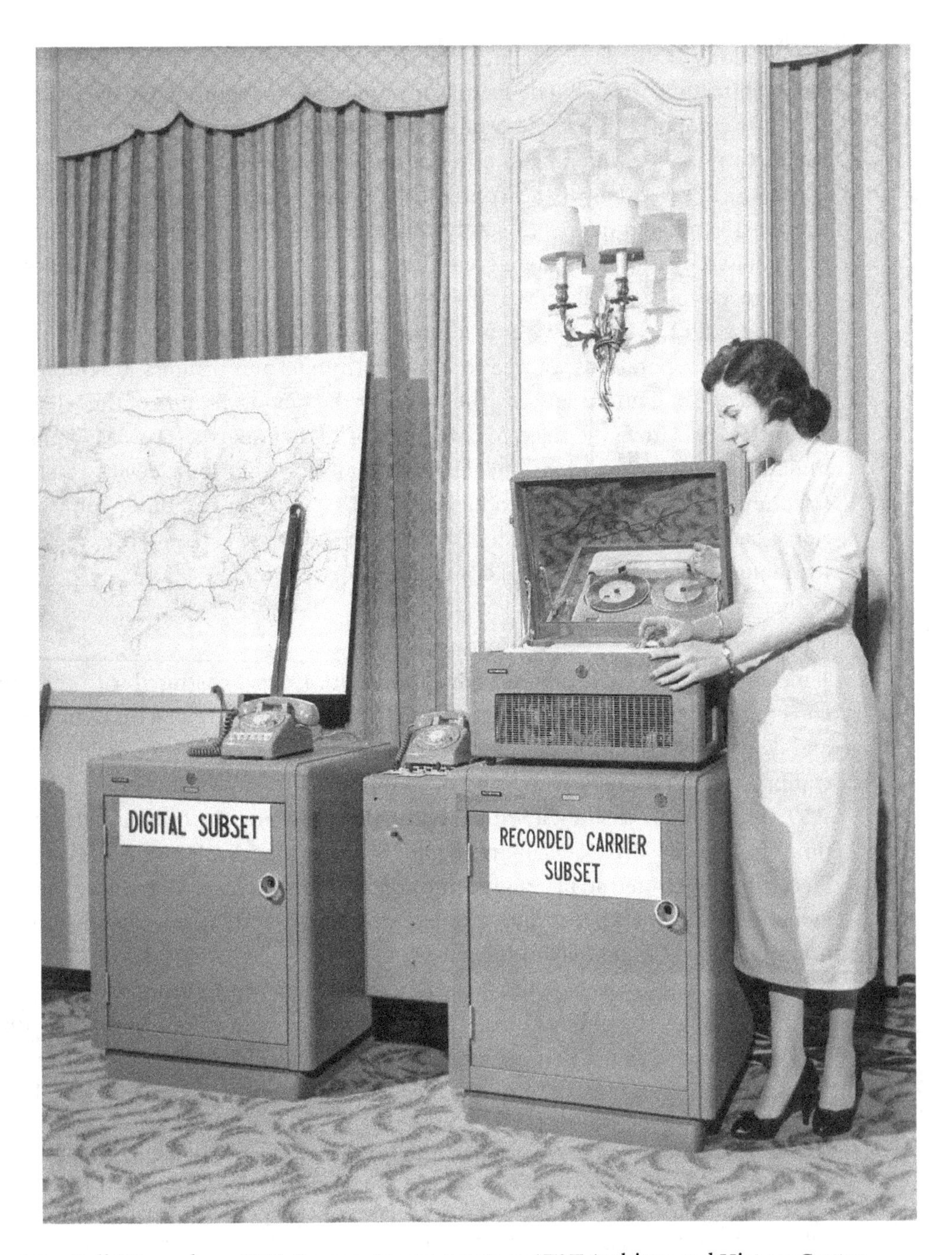

Figure 1.3 Bell 101 modem, 1958. Source: Image courtesy AT&T Archives and History Center.

corporations of the day.[31] The mainframe era has clear roots in the technologies and architecture of SAGE. The mainframe architecture featured one big computer, the Host computer that sat in a raised-floor, air-conditioned, often high-security room. Terminals, printers, and other peripherals were directly wired to the Host computer in essentially a star configuration. The host, or Big Blue, was thought the "boss" and all other devices were "slaves."[32] This centralized architecture was perpetuated by IBM and gave a great deal of power to their corporate clients, the Data Processing or Management Information System departments.

At first, all the slave devices were local, but following the success of the IBM System/360 corporations wanted to locate terminals and printers at remote locations. To do so required sending the bits over the analog circuits of the telephone network. That drove the need for modems of higher speeds (bps). Modems and multiplexers—products that enable more than one computer device to share a telephone circuit—were the products of the first wave of computer communications: data communications. Modems and multiplexers were highly co-evolving technologies, yet only a handful of firms mastered both.

1.4.4.1 Time-sharing

Time-sharing as an idea first surfaced in the late 1950s. Frustrated with the time-consuming method of batch processing, where jobs were created on punch cards and delivered to a computer operator who would run the job later, scientists and computer programmers sought ways to interact directly with the computer. In 1959, Christopher Strachey, a British mathematician, gave the first public paper on time-sharing at a UNESCO congress; and, working independently, Professor John McCarthy distributed an internal memo about time-sharing at MIT. Under the leadership of Professor F.J. Corbato, time-sharing was first demonstrated at the MIT Computational Center in November 1961.

Time-sharing might have lingered there were it not for the visionary leadership of Dr. J.C.R. Licklider and his license to invest government funds. In October 1962, Dr. Licklider became the first director of the newly created Information Processing Techniques Office (IPTO) of the Advanced Research Projects Agency. His charge

31. The market-structure of first-generation mainframe computers (1950–1959) consisted of only seven companies and 31 computer models. Other companies developed computers but they did not sell them commercially. Research and development funding came almost entirely from the U.S. Government. Although a commercial computer market existed, it was far from clear what its economic potential might be.

32. For recent discussions around eliminating the once-conventional "master/slave" terminology, see Elizabeth Landau. 2020. Tech confronts its use of the labels 'master' and 'slave.' *Wired* July 6, 2020, https://www.wired.com/story/tech-confronts-use-labels-master-slave/.

was to invest in advancing information technologies. Based on his experiences at MIT Lincoln Labs and Bolt, Beranek & Newman, and his vision of man–machine interactions, too briefly summarized as interactivity, he prioritized funding to time-sharing projects. And if projects didn't exist, he created them. For example, at MIT he helped create Project MAC (for machine-aided cognition or multiple-access computer) under the leadership of Professor Robert M. Fano, and approved $3 million a year in funding for the project. It would become the most influential effort in time-sharing. In 1967, IPTO funding to over a dozen time-sharing projects, at both universities and research organizations, exceeded an estimated $12 million.

Time-sharing required new software and hardware, as well as the most challenging innovation—an operating system that could support many simultaneous users and create the illusion that each user had exclusive control of the computer. The speed of the computer made this sleight of hand possible: if the computer could switch back and forth between programs fast enough, users perceived that they had both real-time and on-line performance. This experience was simply impossible in operating systems designed to process programs in batch fashion.

The first computer company to embrace time-sharing was General Electric (GE). In May 1964, a GE computer was used in a time-sharing demonstration at Dartmouth College. That summer, GE announced its 600 series computers would all support time-sharing, using software developed at Dartmouth. And that fall, MIT surprised everyone when it announced it would buy a GE computer for use as the main computer for Project MAC. IBM, which had abandoned internal efforts to develop a time-sharing system and did not support time-sharing in its initial releases of System/360, had jeopardized its valuable connection to MIT. Support for time-sharing was added when IBM released the TSS/360 time-sharing operating system for the 360 model 67 released in 1967 and later the System/370 announced in 1970.

As time-sharing spread, so did the demand for the required communications hardware, such as modems, multiplexers, and communications processors to transmit data between terminals and mainframes.

1.4.4.2 Minicomputers

The roots of minicomputers can also be found in the SAGE Project. In 1953, Kenneth Olsen, a recent graduate of MIT and one of 400 engineers hired to staff the SAGE Project, was reassigned to work as a liaison to IBM, the firm contracted to manufacture the SAGE computers. When it was time for a new assignment, Olsen went to work for an advanced engineering group at MIT Lincoln Labs led by Wes Clark. Clark had approval to build a transistorized computer, the TX-2. The contrast between the working environments of IBM, where development was slow and subject to heavy bureaucracy, and the lively pace of research and collaboration at Lincoln Labs, made a lasting impression on the young Olsen, who was inspired to recreate the research lab culture in his own business. In early 1957, Olsen left MIT to test his entrepreneurial skills and, together with Harlan Anderson, and supported by venture capital from American Research & Development, they founded Digital Equipment Corporation (DEC) in August 1957. Their first product, the PDP-1, released in 1959, borrowed significantly from the TX-2. In the fall of 1965, DEC introduced the first commercially successful minicomputer: the PDP-8. In 1966, DEC went public with a valuation of $77 million, 770 times its founding valuation. In the few years that followed, venture capital investors eager to discover the next DEC funded an explosion in the number of minicomputers.

It was not until DEC introduced their PDP-8 that businesses began to use the minicomputer as a smaller version of a mainframe computer. For smaller companies, minicomputers would soon occupy the central role that mainframes occupied. They were the repository of all the accounting and operational data and enabled printing of timely reports. Eventually, they performed the same role with manufacturing data, such as inventory levels and purchasing information on vendors and orders outstanding. The next stage was integrating all the manufacturing data and information into what became known as MRP systems (initially Material Requirements Planning and later, as the software became more inclusive and sophisticated, Manufacturing Resource Planning). It took roughly a decade for third-party software vendors to emerge and create, sell, and support software that even the minicomputer companies had a hard time creating. In the interlude, minicomputer companies found a welcome home focusing on the fast-growing data communication market, providing statistical and time division multiplexing functions, acting as communication processors, or becoming a building block of private networks.

Minicomputers were also used as time-sharing computers. DEC's first computer to support time-sharing was the PDP-6, released in 1964. The DEC time-sharing operating system TSS/8, which ran on the PDP-8, was released in 1968. Later in the mid-1970s, Hewlett-Packard introduced their HP 3000, another popular minicomputer that supported time-sharing.

1.5 Venture Capital and Public Capital Markets

The success of an entrepreneurial endeavor often hinges on the availability of capital needed to fund the proposed business idea. Traditional sources of start-up funding came from institutional loans and wealthy families, but in the late 1960s venture capital partnerships were beginning to emerge as an alternative source of risk capital for early-stage start-ups.

The modern venture capital industry is generally considered to have begun with the founding of American Research and Development Corporation (ARD) in 1946 by Georges Doriot, a former dean of the Harvard Business School who many consider the "father of venture capitalism," with Ralph Flanders and Karl Compton (a former president MIT) and other distinguished leaders from the Boston area. ARD is considered the first major venture capital success story with its initial investment of $70,000 into the founding of DEC for 70% of the ownership in 1957. DEC's initial public offering in August 1966 was considered a "wild" success story, valuing DEC at $8.25 million.[33] The success of ARD's "long-tail" investment strategy, in which one or a few high performing outliers in the "long-tail" of the distribution curve increased fund returns significantly, proved the viability of a well-managed portfolio of early-stage equity investments.

Another important influence in the development of the modern venture capital industry came in the form of government policy, when in July 1958 President Dwight D. Eisenhower signed into law the Small Business Investment Act. The act licensed private, Small Business Investment Companies (SBICs), and made available Small Business Administration loans to leverage a company's pool of capital by up to 4 dollars for every 1 dollar of private investment. More than 500 SBIC licenses were issued by the end of 1961.[34] The majority of SBICs invested in debt financing or real estate, but many invested in private companies, including the growing number of semiconductor manufacturers and other technology start-ups that were founded in the 1960s. Prominent SBICs that made investments in early technology start-ups included Continental Capital Corporation, founded in 1959 by Frank Chambers, and Boston Capital Corporation, founded in 1960, the largest SBIC at the time, with an investment pool (including government loans) of about $100 million ($810 million in current dollars).[35] Some notable companies that received SBIC funding included American Microsystems Inc., Intel, and ROLM. The growth in private investment companies as a result of the SBIC Act helped many young investment professionals gain experience and capital, inspiring several to form new venture partnerships. William Draper, III, and "Pitch" Johnson formed their SBIC, Draper & Johnson, and went on to build successful venture partnerships Sutter Hill and Asset Management Company.

The 1960s saw the formation of influential venture partnerships such as Greylock Partners, founded in 1965 by former ARD vice president William Elfers, and

33. "Digital equipment markets its shares," *New York Times*, August 19, 1966, 42.

34. John W. Wilson. 1985. *The New Venturers—Inside the High-Stakes World of Venture Capital*. Addison-Wesley, 21.

35. Tom Nicholas. 2019. *VC: An American History*. Harvard University Press, 136–140.

Venrock Associates, by Laurance Rockefeller in 1969, both prominent East Coast examples, while on the West Coast Draper, Gaither & Anderson was the first limited partnership, started in 1959. One of the most successful venture capitalists in the early tech industry was Arthur Rock. Rock and Tommy Davis started their limited partnership Davis & Rock in 1961. Rock's investments in Scientific Data Systems, Fairchild Semiconductor, and later Intel were among the legendary investments of early Silicon Valley history.

The sustained growth economy of the United States that began in the early 1950s had neither the breadth nor legs to support the policies and actions of the Federal Government during the 1960s. The simultaneous spending on both "guns and butter"—the Vietnam War and the "Great Society"—forced the government to issue excess money. Perceived by a growing number of professional fund managers as a certain prescription for inflation, they sought new ways to increase their investment returns to offset the erosive potential of inflation.[36] Seeking higher returns than could be earned by investing in bonds, the fund managers began investing in stocks, and were amply rewarded on January 10, 1967. On that day, following President Lyndon B. Johnson's State of the Union address, buying stocks for their growth potential turned into a stampede when the third largest volume of shares at that time were traded on the NYSE. A two-year bull market ensued. The most desired stocks were the "glamour" stocks or "Houdini issues": IBM, Xerox, Polaroid, and Kodak.[37] Stock prices traded as high as fifty times next year's projected earnings.

Investor appetite and willingness to pay high prices for technology companies induced private technology companies to go public in order to raise always-needed cash and create desired liquidity for shareholders. Computer leasing companies proved an immediate favorite. By June/July 1967, investor actions resembled a "speculative orgy" according to *Business Week* with the AMEX up 50%. By August it would be up 70%. It seemed as if all a company had to do was embed "tronics" in its name, and it became a "high-flyer." The markets peaked in September 1967, then regained momentum in the spring of 1968, opening another market window for technology companies, especially those that were computer related.[38]

The "hot" market for technology stocks induced the transformation of venture capital from largely an activity of wealthy families to one of professionally managed fund partnerships like ARD. Investors, having made money on their private investments that went public, wanted to reinvest their capital gains in other new, private technology companies. The goal was to achieve 10 to 20 times their investment

36. "The market warms up," *Business Week*, January 21, 1967, 25.

37. "Pension advisors play it cool," *Business Week*, April 1, 1967, 116.

38. "Speculative spree alarms AMEX," *Business Week*, July 15, 1967, 36.

in three to five years. A new breed of venture fund managers emerged in response. Unprecedented sums of money began flowing into venture capital. By 1970, the first year for which records were kept, $83 million was invested, up from $10 million (by estimate of the authors) in 1966.

1.6 The Early Entrepreneurs of Data Communications

Entrepreneurs have always played valued roles in human societies. Why? Because societies have always confronted problems, and curious individuals enjoy the challenge of solving them. But to be successful, entrepreneurs must have more than curiosity; they must possess the unique combination of vision and leadership. They must envision a new way of doing things and be capable of attracting others to help them achieve that vision. Very few entrepreneurs have all of the resources at their disposal to solve their problems of choice—so the help of others is essential. Beyond the initial idea for a business, the entrepreneur or co-founders need to build a team, raise the necessary capital to develop the technical product, and build a successful model for generating business revenue.

As important as the vision and leadership of individual entrepreneurs is the environment in which they act. The massive government investment in technology following World War II resulted in an unprecedented scale of technological innovation and created the building blocks for many of the entrepreneurial innovations of the emerging information economy. When combined with changes in regulatory policy favoring competition and the growth in the availability of venture capital, the time was ripe for those with entrepreneurial aspirations. The pioneers in the early evolution of computer communications paved the way for the flourishing entrepreneurial culture of the late 1960s, 1970s, and 1980s. The work of Thomas Carter, William Shockley, Kenneth Olsen, and many others of this time marked the first wave in the explosion of new products, new methods of production, and the formation of new industries.

1.6.1 Codex

Entrepreneurship does not always begin with a grand vision of the future. Sometimes the motivation can simply be a desire to do what one enjoys most, to escape an unpleasant work environment, or being forced to try something different. Such was the case for Jim Cryer and Arthur Kohlenberg in 1962 when their employer, Melpar Electronics, informed them that they were closing the advanced research laboratory they had been running as director and chief scientist, respectively. Even though offered the option to move to Virginia, both men had little desire to leave the Boston area. They believed that on their own they could win technology development contracts being let by government agencies. So they incorporated a new company, Codex, and joined thousands of other companies swept up in the federal government's funding of technological innovation that included large defense projects following SAGE, and newer ones like NASA's Apollo project.

Cryer and Kohlenberg knew just such an opportunity: the Air Force wanted better error-correcting codes for digital transmission over telephone lines. They also knew that Robert Gallager, then a young professor at MIT, and his graduate student, Jim Massey, had developed new error-correcting techniques, thought a sure bet to secure a development contract. Their instincts were right. Soon they had a contract to develop exotic error-correcting codes for the Air Force's Ballistic Missile Early Warning System, the successor to SAGE. Error-correcting codes were needed to restore the lost data. Better codes required more of the total capacity of the communication lines, or bandwidth, leaving less bandwidth for radar data. More powerful codes also required faster modems.

Even before taking possession of their first AT&T modems in the 1950s, the Air Force wanted faster ones. The need for speed came from wanting to create and maintain a worldwide command and control system for air defense. Brigadier General H.R. Johnson, Director of Point-to-Point Planning for Headquarters Airways and Air Force Communications Systems (AFCS), USAF, from 1950 to 1955, remembers a senior member of his technical staff, Bill Pugh, calculating: "a suitable goal would be 10,000bps in a voice band" for modems. That goal was then set forth in 1956 in: "the proposed General Operational Requirement that AFCS sent to the Air Force, which subsequently became the research document for the Air Force Communications System."[39] Yet a decade later, reliable modems operating at that speed remained an elusive goal.

Such was the background in 1966 when Cryer and Kohlenberg began taking seriously the idea of Codex developing a leased-line modem to sell to the Air Force. That they knew the Air Force yearned for higher speed modems for their air defense system made the opportunity seem a sure bet. But there was a problem: up to that point Cryer and Kohlenberg had little experience, or for that matter any real interest, in selling products. Their competence lay in solving difficult technical problems, not in managing what they imagined as the boring business of stamping out the same products, day-in, day-out. The very prospect demeaned Codex's proud corporate ethos of: "if not technically challenging, it was not worth doing."[40]

39. Harold Richard Johnson, oral history interview by James L. Pelkey, May 3, 1988, Cupertino, CA. Computer History Museum, Mountain View, CA. Available from https://archive.computerhistory.org/resources/access/text/2016/04/102738128-05-01-acc.pdf.

40. Art Carr, interview by James L. Pelkey, April 6, 1988, Newton, MA. Computer History Museum, Mountain View, CA. Available from https://archive.computerhistory.org/resources/access/text/2015/10/102737982-05-01-acc.pdf.

Even so, Cryer and Kohlenberg worried about Codex's dependence on the feast-or-famine nature of government contracts, when sales could be $1 million one year and nothing the next. Selling a product, such as modems, did have prospective advantages.

In discussing the subject with MIT's Gallagher, Cryer and Kohlenberg learned that a high-speed 9,600bps modem—four times faster than the fastest commercial modem then available from AT&T—was possible. Wanting to know how, they pressed him further. Gallagher then told them about Jerry Holsinger, a 1965 MIT Ph.D. graduate whose thesis had been on high-speed data transmission over telephone lines. He last heard Holsinger had left MIT Lincoln Labs and was employed by a small R&D shop on the West Coast named Defense Research Company. Intrigued, Cryer and Kohlenberg convinced themselves that a 9,600bps modem would give Codex the competitive edge and hopefully the financial security they needed to be successful while upholding their proud tradition of solving hard problems.

On meeting Holsinger in early 1967, Cryer and Kohlenberg discovered he had already formed a company, Teldata, and was soliciting investment from venture capitalists or anyone else who had money. Holsinger claimed he had a working prototype of a 9,600bps modem, one developed at Defense Research Corporation with funding from the NSA. He confided his original design had not worked on normal telephone lines, but he had perfected the design and had a working breadboard prototype. All he needed to do was convert his modem to printed circuit boards to have the world's first 9,600bps modem.

Holsinger thought of himself as an entrepreneur, not an employee working for a salary or as a research scientist, but he was having trouble convincing others that they should invest their money with him—not surprising given he lacked business experience and was only two years out of graduate school. Holsinger remembers how green he was: "If somebody like me were coming to me now, I would probably tell them the same thing. Go belly up to somebody." It didn't take long for him to realize: "it wasn't really what I wanted to do. I thought that I wanted to run a business, but it wasn't in the cards at that point, so I ultimately got together with Codex and they bought out the rights of the people on the West Coast, and they effectively got me and a production-prototype modem design in that process."[41]

Cryer and Kohlenberg persuaded Holsinger they were serious about building a modem business and, lacking an alternative, Holsinger agreed to sell Teldata to

41. Jerry L. Holsinger, oral history interview by James L. Pelkey, April 6, 1988, Westborough, MA. Computer History Museum, Mountain View, CA. Available from https://archive.computerhistory.org/resources/access/text/2016/04/102738129-05-01-acc.pdf.

Codex in May 1967. Codex acquired 82.36% of Teldata's shares for $94,000. Securing the technology for its first product accomplished, Codex engineers turned to the task of developing the actual product. As often is the case with cutting edge technologies, the process was fraught with challenges and setbacks.

1.6.2 Milgo

Codex embarked on its journey into modems by way of acquisition. Many other defense contractors and electronics companies, like Rixon Electronics, Collins Radio, and Stelma, began selling modems, like AT&T had, by using technology they developed for the government. The first independent company to really challenge AT&T, Milgo Electronics Corporation (Milgo), hired a talented individual, Sang Whang, and funded the project internally.

Monroe Miller and Lloyd Gordon, the "Mil" and "Go" of the name "Milgo," had served the defense agencies and NASA ever since founding their company in 1956. They, like Cryer and Kohlenberg, learned that NASA and military agencies wanted faster modems. In 1965, they hired Sang Whang out of Brooklyn Polytechnic Institute to develop a line of modems to sell to the Kennedy Space Center for downrange instrumentation. In 1967, Milgo introduced its commercial 2,400bps modem, the 4400/24PB. Edward Bleckner, head of Milgo's efforts to enter the modem business, hired an executive search firm to find a seasoned sales/marketing executive with modem experience. They luckily caught up with Matt Kinney on the telephone as he was stranded by a snowstorm at LaGuardia airport. He remembers: "They asked me if I'd like to come and talk to them about a job, and I said, 'Where are you?' They said, 'Miami, FL.' The answer: 'You bet your sweet life!'"[42]

In joining Milgo in January 1968, Kinney brought to Milgo needed experience in selling commercial data communication products and an understanding that significant changes might soon propel the demand for data communications; that is, if Tom Carter won his case against AT&T. Kinney remembers: "Tom Carter is one of my oldest and dearest friends. Hell, I knew in '66 that if Carter prevailed, which seemed highly unlikely at the time, that the industry would take off."[43]

Carter's chances depended entirely on the willingness of federal regulators to reexamine the fundamental assumptions upholding AT&T's monopoly.

---

42. Matt Kinney, oral history interview by James L. Pelkey, March 9, 198, Sunrise, FL. Computer History Museum, Mountain View, CA. Available from https://archive.computerhistory.org/resources/access/text/2017/10/102738573-05-01-acc.pdf.

43. Kinney interview, Computer History Museum.

1.6.3 Bernard Strassburg

In entrepreneurship, it is not only the case that the motivation needs be economic or defined by the starting of a company. Accordingly, our usage of the term comes from our recognition that entrepreneurs exist in all elements of society. To restate what we said in the Introduction, we follow Joseph Schumpeter's definition of entrepreneurship: "The typical entrepreneur is more self-centered than other types, because he relies less than they do on tradition and connection and because his characteristic task—theoretically as well as historically—consists precisely in breaking up old, and creating new, tradition." The last entrepreneur we will mention here is not an entrepreneur from the business sector, but one from the government regulatory sector who, nevertheless, acted with similar foresight and vision in relation to the emerging technologies of computer communications. The emergence of the new market-structure of data communications was fueled by technological innovation as well as acts of entrepreneurship from multiple individuals across multiple sectors. In an area that was heavily regulated, *policy* entrepreneurship was complementary to the efforts of entrepreneurs in companies such as Codex and Milgo—and, arguably, every bit as creative and significant.

Before 1965, Bernard Strassburg, Chairman of the CCB of the FCC, viewed the relationship between AT&T and the FCC as collaborative: "It was truly a symbiotic relationship. The regulated monopoly operated in what was considered to be the public interest and, in turn, was shielded against incursions by rivals and competitors, including the possibility of government ownership."[44]

By late 1966, however, Strassburg had radically rethought his view as he began to understand the importance of computers. Upon learning about developments in data communications in 1965, he recalled that he "assembled a task force, a small group of staff members to sort of take an overview of the various dimensions of data communications; what the problems seemed to be, if any, and what we should do about them."[45] Knowing he had to educate the Commissioners to the needs of computers, he also contacted the Institute of Electrical Engineers (IEEE) to give a series of lectures to the Commissioners. One of the lecturers was Paul Baran, who Strassburg knew, and as future chapters will make clear, was a dominant figure in the history of computer communications.

Strassburg's revised understanding of emerging computer technology was due in large measure to the research of economist Manley Irwin, who consulted with the FCC in 1966 and who was assigned to draft a speech Strassburg was scheduled

44. Henck and Strassburg, *A Slippery Slope*, xi.

45. Strassburg interview, Computer History Museum.

to make at American University on the subject of computers. Irwin's paper outlined the developing trend: computer technology required a method of sharing data over large distances, and the method in use at the time was via telephone lines and modems. In addition, AT&T employed an increasing amount of computer technology in their own operations, both for processing internal data and for switching in their telephone networks.

What Irwin saw was the coming convergence of the computer and communications industries. Strassburg realized the importance of Irwin's ideas and recognized that he would do well to get out in front of the potential for conflict between the two evolving industries.

Strassburg realized computer users would want to interconnect terminals and computers over the telephone network in ways certain to be resisted by AT&T. In a speech to an audience of computer professionals on October 20, 1966, he declared, "Few products of modern technology have as much potential for social, economic, and cultural benefit as does the multiple access computer."[46] One obstacle to this potential was economic—the problem of market entry: Who would be allowed to sell what products and services? Did AT&T have the right to monopolize products and services others wanted to sell? Strassburg was about to test the waters to see how serious the problem of convergence was. He remembers: "I decided that we ought to formalize this thing. We sensed enough ferment out there to say: 'Well, look we're going to encounter some problems here, and let's get on top of them sooner, rather than later, and for once let a regulatory agency be out in front, rather than trying to shovel up the mess that's left behind."[47]

Consequently, Strassburg and Irwin led the FCC in initiating a formal proceeding on November 9, 1966, when the FCC announced that CCB would hold a public inquiry titled: "Notice of Inquiry, In the Matter of Regulatory and Policy Problems Presented by the Interdependence of Computer and Communications Services and Facilities (Docket F.C.C. No. 16979)."[48] The Notice of Inquiry, also written by Irwin, read: "We are confronted with determining under what circumstances data processing, computer information, and message switching services, or any particular combination thereof—whether engaged in by established common carriers or

46. Strassburg, "The marriage of computers and communications."

47. Strassburg interview, Computer History Museum.

48. Strassburg remembered: "I decided that we ought to formalize this thing. We sensed enough ferment out there, or enough concern, to say: 'Well, look we're going to encounter some problems here, and let's get on top of them sooner, rather than later, and for once let a regulatory agency be out in front, rather than trying to shovel up the mess that's left behind." Strassburg interview, Computer History Museum.

other entities—are or should be subject to the provisions of the Communications Act."[49]

In anticipating the challenges brought on by the emerging field of data communications, Strassburg had acted, in fact, as an early entrepreneur of the same industry. His vision of the coming demand for new technologies and innovative ways of using existing technologies helped open areas of opportunity for many others.

1.7 Emergence of the Data Communications Market-Structure

The technologies and early products of data communications were well developed by the late 1960s and had formed the beginnings of a viable market, mainly to government agencies and institutions that leased private access to AT&T's telecommunications network. The entrepreneurs of the leading companies in the field, Codex and Milgo, both made the important decision to expand beyond their reliance on government contracts and to focus on developing and selling new products to commercial customers. The timing was important, for having the foresight to see the coming of deregulation their early moves in developing commercial products and establishing sales and distribution put them ahead of the pack when the rush to start companies began at the close of the decade.

1.8 In Perspective

There were multiple forces of dynamism in American communications and computing in the decades after World War II. Massive federal investments drove advancements in the technological underpinnings of electronics and computing. Individuals working in a number of different settings—established corporations like IBM and new companies like Codex and Milgo, and researchers at MIT and other universities—seized the moment to create new opportunities. Even in an industry that appeared to be stable, the telephone industry monopoly, the incumbent monopolist was under increased attack, forced to defend itself from antitrust officials, FCC regulators, and entrepreneurs who aspired to be AT&T's competitors.

The year 1968 was shaping up to be a very busy and potentially transforming year for the FCC and CCB. While FCC Examiner Naumowicz had issued his initial decision in August 1967 that the Carterfone did not pose a threat in connecting to the telephone system, the debate continued over the wider implications of allowing users permission to interface with AT&T's network. On the matter of MCI, after Scharfman's initial response in favor of approving MCI's license, the FCC, at the time operating with six commissioners after the retirement of commissioner

49. Computer I, Docket No. 16979, NOI 7 FCC 2d 19 (1967).

Loevinger, was split along party lines with the three Democrats in favor and the three Republicans against. Their final decision would not be made until after the politically auspicious appointment of commissioner Rex Lee by President Johnson, which was made in late 1968, before the election of Richard Nixon. By the end of 1967, Strassburg and the CCB had received responses to the Notice of Inquiry and, as we shall see in the following chapter, it was to be the tip of an iceberg heralding an unforeseen demand for communications technology.

In addition to the key events at the regulatory level, private firms like Codex and Milgo were poised to take advantage of a rush of new interest and investment in technology, giving rise to many garage tinkering start-ups as well as well-funded ones like Intel.

Onset of Competition: Data Communications, 1968–1972

2.1 Overview

The year 1968 would prove to be one of the most contentious and violent years in US history. Riots erupted in the wake of the assassination of Martin Luther King, Jr., in April. Robert F. Kennedy was killed a few months later. Demonstrations at the Democratic National Convention in August also turned violent as the Chicago Police and National Guard clashed with demonstrators protesting against the Vietnam War. A sense of turmoil permeated all aspects of American society. With the backdrop of so much political and social unrest, it is not surprising that the decades-long regulatory policy of upholding AT&T's stranglehold on the communications industry would be seen in new light—albeit in much less violent fashion. In the face of unprecedented technological advances in the processing, storage, and transmission of information, users demanded access to the telecommunications network in ways that challenged the existing regulatory guidelines.

The actions of the FCC in light of these new demands had a profound effect on the development of the data communications market-structure. Their response addressed several challenges to the existing regulations of AT&T's monopoly, including competition in the market for microwave telecommunications, regulation of telecommunications services for the purpose of data transfer, and the attachment of electronic devices to the network for controlling and facilitating data communication. Of key importance to the regulators was adherence to their initial mandate of protecting the public interest and the interest of commercial development.

The decisions of the FCC and the courts regarding AT&T gave a clear signal to entrepreneurs of data communications products to move forward or be left behind. In the brief period of 1968–1972, over 100 start-ups and existing companies brought to market products for this new industry. In addition to market leaders Codex and Milgo, this chapter introduces seven influential data communications start-ups founded in 1968–1969. Their founding stories follow, including the challenges they faced bringing their products to market and navigating the roadblocks the monolithic incumbent AT&T tried to place in their path. This was a period of rapid growth for successful start-ups in data communications, but with it came a rush of competition.

2.2 Government and AT&T

2.2.1 Computer Inquiry I

By the fall of 1967, responses to the Notice of Inquiry had been pouring into the FCC. To the FCC's Bernard Strassburg, who had wondered how real the interest in data communication was, it was as if a sensitive nerve had been struck. Furthermore, corporate users were eager to criticize AT&T. An already burdened CCB could not ignore thousands of pages of input and exhibits. As CCB staffers began leafing through the materials, two subjects came up again and again: the prohibitions on foreign attachments were unduly restrictive, and the telephone rate structures were designed for voice, not data, communications. The CCB had neither the staff nor the requisite expertise to properly interpret the 55 responses. So, the Bureau contracted the Stanford Research Institute, International (SRI) to do the analysis. Unmistakably, changes in market conditions and technologies were sending shock waves through the industry.

2.2.2 MCI and Carterfone

The FCC's initial decision to approve MCI's application for a microwave network was an opportunity for the FCC to open the door to new players in the communications industry. Likewise, the Commissioners would employ that same logic in the case of Carterfone. On June 27, 1968, in a surprising and unanimous decision, and despite last minute lobbying by AT&T and General Telephone & Electronics (GTE) that "the integrity of the telephone system necessitated the use of only carrier-supplied attachments,"[1] the FCC ruled in the Carterfone case that the tariff restrictions:

> ...are, and have since their inception been, unreasonable, unlawful, and unreasonably discriminatory under the Communications Act of 1934.[2]

1. S.L. Mathison and P.M. Walker. 1972. Regulatory and economic issues in computer communications. *Proceedings of the IEEE* 60 (November 1972), 1266.

2. Mathison and Walker, "Regulatory and economic issues in computer communications," 1266.

Because the tariff prohibited the use of "harmless as well as harmful devices," it placed an improper burden on the manufacturers and users of such devices. The Commission did allow that the carriers could submit new tariffs to protect the telephone system, including technical standards for any devices attaching to their system.[3]

In August 1968, *Datamation* reported the FCC decision

> the ruling, if it stands, breaks the market for modems wide open, and provides a major opportunity for independent manufacturers in areas like touch-tone keyboards and picture-phone type units. There are no authoritative figures on the number of Western Electric's modems in the dial-up network, but one manufacturer says that's where 90% of the business is. Among data set suppliers are General Electric, which announced an extensive line late last year, Automatic Electric, Milgo, Rixon, Collins Radio, and Ultronic.[4]

Thus began a back-and-forth process in which the regulators sought to encourage developments in the promising new markets of computer communication technologies, while the heads of AT&T tried to maintain their control. That same August, AT&T leadership proposed a

> new "Data Access Arrangement," under which independently manufactured terminals could be coupled electrically, inductively, or acoustically to the public telephone system through a "protective device" and a "network controller." The data communications user would pay $10 to have the protective device installed, and $2 a month for the service. . . Both devices are to be supplied exclusively by the Bell system, and no one else apparently will have any say in their design.[5]

In September, the FCC asserted its decision: devices that did not adversely affect the telephone company's operations, or the telephone system's utility for others, could be connected to the interstate telephone system.[6] AT&T soon responded by filing new tariffs that allowed customers to directly connect terminal equipment to the public switched network provided they connect using an AT&T supplied protective connecting arrangement (PCA) (see Figure 2.1). That this tariff applied to

3. *Hush-A-Phone v. United States*, 238 F.2d 266 (D.C. Cir. 1956).

4. *Datamation*, August 1968, 86–87.

5. *Datamation*, August 1968.

6. Fred W. Henck and Bernard Strassburg. 1988. *A Slippery Slope: The Long Road to the Breakup of AT&T*. Greenwood Press, 106.

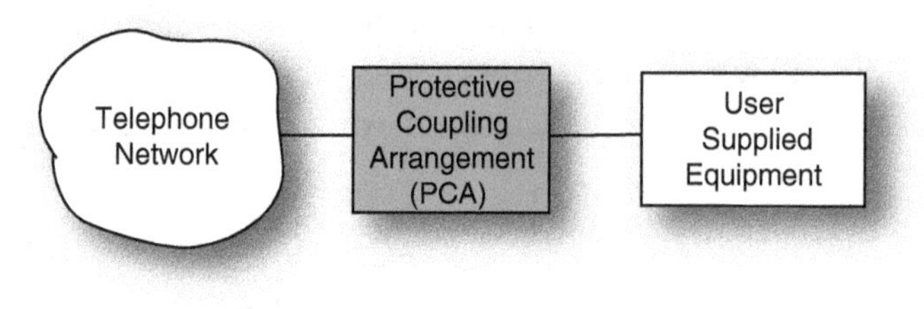

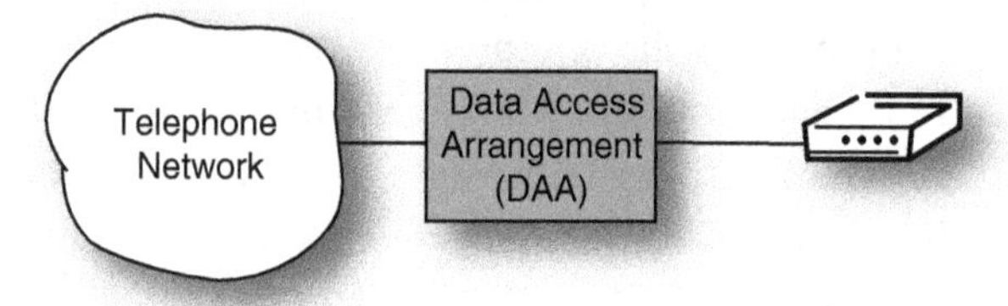

Figure 2.1 AT&T Carterfone tariff. Source: Illustration by James L. Pelkey and Loring G. Robbins.

anyone wishing to connect equipment to the network far exceeded the expectations of the FCC for a tariff specific to Carterfone. The FCC ruled that the new tariffs would become effective January 1, 1969.[7]

Once the new tariffs became effective, AT&T announced that the PCA for modems would be called a Data Access Arrangement (DAA). DAAs had two primary functions: assure telephone network integrity by limiting the signal power of attached modems and maintain exclusive Bell control of all network signaling functions.[8] To be installed only by Bell personnel, and to rent for $2 to $4 per month, DAAs were a single circuit board that came with a separate telephone set having a voice/data key. There were no provisions for either automatic dialing or unattended answering—even though Bell modems already had these functions. So, while the DAAs made it possible to connect independent manufacturers' modems to the switched telephone network, they severely constrained modem functionality and introduced additional costs.

Immediately there were protests. Why should independent modem manufacturers face extra costs and reduced functionality? Bell was up to its old tricks again.

7. Shortly after the tariffs went into effect, accepted by the FCC, the parties to the Carterfone antitrust lawsuit settled out of court. Carter et al. received a reported $375,000; they had sued for $1,350,000. A little over a year later, Carter left his firm to consult. Henck and Strassburg, *A Slippery Slope*, 107.

8. Data Pro 1970, Computer Conversions Inc., All About Modems, 70F-300-01b.

What seemed particularly preposterous to those independent modem manufacturers selling modems to telephone companies was that they would now have to re-engineer them to work with DAAs. This shaky logic made it possible for them to sell a modem to a telephone company, which could sell it to a customer, but the modem manufacturer could not sell to that same customer? In response, AT&T claimed: "If we provide it, we maintain it and we know it's going to work right. If the customer provides it, he might not maintain it, and a short might cause a voltage surge on the line which might kill somebody."[9]

The new tariffs were already more liberal than anyone would have thought possible only months earlier. Strassburg responded to the independent manufacturers' complaints, telling them, "Well, you may be right, but this is where it is right now, and until we find a better alternative, this is where it's going to stay, because we're not going to open up the network to indiscriminate connections for fear that this would degrade the performance of the network."[10]

The CCB now wanted independent assessment of alternatives to PCAs. Seeking the most impartial, technically competent organization, the FCC contracted with the National Academy of Sciences (NAS) to study the tariffs and to recommend alternatives.[11] In February 1969, a month earlier than expected, the FCC received the analysis, which was conducted by the SRI.[12] The report was too technical and detailed to be understood by anyone at the FCC or CCB. Once again, Strassburg sought out Baran, who had since left Rand and started the Institute for the Future (IF). Presumably by coincidence, Romnes of AT&T was a member of IF's Board of Trustees. Baran initially agreed to interpret the report.

9. Thomas Thompson recalled, "This is the type of horror stories they always raised. So that was what we were stuck with. We were stuck with the DAA." Thomas Thompson and Robert Smith, oral history interview by James L. Pelkey, March 11, 1988, Middlebury, CT. Computer History Museum, Mountain View, CA. Available from https://archive.computerhistory.org/resources/access/text/2017/11/102738591-05-01-acc.pdf.

10. Bernard Strassburg, oral history interview by James L. Pelkey, May 3, 1988, Washington, DC. Computer History Museum, Mountain View, CA. Available from https://archive.computerhistory.org/resources/access/text/2015/11/102738016-05-01-acc.pdf.

11. Henck and Strassburg, *A Slippery Slope*, 107: "NAS had its Computer Sciences and Engineering Board set up a fourteen-member panel to analyze the considerable amount of written material submitted to the FCC. The fact that panel members were not 'pure' scientists in the sense that they drew paychecks immediately caused criticism. It was a symbol of changing attitudes that most objections were raised because two of the fourteen panelists were officials of the Bell System. The others were employed by nonprofit and/or government organizations, non-Bell manufacturers, independent telephone companies, or large users of communication services."

12. Stanford Research Institute, "Policies and Issues Presented By the Interdependence of Computer and Communications Services" (Report Nos. 7379B0).

However, shortly after taking the assignment, AT&T offered Baran's IF a lucrative, and interesting, consulting contract. Needing the work, Baran notified the FCC of his potential conflict of interest and ceased being a consultant.[13] The AT&T assignment was to study its management practices. Baran identified entrepreneurs in data communications as a constituency that now wanted their voices heard in the discussion over AT&T's tariffs.

Baran remembers his conclusion: "The old constituency in the past was never big enough, or had enough interest, to attend hearings or doing anything, but now you have these new entrepreneurs coming along and that you're probably better off giving in to them and not threaten the rest of your system."

With Baran's help as a "general consultant," in May the FCC issued a *Report and Further Notice of Inquiry* to solicit opinions on the SRI study. Respondents' comments added little to the FCC's understanding.[14] The CCB now had the task of deciding what actions they should, and would, take. Strassburg remembers his perspective changing during this period:

> Bell couldn't be all things to all people for all times. The environment had changed, or was changing. . . innovation and creativity didn't all start within the walls of Bell Labs, and all the wisdom wasn't necessarily in Bell Labs. We were also concerned, I was concerned, that AT&T was beginning to grow big, in terms of not only revenue—they had always been dominant as a corporate

13. Baran recalled: "Here I was working for the FCC and along came this contract from AT&T, for the Institute for the Future, and we needed that work, so I told my friends at FCC that I would no longer be able to be a consultant to them, and they said: "Well, we understand, but why don't you become a general consultant to us on research and development, because we're not doing a very good job with research and development at the FCC and we could use some help, and that should be clean and shouldn't give you any problem with conflict of interest." So I said, "OK." And I said: "First of all, how much are we paying, what would have been the Chief Engineer." They said $25,000. And I said: "Well, that's not enough money to get the sort of person you really need for that top position." They said: "We know, but the Congress dictated that. It's in the legislation, and that was done purposely, because about 25% of the congressmen had some interest or other in a broadcast station, or TV, a very high correlation. It was very important to their political position. So, there was a nice strong political constituency that wanted to see the FCC weak for some time, and so that was a constraint. So I said: "Well, no, until you get this problem fixed, there's hardly very much you can do," cause the people they had were just, they were technicians. So I didn't do a lot more consulting after that one." Paul Baran, oral history interview with James L. Pelkey, January 12, 1988, Campbell, CA. Computer History Museum, Mountain View, CA. Available from https://archive.computerhistory.org/resources/access/text/2017/09/102740210-05-01-acc.pdf.

14. Mathison and Walker, "Regulatory and economic issues in computer communications," 1256.

power—but at this time it was getting awfully big, so was there room for other participants in this marketplace called communications?[15]

On April 3, 1970, the FCC issued its "Tentative Decision," popularly known as the "Computer Inquiry."[16] The Tentative Decision addressed four key issues: Data Processing Computer Services, Common-Carrier Provision of Data Processing Services, Store-and-Forward Message-Switching Services, and Hybrid Services.[17] On the whole, the picture that emerged from the FCC's Decision was more complex than the regime of regulated monopoly that had prevailed since 1913. In some areas, such as data processing computer services, the FCC found little need to assert its regulatory authority. But in areas such as hybrid services and common carrier provision of data processing, the regulatory issues were more subtle and complex. Most important, there were several suggestions that the FCC was more willing to entertain competition than in the past.

In September 1970, the FCC heard oral arguments from 20 interested parties. The FCC continued to collect information, including the June 1970 report from the National Academy of Sciences. The NAS report concluded that uncontrolled interconnection could cause harm to personnel, network performance, and property. Protective couplers and signal-level criteria could provide an acceptable way of assuring network protection, albeit with increased overall costs. Another acceptable way to assure network protection would be to establish a regime of standards and enforced certification of equipment.

A subsequent study commissioned by the FCC to computer consultant Dittberner Associates concluded that manufacturers of data modems and other types of interconnected customer equipment could easily build into their equipment the necessary circuitry to protect the telephone network—the common carriers need not be the only ones providing network protective couplers.[18] Furthermore, a program of standards and certification would be an inexpensive way to extend interconnection privileges without harm to the common-carrier network.

Both the NAS and Dittberner reports agreed that safe attachment of customer-provided equipment could be accomplished without the objectionable carrier-supplied access arrangements or PCAs. Knowing an alternative to the PCAs existed, the CCB needed a plan of action. Due to manufacturer and customer interest,

15. Strassburg interview, Computer History Museum.

16. *Tentative Decision and Notice of Proposed Rulemaking*, 28 F.C.C. 2d 291 (1970). The FCC later held two successor Inquiries, at which point the 1970 decision became referred to as "Computer Inquiry I."

17. Mathison and Walker, "Regulatory and economic issues in computer communications."

18. Dittberner Associates, Interconnection Action Recommendations, Rep. to the FCC, Sept. 1970.

the FCC established a Public Branch Exchange (PBX) industry advisory committee in March of 1971 with 30 members representing carriers, equipment manufacturers, and users. This committee had the responsibility to devise technical standards as well as certification and enforcement procedures permitting direct connection of PBX equipment—without using PCAs.[19] As we will see in later chapters, the evolution of the PBX, and in particular the data PBX and CBX (computerized branch exchange), will have significant impact on the data communications and networking industries.

In that same month, on March 18, 1971, the FCC, in a divided 4 to 3 vote, rendered its Final Decision.[20] In it, the FCC introduced the concept of "maximum separation"[21] to solve the problem of common carriers wanting to provide data processing services. To compete in the *unregulated* field of data processing services, common carriers needed separate subsidiaries with separate books of account, separate officers, separate operating personnel, separate equipment, and facilities devoted exclusively to the rendition of data processing services.[22] These subsidiaries would lease communication services from carriers (the parent company or any other carrier) under public tariffs, just like competing suppliers of data-processing services.[23] Except for "hybrid services," the regulatory issues between data processing and communications seemed settled. (The Second Circuit of the US Court of Appeals later supported the commission's determinations in a February 1973 decision.[24])

19. Mathison and Walker, "Regulatory and economic issues in computer communications."

20. Common Carrier, pg. 191 (Final Decision, 28 FCC 2d 267 (1971)).

21. Bernard Strassburg. 1973. The Computer Inquiry—The regulatory results. *Computer Law Service, Callaghan & CO*, 2–3: "Thus, the commission invoked the doctrine of 'maximum separation' by which to insure that the regulated activities of the carrier are in no way commingled with any of its non regulated activities involving data processing........Essentially, the degree of separation required by the commission was premised on the following regulatory concerns: (1) that the sale of data processing services by carriers should not adversely affect the provision of efficient and economic common carrier services; (2) that the costs related to the furnishing of such data processing services should not be passed on, directly or indirectly, to the users of common carrier services; (3) that revenues derived from common carrier services should not be used to subsidize any data processing services; (4) that the furnishing of such data processing services by carriers should not inhibit free and fair competition between communication common carriers and data processing companies or otherwise involve practices contrary to the policies and prohibitions of the antitrust laws."

22. 28 FCC 2nd 267, at 270.

23. Mathison and Walker, "Regulatory and economic issues in computer communications."

24. Common Carrier, pg. 191. GTE Service Corp. v. F.C.C., 474 F. 2d 724.

As much as the FCC wanted to proceed in an orderly fashion, events soon proved messy. The immediate cause was two proposed tariffs filed by AT&T in late 1971. The first tariff mandated use of DAAs on leased lines that had to-date been exempt from the PCA tariffs. Interestingly, leased lines were also the facilities experiencing the most competition from the independent modem manufacturers, a connection not lost on the modem manufacturers. The second tariff lowered modem rental rates.[25]

Michael Slomin, a lawyer at the FCC working closely with Strassburg, remembers the complaints of the Independent Data Communications Manufacturers Association (IDCMA), a recently formed cooperative of independent modem and other data communication manufacturers (discussed in more detail below):

> This is manifestly anti-competitive. This is evidence of a grand master plan to wipe us out, and furthermore, it's predicated on a false premise anyway. This data access arrangement is ridiculous. It's not needed. Our devices are designed properly to work with the telephone network, indeed, our companies sell them to about a hundred governments abroad for use with their telephone networks and there's no problem whatsoever. And finally, the data access arrangement is a Cadillac when a Chevy would have done the job. It has extra functions and, on top of all else, it impairs our communications. It introduces its own aberrations and makes our communications service stinky. Do something about this, FCC.[26]

Competitive outrage could no longer be contained. Independent manufacturers began clogging the courts with antitrust lawsuits. The FCC was stretched beyond its capacity to regulate the communications monopoly while fostering independent growth in new communications technologies. Each party played to their strengths: the entrepreneurs banded together to force change while the monopolist threw obstacles in their way. The battleground would soon move to Congress.

2.2.3 William McGowan and MCI

MCI's application for a license to offer microwave communication services was still ongoing. While the FCC had initially recommended approval of the license

25. "All About Modems," *Datapro*, 1971, pg. 01c.

26. Mike Slomin, oral history interview by James L. Pelkey, March 10, 1988, Allentown, NJ. Computer History Museum, Mountain View, CA. Available from https://archive.computerhistory.org/resources/access/text/2017/09/102740208-05-01-acc.pdf.

in 1967, additional hearings consumed another 2 years before a final decision was made. In this period MCI struggled to raise funds.

William G. McGowan joined MCI in 1968 with an investment of $50,000 that gave him 50% ownership of the newly incorporated company, MCI Communications. McGowan already had a reputation for guiding businesses to success as a young consultant in New York City, but his role in guiding the upstart company into battle with AT&T made him one of the most influential and successful entrepreneurs of his day.[27]

When he joined MCI, the company was waiting for FCC approval for a radio transmission line between St. Louis and Chicago. The company planned to offer private radio communication to trucking and shipping companies using microwave radio transmission towers and local telephone lines. The plan would bring MCI into direct competition with AT&T. Where others feared the overpowering monopoly of AT&T, McGowan saw opportunity and an irresistible challenge.

In 1969, MCI received approval from the FCC. Of course, AT&T appealed the decision. Nevertheless, McGowan and MCI began building microwave towers as fast as they could. McGowan fostered a spirit of passion and excitement in his employees as they set about changing the face of the communications industry. MCI quickly built out its radio tower network, filing applications through subsidiary companies to create microwave communications lines between other major cities in the country. In 1971, they began selling a data transmission service to customers.

While AT&T fought MCI every step of the way, including raising rates and assessing fees MCI had to pay to access AT&T's local lines, MCI was able to win support from the FCC and was effectively sanctioned as a long-distance carrier. The fight between the David and Goliath of telecommunications lasted into the 1980s.

Without Bill McGowan taking on AT&T, the communications market may have looked very different. Not only did he see and pursue an opportunity to provide a service people wanted (lower long-distance rates), which alone would have qualified him as a true entrepreneur, but he did so in spite of significant market challenges. While the technological advances, regulatory policy, and economic environment were ripe for the data communications market to emerge, it was the bold vision and action of a few key pioneers like McGowan that accelerated its evolution by years and perhaps decades.

27. For more on MCI, see Philip Louis Cantelon. 1993. *The History of MCI 1968–1988: The Early Years*. Heritage Press.

2.3 IBM and Computing

2.3.1 Mainframe Computers and Time-Sharing

Demand for modems and multiplexers surged from 1968 to 1970 due to the huge success of the terminal-based IBM System/360 introduced in 1965 and the wider commercialization of time-sharing. And although time-sharing would suddenly collapse in 1970–1971, the sales of mainframe computers expanded from 5,700 units in 1970 to 14,000 units in 1973. Data communication products continued to grow at rates above 30% per year. The transition to terminal-based, on-line, real-time computing had happened, and, combined with the increasing use of remote terminal access, data communications had become a rapidly growing business.

One way competitors tried to differentiate their products from System/360 was time-sharing—largely because IBM did not support time-sharing in the System/360. IBM was late to the table with time-sharing and left this market open to other computer companies. DEC (PDP-10), GE (600 Series), and Scientific Data Systems (SDS 940) all had active presence in the time-sharing market by 1966. These companies supplied systems for many of the time-sharing projects funded by the Information Processing Techniques Office (IPTO) of ARPA. These government projects, such as Project Genie at UC Berkeley, which utilized the SDS 940, gave other computer companies a needed boost in the IBM-dominated market. The internal conflict within IBM over time-sharing vs. batch processing was an example of the type of inflexibility that so often hinders a large corporation from adapting to new technology in the industry and new demand in the marketplace.

2.3.2 Mainframe Market-Structure

In 1969, seven companies contested IBM in mainframe computers: GE, RCA, Burroughs, Control Data, Honeywell, NCR, and Sperry Rand's Univac division. Known as the "Seven Dwarfs," none believed they could unseat IBM, nor was that necessary to their survival and success. What each had to do was carve out enough market share, perhaps 10%, to become number two to IBM. And since none of them held more than a 5% market share, the challenge was to double their respective size by taking share from IBM. Two examples of such companies were GE and RCA, both industrial giants with the resources and commitment to succeed.

By the middle of 1969, GE's strategy had two components: dominate time-sharing and build a new line of computers compatible with the System/360. Time-sharing was the easy part. Management believed that they controlled 40% of the time-sharing market—through both its time-sharing services as well as leases, or infrequent sale, of mainframe computers—and, if time-sharing would come to represent as much as three-fourths of the market, as they believed, all they had to do was maintain their current share and they would be successful. Two assumptions drove their confidence in time-sharing: "by the late Seventies from one-third to one-half of all computer power in the US will be used for corporate strategic planning" and "within a couple of decades it will be as rare to find an in-house computer as it is to find a company-owned electric generating plant."[28]

The second leg of GE's strategy was formulated after March 1969. GE had to respond to the System/360 and developed a plan to do so, code named Project Shangri-La. "Project Shangri-La very likely produced the most comprehensive and boldest master plan for an assault on IBM ever prepared," wrote W. David Gardner in a 1970 *Datamation* article. GE was the only one of the Seven Dwarfs with the resources and size to take on IBM. The cost of implementing the master plan represented a significant investment, even for GE. Conservative estimates ran $450 to $500 million over 6 or 7 years, covering machine design and development as well as marketing development.[29] In September 1969, GE executives, emboldened with their new strategy, reaffirmed their commitment to the computer business.

RCA also premised their strategy on taking business from IBM. L. Edwin Donegan, Jr., an ex-IBM sales manager, who became vice president and general manager of RCA's Computer Systems Division on January 1, 1970, said: "We have two options if we want to get 10% of the market. We can get a little out of the hide of each of the other Dwarfs, or we can get it out of IBM's hide. It's easier for us to get after IBM."[30] RCA aimed to out-IBM IBM.

Once he became general manager, Donegan prioritized the need for a new line of computers within the year. On learning R&D would be of no help, the advanced computers they were developing would not be ready for at least 2 years, he decided to take their current Spectra series of computers, change the covers, add more memory, and introduce them as a new line. The scheduled introduction date was September 1970.

But on May 20, in "possibly the most startling event ever to occur in the computer industry,"[31] or so claimed *Datamation* in July, Honeywell announced it was acquiring all of GE's computer operations except the time-sharing division.

28. "It is hardly a coincidence that General Electric, the company that controls 40 percent of the time-sharing market, has also the longest and strongest commitment to management science." Tom Alexander. 1969. Computers can't solve everything. *Fortune* Oct 1969, 171.

29. W. David Gardner. 1970. Anatomy of a merger. *Datamation* Nov 15, 1970, 25.

30. W. David Gardner. 1972. Curtain act at RCA. *Datamation* March 1972, 36.

31. *Datamation* July 1970, 80.

(GE management refused to sell their last toehold in computers even though offered as much as $200 million.)[32] In exiting the mainframe computer business, GE had effectively conceded that IBM held too big a lead. The investment required was simply too large and too risky. Market consolidation, a sure sign of dominant designs and immensely powerful firms, had begun.

On June 30, 1970, IBM announced the System/370 line of computers. The System/370 represented incremental improvement along the technology trajectory established by the 360. A 1970 article in *Datamation* entitled "IBM's System/370 surfaces, but is that all there is?" points out that "perhaps that should not have been surprising, for it is unlikely that any company—least likely IBM—will ever shake the foundations of its user audience as profoundly as IBM did with the introduction of the incompatible S/360 series."[33] *Datamation* went on to say that RCA, Honeywell, and NCR had terminals and systems ready to respond to IBM's announcement. But nobody seemed to grasp that the scale and scope of response was insignificant, given the advantages IBM had been accumulating ever since the announcement of the S/360 in 1964.

In September 1970, RCA announced their new Spectra family of computers—believing they had priced their line very attractively to IBM's announced and to be announced products. Only, RCA misfired. The machines they announced to take control of IBM's market were obsoleted in less than a week when IBM announced the System/370-145 that had more memory and was lower priced than RCA had anticipated. The System/370-145 was the first commercial computer to ship with not only semiconductor memory but with virtual memory, which greatly expanded the effective memory the computer had.[34]

Undaunted, in March 1971, at the annual meeting, Robert Sarnoff, RCA's Chairman, told shareholders: "Our highest priorities today are the establishment of a profitable computer business and capture of the domestic industry's No. 2 position. RCA has made a greater investment in this effort than in any prior venture in its history, and we are convinced that the returns will be substantial."[35] RCA's computer revenues had grown from $14 million in 1960 to $257 million in 1970.

Just 9 months later, RCA abruptly, and without any counsel from those in its computer division, threw in the towel. Univac would buy its customer base of roughly 1,000 machines and 500 customers for $70 million and the potential of

32. Gardner, "Anatomy of a merger," 22.

33. "IBM's System/370 surfaces, but is that all there is?", *Datamation* Aug 1, 1970, 58.

34. *Datamation* March 1972, 37.

35. *Datamation* March 1972, 36.

another $30–60 million over the next 5 years.[36] It made little difference to the competitive dynamics of the market-structure for IBM was solidly in control.

In the early 1970s, the mainframe computer market-structure had become an oligopoly of one—IBM. The two potential alternatives, time-sharing or a better mainframe, proved false hope. Time-sharing could never overcome the overhead of communication costs—once terminals were over 100 miles from the computer telephone line charges made time-sharing unprofitable.[37] And as for a better mainframe, IBM had an 8 year advantage and an insurmountable lead.

2.3.3 Unbundling Software and Services

In January 1969, IBM announced record earnings of $871 million—a 34% increase. Revenues had increased by $1.5 billion to $6.8 billion. The very next day, on their last day in public office, January 17, 1969, Attorney General Ramsey Clark and his chief, Edwin M. Zimmerman, filed a major antitrust suit against IBM. The Justice Department was not the first to act, for in December 6, 1968, Control Data Corporation filed a suit charging IBM with violation of the Sherman Antitrust Act. Then earlier in January, Data Processing Financial & General sued IBM for violation of "antitrust laws, the Consent Decree of 1956, and state unfair competition laws."[38]

The Justice Department's suit focused on the sale and leasing of general-purpose digital computers. The complaint, in spelling out the extent of IBM's dominance of the computer market, seemed compelling. Every year from 1961 to 1967, IBM represented between 69% and 80% of the sales of computers. In 1967, while computers and related products only accounted for 43% of IBM's revenue, or $2.3 billion, IBM constituted 74% of the total computer market. And the nearest rival held but a 5% market share, or revenues of $165 million.[39]

According to *Business Week* of January 25, the Justice Department accused IBM of: "obtaining a "monopoly" by practicing manufacturing and marketing policies that deny competitors adequate opportunity in the computer market." The article goes on to identify four types of activities that IBM engaged in to effectively prohibit competition: A single price policy for equipment, programming, and "related support," including service personnel; domination of the software environment

36. *Datamation* Jan 1972, 53.

37. Manley R. Irwin, "The Computer Utility," *Datamation* Nov 1966, 26.

38. Data Processing Financial & General Data Corp. asked for more than $ 1 billion in damages. "Data Processing claims that IBM's business practices, particularly its sale and lease prices on new computers, injure computer equipment leasing companies. The complainant is a an eight-year-old operation that had 1968 revenues of $16.7-million. More than 99% of the equipment it leases was made by IBM." *Business Week* Jan. 11, 1969, 38.

39. *Business Week* Jan. 25, 1969, 37.

and related support; introducing low-profit lines of equipment and announcing new models earlier than they can deliver; and discriminatory pricing and price allowances to colleges and universities.

Once the Justice Department's lawsuit had been filed, Applied Data Research Inc. and Programmatics Inc., both software companies, filed as well.[40] They also targeted IBM's practice of not separately pricing hardware and software nor charging for software programming services. Since customers were forced to pay for IBM's software, whether used or not, it made it extremely difficult to convince customers to then pay for third-party software. Unless customers had the choice of *not* paying for IBM's software, they argued the software market would be stunted in growth.

While denying any connection, IBM announced on June 23, 1969, that as of January 1, 1970, it would unbundle hardware and software pricing, charge for programming services, service IBM equipment no matter how the customer acquired it, and charge for education courses.[41] There remained the question of IBM's market dominance, but it had eliminated many objectionable practices. Clearly the burst of lawsuits had, if not changed IBM managements' attitudes, forced to make them public. All competitors now had reason to rejoice as the rules of competition had now changed in their favor.[42]

2.3.4 Minicomputers

The market for minicomputers, still dwarfed by mainframes in terms of revenues, was now entering a time of rapid growth. Dominating the firms in this market was DEC and its flagship mini, the PDP-8, released in 1965. Dominance by DEC was short-lived, however, for between 1968 and 1972 ninety-two competitors entered the market.[43] The barrier to entry was low as new companies tapped technological advances in integrated circuits and cheaper methods of manufacturing at a time when the demand for lower-cost computing was expanding rapidly. The most important were Computer Control Company (3C)/Honeywell, Hewlett-Packard (HP), Data General, Prime, and finally IBM.

Honeywell built its minicomputer effort around 3C, an early entrant in the minicomputer market, known for its Digital Data Processor (DDP) series of minis. Introduced in 1963, the DDP-116 was the first 16-bit minicomputer. It sold for $28,500 and

40. *Datamation*, Jan. 1970, 89.

41. "Where investors get a run for the money," *Business Week* June 1, 1968, 104.

42. Martin Campbell-Kelly. 2004. *From Airline Reservations to Sonic the Hedgehog: A History of the Software Industry*. MIT Press, 109–119.

43. Chester Bell. 1984. The mini and micro industries. *Computer* 17 (November 1, 1984), 14–30.

was designed by Gardner Hendrie, who later designed computers for Data General. The company was purchased by Honeywell in 1966 and became its Computer Controls division. A version of the DDP 516 was adapted by Bolt, Beranek and Newman (BBN) as the first ARPANET Interface Message Processors in 1969.[44] Honeywell continued the DDP line until 1970 when they purchased the computer division of GE and decided to focus on larger time-sharing systems.

After rumors of a failed attempt to buy DEC in the early 1960s, HP entered the minicomputer market in 1966 with its first minicomputer, the 16-bit 2116A, which sold for $22,000. It was designed to be used as an instrument controller to interface in real-time with HP's many instrument products. Later, this same model was also widely used for time-sharing. Subsequent minicomputer products included the successful HP 3000 series, which poached some IBM mainframe users.

Data General was founded in 1968 by three former employees of DEC, Edson deCastro, who had managed development of the PDP-8 minicomputer, and two engineers, Henry Burkhardt, III, and Richard Sogge. A fourth founder, Herbert Richman, left a marketing position at Fairchild Semiconductor. Data General released the Nova computer in 1969, which quickly became a success with scientific laboratories due to its speed and low price. In designing the 16-bit Nova, deCastro minimized the amount of wiring required in its assembly by using a single printed circuit board for the backplane, greatly reducing the cost of manufacturing and assembly. The Nova line provided significant competition to both DEC's PDP-8 and later PDP-11.

Prime Computer co-founder William Poduska had been involved with the early development of time-sharing at MIT. Founded in 1972, Prime developed a series of minicomputers and made significant early developments in computer networking with its PRIMENET.

Finally, IBM offered products in the minicomputer market with its early lower-priced model computers, such as the 1130, introduced in 1965, but didn't become a major threat to the early minicomputer leaders even after it introduced the Series/1 minicomputer in 1976.

The rapid growth in the number of minicomputer manufacturers between 1968–1970 was a key factor in the growth of the data communications market during the same time period. The access to cheaper computer power, coupled with a huge demand for computers from businesses, universities, and government, meant many players could enter the field and gain significant market share without

44. Bolt Beranek and Newman, "Proposal: Interface Message Processors for the ARPA Computer Network," 6 September 1968, page 11, available from https://historyofcomputercommunications.info/assets/pdf/bbn-arpanet-prop-ocr.pdf#page=11.

much in the way of competition. The abundance of early entrants in the minicomputer market-structure was typical of an emerging market, with companies earning large margins and experiencing rapid growth.

More fuel came from the fact that over-the-counter stocks were soaring in 1968 and 1969, leading to one of the hottest new issues markets ever. Nearly 1,000 small companies offered their stocks to the public. Underwriting of small company stocks reached $1.4 billion. Opportunities to invest in early-stage private companies and to cash out in public offerings seemed endless. It was a propitious time for entrepreneurs interested in data communication technologies.[45]

2.4 Early Data Communications Leaders: 1968–1969

2.4.1 Codex

By June 1967, Jerry Holsinger, now an employee of Codex, began the challenge of converting his prototype leased line modem into a shippable product. A year later, in May 1968, Codex introduced the AE-96, the world's first 9,600bps leased line modem. It weighed approximately 125lbs and consisted of 66 printed circuit boards of RTL semiconductor logic. When installed, each pair of modems needed to be manually "tuned" to the telephone circuit, and when the line characteristics changed, as they invariably did, the modems had to be re-tuned. Re-tuning required qualified personnel to make adjustments to the modems at both ends—a serious problem when customers wanted to use the modems on expensive international circuits. As was true for many early electronic products using RTL logic, the AE-96 generated troublesome heat. Since each end of the circuit required an AE-96, the total cost to a customer was $46,000.

The Codex Board of Directors knew they needed to hire personnel with commercial experience. President Jim Cryer felt the highest priority was finding a vice president to head sales and marketing. The executive search firm he hired quickly focused on Art Carr, director of marketing for the minicomputer company 3C.

Carr needed little persuading for he had recently completed an assessment of the opportunities in data communications and had recommended that 3C make data communications a strategic focus. Honeywell had acquired 3C in 1966 and now greatly influenced strategic decisions, and Carr's recommendations were not adopted. Hence, the timing could not have been better for Codex as Carr was more than ready to leave 3C.

45. William D. Bygrave and Jeffry A. Timmons. 1992. *Venture Capital at the Crossroads*. Harvard Business School Press, 22.

Quickly coming to terms, the outwardly calm yet intensely competitive Carr joined Codex as Vice President of Marketing at the end of July. Decades later, he still remembered his first day with the company:

> Jim Cryer, the founding president of Codex, was a fine man, but he was the world's greatest optimist. It's just beyond my ability to describe it to you, but I can give you an example. He had a memorandum waiting for me the day I started that was about four or five pages long that added up to six or seven million dollars of business that was about to close, and the very first thing I did was take a two-week vacation. I said to him: 'If you've got all this business lined up, I was going to go down to the Cape this year.' And he said: 'Oh, yeah, no problem.'[46]

Cryer next recruited James Storey to be the vice president of administration. The staffing costs soon strained Codex's financial resources. Without more money, its efforts at self-transformation might mean accelerated bankruptcy. The good news was that the prospects of the AE-96 had investors and investment banks claiming they could easily raise ample money. The phenomenal success of computers—and technology in general—kept investors salivating for the next great product opportunity.

2.4.2 Milgo

By early 1968, Milgo management had reason to celebrate. Their recently introduced 4400/48, priced at $5,885 each, proved to be the first reliable 4,800bps leased-line modem to work over standard grade, private telephone lines. The 4400/48 was an instant hit. Investment bankers began selling management on the idea of going public; the market for technology stocks that had been so hot through most of 1967 looked to be returning. Needing cash to finance its growth, Milgo filed to go public in May 1968. Their timing could not have been better. In the first month of trading Milgo's stock price doubled.[47] Then in August, Milgo signed an agreement with Racal Electronics Limited (Racal), a United Kingdom corporation, to sell Milgo modems internationally, raising another $250,000.[48] By October it had

46. Art Carr, interview by James L. Pelkey, April 6, 1988, Newton, MA. Computer History Museum, Mountain View, CA. Available from https://archive.computerhistory.org/resources/access/text/2015/10/102737982-05-01-acc.pdf.

47. "Market briefs," *Business Week* May 18, 1968, 128.

48. In August 1968, they agree "to form a jointly owned United Kingdom corporation to be named Racal Milgo Limited (Racal Milgo). Racal agreed to pay to Milgo the sum of $250,000 in exchange for one half the manufacturing and marketing rights to the data modem product line in Europe, Australia, New Zealand, and the Union of South Africa." Milgo Annual Report 1968, pg. 10.

become clear that the data communication business needed to stand on its own, not as a wholly owned subsidiary of Milgo. So, a new company—International Communications Corporation (ICC)—was chartered with 3% of the stock distributed to employees.[49] (Our convention will be to use Milgo, not ICC, as the corporation name, for eventually that will become the industry practice.) Modem sales for Milgo in 1968 would total $1.1 million, second only to AT&T.

2.4.3 Codex

Fortunately for Codex management, the "feeding frenzy" for stocks of young technology companies continued. With promises for the future more important than current operating results, and with the performance of Milgo's stock on record, Codex went public on December 23, 1968, raising $2.1 million, with a post-money valuation of $12.5 million. The success of the offering rested entirely on the excitement generated by the revolutionary AE-96, not the low margin, unpredictable government R&D operations. Sales of $1.3 million for 1968, however, included no modem sales.

In early 1969, Codex used money from its public offering to fund a promotions campaign for its AE-96 modem. Mindful that if they could sell 50 modems in the coming year that they would equal all of last year's sales, they were both stunned and ecstatic when they received 8,000 inquiries. It seemed as though all they had to do was scale up manufacturing and begin filling orders. That was until they had experience with customers using their modem. The AE-96 would not stay working. Carr remembers: "We used to joke that we had made something less than 100 AE-96s and shipped several hundred of them, because they kept coming back and going out and coming back and going out again."[50]

With each passing month, Carr bore the brunt of Jim Cryer's frustrations. Cryer, Carr's boss and President, read the overwhelming interest in the AE-96 as customers ready to buy and didn't want to hear Carr's excuse of "but it doesn't work" for not meeting sales objectives. Since it had been Cryer's decision to bet the future of Codex on the AE-96, he leaned on his management to get results. But results were

49. Again from the 1968 Milgo Annual Report: "The Company believed the formation of ICC to be in its best interests, and that the grant of stock bonuses to the selected officers and key employees would enhance the probability of the Company's retaining these persons in its employ. The Company believes the retention of these persons to be important to its future.......At this time, ICC performs marketing and engineering functions in the data communications field and utilized the Company's manufacturing facilities for its manufacturing needs." The three percent it distributed was much less than the twenty plus percent common for independent companies.

50. Carr interview, Computer History Museum.

not forthcoming. They were quickly depleting their cash. A gloomy cloud hung over every conversation and decision.

Solving the cash crisis meant solving the AE-96 problem. No one understood the problem, much less the solution. Holsinger was stumped. Kohlenberg, bereft of ideas, turned in frustration to Dave Forney, who worked exclusively on R&D development contracts, and asked him to drop what he was doing to help. Forney earned his Ph.D. from MIT in information theory and had virtually no modem experience.

A frustrated Holsinger identified the problem of the AE-96 as "phase jitter." Phase jitter, while endemic to telephone lines, remained largely unrecognized for it had no effect on voice communications or the slower-speed modems of the day. Since telephone lines were not controlled for phase, every circuit could differ as to being either in phase or not. Phase fluctuations—hence jitter—caused modems to lose equalization. The AE-96s could neither detect nor correct phase problems, if phase jitter occurred, so they ceased working.

Forney quickly, and cleverly, conceived of how to detect and correct phase jitter errors to stabilize the performance of the AE-96. With Forney's innovation, the AE-96, once equalized to a circuit, could adapt to subsequent phase jitter. The required electronics forced the addition of another printed circuit board that had to be hung under the lid of the modem for lack of space. Named the Threshold Decision Computer (TDC) for marketing reasons, it pulled out as if from a drawer and had a red light that flashed every time it corrected an error. Carr recalls: "Well, it worked. In fact, I remember going to Air France in Paris, which was the first transatlantic installation of 9600 bit per second traffic, and they used to run it with the drawer out all the time because it somehow gave them comfort to see this red light blinking."[51]

John Pugh, Director of Product Marketing since January 1969, wanted to include the TDC with every AE-96 without charge, arguing that the modem did not work without it. But Cryer, facing a survival-threatening cash crisis, insisted it be sold as an extra. So the TDC, which made for a stable and working AE-96, sold for $2,000 and shipped with every modem.

Next, working AE-96s made obvious the problem that commercial customers did not have peripherals that communicated at 9,600bps. Recalling their days at 3C when they sold minicomputers to multiplex many incoming communication lines to host computers, Carr and Pugh turned to the idea of using a multiplexer. If Codex had a small, inexpensive multiplexer for eight 1,200bps lines, or four 2,400bps lines, then the AE-96 would provide the transmission speeds customers wanted. As if by magic, a multiplexer of eight or four lines solved another problem: The added

51. Carr interview, Computer History Museum.

expense of the multiplexers, as well as the premium paid for the AE-96s, were recovered easily through reduced telephone line costs since only one telephone line would be needed.

Carr and Pugh contacted ADS hoping to buy multiplexers, but ADS had absolutely no interest in an OEM arrangement, strained as they were to engineer all the products in their development queue. Carr and Pugh then began arguing their case to Cryer and the engineers. Relieved to have at least a reason for optimism, Cryer authorized an internal development effort to develop a multiplexer.

Carr next pressed his case for a 4,800bps modem, but this time his reasoning fell on deaf ears. Carr refused to give in; every day his salespeople complained of having sold customers on upgrading to higher-speed modems, only to have them buy less risky 4,800bps modems, often from Milgo, their competitor and a growing concern to Carr. Certain he was right, Carr pressed Cryer at every opportunity: "A, it will work. B, I can sell it, and it would be nice if we had some money coming into the place!"[52] Cryer remained unyielding.

By November, Holsinger no longer could repress his inner calling to start his own company, and he resigned from Codex. The man who first proved a 9,600bps modem was possible had seen his knowledge and expertise institutionalized as Codex's growing engineering department. Lacking challenges and sensing a boring future engineering slower-speed modems, Holsinger concluded he could do the same in a company of his own. In 1970, using the profits from the sale of his Codex stock, Holsinger, the entrepreneur, joined a long list of start-ups by founding Intertel.

2.4.4 ADS

In the spring of 1968, Art Wilkes' neighbor, John Kinmouth and a group of his friends invested $100,000 in ADS. Wilkes and Bob Schaaf next began pounding the pavement for a first customer while Bill Norred continued to labor in Wilkes' garage to finish a working prototype of their time division multiplexer (TDM). The more people Wilkes and Schaaf talked to, the more they believed their window of opportunity would be brief. If they could just secure IBM's time-sharing operation—Service Bureau Corporation—as a customer, then they could withstand any competitive onslaught, or so they thought.

Summer turned to fall before the ADS-660 shipped. Even so, it could multiplex three times as many terminals—45 as opposed to 15—as the most competitive frequency division multiplexer. They knew they had a winner and so did IBM, which signed a $1 million contract. Norred remembers: "It was a big hit mainly

52. Carr interview, Computer History Museum.

because the timing of it was coupled with the time-sharing industry really starting to emerge."[53]

For 1968, ADS had sales of $750,000; 1969 looked to be a blockbuster year. It had a head of steam entering 1969 with an innovative TDM and a contract with IBM. In having built diagnostics into the ADS-660, ADS had found a way to wedge itself successfully between AT&T and IBM.[54] So while it made for an uncomfortable existence, it offered fertile ground to grow before the behemoths took notice.

In fact, sales, and thus the need for working capital, were growing so rapidly that ADS was strapped for cash. Unfortunately, in early 1969, selling stock to the public was no longer an option. Instead, ADS began to explore the idea of a partnership with The Automatics Division of North American Rockwell (Rockwell), a major defense and space contractor. Rockwell had developed an automatically equalizing 4,800bps modem under military contract and now wanted to sell it commercially. ADS had been selling 4,800bps modems through OEM arrangements with Milgo, but like the Codex AE-96 the modems had to be manually equalized.[55] Just as Codex had found, Wilkes knew that the ability to sell a reliable high-speed modem gave ADS's customers added incentive to buy their multiplexers. "The more modems, the more multiplexers we could sell; 4800 we could really sell."[56] So when ADS management learned of Rockwell's new modem technology, they couldn't believe their good fortune.

After hasty negotiations, an agreement was reached. Rockwell would sell their technology to ADS for $2 million. In return, Rockwell would invest more than $2 million in ADS and guarantee a line of credit in return for 25% ownership, leaving management and existing investors with 75% ownership.

---

53. William (Bill) Norred, oral history interview by James L. Pelkey, April 27, 1988, Simi Valley, CA. Computer History Museum, Mountain View, CA. Available from https://archive.computerhistory.org/resources/access/text/2018/07/102738827-05-01-acc.pdf.

54. Norred recalled: "The ADS multiplexer used to get so hot, people used to joke about being able to fry eggs on the front panel, and in fact we tried to do without fans for years, but we finally had to give up and put fans in the unit because it would just get so hot that the front panel would almost melt. It literally had all these 28 volt lamps in it, but it was the beginnings of diagnostics." Norred interview, Computer History Museum.

55. Norred recalls: "Most of our links were 4800, and the dominant supplier at that time, of course, was Milgo. Milgo, for all intents and purposes, in the beginnings around '69, was the dominant supplier of high-speed modems. They had this manually equalized 4800 bit per second modem." Norred interview, Computer History Museum.

56. Art Wilkes, oral history interview by James L. Pelkey, May 9, 1988, Chatsworth, CA. Computer History Museum, Mountain View, CA. Available from https://archive.computerhistory.org/resources/access/text/2018/07/102738826-05-01-acc.pdf.

Before year-end 1969, ADS shipped the Rockwell-designed modem. It was a disaster economically, however, costing as much to make as the price for which it could be sold. Without any good alternatives, management decided to sell the existing version until a modem built with new semiconductor chips from Rockwell could replace it. Then the projected cost of the modem would drop from $2,000, to $600 a unit, turning the corner on profit.

Heady from being uniquely positioned as the only company selling both TDMs and high-speed modems, ADS management aimed to become the dominant supplier of all products needed to connect computers and remote peripherals, including IBM 2260 compatible controllers, computer-based front-end processors, CRT terminals, and terminals to replace either teletypes or IBM 2741 terminals. Bill Norred, head of engineering and manufacturing, began ramping up the engineering organization and, before the end of 1969, had a staff of nearly 300. ADS had close to 400 employees. Norred remembers: "The idea was that we would literally provide everything from the computer interface all the way out to the terminal, except the telephone lines. . . I'll never forget running this big multi-page ad, based upon the American Flag, that showed we provide everything but the computers and the telephone lines."[57]

Propelled by the demand for their TDMs, ADS's revenues soared to nearly $5.0 million in 1969. ADS became the runaway success of data communications.

2.5 A Swarm of Data Communications Start-ups: 1968–1970

The period of 1968–1970 saw the founding of dozens of new data communications companies. This Schumpeterian swarm was a sure sign of the start of the competition stage of a market-structure. In many cases, these start-ups were founded by engineers who left companies that had recently been acquired by larger companies where the prospects for innovative and stimulating work were lacking. In several instances, these new companies started out as OEM manufacturers for Western Union. What follows briefly are the early histories of the entrepreneurs of seven other leading firms in data communications formed between 1968–1970.

One company that will play a continuing role that was founded in 1968 is Infotron. Five other leading data communication firms were founded in 1969: General DataComm (GDC), Timeplex, Paradyne, Vadic, and Universal Data Systems (UDS). The last successful data communications company, Intertel, was founded in 1970.

57. Norred interview, Computer History Museum.

2.5.1 Infotron

In 1967, an eager Stan Hunkins challenged his boss, the vice president of engineering of Ultronic Systems. Hunkins said he could assemble a volunteer team and design a stock-quote desk system in 2 months, a task the company had not been able to accomplish in over 2 years. Given a green light, they succeeded. Afterwards, the team members hungered for more opportunities. However, the acquisition of Ultronic by GTE, a $2 billion company, portended more bureaucracy and less freedom. The conversations of the group soon turned to forming their own company. In September 1968, Hunkins, Jim Hahn, Joe Andrews, and Tony Barbaro launched Infotron in Hunkins' basement. From their Ultronic background, they knew that companies wanted to interface large numbers of asynchronous terminals to computers. So, they decided to innovate a TDM. In 1969, they introduced their TL110, so named because it multiplexed teletype machines that ran at 110 bits per second.

2.5.2 General DataComm

Like the founders of Infotron, Charles P. Johnson did not need others to convince him of the opportunities in data communications. Working early in his career at Illinois Bell Telephone, then selling telephone services to the SAGE project for International Telephone and Telegraph, and finally working for the military contractor Stelma, Johnson understood the need for modems and multiplexers. After Data Products Inc. acquired Stelma in 1968, Johnson decided it was time to strike out on his own. Needing a team, he approached others dissatisfied with the Data Products acquisition. Over the winter of 1968, Johnson, Robert Smith, Tom Lehrman, and Jack Arcara wrote a business plan. In 1968, there were primarily two types of communications lines available: PSTN phone lines from AT&T and private-line teletype networks supplied by AT&T or Western Union. When customers had problems, they called Western Union or AT&T and waited for them to be fixed. That might have been acceptable for administrative teletype networks, but for remote users trying to connect to a central computer, the problem needed immediate attention. Smith remembers: "We wanted to provide modems and multiplexers that not only could pass data through, link to link, but also have some diagnostic capability. We wanted to provide the user with some information as to what was happening."[58]

In 1969, the Johnson-led team formed General DataComm Industries Inc. (GDC) and raised $1.5M of venture capital. Incrementally innovating on the widely successful ADS-660 TDM, they introduced their TDM at the International Communications Association trade show in 1970. GDC had sales of $160,000 in 1970 with

58. Thompson and Smith interview, Computer History Museum.

a loss of $676,000. Western Union would be its first customer and remained its most important customer for many years. They next introduced low-cost dial-up modems.

2.5.3 Timeplex

In 1969, Ed Botwinick, an analyst with the investment bank Goldman Sachs, came across a business plan written by a group of engineers wanting to leave Western Union (Sidney Kaplan, Richard Schmal, and John Elich). Having passed on making an investment in ADS a year earlier, Botwinick had maintained an interest in TDMs and met with the engineers. He remembers: "Their business plan didn't really make sense, but their product plans did, so I became a member of the founding group, and I rewrote the business plan and raised all of the start-up capital."[59]

With an initial investment of $210,000, Timeplex began operations in 1969. In 1970, struggling to make sales, Timeplex signed a take or pay agreement with industry-leader Milgo to supply their TDMs. They ended 1970 with sales of $109,000 and a loss of $205,000.

2.5.4 Paradyne

In 1969, a group of engineers led by Joe Looney left Minneapolis-based Control Data Corporation and founded Paradyne. Backed by venture capitalists, they pursued a product strategy of building modems and front-end data communication processors to be connected to mainframe computers. Within 5 years Paradyne would become a leading modem manufacturer.

2.5.5 Vadic

In early 1969, Kim Maxwell and six others founded Vadic, one of dozens of companies that would jump into the dial-up modem business. At first, Vadic planned to develop both control systems and modems because they had one person who knew a little about each. But they soon realized they needed more focus and collectively decided it would be modems. After realizing the opportunity that had developed from the Carterfone decision, Maxwell remembers asking potential customers: "'What kind of modems would you like?' Well, people said things like Bell 103s. So we decided we better go find out what a 103 was. We bought the technical book from AT&T and we read through it. Now that tells you the level of knowledge

59. Edward Botwinick, oral history interview by James L. Pelkey, March 10, 1988, Woodcliff Lake, NJ. Computer History Museum, Mountain View, CA. Available from https://archive.computerhistory.org/resources/access/text/2018/02/102738718-05-01-acc.pdf.

and sophistication of this company that created the dial-up modem business."[60] Within a few years, Vadic would challenge AT&T as the leading innovator of dial-up modems.

2.5.6 Universal Data Systems

In 1969, Mark Smith, an engineer with SEI Systems, a government contractor, realized he did not want to work in an engineering job shop forever—he wanted to create products to sell. He too began reading about Carterfone. Knowing nothing about modems, he contacted Bell South to speak to a modem salesman. Smith remembers: "When the, quote, 'salesman' came out and explained to me the reason that AT&T's unit was more expensive and five times as big as the other units that were starting to show up on the market was that it had more resistors and capacitors in it, I figured that this might be a good business opportunity."[61]

Later that year, Smith and a friend, John Howell, decided to start UDS. Having but $30,000 between them, they kept their jobs and worked nights and weekends to build their first product, a Bell 202 leased line modem. Smith remembers: "We did the Bell 202 modem simply because it was conceptually, in every way, the simplest possible thing you could do, and we wanted to get started with something. By August of '70, we had ten units that were basically complete. So we had our show and tell units." On August first, Smith resigned. "We still had 25 of our $30,000 left by that time."[62]

Hustling whatever opportunities they could find, they soon bid on a large job for the Southern Company, a major utility in the southeast. In October they were notified they had lost the bid to ADS. Nearly out of cash and close to the end of their entrepreneurial aspirations, they received an unexpected phone call in December. The Southern Company program manager had gotten upset with ADS. Smith remembers the problem: "Part of it was they had called a meeting and [ADS] had called and said they couldn't come because they had an earthquake in California. He asked us if we'd like to supply the modems. We said: 'Heavens, yes!' So we got a contract for maybe $200,000, and, in addition, we got a $50,000 advance. That put us in business."[63]

---

60. Kim Maxwell, oral history interview by James L. Pelkey, July 19, 1988, Palo Alto, CA. Computer History Museum, Mountain View, CA. Available from https://archive.computerhistory.org/resources/access/text/2017/09/102740207-05-01-acc.pdf.

61. Mark Smith, oral history interview by James L. Pelkey, November 28, 1988, Huntsville, AL. Computer History Museum, Mountain View, CA. Available from https://archive.computerhistory.org/resources/access/text/2017/10/102738572-05-01-acc.pdf.

62. Smith interview, Computer History Museum.

63. Smith interview, Computer History Museum.

2.5.7 Intertel

Intertel was founded by Jerry Holsinger, who had initially started out building a company (Teldata) around his design for the first 9,600bps modem before he merged his company with Codex. After witnessing the rush of venture capital into the technology industry, and the success of Codex's IPO, Holsinger had come to the conclusion that he would rather return to running his own company than continue as an employee. So, he and two other former Codex employees, Andy Toth, who had worked for Holsinger as an engineer, and Bill Menges, a project coordinator, founded Intertel in 1970 with money they had from the sale of their Codex stock. After talking with many of the Boston area technologists, they decided on building modem boards to sell through OEM deals with other manufacturers. Their first successful products were 1,200bps modem boards for both leased and dialup lines. After funding the company for the first year, they eventually succeeded in finding venture funding through investors Walt Winshall and Jim Blair. In contrast to his experience with Teldata, this time Holsinger was more successful as an entrepreneur.

2.6 1970: A Pivotal Year for Codex and ADS

Sensing that his days with Codex were numbered, Carr knew he had to deliver—Cryer had made that abundantly clear. Carr's ears rang from Cryer's blistering tirades: "I want to see results and I don't want to hear again about needing a 4,800bps modem."[64] Carr understood that Codex faced a cash crisis, but he expected a little empathy for the uphill battles he and his salesmen waged every day. Competition had never been more intense and if rumor had it correctly, Milgo would soon introduce a 9,600bps modem, eliminating Codex's one unique advantage. Carr remembers: "What was happening was Bell people would go around and say: 'Look, if 9600 was possible, AT&T would have done it. We have Bell Labs.' Scared the hell out of the customer. Milgo would go out and say: 'Don't buy two of these spooky things, buy four 48's.'"[65]

In February 1970, Carr and Pugh scheduled a product-planning meeting to discuss the future of the AE-96. No one anticipated anything more than a routine scheduling meeting, but history would judge differently—for the meeting would set Codex on the path to becoming the world's largest independent data communications firm.

Refreshingly, after so many meetings devoted to yet another AE-96 crisis, the subject concerned the future and what Codex should do as an encore now that

64. Carr interview, Computer History Museum.

65. Carr interview, Computer History Museum.

they had a product that worked. After some light-hearted banter, and before the conversation could turn serious, Carr turned crusader once again, arguing that the sales force did not need an improved 9,600bps modem, but rather they needed more products to sell—specifically a 4,800bps modem. Cryer, as stubborn as Carr, repeated the obvious: they had barely enough cash to survive selling the products they had and certainly not enough to develop and launch a new product. He concluded with the now expected speech that the credo of Codex was to advance the state-of-the-art. And furthermore, how could Codex sell me-too products if they couldn't even sell the world's most advanced modem?

Before the meeting could turn into another pointless standoff, Forney, who had become involved with modems again after Holsinger's departure, suggested that maybe it need not be an either-or choice. He described a new technology being developed by Gallager, code named Modem-X, which was very different than the single sideband technology used in the AE-96—a technology with which a competitive 4,800bps modem could not be built.[66] Forney believed the Modem-X technology, which would become known as Quadrature Amplitude Modulation (QAM), could be the basis for both a better 4,800bps and a significantly improved 9,600bps modem.

After a lengthy discussion, Cryer relented, authorizing Forney to lead an effort to build first a 4,800bps and following that a 9,600bps modem using the Modem-X technology. Why did Cryer finally give in? Carr recalls: "Just incessant pressure from me, and the fact that we had a very bad year in '69. We were losing money. . . And I said: 'Look, one thing about this, whether it's challenging to you or not, Jim, I can sell it. I can collect from people for it without umpty-ump months of testing.'"[67]

Unknown to Carr, Cryer had already concluded that Carr had to be fired. However, he also knew he had to raise more money, and firing the VP of sales immediately prior to a financing was a sure way to stall investors' decisions, a delay he could not afford. He also did not want to hear potential investors parrot Carr's insistence on the need for a 4,800bps modem. Fortunately, Forney had proposed a most ingenious solution: a potentially radical new technology to advance the state-of-art of 9,600bps modems, and also a virtually risk-free means to innovate a superior 4,800bps modem.

---

66. Carr remembers Modem-X as: "It was intended to create a modem consistent with Codex's theory, something way beyond 9600 bits per second, whatever that was. Nobody knew what it was. Since we now were making a 96 that kind of worked when the red light blinked, we're now going to take on this new challenge thing." Carr interview, Computer History Museum.

67. Carr interview, Computer History Museum.

Pugh charged off to create both product specifications. Benefiting from the year of selling—and not selling—the AE-96, the specifications would focus on ease of installation, use, and service. Able to specify precise performance and quality measurements, Pugh set technical objectives that would make the new modems significantly better than the AE-96. Pugh also needed to project how many of each modem would be sold. Carr remembers his reactions to Pugh's forecast:

> I asked John Pugh to produce a forecast for how many 9600s we could sell, and his forecast was 465 for the life of the machine, and we all sat around my conference table and howled laughing. We thought, and I'll never forget it, I can see it like it was yesterday—we had sold and made 70 some AE-96s, so he was talking something like four times what we had done, and we thought it was so goddamned hilarious. We could believe that kind of a number for 4800s, and Storey ridiculed the hell out of him. It's a legend around Codex about this meeting, where we all laughed at John.[68]

Forney started work immediately, knowing Codex's future depended on his success. Sales of the existing AE-96 were not generating sufficient revenue. Government contracts were a luxury of the past, and financial projections indicated Codex would be out of cash in a few months and unable to meet their bank's requirements to borrow money.

Lacking alternatives, Cryer and Storey began discussions with their investment bankers, Kuhn, Loeb & Co., hoping to raise the equity capital needed to finance operations. By the end of March, terms were finalized and the closing scheduled for April 6th. With their money problems soon to be over, management gave a collective sigh of relief.

Carr then left for Hawaii to attend a military conference. He had been trying to sell the military a way to create more communication circuits, or channels, from existing circuits—the military had a desperate need of more international circuits as a consequence of the Vietnam War. Carr believed if he could sell the "channel packing" concept, it might generate desperately needed revenues and cash flow. Since most of those in the chain of command he needed to convince were attending the Hawaiian conference, he hoped he might pull one more order out of the military, an order that would give Codex some breathing room.

After encouraging meetings, Carr returned home on Sunday April 5th to be available, if needed, for the closing of the financing on Monday. Tired from the long trip, he was greeted at his front door by an anxious babysitter with a handful of phone messages marked Urgent. His first call back left him stunned. Earlier

68. Carr interview, Computer History Museum.

that day, Jim Cryer had died from a heart attack while playing tennis. An emergency Board of Directors meeting was scheduled for the next day.

That Monday morning the shock of Jim's death cast a pall over the boardroom. No one knew what to say. The Board members offered their condolences to the staff, and awkwardly drifted into the conference room, trying to collect their thoughts before the meeting began. Kohlenberg, weakened by Hodgkin's disease, came in, knowing the company he helped found was deep in crisis.

Once the meeting was called to order, the representatives of Kuhn, Loeb & Co. explained that under the circumstances it would be impossible to close the financing. A new investment memorandum had to be written and circulated. Realistically, it would be months before a financing might close. After a few blank stares, the bankers left, and the conversation turned to: Who was to run the company? What was to be done about cash? Carr remembers what happened then:

> I found out, much to my surprise that day, that I was right at the top of the shit list, that I was about to be fired because the view of the board was that I had joined the company and I had pissed all this money away and not brought in any business, which was accurate, although there were, God knows, an awful lot of other flaws in the company, like the product didn't work and we couldn't build it and a few other trivial things like that. But just about every VP of sales along Route 128 was being fired anyway, in those days. So I was literally within days of being canned when poor Jim dropped dead.
>
> So I walked into this board meeting, but hardly anybody was talking to me. And I'll never forget, Arthur [Kohlenberg] came in that day, because of this tragedy, and the man was shaking like a leaf. He was in terrible shape. He was watching all of this, and after a while—and he was always known as Arthur and I was always known as Art. He said: "You know, there's something I don't understand here. Why are you being unpleasant to Art?"
>
> The guy that was called the chairman, a fellow named Tom Meloy who was a legend in his own right, launched into this: "He's pissed away all this money and not sold anything," and Arthur really lit into him, that they didn't know what was going on, that you can't sell something that doesn't work. He told them about the equalizers that didn't converge and the whole nine yards, and when he got all done, probably a three or four minute monologue, he was so exhausted that he had to leave, and he said something like:
>
> "You stick with this guy. It's not his problem," and so on, and he left. That was the last time I ever saw him alive, because he died that July. He was never able to come back to work after that meeting.[69]

69. Carr interview, Computer History Museum.

The Board elected Jim Storey Chief Financial Officer. Carr was neither fired nor made to feel welcomed. After Kuhn and Loeb backed out over concern that the company was not marketable in its current state, Carr and Director Fulton Rockwell were left to raise the needed capital on their own. In the face of a bleak economy the prospects were grim. They appealed to their bank, First of Boston, repeatedly to loan them enough for payroll, but eventually the bank insisted they put the company up for sale. Carr remembers: "We offered the company to Raytheon. We offered the company to Milgo. We offered the company to Daman, who was in the medical lab, blood analysis business; Christ, a rubber company in Muskegon; Andag, that made retreaded tires. Anybody the bank wanted us to talk to, we would."[70]

Forney gave the Milgo executives a briefing and demonstrated the Modem-X, or QAM, technology. He remembers: "But they turned us down anyway." ADS executives also investigated Codex before passing on the opportunity. (ADS and ESE had used a similar 16-point QAM in their 4,800bps modems as early as 1970.)[71] It was understandable why ADS was not interested given they had a similar technology, but Milgo passing is mystifying with the reasons lost to time.

Meanwhile Forney had a working 4,800bps modem, albeit only a breadboard prototype, one still a long way from a shippable product. But the prototype worked, and given everyone's somber mood, this success represented a small ray of hope. A working prototype was also the kind of promising news that might impress a potential acquirer of the company.

Near the end of August 1970, a financing appeared possible. The partners of a new venture capital partnership, the Becker Technology Fund, indicated a strong interest in investing $300,000. Their conditions were that Carr take over the company and invest some of his own money and that they find additional investors to bring the investment to a minimum of $600,000. With the help of Kuhn and Loeb, they were able to raise $1,250,000. As a result of the reorganization, Jim Storey had to step down as COO to become Executive VP. Carr remembers:

> He [Storey] and I had a meeting the night before we signed the papers for this million-two, and shook hands on the deal, where I'd be one and he'd be two and we'd not let each other down, even if this thing went astray. We had been basically enemies up until that time because he was really trying to hang me out to dry. But it was a great exercise in emergency behavior...

70. Carr interview, Computer History Museum.

71. G. David Forney, Jr., Robert G. Gallager, Gordon R. Lang, Fred M. Longstaff, and Shahid U. Qureshi. 1984. Efficient modulation for band-limited channels. *IEEE Journal on Selected Areas in Communications* SAC-2, 5 (Sept), 632.

> Storey and I became a team that September, and that team was inseparable for the next fifteen years.[72]

In December 1970, at the fall Joint Computer Conference trade show in Houston, TX, Codex introduced their 4,800bps modem based on the QAM technology. They boldly named it the "4800," as if setting the standard to which all others had to conform. It was an immediate hit. Once they began demonstrating the 4800 on customer telephone circuits, it seemed that no matter how bad the circuits were the modem worked perfectly.[73] Codex began shipping the 4800 in January 1971 and couldn't build units fast enough to meet demand.[74] The timing was perfect, since sales in 1970 were only $1.1 million, down nearly 50% from 1969. Codex lost $3 million. If Forney had not succeeded, Codex would surely have gone under. Instead, in 1971 it had sales of $2.5 million, up 120%, albeit it still lost $2.0 million.

Milgo, which had sales of nearly $14 million in 1970, its second straight year of high double-digit growth, would be the most impacted by Codex's success. Milgo's sales in 1971 dropped 35% to $9 million.

---

72. Carr interview, Computer History Museum.

73. Pugh remembers: "We took it out on lines that nobody could run on, and that modem would run 10 to the eighth. It would never make an error. It was so resilient to all the parameters—I remember I came back from the first demonstration, it was a circuit that was out at Interdata in Waltham. They were a financial timesharing service of some kind. And they had a line that nobody could run on. And we took that modem out and measured the parameters on it and put the modem on it and [snaps fingers] just like that, it ran. And the guy out there was a guy by the name of Norm Daggett. He could not believe it. He became one of our major references that we would subsequently use for getting more money. And also, he spread the word around that if you got a tough circuit, the only place to go is with Codex. When I brought the modem back that day, and I talked to Forney, I said, "You know, this thing ran perfect." And he said, "What were the parameters?" And I told him, and he said well, "Naturally, I would expect it to." It was no surprise to him. [Laughter] So the 4800 was an immediate success. We just couldn't build it fast enough. And it was going primarily into applications of RJE terminals." John Pugh, oral history interview by James L. Pelkey, February 25, 1988, Canton, MA. Computer History Museum, Mountain View, CA. Available from https://archive.computerhistory.org/resources/access/text/2016/03/102738098-05-01-acc.pdf.

74. In pricing the 4800 at $5,575, slightly below Milgo's 4,800bps modem at $5,885, Codex intentionally tried not to provoke a price war. Codex's actions mimicked those of Milgo, which months earlier had priced their 9,600bps modem, the 5500/96, at $11,500 compared to then pricing of the AE-96 at $13,975—Codex had lowered the price from $16,000 in anticipation of Milgo's entry. In acting prudently and realizing neither had to use price to compete, both Codex and Milgo protected their product margins, which helped them achieve and maintain profitability. (Management of both organizations held the same rule-of-thumb of pricing modems for one dollar a bit, or $4800 and $9600, as the eventual goal.) Product pricing information is from *Datapro* reports unless otherwise stated.

2.6.1 ADS

For ADS, 1970 qualified as a nightmare. Coming off a spectacular 1969, when revenues were $5 million, everyone expected 1970 to be a gangbuster year and geared up accordingly. However, products were late, the market for time-sharing stalled, and it seemed everyone who could use a TDM multiplexer owned one. On top of that, the modem chips from Rockwell for the "killer" 4,800bps modem could not handle frequency translation and phase jitter. Sales were down while expenses continued to grow. In September, the Board elected a Rockwell executive to replace Wilkes.

Norred recalls:

> I remember the third year because I used to keep a forecast of around $32 million pinned on my wall, and I think we ultimately did about three or four or something. But that was 1970 when the world came to a screeching halt. One of the reasons was the modem. We actually shipped somewhere close to between 200 and 400 modems to the field, these automatically equalized modems, to find out that it had flaws we didn't understand. . . We were shipping to customers who were trying it saying: "Boy, we have a big requirement," and unfortunately the modem just didn't work well.[75]

Frequency translation and phase jitter haunted ADS, just as it had stumped Codex, and as it would challenge every firm trying to innovate a high-speed modem. Few succeeded, having to wait for the solution to become public knowledge before they could introduce competitive products.

Had ADS fatally overreached, or would it right itself?

2.7 The Creation of the IDCMA

For Carr and Codex, the upcoming ICA trade show in Atlanta in June 1971 was well-timed. By far the largest industry trade show, the ICA served as a giant magnet to decision makers contemplating the use of data communication products. With every significant vendor assembled under one roof, customers could comparison shop, viewing the latest and greatest products every firm had to offer, especially those from firms not yet advertising or too small or too new to have established adequate product distribution. And for those attendees simply trying to make sense of the dazzling explosion of products promising to save money, improve performance, or revolutionize how corporations used computers, seminars and tutorials conducted by company representatives or industry consultants ran back-to-back

75. Norred interview, Computer History Museum.

from morning to night. In compressing the normally diffused interactions of buyers and sellers into a three-day public fishbowl, a young company's future could easily depend on the outcome of this one show, and Carr intended to make ICA an unqualified success for Codex and the 4800.

However, AT&T's proposed private-line modem tariff announcements drowned out any hopes that the 4800 would dominate the buzz of ICA: AT&T wanted all customer-supplied private-line modems to use DAAs, and it intended to slash the lease rates of its modems. Since third-party modems had been safely connected to private lines for years, show goers wondered why the sudden change in AT&T policy. One question dominated every conversation: What could, or would, the independent modem manufacturers do to fight this blatant attempt to squash competition?

The small dial-up modem manufacturers couldn't have been happier and did all they could to stir the controversy. Maybe now the larger leased line modem firms would join their fight, finally realizing that if they did not fight AT&T tooth and nail they might all be put out of business. It seemed that no matter where one turned, the conversation remained the same: What could be done?

Carr tried to remain focused, knowing if he didn't capitalize on the early success of the 4800 before competitive products emerged it mattered little what AT&T did because Codex might not be around. Still losing money and having invested time and scarce resources into having a new 9,600bps modem, Carr argued that as onerous as the proposed tariffs were, they had little real effect on Codex. Even if you added $10 a month to the cost of buying a $5,000 modem, it did not change the significant economic advantages of ownership. Equally, AT&T could lower their lease rates as called for in their new Information System Access Line pricing, but their new 4,800bps modem did not even bear comparison to Codex's 4800. Moreover, AT&T did not offer a 9,600bps modem. So yes, AT&T needed to be reined in, but for now that had to be left for others as Carr had neither the time nor money to join the fight.

Edward Bleckner and Matt Kinney, President and Vice President of Sales of Milgo, on the other hand, aggressively lobbied modem manufacturers to protest AT&T's filings with the FCC from the start and now carried their crusade to the floor of the convention.[76] As executives of the largest independent data communications company—sales of modems were $9.8 million in 1970 out of total revenue of $14 million—they knew they did not have the means to fight AT&T on their own, but would have to assume a leadership role if any coordinated response was to be

76. "PBX suppliers face stifer AT&T policy," *Electronic News*, June 7, 1971, 1.

made. But how were they going to stimulate collective action of competitive firms without running into legal problems?

As Bleckner and Kinney canvassed the other firms, they quickly found allies in Chuck Johnson and the executives of GDC. Since GDC also sold dial-up modems, they already fought the use of DAAs and welcomed the idea of new comrades in arms. When Bleckner and Kinney approached Joe Looney, President of Paradyne, they found him receptive, but with little time or money to contribute since Paradyne had just begun selling product. Looney agreed that if AT&T had its way, Paradyne might not have a future. So, yes, he was interested enough to listen to what might be proposed. Even Carr conceded the importance of unanimity and agreed to attend a group meeting.

Wanting to reach agreement on a plan of action before the show ended, Bleckner and Kinney invited executives of the other modem manufacturers to join them in their hotel suite after the close of the exhibitions one day. In an act of true mutualism, nearly a dozen firms agreed to form a trade association called the Independent Data Communications Manufacturers Association, or IDCMA. The purpose of the IDCMA would be to fight AT&T and lobby for market competition. Four companies, Milgo, GDC, Codex and Paradyne would be the four founding members with Bleckner, Johnson, Carr, and Looney serving as the initial Board. One of their first acts would be to hire legal counsel and contest AT&T's intentions to require DAAs for private-line modems—AT&T soon withdrew its filing. The IDCMA proved essential to the growth of the data communications market-structure and to the repeal of the DAA tariffs.

In the following year, a similar organization would form to promote fair competition in the computer industry. Founded in 1972, the Computer Industry Association represented a collective of plug-compatible computer peripheral manufacturers initially concerned with opposing the monopolistic practices of IBM. Its board featured the CEOs of Digital Communication Associates and GDC (John Alderman and Chuck Johnson, respectively). The organization would later change its name to the Computer and Communications Industry Association and take on AT&T as digital technology became more important in the communications industry. The spirit of cooperation exhibited by the formation of the IDCMA did not affect the month-to-month slugging it out for sales, however, and 1971 proved a struggle for the nearly 100 firms competing in the data communications market-structure.[77]

77. "The data communications market: Modems, multiplexers, and communications processors," Frost & Sullivan Inc., 189. https://historyofcomputercommunications.info/assets/pdf/FrostAndSullivan_Report.pdf.

2.8 Strategic Partnerships in the Data Communications Market-Structure: 1971–1972

Codex fared better than most with a 126% increase in sales to $2.5 million, largely on the back of the 4800, while losses were commensurably cut by a third to $2.0 million. In October 1971, just after the close of the fiscal year, Codex introduced the QAM-based 9600, the long-awaited successor to the AE-96, priced at $11,500. The QAM technology gave Codex a significant advantage in the market, as Pugh explains:

> When we came out with the AE-96, which was a suppressed carrier, single side band modulation, a lot of people moved in and copied that, which was a mistake for them, because we had the QAM modem on the drawing boards. And about the time that Milgo came out with a single side band machine, AT&T came out with a single side band machine, and we had then announced our 9600, which was a QAM machine. We had the market all to ourselves for several years because it took them that long to catch up. That modem lasted for four or five years, and it was a marketing game. The 9600 became an instant hit![78]

Codex had cleared a major hurdle by successfully innovating its second-generation 9,600bps modem technology.

Early in 1972, it received the news they had been hoping to hear for 4 years: Codex had won the channel packing contract. First proposed to the Defense Communications Agency (DCA) in 1968, and the occasion of Carr's trip to Hawaii in 1970, the DCA had bureaucratically decided to ask for competitive bids for the contract, soliciting bids from 44 firms. Two firms, Harris Corporation and Codex submitted bids, and Codex won the $7.5 million contract by a margin of less than one percent of the total price. Before the joy of victory could be savored, however, there remained one small problem: Codex did not have the money to buy the parts, build the units, or finance the receivables. The contract, three times their previous year's sales, totally dwarfed Codex's dwindling resources. Cash at fiscal yearend 1971 totaled but $20,000. With a history of raising money under dire circumstances, management presumed the channel packing contract could make a financing a slam dunk. So Carr promptly contacted their investment bankers, Kuhn Loeb, who agreed, and began writing a prospectus for a public equity financing.

As Carr's back began aching, he soon guessed financing problems were imminent, for every past financial crisis had precipitated back problems. Sure enough,

78. Pugh interview, Computer History Museum.

Kuhn Loeb called requesting a meeting. In the course of their due diligence, they had discovered a report by the prestigious consulting firm of Arthur D. Little (ADL). The modem, according to ADL, would soon be made obsolete by the all-digital data networks announced by AT&T and competitors such as Datran. Clearly, Kuhn Loeb could not sell stock to the public given such a bleak prognostication. Carr and Codex management, in shock, argued vainly as the bankers simply pleaded ignorance and left the meeting suggesting Carr write a report refuting the ADL conclusions, which they could review.

After the day-to-day struggles for survival, Carr and the rest of management were forced to pause and examine the industry's prospects. In doing so, they came to two conclusions, one comforting and one startling. First, they persuasively argued that the threat posed by all digital data networks was overstated and the future was promising for modems. The conclusion was eagerly accepted by Kuhn Loeb—for no financing meant no fees or trading profits. The second conclusion remained private and came as a cold shower to management. If they, Codex, did not act quickly to engineer Large-Scale Integration (LSI)-based modems their QAM-modems would soon be uncompetitive because LSI semiconductor technology promised to dramatically transform the size, power requirements, performance, and pricing of all integrated circuit products. In mulling over this conclusion, Carr remembered his recent meeting with Norred who was trying to sell the assets of ADS.[79] Carr decided that maybe he ought to contact Rockwell, the owner of ADS. Certainly, Rockwell had the requisite semiconductor technology, and if Codex was going to engineer LSI-modems they would need a strategic relationship with a supplier.

Kuhn Loeb, satisfied as to a future—or at least the reasonable possibility of a future—for modems, completed the prospectus and filed it with the Securities and Exchange Commission (SEC). Proving the adage "Never count a financing done until the cash is in the bank," in 1972 the SEC informed Kuhn Loeb and Codex that since they had raised money in a private placement within the last 12 months, they could not now do a public financing. It violated a rule outlawing private placements in anticipation of a public offering. Since Codex traded over-the-counter, the whole matter was referred to a NASDAQ appeals board for resolution. Carr remembers pleading their case: "Basically, all BS aside, we have to do this public offering to finance that contract. There is no conceivable way on God's earth that we could

79. The implication was so unsettling because Codex management thought when the competition had introduced the older single sideband technology modems that they had won the day with their QAM modems.

have known we were going to be given this award, therefore we couldn't have known we were going to do a public offering when we did the private placement."[80]

The appeals board adjourned after hearing Carr's testimony and returned in a matter of minutes with the decision: Codex was allowed to proceed with their offering. On October 4, 1972, Codex raised $2,432,000 with a post-money valuation of $22.8 million. For fiscal year 1972, revenues totaled $4.0 million with a profit of $561,000. Codex had achieved another important milestone.[81]

Unfortunately, the same could not be said for ADS. Hit simultaneously with plummeting multiplexer sales due to a weakening time-sharing market and struggling unsuccessfully to perfect its automatically equalizing 4,800bps modem, ADS reeled under a succession of bad results turning worse. By the September 1971 Board of Directors meeting, everyone expected management changes. Rockwell, asserting its ownership rights, replaced the President named the prior year with another Rockwell executive and fired co-founder Schaaf. The discouraging results from ADS did not deter Rockwell in September 1971 from acquiring controlling interest in Collins Radio, an organization that, in theory, competed with ADS and had estimated sales of modems and multiplexers of $2 million in 1972.

In 1972, ADS sank ever more deeply into the ranks of the also-rans. After the habitual ax-wielding September Board meeting, Rockwell executives had had it. They fired Wilkes, cut the company back to a bare minimum, and tasked Norred with selling the shell of a company to whomever for whatever. ADS, the first true star of data communications, had overreached by trying to do too many things without sufficient capital, management, and engineering.

2.9 Data Communications Market-Structure

2.9.1 By 1972 the Data Communications Market-Structure had Emerged

As of year-end 1972, AT&T continued to dominate data communications although its estimated share of the modem market had dropped to 70%.[82] Not until early 1972 did AT&T offer a high-speed modem: its 4,800bps leased line 208A Data Set. AT&T did not compete in the multiplexer market.

The leading independent modem firm, Milgo, had sales of $12 million, or more than 25% of all modem sales and more than 50% of high-speed modem sales. Milgo

80. Carr interview, Computer History Museum.

81. Other facts from the prospectus were that Codex had 156 employees, 30 of whom were in product development, and they had approximately 70 customers.

82. All data in this section from the Frost and Sullivan report "The Data Communications Market: Modems, Multiplexers and Communication Processors," December 1972.

did not compete in the multiplexer market, having ended its OEM relationship with Timeplex. Milgo's success stemmed from having a broad modem product line and a sales distribution strategy using manufacturing representatives rather than its own sales force. (Manufacturing representatives are independent organizations that sell the products of many manufacturers to end-users.)

Codex had captured the role of technological leader with the introduction of its QAM-based 4,800bps and 9,600bps modems. Even so, since it declined to participate in the lower-speed modem categories, Codex would not overtake Milgo as market leader for many years. Codex was, however, the only company to innovate both high-speed modems and TDMs. (See Table 2.1 for a sample of the diversity of product offerings.)

Two of the new data communications start-ups, GDC and Timeplex, strengthened their positions behind the two market leaders, Milgo and Codex: GDC went public in 1972. That year, 70% of GDC's sales would be to common carriers (telephone companies) and only 30% to end users. Sales to Western Union would account for 42% of sales. GDC had not yet broadened their product line to include modems. Timeplex's sales for 1972 doubled those of 1971, and, in February 1973,

Table 2.1 **Data communications firms and products**

Company	Year founded	300bps modems	300–4,800bps modems	>4,800bps modems	FDM	TDM	Comm. Proc.
AT&T	1880	X	X				
IBM	1911		X			X	X
Milgo	1955		X	X			
Codex	1962		X	X		X	
ADS	1968	X	X	X	X	X	X
Infotron	1968						
GDC	1969	X	X		X	X	
Paradyne	1969			X			
Timeplex	1969					X	
UDS	1969	X	X				
Vadic	1969	X	X	X			
Intertel	1970		X	X			
# of firms selling		57	53	19	20	19	55

FDM: frequency division multiplexer; TDM: time division multiplexer; Comm. Proc.: communications processors.

Source: Adapted from "The Data Communications Market: Modems, Multiplexers, and Communications Processors," Frost & Sullivan, Inc. 190–193. Used with permission.

Timeplex would also become a public company in one of the last technology IPOs before the market soured.

Uncertainty was common in the early data communications market, as the performance of other early entrants revealed: ADS, the early star of data communications, was firmly under the control of North American Rockwell by year-end 1972 and faced an unclear future. Other start-ups, Infotron, Paradyne, Vadic, UDS, and Intertel, remained modest companies struggling to survive. At the same time existing firms also competed in the data communications market: Ultronic Systems had estimated sales of modems and multiplexers of $12 million; Western Union continued to be a purchaser of product used in its networks; and Stelma's sales persisted flat at roughly $15 million.

Finally, the battle projected between AT&T and IBM heated up when IBM entered the data communications market in December 1971 with a line of modems and communication processors. AT&T continued to dominate the market for computer terminals through its Teletype division of Western Electric. IBM was second.

In 1972, modem sales, exclusive of telephone companies, were estimated at $38 million and multiplexer sales at $21 million. Total sales of $59 million were up more than six times those of 1968, or a compounded annual growth rate of 55%. Ninety-seven companies sold modems, only nineteen sold high-speed modems (4,800bps or higher). Nineteen companies sold TDMs and twenty companies sold the older technology frequency division multiplexers (five companies sold both types of multiplexers). Twenty-two companies sold both modems and multiplexers. The market research firm Frost and Sullivan forecasted in 1972 that modem sales would peak in 1976 at $67 million and multiplexers would peak in 1977 at $75 million. When we return to the data communication companies, we will follow the story of how these firms weathered an economic downturn, lack of investment capital, and an increasingly competitive market.

2.10 In Perspective

A combination of incentive and opportunity opened a market window for entrepreneurs in data communications between 1968–1972. The results: a burst of new firms introducing modems and multiplexers. Thus, in four short years data communications went from domination by one firm, AT&T, offering a minimal number of products, to nearly 100 firms and over 200 products. The economic opportunities in data communications were a result of the increasing use of computers by corporations, the opening of market competition in telecommunications, and the unprecedented capital available for investment in high technology companies, all combining to fuel entrepreneurial ambitions.

Innovation in data communications products did not have to be disruptive to be successful. Many of the new start-ups in modem technologies, such as Vadic and UDS, made incremental innovations on existing Bell modems and were able to capture meaningful market share from the incumbent, AT&T. A rapidly growing market for products, combined with low costs of entry, brought many entrepreneurs early success, before competition began to shape the market dynamic.

Two new market-structures emerged in the four short years beginning in 1968: data communications and minicomputers. They were closely intertwined, for as the number of computers increased in the workplace, so too did the need to connect them. At first, time-sharing promised to be a growing market for communications products, but when that model of computing proved too costly for long distances, other markets emerged: connecting terminals to host computers became more important as more users in the workplace needed to connect to data sources in central locations.

As busy as the datacom players were, they couldn't help noticing the interest in a new computing project making waves in academic computing centers. The ARPANET, which was demonstrated to an enthusiastic reception at the 1971 ICC conference, represented a novel solution to the challenge of communications between computers. However, just as AT&T was slow to adapt to innovations in data communication, and IBM missed an early opportunity to embrace time-sharing, the data communication firms were too busy with their own customers and products to pay this new academic network much attention. We will leave them with their balance sheets and turn now to the exciting story of the beginning of the "intergalactic network..."

Packet Switching and ARPANET: Networking, 1959–1972

3.1 Overview

In the previous chapter, we saw how AT&T, federal regulators, and entrepreneurs struggled to define the future of data communications and its new enabling devices. Companies such as Codex, Milgo, and ADS sought to raise capital, ship products, and create a new market-structure. Between 1968 and 1972, companies waged the battle over technological leadership incrementally, through devices that could transmit data at slightly faster speeds for a slightly better customer value proposition.

During these same few years, a different set of individuals charted a radically different technological future. These individuals operated outside the rules and regulations defining AT&T's struggle with the federal government. And they operated outside the conventions of sales, manufacturing, and venture capital. They were outliers whose ideas soon would become mainstream.

Many readers will recognize their names—J.C.R. Licklider, Paul Baran, and Larry Roberts—and the fruits of their work, namely, packet switching and the ARPANET. In this chapter, we recast their stories emphasizing the three key themes in this book, *entrepreneurs, market-government boundaries*, and *learning*. Entrepreneurial activities abounded—people starting companies, launching initiatives within existing organizations, and devising strategies to marshal resources behind their ideas. The theme of market–government boundaries also looms large in this chapter, with government investments (research grants and contracts) in the US and England for technologies that had not been developed by market participants. In this chapter, we'll see the importance of both the formal and informal aspects of learning. The *formal* aspects include degree programs at universities, as well as professional seminars and conferences. The *informal* aspects include learning-by-doing, the application and communication of tacit knowledge, and the process of peer learning—in other words, picking up tricks and insights from friends, coworkers, and even rivals.

3.2 The Intergalactic Network

In October 1962, Dr. Licklider became the first director of the Information Processing Techniques Office (IPTO) of the Advanced Research Projects Agency (ARPA). His charge was to invest in advanced information technologies. Licklider already had a reputation for promoting leading-edge computer research, such as time-sharing. And he was also an advocate for "interactive computing" that would provide instant feedback for users. Both visions were in sharp contrast to the prevailing modes of computer use. Existing mainframes were single-user machines that operated through batch processing: someone would submit a set of instructions and data on cards into the computer and receive the results at a later time. Licklider, a psychologist by training, had been involved with human factors at MIT during the development of SAGE—an experience that made a powerful impact on his view of computing.

In 1963, as the Director of IPTO, Licklider wrote a memo playfully addressed to his research community as "Members and Affiliates of the Intergalactic Computer Network." The memo outlined Licklider's overarching vision of human–computer interaction, time-sharing, and computer networks. Perhaps anticipating some concerns that a military patron was driving the community's research agenda, Licklider emphasized that "many of the problems will be essentially as important in the research context as in the military context." In other words, he was aiming for advances in computing that would likely impact all aspects of society.

Licklider told Pelkey in 1988, "The term 'Intergalactic Network' was a kind of intentionally grandiloquent way to express the idea, because we didn't really expect to get at that right away. It was all we could possibly do to make time-sharing systems work."[1] Licklider conceived a future of networked computers when few computers supported more than one user at a time. It required true imagination to see beyond the paradigm of batch processing, where users passed decks of computer cards to trained operators and sometimes waited days to receive their results.

By dint of his energy, enthusiasm, and leadership, Licklider's dreams became the founding vision for computer communications. He prioritized funding for time-sharing projects, and prodded researchers to think big. For example, at MIT

1. J.C.R. Licklider, oral history interview by James L. Pelkey, June 28, 1988, Arlington, MA. Computer History Museum, Mountain View, CA. Available from https://archive.computerhistory.org/resources/access/text/2016/03/102717159-05-01-acc.pdf.

he helped create Project MAC under the leadership of Professor Robert M. Fano. He then provided $3 million a year in funding, which helped Project MAC become the most influential effort in time-sharing. In 1967, IPTO funding to over a dozen time-sharing projects, at both universities and research organizations, exceeded $12 million.

Licklider also understood that his vision required vast numbers of researchers. To that end, Licklider supported some of the first doctoral programs in computer science at "centers of excellence" like MIT, CMU, Stanford, and UC Berkeley.[2] This is a clear example of Licklider operating as an entrepreneur—directing resources and investments toward activities that he hoped would bear fruit in years to come.

For the self-effacing Licklider, computer networking came naturally—as did the nurturing of a community of researchers, an "intergalactic network." A gracious man with endless enthusiasm for new ideas and the will to implement them, many people remember Licklider's gift for connecting with people. Licklider's insatiable quest for new ideas brought him into contact with the finest computer scientists of his day. Everywhere he went in the 1950s and 1960s—including MIT, Harvard, Bolt Beranek and Newman (BBN), IPTO, and IBM—he sought to create environments for exploring how computers could be made more ubiquitous and useable, and therefore advanced the state of many basic ideas.

Once at ARPA, Licklider mobilized his network of individuals as well as a number of forward-thinking corporations. For the most part he was successful, but not always. He was unable to draw in AT&T and its Bell Labs, as he told Pelkey: "The telephone company wasn't interested. Well, Buick used to have the expression: 'When the better cars are built, Buick will build them.' I have a feeling the telephone company felt: 'When there's a time for networks, we'll know about it.'"[3]

In July 1964, after only 2 years, Licklider left ARPA for IBM to assume a role he later described as more promoter than scientist or researcher. In September, Dr. Ivan Sutherland, a brilliant young computer scientist who Licklider had supported with ARPA funding, took over as the new Director of IPTO. One of his first decisions was to fund the work of his friend Dr. Lawrence G. (Larry) Roberts, a principal investigator at Lincoln Labs. Roberts, who was to become one of the giants of computer communications, told Pelkey: "Nobody knew what anybody should be doing with the computer. When Ivan went to ARPA, we worked together to supply money to

2. Robert Taylor. 1990. *In Memoriam: J. C. R. Licklider, 1915–1990*. Digital Systems Research Center, Palo Alto, CA.

3. Licklider: "The telephone, that was the object of their [AT&T] research, was a physical system that kind of stopped with the microphone on one end and the earphone on the other." Licklider interview, Computer History Museum.

the group, and as a result, I wound up being in charge as the contract monitor for ARPA."[4]

Roberts and Sutherland had known each other since entering the MIT doctoral program in 1959. They quickly became friends, sharing both an office and a passion for computer graphics. When preparing their computer demonstrations to complete their degree requirements, they used the TX-2 computer at Lincoln Labs on alternate nights. In their final exams, each demonstrated algorithms that became foundations of computer graphics.[5]

In November 1964, Licklider, Sutherland, and Roberts were among a contingent of ARPA scientists traveling by train to Hot Springs, VA, to attend the Second Congress of the Information System Sciences sponsored by MITRE Corporation.[6] The trip afforded the rare opportunity to interact as a group, and they crammed every minute with conversations later characterized by Licklider as intense and spirited. When the trip began Roberts had only a modest interest in computer communications. He remembers:

> I concluded that the thing to work on would be the communications between computers and to computers, because the computer stuff itself was a big team activity at that point, and one that I thought I knew how to handle anyway. The real challenging task was to try to interlink these systems.[7]

3.2.1 How to Design a Data Network

By early 1965, Sutherland decided it was time to begin exploring the issues faced in interconnecting computers. In February, Sutherland turned to Roberts, who always had the time and energy to tackle something new, and authorized an experiment to study how to interconnect computers. Roberts turned to Thomas Marill, founder of the time-sharing company, Computer Corporation of America, to devise a network experiment. Marill, a former student of Licklider's, also was motivated by Licklider's Intergalactic Network vision. In October 1965, Roberts and Marill connected a TX-2 computer at MIT Lincoln Lab with a Q-32 computer at System

4. Lawrence Roberts, oral history interview by James L. Pelkey, June 17, 1988, Burlingame, CA. Computer History Museum, Mountain View, CA. Available from https://archive.computerhistory.org/resources/access/text/2013/04/102746626-05-01-acc.pdf.

5. For Sutherland it was Sketchpad, and for Roberts it was a hidden lines algorithm that was minor to his thesis.

6. MITRE was another organization associated with MIT and a technology prototyping organization doing work for government agencies, especially the Air Force.

7. Roberts interview, Computer History Museum.

Development Corporation in Santa Monica, CA, using a leased line from the telegraph carrier Western Union.[8] The simple yet pathbreaking experiment proved that the computers could run programs and retrieve data on remote machines, but the existing communications infrastructure presented problems. Roberts remembers: "And what we found is that you can connect the computers fine internally and the time-sharing systems both could call on each other, but the communications was slow and unreliable and difficult—and made the whole process so slow it wasn't very attractive."[9]

The telephone network had been designed for voice communication. Its underlying technology was circuit switching. Every telephone has a line, or circuit, that connects physically to a telephone switch. Both the person making the call and the person being called are connected to the same switch. The connection is maintained until one person hangs up, at which time the switch terminates the connection, freeing lines for other calls. Circuit-switched communications on dedicated lines are robust and costly. Since switches were expensive, telephone companies recovered their investments by levying a minimum charge for every telephone call, generally 3 minutes. For longer voice calls, a minimum charge was rarely an issue. But communications between computers often last seconds, which made it difficult to imagine how circuit switching could work efficiently.

Although these issues were generally understood, Roberts and Marill in 1965 raised these problems in the new context of ARPA's mandate to develop new command and control systems. The experiments also made it abundantly clear that the problems confronting computer communications also existed in the design of mainframe computer hardware and software. Host operating system software assumed there was only one Host and all connecting devices were as if "slaves." Hosts were not designed to recognize or interact with peer-level computers; the concept of peer-level computing did not yet exist. Thus, in interconnecting two computers, one had to be master and one slave. The problem only became worse if more than two computers wanted to interconnect and communicate. Nevertheless, the problem of Host software was considered to be solvable if a suitable communication system could be designed and made to work. Fortunately, an inquisitive scientist named Paul Baran had already explored these problems.

8. Roberts and Marill documented their work in 1966. Thomas Marill and Lawrence G. Roberts. 1966. Toward a cooperative network of time-shared computers. In *Proceedings of the November 7–10, 1966, fall joint computer conference (AFIPS '66 (Fall))*. Association for Computing Machinery, New York, 425–431. DOI: https://doi.org/10.1145/1464291.1464336.

9. Roberts interview, Computer History Museum.

3.2.2 Paul Baran

Paul Baran exemplifies the principle that if one must work, he or she must find something really important to work on. Ever exuding a quiet, even polite, intensity that speaks of someone who is confident of what he is thinking, by 1959, just 10 years out of college, Baran already had discovered his. Baran wanted to prevent a nuclear holocaust, not for money or fame, but from personal angst. After graduating from Drexel Institute of Technology, he went to work for the computer start-up Eckert-Mauchly Computer Company before moving on to Raymond Rosen Engineering Products. A few years later, he moved to California and landed a job with Hughes Aircraft as a junior engineer on the Minuteman missile control system. These experiences taught him digital design and implementation. While at Hughes, he attended UCLA graduate school at night where he earned his master's degree in engineering. Baran then joined RAND where he dedicated himself to solving the problem of nuclear missile command and control. At the time, he had absolutely no concept that his solution would one day be the foundation of a global communications revolution.

RAND, short for "research and development," was formed at the end of World War II to preserve the operations research capability developed by the Air Force during the war. It first tucked under the protective wing of Douglas Aircraft Corporation in California. However, a research organization managed by a manufacturing organization proved an uncomfortable fit. To secure RAND's autonomy, the Ford Foundation advanced seed money to convert it into an independent, nonprofit research organization chartered to work on problems of national security. Ideas developed by its staff only could be implemented by other organizations—a true think tank. An exception came early, when MIT Lincoln Labs subcontracted computer programming for the SAGE project to RAND. In two short years, RAND would divest the effort to the Systems Development Corporation, better known as SDC.

One way the Air Force made RAND researchers aware of its needs was to distribute a weekly list of requests for study.[10] Baran, in search of a project, discovered

10. Baran remembers RAND as "a neat place:" "It was multi-disciplinary, and the reason its output was as productive as it was, it had the neatest way of allowing people to do pretty much what they wanted to do. They picked very good people to start with, were able to pick those they wanted, and they guaranteed them continuity and no interference, and then they'd restrict the output flow, so any briefing had to go through a tough review process. Before anything became a RAND report, it went through a very, very careful review process, so all the failures, all the nonsense got filtered out, and as a result, you know, my God, you got some very high-quality output. So, it was the ability to bury bad work easily that I think made for a lot of success." RAND, at the time, was funded by the Air Force, and the Air Force was synonymous with the national

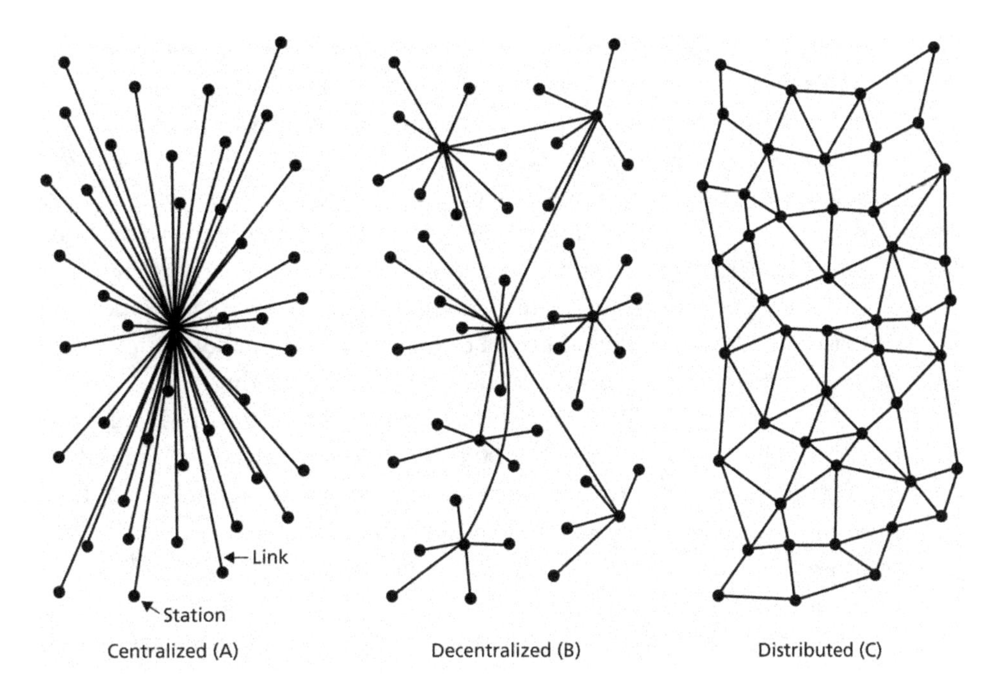

Figure 3.1 Centralized, decentralized, and distributed networks. Source: Paul Baran, *On Distributed Communications Networks* (Santa Monica, CA: RAND Corporation, 1962), 4, https://www.rand.org/pubs/papers/P2626.html. Used with permission.

a project concerning the survivability of the military's strategic command and control system. Baran began by studying the survivability of the AT&T telephone network—the communication system the Air Force depended on. He concluded it was a disaster: a few well-placed bombs could disrupt communications throughout the country. Baran had found his focus: "How to build a robust communications network that could survive an attack and allow the remainder of the network to behave as a single coordinated entity?"

AT&T's telephone network vulnerability came from its highly centralized design. In general terms, networks could be designed to be either centralized or decentralized. In centralized networks, all end points (nodes) connect to one central switching point. In decentralized networks, clusters of smaller centralized networks are interconnected to form one large network, thus mitigating some risks of a single point of system failure (see Figure 3.1).

defense, 'cause what the hell was national defense, then. You had airplanes and they carry a bomb and that was national defense." Paul Baran, oral history interview with James L. Pelkey, January 12, 1988, Campbell, CA. Computer History Museum, Mountain View, CA. Available from https://archive.computerhistory.org/resources/access/text/2017/09/102740210-05-01-acc.pdf.

Baran wondered if there was another, more robust way to design a network. In his investigations, he was strongly influenced by his understanding of how the brain worked. He had numerous interactions with Warren McCullough of MIT, an influential cognitive scientist. Inspired, Baran examined *distributed* networks, where every node connected to every other node, but found little research on the subject. To discover how distributed networks behaved under disruptions, Baran modeled various configurations and simulated attacks against the network. He concluded: "A critical mass of the structure occurred when a network reached about 15 to 20 nodes in width and used a redundancy level of about three times as many links as the minimum needed to tie all the nodes together."[11]

As how to build such a network, Baran recalls taking on the problem of "getting signals through this fishnet type of network." Given the rapid deterioration of analog signals when many links are in tandem, Baran concluded that he would need to use digital signals. He "initially thought in terms of 'minimal essential communications'" and built on an earlier proposal from Frank Collbohm, the President of RAND Corporation, to relay teletype signals between AM broadcast stations. "Unlike skywave HF transmissions," Baran told Pelkey, "AM broadcast ground wave signals did not depend on the ionosphere for propagation." One "limitation" of Collbohm's idea, as Baran put it, was that there was "no intelligence to relay signals. I proposed merely to flood the network where subsequent messages wash out the older messages."[12]

Baran presented his solution to the Air Force. He was told that while his proposal might take care of the President, it lacked the capacity that the Air Force and other military branches would need to communicate with field personnel. So he continued working, and in November 1962 Baran presented a paper titled "On distributed communications networks."[13] In it, he proposed alternatives to traditional communication networks. The first element in his proposal was a standard message block, in contrast to a continuous circuit designed for voice communications:

Baran presented a creative idea for passing messages, which deserves extended quotation:

> Torn-tape telegraph repeater stations and our mail system provide examples of conventional store-and-forward switching systems. In these systems,

11. Baran interview, Computer History Museum.

12. Baran interview, Computer History Museum.

13. The paper was presented at the First Congress of the Information Systems Sciences, sponsored by MITRE.

> messages are relayed from station to station and stacked until the "best" outgoing link is free. The key feature of store-and-forward transmission is that it allows a high line occupancy factor by storing so many messages at each node that there is a backlog of traffic awaiting transmission. But the price for link efficiency is the price paid in storage capacity and time delay. However, it was found that *most of the advantages of store-and-forward switching could be obtained with extremely little storage* at the nodes.
>
> Thus, in the system to be described, each node will attempt to get rid of its messages by choosing alternate routes if its preferred route is busy or destroyed. Each message is regarded as a "hot potato," and rather than hold the hot potato, the node tosses the message to its neighbor who will now try to get rid of the message.[14]

Baran remembers conducting 40 or more briefings around the country to government and research organizations. The reception was mostly positive: "Many who were proficient in computer technology felt the concepts to be viable." But this reception was not universal, especially among audiences that "were familiar only with conventional analog transmission." In particular, "AT&T that held the monopoly for telecommunications at the time was among the most negative."

Baran published his paper in the *IEEE Transactions on Communications Systems* in March 1964. A few months later, RAND Corporation published the much more extensive *On Distributed Communications*, in 11 volumes. Destined to be a landmark, *On Distributed Communications* set forth the concepts of how communication networks could be designed as a message-based, distributed system.

Yet it remained only an idea. To really see if it worked, a message-based system needed to be built. In 1965, the opportunity seemed to present itself. The Air Force asked MITRE Corporation to organize a review committee, which supported putting the idea into action. "Then came one of those brilliant strokes of higher-level management," Baran noted sourly. "The Department of Defense ruled that the agency that should be building the system was the Defense Communications Agency (DCA), not the Air Force, since it would be used by more than one service."[15] But since the DCA had no computer or digital experience, Baran recommended the project be shelved. The ideas were tenuous enough, and important enough, that he preferred to wait for the right group.

---

14. Paul Baran. 1962. *On Distributed Communications Networks*. RAND Corporation, Santa Monica, CA, https://www.rand.org/pubs/papers/P2626.html.

15. Baran interview, Computer History Museum.

3.2.3 Donald Davies Davies—1965–19661

In 1965, Donald Davies, Deputy Superintendent of the Autonomics Division of the National Physical Laboratory (NPL), London, attended an International Federation for Information Processing (IFIP) Congress meeting in New York City. The IFIP meeting started Davies down a path of discovery similar to Baran's, although with special twists.

At the time, the future seemed to be time-sharing. Davies arranged a seminar at the NPL in London on November 2 and 3 with scientists from MIT to discuss Project MAC. Larry Roberts attended. Davies remembers that the conversation dwelled on the concept of time-sharing. At points, the discussion connected communications and time-sharing. Davies recalled, "Nothing very much in detail was said at that meeting about solutions to the problem, but several people said how difficult it was: how you could get hour-long telephone calls in which not very much data was transmitted, what you could do about making communications more efficient, and so on." The conversation led Davies to think about treating information as short messages, using a store-and-forward approach. He recalled:

> I simply sat down and did a few samples on the back of an envelope, literally, to see how this would work out. My first thought was that if you had to store messages and transmit them, there must be a delay, and this might defeat the whole purpose of the thing, which was to have rapid communications. It soon became obvious that this wasn't so, and that if you chose fairly high data rates, by the standards of the day, and fairly short messages, the storage time was so short that it didn't really affect your communications. Simple idea. I began to work this out.[16]

A week later, November 10, 1965, Davies wrote a short paper titled: "Remote On-line Data Processing and its Communication Needs." He concluded that the delays inherent in a store-and-forward system did not need to conflict with the objective of instantaneous communications, as long as the line speed was at least 10,000bps.

Davies, like Baran 5 years earlier, brought to the problem a background in digital technology. Having experience with the earliest stored-program computers (1947–1951), Davies instinctively turned to the same "message block" solution formulated by Baran. To Davies, it was an obvious solution to the mismatch

16. Donald Davies, oral history interview with James L. Pelkey, May 27, 1988, London, England. Computer History Museum, Mountain View, CA. Available from https://archive.computerhistory.org/resources/access/text/2017/11/102738594-05-01-acc.pdf.

between the "voice" telephone circuit and the needs of computer time-sharing. In his words:

> A lot of effort in time sharing systems had gone into avoiding the waste of the computer's time while it waited on the user, the thinking time, but the telephone network's contribution to the cost had been ignored. Essentially, the communication network gave the user transmission capacity while the computer dealt in blocks of information, mostly in short units. This was the mismatch that set me thinking.[17]

On December 8, Davies circulated an eight-page "Proposal for the Development of a National Communications Service for On-Line Data Processing" to the British Post Office and others interested in telecommunications. Davies remembers that the comments were neither "destructive" nor "very enthusiastic." The most common response was that message switching would probably work well—but "nobody could build the necessary 'message switches.'" Encountering no strong opposition, Davies continued work by attaching the proposal to a research program called "programming research" in order to avoid attracting too much attention.[18]

On March 16, 1966, Davies gave a public lecture titled: "The Future Digital Communication Network." Typically, 20 to 30 people attended such talks. A standing-room-only crowd of at least 120 people showed up, mostly from the British Post Office and various telecommunications manufacturers. In the spirited discussion that followed, a few people from the Post Office formed a nucleus of opposition to Davies's proposal to build a message-based experimental network for the Post Office (just as Licklider had been frustrated in the United States). Davies' lecture was published in June 1966 as a 25-page report titled "Proposal for a Digital Communications Network."

When Roberts read Davies' report, he sent Davies a copy of Baran's internal RAND report from August 1964. Davies remembers feeling "fortunate not to have read Paul Baran's paper when it was published because I might have considered the concept as 'well-known' and done nothing more." But there was one significant addition. In his report, Davies used the word "packet" for the first time to refer to the messages circulating over the network. He unintentionally coined a name for the new approach: "packet switching."[19]

17. Davies interview, Computer History Museum.

18. Donald W. Davies. 1986. A personal view of the origins of packet switching. In L. Csaba, et al. eds., *Computer Network Usage: Recent Experiences: Proc. of the IFIP TC 6 working Conference COMNET '85*, Budapest 4–7 Oct. 1985. Amsterdam, S, 1–13.

19. Davies interview, Computer History Museum.

3.3 ARPANET: The Planning Phase

In 1966, Robert (Bob) W. Taylor succeeded Sutherland as Director of the IPTO. He faced the essence of the problem every day in his office: he had three different computer terminals because he needed access to three different computers. Taylor remembers:

> By late '65, early '66, there were a number of ARPA-sponsored research groups that had built for themselves, and were using in their own work, some of the first time-sharing systems. So, it occurred to me, sort of taking off from this tongue and cheek "Intergalactic Network" phrase of Licklider's, that the next thing to do was obvious, and that is—if we had singular communities who could interactively communicate through a time-sharing system that they were all members of, why couldn't we have clusters of communities interact, members of one community could interact with members of another community, as though they might be sharing a single time-sharing system.[20]

In February 1966, influenced by the networking experiments at Lincoln Labs, Taylor decided the time had come for ARPA to bring time-sharing systems into an ARPA scientific community. Not having the money to launch a new project, he approached Charles Hertzfeld, Director of ARPA.[21] He remembers explaining to Hertzfeld:

> There are certain experts in certain fields who sit in California, and there are other experts in that same field who sit in Massachusetts or someplace else, and if we can make this work, we can have a medium through which they can work cooperatively, and so we get amplification of ideas. Another advantage of tackling this problem is that we might be able to achieve some fail-soft characteristics in any collection of computing that the Defense Department would especially be interested in.
>
> So, that discussion probably lasted 15 minutes, and he immediately was excited about it, and he said: "You've got the money. How much do you need to get started?" I gave him a number, and he pulled it out of another one of his ARPA projects, and said: "Go."[22]

20. Robert W. Taylor, oral history interview with James L. Pelkey, June 16, 1988, Palo Alto, CA. Computer History Museum, Mountain View, CA. Available from https://archive.computerhistory.org/resources/access/text/2017/12/102738691-05-01-acc.pdf.

21. He knew that in addition to the advantages of having the communities linked, they would have to figure out how to make heterogeneous systems communicate.

22. Taylor remembers the amount to have been about $1 million.

Taylor next needed a program manager. His first choice was Roberts. Roberts, however, wanted nothing to do with becoming a program manager or of moving to Washington. Unable to think of anyone as qualified as Roberts, Taylor kept asking and Roberts kept declining. Taylor remembers the ruse that won the day:

> In September or October of '66, it dawned on me that ARPA supported 51%, or thereabouts, of all of Lincoln Lab's work. So I went to see Hertzfeld and I said: "Charley, is it still true that ARPA supports 51% or more of Lincoln Lab," and he said: "Yeah." I said: "Well, you know this network project that I'm trying to get off the ground?" He said: "Yeah." I said: "Well, there's a guy at Lincoln Lab that I want to be the program manager for it and I can't get him to come down here. His name is Larry Roberts. I'd like for you to call the Director of Lincoln Lab and tell him that it would be in Lincoln Lab's best interest and Larry Roberts' best interest if the Director of Lincoln Lab encouraged Larry Roberts to come down to Washington and be the program manager for this project." Charley said: "Sure," and he picked up the phone with me in his office, and he called the Director of Lincoln Lab and had a short conversation and he hung up the phone, and about a month later Larry accepted the job. In Christmas of that year, he came down with his family and they stayed at my house over the holidays because they didn't have a place to live yet. I blackmailed him into fame.[23]

With Roberts aboard as program manager, Taylor began visiting various ARPA contractors, explaining the purpose of the network. Not wanting to give others access to their computers, most of the contractors resisted. It became very clear that the challenge of bringing into being the world's first computer communication system would involve more than just technology. Taylor and Roberts would have to rely on the community cohesion that Licklider stimulated. But, perhaps more important, they learned to use the leverage ARPA had as a powerful source of funding.

With his legendary intensity, Roberts tackled the challenges of bringing into being a network to interconnect the ARPA community. To him, Baran's and Davies' concept of communications by exchanging messages or packets was simply a logical extension of how computers communicated internally—exchanging blocks of data.

Roberts remembers the beginnings of building a computer network:

> All of us in computing were clearly not going to go after it on a circuit switched basis. We were all thinking in blocks. That's the way computers

23. Taylor interview, Computer History Museum.

> worked. So we approached it very differently than the communications people. We thought in terms of: "How can we do this such that it will be a functionally useful service for the computers?" I got together groups and committees of the ARPA people and started working on it.[24]

After numerous conversations, Roberts concluded his first major decision had to be the *network topology*; how to link the computers together. Interconnecting each computer to every other computer didn't make sense, based on the results of his experiment at Lincoln Labs and the absurdity of projecting hundreds of computers all interconnected to each other. The number of connections would explode as the square of the number of computers divided by two [actually $n * (n - 1)/2$].

Two alternative architectures for a shared network emerged: a star topology or a distributed message switched system. A star topology, or centralized network, would have one large central switch to which every computer was connected. It represented the least development risk because it was well understood. However, it was also known to perform poorly given lots of small messages—the precise condition of packet messaging. On the other hand, a distributed message switching system as proposed by Baran and Davies had never been built, but it held the theoretical advantage of performing best given lots of small messages.[25] With a choice needing to be made, the upcoming annual meeting of ARPA contractors seemed an ideal time to reach a decision.

Wes Clark, then at the University of Washington in St. Louis, was at the meeting and remembers: "Towards the end of the meeting it became clear to me what the problem was. So, I slipped a note to Taylor stating 'I know what to do.' Taylor probably didn't look at my message until after the meeting. It was fairly obvious to me to put the communication functions in a separate, smaller computer outside the computer 'network.'"[26]

---

24. Roberts interview, Computer History Museum.

25. "Star systems perform satisfactorily for large blocks of traffic, but the central switch saturates very quickly for small message sizes... (The) alternative to the Star, suggested by the RAND Study 'On Distributed Communications,' is a fully distributed message switched system. Such a system has a switch or store and forward center at every node in the network. Each node has a few transmission lines to other nodes; messages are therefore routed from node to node until reaching their destination." Lawrence G. Roberts and Barry D. Wessler. 1970. Computer network development to achieve resource sharing. In *Proceedings of the May 5–7, 1970, spring joint computer conference (AFIPS '70 (Spring)*. Association for Computing Machinery, New York, 543–549. DOI: https://doi.org/10.1145/1476936.1477020.

26. Wesley Clark, oral history interview with James L. Pelkey, July 11, 1988, New York, NY. Computer History Museum, Mountain View, CA. Available from https://archive.computerhistory.org/resources/access/text/2017/11/102738606-05-01-acc.pdf.

After the meeting, Taylor, Roberts, Clark, and Dave Evans shared a taxi to the airport and discussed the network topology decision. Taylor remembers:

> Larry, prior to this taxi ride, was thinking of a network controller in a centralized sense; something in the center of the country, a large machine, that would control the network, and I was nervous about that. I talked to Licklider and to Wes about it, separately, and Larry wasn't irrevocably wedded to the idea, but that was his model at the time. In the cab to the airport after this meeting, I got Wes talking about it. Whether he had sorted it all out prior to that cab ride or whether he sorted it out based spontaneously in the conversation in that cab, I don't know. But he said: "Why have a central control. Why not have small machines?[27]

Clark remembers:

> I think it was fairly obvious. I think somebody else would have come to it with a little more time. Let those little computers talk to one another and serve as terminals to which the big machines would talk. In a sense, that took the big machines outside the network. The concept up to that point was that the network was the big machines plus all the interconnections, and my sudden realization at the meeting was that you wanted the [big] machines outside the network, not inside it. Larry or Bob asked me how to get these little small computers built and I said I thought there was only one person who could do that job in the country, namely Frank Heart.[28]

Back in Washington, Roberts and his staff concluded that Clark's idea of a separate computer located at each site handling the network functions was an ingenious solution. In addition to its technical merits, it allowed the network to be designed and built independently of host computer hardware and software, greatly simplifying project management. The small computers, to be called interface message processors (IMPs), together with the telephone lines and the modems would constitute the message-switching, communications network, or "subnet" (see Figure 3.2).

Roberts understood a deep and important dilemma of the evolving network. Computers wanted to communicate in message sizes very much larger than ideal for a packet network. This meant an IMP would receive a message from its Host computer that it would have to parse into packets to traverse the subnet. The packets would then have to be re-assembled into the message before being sent to the

27. Taylor interview, Computer History Museum.

28. Clark interview, Computer History Museum.

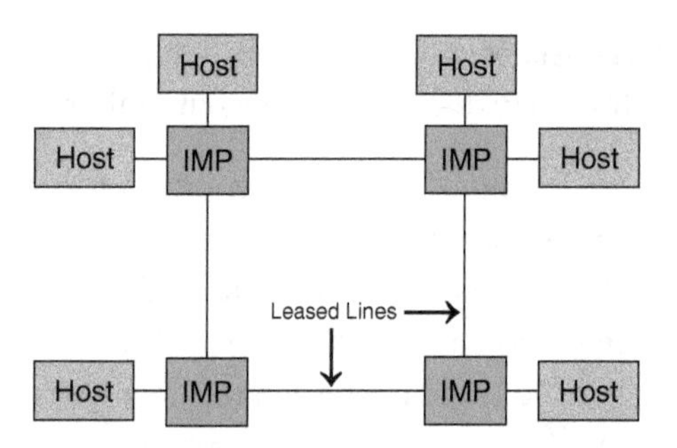

Figure 3.2 The ARPANET subnet and hosts. Source: ARPANET Completion Report, F. Heart, A. McKenzie, J. McQuillan, D. Walden, Washington, D.C., 1978.

Host. Realistically, that implied that the IMPs would have to store packets before forwarding them. Such a network had never been designed, much less built.

Roberts remembers:

> What we concluded was that you wanted to not store the whole message and forward it, and you couldn't have a perfect virtual cut-through where you sent every block immediately synchronously because it might interfere with the next message. So you had to do it in some smaller breakdown, which is like a packet, or whatever, which, of course, is the size lump you're in anyway, because you've got to put sum checks on it every interval. So, there wasn't any question about packets—and clearly Donald gave it the name—that we had to be in that sort of size.[29]

Roberts sought help from Leonard Kleinrock, his former officemate from MIT and now on the faculty of UCLA.[30] Even though Kleinrock was not working on network theory at the time, he had shown in his Ph.D. thesis that a large store-and-forward approach could work.

During this period, Roberts was coming to the opinion that a limited experiment would not be very meaningful. But that introduced the problem of how to convince the many more potential computer sites to devote resources to the network, as opposed to their chosen priorities. In 1988, Licklider told Pelkey:

> I have the strong impression that Larry thought there was no little experiment that would be very helpful; that he had to have a network with many nodes—a dozen anyway and probably 100—and that it had to be used for serious purposes, and that his problem was—what he had to excel at as a

29. Roberts interview, Computer History Museum.

30. Before moving to California to join the faculty of UCLA in 1963, Kleinrock added to the long list of computer scientists who spent time at Lincoln Labs.

manager was actually getting this whole ARPA community to make ten or fifteen percent of everybody's effort to get the network to go. He thought he was in a good position, that he had not only the people who could build it but enough people to use it, if he could only get them really focused and interested.[31]

Then, in another important community event that caused historical course-corrections, came the ACM Symposium on Operating System Principles in Gatlinburg, TN, October 1–4, 1967. In "Multiple computer networks and intercomputer communications," Roberts lamented the deficiencies of dial-up telephone circuits yet nevertheless concluded that the communication links between IMPs would be 2400 bit/second dial-up circuits.[32] That constraint would not last very long, however, for another speaker, Roger Scantlebury, described a local network being developed at NPL based on Davies' ideas and employing much higher speed circuits.[33] (On returning to the UK, Scantlebury reported: "It would appear then that the ideas in the NPL paper at the moment are more advanced than any proposed in the USA.[34])

Roberts took the findings of the NPL team seriously: "The NPL paper clearly impacted the ARPANET in several ways. The name 'packet' was adopted, a much

---

31. Licklider interview, Computer History Museum.

32. "Current automatic dialing equipment requires about 20 seconds to obtain a connection and a similar time to disconnect. Thus, the response time is much too long assuming a call is made only after a message arrives and that the line is disconnected if no other messages arrive soon. It has proven necessary to hold a line which is being used intermittently to obtain the one-tenth to one second response time required for interactive work. This is very wasteful of the line and unless faster dial up times become available, message switching and concentration will be very important to network participants." Lawrence G. Roberts. 1967. Multiple computer networks and intercomputer communication. In *Proceedings of the first ACM symposium on Operating System Principles (SOSP '67)*. Association for Computing Machinery, New York, 3.1–3.6. DOI: https://doi.org/10.1145/800001.811680.

33. D.W. Davies, K.A. Bartlett, R.A. Scantlebury, and P.T. Wilkinson. 1967. A digital communication network for computers giving rapid response at remote terminals. In *Proceedings of the first ACM symposium on Operating System Principles*. Association for Computing Machinery, New York, 2.1–2.17. DOI: https://doi.org/10.1145/800001.811669. Shortly after Davies' lecture in June 1966, Davies and Derek Barber decided it was necessary to build a model "interface unit" and use it as a local network within NPL. To study issues introduced in a "multi-interface" network such as routing, flow control and congestion, they decide to use simulation. In August of 1966, when Davies became Superintendent of the newly named Computer Science Division, he authorized two teams, one to work on each project.

34. Davies, "A personal view of the origins of packet switching." The NPL Data Communication Network would not become operational until June 1973.

higher speed was selected (50 Kilobit/second vs 2.4 Kilobit/second) for internode lines to reduce delay, and generally the NPL analysis helped confirm the concept of packet switching."[35]

Also at Gatlinburg, Roberts and Baran finally found time to talk. Roberts remembers: "The RAND work was very detailed, since it covered the whole network including microwave and one valuable analysis on routing. The hot potato routing algorithm was a useful starting point for the ARPANET routing design."[36]

With these elements clicking into place, Roberts began to write a Request for Quotation (RFQ) to solicit bids. He also began selling the network to ARPA contractors, all of whom were stretched thin for resources and were disinclined to reallocate 10% to 15% of their budgets to a network project. For those sites not willing to cooperate, Roberts was willing to exercise his power if needed. He remembers: "we just convinced them all they weren't going to get any computer funding anymore unless they cooperated."[37]

At the same time, Licklider and Taylor pressed the case to the general public. In an article published in *Science & Technology* in April 1968, Licklider and Taylor wrote of a future day "when people of similar interests will work with each other through a network of computers—even when they are in the same room." Later in the article, they predicted: "What will on-line interactive communities be like? In most fields they will consist of geographically separated members, sometimes grouped in small clusters and sometimes working individually. They will be communities not of common location, but of *common interest*. In each field, the overall community of interest will be large enough to support a comprehensive system of field-oriented programs and data."[38]

When distributed in July 1968, the RFQ specified a four-node network with the potential to be expanded to 35 sites. The first nodes would be UCLA, SRI, UCSB, and the University of Utah. UCLA would be installed in September 1969, with successive sites to be added monthly (see Figure 3.3). The minicomputer-based IMPs were to be interconnected by 50 kilobit/second leased lines. The network transport mechanism was to be packets but the IMPs would communicate with the Host computers using messages. The RFQ outlined what the network was supposed to do, both structurally and functionally, without specifying how to do it. It would be the

35. Larry Roberts. 1986. The Arpanet and computer networks. In *Proceedings of the ACM Conference on The history of personal workstations*. Association for Computing Machinery, New York, 51–58. DOI: https://doi.org/10.1145/12178.12182.

36. "The first time we really sat down and talked about the network in detail was at the Gatlinburg conference." Roberts interview, Computer History Museum.

37. Roberts interview, Computer History Museum.

38. J.C.R. Licklider and R.W. Taylor. 1968. The computer as a communication device. *Science and Technology* 76, 21.

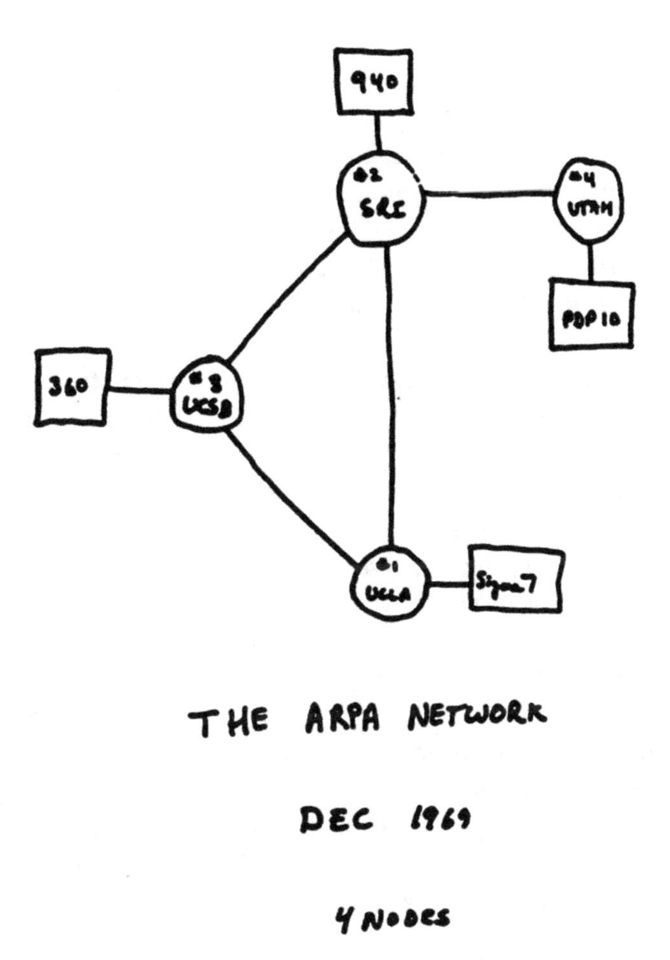

Figure 3.3 Initial ARPANET nodes. Source: Illustration courtesy of Alex McKenzie.

responsibility of the winning contractor to mold the concepts in the RFQ into a working system. Clearly, it was hoped that some of the uncertainty of the design would be clarified in the responses to the RFQ.

Twelve firms responded to the RFQ. IBM, the largest computer company, did not respond, despite Licklider's evangelizing. Neither did AT&T. Four contenders held supplementary technical briefings and final negotiations were conducted between two finalists—Raytheon and BBN.

When ARPA released the RFQ in July 1968, BBN had assigned the responsibility of preparing its response to Frank Heart, the head of Division 6. Heart had extensive experience with computer communications including the SAGE system at Lincoln Labs. Heart also enjoyed personal relationships with many of the ARPA personnel, including Roberts. Recall that, after the Michigan meeting in 1967, Clark had recommended Heart as the one person who could connect the computers together.

Heart recalls attaching no special importance to the project: "No one realized at this stage how big it was to be. After all, it was just to build a four-node network. We did not know it was going to start a revolution!"[39] Heart's core team was made up of former Lincoln Labs employees who had followed him to BBN. Severo Ornstein, who had once worked for Wesley Clark, had responsibility for the hardware design. Will Crowther was the principal software designer, and Dave Walden worked for Crowther.

Robert Kahn, another key contributor, was loaned to the team from BBN Division 4, the division responsible for time-sharing and computer research. A man of inexhaustible energy, Kahn served as a member of the technical staff of AT&T's Bell Labs while a graduate student at Princeton University. After completing his Ph.D. in electrical engineering in 1964, Kahn joined the faculty of MIT. In 1966, he left MIT for BBN where he reported to Jerry Elkind. Elkind believed that designing a computer network was of national importance, encouraging Kahn in that direction.

Heart emphasized to Pelkey the importance of his team's shared experiences building real-time computer systems at Lincoln Labs: "At that time, very few people understood how to build real-time computer systems. That was one of the things that the people who worked at Lincoln had learned, that when you're building radar systems, or the SAGE system, or systems to handle seismic data, or radio telescope data, performance was very critical." Roberts, himself having thrived at Lincoln Labs, did not ignore the advantages of working with others so trained. He recalls:

> Raytheon had a good proposal that competed equally with BBN, and the only distinguishing thing in the long run for my final decision was that BBN had a tighter team organized in a way that I thought would be more effective than a very steep commercial structure with lots of managers.[40]

The week before Christmas 1968, BBN learned it had won the ARPA contract. While pleased, the team knew the real work now began. There was one light moment: before receiving their formal notification, Senator Edward Kennedy

39. Frank Heart, oral history interview with James L. Pelkey, July 11, 1988, Cambridge, MA. Computer History Museum, Mountain View, CA. Available from https://archive.computerhistory.org/resources/access/text/2017/12/102738689-05-01-acc.pdf.

40. Roberts interview, Charles Babbage Institute.

telegrammed BBN, congratulating them on having won the "Interfaith Message Processor Project."[41]

3.4 ARPANET: Design, Implementation, and Administration

In January 1969, the effort to build the ARPANET started in earnest. BBN had won the right to build the IMPs that would be interconnected using leased lines from AT&T to create the communications network, or subnet. Now the many design issues left open had to be decided.

3.4.1 Subnet Design and Implementation

The BBN team began the painstaking tasks of fleshing out the design of the communications subnet. It had been agreed that the subnet would consist of minicomputer-based IMPs interconnected with leased telephone lines. Hosts would communicate with other Hosts by sending messages over the subnet. IMPs then routed a message by parsing it into up to eight packets with the destination IMP reassembling the packets into the message before delivering it to the destination Host. A message could consist of up to 8,000 bits, while a packet was limited to 1,000 bits. Exactly how this was to work, reliably and error-free, was now the challenge. ARPA personnel had oversight for IMP to IMP links, and personnel at the Host sites had oversight for connecting Hosts to IMPs.

Given this architecture, a number of important issues remained to be specified, such as a routing mechanism. BBN called somewhat vaguely for the "shortest-path routing, with certain metrics," which was how it chose to express, in Kahn's recollection, the simple fact that "we wanted to do more research." BBN found Baran's ideas about "hot potato" routing to be interesting but limited. Kahn believed that Baran was "talking about switches that were low-cost electronics. The idea of putting powerful computers in these locations hadn't quite occurred to him as being cost effective. So the idea of computer switches was missing. The whole notion of protocols didn't exist at that time. And the idea of computer-to-computer communications was really a secondary concern. What finally happened in networking was, in fact, very strongly derivative of what Baran was talking about, but he had not really laid a clear template for what it was."[42]

41. Vint Cerf: "They were actually congratulated on their ecumenical effort." Vinton Cerf, oral history interview with James L. Pelkey, February 8, 1988, Reston, VA. Computer History Museum, Mountain View, CA. Available from https://archive.computerhistory.org/resources/access/text/2015/11/102738017-05-01-acc.pdf.

42. Robert Kahn, oral history interview with James L. Pelkey, February 22, 1988, Reston, VA. Computer History Museum, Mountain View, CA. Available from https://archive.computerhistory.org/resources/access/text/2016/10/102717241-05-01-acc.pdf.

Other issues that concerned Kahn, the principal architect, were congestion control, independence, and deadlocks: How could the network be kept from being congested by too many packets? How do you build a system where each of the nodes would act independently and still talk to each other without requiring global control? How to keep the network from coming to a grinding halt? The last concern, deadlocks, became "contentious."

Roberts and Frank Heart benefited from being from organizations that gave managers the "room to make it happen." For when they made a decision, that was it. No other approval was needed. The high level of trust between the two organizations—grounded in the relationships among the many individuals who had been members of not only ARPA and BBN but also MIT and Lincoln Labs—facilitated project management. Roberts and Heart knew each other and knew they would be working with each other in the future. These cultural and organizational attributes became critical as Roberts and Heart pushed to complete the subnet on schedule. Heart opines:

> Larry at his level in ARPA, was very much in charge. Almost nobody was looking over his shoulder closely and, at BBN, I was a free agent. There was nobody looking over my shoulder either. So projects like this that are this hard, it's very critical not to have too much back seat driving, and that's one of the things about this project that was very unusual.[43]

ARPA's schedule called for UCLA to receive the first IMP since UCLA, under the supervision of Kleinrock, was creating the software and hardware needed to measure network performance. Since no network like the ARPANET had ever existed before, measuring its performance was crucial and, by so doing, knowing when and how to expand the network without inducing catastrophic problems. In recognition of its critical role, UCLA became known as the Network Measurement Center or the NMC.

As the NMC, UCLA's responsibilities ranged from working with BBN to make sure the necessary measurement capabilities were designed into the IMPs, to providing constant network monitoring and analysis once the network was operational. Knowing Roberts wanted to expand the number of sites connected to ARPANET as quickly as possible, the NMC plan called for 3 months of tests with the first four IMPs.

A UCLA graduate student named Steve Crocker took up general management of UCLA's site preparation. Much to his surprise, BBN managed to ship the first IMP

43. Heart interview, Computer History Museum.

on time (see Figure 3.4). Crocker remembers: "it wound up on our loading dock on Saturday, the end of August, and on the same day somebody showed up and wheeled it in and plugged it in and the program kept running from when they had unplugged it, and they had a working IMP."

Figure 3.4 Interface Message Processor. © Mark Richards. Courtesy of the Computer History Museum.

Kleinrock also recalls timely arrival: "Well, to BBN's credit, they connected this thing up, and that day we had bits moving back and forth. I think the next day we had packets moving back and forth and messages worked. It came in and the damned thing worked!"[44] A milestone, one that even weeks earlier had seemed out of reach, had been achieved. BBN delivered the second IMP to SRI in early October, and UCSB and the University of Utah received theirs in November and December, respectively.

In September 1969, just as the ARPANET project began to take off, Taylor resigned from his position as Director of IPTO and Roberts became the next director. The transition proved seamless, as Roberts had by then already been given most of his new responsibilities. His expanded budgetary clout would help him persuade Host site personnel to make the network a priority—a clout very much needed. However, with each new responsibility, he was challenged to make time available for ARPANET. His solutions: to assign some of the ARPANET workload to Barry Wessler, who he had recruited from the University of Utah to be his assistant, and to simply work more hours himself.

A person less competent, committed, or able to maintain such a punishing schedule would have had to give up active involvement with ARPANET. But not Roberts. In fact, Roberts was a highly effective entrepreneur, as evident in his accomplishments that would follow. Indeed, the additional authority and budget power that came with the directorship gave Roberts even more clout to command the attention and cooperation of the sites connecting to the ARPANET—leverage that would become critical as Roberts pushed to get ARPANET not only up and running but indispensable to the fabric of the ARPA community.

During the summer and fall of 1969, Roberts struggled with the issue of network topology: the interconnection of nodes. He began simulating network topologies on a computer and quickly concluded he needed expert help. Roberts turned to Dr. Howard (Howie) Frank. Frank had founded Network Analysis Corporation, a company specializing in topological design based on his groundbreaking work at the Office of Emergency Preparedness. Frank remembers Roberts' call requesting a meeting, where Roberts was stumped about how to extend the simple, four-node network across the country to the East Coast.

> He needed to order communication lines for that, and he said: "I don't know what I'm doing. I'm just drawing these lines. Could you figure out a way to do this better?" So, we wrote him a proposal, and we started our contract in

44. Leonard Kleinrock, oral history interview with James L. Pelkey, April 27, 1988, Los Angeles, CA. Computer History Museum, Mountain View, CA. Available from https://archive.computerhistory.org/resources/access/text/2015/12/102738036-05-01-acc.pdf.

> October 1969. Larry had a deadline. It was a real deadline. He said: "I can cancel the orders by this date." We analyzed the configuration that he had given us, and we developed the very first techniques for designing distributed computing systems, which were primitive compared to the ones we subsequently developed. I would say that within a period of 2 to 3 months—no more than that—we came back with a design which was something like 25% cheaper and had 40% more throughput than the one that he had come up with. We worked like a bear because it was truly a hard project.[45]

At the same time, the teams at UCLA and BBN established a collaboration—sometimes awkward or tense—to analyze network traffic. In December 1969, after all four IMPs had been installed, Kleinrock instructed the NMC to generate weird configurations of data traffic. His goal was to stress the subnet to the point where it would stop functioning. This experiment put the NMC on a collision course with BBN, since BBN had to correct the problems. Kahn of BBN had concerns of his own, especially regarding potential "deadlocks," when the network simply froze and would not function. Kahn recalls the difficulties he had convincing others to pay attention to the issue of deadlocks—so he ran a test when he traveled to California to visit the NMC, hoping that a demonstration would get his message across.

At this time, a long lasting professional and personal friendship began between Kahn and Vint Cerf, who was at that time a promising Ph.D. student at UCLA. Cerf remembers:

> The whole system was largely Bob's architecture, and he came out to UCLA to go and find out, by kicking the tires, how this thing would really perform. He had some theories about places where it would break that not everyone agreed with him about, but he said he was going to go and prove that it would break in certain ways by generating traffic at UCLA and forcing it through this four node network in various and sundry ways. So, he and I worked together, me doing the traffic generation and measurement software and he was figuring out what experiments to perform for three or four weeks at UCLA. That's a collaboration that has gone on ever since![46]

The experiments, in Kleinrock's recollection, generated a new understanding of the phenomenological behavior of networks. Kleinrock recalled, "We had a whole

45. Howard Frank, oral history interview with James L. Pelkey, May 2, 1988, Washington, DC. Computer History Museum, Mountain View, CA, Available from https://archive.computerhistory.org/resources/access/text/2016/02/102738078-05-01-acc.pdf.

46. Cerf interview, Computer History Museum.

catalog of degradations and deadlocks which BBN eventually fixed. Those things are still present in every network today."[47]

Despite lingering problems and differences of opinion, the network worked. By June 1970, the network included SDC and RAND on the West Coast, and BBN, MIT, and Harvard on the East Coast. All the while, network performance testing continued uncovering problems, most of which would be corrected, including some thought intractable.[48] By mid-year, a rudimentary version of the Network Control Center was established at BBN.[49] Four more nodes were added by the end of the year: Stanford, Lincoln Labs, Carnegie Mellon, and Case Western.

3.4.2 Host-to-Host Software and the Network Working Group

With these advances in network implementation and measurement, the number of people working on the ARPANET (Licklider's "Intergalactic Network") increased. One essential challenge that faced the group was to design network protocols to facilitate data transfers between hosts—hence their name, "host-to-host" protocols or software. Personnel from the Host sites had been meeting since mid-1968 to craft the host-to-host protocols that would function over the subnet, yet they remained unsure of how much authority they had to make decisions.

Roberts always assumed that each site would have to connect its computer to the subnet. The problem was the perception of who was in control. In other words, to convince sites that an outside contractor would be responsible for software residing on "their" computers was a thought so top–down as to undo the very heart of ARPA management practices, that is, hire the best and leave them alone. He needed the ARPANET to be seen as the users' creation, not a straitjacket imposed from on high. Thus, the Host sites had to create the architecture and software that would make the ARPANET a functioning network.

So, concurrent with the release of the RFQ in June 1968, Roberts asked Elmer Shapiro of SRI to organize representatives from the initial four sites to begin working on the host-to-host issues. Shapiro chaired the first meeting in early July 1968. This meeting began a process that would become even more problematic than the

47. Kleinrock interview, Computer History Museum.

48. "In late 1971, it became apparent that serious problems were being encountered with the flow control system. BBN set about to design a new flow control system. By mid-1972 the revised system was ready for installation after undergoing extensive testing in the laboratory on a small-scale network (3–4 nodes)." Paul Baran, et al. 1974. *ARPANET Management Study*. Cabledata Associates, Palo Alto, CA, 9.

49. Frank Heart, Alex McKenzie, John McQuillan, and David Walden. 1978. *ARPANET Completion Report*. Defense Advanced Research Projects Agency, Washington, DC, III-55.

subnet development. Steve Crocker,[50] who attended as the representative of UCLA, remembers:

> The first meeting was seminal. We had lots of questions—how IMPs and hosts would be connected, what hosts would say to each other, and what applications would be supported. No one had any answers, but the prospects seemed exciting. We found ourselves imagining all kinds of possibilities—interactive graphics, cooperating processes, automatic data base query, electronic mail—but no one knew where to begin. We weren't sure whether there was really someone from the East that would be along by and by to bring the word. But we did come to one conclusion: We ought to meet again.[51]

Around the same time, Taylor initiated an annual meeting of graduate students working on ARPA contracts, parallel to the annual principal investigators conference. The first meeting was held in July 1968 at the University of Illinois, chaired by Barry Wessler, Roberts' assistant since early 1968. Crocker attended as the MIT representative, and Alan Kay and John Warnock showed up from Utah. Vinton Cerf, a high school buddy of Crocker's who had worked for IBM and was now in the Ph.D. program at UCLA, represented UCLA. Crocker recalls that Barry Wessler kept trying to get the group interested in the network and associated issues like file sharing. But the group's interests veered elsewhere, toward "artificial intelligence and graphics systems and other topics that were hot at the time, [so] there wasn't a lot of response. It just sort of fell flat. So, the one thing that was true was that the community was not keenly involved in networking, and not really responsive. On the other hand, ARPA was pushing it and it was a serious vision."

During the summer and fall of 1968, Crocker, Carr, and Jeff Rulifson began meeting as ARPANET site representatives. Crocker remembers:

> We didn't have a charter. There wasn't any agenda. There wasn't any mandate to go forward. There wasn't any organization imposed. There wasn't even any authority to do anything. We had been told, basically, that these IMPs were coming and we would get connected, and that was all the structure there was.[52]

50. Crocker, technically a graduate student at MIT, had returned to his undergraduate UCLA to work with Professor Jerry Estrin to develop software measuring operating system performance. The others attending Shapiro's meeting were Steve Carr from the University of Utah, Ron Stoughton from UCSB, and Jeff Rulifson from SRI. All had an interest in networking.

51. Steve Crocker, oral history interview by James L. Pelkey, April 26, 1988, Washington, DC. Computer History Museum, Mountain View, CA. Available from https://archive.computerhistory.org/resources/access/text/2017/12/102738690-05-01-acc.pdf.

52. Crocker interview, Computer History Museum.

In February 1969, Heart convened a meeting at BBN of site representatives so they would be ready to connect IMPs when they were installed later in the year. Crocker, Carr, and Rulifson attended hoping to be told "what to do." Crocker remembers, "I don't think any of us were prepared for that meeting." The BBN team, which included Frank Heart, Bob Kahn, Severo Ornstein, and Will Crowther, found themselves talking to a crew of graduate students. And the graduate students, in turn, found themselves talking to "people whose first concern was how to get bits to flow quickly and reliably," but, unlike the students, hadn't "spent any time considering above the link level."[53]

BBN concluded that they had to provide information to the host sites so that the sites could develop the hardware and software needed to interface with the IMPs. Kahn assumed responsibility for creating a document specifying the IMP interface, a document that would become a de facto standard as BBN Document #1822.

Thanks to the February meeting, Crocker, Carr, and Rulifson realized that they were the leaders. If the sites were going to connect to the subnet, they had to make some decisions and get to work. At their March meeting, they decided to begin documenting their conversations, not as formal minutes but as notes, a trail of thoughts, to which they gave the name Request for Comments (RFC). Crocker, who had become de facto chairman of the small group of site representatives, submitted RFC 1—Host Software, on April 7, 1969.

In RFC 1, Crocker described how the IMP software worked and its implications for Host software. Significantly, he described that when a Host wanted to initiate a connection with another Host, it did so by sending a link code that the IMP would use to establish a link with the intended Host. A second message could not be sent over an established link without receiving an RFNM (Request for Next Message). Each Host would have a limited number of links with each other Host. The creation of connections using links was tantamount to establishing virtual circuits between Hosts. Hence, while the subnet functioned by routing packets, Host connections functioned by sending messages over virtual circuits. This distinction and its implications—that is, the distinction between virtual circuits and "connectionless" packet switching—would embroil the computer communication community for over a decade.

Another point Crocker made in the RFC was the desire for some host-to-host error checking. BBN made it clear that no checking was needed as the subnet would provide sufficient error-correction. This assumption would prove inaccurate and,

53. Stephen D. Crocker. 1987. The origins of RFCs. In Joyce Reynolds and Jon Postel, eds., *The Request for Comments Reference Guide*, RFC 1000, https://datatracker.ietf.org/doc/html/rfc1000.

combined with the fact that no host-to-host checking would be built-in, caused many future problems.

In June 1969, BBN distributed Document #1822 to the sites and their representatives. It defined the physical, link level, and packet level interfaces to the IMPs. With only 3 months to go before the sites began receiving their IMPs, site personnel needed help. Heart recalls:

> BBN put a great deal of energy into helping the host sites. We not only wrote 1822, but we didn't just go and leave it. We went and involved ourselves with every single site in those days, talked to the people designing the hardware and software, helped them over rough spots. We put a lot of energy into working on the host side of it. It was an important issue, and of course ARPA also was very anxious to make it happen, and encouraged us to do that.[54]

The host-to-host group kept growing in members as more sites began to take connecting to the ARPANET seriously. While a core group of graduate students and computer scientists met irregularly, nearly 100 participants attended bi-annual meetings held on the East and West Coasts. These meetings were marked by serious arguments, some so heated that the only way to be heard was to shout down the objections of others. There were no answers and even the questions sometimes eluded coherent articulation.

Crocker recalls: "We wanted a generic underpinning, but we didn't know quite how to get there. We were struggling with it, so the first design we came up with, which we were by this time under some pressure to have, was a specialized design that would allow you to log-in from one place to another, but that was pretty much it."[55]

On November 21, when Roberts and Wessler witnessed an initial demonstration of the protocol software by the host-to-host group at UCLA, Roberts could not hide his disappointment. He challenged them to be more aggressive and imaginative. He knew that to win support from reluctant sites for an expanded network would require more functionality than simply logging onto computers at other sites. Remote login was not a compelling application. He had to create a sense of urgency, and more ambitious goals, if the network was to become a reality.

The group's response had technical and administrative aspects. On the technical side, they designed a symmetric host-to-host protocol called the Network Control Program (NCP). NCP was a novel step because it disregarded the common

54. Heart interview, Computer History Museum.

55. Crocker interview, Computer History Museum.

master–slave paradigm of protocols from the mainframe computer world. Crocker recalls,

> a general-purpose interprocess communication facility was definitely needed, and then you'd build things up on that. We knew we needed layers, but having a number wasn't important. The fact was that things were built on top of each other, that you had the least commitment at a certain level and then you could build on top of that. Then all of the advanced ideas about how to get computers to cooperate on various tasks could be implemented. Those were the days when, instead of viewing the network as an electronic mail system, which was kind of an afterthought in a way, there were all these visions of shared databases and load balancing, or jobs would be shifted from one machine to another.[56]

From an administrative standpoint, this small design group decided to formalize itself. By early 1970, the host-to-host group (that had begun as a few graduate students meeting and freewheeling about how the ARPANET might be used) had evolved to a network of over 100 participants confronting the need to make ARPANET functional. The need for more formality included recognizing the importance of the host-to-host group. This prompted a name change to the Network Working Group (NWG).

Indicative of the growing awareness of the ARPANET was the involvement of Robert Metcalfe with NWG in 1970. Metcalfe, a graduate student at Harvard looking for a topic for his Ph.D. and a job to make some money, had a friend on the MIT Project MAC offer him a position building memory or working on connecting computers to the ARPANET. Having been told that networking was "hot" as ARPA was pumping a lot of money into it, Metcalfe remembers: "I had no idea what a network was!"[57] He couldn't persuade Harvard that he should oversee a big project with their PDP-10, but he was able to do "some wheeling and dealing" that got him invited to Crocker's meetings as a representative of MIT.

Distributed computing over the ARPANET required the communication protocols being created by an overworked NWG. The March 1970 NWG meeting at UCLA began with a presentation of the host-to-host protocols and highlighted the critical open issue: how to pass a connection from one computer to another? A heated discussion followed. Crocker and the members of the NWG, who now had been

56. Crocker interview, Computer History Museum.

57. Robert Metcalfe, oral history interview by James L. Pelkey, February 16, 1988, Portola Valley, CA. Computer History Museum, Mountain View, CA. Available from https://archive.computerhistory.org/resources/access/text/2013/05/102746650-05-01-acc.pdf.

attending meetings for 2 years, believed in distributed computing: processes or programs executing in one computer should be able to pass connections automatically to another computer. One computer might serve as the log-in center, for example, to perform authentication and security before granting users access to the system. Once authenticated, the log-in computer would then connect users to their requested computer instantly. While seemingly a simple task, in a network consisting of a large number of computers and users, the complexity of assuring error-free connections was significant.

The institutional uncertainty felt by members of the NWG regarding their role and authority complicated the creation of the host-to-host protocols, especially for Crocker whose role had yet to be formally recognized. Crocker hesitated to raise these issues with Roberts, sensitive to being only a graduate student. He believed Roberts had more important priorities. Adding further confusion, Crocker thought he reported to Kleinrock. But since the issues of the NWG were not Kleinrock's concern, and Kleinrock had other pressing matters, Crocker remained unmanaged. This lack of management accountability exacerbated the tendency of an inexperienced, creative engineer to seek a better solution at the expense of task completion, and Crocker proved no exception. Against this ambiguous formal structure was set the resistance of the ARPA sites to the whole undertaking.

A crucial meeting of the NWG in Atlantic City in May 1970 did little to resolve the uncertainty of the group. Crocker asked Roberts how official was the NWG and his role. Crocker recalls Roberts telling him in front of others: "Well, what's your problem. You're in charge." This was problem resolution, ARPA style. At the same time, the papers presented at the meeting revealed the deep and innovative thinking that was developing within the group.[58]
Crocker remembers:

> I remember Frank Heart put up some diagram that had sort of the spectrum of the problem and the host-to-host protocols were a thin little sliver on one end and the data communications, the long distant telephone lines were the other thin sliver, and the IMPs solved this problem that was really right in the middle. I remember looking at it and: "Well, that's your point of view."

58. The presentations included: Roberts and Wessler, "Computer network development to achieve resource sharing"; Heart, Kahn, Ornstein, Crowther and Walden, "The interface message processor for the ARPA computer network"; Kleinrock, "Analytic and simulation methods in computer network design"; Frank, Frisch, and Chou, "Topological considerations in the design of the ARPA computer network"; and Carr, Crocker, and Cerf, "Host–host communication protocol in the ARPA network."

> From my point of view, all that lower-level stuff was the bottom layer and then we had this vast territory to try to untangle.[59]

As meetings continued without resolution, Crocker began receiving direction. On August 5th, Wessler visited Crocker and finally gave him a direct order: "This is not going well, drop that portion of the protocol." Later in August, Crocker visited ARPA, and Roberts offered him a job at IPTO. During the year it took to finalize the terms of his employment, Crocker continued to run the NWG. To assist sites that had not yet interfaced their computers to the ARPANET, he organized a team of facilitators, including Metcalfe and Jon Postel, to provide expert help on demand.

A breakthrough came in mid-February 1971 at a meeting at the University of Illinois. A subcommittee known as the "host-to-host protocol glitch cleaning committee" was formed. They essentially settled the design of the host-to-host protocol.[60] But documenting the protocols so that user sites could code and implement the protocols was a very different matter: documentation had yet to be completed and implementation could take a very long time. The ever-impatient Roberts wanted sites to finish their implementations as soon as possible and become active ARPANET nodes. To eliminate the impasse of documentation, at the NWG meeting in May 1971, Alex McKenzie, of BBN, "took on the task of writing a definitive specification of the host-to-host protocol—not to invent new protocol, but to write down what had been decided."[61] With this document, each site could then begin creating the computer code needed for their computer(s) to communicate with other computers connected to the network.

3.5 Uncertainty and the Emergence of a Dominant Design, 1969–1972

3.5.1 Early Surprises

Great promise, modest functionality, pleasant surprises, and bureaucratic uncertainty marked the early days of ARPANET. The vision of distributed computing as users and programs utilizing multiple, distributed, concurrent resources, remained elusive. The lack of host-to-host protocols, the foundations on which the higher-level functions of distributed computing were to be built, limited network functionality. In fact, the only real application remained a primitive version of remote login. Even so, early surprises proved the value of the network.

The first surprise was that a user could switch terminal connections between local host computers connected to the IMP simply by issuing a command to the

59. Crocker interview, Computer History Museum.

60. *ARPANET Completion Report*, III-64.

61. *ARPANET Completion Report*, III-65.

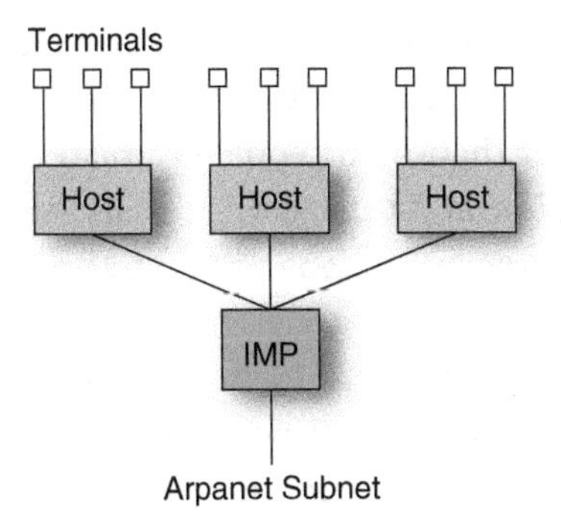

Figure 3.5 Intra-IMP Traffic. Source: Illustration by James L. Pelkey and Loring G. Robbins.

IMP. Most terminal traffic never accessed the subnet but stayed within the host site. (see Figure 3.5) Easily switching a terminal connection between local computers was a great benefit to those who needed access to multiple computers.

A second surprise was that network users were not frustrated by the lack of functionality; for that is all they wanted—terminal access to remote computers. At the beginning of the project, Roberts expected computer-to-computer traffic that could transfer software, allow remote interactions, and activities that would give users the illusion of using the resources of another machine. But most users didn't start this way, they simply viewed machines across the network as remote terminals. Roberts recalls, "the concept of distributed computing was a future concept in a lot of respects." The more immediate need was to provide "a much better communication system to get people to their remote computers."[62]

To meet this goal of terminal access, a second type of IMP was developed—the Terminal Interface Processor, or TIP. The advantage of TIPs was that terminals could connect directly to the network. Since computer terminal ports were limited and expensive, tying them up with terminals solely needing network connection was wasteful. BBN received the contract to develop a TIP in mid-1970 and delivered the first TIP in August 1971. Once available, TIPs also gave sites without computers access to the ARPANET.

A third surprise was electronic mail, or email. While Roberts believed electronic mail would be an important network application, it never appeared in any of the original specifications. According to Kahn, there was "a lot of early experimentation, moving graphics back and forth," but "in terms of total number of actions people took, there was probably more electronic mail activity, even though some of the other activities probably transmitted more bits."[63]

62. Roberts interview, Computer History Museum.

63. Kahn interview, Computer History Museum.

At first, email consisted simply of a message from one person to another person. Roberts coded one of the first improvements: a "TECO hack" that allowed a user to select which message to read rather than being forced to read messages only in the order received. (TECO [Text Editor and Corrector] was an early editor language. Hack refers to an innovative, yet largely unsupported software program, and is generally a term of respect.)

Dan Lynch, the director of computing facilities at SRI in the 1970s, remembered when Ray Tomlinson and Dan Murphy, both of BBN, wrote the original Email program as a side project, a way to document their development of TENEX.

> Tomlinson and Murphy created Email because they had a PDP10 to themselves to do development of TENEX. They had one machine, a BIG thing, right. Two guys, one machine, and they worked in shifts, I mean they basically worked twelve hours. Twelve on, twelve off, and sometimes they'd overlap, physically, and sometimes they wouldn't. As soon as they got the file system to the point where it actually would stay together, they started writing notes to each other and leaving them in a place on the disk, and, you know: "I did this. This now works." Just little notes back and forth and it kept the history. When they reached the point where they had to interface the system to the ARPANET, they said: "Oh, well, let's do it so it works from one machine to another." They made that leap because they were writing the network code as well.[64]

Email represented a new mode of interaction and communication: convenient, able to be left by the originator and picked up by the receiver at their convenience, and one did not have to respond immediately to a comment but rather could first give it thought. From the start, email was an informal mode of communication. No one worried about typos or structure. Communications that were short and to the point mattered most.

So even though the early ARPANET fell short of the embodiment of a new paradigm of distributed computing envisioned by Roberts, it did immediately demonstrate that packet switching worked. And, once users were connected by a packet-switched network, the "Members and Affiliates of the Intergalactic Computer Network," as Licklider imagined them, discovered that the network could facilitate surprises and serendipity. In short, it built and sustained a digital community.

---

64. Daniel Lynch, oral history interview with James L. Pelkey, February 16, 1988, Cupertino, CA. Computer History Museum, Mountain View, CA. Available from https://archive.computerhistory.org/resources/access/text/2016/02/102717120-05-01-acc.pdf.

3.5.2 Parallel Experiments in Hawaii and London

ARPANET was not the only computer network experiment underway during the late 1960s. Two others were the ALOHAnet led by Norm Abramson in Honolulu and the NPL network under the leadership of Donald Davies in London. Both would have lasting impact on the history of computer communications.

The story of ALOHAnet begins in 1966 when Norm Abramson joined the faculty of the engineering department of the University of Hawaii. He thought he was taking a "big gamble," for although he would be able to continue his engineering research, he was giving up the intellectual stimulation of Harvard and Stanford where he had spent the last 7 years. In addition, he had the challenge of finding his own funding. Then fate smiled on Abramson as he found funding that would lead to his making a permanent contribution to the development of network technologies with his radio packet switched network: ALOHAnet.

Learning of a newly created ARPA program named THEMIS—whose mission was to support research at "second tier" universities—Abramson and two of his fellow professors, Wes Peterson and Ned Weldon, joined forces to create a team with both communications and computer background. Abramson recalls:

> So we cast about for a research topic that we thought would make sense to the Department of Defense, that we would be interested in, and said: "Well, communications for computers makes sense." The telephone system appeared not to make sense at that time, especially in Hawaii, and we thought we had something which was intellectually stimulating and a package that we could sell to ARPA.[65]

In 1967, Abramson arranged a meeting with Bob Taylor, who was Director of IPTO. Abramson recalls blowing the opportunity, however: when asked precisely what they wanted to do, Abramson could do little more than shrug. Abramson got another shot in 1969, when he met with Taylor and Roberts. He remembers expressing frustration about the limited capacity of radio channels: "Something much more sensible for radio can be done here than assigning a single channel for every user in the network. That's crazy. That won't work!"[66]

Where one person's ideas began and ended is now a blur. What is clear is that at a meeting held later in 1969, without the participation of Taylor or Roberts, the important decision to directly transmit user information in a single high-speed

65. Norm Abramson, oral history interview with James L. Pelkey, October 13, 1988, Menlo Park, CA. Computer History Museum, Mountain View, CA. Available from https://archive.computerhistory.org/resources/access/text/2013/05/102746645-05-01-acc.pdf.

66. Abramson interview, Computer History Museum.

packet burst, now known as an ALOHA channel, was made. That is, every terminal would transmit its data to the host using the *same* radio channel. If collisions occurred, a terminal would not receive an acknowledgment and would re-transmit. No terminal had its own dedicated broadcast channel: all terminals would use the same channel. Abramson and his colleagues wanted to push beyond conventional point-to-point modes of frequency-division multiple access (FDMA, or FDM) or time-division multiple access (TDMA, or TDM) manner. He later wrote that the alternative was simple: "Some form of sharing of a common communication channel resource appeared necessary."[67]

Once again, the intermittent operation of interactive computer terminals was causing communication system architects to rethink how to construct a data communications network. But what a preposterous notion—that all terminals share the same channel simultaneously! The next step was to build a demonstration. Two graduate students under the supervision of Abramson, Charlie Bass and John Davidson, both of whom will become important to the history of computer communications, gained important experience working on ALOHAnet. Maybe the most unlikely source of help, considering the demands on his time, was Roberts himself. Something about the project captured his imagination, to the point that Abramson thought of Roberts not merely as a sponsor but also as "another member of the research staff of the project, contributing a number of major technical results (including the first derivation of the capacity of the slotted ALOHA channel and the first analysis of the capture effect in ALOHA channels).[68]

ALOHAnet had a centralized, star topology consisting of remote terminal sites all connected by radio channels to a host computer at the University of Hawaii. All users transmitted on one frequency and received on another. At its peak, ALOHAnet supported 40 users at several locations on the islands of Oahu and Maui. User terminals connected to the host computer via a terminal control unit that communicated at 9,600 bits per second. With his success in radio, Abramson in 1972 applied the ALOHAnet concepts to satellite channel communications. On December 17, 1972, an IMP connecting the ALOHA host to the ARPANET by satellite channel was installed.

On the other side of the globe, in England, Donald Davies continued to explore packet switching ideas. In August 1966 he became Superintendent of the Computer Science Division of the National Physics Laboratory, giving him the budgetary power to bring into being a network exploring the packet switching ideas. But

67. Norm Abramson. 1985. Development of the ALOHANET. *IEEE Transactions on Information Theory* 31 (March 1985), 119–123.

68. Abramson, "Development of the ALOHANET," 121.

Davies recognized that he could "never build an ARPANET. We had no mandate for building a nationwide network and couldn't imagine who would use it. We had nothing like ARPA to act as our community."[69]

In searching for network design objectives, his team realized they had to look no further than a problem they confronted every day in their laboratory: How to provide common computer access for their growing proliferation of computer terminals? Their solution, a computer called an interface processor, was essentially a terminal multiplexer much like the TIPs of ARPANET. Only the NPL interface processor connected up to 512 terminals to a local computer at a combined data rate of up to one megabit per second.[70]

Once the interface processor had been conceived, the NPL researchers questioned whether there might be more to gain than simply terminal connections. For as with all new "black boxes," their existence opens up possibilities not contemplated in their original design. In the case of the interface processors, Davies' group recognized that they could share more than just common terminal access. Their motivation was partly driven by the high cost of adding capabilities to small computers, as Davies summarized in an interview: "you had to add disk stores, which in those days were great big cabinets that cost you more than the computer itself. So what we said was that what we can do for all our mass of small minicomputers, PDP-8s and things around the laboratory, was provide them with a central storage facility, a file server, using the latest technology." Davies and his group built a file server to test their network, which led them to another important first in networking history—the concept of "local area networks," or, in other words, "local" computer-to-computer and terminal-to-computer interconnection. Again, history shows that Davies had coined a phrase, "local area networks," much as he had earlier with "packet switching."[71]

When the network first worked in 1971, the simple host-to-host protocol proved inadequate and had to be completely re-written in order to speed up packet transmission. Once the new protocol software was installed in 1973, the network handled over one million packets a day.

3.6 ARPANET Meets the Public: ICCC Demonstration, 1972

As we have discussed, the theme of "learning" can cut several different ways. It includes the formal education of students, such as in the crucial graduate

69. Davies interview, Computer History Museum.

70. Terminal addresses were organized hierarchically with three levels of branching and eight nodes at each branch; hence, the address limitation of 512 devices.

71. Davies interview, Computer History Museum.

programs at UCLA and MIT. It also captures the process of informal learning, as scientists and engineers involved in all phases of the ARPANET project were encountering new ideas about networking and computers. Finally, leaders and researchers involved with the ARPANET project also faced the continual need to educate—or provide information to—various constituencies, including their supervisors in the government and universities, contractors, international partners, and so on.

It is this latter meaning of learning—dissemination of knowledge about the ARPANET—that was on Robert Kahn's mind in mid-1971 when Larry Roberts was venting about the ARPANET being slow to arrive into full operation. The lack of host-to-host protocols loomed as the largest problem. But other problems existed as well, such as convincing new sites to accelerate activities required to connect their computers to the network.[72] While every site confronted similar problems, each site was also unique, and few acted with Roberts' sense of urgency.

Kahn's idea was to hold a public demonstration. It could serve two functions at once. First, it would provide a deadline for the Host sites to get their acts together. After all, very few things are as motivating as the prospect of public embarrassment. Second, Kahn imagined a public demonstration could be a coming-out party: it could educate researchers and partners about the ARPANET and its capabilities and encourage new partners. Roberts liked the idea and asked Kahn to manage the effort. Kahn recommended that the demonstration be held at either a Spring or Fall Joint Computer Conference. Roberts, however, preferred a brand-new conference, the International Conference on Computer Communications (ICCC), to be held October 24–26, 1972, in Washington DC. The ever-persuasive Roberts prevailed.

From mid-1971 until the ICCC, Kahn spent virtually all of his time organizing the demonstration. He recruited Al Vezza of MIT's Project MAC to help him, and they soon would involve others. The NWG contributed by holding a game, or "fly-off" at their fall NWG meeting held at MIT. As Crocker remembers it, the concept of the game was for everybody to try to log into all the other hosts by initiating remote login (Telnet) sessions. It proved to be a useful occasion for all the sites to demonstrate their capabilities, with one exception: "SDC distinguished themselves by being completely out of it and having nothing ready. Everything else kind of worked."

72. During this period, the Host-to Host protocols assumed the name Network Control Program, or NCP, which was originally the name of the software that enabled hosts to talk to IMPs The name change reflected the importance and significance of the Host-to-Host software, a subject to occupy an important role in future chapters.

The "fly-off" provided a useful taste of what was to come. Kahn's plan for the ICCC demo called for a TIP with a full complement of computer terminals be installed at the Hilton Hotel in Washington D.C., the site of the ICCC. Interested conference participants could then log-on to one of the ARPANET Hosts and run an application on-line. That meant, however, that interesting practical applications, to be known as "scenarios," had to be created and de-bugged or, if an application already existed, to make it network usable. Another task was to arrange for computer terminals to be installed and working. Kahn used this opportunity to convince terminal manufacturers to loan terminals to ARPA, and to help make sure they were configured to talk to the TIP. A third major task was to get the room ready for the demonstration, including making arrangements with AT&T for the leased lines.

To help Host sites connect their computers to ARPANET and create scenarios, Kahn organized a group of about 50 facilitators, including Cerf, Metcalfe, and Postel. This new group relieved the NWG of any continuing involvement for the demonstration, allowing it to focus its efforts on implementing higher-level protocols, including those needed for distributed computing applications. Around this same time, Crocker dramatically reduced the time he devoted to ARPANET, working instead on other ARPA projects.

In September, Kahn asked Metcalfe to work with the NIC at SRI to document the working scenarios and create a manual for ICCC participants. Metcalfe spent 2 weeks at SRI pulling together 19 scenarios "to exhibit variety and sophistication, while retaining simplicity."[73]

The ICCC would prove to be for packet switching what the Centennial Exposition in Philadelphia in 1876 was for the telephone: the public unveiling of a technological discontinuity. For the 800 computer communication professionals, government employees and academics attending the ICCC, seeing the TIP on a raised floor in the middle of the room with 36 connected computer terminals circled around it and dozens of ARPA scientists milling about, eager to show off their pride-and-joy, the scene must have seemed like a sideshow at some alien world's carnival. And then to sit at a terminal, and with but a few key strokes be connected through a computer at UCLA to one at MIT and instantly be using an application, and then just as easily connect to any one of the other participating computers, the disorientation must have felt as if truly on that alien world—no wonder the most accessed scenario was weather conditions around Mother Earth. To most, a computer was a single machine safely stored in an air-conditioned, secured room.

73. Scenarios for Using the ARPANET at the Int'l Conf. on Computer Communication. NIC No. 11863. Network Information Center, Washington, DC, Oct. 1972.

The idea of accessing computers around the country from a conference room in a Hilton Hotel was simply unheard of. And as for the ARPA scientists, the bonds formed from staging the demonstration and living around the clock with their creation left them heady and optimistic about the computing future they were creating.

Many of the protagonists of the event shared their perspectives with us—these capture the spirit of the day.

Kahn has maybe the best perspective of the event.

> It was kind of a tour de force to actually make it happen. I forget which day of the week that the conference started on, but we didn't actually have access to the room until something like 7:00 on the day it had to work. Now you have to imagine what it's like building a whole computer installation when you have something like five or six hours to actually do it. People were going to show up in the room to use the network that afternoon. And so we had to lay the false floor and we had to get the long-distance telephone lines, get all the terminals installed and do that all in the compact space of six hours. It worked like a charm. It was just all ready.

> The TIP was right in the middle of the ballroom, and it was on a raised floor. We had ramps all around it to get people in and out and to handle the cabling. It was structured so that people could walk through the ballroom and see all the demos. People could sit down at the terminals, and they'd pick a scenario and they'd do it. There were booths on the sides as well as in the center. Each of the booths had somebody assigned to them and then people responsible for regions of the ballroom, like Bob Metcalfe, Vint Cerf or Jon Postel. They would kind of roam around and just help out wherever they were needed. There were probably at least thirty people involved. We also had demos outside the ballroom, staff at the doors, and we had a separate room where we were showing a movie.

> For the first couple of days when it was up and running before the conference started—all these network experts were there trying to get their demos to work. When you've got a hundred or so of the best computer people in the country and they're all in one room, any question that you want to ask can probably be answered by somebody in that room. People weren't leaving the room until well after midnight every night. I mean, nobody wanted to leave that room. If we didn't decide to shut the doors and lock it up, they might

> have stayed there all night for a whole week. Then at the end we just tore it down without ceremony.[74]

Metcalfe remembers an incident:

> They gave me the job of escorting ten AT&T vice-presidents around. So I was demoing the system, and for the only time in that whole show, the TIP crashed. The only time. It went down for about ten or twenty seconds. It finally came back up again. We reestablished connection and it never went down again. But this was a very enlightening moment for me because when I looked up, you know, they were happy that it crashed. They made no point of hiding their joy. Because this confirmed for them that circuit switching was better and more reliable than packet switching, which was flaky and would never work. And I had been working on this for 2 or 3 years, and it really pissed me off.[75]

Davies attended the ICCC and remembers the impact of seeing everyone gathered together:

> The ARPANET was key because it demonstrated the concepts of packet switching on a large scale. The ICCC meeting in Washington, DC, was absolutely crucial because, for the first time, you could see a large community of people all working together. That was a watershed, because that was the first time that you had lots of people together, all of whom were convinced that it was all going to work and be significant. Before that time, whenever I talked about it, I was always defending it and saying: "Yes, in spite of what you say, it's going to be important!"
>
> At the ICCC there was tremendous enthusiasm. There was enormous intellectual power there; all these people concentrating on doing things. It wasn't one or two oddballs like myself and Larry Roberts. People were talking about the possibilities. It wasn't just academic anymore; it was real working stuff. So there was a tremendous difference. I think everybody was very much affected by the success of that as a demonstration.[76]

The clash of the two cultures—circuit switching versus packet switching—had begun. Events still to unfold could never have been predicted, even with the insights gained from those momentous years. For this small, yet growing community of network advocates, change was both certain and welcomed. In fact, the

74. Kahn interview, Computer History Museum.

75. Metcalfe interview, Computer History Museum.

76. Davies interview, Computer History Museum.

coming out party for ICCC was also a going away party. Crocker, now at ARPA, would essentially exit the world of communications. Kahn had accepted a position at ARPA and left BBN shortly after ICCC. Taylor moved from the University of Utah to Xerox PARC and recruited Metcalfe to join him. Cerf had accepted a position at Stanford University and his last act at UCLA was participating in ICCC. And while Postel stayed on at UCLA to complete his Ph.D., he began working with Dave Farber, an important scientist in our coming story. Roberts puts the successful demonstration of ARPANET in perspective:

> Clearly, I was influenced by the whole community in that I talked to everybody and tried to collect ideas. I think that one has to look at the follow through; what is it that makes it happen, the whole process? I've seen lots of people with ideas, and they mention them and no one picks them up and they don't carry them forward. You've got to then believe and see that it's economically attractive and viable and have enough confidence in that to carry it through, and that's really what happened with the ARPANET. I don't think it was an invention; it wasn't a theory breakthrough like Einstein. It was a collection of ideas that were around at the time. The computer people had always had blocks and lines were always around; that was nothing new. In fact, I really don't believe that Paul Baran or Donald Davies influenced the design all that much, because they were hardly involved. Donald did in the sense that he got me to use higher speed lines than I would have used and Paul had done the "hot potato" routing and we looked at that first as a good example and proceeded from there. So, those were pieces that we applied, but the real issue was to carry through and see that it was important and it was economic and it was going to have an influence and make sure it happened.[77]

3.7 In Perspective

The public demonstration of ARPANET at the ICCC marked a magical and exciting time, when a powerful new idea—packet switching—proved real and a torrent of activity and thinking was unleashed to reshape the way computers would communicate. It proved that with a few simple keystrokes one could access widely dispersed computers from the same computer terminal without having to establish new connections with each computer. Even as 35 other users at terminals shared the same TIP accessing different computers, or even the same computers—each believing they had sole use of the communication network. Regardless of how mundane an accomplishment this seemed to Roberts, it represented a watershed

77. Roberts interview, Computer History Museum.

in computer communications. The revolutionary concept of computers communicating simply by sending packets of data whenever desired over a shared communications network versus having to establish a circuit, send data, and terminate the circuit, had been proven. ARPANET, the first packet-switching network, forever changed how computer communications would evolve.

Although the many computer scientists who had been involved with ARPANET dispersed after the ICCC, they took with them the seminal ideas and optimistic energy of those special days. Soon, many were improving computer communications in ways that could never have been predicted. The story of one such innovation—local area networking—specifically Ethernet—will follow. But first comes the story of how the data communication *companies* responded to the growing need to interconnect computers.

Even though at first information was available only to the most interested, ARPANET would become widely known. In other words, the various strategies for education devised by ARPA program managers—Licklider, Taylor, Roberts—worked. Those heavily invested in circuit switching, such as the firms designing and building modems and multiplexers, charged on in their own world, ignoring the coming of packet switching. It was not that they did not see the growing computerization of corporate America, they did. Only they saw immediate products, revenue, and success from doing what they knew how to do. The next chapter tells the story of data communications from 1973 through 1979.

Market Order: Data Communications, 1973–1979

4.1 Overview

While the ARPANET community was busy proving the viability of packet-switched networking, the entrepreneurs of data communications were experiencing their own success selling products that connected computers using existing technologies. Their customers couldn't get enough of these devices. For the nearly 100 modem and multiplexer start-ups, the market for communications products was growing rapidly. For some companies, the competitive phase of the market-structure would become fatal if they were unable to generate sufficient profits to sustain growth. For a few—some on the brink of collapse—the right combination of engineering, luck, and a keen eye for realizing opportunity would propel them to positions of market leadership.

In this increasingly competitive stage of the data communications market-structure, the government continued to influence market dynamics, both through antitrust litigation against both AT&T and IBM as well as through changes in telecommunications policy. The FCC further defined the separation between voice and data services over the telephone network. These new regulations had significant impact on AT&T especially, restricting them from competing in the data services markets unless as separate subsidiaries.

Entering 1973, industry analysts expected the robust growth of data communication revenues to continue at 40–50% per year. Lower prices and increased competition, especially in the high-speed modem category where AT&T had finally introduced products, drove demand. But by 1974, a sagging economy and merciless competition had firms struggling to break even. Sales of modems were projected to be flat. No one imagined that just a few years after its announcement in November 1971, the microprocessor would energize unprecedented opportunities.

For the early data communications start-ups, adaptation to the increasingly competitive market required strategic decisions on new product development, selling to new niches in the market, and innovations in marketing and distribution. The executives in charge of the companies responded to competitive pressures with unique plans for growth based on their company's strengths and specific position in the industry. As we shall see, many of their decisions had profound impacts on their companies and the entire data communications market-structure.

4.2 Regulatory Challenges to IBM and AT&T

As late as 1968, information technologies seemed securely controlled by IBM and AT&T. If they had had their way, any new firms challenging their market dominance would have been severely constrained. The efforts of the Federal Government, by way of the Justice Department, to foster competition in the markets for computers and communications intensified in 1969 with the filing of an antitrust lawsuit against IBM. By 1973, a number of corporations joined by filing antitrust lawsuits as well, and, if nothing else, IBM was on its best behavior—witness its decision to unbundle its software in the sale of computers. As we saw in Chapter 2, AT&T's monopoly also was contested by competitors as well as regulators in the FCC. These issues framed the macro-conditions of data communications.

In September 1973, John D. deButts was Chairman and CEO of AT&T, having succeeded H.I. Romnes. Unlike Romnes, deButts had risen through the operating companies and wanted to return AT&T to the glory days of Theodore N. Vail's "One System, One Policy, Universal Service." He soon delivered a fiery speech entitled "An Unusual Obligation" to the National Association of Regulatory Utility Commissioners (NARUC). In words no one could misunderstand, deButts aimed to "take to the public the case for the common carrier principle and thereby implication to oppose competition, espouse monopoly."[1]

He knew his speech would inflame many in government. He couldn't have cared less, having the appetite for a fight. DeButts got his wish in March 1974 when MCI filed an antitrust lawsuit charging 22 counts of unlawful activity. Then Congress acted. In 1974, Senator Phillip A. Hart, Chairman of the Senate Judiciary Antitrust and Monopoly Subcommittee, held hearings on restructuring seven industries—including telecommunications. Clay T. Whitehead, Director of the Office of Telecommunications Policy, testified: "A restructuring of the

1. Peter Temin with Louis Galambos. 1987. *The Fall of the Bell System: A Study in Prices and Politics*. Cambridge University Press, 96.

communications industry may be necessary if competition and monopoly are to coexist constructively."[2]

Big business was falling under public scrutiny. The persistent agony of Vietnam, the threat of President Richard M. Nixon's impeachment (Watergate), and mounting inflation all contributed to a social climate where people lost faith in organizations and institutions. Within the Federal Government this had the effect of weakening the authority of political appointments and strengthening the power of permanent staff. Justice Department staff members, recalling the 1956 AT&T Consent Decree, saw an opportunity to seize the initiative. President Ford echoed the sentiment on October 20, 1974, in a speech calling for tougher antitrust enforcement.[3]

A month later, the Justice Department initiated its fourth major antitrust assault on AT&T in United States v. AT&T Co.[4] More extensive than the 1949 suit, the broad complaint charged that AT&T had monopolized and conspired to monopolize various telecommunication markets including customer-provided equipment.[5] The relief sought was for AT&T to divest itself of Western Electric (WE), for WE to be divided into multiple companies, and for some or all of the Bell Operating Companies to be divested from AT&T Long Lines. Chairman deButts wrote shareholders that AT&T would fight it to the end.

In November 1975, AT&T responded by championing an amendment of the Communications Act of 1934. Carrying the formal title of the Consumer Communications Reform Act and known as the "Bell Bill," it aimed to return telecommunications and AT&T to the nostalgic state existing before Carterfone. Heavy-handed and showing no room for compromise, the bill nevertheless received respectable support.[6] The antitrust lawsuit would continue to progress slowly, victim to legal maneuverings.

As a complement to aggressive actions from the Justice Department, regulators at the FCC revisited the rules governing the attachment of customer premises equipment (CPE) to AT&T's network. The rules governing the connection

2. Alan Stone and William L. Stone. 1989. *Wrong Number—The Breakup of AT&T*, Basic Books. 283.

3. Stone and Stone, *Wrong Number*, 284.

4. The first three assaults were the Kingsbury Commitment, the Special Telephone Investigation, and United States v. Western Electric.

5. "The charges included that (1) Western Electric supplied the telecommunications equipment needs of the Bell system, thereby eliminating competition from other manufacturers and suppliers; (2) AT&T obstructed the interconnection of SCCs and other carriers; and (3) AT&T obstructed the interconnection of customer-provided CPE into the Bell system." Stone and Stone, *Wrong Number*, 288.

6. Legislation would remain undecided until 1985, before dying a quiet death.

of specialized common carrier networks to, and through, AT&T's network were also under scrutiny, as were the rules governing the boundary between communications and computing. An overriding concern was—which market-structures would be regulated and which would be shaped by market competition?

FCC Common Carrier Bureau chief Bernard Strassburg knew the fight over foreign attachments was far from over with AT&T's filing of tariffs for Protective Connecting Arrangements (PCA) on January 1, 1969. Given that the FCC only had regulatory authority over interstate telecommunications, he foresaw similar struggles between state Public Utility Commissions and local telephone providers. The reason was no big mystery. If customers purchased their own CPE, modems or PBXs for example, or connected to an alternative carrier, such as MCI, then telephone companies lost revenue and local telephone rates would surely have to go up since local telephone rates were subsidized by the profits AT&T made on customer CPE and interstate telephone calls.[7]

In an effort to pre-empt state actions, Strassburg announced a Joint Proceeding with NARUC on June 14, 1972. The objective was not to review Carterfone. That had already been decided—tariffs now allowed connection of customer-provided CPE with the use of PCAs.[8] The issue was whether, and under what conditions, customers would be permitted to provide their own PCAs. Strassburg recalls: "The Joint Proceeding would consider the recommendations of the National Academy of Sciences, the Advisory Committees, the Chief Engineers Office, and any other comments. It was to be the forum for formally resolving the PCA issues and registration—or any other alternatives to PCAs."[9]

NARUC and the individual states were not content to leave all to the Joint Proceeding, however. NARUC and 17 state PUCs conducted their own investigations of the damage from the interconnection of customer-owned and maintained terminal equipment. To get data required requesting it from AT&T, which wanted to support NARUC's concerns and, ideally, *reverse* the Carterfone decision. In April 1973, they publicized their results. After studying 1,523 cases of CPE problems, they concluded: "It is clear that the interconnection of subscriber-provided equipment

7. This issue, separations, is critically important and will not be but touched on in this discussion. It is core to understanding the interconnections, and how they were accounted for, that made organizational and institutional structure so difficult to change. See Temin, *Fall of the Bell System*, for the best discussion—one involving over 100 interviews of AT&T executives during this period.

8. Docket 19419, Interstate and Foreign MTS and WATS, 35 F.C.C.2d 539 (1972).

9. Bernard Strassburg, oral history interview by James L. Pelkey, May 3, 1988, Washington, DC. Computer History Museum, Mountain View, CA. Available from https://archive.computerhistory.org/resources/access/text/2015/11/102738016-05-01-acc.pdf.

has had adverse effects to date on the quality of telephone service."[10] Five weeks later, the FCC reported that in reviewing the data "statistically meaningful differences" between customer-provided and telephone-company provided equipment could not be demonstrated.[11]

Next, North Carolina directly challenged the authority of the FCC to proscribe intrastate telecommunications policies and tariffs (Telerent Leasing). Then the public utility commission of Nebraska declared any PBX connected to intrastate lines a common carrier, needing to get a certificate of convenience and necessity, which, obvious to all, would take a long time. Where North Carolina took the battle to the courts, Nebraska waged war administratively. Throughout this period, AT&T continued to implement their PCA program, and, increasingly, defend their policy from charges of monopoly. (By July 1978, 160,000 PCAs would be in use.)[12]

On January 1, 1974, Strassburg retired and Walter R. Hinchman became the new Chief of the Common Carrier Bureau. In March 1974, only months after retiring, Strassburg gave a speech to the North American Telephone Association, the group of independent manufacturers of CPE organized by Tom Carter of Carterfone. Strassburg advised them that they "must look elsewhere than to regulation for a solution."[13] Given the knowledge and insight of someone so respected, it is small wonder private antitrust suits were soon filed in record numbers (see Table 4.1).

In early 1976, the Fourth Circuit Court ruled that the FCC could pre-empt state jurisdiction to impose nationwide telephone standards. Before the end of the year, the Supreme Court refused an appeal for review. In March 1977, the Fourth Circuit Court ruled that the FCC's regime for equipment registration and certification was legal. Six months later the Supreme Court again denied a writ of certiorari. AT&T now had to certify its products as well.

Another open issue between the FCC and AT&T was that of hybrid services from Computer Inquiry I. Hybrid services were defined as those that had both data processing and message-switching components. This definition had become critical for AT&T as it clearly wanted to enter data processing markets and chafed under the proposed separate affiliates solution. On August 9, 1976, the FCC issued a Notice of Inquiry and Proposed Rulemaking. It became known as Computer Inquiry II.

---

10. United States v. AT&T, Defendants' Third Statement of Contentions and Proof, Vol. II, pp. 1149–1150.

11. Fred W. Henck and Bernard Strassburg. 1988. *A Slippery Slope: The Long Road to the Breakup of AT&T*. Greenwood Press, 134.

12. Third Statement, p. 1174.

13. Henck and Strassburg, 134. This subject is discussed in the next section. See, for example, Table 4.1, Number of active antitrust cases pending against AT&T.

Table 4.1 **Number of active antitrust cases pending against AT&T**

Year	Number of cases	Year	Number of cases	Year	Number of cases
1960	1	1968	15	1976	47
1961	2	1969	13	1977	50
1962	3	1970	21	1978	54
1963	3	1971	26	1979	50
1964	5	1972	31	1980	51
1965	8	1973	29	1981	60
1966	9	1974	38	1982	59
1967	14	1975	47		

Source: Based on Alan Stone, *Wrong Number: The Breakup of AT&T* (New York: Basic Books, Inc., 1989) 154; Antitrust at a Glance (AT&T Report) (December 15, 1982), in AT&T Archives & History Center.

Three years later, in May 1979, the FCC released its Tentative Decision for Computer Inquiry II. Voice services remained regulated, while basic non-voice services (read data processing), were unregulated. "Dominant" carriers could offer basic non-voice services but only through separate subsidiaries. AT&T objected to separate subsidiaries. The Justice Department objected to the very concept of the FCC trying to expand its authority under the Communication Act to include structural issues. The FCC took these and other comments under advisement.[14]

In the summer of 1978, poor health forced reassignment of Judge Joseph C. Waddy's cases. The AT&T case was assigned to a newly appointed District Judge, Harold H. Greene. In September 1978, Greene issued orders for a trial to start in September 1980. Showing no signs that it was going to be denied control of data communications, AT&T announced its Advanced Communications Service (ACS), an intelligent data network intended to be as easy to use as telephones.[15] ACS would obviate the need for modems or for any user to worry about interconnecting incompatible computer devices.

In February 1979, Charles L. Brown succeeded deButts as Chairman and CEO of AT&T. Renouncing combativeness, Brown announced a new management philosophy acknowledging and accepting competition: "I am a competitor and I look forward with anticipation and confidence to the excitement of the marketplace."[16]

As slowly as the AT&T lawsuit had been progressing, the one filed against IBM seemed motionless in 1979. Numerous corporations had joined the fray: Telex,

14. Temin, *Fall of the Bell System*, 191–194.

15. "Seeds of network change planted during past year," *Datamation*, December 1978, 37–38.

16. Temin, *Fall of the Bell System*, 175.

Greyhound Leasing, Hudson General, Transamerica, Memorex, and Forro Precision.[17] Only the Telex case had been decided, in favor of IBM. An appeals court also overruled in the Greyhound Leasing case, but this time against IBM. The message, in either case, remained unclear. As of year-end 1979, the Justice Department still had controversial antitrust cases against the two dominant companies in computer communications: AT&T and IBM.

4.3 Data Communications Market Leaders in the Early 1970s

Against this backdrop of macro-level conditions—regulations, politics, and two massive incumbent firms—were the micro-level actions and conditions of the data communication firms. Start-ups labored to combine technological innovation and product selection with available channels of distributions. To succeed meant incorporating LSI technologies, innovating network management and, in the case of multiplexers, harnessing the computational power of microprocessors and software design. These product advances would enable corporations to integrate their ad hoc point-to-point networks into more robust networks that could support their burgeoning distributed data processing. Not all firms would clear these hurdles. Codex succeeded but ADS stumbled, unable to master the technologies needed to bring products to market and suffering from the sudden decline of time-sharing.

With the increase in competition, the more successful firms sustained profitability by creating new products and new sources of revenue at higher gross margins. In the special case of data communications, there were two main product categories, modems and multiplexers, and often a third, communication processors. With both dial-up modems and leased line modems, higher speeds generally required expertise that proved to be significant barriers to entry. Likewise, even though a firm learned to master frequency division multiplexers, this was no guarantee that it could innovate time division multiplexers, or the even more complex statistical multiplexers.

Other elements that influenced which firms succeeded and which ones struggled and failed were the movement of people, especially CEOs and talented engineers; their ability to forge successful competitive and cooperative relationships; the management of financial resources, especially maintaining enough cash to finance growth; and making the right strategic acquisitions and avoiding pitfalls. A final important factor was the reduction in the number of firms, largely the failure of the most recent and thinly capitalized entrants. Up to 70% of the firms in business at the peak of the emergent phase would be gone by the end of the competitive

17. *Datamation*, January 1978, 91.

phase—hence the name. Now to observe how some of the more successful firms managed the challenges.

4.3.1 Codex: Modems, Multiplexers, and Competition, 1973–1976

In early 1973, Carr found himself in unfamiliar territory. Codex was profitable, demand was strong, and the 1972 year-end public offering had provided ready cash. Existing contracts and changes in lease accounting virtually guaranteed near-term revenue growth. Thus, freed from the stresses of having to manage every day as if it might be the company's last, Carr turned his attention to the threat of LSI semiconductor technology and decided it was time to contact Rockwell, a firm he knew was interested in modems from their having tried to sell Codex their failing subsidiary ADS.

Exploratory telephone conversations confirmed Rockwell's interest. They wanted to fabricate a 9,600bps modem chip to sell to Japanese facsimile manufacturers.[18] Rockwell had no intention of selling stand-alone modems. The opportunity seemed too good to be true. So Carr, Storey, and Forney arranged to visit Rockwell. In a pre-meeting strategy session over breakfast at their hotel, Forney told Carr and Storey that his Rockwell contact made it clear that they had no interest unless Codex committed to buy a minimum of 5,000 chips. How easily hope turned to despair. The idea seemed preposterous: 5,000 chips meant 5,000 modems when only 18 months earlier they all remembered laughing so hard they cried when Pugh projected selling 400 modems. Fear, however, makes the impossible seem doable, especially for someone like Carr. Carr could not dismiss the rumors that Milgo, and others, had LSI modems under development. So Carr proposed:

> "Look, if we go in and we tell this guy that we'll commit to 10,000 and he buys the deal, we'll get started." So we went in and we had the meeting and we committed to 10,000 modems, and he took it with a pretty straight face, and I gave it to him with a straight face, and we cut a deal.[19]

After months of negotiating a contract, including the thorny issue of circumventing antitrust regulations, the difficult and time-consuming work of designing and fabricating the chip began.[20] Carr's immersion into the rapidly advancing world of semiconductors gave him valuable insight. Discussing this knowledge

18. Collins Electronics, an acquisition, did not have the requisite 9,600bps expertise.

19. Art Carr, oral history interview by James L. Pelkey, April 6, 1988, Newton, MA. Computer History Museum, Mountain View, CA, https://archive.computerhistory.org/resources/access/text/2015/10/102737982-05-01-acc.pdf.

20. Each party wanted to prevent the other from selling the modem chips to its respective competitors, such as Rockwell selling the chips to Milgo.

with Pugh, they wondered if it was time to start development of a computer front-end communication processor. Their 3C experiences—when they sold minicomputers as communication front-ends for mainframe computers—informed their instincts. Might substituting microprocessors for minicomputers yield a new product line? Developing computer technologies would also force Codex to overcome a lack of knowledge that concerned both men.

Then, as if a prayer had been answered, James Vander Mey, a professor at the University of Illinois, asked Jim Rothrock at a Codex trade show booth if they had any interest in front-end communications products. Rothrock forwarded the inquiry to Forney who discussed the issue with Carr. Soon, Carr and Forney were making trips to Illinois to sell Vander Mey on joining Codex. In May 1973, Vander Mey and a handful of his best students became Codex employees.

While Forney investigated the technology, Pugh began assembling a marketing team by raiding Memorex, the only company offering a competitive product to IBM's best-selling 2703 front-end processor. Soon, marketing was specifying product requirements for engineering. It didn't take long, however, for Pugh to conclude he and Carr had significantly underestimated the commitment required to compete against IBM. For one thing, Codex had no experience creating and supporting host computer software. A cautious Pugh recommended ceasing all development and Carr soon agreed. By then, however, Vander Mey and his team had so impressed Forney, Pugh, and Carr that they wanted to find another project for them to work on. It would be a statistical multiplexer.

Wesley Chu and the Statistical Multiplexer, 1966–1975

Statistical multiplexing is the third important innovation in the technology trajectory of multiplexing, after frequency division (FDM) and time division multiplexing (TDM). Wesley Chu's theoretical work in statistical multiplexing began in 1966 after he earned his Ph.D. in electrical engineering from Stanford University. He then joined a new computer communications studies group at Bell Labs (AT&T). The study group began investigating terminal-to-computer communications from traffic measurements. They learned terminals typically used only about 5% of the bandwidth of communication lines. The question was: How to multiplex the traffic of many terminals over a communication line to use the bandwidth of the circuit?

Chu first turned to improving TDM. In TDM, each terminal connected to the multiplexer has full use of the communication line on a rotating basis. While a significant improvement over FDM, TDM still suffered inefficiencies because rotating terminals frequently had no data to transmit.

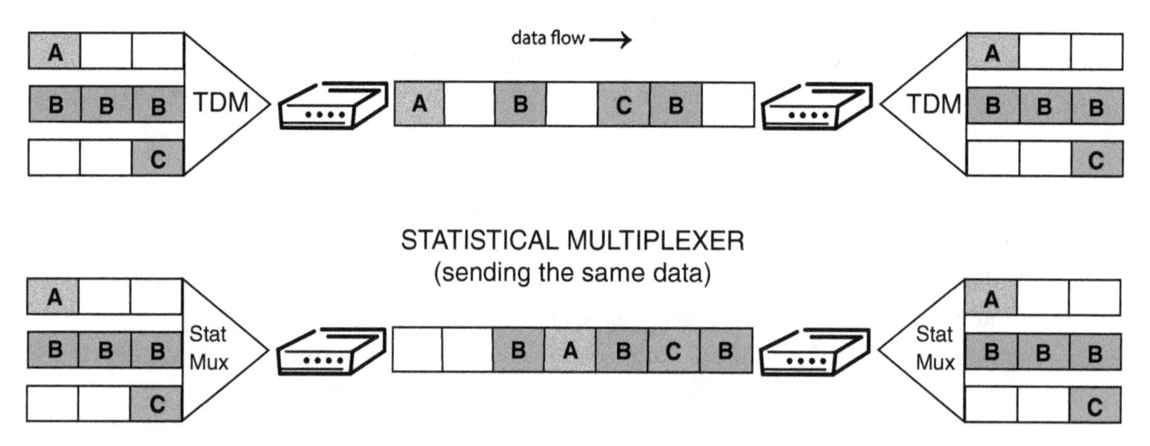

Figure 4.1 Statistical & time division multiplexing. Source: Illustration by James L. Pelkey and Loring G. Robbins.

How then to always give terminals with data control of the communication line? (See Figure 4.1.) A solution required intelligence—the multiplexer had to determine which terminals had data to send and how to queue the terminals so as to optimally serve all terminals.

In 1969, Chu left Bell Labs to teach at UCLA. While he continued to investigate statistical multiplexing, the prohibitive cost of hardware precluded any immediate practical application. When Intel introduced the 8008 in 1972, Chu converted his design to the eight-bit microprocessor and began experiments using 64 terminals. He found one chip did not provide the needed computational power, so he redesigned his system using two 8008s and by 1975 had a working statistical multiplexer supporting 64. Chu filed successful patent applications in 1976 and 1977. As it turns out, neither he nor UCLA ever asserted their rights.

By year-end 1974, Carr and Pugh's decision to investigate LSI semiconductor technology took on new meaning. First, AT&T finally introduced a 9,600bps modem that leased for $230 per month. Two other competitors also began selling 9,600bps modems: Paradyne ($6,500) and ESE Ltd., a Canadian corporation ($7,000). The crowded 4,800bps modem market numbered at least a dozen competitors including new entrants IBM and Intertel. No longer did Codex and Milgo control high-speed modems. Also of concern was IBM's announcement of its Systems Network Architecture (SNA) providing a single standard access method and link control for terminals connected to IBM host computers.[21] While not an immediate threat, it implied computer firms sought control of data communications. The future looked bleak for independent modem manufacturers.

Despite these worries, Forney had committed to having the LSI modem ready for introduction by the fall, hopefully before the Milgo announcement. As a reminder that they were not alone in anticipating the importance of LSI technology, in April 1975, Paradyne announced an all-digital 9,600bps "stripped down" modem for its digital data network.[22] It would be sold through OEM contracts for as low as $2,000. Forney lost little sleep over this announcement since he knew his technical team had conspired with their counterparts at Rockwell to significantly upgrade the C series design, not simply converting the C design to LSI as had been negotiated by the "business people."

At the fall 1975 Interface trade show, Codex, with full fanfare, introduced their L series modems. They caught the world by surprise: here was a 9,600bps modem (LSI 9600) the size of a shoebox for only $8,500. Carr remembers with excitement: "We expected we were in a death race with Milgo. In fact, we went to the show sure we would see theirs, and we were going saying: 'Whew, at least we're going to be in the same show,' and they didn't have anything for over a year after that, and we just—I mean, it just wiped them out."[23]

But the fear that Milgo would beat them to market had blinded Codex management to the impact that announcing the L series would have on their existing C series modem sales. Carr recalls: "The problem we had was we introduced the L-series in the fall of '75... and all the C-Series business dried up. Everybody wanted the L's. It was a very hard lesson, but we just didn't think we dared wait. Then we found out, much to our chagrin, we were a year early."

In 1976, the QAM technology that Codex had developed would become the CCITT international 9,600bps private line standard. While this made the QAM

21. "Before the introduction of SNA, IBM had more than 200 communications products requiring 35 teleprocessing access methods, and 15 different data link control procedures. The goal of SNA was to provide a unified approach to IBM networking by introducing a single standard host access method and link control procedures. The use of these standards would achieve terminal compatibility at the communications line level as well as independence between network devices (e.g., terminals) and host applications. This represents a major step forward in IBM's recognition of networks as a vital element of future computing systems." "Data communications in the '70s: A decade of birth," *Computerworld*, Jan. 7, 1980, 41.

22. *Electronic News*, April 21, 1975. This modem was the result of the development agreement with Datran.

23. Carr interview, Computer History Museum.

technology public, and thus invited competition, it also confirmed Codex's technical leadership and was a coup over AT&T.

In early 1974, after Carr had authorized the development of a statistical multiplexer, Vander Mey recommended a multi-microprocessor architecture, but changed his mind as to which microprocessors to use. This led to delays and mounting stress.[24] The one who felt the most stress was Forney. With a highly talented team working for him, Forney began questioning his management abilities.[25] Carr, however, would have nothing of Forney's self-doubts. Forney didn't want confidence boosts but rather help in bringing an end to an "extremely painful development." By the fall of 1975, he concluded Vander Mey's team did lack practical engineering experience, like knowing how to release a product to manufacturing, or knowing how to eliminate noise from their design. So Forney hired expert consultants when possible. Vander Mey and his team forecasted a spring 1976 manufacturing release.

Based on a spring release, marketing kicked off the launch of the statistical multiplexer in early 1976. Management's first goal was to stimulate customer interest in their innovative—and expensive—new product. A second goal was to train the sales force in how to sell a product requiring customization, a far more complicated sale than selling modems off a price sheet. Codex began making customer presentations, leaving customers product data sheets and other information for review. By February, TDM competitors had copies of Codex's literature, and while the expected price of $25,000 to $50,000 meant they posed no immediate threat to their less expensive TDMs, many competitors recognized that they too would have to follow Codex's lead.

By mid-1976, Codex was no nearer to shipping product. Frustrated, Carr hired Lowell Bensky, a former engineering manager he had worked with at 3C, to conduct a program review. After meeting with Bensky, who gave Carr an estimate of over a year to get the product to market, Carr was at his wit's end. He remembers telling Bensky: "'Does it work? You tell me, yea or nay, does it work?' 'Yes, it works, but it doesn't have this and that and this part of it is shaky,' and I said: 'Then we go, and we will work night and day in some customer facility, if that's what it takes.' And that's what we did."[26]

---

24. Vander Mey began with Intel 4004s, switched to 8008s, then 8080s and next to Motorola's 6800s, and finally to Advanced Micro Devices' 2900. They stayed with the 6800s.

25. Others who worked on this project who went on to distinguish themselves both at Codex and other companies were Steve Finn (founder of Bytex), Jim Hart, Bill Tao (founder of Ztel), and Larry Krakauer.

26. Carr interview, Computer History Museum.

In September 1976, Codex introduced the first two models of their 6000 Series statistical multiplexers: the 6030 and 6040. The Model 6030 supported 124 terminals and cost up to $30,000 and would ship by yearend 1976. The Model 6040, to ship May 1977, supported 248 terminals and cost up to $60,000. As Forney recalls: "It was a fantastic tour de force in computer architecture; but in retrospect, we undoubtedly aimed too high."[27]

Carr may have hoped his biggest problems were behind him when he forced the Model 6030 out the door, but as things turned out, he had swapped them for new, no less challenging problems. Selling the statistical multiplexer, a "computer thing," was a challenge to their regional sales managers, many of whom had to be replaced. Carr explains: "they could sell modems like falling off a log, and the SM [statistical multiplexer] needed support help and you had to work with the customer and you had to configure systems and you had to bid it and the whole nine yards, and it was just too damned hard. We had quite a year, a big, big field turn over year."[28]

By the end of 1976 competition began emerging, in part because Codex had given their competition warning through their early marketing to customers. Codex would meet the challenge, however. In mastering statistical multiplexing, Codex had established a second strong product line alongside its new LSI modems.

4.3.2 Milgo Defends Its Position

Throughout the 1970s, Milgo remained market leader in modems due to early "entrance advantages" and not making mistakes. Matt Kinney saw firsthand the transition from the early high growth period to the eventual rise in competition: "the market was so damn big, and there was so much potential that there was no way that one single organization could grow fast enough to accommodate the entire thing. You could not move fast enough to dominate it. There were literally a few years when Codex's sales group and our sales group never saw one another at all." But then came Paradyne: it "did what most latecomers do, and started slashing, cutting, burning the prices. So that opened up the users' awareness that they can get equivalent products for a lot less money. So they started playing us one

27. G. David Forney, Jr., oral history interview with James L. Pelkey, July 28, 1988, Boston, MA. Computer History Museum, Mountain View, CA. Available from https://archive.computerhistory.org/resources/access/text/2016/04/102738110-05-01-acc.pdf.

28. Carr: "It was interesting, some years later, Infotron, which was in the mux business, went into the modem business probably '79 or '80, and their VP called John Pugh up and said: "Maybe you can tell me something. You've got these mixed product lines. Can you tell me how to get mux salesmen to sell modems?" And John just lost it, because we had been at the end of three years trying to get modem salesmen to sell multiplexers." Carr interview, Computer History Museum.

against the other as you would expect, and competition became a real factor in the industry."[29]

Milgo was not averse to pressing its own advantages. As early as July 1971 Milgo had attempted to forestall competition by filing a patent lawsuit against Rixon Electronics, claiming three of its modem patents had been infringed upon. Others could play the same game. In December 1974, WE, a division of AT&T, sued Milgo, claiming ten modem patent infringements.[30] In February 1975, after conferring with the Justice Department, Milgo countersued WE charging violation of the 1956 Consent Decree involving patent royalties on the manufacture of modems.[31]

Codex unintentionally added to the confusion after receiving their QAM signal structure patent in 1975.[32] After making an attempt to discuss with Milgo what Codex considered patent infringement, they were eventually sued by Milgo. In January 1976, the court awarded Milgo a victory in its patent suit against Rixon et al.[33] Ten days later in February, Milgo sued AT&T, asking for injunctions stopping WE from manufacturing and AT&T from distributing its 4,800bps and 9,600bps modems. Milgo also sued Yellow Freight Systems of Kansas, a user of Codex 9,600bps modems, claiming they had violated its patents. Thirdly, Milgo sued Codex seeking "declaratory relief" since Codex patents violated Milgo's patents.[34] Codex responded almost immediately by filing lawsuits against Milgo in Miami and Boston in March. In reflecting on Milgo's behavior Forney offers: "Their concern was almost entirely for AT&T, but secondarily, they had a problem with Codex's patent on the signal structure... They had lots of hooks in AT&T, and they hassled them to death. We were, it turned out, a much more formidable foe for them."[35]

Later that same March, the Federal Court sided with Milgo and ordered WE to defend itself against Milgo's claims of violations under the 1956 Consent Decree before it would hear WE's suit against Milgo.[36] In April, Milgo asked the Federal Court for $44 million in damages it claimed "to have suffered as a result of alleged

29. Matt Kinney, oral history interview by James L. Pelkey, March 9, 1988, Sunrise, FL. Computer History Museum, Mountain View, CA. Available from https://archive.computerhistory.org/resources/access/text/2017/10/102738573-05-01-acc.pdf.

30. "Milgo charges violation of court ruling by WE," *Electronic News*, Feb. 3, 1975. The WE suit was probably prompted by the fact that AT&T had OEM Milgo's 4,800bps modem before coming out with its own.

31. "Milgo confers with Justice," *Electronic News*, Jan. 6, 1975.

32. The patent was for its Double Side Band-Quadrature Carrier modulation.

33. "Milgo wins patent suit covering data modems," *Electronic News*, Jan. 26, 1976, 2.

34. "Milgo sues AT&T, users on modems," *Electronic News*, Feb. 2, 1976, 1 and 16.

35. Forney interview, Computer History Museum.

36. "WE to go on trial on Milgo patent charges," *Electronic News*, March 29, 1976, 2.

antitrust violations and unfair competition by WE, AT&T, and the Bell System in the licensing of modem patents and the sale and rental of modems."[37]

Then, as if Milgo did not have enough legal concerns, on November 8, 1976, Applied Digital Data Systems (ADDS), a computer terminal manufacturer with sales of $17.8 million, thought they saw a unique opportunity. So they announced a takeover attempt of Milgo, offering a swap of stock valued at roughly $50 million—a $15 million premium over Milgo's public valuation.[38] The much larger Milgo, seen as struggling after a 56% drop in earnings for fiscal year 1975, rejected the offer 2 days later claiming it was "not in the interests of the shareholders and does not reflect the long-term prospects of the company."[39] After weeks of jockeying, on December 1, Milgo, in a maneuver to fight ADDS' intentions, announced its intentions to sell 312,000 shares of stock to its UK partner, Racal Electronics. ADDS immediately filed a restraining order to block the sale that the court issued on December 9. Jockeying continued and by February 7, 1977, Racal and ADDS each claimed 45% ownership of Milgo's stock. By the 18th, Racal appeared to control over 50% of Milgo's stock, and on the 23rd, ADDS tendered its stock to Racal, ending the hostile action, and giving Racal subsequent ownership of Milgo for $62 million.[40] (Milgo's other legal battles ended with an out-of-court settlement with AT&T, and in June 1981 they would lose their lawsuits with Codex.)

4.3.3 ADS: Rebirth as Micom, 1973–1976

In March 1973, Rockwell management, tired of a business without any prospects of generating income, discharged ADS into a let's-get-it-over-with Chapter 10 bankruptcy.[41] Rockwell flew an executive to London to inform their UK distributor, CASE Ltd, their one important customer.

37. "Milgo seeks $44M in suit against WE/Bell System," *Electronic News*, April 12, 1976, p. 1 and 14.

38. "Applied Digital sets a stock-swap offer for Milgo Electronic," *The Wall Street Journal*, Mon. Nov. 8, 1976. The data to follow all comes from the Wall Street Journal articles over the period of the transaction.

39. *Wall Street Journal*, Nov. 10, 1976.

40. "Applied Digital tenders its 47.8% stake in Milgo to UK's Racal for $29.7 Million," *Wall Street Journal*, Feb. 23, 1977, 8. Based on prior fiscal year revenue and net income, Codex sold for 2.9 times sales and 24 times net income and Milgo sold for 1.5 times sales and 26 times net income.

41. Norred: "The problem was that the company had so much debt that, as a result of the interest on the debt, it was causing the company to lose lots of money. If you could take the debt away, it was a very profitable business at that time, but with the debt, Rockwell just finally got tired of it. They saw that they didn't want to put more money in it. They didn't see it working its way out of it. They couldn't find anybody to buy it." William (Bill) Norred, oral history interview by James L. Pelkey, April 27, 1988, Simi Valley, CA. Computer History Museum, Mountain View, CA. Available from https://archive.computerhistory.org/resources/access/text/2018/07/102738827-05-01-acc.pdf.

For Roger Evans, the CASE executive responsible for data communications, the first reaction was dismay. Evans had been expecting to hear that CASE and ADS had won a multimillion-dollar order for ADS 670 multiplexers from the British Post Office (BPO, to become British Telecom).[42] Evans quickly reasoned, however, that if CASE bought the rights and assets to the multiplexers from Rockwell, then CASE eliminated BPO's sole objection: the multiplexers were not sourced or manufactured in the UK. It would also initiate CASE's metamorphosis from distributor to manufacturer. Evans had to see Norred; for any plan to work, CASE needed Norred's cooperation.

Norred also considered picking up the pieces of ADS and moving forward, somehow. With bankruptcy wiping out the debt there just might be enough revenue to generate a small profit. The critical assumption hinged on CASE, for without their business the numbers simply did not compute. His thoughts generally ended there. The conservative engineer in him called for an end to such daydreaming, reminding himself he needed a job. He figured that he had better call Carr at Codex, who he knew from trying to sell him ADS, and who had left him feeling that he would hire him if given the chance. Then the phone rang: Evans wanted to see him.

Evans and Norred quickly cut to the chase. Evans sought Norred's help. He proposed Norred assist Evans and CASE's lawyers to specify the assets and intellectual property needed to satisfy the on-going needs of CASE and the hoped-for contract from BPO. CASE would assume all the costs and legal responsibilities of working with the bankruptcy court and, if successful, CASE would then contract with a company Norred would form. As the weeks passed, their hope began to fade. Norred recalls: "Almost as a final ditch effort, we proposed the receiver buy half of the inventory and acquire a non-exclusive manufacturer's license for the product line. He accepted it."[43]

On hearing the good news, Norred and Evans met in Evans' hotel in Woodland Hills to celebrate. Evans wanted to return to England as soon as possible with a contract executed with Norred's new company to show BPO and secure their contract. Evans pressured Norred to name his company so a letterhead could be created on which to document their relationship. Exasperated, Norred said, "Why don't I just call it my company? Evans then shortened it to Micom." Norred remembers: "It was just a business opportunity, with no real business plan whatsoever. I owned

42. Evans had reason to be optimistic as this new order followed a $2 million dollar procurement by BPO of ADS 660s let in October 1971; one of the largest orders ever received by ADS.

43. Livermore Data Systems also acquired rights to ADS's product line. (Datapro, September 1973, pg. 70G-500-01b.)

100% of the company and put a little cash into it, I think $20,000, just so it would have a little equity on the balance sheet, and the company literally was a company in support of CASE."[44]

For the next two and a half years, Norred and his small company, never more than a dozen employees, survived by manufacturing and servicing ADS products for CASE while they "Dabbled and diddled around with some microcomputer-based products as well as other communications interface products that we tried to sell, not terribly successfully, frankly."[45]

Desperate to find products to create and sell, Norred turned his attention to products interconnecting the multiplexers he already sold. But any designs to add functionality to existing multiplexers were limited by a lack of experienced software engineers.

By late 1974, Norred was thinking hard about leaving data communications, but as he tried other ideas on, he kept returning to what he had been doing for the last 6 years and decided that the opportunities in data communications were simply too "interesting." Resolved to grow Micom, he again tried to raise venture capital. The availability of venture capital in the mid-1970s was tight, however, and Norred had difficulty presenting Micom as anything other than a "me too" business with minimal potential for revenues and growth. So he focused on finding a strategic partner instead: "The strategy was to find people who would be willing to pay us for the development of a product that they couldn't buy on the open market but needed badly enough that they were willing to pay somebody else to design it and manufacture it for them. The first one of those was a company called Datran."[46]

Norred knew marketing and selling were not his strengths. Yet neither could he find someone to hire; everyone he talked to sounded all too willing to spend money he did not have. So while he sought new customers to fund new products, his most reliable source of revenue and new product ideas remained CASE's. Fortunately for Norred, CASE was looking to distribute its products in the US. Evans remembers: "I was concerned that we were becoming unacceptably dependent on the R&D coming from Micom, and Bill was having a hard time putting a real company together. He never really found a marketing guy before that he felt he could work with the way he felt he could work with me." Evans and Norred worked together to craft a deal in which CASE would invest in a minority stake in Micom with other European investors, in which CASE would sell products through Micom in the US. Evans would relocate to the US to oversee the investment.

44. Norred interview, Computer History Museum.

45. Norred interview, Computer History Museum.

46. Norred interview, Computer History Museum.

Evans joined Micom in May 1976, shortly before the scheduled closing of the CASE-led investment. Norred shares what happened next: "I can recall very clearly looking out the window one day and seeing Derek Levell, who was the joint managing director of CASE, coming up the parking lot to Micom, and I wasn't expecting Derek." Levell was there to inform Norred that CASE had run into financial difficulties and that "they would not be making the investment in Micom, and that, because of their financial difficulties, they were going to be curtailing or eliminating a substantial number of the development contracts that we had with them."[47]

As a founder of CASE, Evans could have returned to England, but: "decided to cut the cord and stay here anyway." He focused on Datran, which quickly became Micom's leading customer. Then on August 26, Datran filed for bankruptcy, owing Micom $110,000, 80% of their accounts receivable. Evans recalls the shock: "The day they filed, we decided we had 2 weeks in order to raise some money or we were out of business."[48]

Norred and Evans scrambled to find capital investors to save their company. Venture capitalists had no interest. Then they focused on finding a corporate investor. They contacted Vadic, a supplier of modems to many of the same manufacturing representative firms they used. Vadic would hire them but had no interest in buying their company. They thought of calling Carr at Codex.[49] Then a business broker introduced them to John M. Thornton, the chairman of the board of Wavetek, a company on a recent spree of acquisitions. Thornton proposed the investment to his board but was turned down. Unwilling to let what he regarded as a potentially good investment get away, he asked for, and received, permission to make a personal investment in Micom. In September 1976, acting as agent for a group of investors including David M. Goodman and Martin B. Ortlieb, Thornton

---

47. Norred interview, Computer History Museum.

48. Roger Evans, oral history interview by James L. Pelkey, January 15, 1988, Simi Valley, CA. Computer History Museum, Mountain View, CA. Available from https://archive.computerhistory.org/resources/access/text/2015/09/102737975-05-01-acc.pdf.

49. Carr remembers: "We saw Norred and Micom as a significant potential acquisition, but we could never quite get him over the threshold. I don't know how many times we romanced in the moonlight and we got to the door and then he kept the key. In fact, the last time, he had a list of people, he told us later, that he was calling to try to raise money, and there was a guy in southern California that was the name above ours on the list, and when he called him, he agreed to guarantee loans for a piece of the company, so he didn't call us, but if John hadn't answered the phone, I'm quite sure that time Codex would have acquired Micom because we were ready." Carr interview, Computer History Museum.

advanced a loan of $35,000, invested $2,160, and made a line of credit of $200,000 in return for 51% of Micom.[50] Norred and Evans had again avoided disaster.

Desperately in need of a successful strategy, they strained to craft a scenario both realistic and likely to succeed. The recent flurry of statistical multiplexer announcements by Codex, Infotron, DCA International, and Timeplex dated their TDMs. To innovate a statistical multiplexer, however, likely meant becoming a systems supplier with large sales and service organizations, a strategy they thought beyond their means and interest. But continuing to do more of the same seemed sure to invite failure. They considered selling inexpensive data communication products by catalog but decided to stay the course for a few months longer while Norred continued working on other potential products. If nothing came of their efforts, they would get into the catalog business.

4.4 The Swarm of Data Communications Firms, 1976–1979

By the mid-1970s, the modem and multiplexer markets were revitalized, not stalling as forecasted by Frost & Sullivan in 1972. LSI semiconductors and microprocessors made possible new product innovations that in turn enabled customers to construct data communications networks. The evolution from point-to-point data communications to multipoint, distributed data processing networks, with management and diagnostics, fitted perfectly with the needs of customers installing more and more computers.

The growth in corporate use of computers began as remote terminal connections to distant computers over low-speed connection to telephone lines. But there were other cases of communications between computers that would require more bandwidth. It happened first on the periphery, as it so often does. This time it was the submarket of engineering workstations. Workstations were designed to transfer data at speeds that would rapidly approach 1Mbps, far exceeding the 10 to 20,000bps of computer terminals.

It was not that executives did not have enough to consider in crafting a winning strategy. Even with high-speed or dial-up modems, there were many factors to take into consideration in crafting a product strategy such as a wide range of transmission speeds, multiple-speed selection, multiple-channel operations, serial or parallel machine interfaces, asynchronous or asynchronous operations, and many other optional choices. Modem pricing tended to reflect those capabilities and would run from $2,000 to $12,000 per unit.

50. Technically, a new corporation, JMT Corp. became the successor corporation and not until November 3, 1977, was the name changed back to Micom Systems Inc.

In March 1977, the headline in one of the largest information technology weeklies read: "Data com, distributed EDP push modems toward $200 M year."[51] Sales of modems for 1976 were reported as $184 million, nearly triple the forecasts from 1972. Sales of high-speed modems alone reached $91.7 million. Little wonder Milgo and Codex were so successful. The article noted growth would come from networking and distributed processing. Each of the leading firms in data communication responded differently to these market dynamics.

4.4.1 Infotron

When James Hahn, founder and president of Infotron, learned of the Codex statistical multiplexer in early 1976, he instantly knew they needed to develop one as well. To do so meant hiring an engineering manager with microprocessor experience. His wife, Leigh, who still worked for Ultronic Systems, the company Hahn had left to found Infotron, recommended Bill Dambrackas, a young engineer who had just developed a specialized terminal using Motorola 6800 microprocessors. Hahn's overture couldn't have been better timed. GTE, under the leadership of Robert Wiggins, was consolidating Ultronic Systems and a number of other companies in California. Dambrackas did not want to relocate. The idea of working just a few blocks down the street, with the challenge of managing a high-profile statistical multiplexer project, made for an easy decision. Dambrackas joined Infotron in March of 1976, charged with having product to ship by year-end.

Dambrackas knew he did not have the luxury of creating an entirely new design and that he had to use as much existing TDM circuitry and packaging as possible. If their existing TDMs were field upgradable into statistical multiplexers, Infotron might just pull the carpet out from under Codex's grand design. The marching orders were clear: keep it simple and get it done on time.

Dambrackas strengthened the Infotron team with some hires from Ultronic Systems and set to work. In October of 1976, they announced their Supermux 780, for a base price of roughly $6,000, for customers with Infotron's existing TDMs. Arguably nowhere near the product of Codex's 6030, it nevertheless gave an interested buyer a much cheaper alternative. Dambrackas remembers: "While Codex did a revolutionary design, where they had a whole fresh start on the whole box, they had a lot of headaches and a lot of start-up problems. So even though they announced the

51. "Data com, distributed EDP push modems toward $200 M year," *Electronic News*, March 14, 1977, 1.

product, we ended up bringing our product to market and beating Codex pretty good. And it was a big hit for Infotron."[52]

Over the next 3 years, over 3,000 Supermuxes were sold compared to 950 Codex's 6030s and 6040s.[53] In dollar terms, however, Codex's sales (roughly $22 million) exceeded Infotron's (roughly $18 million). Dambrackas saw the evolution of the statistical multiplexer market becoming competitive almost as soon as it had started: "Codex quickly made a 6010 which moved down into the lower price range. It was cheaper and simpler. But they started off, I guess, saying that statistical multiplexers would be sold like a very special thing... they didn't realize it would drop down into the dirt so quick and end up being the bricks and mortar of getting data around."[54]

Under Dambrackas' leadership Infotron would introduce a range of statistical multiplexers over the next few years—the first being the Supermux 780, introduced in October 1976. Then in early 1979, headhunters called him with another opportunity. In June 1979, Dambrackas would leave Infotron to head Milgo's efforts to develop its own statistical multiplexer.

4.4.2 General DataComm

In 1973, General DataComm (GDC) began exploring if they could OEM 201 modems from Intertel, the start-up that spun out of Codex in 1970. However, the deal had exposed Intertel to GDC's diagnostics card product and the following year, at the ICA tradeshow in New Orleans, Robert Smith noticed similar products on display by Intertel. Eventually the two companies would compete fiercely in the new category of networking modems with diagnostic capabilities. One such bid was to Manufacturers Hanover Trust Company, which GDC lost to Intertel. Smith remembers: "We bid that job against them and lost by a big number of dollars, and I was later told that they bought that job because they wanted the contract. The history is that Intertel became very successful on Wall Street. They owned the Wall Street community in terms of data communications."[55]

Recognizing the importance of diagnostics from their earliest days, GDC management invested in new products. Yet engineers move from company to company,

52. William (Bill) Dambrackas, oral history interview by James L. Pelkey, March 9, 1988, Ft. Lauderdale, FL. Computer History Museum, Mountain View, CA. Available from https://archive.computerhistory.org/resources/access/text/2018/10/102740438-05-01-acc.pdf.

53. Datapro, "Multiplexers—Basic characteristics and equipment specifications," October 1979.

54. Dambrackas interview, Computer History Museum.

55. Thomas Thompson and Robert Smith, oral history interview by James L. Pelkey, March 11, 1988, Middlebury, CT. Computer History Museum, Mountain View, CA. Available from https://archive.computerhistory.org/resources/access/text/2017/11/102738591-05-01-acc.pdf.

often taking ideas with them, or companies incrementally innovate on the success of others. Smith offers his perspective on the new market:

> I interviewed a guy who was working at Bell Laboratories. The story as he tells it is: "We look out in the world and we see this company, Intertel, selling all these diagnostic systems, and we did a study. We decided that the market really could use a good diagnostic networking modem," so they proceeded to develop Dataphone II. It is my conviction that the Paradyne Analysis, AT&T's Dataphone II, the Intertel DMS and then the competitors like Milgo and Codex, seeing this coming along, all started here at General DataComm.[56]

Although primarily a modem company, GDC began introducing TDM multiplexers in 1970 and introduced two statistical multiplexer models in 1979.

4.4.3 Timeplex

At the end of 1973, Timeplex became one the last technology companies to go public. Even so, the cash raised did not ensure Timeplex's success. Botwinick remembers that by June of 1976 the company was essentially insolvent: "What had happened was that the auditors had come in and finally figured out that the assets were significantly overvalued. All of the profits were sitting in overstated assets, and there was no management. It was as simple as that."[57]

Timeplex struggled through 1976, with their investor Allen & Co "pounding on Chemical Bank to keep the doors open." In order to keep the bank happy, an effort was made to sell the company. Codex came to look the company over, as did Milgo. Neither saw enough value to make a bid. However, neither Timeplex's poor financial performance nor lack of interest on the part of potential buyers prevented a power struggle for corporate control from developing between the investment bankers, Allen & Co., company management, and eventually a group led by Botwinick. By the spring of 1977, Botwinick had exhausted his financial resources in buying enough shares of Timeplex' public stock to end the standoff. On June 27, 1977, he became Chairman of the Board and Chief Executive Officer. Botwinick remembers:

> The second week I was here, I went out to lunch with the guys from Chemical and United Jersey banks, and at the end of the lunch they said to me: "This is all very interesting. You're the first guy we've ever talked to in this

56. Thompson and Smith interview, Computer History Museum.

57. Edward Botwinick, oral history interview by James L. Pelkey, March 10, 1988, Woodcliff Lake, NJ. Computer History Museum, Mountain View, CA. Available from https://archive.computerhistory.org/resources/access/text/2018/02/102738718-05-01-acc.pdf.

> company that seemed to know what he's talking about, but we've had it. You have 60 days to tell us how we're going to get our money back or else." I don't know what the "or else" would have been, because there was nothing to have if they wanted to shut it down. So I didn't take that terribly seriously. On the other hand, I was in imminent danger of going broke personally.[58]

Botwinick immediately began aggressively collecting overdue receivables to raise desperately needed cash. In doing so, he learned the company had shipped defective product in order to record sales, defective product that would need to be replaced. He then began selling whatever assets had any value. Combined, Botwinick recovered enough cash to create some breathing room. He then took a hard look at the recently introduced Dynaplexer, a statistical multiplexer hub that worked with its TDMs but had no terminal or computer ports. While offering their large installed base the option of upgrading to the latest multiplexer technology, Botwinick remembers: "I got a close look at the Dynaplexer and I realized that it was conceptually flawed. First of all, they had no capabilities to develop it. It was too complex. Second was that the concept was flawed, because the old TDMs that were in the remote sites were all hard wired. There was no way to configure them remotely."[59]

Realizing the Dynaplexer was not saleable, and might never be, Botwinick turned his attention to developing a microprocessor-based stand-alone statistical multiplexer. Investing long hours, Botwinick and his new engineers innovated their Series I Microplexer that was introduced in 1978. Then, in one of those strokes of good fortune, Western Union, literally up the road, decided to end their efforts to develop a statistical multiplexer to compete with Codex. Botwinick leaped on the opportunity and hired a trained team that immediately started developing a product to replace the feature-weak Series I Microplexer. In addition to the forthcoming Series I and II Microplexer(s), soon to be introduced by yearend 1979, Timplex reduced the number of TDMs they supported from nine to five in the prior 2 years, as well as ceasing sales of the Dynaplexers. The Series II Microplexer was introduced in 1979. Botwinick remembers: "Series I came to market and it held the doors open. In fact, it stimulated sales of our old TDMs, which were still the bulk of our business. At that point, we did get some people from Western Union... They came in and did the Series II. Now, the Series II was the first networking unit that we did, and that's what we built the company on."[60]

58. Botwinick interview, Computer History Museum.

59. Botwinick interview, Computer History Museum.

60. Botwinick interview, Computer History Museum.

4.4.4 Paradyne

In 1972, Paradyne management signed a joint development agreement with Datran to create an all-digital 9,600bps LSI modem—months before Codex entered into their relationship with Rockwell.[61] By the end of 1973, the Board recognized the need to find a seasoned president. In hiring Robert Wiggins in April 1974, they made a brilliant decision. Wiggins would lead Paradyne for over a decade. With 13 years of marketing and product development experience with IBM, having worked for a time-sharing company, and most recently having headed the Information Systems division of GTE, Wiggins fully understood the importance of a 9,600bps LSI modem.

In 1974, they began selling a 9,600bps modem, the M-96, which listed for $6,500, significantly less than the competitive modems of Codex ($ 8,500) and Milgo ($8,350). The following year, Paradyne began shipping modems to Datran, resulting in a $5.2 million contract extension. To take advantage of the emerging opportunities, Wiggins hired a seasoned vice president of corporate marketing, Jay Hill, who shared his views as to how to build a successful company. In early August 1976, Hill, who had been with IBM before building a successful career in sales and marketing at the data processing firm, Inforex, came aboard full of a newcomer's enthusiasm. Within days he received a rude awakening. Hill remembers: "I didn't quite understand the significance of the problem when they were running around the halls saying, 'Oh my God, Datran just filed for bankruptcy.' Bob came into my office and said, 'We've had a very unfortunate thing happen to us. Our largest customer is gone and you have to make up for it. Get going.'"[62]

The ever-composed Wiggins never lost his confidence: "We had an LSI technology where we could build a 9,600bps modem, I believe, less expensively than anyone else, and we were very aggressive in pricing those products, because technology permitted it, and we needed to gain market share, because we had to have business."[63]

While the loss in sales was significant, it was not devastating for Paradyne, for they retained the product rights to the 9,600bps modem. Paradyne subsequently introduced an all-digital LSI-96 modem, a "stripped down" version of the modem they were developing with Datran. It carried a list price of $4,500.

61. "Datran LSI modem contract," *Mini-Micro Systems*, May 1976, 29.

62. H. Jay Hill interview, oral history interview by James L. Pelkey, July 27, 1988, Waltham, MA. Computer History Museum, Mountain View, CA. Available from https://archive.computerhistory.org/resources/access/text/2015/10/102737986-05-01-acc.pdf.

63. Robert (Bob) Wiggins, oral history interview by James L. Pelkey, November 29, 1988, Fort Meyers, FL. Computer History Museum, Mountain View, CA. Available from https://archive.computerhistory.org/resources/access/text/2017/09/102740209-05-01-acc.pdf.

Over the next 2 years, Hill began building an "IBM-like" sales team focused largely on the rapidly growing market for high-speed point-to-point modems.[64] Then by late 1977, engineering not only delivered a series of network-oriented 4,800 and 9,600bps modems, with names such as Line Sharing Devices and Micro-Processor modems, they also delivered an entirely new product that allowed Paradyne to sell networks of modems with network management and diagnostics. The Parallel Interface Extender (PIX) initially provided communication functions that enabled the users of IBM System 360/370 to perform remote processing over dial-up, private line, digital networks, or satellite facilities, with no communication software required. In addition to the PIX communication products, the Analysis Network Management System provided network control capability and catapulted Paradyne into the role of supplier to the then emerging need of large corporations to tie together their far-flung computers and peripherals into on-line networks. Hill remembers Analysis as being "the breakthrough and one of the things in Paradyne's history that really gave it a big lift." He elaborates:

> After 1978, we would sell one Analysis to a major insurance company like Hancock, and 100, 200, 300 modems would go out, and at that time, pricing of modems played a very key role in Paradyne's success. The list price on a 4800 modem back then was $3,000, and we would sell them in any reasonable quantity, at $2,400 per copy, and an aggressive bid... we would just get below $2,000, and our gross margins never on a sale like that, got down to 50%.[65]

Success in modems did not translate to mastering statistical multiplexing, however. Paradyne formed a relationship with CASE, the firm Evans of Micom once worked for and whose multiplexer technology had originated with ADS. Paradyne supplied modems to CASE for their European market and CASE supplied multiplexers for Paradyne to sell in the US. Paradyne was diversified enough to appeal to investors and in July 1978, Paradyne went public—selling stock for $10.00 per share and raising approximately $5.9 million with a market valuation of $30 million.

4.4.5 Vadic

In June 1972, Maxwell hired John Bingham who brought with him the ideas for how to build a robust full duplex 1,200bps dial-up modem. Bingham had tried unsuccessfully to convince his previous three employers to develop his idea. As often is

64. Paradyne had a second modem-type product named PIX that accounted for roughly 50% of their sales.

65. Hill interview, Computer History Museum.

the case in a new industry, young innovators must break from established companies to pursue their ideas. Maxwell realized the opportunity Bingham could offer Vadic to be among the first to develop this speed in the dial-up category. Nevertheless, a rash of mistakes prompted the Board to demote Maxwell to the engineering and marketing ranks.[66]

Bingham, with the help of Maxwell and others, enabled Vadic to introduce the first successful duplex 1,200bps dial-up modem in May 1975. Although there were some issues, none would be as serious as when AT&T, in September 1976, introduced their rival backward-compatible 1,200bps full duplex dial-up modem, the Bell 212. Bingham, Maxwell, and the other engineers were thrust into scramble mode. They proved up to the occasion, fortunately, and introduced their wildly successful VA3467 "triple modem" in June of 1978, so named because it was compatible with three modems: the VA3400, the Bell 212, and the Bell 103 modems.

Despite the triple modem's success, the company continued to have other problems. Finally, significant disagreements among the members of the board and management led to the board selling Vadic to Racal Electronics in 1978 for $20 million. At that time, Racal-Vadic considered AT&T, UDS, GDC, Rixon, Penril and Anderson Jacobson to be their principal competitors.

4.4.6 Universal Data Systems

From the large number of data communications start-ups of the early 1970s, Vadic and UDS would dominate the low-speed dial-up and leased line modems and OEM markets. When asked the key to success, co-founder and president Mark Smith points to UDS's ability to keep overhead low and maintain profitability:

> I think that the biggest single thing influencing our success was not being able to raise capital... By not raising the money, by not being able to, then the only alternative was for us to generate a profit... The only way you can do that, of course, is to be low cost, low overhead, and efficient. That fit real well with the low-speed business; it fit very well with the OEM business. We picked up about all of the modems, in the early years, from Texas Instruments, NCR, just a whole bunch of OEM accounts that, as their products grew in volume, they did very, and we did very well.[67]

66. Kim Maxwell, oral history interview by James L. Pelkey, July 19, 1988, Palo Alto, CA. Computer History Museum, Mountain View, CA. Available from https://archive.computerhistory.org/resources/access/text/2017/09/102740207-05-01-acc.pdf.

67. Mark Smith, oral history interview by James L. Pelkey, November 28, 1988, Huntsville, AL. Computer History Museum, Mountain View, CA. Available from https://archive.computerhistory.org/resources/access/text/2017/10/102738572-05-01-acc.pdf.

UDS had only one salesman who had set up the entire manufacturing representative organization that remained UDS's primary sales organization for many years. In the early years all senior management had responsibility for specific OEM accounts. George Grumbles, who eventually became UDS's first vice-president of sales and marketing, and would succeed Mark Smith as president, remembers: "Prior to the mid to late '70s, we had been very successful in the OEM area, and at some time in there I would say we had 60, 70% of all the OEM volume; if one does not include the Rockwell OEM modem chips that Rockwell sold to Codex."[68]

UDS's initial OEM contracts were for both dial-up and leased line low-speed modems. Milgo and Codex had captured the higher speed leased line customers. Then once Vadic innovated the 1,200bps modem, UDS quickly followed with its 1,200bps leased line modem that became one of its bestselling products. Again, Smith remembers: "We went from a 202 up to a 201, and 1200. The 1200s were a reasonably high speed because the 4800s and 9600s, at that point, were enormous things, and didn't work very well... During the mid '70s, the 1200 became, then, our big product. It was the big money maker."[69]

UDS and Vadic continued to dominate the lower-speed modem market as Grumbles recalls: "When things settled out, Vadic and UDS were typically the two principal OEM suppliers in the industry, and we were, in those early days, nose to nose in nearly every account. We would win one; they'd win one."

In November 1975, the FCC determined that certified equivalent hardware could be used when connecting to the telephone network in place of the Data Access Arrangements (DAAs).[70] UDS took advantage and produced DAAs themselves. Grumbles remembers: "We probably were one of the largest suppliers of DAAs. I remember when DAAs could be built by other than the telephone company. We were at probably an Interface Show in New York, and we received an order for 50,000 DAAs from a company... We delivered tens of thousands of DAAs."[71]

UDS joined other independent modem manufacturers in forming the Independent Data Communications Manufacturers Association (see Chapter 2) to fight AT&T's restrictive and anti-competitive policies, especially the DAA. UDS was significantly affected: "The dial-up market was so terribly impeded with the DAA in the

68. George Grumbles, oral history interview by James L. Pelkey, November 28, 1988, Huntsville, AL. Computer History Museum, Mountain View, CA. Available from https://archive.computerhistory.org/resources/access/text/2017/10/102738571-05-01-acc.pdf.

69. Smith interview, Computer History Museum.

70. For background on DAAs, see Ken Krechmer, oral history interview by James L. Pelkey, January 6, 1988, Menlo Park, CA. Computer History Museum, Mountain View, CA. Available from https://archive.computerhistory.org/resources/access/text/2016/04/102738107-05-01-acc.pdf.

71. Grumbles interview, Computer History Museum.

early years. We did a Bell 103, which was dial-up oriented, but a DAA would lease for $7.50, which is about what one should lease a complete Bell 103 for. The net of it was that it was just an uneconomical situation."[72] Smith's frustration exemplified the opinions of many of the entrepreneurs in data communications eager to loosen AT&T's stranglehold. Not only were the pricing structures prohibitive, the technical challenges presented by DAA hardware were formidable: "The DAA itself also introduced distortion and generated its own unique set of problems." In an attempt to avoid the restrictions still present in the dial-up market, Smith and GDC decided to develop a Bell 201-compatible leased line modem.

The competition between UDS and Vadic soured when Vadic sued UDS in 1975 for patent infringement over their design of the 1212 modem, which took advantage of similar technology to Vadic's 3400 full duplex 1,200bps modem. The suit lasted over 4 years and was a financial drain and distraction for both companies. UDS finally won, based on the fact that Vadic had filed their patent 2 years after the initial product had been on the market.

4.4.7 Intertel

In early 1973, Jerry Holsinger started asking how Intertel, the company he founded in 1970, was going to be successful against competitors such as Codex or Milgo. Doubting his original business strategy of OEM sales, he began asking some large end-users if they had problems that were not being solved. From Manufacturers Hanover Trust Company and Eastern Airlines, one rather significant problem emerged. Holsinger remembers:

> In the old days of point to point, there were skilled people at both ends of the line. If you have a problem, you call the guy up at the other end and he gets out his patch panels and his test equipment and you work on it. In a multipoint network, you have operators at the remote end on terminals. They don't know "nothing from nothing." So you were now operating in an environment where the only technically skilled people were at the computer site, and in the meantime, these were on-line networks where, if it was down, it wasn't like: "Oh well, what the hell, we don't run our batch today, we'll run it tomorrow." It was like: "Hey, they're not working." The bank wasn't doing transactions or the airline wasn't making reservations, and that's really how it was. People were starting to understand they've got problems.[73]

72. Smith interview, Computer History Museum.

73. Jerry L. Holsinger, oral history interview by James L. Pelkey, April 6, 1988, Westborough, MA. Computer History Museum, Mountain View, CA. Available from https://archive.computerhistory.org/resources/access/text/2016/04/102738129-05-01-acc.pdf.

Working with Gunther Kempin, their contact at Manufacturers Hanover, Intertel engineers designed a diagnostic card that would also have dial back-up capability to restore malfunctioning lines. Kempin "was a real pioneer. You know, all this leading edge stuff you sell to pioneers, the guys that want to do the leading edge kind of thing, and they get excited because they are influencing your product, so if you get the right guy, then it is a dynamic interaction, and then he's really hooked. So in 1973, we sold our first stuff to him."[74]

At first selling network control products proved very difficult. Sales remained flat in 1973 at $3.4 million. In 1975, network products began having market traction and 1976 and 1977 were great years, with sales approaching $20 million. Intertel had established itself as leader in networking modems. In 1978, they ran an ad that came out just before the TCA trade show challenging customers to ask their Codex, or Milgo or Paradyne salesmen if they could match the features of Intertel modems. Matt Kinney of Milgo remembers thanking Holsinger: "When we got to this show, I made a bee line to go and thank him for legitimizing my company in the network management business, because the leader of the network management business said that we were in it. I chased down Art Carr and the two of us went off and we had a beer together and roared."[75]

By now, however, Holsinger had decided he had had enough: "I said, after a lot of soul searching: 'I want to go out and get a president, a guy that's a good marketer, experienced manager and all that good stuff, and let me go back and dream up new things.'" After searching for over a year, they thought they had found the perfect candidate, "with an IBM background in marketing, Harvard MBA. So this guy on paper was perfect, smooth, polished, the whole thing."[76] Sy Rosen took over in May 1978 but within 9 months Holsinger, still Chairman and CEO, knew he had made a mistake: "It was clear that either he went or the company was going under. So I did my thing and he left and I stepped back in. It was painful because I didn't really want to go back in at that time."[77]

While Intertel had made the transition to a new product line successfully, the challenges of surviving the competitive phase of the market were not only technical. As Holsinger had discovered, insight and innovation were only part of the requirements for success in a highly competitive market.

74. Holsinger interview, Computer History Museum.

75. Kinney interview, Computer History Museum.

76. Holsinger interview, Computer History Museum.

77. Holsinger interview, Computer History Museum.

4.5 Micom's Breakout Product, 1976–1979

After the last-minute financing in September 1976, Evans knew he needed to find a viable product opportunity if Micom was to survive. He began making calls with his manufacturing representatives. He soon learned that Gibraltar Savings and Loan in Los Angeles had a Data General minicomputer and wanted to support offices in San Francisco and Fresno by generating mortgage and trust deeds on-line. The manufacturing rep had sold the account on using Micom's TDMs, claiming they would support three terminals and a printer in each office. Evans, realizing the problem of transmitting entire documents without error control, informed the customer that using TDMs would not work. He tells what then happened:

> So I ended up walking away, first of all having made a friend for life because the customer had actually for the first time talked to a salesman who had sold him *off* something, rather than onto something. Secondly, I walked away saying: "If we could solve this, we'd have a real business here." Third, I had at least learned enough from this guy to know that there were quite a number of other guys in the area planning to do similar things.[78]

Evans had been shocked to realize how many businesses had started using minicomputers for many of their business tasks, and the number was "growing like wildfire." They were already using existing multiplexers to achieve cost reductions on communications lines, but they were desperately in need of retransmission on error. Unlike the large companies connecting mainframe to mainframe, with high-volume traffic and willing to spend extra for features, Evans saw the usage of these terminals and realized another difference specific to this customer: "They were paying an arm and a leg for 9,600bps modems to be cut up into four 2,400 bit channels where the terminals were hunt and peck in one direction and only sporadically used in the other direction. So the data traffic was minimal, and it was the classic case where a statistical multiplexer comes into its own."[79]

In a flash of insight, Evans envisioned selling statistical multiplexers to minicomputer users. His instincts were so strong and certain, he assumed others had seen the opportunity as well. The sheer volume of what he didn't know, what he had to know, began to consume him. As for details, such as having to find a customer who would fund the development and not retain product rights (for Micom had no cash to develop and launch a statistical multiplexer) well, they were just details, and

78. Evans interview, Computer History Museum.

79. Evans interview, Computer History Museum.

would be sorted out in due time. To be so certain yet faced with so many uncertainties might have stopped a less streetwise, self-confident entrepreneur, but Evans knew he had a winner.

Evans first sought to confirm that the Gibraltar situation was not unique, that the growth in use of minicomputers to support remote locations was substantial and unaddressed by other multiplexer vendors. To his amazement, the potential appeared much larger than he had first thought. He also learned system integrators sold and installed most minicomputers and they required a margin of 40% off list price—a discount structure he assumed Micom would have to offer as well. Furthermore, the telephone circuits between terminals and computers tended to be much shorter with minicomputers than with mainframe computers. Shorter telephone circuits meant less expensive lines and reduced savings to justify purchase of a statistical multiplexer. Evans recalls:

> As I talked to potential customers, I ended up concluding that the real market probably lay with a list price around a couple of thousand dollars for a four-channel box. We also realized that, whereas Codex and Milgo expected to install their equipment with an engineer that understood communications, we were going to be reliant on systems integrators or the end user himself, neither of whom knew anything about communications. So ease of use and built-in test facilities were absolutely key, and do it yourself installation was much more important than anything else.[80]

Next came the challenge of finding a customer to fund development. In a stroke of good fortune, an existing customer, Reynolds & Reynolds (RR) of Dayton, OH, sought a device that would connect terminals in their automobile dealerships to their minicomputers. They had a potential supplier of a "very dumb" product that might work but were willing to work with Micom if they could provide a better solution. If Norred and Evans had any questions as to the viability of the market they were contemplating, they were soon dispelled: when they asked RR how many boxes they were interested in buying. Norred remembers: "They said: 'Well, certainly we're going to need at least a thousand.' To us, a thousand of anything was just mind-boggling. You just didn't sell a thousand of anything in our business."[81]

Norred began evaluating design options, turning first to the problem of "flow control." When too many terminals wanted to send data at the same time, a solution was needed to store the "overflow" data. To Norred's surprise, minicomputers had a "stop terminal" command that stopped terminals from sending more data.

80. Evans interview, Computer History Museum.

81. Norred interview, Computer History Museum.

It was then that Norred began to believe a low-cost statistical multiplexer, or "concentrator" as Micom would name it, was possible.[82] Norred remembers: "It was that breakthrough, in my mind, that was the biggest, most significant element of why we could build a concentrator and make it a viable product."[83]

Norred's first design for RR proved too expensive. In reviewing how much cost had to be eliminated, both men doubted it could be done. Fortunately, Norred had designed in a microprocessor, the Zilog Z-80, that allowed them to substitute software for logic chips, and as Evans summarizes: "We threw out a chip here and a chip there, and then ended up concluding we still hadn't thrown away too many chips to be able to implement statmux [statistical multiplexing] code and make it work."

By late summer of 1977, Norred and Evans knew that their concentrator would be ready to ship in early 1978. To their surprise, no competitor had announced a similar product. Evans remembers his willingness to bet the farm:

> We said, "If, when we're ready to launch the statmux it looks like we really have the field clear, we'll stop everything, focus on the statmux, and become a one product company for as long as it takes for us to dominate and have resources to spare, because the rest of the world's being stupid enough not to see the opportunity now, but they sure won't be once we bring the product to market."[84]

In January 1978, Micom introduced the revolutionarily modest Micro800 Data Concentrators, priced from $1,650 to $2,750. They were instant hits.

Within weeks, Ed Botwinick, president of the struggling Timeplex, called saying he was in the neighborhood and wanted to visit. Evans remembers: "Ed Botwinick came by to say he had heard about our product and it certainly sounded very interesting. Of course, it was very unfortunate that we had no sales and marketing capability, and, therefore, we were really going to have a hard time doing justice to this product—but he had the perfect solution." Evans and Norred were not interested in discussing any type of relationship with Timeplex. Evans remembers their response: "We said that we did have a pretty clear understanding of how we were going to take this product to market. In considerable irritation, he then moved into threat mode."[85]

82. He soon learned all minicomputer manufacturers had provided for flow control: For example, Hewlett Packard called it "Xon/Xoff" and Data General used "Data Terminal Ready.

83. Norred interview, Computer History Museum.

84. Evans interview, Computer History Museum.

85. Evans interview, Computer History Museum.

Botwinick recalls his position: "I wanted to buy them. They had announced their product and we had not yet announced our Series I. I told them about it and I figured it might shake them a little bit, but they decided to go their own way."[86]

Norred and Evans had expected competition. What they did not anticipate, however, was that the combination of having no money, no installed base of customers or committed channels of distribution, and a high degree of confidence in knowing who would be buying their product caused Micom to introduce something far more than simply a very clever product. They innovated an entirely new way of marketing and selling data communication products.

That prior fall, when Norred and Evans made the data concentrator the focus of Micom, they agreed their ship-and-use statistical multiplexer would be sold to minicomputer users through broad-based distribution. A $2,000 list price provided for both a 40% discount and a healthy gross margin for Micom. Evans remembers the problem of creating credibility:

> Timeplex had been in the business for years and was nowhere close to shipping a product it had been claiming it was going to deliver for 2 years. . . GDC had done exactly the same. Codex was the only guy out there, and they were losing money because it had proven to be a much taller order than they realized. And we were going to come out with a product at TDM prices and we ran the risk of having people laugh at us, just kill themselves laughing, that some start-up comes out with a product that offers all this capability for no money—you've got to be crazy.[87]

To overcome disbelief, Evans invested his entire year's marketing budget in a product brochure. He imagined a design "so quality and Fortune 500 in its feel, that nobody could even question whether this company was for real." A photograph of an orange juice can next to an orange was the cover shot: "The orange being the old-fashioned way to start your day, and the concentrate can being the new, efficient way to get your orange juice in the morning. Hence the analogy: the old-fashioned way of transmitting data being the orange and the newfangled way, or the efficient new way, being the concentrate in the can."[88]

Evans spent the money on the brochure (see Figure 4.2), and within 6 months, almost everywhere he went, people would say: "'Oh, you're the guy from the orange juice company.' The oranges made an incredible impact because, for a company in our kind of business, it was unheard of to do that kind of thing. So it became

86. Botwinick interview, Computer History Museum.

87. Evans interview, Computer History Museum.

88. Evans interview, Computer History Museum.

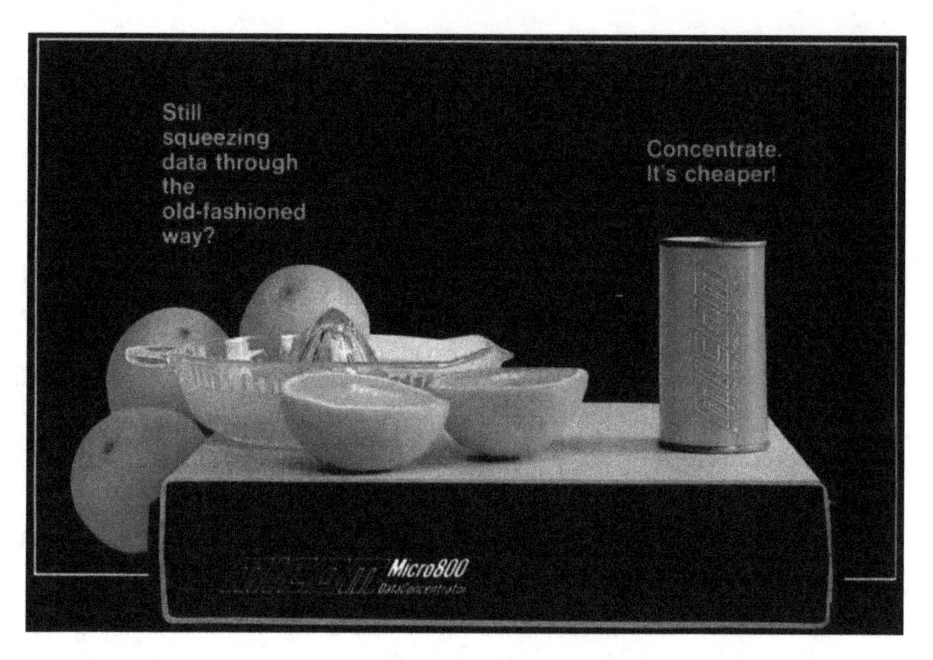

Figure 4.2 Micom Micro800 Data Concentrator ad. Source: *Computerworld* (December 24, 1979), 20. Used with permission.

a fundamental part of Micom and what we stood for."[89] Micom also held product seminars for buyers, not "techies." It proved a winner, broadcasting Micom's success as if inviting competition.

Infotron responded first, just as they had done to Codex. In early 1978, an Infotron customer, Bank of America, showed Dambrackas, director of multiplexer engineering, a Micom Data Concentrator. On seeing the "little plastic box you could put in an attaché case," he thought it "cute" but wondered: "Why such a small number of channels?"[90] Not posing any competitive threat to Infotron's products, he quickly forgot about it. But not for long, for it soon seemed as though every conversation ended up involving Micom and their strange little plastic box. Dambrackas bought a couple. In playing with them, he soon "got very excited," and saw ways to make improvements—largely from using the recently introduced Motorola 6502 microprocessor. In December 1978, Infotron introduced their Supermux 480: four channels for $1,725 and eight channels, for $2,725. They didn't, however, change their distribution or marketing practices, simply listing the Supermux 480s in their standard product catalog; revealing they saw only the technology and

89. Evans interview, Computer History Museum.

90. Dambrackas interview, Computer History Museum.

not the important new market of results-oriented minicomputer users opening up—users who did not buy data communication products in the then-traditional manner.[91] Infotron would not be alone in making this mistake. By mid-1980, six other firms would announce low priced statistical multiplexers—none would challenge Micom's market dominance.

Micom's sales nearly doubled to $1.5 million in 1978 and then grew an astonishing 250% in 1979 to $5.3 million. By 1980, Micom's sales of $15 million equaled those of the two leading multiplexer companies: Timeplex and Infotron. Norred recalls: "The growth of the Data Concentrator was so far beyond our expectations. We ran for almost 3 years trying to figure out ways to get manufacturing big enough to deal with the orders."[92]

Norred and Evans made yet another prescient decision in mid-1978 when they decided to OEM the Data Concentrator to other data communication firms. Their strategy was to increase their volume to the point where their manufacturing costs were radically reduced, and to exploit their early lead in the market. Evans remembers an additional element of their sales strategy: "We also were convinced that we were clearly going after a target market that had never heard anything about Codex or GDC or Paradyne, and that those guys could take product from us and it would be totally incremental to what we'd be sending through our channels."[93]

Evans' instincts that the high-end multiplexer companies wouldn't be able to compete with a low-end multiplexer "without totally changing their strategy" proved accurate. Codex introduced Micom products resold through OEM arrangements in July 1979, as did GDC later that year. Paradyne would follow in 1980. (In 1980, one-third of Micom's sales would be OEM.)[94]

By 1979, Micom's strategic focus on dominating low-cost statistical multiplexers appeared to be working like a charm. They held an amazing 80% market share. However, some critics questioned whether Micom was missing out on the emerging demand for networking systems. Evans' characteristic response to Micom's

91. Evans: "We hadn't done anything that, once people could look at our box and see what we had done, it wouldn't be that tough for them to emulate it. In fact, everybody that did try to emulate it was stupid enough to look at our list price and say: "Hey, we could make a lot of money doing that." Our planning was always based on 40 off list, because that was what we expected to get for our boxes. Everybody that came in told their engineers to build a product where they could make their margin at list, which is why nobody ever came close, from a product cost standpoint, to meeting what we had done." Evans interview, Computer History Museum.

92. Norred interview, Computer History Museum.

93. Evans interview, Computer History Museum.

94. Micom prospectus of June 19, 1981, p. 15.

critics was: "We may be unique in the business today with no systems orientation. Some say it's our fatal flaw, but I prefer to think we know something they don't."[95]

Micom's meteoric success had venture capitalists pounding on their door, begging the company to take their money. However, Micom didn't need money; tight-fisted expense management, exceptional profitability—in 1979 pre-tax profits were 27% of sales—and the ability to dictate terms of sale to its channels of distribution, all helped minimize cash requirements.

Numerous companies had designs on acquiring Micom. Dave Goodman, one of the outside directors of the board, sensed that Norred and Evans might be tempted to sell the company prematurely, or would become gun-shy of growing the company aggressively for fear of risking their existing paper capital gains. He proposed they sell some of their stock to eager-to-invest venture capitalists. Goodman also argued that if Micom ever sold stock to the public, they would benefit from the advice and cachet of venture capital investors. Norred remembers: "The driving force, as much as anything, wasn't to bring money into the company; it was so Roger and I could both sell some stock and put a little away before we screwed the company up. There was also an element of listening to people—it would be important to us to get other people involved that could help us."[96]

In November 1979, Micom sold 796,000 shares for $3.021 per share; the company raised just shy of $1.6 million and the selling shareholders received nearly $800,000. Micom's new market value: $16.6 million. Three years earlier the company had been valued at less than $500,000. On paper, Norred and Evans were multimillionaires.

The financing changed the conservative management style of Norred and Evans in two important ways. First, in allowing each to take some of their personal money off the table, they no longer lived under the threat of losing everything if Micom's fortunes declined; in fact, the money they received from the sale was already close to their original hopes/expectations. As a consequence, they became motivated to make their remaining shares worth as much as possible, including growing Micom large enough to go public—a goal reinforced by the new venture capital shareholders. A second effect of the financing was to further reduce the risks of either the company running out of cash or being unable to finance accelerated growth. They could also afford the expenses of additional management needed to free Norred and Evans so they could concentrate on strategy and growth. One of the first acts was to initiate a search for a vice president of engineering so Norred could focus on being president.

95. Evans, quoted in *Electronic News*, March 26, 1979, 36.

96. Norred interview, Computer History Museum.

4.6 Market Leaders Are Acquired

In mid-1976, amidst the continuing challenges of ramping production of the L-series modems, finishing the statistical multiplexer, expanding their line of TDMs and wondering if business conditions would ever improve, Carr had a visit from Keith Bane, director of corporate development of Motorola. Carr recalls: "Bane gave me this pitch why we ought to be bought by Motorola, and I showed him the door. On the way out he said: 'If I come up with a good plan, can I come back?' and I said: 'Yeah.'"[97]

Carr's chilly reception masked his own gnawing concerns of how best to steer Codex through an increasingly complex environment. Gone it would seem were the days of almost gentlemanly competition among a handful of well-known-to-each-other firms. Now each week brought new surprises, and fateful signs that the lumbering AT&T and the expansive computer companies saw data communications as another means to achieve market domination. Was there a future for independent data communication companies? Or were they destined to be scooped up by the larger, more bedrock firms? Carr decided to engage his senior managers in serious reconsideration of assumptions long held inviolable.

A dispassionate evaluation of modems came first. Fortunately, they had seen the implications of semiconductor technologies. To believe the press, every high-speed modem competitor had LSI modems under development.[98] The first to announce an LSI modem, Paradyne, had set the tone with aggressive pricing. (Although the August bankruptcy announcement of Datran threatened the undoing of Paradyne and a return to more traditional market behavior, or so Codex management hoped.) Semiconductor microprocessors introduced another uncertainty. For example, Milgo had recently introduced Fairchild microprocessor-based modems. Would the programmability of microprocessors prove more important than the speed and costs of LSI custom designed circuits? Another new development, initiated by the Codex-spinout Intertel, emphasized the integration of network control and diagnostics into modems. Then there was the advent of multipoint modems, modems that shared the same telephone circuit, thus dramatically cutting communication costs. How would Codex fare in the face of such diverse innovations?

As confused as the future of modems appeared, it seemed comparatively certain against the nightmare of deciding what products to offer after multiplexers. Multiplexers were an obvious choice as they made modems much more cost effective. Many thought computer terminals were logical products to sell as almost every

97. Carr interview, Computer History Museum.

98. See "Modems—Big battle shaping," *Electronic News*, March 15, 1976, 44–46. This article provides an excellent overview of many trends in data communication.

data communication application involved connecting remote terminals to host computers. However, terminals, historically decidedly low-tech, were becoming intelligent, which probably meant rapid product development cycles. Competition was fierce—every major computer company, including AT&T, sold terminals as did countless independent firms—and servicing mechanical products in the field was a real headache. Many potential products, like the previously considered front-end processor, would involve a massive software effort, a competence Codex did not have.

More threateningly, the computer companies now sold data communications products and were introducing networking software. IBM had started the trend in 1974 with its SNA. In 1976, they significantly enhanced SNA to include support for multiple computers. In reaction, every major computer company announced similar products, including DECnet in 1976. If the challenge of developing host computer software had seemed daunting before, it had now become a seemingly impossible undertaking. The question facing the data communication companies had suddenly switched to: How not to be locked out by the computer companies?

Any contemplation of the future had to include AT&T. The DAA was going to become a relic of the past, although not until June 1977. Not to be counted out, however, Pacific Bell had publicized the misbegotten idea of "connecting blocks," another way AT&T could charge for interfacing foreign attachments to their network. However ill-conceived, AT&T's shenanigans could not be easily dismissed for it had the technological and financial muscle to wipe out the independent manufacturers.

Then, in a stark reminder of the unforgiving nature of markets and the volatile state of data communications, on November 8, 1976, ADDS announced a takeover attempt of Milgo. Could Milgo escape the embrace of the unwanted suitor? Codex management had to wonder if they were to endure the same fate with Motorola.

In December, Bane returned with a new plan of acquisition. Carr considered it only marginally better and bluntly said so. Bane would not be denied, however, and persuaded a curious Carr to meet Robert Galvin, Motorola's CEO. Carr, having reviewed Codex's options with management, and stunned by the victimization of Milgo, realized he felt far more disposed to the idea of being acquired than he had assumed. He had to chuckle thinking of the trials of the past year: they were enough to cause anyone to question why they would want to be president of a young technology company. Carr recalls:

> Then, here came Motorola and said: "If you're buried in Motorola, you're not going to be visible. You don't have to perform every quarter. We can fund you. Our interest is in making you the foundation of a new business that we're

> willing to fund. Your interest is in dominating your marketplace. With us, you can do more than one thing at once.'"
>
> We started thinking about how much capital we could raise, and we thought we could raise a lot of capital, but we didn't see how we could manage the P&L profit and loss statement). We used to have an analyst meeting every quarter, and we had analysts who stood up and were unsatisfied with 36% pre-tax. They'd say: "You've been doing 36% for six quarters now. When are you going to improve it?" And the board, believe it or not, was giving us the same routine. "Why don't you crank up earnings per share?"'
>
> So the insiders, Storey, Forney, and I, finally decided that, from a strategy point of view, we believed we could advance the fortunes of Codex more significantly being buried in Motorola and drawing on their resources than we could by being a free-standing company and having to dance the quarter-by-quarter tune.[99]

On February 7, 1977, Motorola announced an agreement in principle to acquire Codex in an exchange of stock valued at more than $80 million. On February 23rd, Racal acquired Milgo for $62 million. The two leading independent data communication firms, and long-time foes, now had to learn if being small entities in much larger corporations gave them the resources and freedom to extend market leadership. A year later, Motorola also acquired UDS.

4.7 The Data Communications Market-Structure: Market Disruption

The competitive phase of the data communications market-structure required companies to introduce new products, as gross margins were eroded by price-cutting competitors. Innovation was essential as the new technology of microprocessors gave innovators more possibilities for added product features. Companies faced the challenges of an increasingly competitive market with different strategies: UDS adapted to a lack of available capital by trimming costs and focusing on their OEM relationships; Intertel discovered new pain points from their banking customers who badly needed reliable connectivity. Disruption in two key areas of the data communications market were Paradyne's low-priced high-speed leased line modem and Micom's low-end statistical multiplexer.

Paradyne succeeded in disrupting the high-speed leased line modem industry with advances in engineering that allowed them to build LSI modems at a significantly lower cost than their competitors. The technology they developed under contract to Datran became the basis for their line of LSI modems at a time when LSI

99. Carr interview, Computer History Museum.

technology was still uncommon in the modem industry. The low price point, combined with the success of complementary products for network controllers, helped Paradyne rapidly gain market share. While the LSI modem was sold in quantity for prices as low as $2,000, Paradyne still maintained a minimum 50% profit margin. It quickly became a favorite for OEM and export sales.[100] Paradyne had radically changed the pricing structure for high-speed modems.

Unlike Micom and GDC, companies that stuck to their bread-and-butter revenues of box products, Paradyne went after networking services. Wiggins was clearly influenced by his 13 years with IBM and its attention to customer retention and service. He remembers:

> Most people were going with distributors and various representative organizations. We decided that we wanted to control our own destiny, so we went with the end-user sales and service organization, feeling that it would be impossible to really grow the company the way we wanted to grow it if we couldn't service networks.[101]

Another innovation introduced by Wiggins was their inclusion of technical support staff in their marketing strategy. McDowell remembers:

> One of the things Bob put in place that set Paradyne apart from any of its competitors at the time was a lot of resource in sales support... We had people that were in product management and product marketing all working together with sales, so the customer was literally exposed almost from the first sales call to some technical people and had the ability to call in. We had technical people putting proposals together, actually laying out their networks, and we won a lot of business that way.[102]

By 1982, Paradyne was the fifth largest high-speed modem manufacturer with sales of $80 million, following only Codex, Milgo, AT&T, and IBM. Between 1975 and 1982 it had a compound annual growth rate of 60% with an increase in revenues from $7.7 million to $207.4 million.[103] The industry growth and standing

100. In 1979, OEM and distributor sales represented 32% of Paradyne's total sales of $41.4 million. Notable customers were L.M. Ericsson, Case, Hewlett-Packard, and General DataComm. L.M. Ericsson alone represented 15% of the company's total sales.

101. Wiggins interview, Computer History Museum.

102. Jerry McDowell, oral history interview by James L. Pelkey, April 10, 1992, San Jose, CA. Computer History Museum, Mountain View, CA. Available from https://archive.computerhistory.org/resources/access/text/2020/01/102740544-05-01-acc.pdf.

103. Paradyne annual reports.

gave Paradyne the credibility needed to become a major player in the networking business.

Micom's introduction of the Micro800 Data Concentrator, its line of low-end statistical multiplexers, marked another inflection point in the evolution of the data communications market-structure. At that time the innovation of the statistical multiplexer had only been implemented in the high-end product category offered by DCA and Codex. They were large, expensive, and complicated to configure and install. For large companies with mainframe computers who wanted to save on long-haul communication lines, the expense was justified. The innovation of the microprocessor was key to developing the software-driven power of the multiplexer, as Wesley Chu had shown. Companies like Codex applied similar multiplexing technology to their high-end products first, bringing them to market through direct sales to large corporations with big budgets.

Micom gained first-mover advantage in the low-end market by understanding that the growing number of minicomputers led companies to need more communications lines. An affordable statistical multiplexer, which could consolidate data into fewer lines, would offer attractive savings on communications costs. Micom's success in capturing and quickly dominating this potential market with their Micro800 Data Concentrator was a result of several key factors. For starters, smart engineering minimized the number of chips required, which allowed Micom to hit their target price point of $2,000. The Micro800 was easy to install, and Micom provided training programs that increased demand and appealed to customers. Together with their robust distribution networks, Micom earned the credibility and brand recognition of an industry leader.

The competition was quick to respond but was unable to capture significant market share from Micom. Competitors responded with products that added features, or were designed with too many components, bringing the cost out of the low-end range, while others simply added low-cost products to their catalogue without marketing them effectively. Companies like Codex, GDC, and Paradyne ultimately chose not to develop low-end products and instead signed OEM agreements with Micom. Others, like Western Union, aborted their efforts to develop low-end statistical multiplexers as they saw the price margins drop with the increase in competition.

From its modest revenues of $1.5 million in 1978, the year it introduced the Data Concentrator, Micom's revenue would grow to $189.5 million in 1986, with worldwide shipments of low-end statistical multiplexers of $58 million, capturing 43% market share in that product category.[104] Micom had succeeded in reshaping the

104. Codex/Motorola Registered Secret Proprietary Document—Appendix B, p. 29.

data communications market-structure and led the surge of companies bringing statistical multiplexer products to market. By 1984 over 50 companies had low-end statistical multiplexers on the market.[105] Much like Paradyne re-structured the modem market by undercutting high-end LSI modems, Micom significantly increased the market for low-end user-friendly multiplexers. In the process, they became an industry leader.

While Micom had initiated a boom in the low-end multiplexing market, effectively creating a new market that had not existed before, Paradyne had achieved rapid growth in market share of an existing market, displacing competitors and raising the barriers to entry in the high-speed LSI modem market. In both the modem and multiplexer markets, competition was becoming more intense. By 1980, Datapro identified 21 companies offering competing statistical multiplexer products, while in the modem market 48 companies were offering 400 products.

4.8 In Perspective

The data communications market-structure progressed from an emergent to a highly competitive phase throughout the mid to late 1970s. To succeed during this time, companies pursued different strategies to gain market share and maintain profit margins. Adaptability was critical. The demise of Datran had a huge impact on both Paradyne and Micom, forcing them to re-focus on new products that would eventually become hugely successful. UDS's inability to raise outside capital was emblematic of the entire computer and electronics industries throughout the 1970s as high capital gains taxes and other regulatory restrictions held venture funding to a minimum. To fund their own growth, entrepreneurs had to have the right mix of innovation, efficient design and manufacturing, and effective marketing. But, to survive this competitive phase meant delivering results on a consistent basis, and for some, like industry leaders Codex and Milgo, management decided that this would be better achieved through merging with a larger parent company.

The increasing pace of innovation in this phase of the data communications market-structure gave a taste of things to come in the new tech economy. Between 1973 and 1979, advances in semiconductor technology, most importantly microprocessors, quickly invigorated the growth of data communication firms. The challenge for data communication companies was how to successfully incorporate these innovations into new products. The answer for many firms was to design software driven analytic and diagnostic tools, features that helped evolve the state of data communications from one of predominantly point-to-point connections

105. Datapro report, July 1984.

to one of interconnecting small networks of devices. Just as the entrepreneurs of data communications were incorporating technological innovation and the continued deregulation in the telecommunications industry, with the successful expansion of ARPANET and the import of packet switching networking, a new breed of entrepreneurs responded to take advantage of these new opportunities.

Protocol Confusion: Networking, 1972–1979

5.1 Overview

At the end of Chapter 3, we saw how the ARPANET's successful demonstration at the 1972 International Conference on Computer Communications (ICCC) was a turning point in the history of computer communications. But as much as the ICCC demo was a crowning achievement of research, it marked only the start of an enormous amount of work to fulfill the vision of the ARPANET's creators. A functional network presented a conundrum: DARPA did not have charter authority to operate a network. With high demand for networking, and the growth of the networking equipment companies documented in Chapter 4, there was a clear need for the ARPANET, or something like it, to support commercial needs. Efforts to commercialize ARPANET technologies were not immediately successful, and networks operated by private companies met some but not all market needs.

Elsewhere, research into packet-switching continued along new paths, propelled by committed teams of researchers in Europe and the United States. In France, Louis Pouzin led a team of researchers in a project called CYCLADES, with the goal of learning from and improving upon the experience of the ARPANET. And in the United States, Robert Kahn worked with other DARPA-funded researchers to devise methods for passing packets from the land-based ARPANET to the radio-based ALOHAnet. They soon realized that they would need a new protocol for transmitting packets, which led Kahn and his collaborator Vint Cerf to develop the Transmission Control Program (TCP) in 1973.

By the mid-1970s, a proliferation of projects and protocols came from American universities, private companies like Xerox, and European research institutes—all seeking to provide the foundations for network interconnection and support robust commercial and scientific applications. Scientists and engineers working in institutions devoted to collaboration—including the International Organization for Standardization and the US National Bureau of Standards—sought to use their institutions to bring some harmonization to terminology and network protocols. In short, all three of our book's themes—*entrepreneurship*, *government–market boundaries*, and *education*—were present in the many efforts to create and disseminate protocols for networking in the 1970s. We explore some of these efforts in this chapter, starting with attempts to commercialize the ARPANET.

5.2 Commercializing ARPANET, 1972–1975

In 1971, Larry Roberts recognized a working ARPANET posed a new problem: ARPA lacked legal authority to operate a communications network. A new custodian, presumably a private organization, would have to be found to take on the responsibility without sacrificing the military's preferential use and control of the network for its on-going research. Roberts approached AT&T and BBN. AT&T rebuffed his inquiry and BBN displayed little interest.[1] Believing he had time to solve this problem, Roberts buried himself and his small staff in the many other Information Processing Techniques Office (IPTO, ARPA) projects such as artificial intelligence, speech understanding, various computer projects including Illiac IV, and other communication projects like ALOHAnet. Why? When viewed through a budgetary lens, ARPANET barely made the list of ARPA's important projects. After 4 years, an estimated $3.5 million had been spent buying Interface Message Processors (IMPs) from BBN to construct the Subnet.[2] (From our interviews, we estimate that ARPA invested roughly $10 million, including the costs of attaching Host computers to the Subnet and IPTO management.) During those same 4 years, ARPA's total spending was $833 million, making ARPANET between 0.5 to 1.5% of ARPA's budget—in other words, a sizable investment, but barely significant in the grand scheme of the American Cold War defense establishment.[3]

Until ARPANET could be divested, however, it required continual expansion and improvement. By June 1974, there were 46 ARPANET nodes.[4] Table 5.1 summarizes the growth in nodes by user type. Government agencies—primarily the military—made up most of the growth between 1972 and 1974. With military usage came all the rhetoric of national security that further complicated divesting ARPANET to the private domain.

---

1. Lawrence G. Roberts. 1978. The evolution of packet switching. *Proceedings of the IEEE* 66, 1310.

2. Paul Baran, et al. 1974. *ARPANET Management Study*, Cabledata Associates, Palo Alto, CA.

3. Burton I. Edelson and Robert L. Stern. 1989. *The Operations of DARPA and its Utility as a Model for a Civilian ARPA*. The Johns Hopkins Foreign Policy Institute, Washington, DC.

4. Frank Heart, Alex McKenzie, John McQuillan, and David Walden. 1978. *ARPANET Completion Report*. Defense Advanced Research Projects Agency, Washington, DC, III-91.

Table 5.1 **ARPANET nodes by date and type, 1969–1974**

As of Date	Number of Nodes	Universities	Government Contractors	Government Agencies	Companies
Dec-69	4	3	1		
Jun-70	9	5	3		1
Dec-70	13	8	4		1
Sep-71	18	9	5	1	3
Mar-72	23	10	6	5	2
Aug-72	29	10	5	12	2
Sep-73	40	12	6	17	5
Jun-74	46	14	7	20	5

Source: ARPANET Completion Report, F. Heart, A. McKenzie, J. McQuillan, D. Walden, Washington, DC, 1978.

Roberts had been around technology development long enough to know that operating and improving a system that in the end would have to be divested was a headache he would like to avoid. So, in late 1971 he pressed BBN to step up to the plate to solve his and ARPA's dilemma. However, BBN saw itself as a government contractor, possibly the seller of product into commercial markets, but never as an operator of a communications network. The mere thought of dealing with the FCC, beginning with the effort to attain approval to operate a network without the burden of regulation, was a daunting barrier to entry. Yet in order to be seen as responsive to Roberts, BBN management created a committee to study the issue.

The institutional noose forcing Roberts to divest ARPANET tightened considerably on March 23, 1972, when a Department of Defense (DOD) directive changed the agency's name to the Defense Advanced Research Projects Agency (DARPA) and made it a civilian-directed agency reporting directly to the Office of the Secretary of Defense.[5] It also limited DARPA's responsibilities to the conduct of "basic and applied research and development for advanced projects." And although never a practice, DARPA was precluded from creating separate Research & Development (R&D) facilities. In addition, limits were set as to the maximum funds any one R&D organization could be awarded in a year. Fortunately, Roberts had already anticipated the hidden-yet-clear message to divest ARPANET, although he lacked a solution other than hoping BBN would come to the rescue.

Roberts' plans to transfer ARPANET suffered a setback when three members of the BBN committee studying whether BBN wanted to commercialize the ARPANET

5. Edelson and Stern, *The Operations of DARPA and its Utility as a Model for a Civilian ARPA*, 6.

became so frustrated they left BBN and announced they were going to start a company offering data communication network services. Their product would be "conceptually similar" to ARPANET. They saw the ARPANET technologies as public property, having been funded with public money, and presumed they would be given rights to the technology because it "theoretically should be available to us and to others." In fact, they even told people that they had "been reassured informally of this by the Defense Dept."[6]

BBN's management felt pressured to act. Needing someone to lead the effort, they began recruiting Roberts to leave IPTO and become President of the Telenet Communications Corp. (Telenet) subsidiary they had created in December 1971. BBN's timing could not have been better. Roberts had decided already that once the fate of ARPANET had been resolved it would be time for him to leave IPTO, having already stayed longer than he would have ever expected and longer than was the cultural norm. So Roberts, in his inimitable style, dove into analyzing the opportunity and concluded that an "optimally cost-effective" nationwide network of roughly 14 moderately sized computers would cost $ 10–20 million dollars of computer-time usage.[7] Convinced of Telenet's economic feasibility, Roberts accepted BBN's offer. But he needed time to avoid any appearances of "conflict of interest;" especially with regard to divesting ARPANET. For help, he suggested that RAND, the research organization, study the alternatives and make a recommendation.

On being offered the assignment, Keith Uncapher, the Director of the Computer Sciences Division of RAND, immediately thought of involving Paul Baran. Baran had left RAND in 1968 to found the Institute for the Future to study the question of how society solved problems with long lead times. Baran readily agreed to consult for RAND. RAND management then realized the March DOD directive had set limits restricting how many dollars could be given to a research institution and RAND had reached their limit. Baran remembers: "So I said, 'Oh, what the heck. I'll start a company, if you don't mind, RAND, and do the study, if DARPA doesn't object, and DARPA wants it.' So that's where Cabledata Associates (CDA) first got started, doing a study on the divestiture of the ARPANET."[8]

---

6. *Datamation*, March 1973, 122.

7. Lawrence G. Roberts. 1973. Dynamic allocation of satellite capacity through packet reservation. *Proceedings of the June 4–8, 1973, national computer conference and exposition*. Association for Computing Machinery, New York, 711–716. DOI: https://doi.org/10.1145/1499586.1499753. His analysis also showed that communication costs as a percentage of computer costs would stabilize at 8%.

8. Paul Baran, oral history interview with James L. Pelkey, January 12, 1988, Campbell, CA. Computer History Museum, Mountain View, CA. Available from https://archive.computerhistory.org/resources/access/text/2017/09/102740210-05-01-acc.pdf.

Baran contacted Cerf, who had just started teaching at Stanford University only a mile down the road. Cerf also took little convincing to help CDA. With Baran serving as principal investigator and Cerf as project scientist, work began by the summer of 1972 with a report due by January 1974.

Yet no sooner had CDA started work than the three ex-employees of BBN, Lee Talbert (President), Ralph Alter (Operations vice-president) and Stephen Russell (Engineering vice-president), founded Packet Communications Inc. (PCI) in July 1972. They announced they had venture-capital backing, had secured rights to the ARPANET technology, and would be submitting their application to offer data communication services to the FCC.

By mid-September, Roberts, frustrated from not having found his replacement and feeling the pressure to join Telenet, took J.C.R. Licklider up on his casual offer to take Roberts' job if he could not find a successor. On October 1, 1972, Roberts announced his resignation from IPTO to become President of Telenet and, on the following day, Telenet filed its application with the FCC. Three months later, PCI submitted their application. Both applications would be approved as regulated common carrier undertakings even though they were going to lease lines from AT&T, itself already a regulated common carrier.

A new market was forming. At first the focus would be selling data communication services. In the future, firms would sell packet switching products.[9] Packet switching services and products would prove less important than another market that would emerge from the new paradigm of packet switching—local area networking. PCI never raised sufficient venture capital and faded away; but Telenet became a public company in December 1977 with a market capitalization of $20.6 million.[10] On June 13, 1979, General Telephone Company, the second largest telephone company, bought Telenet for approximately $58 million. BBN received $13.9 million for their cumulative investment of $5.3 million.[11]

9. Roberts, "The evolution of packet switching"; Marvin A. Sirbu and Laurence E. Zwimpfer. 1985. Standards setting for computer communications: The case of X.25. *IEEE Communications Magazine* 23 (March 1985), 35–45.

10. BBN Annual Report 1979, p. 22.

11. Pelkey interview with Roberts: "Well, GTE got interested in getting into the business, and so they came after us and they told us that they had learned their lesson with several other companies they had bought and they would never do it again. They'd let us do our own thing and everything would be fine. That lasted for 1 year and then after that the management changed every few months and they kept on trying to figure out how to position it within their organization." Lawrence Roberts, oral history interview by James L. Pelkey, June 17, 1988, Burlingame, CA. Computer History Museum, Mountain View, CA. Available from https://archive.computerhistory.org/resources/access/text/2013/04/102746626-05-01-acc.pdf.

By the time CDA submitted its recommendation on January 14, 1974, the horse had clearly left the barn. Even so, and reflecting CDA's deep concern if a few firms came to dominate packet switching as an oligopoly, they recommended a new institutional form, a consortium, that would provide "three essential functions":

- A clearinghouse mechanism for transferring payments among cooperating entities.
- A mechanism for creating and enforcing common industry standards.
- A mechanism to allow continuously free and open entry, to avoid the formation of any closed oligopolistic structure that would demand close governmental supervision or regulation.[12]

The DOD had its concerns as well and after another year of meetings exploring alternatives, including the recommendations of CDA, the management of ARPANET was transferred from DARPA to the Defense Communications Agency (DCA) on July 1, 1975. Although this arrangement did not provide a commercial home for ARPANET technologies, it did relieve DARPA of the burden of managing the ARPANET while, at the same time, enabling the ARPANET's sponsors at the DOD to use the network for the defense communications functions that it had envisioned initially.[13]

5.3 Packet Radio and Robert Kahn, 1972–1974

Shortly after the ICCC in the autumn of 1972, the indefatigable Robert Kahn left BBN for DARPA to begin planning the world's first packet radio network. The consummate engineer, he had the experiences of both ARPANET and ALOHAnet to inform his judgment. Kahn later summarized his experience by noting that "the ALOHA system was to packet radio like the original time-sharing computer was to ARPANET."

Kahn soon convened an informal working group, including Vint Cerf and Robert Metcalfe, to stimulate his thinking and engage their interests. Two challenges had to be met if they were to interconnect the packet radio network with the ARPANET. First, known problems with the communications protocol of

12. Baran, et al, *ARPANET Management Study*, iv.

13. On the transition of the Arpanet to the DCA, see Bradley Fidler and Andrew L. Russell. 2018. Financial and administrative infrastructure for the early Internet: Network maintenance at the Defense Information Systems Agency. *Technology & Culture* 59 (October 2018), 899–924.

ARPANET—the Network Control Protocol, or NCP—had to be solved. Second, a means to interface a packet radio network to ARPANET had to be conceived.

The most glaring problem with NCP was the lack of end-to-end, or Host-to-Host, error-correction. In the ARPANET, NCP error correction was provided for packet routing between the IMPs but not for messages passed between the Hosts and the IMPs. Yet in operation errors did occur and thus no end-to-end reliability in ARPANET existed. The probability of errors from a roaming packet radio terminal would be significantly greater than the hard-wired terminals of ARPANET. In a radio network, signals could be affected by static in the air or other radio signals, or be disrupted when communicating terminals entered tunnels or buildings. There were other functions subsumed within NCP that also needed to be elevated to the Host level such as flow control and packet segmentation. So NCP needed to be redesigned both for a better functioning ARPANET as well as to support interconnection of a radio network.

The second challenge was how to interconnect the comparatively slow ARPANET to a fast packet radio network. ARPANET was designed assuming link speeds of 50 kilobits per second (kbps). A packet radio network would operate at 100 to 400kbps. At first the mismatch in operating speeds seemed to have an easy solution: create a gateway between the two networks that converted the messages from one network into acceptable messages for the other network. A gateway had its problems, however, especially if there were many gateways/networks and terminals roved from one to another. NCP assumed there was only one network much less gateways or the even more complicated situation of a terminal sending a message to one gateway and expecting an answer on another, potentially not predeterminable, gateway. All signs pointed to the need for NCP to be re-thought, and perhaps replaced altogether.

In June 1973, at the American Federation of Information Processing Societies–National Computer Conference in New York City, Kahn chaired a meeting to discuss the Host-to-Host protocol issues. Following the meeting, Kahn and Cerf began the uncertain task of redesigning NCP.

5.4 The CYCLADES Network and Louis Pouzin, 1971–1972

In November 1971, Louis Pouzin joined the Delegation a l'Informatique, an agency of the French government responsible for coordinating all activities related to computing. He would be responsible for creating France's first computer communication network. His first official act was to travel to the United States and re-establish contacts he had made when at MIT (1962–1965), and to better understand the mysterious ARPANET.[14] Pouzin recalled that he met the "major ARPANET developers" on his trip, including people at BBN, Larry Roberts, Vint Cerf, the people at SRI, and Len Kleinrock. Pouzin had read the papers on ARPANET before his trip, but his visit and meetings made the ARPANET feel much less abstract and much more real. Over the course of his visit, he came to a better understanding of the origins, organization, goals, and deficiencies of the ARPANET project. Pouzin remembers:

> They explained to me all their compromises and the unfinished things they had encountered. We started discussing how to improve that. They understood that I intended to build another network but they really didn't believe it. They had this feeling that the ARPANET, this kind of complicated system, could only be implemented in a country like the States due to money, expertise and so on. They didn't believe Europe could bring something like that up.[15]

But Pouzin was determined to make it happen. After returning to Paris, Pouzin began designing the computer communications network and organizing a conference of Europeans interested in networking. Most participants attending the June 1972 meeting were French. Notable exceptions were Steve Crocker of DARPA, Donald Davies of the NPL, and Peter Kirstein of University College, London. Two decisions came easy. First, they agreed they needed to meet again and function much like the Network Working Group, NWG, of ARPANET. They agreed that a suitable name would be the International Network Working Group, or INWG. Second, they agreed that the institutional conditions of Europe were very different from those in the United States. How to work with the all-powerful Public Telephone and Telegraph companies (PTTs) and their omnipotent standards-making body, the International Telegraph and Telephone Consultative Committee (CCITT), was bound to be complicated and time consuming. Unlike the regulatory scrutiny that AT&T was facing in the United States, the incumbent telephone monopolies had no independent regulator watching over them—akin to a merger between AT&T

14. "Newsmaker: Louis Pouzin," *Data Communications*, May 1978, 35–36. See more generally Andrew L. Russell and Valérie Schafer. 2014. In the shadow of Arpanet and Internet: Louis Pouzin and the CYCLADES Network in the 1970s. *Technology & Culture* 55, 880–907.

15. Louis Pouzin, oral history interview with James L. Pelkey, November 28, 1988, Ft. Lauderdale, FL. Computer History Museum, Mountain View, CA. Available from https://archive.computerhistory.org/resources/access/text/2017/12/102740273-05-01-acc.pdf. Readers may be interested to compare Pelkey's 1988 interview of Pouzin with Russell's 2012 interview, 24 years later. Louis Pouzin, oral history interview with Andrew L. Russell, April 2, 2012, Paris, France. Charles Babbage Institute, University of Minnesota, Minneapolis. Available from https://conservancy.umn.edu/handle/11299/155666.

and the FCC. To confront the European telephone monopolies, most attendees believed they needed the credibility and authority of an existing organization. Pouzin, a member of the newly created International Federation of Information Processing (IFIP) Technical Committee 6 (TC 6) on Data Communications, suggested INWG look into affiliating with IFIP, a body of computer scientists interested in international harmony and information sharing. The INWG members authorized Pouzin to talk with Alex Curran, chairman of IFIP TC-6. They also scheduled the next meeting for November at the University of Kent, England, after the upcoming ICCC demonstration in Washington, DC.

After the meeting, Pouzin returned to his task of designing a simpler packet switching network than ARPANET. In the process, he spent time studying the NPL network and, to the extent he had access to information, the MERIT, TYMNET, and INTENET networks.[16] Pouzin was certain networking would evolve differently in Europe due to the power of the PTTs—whereas the monopolistic powers of AT&T were being weakened, the monopolistic PTTs remained unchallenged. To think a distinct communications network could be superimposed on top of the PTT networks, as ARPANET was on AT&T's, seemed naive.

In November 1972, just weeks after the heady experience of ICCC, the workshop at the University of Kent convened. With the ARPANET success serving as both an inspiration to those with computer communication ideas and a proof of principle to be improved upon, workshop organizers hoped to foster new collaborations. Participants from the United States, Canada, Japan, and several European countries heard presentations on ARPANET, the NPL of Davies, and the network Pouzin was planning called CYCLADES.

CYCLADES was to be a pure datagram network. CYCLADES would consist of Host computers connected to packet switches that interconnected using PTT-provided telephone circuits. Software in the Host computers would create virtual circuits between Hosts on the network and partition the data to be communicated into datagrams. Hosts would then send the datagrams to their packet switches that forwarded them to the appropriate packet switches that in turn passed the datagrams to their Hosts. The packet switches and the network links were called Cigale, which was equivalent to the ARPANET's subnet (Figure 5.1). CYCLADES differed radically from ARPANET in that Hosts sent datagrams directly between Hosts and provided end-to-end error correction. Pouzin used a datagram scheme knowing there was simply no way to impose error correction, or ordering of packet

16. Louis Pouzin. 1973. Presentation and major design aspects of the CYCLADES computer network. *Data Networks: Analysis and Design Third Data Communications Symposium*, Nov. 1973, 80–85.

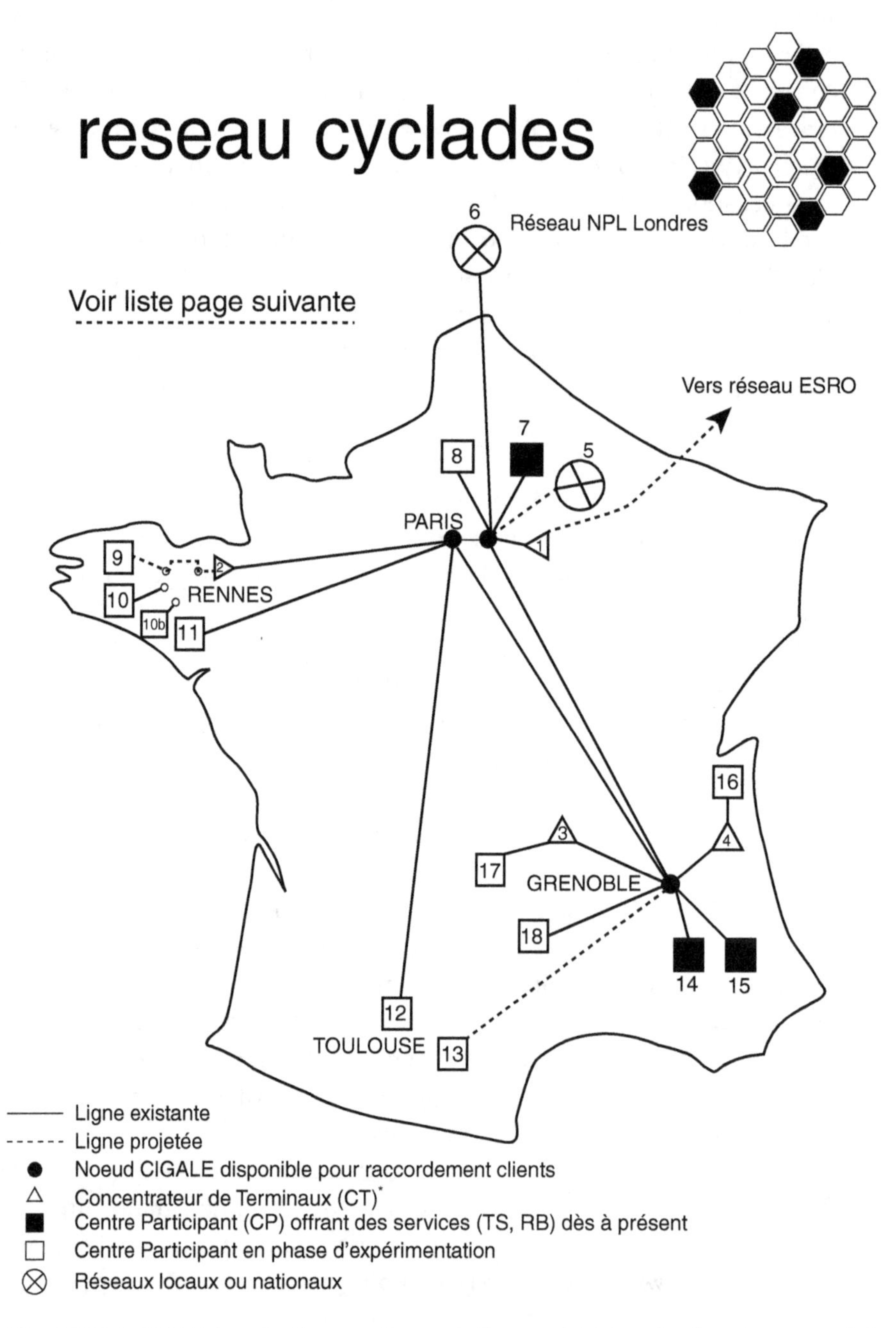

Figure 5.1 The CYCLADES Network. Source: Presentation and Major Design Aspects of the CYCLADES Computer Network by Louis Pouzin, Institut de Recherche d'Informatique et d'Automatique (IRIA), Rocquencourt, France. Used with permission.

responsibilities, onto the PTTs. And as had been learned in ARPANET, even if the packet switches communicated error-free, there could be no guarantee that errors were not introduced by communications between the Hosts and the packet switches. Pouzin's elegant technical design also was a precise political defense: it isolated CYCLADES from the authority and complications of the PTTs.

In placing responsibility for reliable end-to-end, datagram communications in the communicating computers, and proving the architecture could work, CYCLADES would have continuing repercussions for the future of computer communications. Pouzin recalls his thinking at the time:

> The inspiration for datagrams had two sources. One was Donald Davies' studies. He had done some simulation of datagram networks, although he had not built any, and it looked technically viable. The second inspiration was I like things simple. I didn't see any real technical motivation to overlay two levels of end-to-end protocols. I thought one was enough.[17]

Pouzin hoped to have CYCLADES working by the end of 1973. Other European projects emerged at the same time. In 1971, the COST 11 Project was a multination European-initiated research network and a virtual copy of CYCLADES.[18] In 1973, COST 11 was renamed the European Informatics Network and Derek Barber of NPL became the project director. The leading computer companies of Europe, including Olivetti, ICL, Siemens, and CII, were closely associated with both projects. These firms were motivated to take part because they recognized that if they did not provide an alternative to the PTT's data communication products they risked abdicating much of their communications futures. These computer manufacturers composed the core of the European Computer Manufacturers' Association (ECMA), an organization coordinating mutually advantageous industrial policies.

Indeed, researchers within the PTTs were developing approaches to packet switching that would keep the new technology within their control. Pouzin's countryman, Rémi Després, managed the experimental packet switched network of the French PTT called Réseaux à Commutation par Paquets (RCP). Announced in November 1973, RCP was based on the PTT provision of virtual circuits, and not just communication links. RCP was to serve as a test bed for the public packet network the French PTT was planning named TRANSPAC. Després would find allies the following year in Roberts and Wessler of Telenet, who had concluded that Telenet's

17. Pouzin interview, Computer History Museum.

18. Cooperacion Scientifique et Technique; Technical and Scientific Cooperation. It was a set of actions that the European community countries had decided to use as an area for cooperation, so they had a number of potential projects, and number 11 was a computer network. Roberts, "The evolution of packet switching," 1309.

packet switching products had to be based on virtual circuits if they hoped to land PTTs as customers. The PTTs could charge more for the reliable transmission of information—that is by providing virtual circuit networks—than simply the provisioning of links.[19]

5.5 Transmission Control Protocol (TCP), 1973–1976

With no clear answer for what the best design would be for a computer communications network—and with rapidly intensifying commercial and political interest—leaders of the international packet-switching community forged ahead. The debate raged within INWG, which, in 1973, became IFIP Working Group 6.1 (WG 6.1) on Network Interconnection.[20] Steve Crocker, chairman of the original ARPANET NWG, recommended Vint Cerf became Chairman, a suggestion readily approved. Quickly the WG 6.1 meetings became a must for anyone wanting to influence computer communications. The core assumption of this group, which was merely a handful of people in mid-1973, became, in the short span of 24 months, received knowledge by nearly all those involved in computer communications: *the world was going to be populated by many computer networks, networks that inevitably would need to be interconnected.* The dilemma that faced the group was clear: how could the complexities of inter-network communications be resolved when there was so much unknown about what the best technical arrangement would look like? Moreover, what were to be the roles of the firms of the two enabling markets: telecommunications and computers? So even though not a standards-making body, for a few critical years the who's who of computer communications debated the future of networks and their coming together at IFIP WG 6.1 meetings. All agreed that the ARPANET represented a good first proof of concept: it was possible to build a better network than one designed using the circuit-switching model of the telephone system. ARPANET had its deficiencies, however, for it was neither a true datagram network nor did it provide end-to-end error correction. So the big question remained: could a true packet network with end-to-end reliability be created? In September 1973, at a meeting in Sussex, England, Cerf and Kahn presented a communication protocol Transmission Control Program, or TCP, that functioned over interconnected networks of many kinds. Their paper was published by the *IEEE Transactions on*

19. Russell and Schafer, "In the shadow of Arpanet and Internet."

20. On INWG, see Alexander McKenzie. 2011. INWG and the conception of the Internet: An eyewitness account. *IEEE Annals of the History of Computing* 33, 66–71; Andrew L. Russell. 2014. *Open Standards and the Digital Age: History, Ideology, and Networks*. Cambridge University Press, New York; John Day. 2016. The clamor outside as INWG debated: economic war comes to networking. *IEEE Annals of the History of Computing* 38 (July–Sept. 2016), 58–77.

Communications in May 1974 as "A protocol for packet network intercommunication."[21] TCP incorporated end-to-end virtual circuits with datagram transmission and gateways between networks.

Generalized from a solution of how to interconnect ARPANET with a packet radio network, Cerf and Kahn proposed different networks be interconnected by gateways with TCP functioning across both networks and gateways. Gateways would receive incoming traffic from one network and perform whatever transformations were necessary in order to send the data over the outgoing network. One transformation would be protocol conversions. Another, more contentious transformation was fragmenting packet or datagram size: if the outgoing network required a smaller packet size than the incoming network, then the gateway would fragment the packet into multiple packets before resending. Only this required receiving hosts to be informed of gateway-created fragmentations in order to reconstruct the fragmented packets into the original transmission. One transmission could span many networks and potentially be fragmented multiple times.

This solution immediately raised red flags for Pouzin and the Europeans. They were skeptical of any network design that forced hosts to have to correct errors introduced by network operators, that is, the PTTs. Coupling the correction of host-to-host errors with network-to-network errors meant that the protocols used by the computers and PTTs also would have to be coupled, and that seemed like a sure way both to cede control to the PTTs, and to end up with a sub-optimum computer communication system. In March 1974, Pouzin responded to the Cerf and Kahn memo with a proposal of his own: "A Proposal for Interconnecting Packet Switching Networks" (INWG60). It stimulated more revisions and proposals by both sides. Then in November 1974, the Europeans' concerns soared when the CCITT announced it would establish a standard interface (to be called X.25) to packet switching networks.[22] In December, in hopes of forging a solution of one internetwork protocol, Cerf, Yogen Dalal and Carl Sunshine submitted document INWG72: "Specifications of Internetwork Transmission Control Program (revised)." The revision set forth a windowing scheme to end the fragmentation arguments. Pouzin worried about the "window scheme," which he characterized as "technically tricky." He believed it was a "smart" design, but he and his colleagues in Europe still had reservations

21. Vinton G. Cerf and Robert E. Kahn. 1974. A protocol for packet network intercommunication. *IEEE Transactions on Communications* Vol. com-22 (May 1974), 637–648.

22. Pouzin interview, Computer History Museum. PTT members began attending WG 6.1 meetings, and IFIP received a level of membership in CCITT that permitted IFIP members to attend CCITT Rapporteur's meetings; both developments adding voices to those advocating virtual circuits.

about how to implement it in the hotly contested market–government boundaries in Europe. Pouzin recalled:

> We thought it was first, too complex in implementation, and much too hard to sell to industry. The second thing is it mingled—it actually handled in the very same protocol, matters that belong to the transport level, and matters that belong to the end-to-end protocol. That kind of coupling was politically unacceptable, because these two levels of system were handled by two different worlds: The PTTs and the other world, the computer people. So obviously it was not acceptable in terms of technical sociology. You could not sell something that involves the consensus of these two different worlds. So we thought that was not a good way of organizing things, even though it was technically sound.[23]

The struggle to find a common solution had sharpened understandings of both how to design a network, be it either datagram or virtual circuit, and an interconnected network of many networks. Cerf characterized those difficult years as a "religious battle between people who had datagram style networks and people who had virtual circuit style nets. The international PTT efforts went down the path of virtual circuits while the R&D community generally stuck with a datagram style of operations." As a result, Cerf saw that the R&D community came to grips with the uncertainties of datagram networks, where the international PTTs found the risks more difficult to accept, and saw virtual circuit designs as offering greater certainty. Cerf recalled:

> So these communities really went in different directions. They used to fight tooth and nail with each other, and I was out there fighting too. I was beating the table saying: "God damn it, it had to be datagrams because that required less of a network and you had to do things end-to-end anyway, because you wanted to have the mainframes assure the other end that they had really gotten the data, and not just that the network thinks that you got it," so there were a lot of arguments along those lines.[24]

But for Kahn and DARPA the debate needed to end. They wanted to code TCP and see if it would work. They were ready to deploy; they weren't particularly interested in resolving the underlying political and technical open questions. In early 1975, DARPA gave three contracts to test whether the TCP specifications

23. Pouzin interview, Computer History Museum.

24. Vinton Cerf, oral history interview with James L. Pelkey, February 8, 1988, Reston, VA. Computer History Museum, Mountain View, CA. Available from https://archive.computerhistory.org/resources/access/text/2015/11/102738017-05-01-acc.pdf.

were detailed and explicit enough to enable different implementations to function seamlessly. The three teams were headed by Cerf at Stanford, Ray Tomlinson and Bill Plummer at BBN, and by Peter Kirstein at University College in London, England. Pouzin understood the significance of implementing TCP:

> After that, they sort of froze their design, but then we started to become disinterested because we didn't think it could really work. So then we started to skirt the issue and considered that as something we couldn't avoid because they had the whole ARPA backing behind them, so we thought we couldn't stop that. On the other hand, we had quite a good feeling that they would not invade Europe very much, so we started to organize our thing in Europe differently.[25]

The European members concluded that they needed the support of a standards making body to advance their cause. Since IFIP was not a standards-making body, they approached the International Standards Organization (ISO) in late 1975.

In January 1976, in an attempt to bridge the differences between the TCP and European communities, Alex McKenzie, of BBN, re-crafted an international protocol to satisfy both the demands of those wanting a total end-to-end protocol and those wanting the end-to-end and network-to-network functions separated. A paper authored by McKenzie, Cerf, Scantlebury, and Hubert Zimmermann discussing the protocol was submitted to the IFIP and subsequently published in *Computer Communications Review*: "Proposal for an international end-to-end protocol." Unfortunately, it proved too little too late. As Pouzin anticipated, the ARPA-funded community and its leaders refused to give in. As Cerf underscores, he could not "persuade the TCP community to adopt the compromise given the state of implementation experience of TCP at the time and the untested nature of the IFIP document."[26]

5.6 A Proliferation of Communication Projects

The idea that a limited number of computers could serve all users—the vision that had inspired the development of ARPANET—no longer described computer conditions in the United States. The success of the IBM System 360/370 Series, the continuing efforts of other mainframe computer companies to establish market presence, and the gathering number of minicomputer companies created a hodgepodge of computer use—and a variety of visions for computer interconnection.

25. Pouzin interview, Computer History Museum.

26. Cerf interview, Computer History Museum. See also Day, "The clamor outside as INWG debated."

Companies, universities, the military, and various government agencies all contributed to the growing diversity of computer networks.[27] Most commercial networks, such as Control Data Corp.'s CYBERNET and IBM's TSS Network, employed traditional data communication products—modems, multiplexers, and front-end concentrators—and continued in the circuit-switching vein. Competitive products from start-ups, such as Tymshare and Telenet, employed variations of packet switching. University networks also tended to employ traditional techniques and, while generally confined to a single campus, multiple universities sometimes joined together to form an "educational computing network," such as the MERIT Network of Michigan State University, Wayne State University, and University of Michigan.

More adventuresome networking projects tended to be funded by either the military or government research agencies. An example of a sophisticated network developed by a government agency was the Octopus system at the Lawrence Berkeley Laboratory. And then there were networking projects funded by government agencies at universities, the most important being a National Science Foundation–funded network at the University of California, Irvine (UCI) conceived and managed by David Farber.

5.6.1 Token Ring, David Farber, UC Irvine, and the NSF: 1969–1974

In contrast to most of those who came to computer communications from 1965 to 1972, David Farber had an extensive background in both communications and computers. In 1956, Farber joined Bell Labs of AT&T, working in communication systems. During his 10-year stay, he learned about computers and the needs of "real users" as director of the computer center at Holmdel, NJ, and secretary to the IBM users' group SHARE. In 1966, he joined RAND where he spent 2 years and came under the influence of Paul Baran's work. Next, he joined Scientific Data Systems (SDS), a division of Xerox, and taught evening courses at UCI. In late 1969, Farber accepted a 2-year appointment as Acting Associate Professor UC Irvine (UCI) and given 2 years to earn a permanent appointment. He was told that he needed to accomplish something important in those 2 years.

One question summarized Farber's interest: "Could I use a whole bunch of these minicomputers together to form a more effective computation environment?" In early 1970, still undecided as to what would qualify as something important, he attended an IEEE conference in Georgia and heard Abramson's first public presentation of the ALOHAnet. Capturing Farber's attention, however, was a talk

27. A survey article of the time: David J. Farber. 1972. "Networks: An introduction," *Datamation*, April 1972, 36–39.

on communication rings by John Newhall and David Farmer of Bell Labs. He recalls:

> What triggered me on, more than anything else, was the notion that there was technology for local networking. So I went back to Irvine and started thinking of a set of objectives, and remember, I have 2 years to come up with a project, to get it funded, and to get enough published on it, enough work done, so in 2 years I could go up for a permanent position. Good Trick! The things that drive technology are always fun.
> During that period, I wanted to see just how decentralized I could make an environment. I knew that I could certainly build something similar to the IBM token passing loops to communicate between processors, and I could certainly build a master/slave processor. I helped do that at SDS. And so the objectives of what became known as the Distributed Computer System, DCS, was to see if we could do total distribution. No vulnerable point of error. With both communications and processing and software that was completely decentralized. We certainly didn't want to duplicate the central control box in the Newhall and Farmer ring.[28]

Farber began "throwing ideas around" with a young faculty member named Rusty Barbero and a couple of graduate students. They were kicking around the token ring concepts elaborated by Newhall and Farmer. Two questions focused their inquiries: "Is it feasible to build a completely decentralized token ring?" and "Can we build a token ring, a communication system, that supports the type of software paradigms that we wanted?" Again Farber:

> In the early days, you talk about specific machines that you communicate with. Well, there was no way we were going to do things different if user software knew about specific machines, even indirectly. So we thought of the idea of having software that would couple together by sending detached messages back and forth to each other. Now that's to my knowledge, the first presentation of message-based processing. Further, if there were going to be messages to pass back and forth, couldn't we do it in such a way that the addresses were independent of the machines that the programs ran on? So we evolved this idea that we were going to have a process structured software system, with messages that were process addressed. So I want to send a message to somebody, to some program, once I knew its name I just sort

28. David J. Farber, oral history interview with James L. Pelkey, March 8, 1988, Wilmington, DE. Computer History Museum, Mountain View, CA. Available from https://archive.computerhistory.org/resources/access/text/2017/09/102740206-05-01-acc.pdf.

> of sent it to that program and the underlying communication system would take care of it for me.[29]

Farber submitted a proposal for funding to the National Science Foundation (NSF) in 1970, asking for about $250,000 a year, a large grant. It was successful, which Farber recalled "surprised everybody including me," so he turned to the work of implementing the idea. The Distributed Computer System would consist of a series of minicomputers, terminal controllers and File Machines interconnected together by a token ring network. Farber initially wanted to buy PDP-11s from Digital Equipment Corporation (DEC) but, fortuitously, ended up using a PDP-11 clone from Lockheed Corporation called the SUE. Lockheed was in the core memory business and began selling computers as a way to put "some iron under their memories." The SUE came with minimal software, forcing Farber's team to write all the software they needed, including a compiler. If they had used the PDP-11s, they "might have ended up with a kludge because there was a fair amount of software for the 11." They would connect each SUE to a shared twisted pair wire using a specially designed token ring circuit board called a ring interface. The inter-device communication architecture mimicked the Bell System digital T-1 specification with the modification of fixed-length messages with a bandwidth of 2.5 megabits per second.

A token ring network interconnects devices as node-to-node connections that close into a ring. Each node consists of a device, such as a computer, with a special hardware interface connecting to the transmission media (see Figure 5.2). In the case of the UCI network, the transmission media was twisted pair wire. The nodes, or stations, of the network are granted the right to communicate by passing a token, a unique bit pattern—usually eight-bits of ones—from node to node. If the node wants to communicate, it waits for the token to be passed to it, which means it is authorized to communicate, then seizes the token and appends its message. Once sent, the token automatically passes to the next node, which repeats the process. If a node has nothing to send, it simply passes the token on to the next node. Since every node receives the token within a known time, bounded by whether all the other nodes have data to communicate or not, a token ring network is, by definition, deterministic.

In February 1973, Farber presented a paper at the International Conference of IEEE Computer Society even though the network did not yet work. He remembers: "A lot of the things back in those days were published before they were built.

29. Farber interview, Computer History Museum.

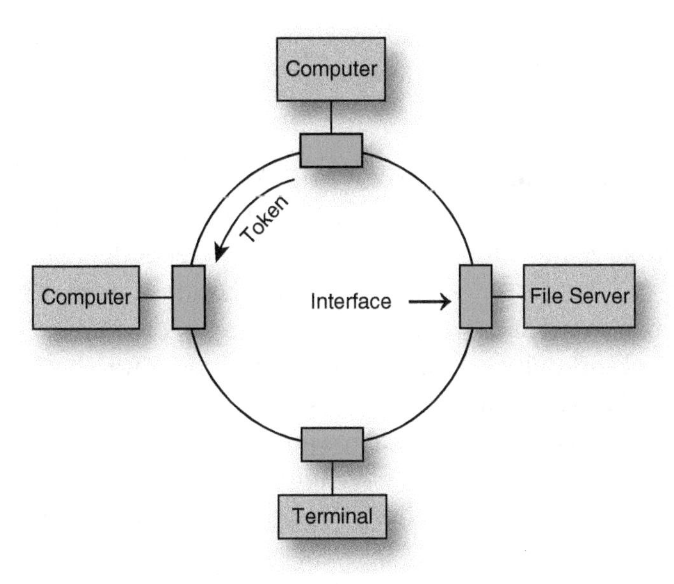

Figure 5.2 Token ring network. Source: Illustration by James L. Pelkey and Loring G. Robbins.

Dangerous game, but quite often, certainly necessary in the academic world."[30] It paid off, and NSF approved the contract renewal.

By late 1973, they completed the software needed to connect a computer to the network. Expecting to take a week or two to get a multinode network functioning, they had a three-computer network passing tokens in a day. As Farber remembers: "It went very fast." By early 1974, they had a semi-stable network. Again Farber: "At that point it got very popular, and it was a very strange situation. People started hearing about it and we would get these phone calls saying: 'We'd like to come down and see it.' We'd say: 'You mean you want to talk?' They would respond: 'No, we want to see it!'"[31]

Farber and his team at UCI proved that another way existed for linking distributed computers. However, their interest was distributed software systems, not in the advancement of computer communications. So they did little to actively promote their token ring technology. But their success would not go unnoticed. In just a few years, their token ring technology—technology funded by the government and thus in the public domain—would be resurrected in response to market

30. Farber interview, Computer History Museum.

31. Farber interview, Computer History Museum.

demands emanating from Xerox's refusal to sell its local area networking technology, a technology developed by Robert Metcalfe at Xerox Palo Alto Research Center (PARC).

5.6.2 Ethernet, Robert Metcalfe, and Xerox PARC, 1971–1975

Last observed at the ICCC demonstration described at the end of Chapter 3, an incredulous Metcalfe couldn't believe the mocking laughter of the group of AT&T executives when the ARPANET momentarily failed. Metcalfe thought them insensitive to all the hard work and hopeful visions he and his colleagues shared—another example of the abusive, arbitrary behavior of those with authority and power. Admittedly, his ire may have been easily provoked for his world had been thrown into disarray by a felt injustice suffered just months earlier. To understand Metcalfe's state of mind and how his unrelenting resolve set him on the course to invent the seminal local area networking technology of Ethernet requires us to return to the end of 1971.

When asked by Kahn to help with the organization of the ICCC, Metcalfe had every reason to feel he had earned his way into the inner circle of those giving birth to the ARPANET. So, despite the fact that the first half of 1972 already loomed as too busy to contemplate—his Ph.D. thesis had to be finished and defended in June and he had to find a job, one that would hopefully start in July—Metcalfe agreed to help. His uninformed decision 2 years earlier to focus on networking, and then to write his thesis on the ARPANET, now seemed uncannily prescient, as if some predestined momentum was sweeping him forward into a larger future.

Interviews confirmed his sense of being part of something important. Most opportunities smacked of bringing others up to speed, of transferring what he already knew and little appreciation for how much needed to be redone. The same could not be said for his interviews with Jerry Elkind and Robert Taylor, dual heads of the Computer Science Lab of Xerox PARC. Elkind and Taylor, formerly of BBN and IPTO, respectively, challenged him not simply to extend his ARPANET experiences but to join a team dedicated to building a new paradigm of "office automation." He liked everything he heard, including the Bay Area location, and agreed to start in July, after defending his Ph.D.

In the early spring, ICCC responsibilities took Metcalfe to Washington, DC, and, as usual, he stayed at the home of his good friend, Steve Crocker. After a customary late evening of spirited conversation, Metcalfe retired to his bed, the living room couch. Restless, he grabbed the *1970 Proceedings of the Fall Joint Computer Conference* off the adjacent coffee table in hopes of reading himself to sleep, but his attention immediately focused on an article by Norm Abramson titled "The

ALOHA System—Another alternative for computer communications." Metcalfe vividly remembers:

> I'm reading this paper about how the ALOHAnet worked, statistically. The model Abramson used was infuriating to me. Infuriating, because it was based on a model that was tractable but inaccurate. In other words, you assume a bunch of things about a system that make the mathematics do-able, but the assumptions are highly questionable. So, I'm reading Abramson's work and it struck me the same way, which is: Assume that you have an infinite number of people sitting at keyboards, and they just type. No matter what happens they just keep typing. Even if they get no answer they just keep typing. Let's see how the system performs. Well, when I read that, I said: "But people don't. They DO stop typing! I mean if they don't get an answer, they wait. This is not accurate." Now it was Poisson processes and exponential distributions and all that stuff that you can just math to death, and it all works out in a beautiful closed form formula. The trouble was, in my mind, that the ALOHA system was not being properly modeled. Mind you at the time, I was a graduate student dying to find some mathematics to put in my thesis.[32]

In June, a confident Metcalfe presented his thesis to his Harvard professors:

> It was rejected, and I was thrown out on my ass! But, imagine the scene—Here's this graduate student who did all of his work at MIT, shows up to defend his thesis among a bunch of professors for whom he had carried no water for the preceding 3 years and they are asked to make a judgment on the intellectual content of my thesis. I got blown out of the water by them.[33]

Metcalfe's thesis was rejected for not being sufficiently mathematical or theoretical. A stunned Metcalfe, doubting he could find the needed new, undiscovered, theoretical or mathematical content in ARPANET, decided he had to go to Hawaii and learn more about the ALOHAnet. Contacting Abramson, he received a gracious invitation. Then he had to convince his new employer to give him the needed time off. On hearing Metcalfe's disappointing news, PARC management couldn't have been more supportive. Other than bringing PARC up on the ARPANET, their IMP would not be installed until October, Metcalfe was given the freedom to do what he needed to do to beef up his thesis and satisfy his commitments to Kahn. In

32. Robert Metcalfe, oral history interview by James L. Pelkey, February 16, 1988, Portola Valley, CA. Computer History Museum, Mountain View, CA. Available from https://archive.computerhistory.org/resources/access/text/2013/05/102746650-05-01-acc.pdf.

33. Metcalfe interview, Computer History Museum.

Hawaii, a serious-minded Metcalfe focused on what he needed to learn and, other than playing a few games of tennis and tipping a few beers with two of Abramson's graduate students, Charlie Bass and John Davidson, he worked and did little else. Abramson remembers: "We went out to dinner a couple of times, that kind of interaction, and he was rather closed-mouthed about what he was doing and I didn't want to push him."[34]

To understand the ALOHAnet, Metcalfe began constructing mathematical models and comparing the results to actual data. He also modeled what would happen if people only typed when they got answers; and when they received no answer, they stopped and waited until they did—a condition known as blocking. Metcalfe remembers that "it became obvious the system had some stability problems." He continued:

> But in the process of modeling that with a finite population model, meaning people stop typing when they did not get an answer, I saw an obvious way to fix the stability problem. I had studied some control theory at MIT, and this was a control problem. That is, the more collisions you got, the less aggressive you should be about transmitting. You should calm down. And, in fact, the model I used was the Santa Monica freeway. It turns out that the throughput characteristics of freeway traffic are similar to that of an ALOHA system, which means that the throughput goes up with offered traffic to a certain point where you have congestion and then the throughput actually goes down with additional traffic, which is why you get traffic jams. The simple phenomenon is that, psychologically, people tend to go slower when they're closer to the car in front of them so as the cars get closer and closer together and people slow down the throughput goes down, so they get closer and closer and the system degrades. So it was a really simple step to take the ALOHA network, and when you sent a message and you got a collision, you would just take that as evidence that the network was crowded. So, when you went to re-transmit, you'd relax for a while, a random while, and then try again. If you got another collision you would say "Whoa, it's REALLY crowded," and you'd randomize and back off a little. So the "carrier sense" expression meant "Is there anybody on there yet?"[35]

Metcalfe did not yet realize that his seminal insight of collision detection would have important implications once back at PARC when confronted with

34. Norm Abramson, oral history interview with James L. Pelkey, October 13, 1988, Menlo Park, CA. Computer History Museum, Mountain View, CA. Available from https://archive.computerhistory.org/resources/access/text/2013/05/102746645-05-01-acc.pdf.

35. Metcalfe interview, Computer History Museum.

interconnecting many computers. Metcalfe presented his findings at a University of Hawaii systems conference.

Returning to PARC, Metcalfe dove into the problems of interconnecting the PARC computers to the ARPANET and writing up the Scenarios for the upcoming ICCC show. When he finally surfaced for air in late October, both projects completed, PARC management challenged him to conceive and develop a communications network able to support the needs of many Altos computers and peripherals such as the also-being-developed laser printers. This "next generation" computing environment posed unprecedented communication requirements because of the use of bit-mapped graphics both as user interface and document output. Voluminous computer communications would be routine, not the exception as with ARPANET. If the required communications could not be reliably supported, PARC's new vision of computing might prove to be just a dream.

Fortunately for Metcalfe, PARC management understood that a proprietary approach to innovation could erect competitive barriers-to-entry that would, in turn, have consequences for the new paradigm of computing. They had no interest in Metcalfe replicating the work of others, encouraging him instead to view the problem with an unbiased perspective and engineer a best solution. For Metcalfe, management's mandate impelled him to treat his growing intuition of computer communications not just as thesis-driven speculation but an opportunity worth seizing. In short, a prepared and motivated individual had encountered inviting conditions.

Metcalfe fully understood the dynamic state of computer communications and scanned the literature for any relevant developments that might influence his work. On learning of Farber's work at UCI, he obtained a copy of his February IEEE paper. (Metcalfe: "We became friendly archrivals.") He also contacted Cerf, an assistant professor now just 10 minutes away at Stanford, and started attending his graduate seminar on networking. In early 1973, Metcalfe participated in the discussions Cerf and Kahn were having as to how to redesign the ARPANET NCP protocol.

On May 22, 1973, Metcalfe distributed a memo marked Xerox sensitive to the ALTO ALOHA team. The subject: Ether Acquisition. The evolution in Metcalfe's thinking is clearly documented:

> While we may end up using coaxial cable trees to carry our broadcast transmissions, it seems wise to talk in terms of an ether, rather than "the cable," for as long as possible. This will keep things general and who knows what other media will prove better than cable for a broadcast network; maybe radio or telephone circuits, or power wiring or frequency-multiplexed CATV,

> or microwave environments, or even combinations thereof. The essential feature of our medium—the ether—is that it carries transmissions, propagates bits to all stations. We are to investigate the applicability of ether networks.[36]

But not everyone was impressed with the scope of Metcalfe's vision. Metcalfe remembers encountering Leonard Kleinrock at Washington National Airport and showing him the mathematics in his Ph.D. thesis. Metcalfe was annoyed at Kleinrock's reaction: "He told me it was: 'Not very rigorous.' He pooh-poohed it."[37]

Metcalfe kept pushing, and by May he had finished adding the mathematics of how the ALOHAnet worked to his thesis and re-submitted it to his new thesis advisor, Jeff Busen. This time it was accepted and Metcalfe received his Ph.D. in June 1973. Metcalfe notes ironically: "Indicative of how I got it—Harvard University did not publish my Ph.D. thesis. It was published by MIT, Project MAC, where I had done all the work. So it was the thesis finished at Xerox, for a Harvard Ph.D. thesis, published by MIT—Mac Technical Report #114."[38]

In June, Metcalfe was given the go-ahead to build a prototype Ethernet.[39] (Since Ethernet will become its known name, our convention will be to use it from the beginning.) Metcalfe remembers:

---

36. Bob Metcalfe to Alto Aloha Distribution, "*Ether Acquisition*," May 22, 1973. "Ethernet Files, Blue Book, announcement NYC," Catalog Number 102740417, Computer History Museum, Mountain View, CA. Available from https://www.computerhistory.org/collections/catalog/102740417. Metcalfe describes the thinking behind the name in his interview with Pelkey: "I had been an MIT student and one of the things we studied in physics was Michelson and Morley's experiment to prove there was no ether, or ether wind, and following that experiment there was no ether so the word ether—the luminiferous, it was now a free word. And what the ether was, the original ether was, was an omnipresent passive medium for the propagation of electromagnetic waves, namely, light. And that word was no longer useful. So what this cable was that we were going to use, the cable was going to be everywhere, totally passive, that is, no switches, no power, just copper and insulation, passive, everywhere, and what was it going to do? It was going to be a medium for the propagation of electromagnetic waves, data packets, hence the cable is the ether... So it was an ether, and so it was a network using an ether, so it was an Ethernet." Metcalfe interview, Computer History Museum.

37. Metcalfe interview, Computer History Museum.

38. Metcalfe interview, Computer History Museum.

39. Kahn opines on Metcalfe's conceiving Ethernet: "Bob was superb in making something like that work simply and effectively. That was his brilliance. It was an engineering coup." Robert Kahn, oral history interview with James L. Pelkey, February 22, 1988, Reston, VA. Computer History Museum, Mountain View, CA. Available from https://archive.computerhistory.org/resources/access/text/2016/10/102717241-05-01-acc.pdf.

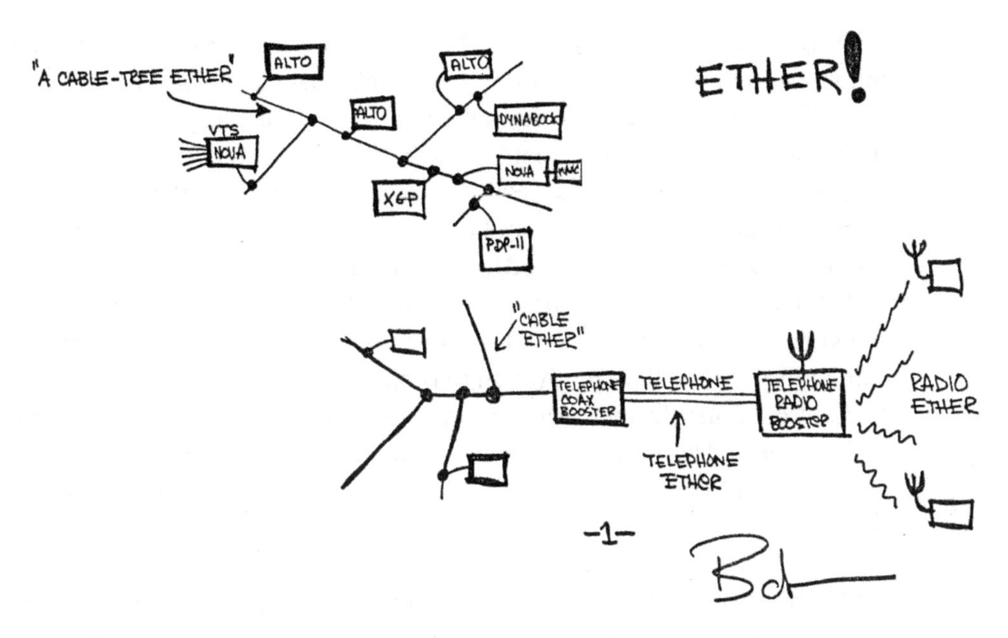

Figure 5.3 Metcalfe's 1972 sketch. Source: Image provided courtesy of the PARC Library.

> I needed to kind of get the project going; do the logic design, build the boards, write the microcode, etc. And I don't like to work alone. In fact, I believe the ideal operating unit is two people. Three is too many and one isn't enough. Two is perfect. So I went out looking for somebody to work with me, and one day, I saw this guy in moccasins with a ponytail down to his back padding his way through Building 34 at PARC. And he didn't look busy. He looked like he didn't have enough to do. So, I checked into it and it turned out he was a graduate student from Stanford who was working for David Liddle. I asked David about him and David said: "Well, why don't you get him to work on your project with you?" So I approached David R. Boggs and propositioned him and we entered into a 2-year long project together.[40]

The Ethernet project required fleshing out Metcalfe's preliminary design, building the hardware to attach the computers to the connecting coaxial cable, and designing and coding the networking protocol so computers and peripherals could share information (see Figure 5.3). Metcalfe realized that he needed a more streamlined communications protocol than the NCP of ARPANET or the new protocol being designed by Cerf and Kahn that had to function over may different kinds of networks.

40. Metcalfe interview, Computer History Museum.

By year-end 1973, as Metcalfe and Boggs progressed from design to implementation, Metcalfe found he had little time to participate in the Cerf-led sessions. He had his own project deadlines to meet that required making choices and reducing those choices to hardware and software. Further constraining Metcalfe's relationship with Cerf was Xerox's confidentiality requirements that restricted what Metcalfe could disclose to Cerf and his colleagues. Without being able to openly discuss his work, Metcalfe derived little benefit from the more academic and open-ended discussions being moderated by Cerf. Because Cerf was acting under the aegis of DARPA, seeking at first to bring about a standard from within a very diverse community, he had little motivation to cooperate or resolve issues in a fixed time frame. Consequently, the early development of local area networking protocols being pioneered by Metcalfe and Boggs proceeded down a very different technical path than Cerf's and Kahn's redoing of NCP, a digression that would soon become important.

Metcalfe's design objective for Ethernet was a communication system that could "grow smoothly to accommodate several buildings full of personal computers and facilities needed for their support." Two secondary, yet desirable, objectives were that it had to be inexpensive and, preferably, distribute control to eliminate the "bottleneck" inherent in centralized control. Metcalfe's design incorporated architectural contributions from ARPANET and ALOHAnet: packet-based communications with broadcast transmission. Beginning with "the basic idea of packet collision and retransmission developed in the ALOHA Network," Metcalfe added his collision detection insight. Computers or peripherals would constantly listen to the communication channel (the "Ether") and only send—broadcast—their messages when they detected a clear channel. If collisions with packets being sent by other stations were detected, all sending stations would stop transmitting, wait intervals of time in proportion to the frequency of collisions, and retransmit. If collisions occurred again, the transmitting computers would wait a longer interval and retry, repeating the process until successful. What makes Ethernet possible is most messages are short, hundreds or thousands of bits, compared to the communication channel bandwidth of 3 megabits per second—the very same principle recognized a decade earlier by Baran and Davies.[41]

The final design of the Ethernet network proved elegantly simple: some hardware to interconnect computers and peripherals so they could exchange bits

41. Robert M. Metcalfe and David R. Boggs. 1976. Ethernet: distributed packet switching for local computer networks. *Communications of the ACM* 19 (July 1976), 395–404. https://doi.org/10.1145/360248.360253.

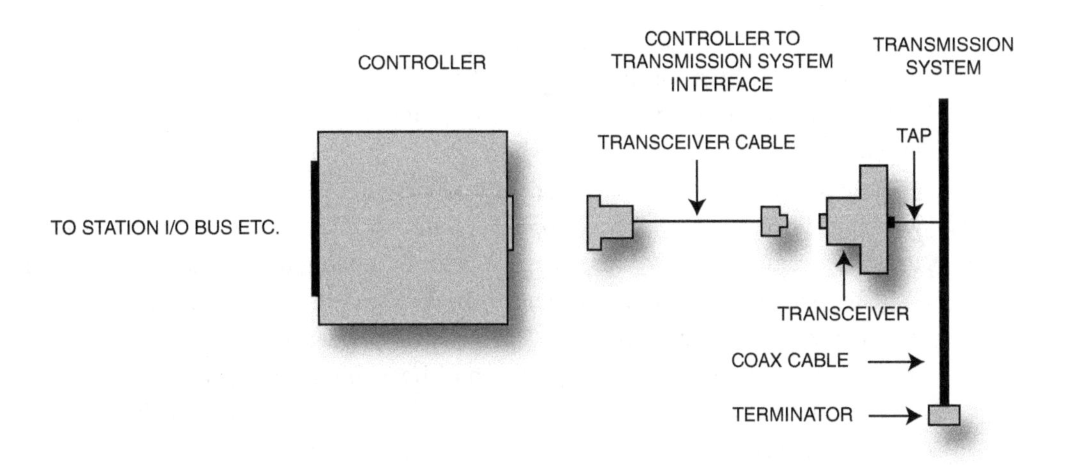

Figure 5.4 Ethernet design. Illustration by James L. Pelkey and Loring G. Robbins, based on Shotwell, Robyn. *The Ethernet Sourcebook.* North-Holland, 1985.

and a networking protocol to make sense of the bits (see Figure 5.4). The hardware consists of interface controllers, transceivers and taps, and a transmission media. An interface controller, or adapter, connects to the backplane, or bus, of computer equipment (Ethernet stations) and sends and receives formatted data to the transceiver. The transceiver converts the digital data coming from or going to an interface controller to analog signals required by the transmission media (communication facility). In effect, the transceiver acts like a modem. Taps are needed to physically connect transceivers to the transmission media with minimal disruption during connecting or disconnecting.[42] And finally, there is the transmission media needed to transport the signals. The first transmission media was coaxial cable, initially with its famous yellow sheathing. To interconnect two or more Ethernets, an additional piece of equipment, a repeater, is needed.

The networking protocol is implemented in software to execute in both the Ethernet stations and the interface controllers and provides the essential services of "error correction, flow control, process naming, security and accounting."[43] The networking protocol Metcalfe and Boggs created—PARC Universal Packet, or

42. In a typical example of collaborative research, Liddle, who had worked for a cable TV company while in school, proposed the use of passive taps as used in cable TV, a technology outside the purview of Metcalfe and a technology that worked just fine at first.

43. Metcalfe and Boggs, "Ethernet."

Pup—leveraged the knowledge and experience gained from ARPA's creation of NCP and its re-creation being led by Cerf and Kahn. Pup was in fact a hierarchy of protocols that enabled end-to-end functionality, including file transfer and email[44].

By late 1974, Metcalfe and Boggs had a 3-megabit per second Ethernet with Pup working. Once successful, Xerox filed for patents covering the Ethernet technology under the names of Metcalfe, Boggs, Butler Lampson, and Chuck Thacker. (Metcalfe insisted that the names of Lampson, the "intellectual guru under whom we all had the privilege to work," and Thacker, "the guy who designed the Altos," both were on the patent.) Once the patent had been filed, Metcalfe and Boggs could publish their work, submitting a paper to the *Communications of the ACM* titled "Ethernet: Distributed packet switching for local computer networks." Published in July 1976, it became a foundational paper for all work on local area networks to follow. By mid-1975, PARC had installed a 100-node Ethernet network that was robust by 1976.

5.6.3 Massachusetts Institute of Technology, 1974–1977

In 1974, the only effective means computer scientists at MIT had to interconnect their computers were two IMPs. This was an increasingly unacceptable solution, especially given what was known about Metcalfe's work, enviously nicknamed "ALOHAnet on a wire." Thus, MIT scientists were challenged to either build or buy local area networks.

The Artificial Intelligence (AI) Laboratory acted first. Taxed by their own research agenda, they had little desire to develop their own local area networking technology and approached PARC about buying Ethernet products. Xerox declined the opportunity. Xerox viewed Ethernet as proprietary and integral to their office systems and not a product to be sold separately. Professor Jerry Saltzer, one of the first to become involved in network development for the Laboratory of Computer Science (LCS), remembers:

> Xerox had invented and built the first version of the Ethernet, but still considered it proprietary and would not allow anyone to use the internal knowledge. The fact that it worked was sufficient for someone else to say: "Well, in that case, we'll build one too." So the AI Laboratory built Chaosnet. The only reason it was invented was because we couldn't use Ethernet. Chaosnet was

44. David R. Boggs, John F. Shoch, Edward A. Taft, and Robert M. Metcalfe. 1980. Pup: An internetwork architecture. *IEEE Transactions on Communications* Vol. Com-28 (April 1980), 612–624.

> essentially another Ethernet that had slight differences, but the differences aren't important enough to worry about.[45]

In 1975, the LCS became serious about local area networking. Michael Dertouzos, the head of LCS, after discussion with Saltzer and Dave Clark, a research associate, directed Ken Pogran to investigate available local area networking technologies. DARPA, learning of LCS's interests, lobbied MIT to import the token ring technology developed at UC Irvine by Farber, rather than creating a new technology.

Pogran visited PARC and spent a day being briefed by a clean-shaven Metcalfe, a business-like contrast to the Metcalfe he had known during the earlier ARPANET days. Pogran then visited Farber and learned of his plans to create a second-generation token ring employing graduate students, not to study token ring per se, but needing an improved token ring to do research in distributed systems.

On his return to MIT, Pogran presented his findings to Dertouzos, Saltzer, and Clark. They decided against Chaosnet, since they knew that future product support and development would be a low priority for the AI Lab, and LCS couldn't replicate the AI Lab's hardware development capabilities. Since Xerox wouldn't share its technology, their only alternatives were either to create a new technology or import UC Irvine's token ring technology. LCS chose token ring even knowing graduate students were developing the version of the product they would use.

LCS began planning what Dertouzos called the "76 Net." Pogran began as project manager but soon took on direct engineering tasks that no one at UC Irvine had either the time or ability for. Despite his efforts, Pogran could not meet the original schedule, but he did finally deliver operational LNIs (Local Network Interfaces) in 1977, supporting a 1-megabit per second token ring network. That same year, 1977, Saltzer, took his sabbatical from MIT, and spent a year working for IBM.

> I was working in White Plains, but I traveled quite a bit, and one of my stops was in Zurich. I discovered that they were interested in token rings, so we proceeded to compare notes, and I basically supplied them with every piece of information we had. The Zurich laboratory had as its charter to do communications, and it was trying to figure out if it could do something useful in the area of local area network communications. At this time, the only local area network in all of Europe was the Cambridge Ring at Cambridge University, U.K. Ethernet was something being done 5,000 miles farther away than

45. Jerome H. "Jerry" Saltzer, oral history interview by James L. Pelkey, March 7, 1988, Cambridge, MA. Computer History Museum, Mountain View, CA. Available from https://archive.computerhistory.org/resources/access/text/2016/10/102717242-05-01-acc.pdf.

> a token ring. Xerox was also a competing company, and it was hard to get inside to look at what they were doing.[46]

Saltzer's opinions, based on his early experience with token ring at LCS, reinforced IBM's historical preference for deterministic, synchronous protocols. The initial diffusion of Farber's and UC Irvine's token ring technology to IBM had occurred months earlier with Phillipe Janson. Clark adds:

> Phillipe Janson, after receiving his Ph.D. from MIT in 1976, joined IBM in Zurich. It's my belief that when Zurich was looking to build a network, and they didn't want to build an Ethernet because they had a strong dose of "not invented here," and Janson was the one that suggested that they ought to build rings based on his experience at MIT.[47]

LCS Network represented an incremental innovation on the token ring technology imported from UC Irvine. For example, concerned with finding wiring faults, the LCS Network connected each network node through a central "wiring closet," giving rise to a star topology that would become standard for future token ring networks.[48]

5.6.4 Metcalfe Joins the Systems Development Division of Xerox, 1975–1978

Despite his success, Metcalfe was frustrated within a strictly research environment. He enjoyed the energy and excitement of engaging in leading edge research, but he also wanted the satisfaction from succeeding in putting ideas to use. He wanted to be more than an engineer. In November 1975, he left Xerox PARC for Transaction Technology Inc., an advanced product development organization of Citibank. In just 7 months, he was wooed back to Xerox by David Liddle to join the newly formed Systems Development Division (SDD). SDD's charter specifically called for the commercialization of the Alto's technologies, including Ethernet.

Commercializing the Alto's technologies required more than simply selling what existed. The entire system, including Ethernet, had to be reengineered to improve performance, reduce costs, and made ready for manufacturing. The initial goal for Ethernet was to increase performance from 3 megabits per second to 20 megabits per second and commensurably improve Pup.

46. Saltzer interview, Computer History Museum.

47. David D. Clark, oral history interview by James L. Pelkey, March 7, 1988, Cambridge, MA. Computer History Museum, Mountain View, CA. Available from https://archive.computerhistory.org/resources/access/text/2018/02/102738738-05-01-acc.pdf.

48. Another important contribution was the symmetry of the starter token. D.D. Clark, K.T. Pogran, and D.P. Reed. 1978. An introduction to local area networks. *Proceedings of the IEEE* 66 (Nov 1978), 1497–1517. doi: 10.1109/PROC.1978.11152.

Liddle remembers the controversy surrounding the decision to increase the throughput, or bandwidth, of Ethernet to 20 megabits per second.

> The people at PARC complained about this a lot, and said: "Why isn't three megabits good enough?" We simply said: "We didn't think three megabits would be good enough over this time horizon," because we thought there would be more movement of big files and databases and printing big images, and the product was really virtually playing almost the role of a bus, not an old-fashion "beep, beep, beep" communication line. This was somewhat controversial because it increased the cost and subtlety of designing some of the components.[49]

By late summer 1976, Metcalfe needed to find someone knowledgeable with the latest in protocol developments, including TCP, to lead the redo of Pup protocol. Metcalfe understood the design of Ethernet inside and out but felt like an outsider looking in when it came to protocol development. Fortunately, just such an experienced person existed, Yogen Dalal. Metcalfe knew Dalal and held him in high regard. Dalal would be completing his Ph.D. under Cerf at Stanford in early 1977.

Hiring Dalal would not be easy for he also was being strenuously recruited by Kahn at DARPA, Tomlinson at BBN, Taylor at PARC, and Steve Crocker at Information Sciences Institute. What gave Metcalfe an edge was Dalal's abiding interest in communication protocols. In 1975, he had been a member of Cerf's team coding and testing TCP. Dalal was also a member of the TCP Working Group and deeply involved in the effort to architect a second version of TCP to reflect what had been learned in the testing and use of the first version.

Independently, in September 1976, Dalal's mentor, Cerf, suddenly resigned both his teaching position at Stanford and Chairmanship of IFIP Working Group 6.1 to join DARPA, where he would manage the packet communication technologies, the Internet project, and the network security program.[50] Cerf's impact on networking would continue both through his own contributions and those of his many students, including Dalal, Carl Sunshine, Richard Karp, Jim Mathis, Ron Crane,

49. David Liddle, oral history interview by James L. Pelkey, October 11, 1988, Mountain View, CA. Computer History Museum, Mountain View, CA. Available from https://archive.computerhistory.org/resources/access/text/2013/05/102746649-05-01-acc.pdf.

50. By late 1976, the ARPA Packet Radio Network, ARPANET, and the Atlantic Packet Satellite Network were connected together using two gateways between the Packet Radio Network and ARPANET and three gateways between the ARPANET and the Packet Satellite Network. The gateways, the store-and-forward packet switches that enable the networks to be interconnected, signaled the emergence of a new class of devices performing internetworking.

Darryl Rubin, John Shoch, and Judith Estrin, the daughter of Jerry Estrin, Cerf's thesis advisor at UCLA.

With Cerf at DARPA, Dalal decided to strike out on his own independent of Cerf. In the end, Metcalfe's offer to create the successor protocol to Pup was simply too good to resist. After joining SDD in 1977, Dalal began assembling his team—including Will Crowther, once a critical member of BBN's ARPANET team, and Hal Murray—and conducting an in-depth review of Pup. Metcalfe also recruited James White, whom he had known from his ARPANET days and who was now working at Stanford Research Institute, to become Manager of the Communications Software Group in 1977.[51] In addition to working on the redesign of Pup, White's Group assumed responsibility for commercializing a PARC-developed, distributed-Ethernet-based electronic mail system called "Grapevine."[52]

By early 1978, with Ethernet working and product sales no closer than when he had joined SDD, Metcalfe found himself frustrated and restless. Wanting to see his Ethernet technology commercialized before others exploited the opportunity, he argued that Xerox should sell Ethernet products unbundled from computer systems. However, management did not see it his way. In the spring of 1978, Metcalfe issued management an ultimatum, with the veiled threat that he would resign unless Ethernet be made available for sale. He remembers:

> When I came back to Xerox in 1976, we were about two and a half years from product shipment, and in 1978 we were about two and a half years from product shipment. And my analysis, at the time amateurish, was that there were things other than engineering that you needed to do right to succeed, and, apparently, since we were so good at engineering, the problems must be in marketing or manufacturing or something, and so I wanted to find out more about those, because I hated failing and we were—WE, not they, WE were failing. Since I was buried in an engineering organization, I gave Xerox 7 months' notice and said I want to at least report to a general manager.[53]

Metcalfe did not get his wish, and true to his word, left Xerox at the end of 1978 to become an independent consultant.

51. White had been recruited to SRI in 1972 by John Melvin, a system programmer whom he had met at NWG meetings. Jon Postel, who joined SRI after receiving his Ph.D. from UCLA and, after a brief detour through MITRE in Washington, DC, worked with White. (During this entire period, Postel retained responsibility for the Request for Comments (RFCs), facilitated by his work at SRI, the Network Information Center (NIC), and repository of all on-line RFCs.) White and Postel worked on a family of protocols that would allow computer procedures to span multiple networks.

52. White would become a key contributor to the standardization of email with ISO.

53. Metcalfe interview, Computer History Museum.

5.6.5 Xerox Network System, 1977–1978

When joining Xerox's SDD in 1977 to lead the re-engineering of the Pup communication protocol, Dalal, like most curious computer scientists, had some knowledge of the breadth of innovations underway within PARC and thus within SDD. However, scant facts woven together with rumor were no match for the actual experience of using a graphic-based Altos computer connected to other Altos/minicomputers, and to peripherals (such as laser printers), using the high-speed Ethernet local area network. Dalal quickly realized the Altos vision was not just another computer innovation but foreshadowed a sea change about to revolutionize computing. He also knew those re-architecting TCP had not contemplated a future populated with thousands, even millions, of networks. Dalal remembers his surprising revelation:

> It became clear to me after I had left Stanford to go to Xerox the impact that local area networks would have on internetworking, and that while the theoretical problems associated with internetworking had been solved in the DARPA context, new light was being shed on what personal computers might want of an internetworking protocol.[54]

As Metcalfe had before him, Dalal tried to participate in both the proprietary, I-am-an-employee-and-am-restricted-in-what-I-can-say, world of Xerox and the academic–government social system driving the creation of TCP. He too found that he had neither the time nor willingness to deal with the conflicts of participating in both communities, and therefore focused on Pup. To that task he brought an extensive knowledge of TCP and used it to influence the redesign of Pup.[55]

By the end of 1977, the first draft specifications for Xerox's next generation communication protocol had been created. To become known as Xerox Network System (XNS), it was designed for the new higher speed Ethernet and extended the datagram architecture in Pup to accommodate gateways, or routers, between networks. XNS separated the functions of routing a datagram (a Pup in Xerox's lexicon) or internet packet through multiple networks from the functions of communicating end-to-end over a network, such as an Ethernet LAN. In XNS, the network layer

54. Yogen Dalal, oral history interview by James L. Pelkey, August 2, 1988, Santa Clara, CA. Computer History Museum, Mountain View, CA. Available from https://archive.computerhistory.org/resources/access/text/2018/02/102738752-05-01-acc.pdf.

55. The flow of knowledge and people between the TCP and Pup communities proved bi-directional. As Dalal left Stanford for SDD, John Shoch left PARC for Stanford to pursue his Ph.D. in computer science. Shoch, fully steeped in Pup and communication protocols in general, became an influential member of the TCP community; one who fully appreciated the coming role of local area networks.

consisted of both an "internet sublayer" and "network-specific sublayer."[56] XNS, like Pup, supported multiple transport protocols, including a virtual circuit protocol as a network-specific-sublayer. This separation of the network and transport functions would ripple through all future networking protocols. A future of multiple heterogeneous networks, especially Ethernet networks that by design involved significant retransmissions, posed serious problems for TCP version 2.

5.6.6 TCP to TCP/IP, 1976–1979

In 1976, DARPA forwarded its newly specified TCP version 2 to MIT's LCS hoping to gain their support for its use. Michael Dertouzos, head of LCS, assigned Dave Reed the responsibility of review and comment. Reed, with help from Dave Clark and others, wrote a memo to DARPA in November 1976, proposing an alternative to TCP they called Data Stream Protocol (DSP). Kahn had absolutely no interest in having one of DARPA's primary research centers develop an orthogonal protocol to TCP and immediately convened a meeting.

Kahn remembers:

> Dave Reed had come up with another protocol because he didn't like TCP. I sat down with Dave and others from MIT, and they described the Data Stream Protocol, and I said: "But that's what TCP is like, with one minor difference." And they said: "No, it isn't. Read what Vint says in this report." And I said: "That's just the way he interpreted it. Go back to our original paper, and you'll see you could interpret it your way too." So even that original paper that we wrote was subject to multiple interpretations about how you actually do the implementation.[57]

Kahn, knowing he had to convince MIT to align behind TCP and abandon DSP, assured them an influential role if they dropped their DSP ideas. Reed and Clark began going to meetings and soon Clark—who was then working on both interconnecting LCS's Multics computer to the ARPANET and developing their token-passing LAN, LCS Net—became a key participant in TCP activities.[58] Clark remembers:

> So we started going to the meetings and, in fact, although Dave (Reed) was the one who wrote the DSP memos, I was the one that got interested in the

56. Yogen K. Dalal. 1982. Use of multiple networks in the Xerox Network System. *IEEE Computer*, Oct. 1982, 82–92.

57. Kahn interview, Computer History Museum.

58. Clark, who had received his Ph.D. in 1973 from MIT with a thesis of pulling the I/O system out of the kernel of the Multics operating system, realized afterwards that he had not solved the problems for multiplexing devices such as networks, and stayed on at LCS as a post-doc to connect a Multics computer to the ARPANET.

> meetings and started going. And during the remainder of the decade, while a lot of local network was going on at MIT, I got more involved in the TCP activities.[59]

Before long, Clark too saw the need to split network-to-network, or internet, functions from the end-to-end, or transport, functions within TCP. Dalal recalls:

> The concept of the datagram evolved out of some gentle hints that were coming out of John Shoch, David Boggs, and myself who were working now on Pup and XNS. Pup was then beginning to be disclosed, but even before Pup had been disclosed, we tried to convince Vint and Jon Postel and others of the importance of breaking things into a datagram (internet) and a session protocol (transport)—primarily because datagrams are useful in local area networking contexts. It was Vint and Dave Clark and Jon Postel that saw that immediately, and slowly started modifying TCP.[60]

In 1978, Clark, Reed, and Kenneth Pogran published an IEEE paper calling for the separation of LAN communication protocols into two layers, calling this a "natural" structure for low-level protocols. In this view, the bottom layer provides the basic function of delivering messages to various destinations, while the higher layer is made available to a variety of protocols.[61]

By 1978, it had become clear that TCP Version 2 had to be changed to accommodate all kinds of network interconnections. Work to split it into two layers, network and transport, began. TCP/IP was first known as TCP Version 4. The new network layer protocols, also to be known as internet protocols (from <u>inter</u>connected <u>net</u>works), enabled seamless interconnection of networks without impacting the internal operations of any network. Jon Postel described the internet layer protocol or IP protocol:

> In summary, the ARPA Internet Protocol (TCP/IP) supports delivery of datagrams from an internet source to a single internet destination. IP treats each datagram as an independent entity unrelated to any other datagram. There are not connections or logical circuits (virtual or otherwise). There are no acknowledgments either end-to-end or hop-to-hop. There is no error control for data, only a header checksum. There are no retransmissions. There

59. Clark interview, Computer History Museum.

60. Dalal interview, Computer History Museum. Cerf adds: "Danny Cohen at ISI who developed two versions of Network Voice Protocol deserves credit also for influencing the separation of IP from TCP." Cerf interview, Computer History Museum.

61. Clark, Pogran, and Reed, "An introduction to local area networks," 1512.

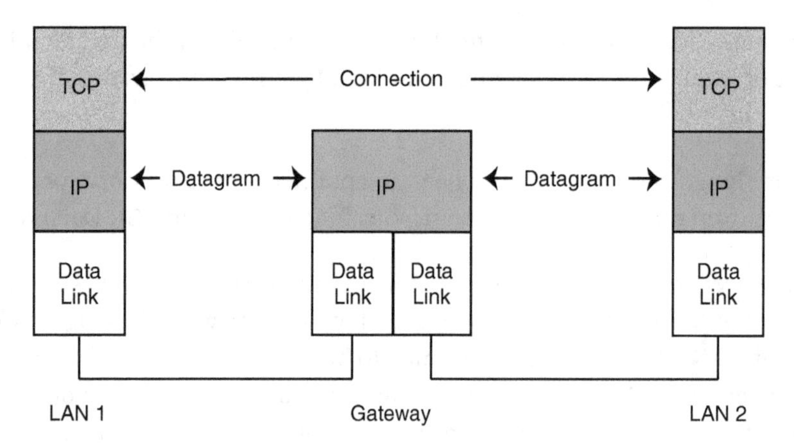

Figure 5.5 TCP/IP transmission model. Source: Illustration by James L. Pelkey and Loring G. Robins, based on personal communication with John Day.

> is minimal flow control. For flexibility, it is explicitly left to higher level protocols to provide these functions.[62]

Gateways, specialized computers used to interconnect networks, routed traffic over the networks using the internet protocols (see Figure 5.5). The separation of the network functions from TCP then enabled the creation of different transport layer protocols including a reliable end-to-end service, such as virtual circuits (TCP).

In 1979, DARPA decided to emphasize the use of DEC's new VAX series computers. Since DEC had already decided to use Ethernet to interconnect their VAX computers and their peripherals, having TCP/IP operate over Ethernet became essential. Only there was first the problem of what operating system to use. Kahn explained, "We came to the conclusion in 1979, with a lot of input from the community, I might add, that what we really ought to do was go with the VAX, since it was the only appropriate machine around. Unfortunately, they weren't very happy with VMS or UNIX."[63]

DARPA awarded a contract to the University of California at Berkeley to take the UNIX system, put it on the VAX, and add all these other features. DARPA awarded a contract to BBN to convert TCP/IP to UNIX. Berkeley was to then take the BBN port of TCP/IP and integrate it with the UNIX port to the VAX. As we will see, this set of actions—federal support to implement TCP/IP in a popular and powerful

62. Postel, Sunshine, and Cohen. 1981. The ARPA internet protocol. *Computer Networks* 5, 261–271.

63. Kahn interview, Computer History Museum.

operating system—would have a significant impact in resolving the proliferation and confusion amongst networking protocols.

The need to separate the network and transport layers made so obvious by LANs also affected protocol development efforts in Europe. That story begins in 1975, when the bulk of researchers in IFIP Working Group 6.1 moved to a new institutional home, the International Organization for Standardization (ISO).

5.6.7 Open System Interconnection (OSI) 1975–1979

In 1975 the European members of IFIP Working Group 6.1 reluctantly concluded that the Americans—specifically those connected to DARPA—were committed to going down the path of TCP. More important, the strategy of the Europeans to influence the CCITT had failed—the CCITT was clearly going down a path of standardizing X.25, a virtual circuit protocol favored by the PTTs.[64] As a result, an X.25 standard would leave computer users without an end-to-end protocol. Frustrated, yet not without fight, they regrouped and approached the International Organization for Standardization (ISO) to argue their case for end-to-end, or host-to-host, communication standards. ISO, the only international standards organization as powerful as CCITT, was organized as a series of technical committees with specialized sub-committees. Data processing and data communications standards rested with Technical Committee 97 (TC 97). Within TC 97, Subcommittee 6 (SC 6) was responsible for data communications standards and the logical home for the members of IFIP Working Group 6.1. Hubert Zimmermann, a close colleague of Louis Pouzin's, experienced member of the CYCLADES team, and senior member of the French delegation and IFIP, recalled:

> We approached Subcommittee 6, explained what we were doing and requested their requirements for going forward with a communication standard for host-to-host communications, or data processing-oriented communications standards. There was a low level of acceptance of the message at that time. We were accepted as people, but the ideas did not really get through![65]

Despite the lukewarm reception, the members of IFIP Working Group 6.1 began working with SC 6, only to find themselves once again embroiled in the politics of technology, not its merits. Again Zimmermann:

64. Larry Roberts and Barry Wessler played important roles in creating the X.25 standard.

65. Hubert Zimmermann, oral history interview by James L. Pelkey, May 25, 1988, Paris, France. Computer History Museum, Mountain View, CA. Available from https://archive.computerhistory.org/resources/access/text/2018/01/102738698-05-01-acc.pdf.

> We worked with Subcommittee 6 on the definition of the HDLC.[66] That was the time when HDLC was just getting out of the oven after 10 years of hard work. Now, there was a fair amount of politics in this, and HDLC had been blocked for some time. Until IBM got SDLC through, HDLC couldn't get through. There was a lot of politics, and we were probably not good enough politicians at that time.[67]

For the Europeans, who hoped TC 97 SC 6 would create end-to-end communication protocol standards, another barrier emerged to test their resolve. Most of them felt they had little choice but to cooperate and push for passage of HDLC, while simultaneously urging SC 6 to take on the challenge of end-to-end protocols. Not all Europeans were prepared to be so compliant, however. Acting independently, the British began lobbying TC 97 members to organize a full subcommittee on end-to-end, or as they would become known, "higher-layer" protocols. With the question of higher-layer protocols scheduled for vote at the upcoming March 1977 SC 6 meeting in Melbourne, Australia, a resolution seemed likely. Unfortunately, the plenary of SC 6—the decision-making body within all ISO committees—rejected the idea, concluding that higher-layer protocols were not mature enough. Then, a week later, in a stunning reversal, the parent organization, TC 97, decided over the opposition of the US delegation that the higher-layer protocols were sufficiently mature to begin standardization, and authorized the organization of Subcommittee 16 (SC 16) on Open Systems Interconnection (OSI)—a subcommittee equal in status to SC 6. The politics of deciding technological outcomes had birthed a new institution. The first task of organizing a new subcommittee required appointing a member organization to be secretariat, and then for the selected secretariat to appoint a chairman. (The secretariat handles all subcommittee administrative responsibilities.) A struggle to be secretariat set the British against the US delegations, with the US delegation winning despite having originally opposed the idea of creating the new subcommittee. (The winning argument was that the US held too few ISO secretariats.)

The American National Standards Institute Committee on Computers and Information Processing (ANSI/X3) represented the US in ISO and thus became secretariat. The Systems Planning and Resources Committee (SPARC) of ANSI/X3 authorized a study group, under the initial leadership of Jerry Foley of Burroughs, to form the delegation to SC 16 and create the initial US position paper. Foley in

66. High-level Data Link Control (HDLC) was originally designed for multipoint circuits before packet switching had been anticipated. SDLC, Synchronous Data Link Control, was IBM's comparable protocol.

67. Zimmermann interview, Computer History Museum.

turn recruited Charles Bachman of Honeywell to the committee, despite his having no prior experience with communication protocols. Bachman, who had just completed chairing a study group chartered to investigate the potential for standardization in the area of database management systems (DBMS), had proved his commitment to standards and Foley believed the committee would benefit from his leadership.

Once constituted, the study group had to convince American computer companies to cooperate and create voluntary standards. While opinion divided as to whether standards helped or hurt the economic fortunes of any given US computer company, most executives thought creating standards was a tactic to give foreign companies an opportunity to drive a wedge into the dominant market share held by US companies. As Bachman recalls:

> IBM and Burroughs weren't sure they wanted standards. Honeywell wasn't sure they wanted standards, except that I said: "You do want standards." When the issue of participation came up, I said: "We should participate." They said: "No, we're not sure we want something which is a worldwide standard," because they were more concerned about losing sales than getting sales out of it. In fact, the way I got Honeywell involved is that I volunteered to be chairman of the committee. IBM said it was inappropriate to have me as chairman of this group because the chairman should be neutral, sit there, and administer the thing and should not be a protagonist for anything. I was an aggressive chairman![68]

Bachman, drawing on his DBMS experience, believed standards should focus on interfaces, where components of systems meet. His philosophy drew substantially on his earlier experiences with the DBMS Framework, where the consensus of the group was to develop standards for interfaces, rather than for how components should work. This modular design approach encouraged simplicity, leaving many important decisions to the companies that would make the components.

68. Charles Bachman, oral history interview by James L. Pelkey, October 26, 1988, Cambridge, MA. Computer History Museum, Mountain View, CA. Available from https://archive.computerhistory.org/resources/access/text/2018/02/102738717-05-01-acc.pdf. Readers may be interested to compare Pelkey's 1988 interview of Pouzin with Russell's 2011 interview, 23 years later. Charles W. Bachman, oral history interview with Andrew L. Russell, April 9, 2011, Boston, MA. Interview # 578 for the IEEE History Center, The Institute of Electrical and Electronics Engineers Inc. Available from https://ethw.org/Oral-History:Charles_Bachman.

Zimmermann, who would become a key member of SC 16, felt resigned to the inevitability of virtual-circuit public data networks.[69] Yet rather than demoralizing him, it became a source of motivation. Cerf remembers 'Zim's' state of mind before SC 16 ever met:

> I can remember walking down the street in Geneva with Zimmermann in 1977, and he was telling me he was going to start out with virtual circuit-oriented stuff because it was the only thing that he could sell in the architecture. He knew, personally I don't know if he publicly admitted it, but I think he knew, and said so privately, that he wanted to introduce the datagram notions, but it would be later, after everybody was comfortable with the architectural model based on virtual circuits. He was much more politically astute than I was at that point.[70]

Bachman and Zimmermann would need all the political savvy they could muster for SC 16 would become not only the venue for waging battle over higher-layer protocol standards but a principal coordinating body forging cooperation between ISO and CCITT. To their advantage, the 40-to-50 engineers and scientists who had trekked from INWG through IFIP to ISO constituted much of the membership of the participating country delegations and had coalesced into a consensus group holding broad agreement on standards-making.[71] Testing their resolve would be the presence of invited representatives from CCITT and ECMA—organizations whose members' economic interests cast shadows over every SC 16 decision and action. SC 16 first convened in Washington, DC, in March 1978. After concluding the necessary organizational issues, each country presented position papers: everyone called for a multilayer protocol architecture. Given the unanimous agreement, they next established four working groups to distribute the work of creating standards (Table 5.2). With much accomplished, Bachman suggested they call it a day.

69. Bachman opines: "Hubert Zimmermann was one of the very most important people on that committee, maybe the most important person, in terms of the contribution to it." Bachman interview, Computer History Museum.

70. Cerf interview, Computer History Museum.

71. Pouzin: "By '77, we had a group of 40 to 50 people in Europe who had been involved in standard making and were also, more or less, a consensus group. So we had a sort of lobby that had started at the academic level and had moved into industry and standard making. This community then agreed very quickly about the very same principles which were the OSI model and the transport protocols." Pouzin, feeling over extended, let others carry his well-accepted ideas forward and remained a member of SC 6. Pouzin interview, Computer History Museum.

Table 5.2 **SC 16 Initial working groups**

Working Group	Responsibilities	Chairman	Country of Chair
WG 1	Overall Architecture	Hubert Zimmermann	France
WG 2	Layers up through Transport	George White	US
WG 3	Upper Layers	Alwin Langsford	UK
WG 4	Network Management	Kenji Naimura	Japan

Source: Andrew L. Russell. 2014. *Open Standards and the Digital Age: History, Ideology, and Networks.* Cambridge University Press, 297–298.

Only Zimmermann, hardened by years of talk and slow action, sought more. He wanted members to commit their agreements to paper and sign the document before the meeting adjourned. Bachman, while thinking the exercise "premature," said if it could be created then OK. Zimmermann remembered their late-night effort:

> We remained there in the evening with a few guys, and we started to cut and paste and write down the things. It was probably a 12-page document in which you had all the basic ingredients of the final version of the Reference Model. We picked seven layers—in some cases some people had organized their stuff in five and six and seven—I think it was the US contribution that put the composition into seven layers. We picked this one because it was not worse than the others, and the others would fit also within this.[72]

The coming-into-being of the OSI Reference Model (see Table 5.3) benefited from all the knowledge amassed creating computer communication protocols since NCP of ARPANET.[73] In segmenting computer communications into logical layers, end-to-end protocols could be assembled by selecting appropriate protocols from each layer to reflect network diversity, while sharing as many intermediate protocols as possible to reduce protocol complexity. Sharing of protocols also meant development and testing could be greatly reduced. The Reference Model recognized distinct transport and network layers, with SC 16 becoming responsible for the top four layers, the higher-layers, and SC 6 retaining responsibility for the three lower-layers. Hence, the critical coordination between the transport and network layers rested in two committees.

72. Zimmermann interview, Computer History Museum.

73. Hubert Zimmermann. 1980. OSI Reference Model—The ISO model of architecture for open systems interconnection. *IEEE Transactions on Communications*, Vol. Com-28 (April 1980), 424–432.

Table 5.3 **The OSI Reference Model**

#	Layer	Function
7	Application	Selects appropriate service for application
6	Presentation	Provides code conversion, data reformatting
5	Session	Coordinates interaction between application processes
4	Transport	Provides for end-to-end data integrity and quality of service
3	Network	Switches and routes information
2	Datalink	Transfers unit of information to other end of physical link
1	Physical	Transmits bitstream to medium

Source: Based on Hubert Zimmermann, "OSI Reference Model - The ISO Model of Architecture for Open Systems Interconnection," IEEE Transactions on Communications, Vol. Com-28, (April 1980), 424–432.

At variance with then existing practices, the Reference Model represented a framework within which communication standards would fit. It was not a technical standard itself. Done for reasons similar to those that had motivated the speedy adoption of the X.25 standard by the CCITT, the Reference Model was seen as a way to direct market actions and head off proprietary vendor—or CCITT—standards. For it was the power of the CCITT to dictate the communication protocols used by computers (over the public data networks) that posed the most serious threat to the interests of the members of SC 16. In creating the X.25 virtual circuit protocol, and formulating a standard for teletext, an end user application, the CCITT seemed well on the way to locking in how higher-layer applications interfaced to the PTT networks and thus dictating forever how computers interconnected over networks. This scenario was more or less the nightmare scenario that Pouzin and his equally independent-minded colleagues were trying to avoid.

In October 1978, the working groups of SC 16 met in Paris to resolve requested changes to the Reference Model and finalize a second version. As with the first meeting, key members pulled a near all-nighter to finish the revised document. John Day, a participant in ARPANET NWG, INWG, and IFIP meetings, was invited by Zimmermann to help formalize the Reference Model for SC 16. Day remembers:

> Standards people met from 9:00 to 4:00 and took their leisurely time, and talked the issues; it was an old-boys club, but at those times, while the standards were important, they didn't have the economic impact, potential economic impact, that this was going to have. The rules had changed substantially. There was big money involved, and everybody knew it. That's where the "electro-political engineering" term comes from. Everybody realized that where we drew the lines for the layers, and how we did the technical

solutions, determined market lines, determined economics, determined money in somebody's pocket. It was no longer this nice old-boys club.[74]

In July 1979, less than 18 months after being formed, SC 16 transmitted the Reference Model of Open Systems Interconnection to its parent organization TC 97 as a Working Draft. TC 97 speedily approved the Reference Model Working Draft before year-end 1979. Then SC 16 began incorporating suggested changes before resubmitting the Reference Model to TC 97 as a Draft Proposal (DP). TC 97 would then have to approve the Reference Model DP before sending it to the ISO as a Draft International Standards (DIS). In an auspicious act of cooperation, the CCITT Rapporteur's Group on Public Data Network Services joined in recognizing the Reference Model. With institutions and markets racing to decide the future, communication protocols had become important.

5.6.8 National Bureau of Standards and MITRE, 1971–1979

The final set of organizations that played important roles in the proliferation of networking protocols in the 1970s were the American National Bureau of Standards (NBS) and a defense contractor by the name of MITRE Corporation. Whereas computer communications over the public telephone networks preoccupied the Europeans, the American standards making body, NBS, focused on the emerging technology of private local area networks. This was not the result of some bureaucratic deliberation but the initiative of largely one man: Robert Rosenthal. After the NBS installed their ARPANET TIP in late 1971, Rosenthal was assigned the responsibility for building instrumentation to measure network performance: not of the network itself, which was being done by the NMC at UCLA, but performance from the perspective of the user. NBS wanted to understand the value of networking in order to recommend its use to other agencies, a responsibility consistent with the NBS charter of "developing federal information processing standards, assisting other agencies deploy technologies that support those standards and conducting appropriate research to assure federal agencies remain on the leading edge in the use of technology."

By 1976, Rosenthal, familiar with the work going on at PARC, began thinking of how he might build local area networks suitable for use in the Federal government.[75] With full support from his superior Dr. Ira Cotton (who, as Rosenthal

74. John Day, oral history interview by James L. Pelkey, July 11, 1988, Canton, MA. Computer History Museum, Mountain View, CA. Available from https://archive.computerhistory.org/resources/access/text/2017/11/102738592-05-01-acc.pdf.

75. Rosenthal recalled: "From my perspective, it was: 'Hey, I've got a group here and I've got to get real smart about this technology.' We had a number of contracts with some other agencies to

fondly remembers, said "Here's some rope, go hang yourself!"), Rosenthal contacted Metcalfe, Boggs, and Shoch at PARC as well as others knowledgeable of networking, such as Charlie Bass then at Zilog. Rosenthal remembers a simple objective, which was to give "dumb" computer terminals to employees all over the Bureau of Standards and let them access the "few very large hosts" that they had available. By 1978, three working prototype boards had been built and a Request for Proposal to build production quantities was let and won by a small company in Florida. In late-1978, as the network boards began being received from the vendor and installed, NBS-Net came into being. Rosenthal recalled that the network was "based loosely on the technology of Ethernet," with some differences from how Xerox approached the close integration of workstations and local network technologies. Rosenthal recalls: "I got so excited about all of this that I thought it would be a good idea to put a workshop together. So I called everybody I knew in local area networking. MITRE was one of the first calls."[76]

MITRE, of Bedford, MA, a government contractor for primarily the Air Force, had installed its ARPANET TIP at the same time as NBS, at the end of 1971. Concurrently, MITRE received one of two contracts let by the Air Force to develop local area networking prototypes and conduct networking studies. The other contract went to Ford Aerospace, of Sunnyvale, CA. By year-end 1972, Ash Dohad of MITRE had working a slotted broadband network named MITRE-Net. MITRE-Net used radio frequency (RF) technology over a cable to create many side-by-side communication channels much like frequency division multiplexing. Broadband differed radically from Ethernet and token ring in that it multiplexed many channels onto the transmission media. Ethernet and token ring created just one communication channel over the coaxial cable or twisted-pair wire.

---

actually install some of the early three-megabit Ethernet devices, and I had put a lab together here with Altos and Dover printers and the like. We also did some work for some people downtown. So we were very much aware of what Xerox was up to. Xerox's mindset, as I recall, at the time, was not to unbundle the LAN technology, but to sell an office system. Our motivation was to unbundle that technology and provide the equivalent of a carrier, but local area networks. At the time—we were forcing definitions like 'locally owned and administered.' All the bad things that we knew about carriers, from a user's perspective—they're not bad; the regulatory kinds of things—we wanted to do without, because we were trying to connect terminal devices within buildings we owned. There was no need for carrier services, so we administered them ourselves, we did everything ourselves. That's what we meant by local networks at the time." Robert Rosenthal, interview by James L. Pelkey, May 4, 1988, Washington, DC. Computer History Museum, Mountain View, CA. Available from https://archive.computerhistory.org/resources/access/text/2020/04/102792038-05-01-acc.pdf.

76. Rosenthal interview, Computer History Museum.

Then in 1976, Greg Hopkins engineered changes to MITRE-Net so one or more channels could service Ethernet-type traffic. Although the performance of the Ethernet-like channels was not impressive—three hundred thousand bits per second—MITRE secured a patent for its contribution. (Their work cites the prior work of Abramson and Metcalfe.) In late 1978, the Air Force requested MITRE investigate the issues of local networking and recommend actions they, the Air Force, should take. Rosenthal suggested a workshop on "Local Network Protocols," scheduled for January 31, 1979, in Columbia, MD. When Rosenthal contacted potential participants, it became very clear that while virtually everyone who had come into contact with local area networking sensed its importance, they all expressed confusion over what it all meant or what to do about it. Perfect fodder for a forum.

5.6.8.1 The 1979 Meetings: Resolution to the Confusion?

The letter that invited participants to the "Local Network Protocols" forum of January 31, 1979, explained that the goal was to provide a mechanism for sharing and obtaining results from the latest research—especially knowledge that was not available in the published literature. The first Forum in January had ten attendees, including David Clark from MIT, three employees from MITRE, two from NBS, two from Prime Computer (which also was developing a token ring network), and Bob Metcalfe, who was by that time an independent consultant. Lee LaBarre from MITRE remembers:

> We actually had come in with some preconceived ideas as to what the issues were, and we discovered that what we thought were the issues were not really the major issues. There were higher level issues that were more important, and a lot of those issues had to do with the upper layer protocol suite. At that time, we were more concerned with the access mechanisms in local area networks, and we grew to appreciate, because the experts that we had brought together had the ARPA experience, the requirement and the necessity for inter working these LAN's, using higher level protocols: XNS, TCP, etc.[77]

This was exactly the kind of realization that Rosenthal hoped to trigger amongst the group. For Rosenthal, the next step was obvious:

> I started working towards a larger conference as soon as the forum was finished because there was a clear message that something important was happening! So we knew there was a real need to start the talk about local

77. Lee LaBarre and Paul Brusil, oral history interview by James L. Pelkey, April 6, 1988, Bedford, MA. Computer History Museum, Mountain View, CA. Available from https://archive.computerhistory.org/resources/access/text/2020/04/102792037-05-01-acc.pdf.

> networks, and we decided to call them local area networks, by the way. I remember Bob Metcalfe always wanted to call them "local computer networks," LACNs, and I wasn't particularly fond of that because of this mindset I had of unbundling this technology, and I always wanted to call them local area networks.[78]

The preference for "local area networks" over "local computer networks" represented a real difference in perspective between those within NBS and MITRE and Metcalfe the visionary. Both NBS and MITRE saw this new technology as a solution to connecting terminals to multiple host computers, particularly to solve the problems and to reduce the costs of stringing computer cable from every terminal to every computer. With a local area network, one cable could traverse an entire facility with all terminals and computers connected to the one "local" cable. While a valid and understandable objective, for someone like Metcalfe, who had seen the future in the form of Altos workstations and believed a computer would soon be on every desktop, the expression "local computer network" better captured the technology's role. Metcalfe's views were not completely disregarded for he won the debates concerning the priority of higher-level protocols—convinced as he was that the lower-level access issues had been solved with Ethernet. To keep the momentum going, NBS and MITRE scheduled a more extensive meetings in Boston in March and May of 1979. The two-day May workshop proved to be most significant. Rosenthal and Meisner called it the Local Area Communications Network Symposium, held at the Copley Plaza Hotel in Boston. It featured five formal sessions, panel discussions, and twelve workshops. Wanting to broaden participation, Rosenthal thought of Charlie Bass and his new firm Zilog from the Bay Area. Presenters or session leaders included: Metcalfe, Saltzer, Pogran, Hunt, Tobagi, Sunshine, Hopkins, Shoch, and Cotton.[79] To everyone's surprise, an estimated 400 people attended! For most, it was unbelievable event, comparable in importance to the ICCC ARPANET Demonstration. Rosenthal, admittedly biased toward the event's success, remembered:

78. Rosenthal interview, Computer History Museum.

79. Tobagi and Hunt presented a paper: Fouad A. Tobagi and V. Bruce Hunt. 1980. Performance analysis of carrier sense multiple access with collision detection. *Computer Networks* 4, 245–259. Kleinrock and Tobagi first coined the expression Carrier Sense Multiple Access, CSMA, in connection with two papers published in 1975. L. Kleinrock and F. A. Tobagi. 1975. Packet switching in radio channels: Part I—Carrier sense multiple-access modes and their throughput-delay characteristics. *IEEE Trans. Commun.*, Com-23 (Dec. 1975), 1400–1416; and F. A. Tobagi and L. Kleinrock. 1975. Packet switching in radio channels: Part II—The hidden terminal problem in carrier sense multiple-access and the busy-tone solution. *IEEE Trans. Commun.*, Com-23 (Dec. 1975), 1417–1433.

> There was electricity in the air. People didn't know what to make of what NBS and MITRE were really up to. You had some of the leaders—you had Bob Metcalfe saying: "The world's going to be a better place. There's a need for this stuff." It was just really exciting. The result of the conference was the kind of exposure that I was real excited about.[80]

With new products and companies announced in the wake of the meeting, no wonder some observers detected sincere demand for local networking. Bruce Hunt of Zilog remembers "just being amazed at how many people were really interested in local area networks," and feeling satisfied that the instinct of the researchers—that they were onto something really important—was validated.[81] Coming a little less than 7 years after the ARPANET Demonstration of October 1972, the Symposium represented a defining moment in the emergence of local area networking. Soon flurries of company and product announcements added credence and substance to the promises of a technology that a few years earlier existed as just a dream of a few visionaries. But even though there was new consensus around the important applications of networking technology, the technical details about how networks would work remained unsettled. As the participants left Boston there was no clear consensus as to the best access method: Ethernet, token ring, or one of a growing number of alternatives. Equally, the protocols required to make networks functional were in their formative stage. And there remained the great divide between those who believed local area networks were primarily for terminal-to-host traffic versus those who championed computer-to-computer traffic.

Nonetheless, the exploding constellation of technologies and economic potential had reached the critical point and the funding and control of government agencies and large corporations no longer could hold the center or channel the flow of ideas and people. Entrepreneurs sensed the time had come to act. And those first to act gave confidence to others. Cumulatively they would give rise to a new market-structure, networking, which would join data communications in the broader sphere of computer communications.

5.7 In Perspective

A functioning ARPANET stimulated a decade of computer communication research and innovation. First came the need to change design choices built into ARPANET and to ready it for interconnection with a packet radio network. To do so meant

80. Rosenthal interview, Computer History Museum.

81. Bruce Hunt, oral history interview by James L. Pelkey, July 21, 1988, Foster City, CA. Computer History Museum, Mountain View, CA. Available from https://archive.computerhistory.org/resources/access/text/2013/05/102746651-05-01-acc.pdf.

both redesigning NCP, which provided neither end-to-end virtual circuits nor true datagram connectivity, and accommodating gateways between networks. Cerf and Kahn put forth a first effort in 1974 with their TCP paper.

Meanwhile, the Europeans were pushing the intellectual and scientific boundaries of datagram networks. The CYCLADES network demonstrated that end-to-end virtual circuits could be fit with pure datagram message delivery. The organization of INWG and its transformation into IFIP WG 6.1 provided a forum where the myriad approaches to computer communications were debated. The presentation of TCP precipitated a flurry of design alternatives and the eventual parting of the two sides of the Atlantic and their desires for an overarching network architecture.

Meanwhile, the proliferation of computers in the United States motivated engineers to solve the problems of fast inter-computer communications, not over telephone circuits but over coaxial cables or, soon, twisted pair wires. First, Farber birthed token ring and then Metcalfe fused the ideas of ARPANET and ALOHAnet into Ethernet. These local area networks required communication software different from TCP or even TCP version 2. XNS helped drive a new design of TCP, one that would become TCP/IP—where the end-to-end transport functionality would be divorced from network connectivity. This layered approached became a standard with the OSI Reference Model in 1979. Yetall of this activity left users swimming in confusion, prompting the NBS and MITRE to call for a workshop in early 1979 to make sense of it all. All too soon entrepreneurs would charge forward to seize the perceived opportunities in local area networking and, in the process, dislodge governments and their institutions from the drivers' seat.

Emergence of Local Area Networks: Networking, 1976–1981

6.1 Overview

In the late 1970s, the second major market-structure of computer communications emerged: networking. For over a decade it co-evolved with, and finally eclipsed, the data communications market-structure before the two influenced the emergence, and evolution, of the third market-structure of computer communications: internetworking. By the end of this book, in 1988, total revenues for the three industries combined were over $5 billion.

In the early 1970s, a number of pioneering engineers began to apply recent learning in the field of networking to innovate the use of networks for their employers' in-house productivity, or as solutions to meet specific customer needs. But while these pioneers proved the technology could work, it would take until the end of the decade before the commercial success of networks could be validated in the market. By then, the explosion in business computing—mainframes and the increasingly popular minicomputer—had created a compelling need to connect computers to other computers, peripherals, and terminals throughout the enterprise. Customers began making demands on their vendors for connectivity.

This demand was on display in May of 1979 at the Local Area Computer Networking symposium presented by MITRE and the National Bureau of Standards (NBS). The result was a watershed moment for the emerging market, which, when combined with the resurgence of venture capital, provided entrepreneurs with the right mix of opportunity and resources. Just 1 month later, in June, three of the leading networking companies, 3Com, Ungermann-Bass, and Sytek, were founded. Each differentiated to take advantage of what they saw as a unique market opportunity. They quickly discovered they did not have the market to themselves, as the existing data communication firms saw the same market signals and responded with products of their own.

6.2 Early Networking Pioneers

The earliest companies to find success in networking, such as Network Systems and Datapoint, found traction in a small subset of the computing market. As the use of minicomputers exploded, the minicomputer companies would face increasing demand to provide solutions for connectivity. This demand surfaced in similar stories throughout the computing companies like Prime Computers, DEC, and Data General.

Undoubtedly, there were many employees like Jerry McDowell who saw the opportunities on the horizon in the field of networking and tried to convince their companies of the commercial potential for networking products. Some, like Bill Farr, were engineers who built networks for computer companies that required one-off products for their customers or for in-house solutions. A few, such as Ralph Ungermann and Michael Pliner, would translate their inspiration and experience to found networking companies that played essential roles in this history. And others, even the ones that failed, helped to build the market to a critical mass.

6.3 Select Computer Companies Introduce LANs, 1976–1978

6.3.1 Prime Computer

Prime Computer Inc. was one of the last of the nearly 100 minicomputer companies founded in the rush of 1968–1972. Many of the seven Prime co-founders had prior experience working on Multics at MIT before then joining Computer Control Company (3C), which had been acquired by Honeywell in 1966. For their first products, they chose to build clones of Honeywell minicomputers. But like many of the later minicomputer start-ups, they found it challenging to find customers. Their strategy had been to offer a better price/performance ratio than their competitors, and to follow the lead of the highly successful leader DEC and focus on laboratory and industrial customers.

In 1974, Prime hired Paul Severino, an engineer at DEC, who had experience designing I/O and data acquisition products. Ironically, it wasn't strategic focus but rather a customer's request to interconnect their Prime computers that motivated Prime to hire Severino. Severino remembers the priority project he was handed in 1976: "Someone had sold a system that had to have two computers that talked to each other. So, what happened was that they threw this specification to me and said: 'OK, we need this done. You know, we're late. The customer wants this. We don't have anything to give him. You've got to do this project.'" The project was to connect two computers via a 16-bit parallel interface. "I got two computers working and then I jumped on to another project. We shipped it. It was fine. There was no real need to do anything more than two at that time."[1]

Fortunately, William (Bill) Poduska, Vice President of Software, instinctively understood the importance of interconnecting computers. Before becoming one of the founders of Prime, Poduska had been a professor at MIT involved with Project MAC and was also familiar with ARPANET. This early exposure to time-sharing and computer communications informed his design decisions and proved instrumental in Prime's eventual success. In late 1974, Poduska gave one of his engineers, William Farr, who had joined Prime in 1972 from Honeywell, some reading material—some of the same material that would be read by many of the early innovators in networking. Farr remembers: "Bill gave me some papers to read to try to generate some ideas, seed my thinking. There were papers by Kleinrock, Abramson, and Kahn, and Metcalfe's Ph.D. thesis. I did a little more literature search and came up with some papers from Bell Labs on SpiderNet, and got really excited about the idea of actually linking computers together in a way that went beyond just serial, RS-232, kinds of communications."[2] Farr developed some early concepts, which turned out to be very limited in functionality, relying on expensive cables and computers located in close proximity. He wanted to explore these new ideas further: "Paul Severino had created the Inter-Processor Communication Controller (IPC) that we were selling. At the same time, I was working on these ideas that had developed from the ALOHAnet papers, Metcalfe's Ethernet papers, and the token ring papers."[3]

Farr analyzed the alternative networking schemes and made several presentations to the engineering staff. Concluding in favor of token ring, he wrote an initial product specification. Poduska wanted to have a working prototype ready for the Spring Joint Computer Conference (SJCC) in June of 1976, but Farr objected on the grounds that working on a prototype would distract them from the work that needed to be done to have a robust shippable product. It would take another year before they had working hardware for the network.

Poduska challenged Farr because he knew, or least sensed, the importance of this project for Prime. Farr remembers Poduska's style of management, one he had experienced before:

1. Paul Severino, oral history interview by James L. Pelkey, March 16, 1988, Cambridge, MA. Computer History Museum, Mountain View, CA. Available from https://archive.computerhistory.org/resources/access/text/2017/11/102738590-05-01-acc.pdf.

2. William (Bill) Farr, oral history interview by James L. Pelkey, April 7, 1988, Boston, MA. Computer History Museum, Mountain View, CA. Available from https://archive.computerhistory.org/resources/access/text/2020/02/102792021-05-01-acc.pdf.

3. Farr interview, Computer History Museum.

> Bill Poduska is one of the most creative people I've ever met. He was able to take an idea and push it way beyond what other people were thinking about and see the value in very practical terms at the same time. He was always pushing. There was never a time when he was satisfied with anything. He would be satisfied with what you had done, but he always realized you could do more if you really wanted to. So there was this constant technological tension that he maintained, but it was a very fatherly type, fostering type. I also worked at DEC in 1961–62 and Ken Olsen was very much the same type of person. As a matter of fact, Ken came around every day and talked to every engineer when I was there. Gordon Bell also was—not quite as social, but very much the same kind of fostering person; very dynamic, generated lots of ideas and encouraged you to pick up on them and continue.[4]

Although Farr was excited about the prospect of Prime's potential networking product, he encountered the resistance of others who did not believe as he did in the promise of the new technology. So, despite rumors that DEC, Hewlett Packard, and Data General had networking projects under development, he ran into an all-too-common resistance from management. Farr remembers the response he got: "We went to our marketing organization and they saw absolutely zero need for this product... I said: 'Can't you see that this is something that is valuable because people can share information at high speeds?' They said, 'Well, people don't need to do that. Nobody's doing that now, so it's clearly not important.'"[5]

Not to be discouraged, Farr convinced his boss, Charlie Smith, to buy enough equipment to build a network to interconnect 16 computers in the engineering department. Farr, Bob Gordon, and Paul Levine then completed a token ring network they initially called PrimeNet. By mid-1978, engineering had become totally dependent on PrimeNet, both for electronic mail and file sharing. Eventually, management was convinced, and the commercial version of the product, named Ringnet, was announced in January 1979, making Prime one of the first minicomputer companies to sell a LAN.[6]

The question of which technology was superior, token ring or CSMA/CD, would embroil the emerging market in debate for years. Not surprisingly, it was at MIT's Laboratory of Computer Science (LCS), where a study comparing the two technologies first took place, financed by ARPA and the IPTO.

4. Farr interview, Computer History Museum.

5. Farr interview, Computer History Museum.

6. A year later, Ford Motor Company bought Prime computers for the first time based on the promise of interconnecting a large number of computers.

6.3.2 MIT—The Laboratory of Computer Science

Michael Dertouzos, Director of MIT's LCS, managed one of the most complex computer environments that existed at the time. As a result of a university gift program begun in 1978, Xerox had donated LCS (along with computer science laboratories at Carnegie-Mellon and Stanford) Altos workstations, file servers, and its experimental 3 megabit per second Ethernet. That gave LCS two networks, Ethernet from Xerox and token ring, Farber's network from UC Irvine, with another CSMA/CD network, Chaosnet, at the nearby AI Labs.

Professor Jerry Saltzer, one of the lead scientists of LCS at that time, remembers the laboratory's complex environment: "And we had Xerox Altos, and we had LISP machines... and the question then of whether or not the computer you're attached to is a mainframe time-sharing system or workstation instantly becomes fairly uninteresting. All you care about is: 'this is a computer and I want it to be on the net.'"[7]

At the same time, DEC proposed giving LCS 20 to 30 DEC VAX 11/750 minicomputers to be used as single-user workstations. As Saltzer remembers, "basically they were offering us the opportunity to live in the future and pretend that you had a workstation with the power of a VAX by giving us a bunch of VAXs and asking that we try to use them as workstations. So, we did that."[8] To make the VAXs effective, however, required interconnecting and integrating them into their existing computer facilities. The most obvious, but not necessarily the best, decision seemed to be to re-engineer a faster, second-generation token ring; a technology unencumbered by the complications of Xerox's uncertain licensing policy.

Serendipitously, Robert Metcalfe was on the hunt for consulting clients. He knew Dertouzos, so he got in touch with him, not as an engineer but to evaluate management practices and recommend changes. He would advocate that LCS agree to DEC's terms and commit to a vision of desktop computing, even if it meant interconnecting the VAXs with token ring and not Ethernet. The decision was made to develop a second-generation token ring network when DARPA, keenly interested in the comparative advantages of the different network technologies, awarded LCS a contract to conduct performance measurements of Ethernet versus their imported token ring network.

Interconnecting the VAXs with token ring required upgrading the performance of their existing 1-megabit network, the Local Network Interface (LNI). To do so

7. Jerome H. "Jerry" Saltzer, oral history interview by James L. Pelkey, March 7, 1988, Cambridge, MA. Computer History Museum, Mountain View, CA. Available from https://archive.computerhistory.org/resources/access/text/2016/10/102717242-05-01-acc.pdf.

8. Saltzer interview, Computer History Museum.

meant finding outside help, for Dertouzos knew LCS did not have the requisite skills to do the re-engineering in-house. Dertouzos contacted Howard Salwen, a former classmate, who had a small company that engineered communication products principally under government contracts. Dave Clark, head researcher on the project, recalls Dertouzos' concern with finding someone with enough technical background and skills to complement their team: "He basically said: 'I know Howard. I've known him for a long time. He's a good guy. He run's this consulting company. We'll give him a contract for $100,000 to do a Version 2 LNI for the Unibus.' And so we wrote him a contract. We didn't do any competitive selection or anything like that."[9]

Salwen and a partner had founded Proteon Associates in 1972. In 1974, health problems forced his first partner to resign, and Al Marshall became Salwen's new partner. Proteon's competence rested largely in designing and building modems. Salwen remembers his early involvement with MIT and the meetings he and Marshall attended to discuss which networking technology to adopt: "Of course, Metcalfe was strongly in favor of Ethernet. There was a group from the Artificial Intelligence Lab arguing in favor of their Chaosnet design. Dave Clark and Jerry Saltzer were in favor of token passing ring. . . And the meetings were very exciting. There was a lot of screaming and yelling in those meetings."[10]

Given Xerox's proprietary attitude regarding their technology, Metcalfe's promotion of Ethernet for the MIT installation might have seemed like a challenge only a masochist would have undertaken. But Metcalfe had two advantages: his own unrelenting drive to materialize his vision, and an ally and friend in Xerox PARC project manager, David Liddle. Liddle supported Metcalfe's efforts at the time: "Bob wanted to somehow stimulate things happening out there. That was OK with me provided Xerox got something out of it." To be constructive to Xerox, any promotion of Ethernet outside of Xerox had to be done in partnership: "He sort of wanted to be the marriage broker of getting Xerox to open up the product to lots of other customers, lots of other companies. My position was: 'No, but a few selected companies that could make really strong partners so we can make people see this as a de facto standard, then that's fine.'"[11]

9. David D. Clark, oral history interview by James L. Pelkey, March 7, 1988, Cambridge, MA. Computer History Museum, Mountain View, CA. Available from https://archive.computerhistory.org/resources/access/text/2018/02/102738738-05-01-acc.pdf.

10. Howard Salwen, oral history interview by James L. Pelkey, January 28, 1988, Westborough, MA. Computer History Museum, Mountain View, CA. Available from https://archive.computerhistory.org/resources/access/text/2020/01/102792007-05-01-acc.pdf.

11. David Liddle, oral history interview by James L. Pelkey, October 11, 1988, Mountain View, CA. Computer History Museum, Mountain View, CA. Available from https://archive.computerhistory.org/resources/access/text/2013/05/102746649-05-01-acc.pdf.

6.3.3 Digital Equipment Corporation

While consulting to LCS, Metcalfe contacted Sam Fuller and Bill Johnson at DEC and was soon retained to work on their 10-year long-range plan (especially in the area of connectivity). Soon after, he met with Gordon Bell, vice president of engineering. Bell, like Poduska at Prime, had experience with ARPANET, including attending some Network Working Group meetings. He took it as a given that computer connectivity was important to DEC, but he differed with those who had architected ARPANET. Bell believed that the functions of the interface message processor (IMP) could be included in the design of the host, as he explains: "All the DEC work was based on the notion that a host could be an IMP. We were building IMP-sized computers, so I didn't care whether you actually computed or did switching and computing. Everybody said: 'No, you can't ever have switching and computing in the same box.'" In addition to believing in the one box concept, Bell realized that it made much more sense in regard to future products: "We're not going to force our users to have a whole switching network of IMPs around. This is crazy."[12]

Bell's first efforts to launch DEC into communications began modestly. In early 1974, he decided to try using a PDP-11 as a new remote job entry station for their DEC System 10. He assembled a three-person team, one engineer each from the PDP-11 and DEC 10 engineering groups and Stu Wecker, his communication expert. Wecker had joined DEC in June 1972 as a researcher and had interconnected three minicomputers. Known as SHARP, for Stu's Homogenous Asynchronous Relocatable Process operating system, the demo so impressed Bell that when he needed a communications expert he turned to Wecker, despite the fact that before joining DEC Wecker had absolutely zero experience in computer communications: "I didn't even know the word 'protocol.'"[13] In 7 weeks the team designed a new communications protocol: DDCMP, Digital Data Communications Message Protocol. DDCMP separated control of the devices at the end of the communications line from control of the communications line itself, a division between the "host-to-host" and network responsibilities and thus a two-layered protocol.

By the beginning of 1976, DEC was challenged, just as Prime had been, by customers wanting to interconnect their computers. At first, the need came from industrial and laboratory customers, requests that Bell forwarded to Wecker. Wecker began talking to customers and soon headed up a small networking

12. C. Gordon Bell, oral history interview by James L. Pelkey, June 17, 1988, Cupertino, CA. Computer History Museum, Mountain View, CA. Available from https://archive.computerhistory.org/resources/access/text/2013/05/102746646-05-01-acc.pdf.

13. Stuart Wecker, oral history interview by James L. Pelkey, October 25, 1988, Sudbury, MA. Computer History Museum, Mountain View, CA. Available from https://archive.computerhistory.org/resources/access/text/2016/04/102738130-05-01-acc.pdf.

committee to determine the specifications for DEC's computer communications network, to become known as DECnet.

Knowing little about networking, Wecker studied material on the ARPANET. Of all the papers and articles he read, two proved essential to DECnet: Bob Metcalfe's Ph.D. thesis and *Communication Networks for Computers* by Donald Davies and Derek Barber. The Davies and Barber book provided the concepts of layering, symmetry, and peer-to-peer networking (key differences from IBM's SNA). The writings of Louis Pouzin, Hubert Zimmerman, Vint Cerf, and Carl Sunshine also influenced his thinking.

DECnet shipped in late 1976, but, due to lack of functionality, such as terminal protocols, customers reacted poorly. Members of top management worried that maybe networks were just too complicated and that DEC should concentrate on minicomputers. But Bell, committed to the importance of the VAX computer project launched in 1975, would have none of it, convinced that communications were essential to computers and that to achieve the VAX goal of a single architecture spanning the entire spectrum of performance would require multi-processor communications.

Fortunately, Bell had maintained his contacts with academia. When Metcalfe and Boggs submitted their paper to the ACM in May 1975, Bell was selected as one of the reviewers. Sensing its implications for DEC, he circulated the paper within DEC, nearly a year before its publication in July 1976, and initiated a number of low-level networking projects. He no longer questioned whether networking would play a role in DEC's future, he just wasn't certain how or when. Meanwhile, customer demand for computer communications kept growing. DEC delivered DECnet Phase II in 1978.

Bell documented his vision of DEC's product strategy in 1978. Known as the Distributed Computing Environment (DCE), it was approved by the DEC Board of Directors in December 1978.[14]

Provide a set of homogeneous, distributed-computer-system products based on VAX-11 so a user can interface, store information, and compute without reprogramming or extra work from the following computer's system sizes and styles:

- via large, central (mainframe) computers or network;
- at a local, shared departmental/group/team (mini) computer;

14. Gordon Bell. 1986. Toward a history of (personal) workstations. In *Proceedings of the ACM Conference on the history of personal workstations*. Association for Computing Machinery, New York, 1–17. DOI: https://doi.org/10.1145/12178.12179.

- as a single-user personal (micro) computer within a terminal;
- with interfacing to other manufacturer and industry standard information processing systems; and
- all interconnected via the local area Network Interconnect, NI, in a single area, and the ability of interconnecting the Local Area Networks (LANs) to Campus Area and Wide Area Networks.

Over time, the DCE would involve interconnected minicomputers, shared network servers, workstations, and eventually PC clusters.

By early 1979, none of the experimental projects he had launched after reading Metcalfe's ACM paper seemed likely to result in the Network Interconnect needed for the DCE. As he put it: "I didn't know what the hell I was going to do. We didn't have any good physical things. I didn't want to go off and make them. We were in the throes of deciding between... There was the ring crowd. The ring looked good to me, but..."[15]

Bell was familiar with token ring and knew both Prime and a start-up of ex-Prime employees, Apollo, were both committed to using token ring. Furthermore, Saltzer and Clark had told DEC that they intended to interconnect the gifted VAXs with their version of token ring. Even so, Bell knew of no large operational token ring networks, whereas Xerox operated a large Ethernet network. But how could he loosen Xerox's ironclad control over their technology? Bell remembers his good fortune: "We had to have it, and we would have invented our own. We had two or three different schemes, and I was just turning to that problem when Bob walks in the door and says: 'Would you be interested in a collaborative effort with Xerox?'" Bell was eager to proceed with the collaboration, but how to get the wheels of the two large companies moving in the same direction? Bell remembers:

> A meeting was held with Metcalfe in a corner room in Parker Street. Parker Street was a prison-like building, a big concrete building. They had been meeting all day when I came into the meeting and said: "OK, where are you guys on this thing?" They said something like: "Well, we'd really like to do something, but it isn't clear." I said: "How do we get this thing going?" They said: "Well, you'd better write a letter to so and so." I said: "this thing isn't moving fast enough. Tell me what the letter should say, and furthermore, we will write the letter right now." So I went next door to a word processing system, and Metcalfe and I composed a letter right then. I wrote: We want

15. Robert Metcalfe, oral history interview by James L. Pelkey, February 16, 1988, Portola Valley, CA. Computer History Museum, Mountain View, CA. Available from https://archive.computerhistory.org/resources/access/text/2013/05/102746650-05-01-acc.pdf.

> to do some kind of a joint venture to get a local area network that would be public, a network that would be used by both companies. I viewed Metcalfe as the behind-the-scenes oiler, greaser that made all of this happen.[16]

The letter was sent to Liddle, George Pagent, and James Campbell. Meanwhile, Metcalfe had begun consulting to IBM. He learned that they leaned towards token ring but had not made any final decision as to the importance of local area networking, or whether to introduce a product of any kind.

6.3.4 Zilog

Ralph Ungermann and Federico Faggin co-founded Zilog in 1974. Early on they recruited Charlie Bass who was on the faculty of the University of California at Berkeley to run the software group, which, along with the hardware and semiconductor groups, reported directly to Ungermann. Bass in turn hired John Davidson from BBN, his friend from the ALOHAnet days, along with Joe Kennedy. In 1976, Bass hired Judith Estrin, a graduate of Stanford with a background in TCP, having worked with Vint Cerf, and very familiar with Ethernet. However, even with this considerable talent, the impetus to start an internal networking project came from a very unexpected source.

Bruce Hunt felt very lucky when Kennedy hired him in May 1977. Only a year earlier, he had been a programmer at the Stanford Linear Accelerator when Joe Wells, the Director of the Stanford Center for Information Processing, asked him: "'Bruce, do you know how much it costs to connect a terminal to our computer system?' that was an IBM 370 system at the time. I said: 'No.' He said: 'About $3,000,' and I thought that was astonishing, since a terminal cost $2,000." Having read Metcalfe's Ethernet paper in the July 1976 issue of the ACM, he began to develop his own ideas about dealing with the issue of communication between computer and terminal. "Just about that time, Bernard Peuto, who was working on the Z8000 microprocessor at Zilog, brought by a copy of the first Zilog SIO specification sheet. I looked at that and said: 'You put these things together and you could actually create a network.'"[17] Hunt continued to work out his idea for a network until he had a scheme for how it could be done.

In landing a job with Zilog, Hunt had the opportunity to see if his ideas would work. That summer of '77 Hunt and Ben Laws, who had come to Zilog from Xerox PARC, collaborated on the project: "We sat down and he did the hardware and

16. Bell interview, Computer History Museum.

17. Bruce Hunt, oral history interview by James L. Pelkey, July 21, 1988, Foster City, CA. Computer History Museum, Mountain View, CA. Available from https://archive.computerhistory.org/resources/access/text/2013/05/102746651-05-01-acc.pdf.

looked at my simple designs and turned them into something that would work, and then we built the stuff. I did all the basic software that made it all work. We had the thing up by the end of the summer." They called the system "Ariel" and Hunt began presenting the results. "I started spending about 60% of my time doing nothing but giving demos of how the system would work, because it really ran."[18]

Hunt's Ariel project then got sucked up into the energy and chaos of Zilog with "some very heated discussions." Ungermann recalls: "We had some yelling and screaming matches where I was convinced that we had to have a low-cost, semiconductor-based interconnect strategy." And an interconnect strategy was only one of many projects, underway or proposed. Zilog had been acquired by Exxon as part of a strategy to enter the office automation market and had given Zilog a huge influx of cash to develop a wide variety of products. As Ungermann remembers: "We were a company that was encouraged by our parent to go in as many directions as possible." The amount of talent under their roof meant many projects were in development at the same time, but few became products. "We had very, very good people, and we did lots of things, but we didn't make lots of money. My sense of Xerox PARC was that there was some kind of overall systems design which they were working towards... Zilog had as much talent and as much energy, but it was more dispersed, and it didn't have any mission or objective or unifying force to it."[19]

Characteristic of the Zilog culture were the frequent parties held by Estrin and her roommate, Barbara Koalkin, who worked at PARC. These parties facilitated a cross-pollination of the PARC/Zilog cultures and activities. Invariably, small groups huddled intensely for hours discussing new technologies just becoming available or even still just thoughts. At one of the parties, Estrin introduced Hunt to Fouad Tobagi, who had just accepted a job at Stanford as assistant professor of electrical engineering. Hunt recalls Estrin's introduction: "'Fouad, you ought to know Bruce. Bruce has built this little network' and Fouad says; 'Wow, you know, I studied networks. That's what I did for my Ph.D. for Leonard Kleinrock. You ought to go look at my papers.'"[20] Hunt and Tobagi then co-authored a paper and Tobagi suggested Hunt return to Stanford as a graduate student. In October 1978, Hunt left Zilog for Stanford. Robert Rosenthal invited Hunt and Tobagi to present their paper at the May LACN (Local Area Communications Network) Symposium.

18. Hunt interview, Computer History Museum.

19. Ralph Ungermann, oral history interview by James L. Pelkey, July 20, 1988, Mountain View, CA. Computer History Museum, Mountain View, CA. Available from https://archive.computerhistory.org/resources/access/text/2018/03/102738765-05-01-acc.pdf.

20. Hunt interview, Computer History Museum.

After the departure of Ralph Ungermann at the end of 1978 over his disagreements with Exxon management, the new Zilog executive team led by Manny Fernandez, who had been recruited from Fairchild Semiconductor, tried to make sense of the company's mission. To strengthen management, Fernandez raided his former employer and hired William (Bill) Carrico to be marketing manager for semiconductors. Fernandez soon asked Carrico to investigate the troubled systems group, the one Ungermann had led. Recognizing the need to bring focus to an ambitious list of development projects, Carrico convened a series of strategy meetings in May–June 1979 attended by Bass, Estrin, Davidson, Joe Kennedy, Dave Folger, and Phil Belanger. Having just introduced their Z8000 microprocessor, much of the discussion centered on issues of connecting microprocessors and microcomputers. After Hunt's departure, Estrin had become the new project leader for Ariel. Folger suggested Ariel be used to interconnect more than just Z80 or Z8000 microcomputers and be re-conceptualized as an "intelligent wire." One use could be to interconnect terminals to Zilog minicomputers as a terminal multiplexer.

6.3.5 The Return of Venture Capital

The economic recession of the early 1970s took the edge off the surge in venture capital that had started in the late 1960s. Throughout the 1970s, the capital commitments to venture capital remained in the tens of millions of dollars. The essentially "dormant" venture capital industry of this period began weighing on the minds of entrepreneurs, venture capitalists, and sympathetic members of Congress. Many wondered openly if the vitality of the American economy itself was at serious risk. The cumulative social pressures led to the passage of the 1978 Revenue Act that resulted in a drastic reduction in the capital gains tax rate from 39.875% in 1977 to 28% in 1979. The result was a tenfold increase in capital commitments the following year, or an increase of $556 million. In combination with the passage of ERISA's "Prudent Man" Rule (1979), the Small Business Investment Act (1980), ERISA's "Safe Harbor" Regulation (1980), and lastly the Economic Recovery Tax Rate (1981) that further lowered the capital gains tax rate from 28% to 20%, all led to an additional tenfold increase in capital commitments to venture capital of $1.3 billion in 1981.

These combined actions ushered in a period of unprecedented commitments in venture capital that continued well into the 1980s (Figure 6.1). It was as if "ignition and liftoff occurred in 1979, and the venture capital industry rocketed into the 1980s."[21] For entrepreneurs needing venture capital it was if the stoplight that had been stuck on red had turned green. The impact on networking was immediate.

21. William D. Bygrave and Jeffrey A. Timmons. 1992. *Venture Capital at the Crossroads*. Harvard Business School Press, Boston, MA, 25.

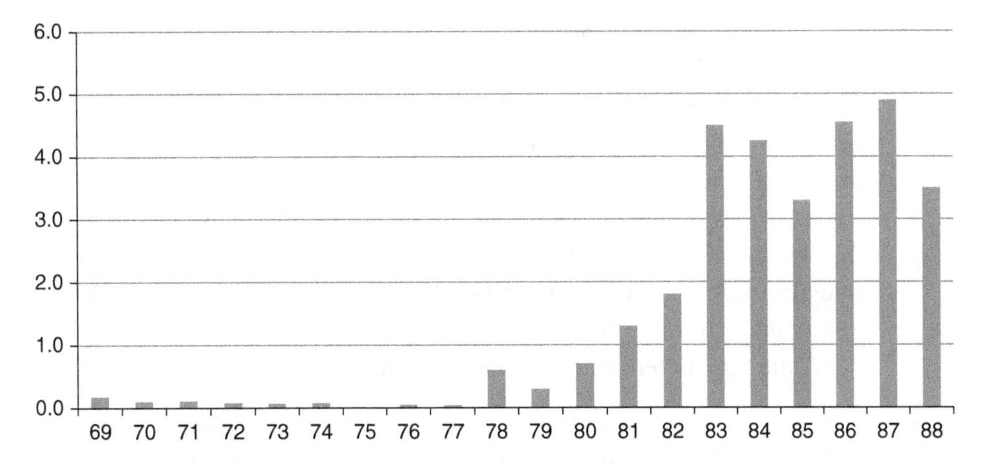

Figure 6.1 New venture capital commitments, 1969 to 1988 ($ billions). Source: Based on William D. Bygrave and Jeffry A. Timmons. *Venture Capital at the Crossroads* (Harvard Business School Press, 1992), 26; *Science and Engineering Indicators, 2002, Volume 1.* National Science Foundation, 2002.

6.4 Early LAN Start-ups

6.4.1 Robert Metcalfe and the Founding of 3Com

Metcalfe left the LACN Symposium more certain than ever that Ethernet had to be freed from the proprietary grasp of Xerox if it was to have a chance of impacting the coming commercialization of networking. After hearing that the letter Gordon Bell of DEC had sent to three Xerox executives had generated interest, Metcalfe facilitated a meeting between Bell and David Liddle. Around the same time, Metcalfe was hired to consult with the NBS. At NBS he was told that a representative from Intel had been there the day before looking for applications for their new 25-megahertz chip technology. Metcalfe immediately got the idea, "Why don't we just build an Ethernet chip with it?"

Metcalfe then organized a meeting at Intel where he met Phil Kaufman, in charge of strategic planning, and who reported directly to Andy Grove. Kaufman was already aware of the potential market for communications controller chips and had been in contact with Bell at DEC. While at Intel, Metcalfe made a presentation to a group of about 30 to 40 people: "So I pitched them on how they ought to develop a custom chip for Ethernet. And the reason they ought to do it is that if DEC and Xerox were going to do this, they're going to need chips and you guys can make the chips for their standard."[22]

22. Metcalfe interview, Computer History Museum.

Kaufman, already a believer that communication chips would be significant "consumers of silicon," was trying to determine which access method would be most commercially viable. If Intel were going to put significant expenditure into manufacturing the first networking chip, it wanted to be sure they could sell lots of them. He remembers his logic: "The one protocol that had actually been used somewhere was Ethernet, as done at PARC. Everything else was inventing on the fly. We took a good look at Ethernet and all the papers that had been written and said: 'It doesn't matter whether it's good or not, it exists and it works. Let's see if we can take off from there.'"[23]

Liddle remembers being contacted by Kaufman:

> Intel contacted me and was interested in making a networking part primarily for IBM. They wanted to make a single part that could do both SDLC and Ethernet... I went to DEC and said: "Intel's interested in working with us too. What do you say we make a three-way arrangement?" My reasoning was very simple: Dr. Wang and IBM and all these people were after us, Xerox, because we had been running these very successful TV ads and were scaring everybody. Competitor claims were getting made that: "Oh yeah, but it's really costly and it always will be." So I said: "If I want to get stuff that's inexpensive, first of all I've got to show that I've got a semiconductor manufacturer who says: 'We'll make all the components so they'll be cheap' and secondly I need a down and dirty equipment vendor who makes modems and terminals and throw-away stuff, which was certainly Digital's reputation at that time. So I thought: this will get away from the image that this is a premium high-end expensive product, and it'll encourage it. I wanted to start an industry at that moment. I didn't want any proprietary network. I wanted to be able to say: "Look, I can hook to all this other gear that other people make." I didn't want to have a post hoc networking industry develop.[24]

Xerox and DEC invited Intel to join their meetings. But legal concerns soon surfaced about any appearance of market manipulation by the three partners. Given the ongoing antitrust lawsuits against AT&T and IBM, the issue had the potential to become a roadblock. Kaufman remembers the attorney's concerns:

---

23. Phil Kaufman, oral history interview by James L. Pelkey, June 17, 1988, Campbell, CA. Computer History Museum, Mountain View, CA. Available from https://archive.computerhistory.org/resources/access/text/2013/05/102746652-05-01-acc.pdf.

24. David Liddle, oral history interview by James L. Pelkey, October 11, 1988, Mountain View, CA. Computer History Museum, Mountain View, CA. Available from https://archive.computerhistory.org/resources/access/text/2013/05/102746649-05-01-acc.pdf.

> What our attorneys essentially told us was that we could not write a three-way agreement to work on the project to develop the technical specification even though we were explicitly going to put it in the public domain, and that we could not have tri-lateral meetings if there were any marketing people present from any company.[25]

Metcalfe soon learned of the impasse. Concerned that lawyers might end the collaboration, he called his former college roommate, Howard Charney, an antitrust expert, who had just finished suing IBM successfully on behalf of Memorex. Armed with the new knowledge that: "All you have to do is have a meeting whose purpose is expansion of markets and making of standards to be publicly disclosed" to avoid antitrust problems, Metcalfe again intervened, facilitating a three-way meeting. Thus began the three-way collaboration of DEC, Intel, and Xerox, soon to be known as DIX.

But freeing Ethernet from Xerox was only one of Metcalfe's concerns that May of 1979. A second and more personal issue was how to avoid being left behind in the coming commercialization of local area networking. As a consulting company of one, he knew he either had to grow a company and begin selling product or become marginalized. For others now believed as he did, with the intention of starting companies to sell local area networking products. How did he know? Others were asking him to join them.

Yet Metcalfe knew his vision of networking desktop computers differed from the views of others—even as he also knew no existing desktop computers needed to be networked. Yet if he did not stake claim to market leadership, the confusion created by others could leave him stranded, left behind and out of luck, an outcome he had no intention of letting happen.

So, on June 4th, 1979, Metcalfe and Gregory L. Shaw incorporated 3Com Corporation (3Com): for computers, communications, and compatibility. Incorporation changed little. Metcalfe knew he needed a client to fund a growth in headcount to add the talent 3Com required to transition from a consulting firm to a product company. Metcalfe contacted General Electric to try to sell them on the idea of creating a home networking product. GE agreed, contracting 3Com to develop a personal computer (which got shelved) and a network system called "HomeNET." In the process Metcalfe was able to expand 3Com and make some key hires: "Consulting to GE is probably the deal that made the company because I was able to expand from one person to ten people, and in particular I was able to add Howard

25. Kaufman interview, Computer History Museum.

Charney."[26] They also hired Ron Crane, an engineer from Xerox PARC who would become a key engineer for 3Com.

In addition to growing 3Com, Metcalfe continued to shepherd the three-way cooperation between Xerox, DEC, and Intel to make Ethernet public. Finally, that fall of 1979, the three firms met in Boxborough, MA. Acknowledging Metcalfe's essential role, he came to the pre-meeting dinner. The following day the technical teams of the three companies met, without marketing people or Metcalfe.

Metcalfe's cares now revolved around 3Com and how to fund products that would conform to the technical specifications he confidently expected DIX would negotiate and then publish. Metcalfe remembers:

> We went from GE to Exxon. Exxon, in a deal that, I don't know how I did it, but we got Exxon to agree to pay us to develop our first three products. We gave them fully paid-up non-exclusive licenses and they allowed us to retain ownership of the technology. The contract was written that they could only use this technology in connection with an Exxon system. The three products were: TCP for UNIX, the Ethernet transceiver, and the Ethernet adapter for the Unibus.[27]

3Com had a contract to build the three essential components for an Ethernet network: an adapter to connect to the computer, a transceiver to connect to the media, and protocol software to enable functionality. The market focus would be interconnecting DEC Unibus computers via Ethernet.[28] And while the UNIX operating system was not as widely used as DEC's proprietary operating systems, UNIX was used often enough, and others had already ported TCP to UNIX. Why TCP for UNIX? Why not XNS, the protocol architecture developed under Metcalfe specifically for Ethernet? Metcalfe explains his rationale: "Vint Cerf persuaded me—it didn't take much persuading—that we should implement TCP, because it was going to be a standard. Now, at that time XNS was a secret of Xerox, and I had just left Xerox. I couldn't do XNS, even if I wanted to, but TCP was public domain. It was to be a standard."[29]

---

26. Metcalfe interview, Computer History Museum.

27. Metcalfe interview, Computer History Museum. The irony is that Exxon had local area network technology in its Zilog operations and yet turned to an outside, start-up company for its technology.

28. A computer bus, or backplane, is the communication network interconnecting the different subsystems of a computer; the subsystems existing as printed circuit boards physically plug into slots interconnected by the bus. Examples of then buses were Unibus, Multibus, and Q-bus.

29. Metcalfe interview, Computer History Museum.

In May 1980, DEC, Intel, and Xerox made it official and announced they would publish their joint specification of Ethernet on September 30, 1980. Metcalfe knew he needed to raise significantly more capital than could be accumulated through profits if 3Com was to make the investments required of a market leader. To raise the capital meant selling equity capital, a percentage of 3Com ownership, to venture capitalists. After writing a business plan, Metcalfe began meeting with VCs. His first meetings were discouraging since venture capitalists refused to properly value 3Com, which was, in Metcalfe's opinion, an established company with three "real" products. They saw the arrangement 3Com had made with Exxon regarding development of the products as a red flag. According to the VCs, Exxon had a fully paid non-exclusive license and could use the technology to compete with 3Com. Metcalfe insisted that the chances of Exxon competing with 3Com were insignificant and that the contract specified that they could only use the technology in an Exxon system. Metcalfe remembers the argument: "They said: 'Ah, no, no, no. You're first round.' And I said: 'No, no. We're second round, and we own all this technology.' 'No, no, you're first round.'"[30]

The crux of the argument: How much ownership would have to be relinquished to raise capital? The venture capitalists argued for as low a company valuation as possible so that their investment would buy the maximum ownership. After all, they reasoned, 3Com's revenue for the fiscal year ending May 1980 totaled only $281,000 and the company had sold rights to its technology to Exxon. So how real a company was it?

On September 30, DIX published the Ethernet specification. Metcalfe, feeling backed into a corner, agreed to accept venture capital on the terms offered. But the venture capitalists made a new demand. They wanted to see an experienced executive hired to bring management competence to the largely engineering-staffed 3Com. Metcalfe, partly defensive and partly desperate to raise money, challenged the VCs to find the successful executive.

Gib Meyers, a general partner of the Mayfield Fund venture capital partnership, responded by asking Metcalfe to meet Bill Krause, a "rising star" at Hewlett Packard (HP). Krause had managed HP's successful minicomputer business from $50 million to $500 million in sales. Krause had also developed a strategy for networking HP's new personal computers using Ethernet. Meyers knew Krause was interested in starting a company. Krause remembers Meyers telling him

> You ought to meet this guy that we've been talking to that's involved in starting a local area network company, and I said: "Fine. Who is it?" And he said:

30. Metcalfe interview, Computer History Museum.

> "It's Bob Metcalfe." I said: "He's the inventor of Ethernet, you know, God, he's an industry leader. I'd love to meet him."[31]

After a series of meetings, Krause made the leap, resigning from HP to join 3Com. He recalls his decision:

> I had not met somebody as charismatic and smart as Bob Metcalfe, with one exception, Howard Charney, and I had not seen as strong a technical group as Ron Crane and Greg Shaw. So the first reason, as is always in venture capital, was the people. The second reason was that Bob and I shared exactly the same vision of how Ethernet was going to eventually be used for PCs. Third is that I really did think it was going to be the third wave of computing and I always thought that if you got in front of the mainstream of something, a lot of the rest was made easy. I had joined HP just as they were getting into the minicomputer business, so that just made me getting on the fast track at HP a lot easier, being in front of something, of the new wave.[32]

With Krause joining as president, and Metcalfe assuming the role of CEO, three venture capital funds, Mayfield, New Enterprise Associates, and Melchor Venture Capital, invested $1.1 million on February 27, 1981. Paul Baran, who had joined 3Com's Board of Directors in March 1980, invested as well. 3Com's post-money valuation totaled $7.6 million, suggesting Metcalfe had prevailed in the battle over valuation. (Post-money valuation represents the total outstanding shares of a company's stock times the share price for the current round of financing. Typically, a first round financing would value the company at less than $5 million and generally less than $2 million.)

6.4.2 Michael Pliner and the Founding of Sytek

Local area networking meant little to Michael Pliner when he joined Ford Aerospace in Sunnyvale, CA, in 1975 to launch an in-house software development effort to win government contract work. Four years later, with a staff of 45 dedicated to networking projects, Pliner needed no one to tell him local area networking was poised to takeoff.[33] Pliner had read all published material on local area networking

31. Bill Krause, oral history interview by James L. Pelkey, August 15, 1994. Computer History Museum, Mountain View, CA. Available from https://archive.computerhistory.org/resources/access/text/2020/01/102740543-05-01-acc.pdf.

32. Krause interview, Computer History Museum.

33. His group had built FordNet, a.8 megabit per second CATV-based network with lineage to MITRENET; Flash-Net Fiber Optic, a high-speed network; and had evaluated local area networking for the Air Force numerous times. Pliner's team presented a paper at the MITRE/NBS Symposium.

and made an effort to meet anyone considered an expert, including Metcalfe and Bass. He also struggled with whether it was time to leave Ford, discouraged by the idea of simply starting a one-person company.

When Pliner confided to four of his staff that he was thinking of leaving Ford, they immediately voiced their desire to join him. Planning began for the new company they would name Sytek. Pliner remembers trying to strengthen his team: "Charley Bass and Bob Metcalfe and I met regularly. We tried to convince Bob Metcalfe to join Sytek and he said: 'No, I want to run my own company.'"[34]

In July 1979, the five founders—Pliner, Ken Biba, Tom Berson, Jack Goldsmith, and Bob Kroll—incorporated Sytek. Like Metcalfe, they started as consultants. Their first client was none other than Xerox, which gave them a $250,000 contract to write the communication protocols for their XTEN Telecommunications Network. Other clients, such as Cox Cable, Hughes, TRW, and several government agencies, quickly followed and before they knew it, they had completed their first year with 14 clients, revenues of $1.3 million, and a bank balance of $300,000 that made possible the exploration of strategy options. Pliner recalls their plan: "In 1980 we took the money we made out of the consulting business, and we said 'let's reinvest it and let's try to build something,' and we decided to go different than everybody else, we went broadband."[35]

Broadband would differentiate Sytek from those firms employing the baseband technology of Ethernet. Broadband technology held the potential to carry both voice and video, in addition to data, and to support multiple simultaneous communication channels. Their competence in broadband represented a diffusion of knowledge from MITRE to Ford and now to Sytek. Lee LaBarre of MITRE remembers: "We went out to Ford Aerospace and talked to them, exchanged things—information. They were interested, of course, in the MITRENET CSMA. And the people who were involved in that effort actually split off and became Sytek."[36]

Their first sale came before they even had a broadband product to ship and would end their friendly relationship with Ungermann-Bass, the third local area networking firm to incorporate that June–July of 1979.

34. Michael Pliner, oral history interview by James L. Pelkey, April 8, 1992. Computer History Museum, Mountain View, CA. Available from https://archive.computerhistory.org/resources/access/text/2018/04/102740326-05-01-acc.pdf.

35. Pliner interview, Computer History Museum.

36. Lee LaBarre and Paul Brusil, oral history interview by James L. Pelkey, April 6, 1988, Bedford, MA. Computer History Museum, Mountain View, CA. Available from https://archive.computerhistory.org/resources/access/text/2020/04/102792037-05-01-acc.pdf.

6.4.3 Ralph Ungermann, Charlie Bass, and the Founding of Ungermann-Bass

Forced out of Zilog at the end of 1978, Ungermann immediately began looking for his next opportunity. His inclinations led him to communications, a field he had been in since the late 1960s, when he served on the staff of Art Collins, the founder of Collins Radio. Ungermann had participated in creating a time division multiplexer cabling system interconnecting much of the equipment in their state-of-the-art semiconductor factory—a precursor of local area networking. Leaving Collins Radio for Western Digital, Ungermann managed the development of the UART (Universal Asynchronous Receiver and Transceiver) semiconductor chip; recognized as the first major communications semiconductor chip, funded by DEC and designed by Bell at DEC. He then joined Intel and created the first USART (Universal Synchronous Asynchronous Receiver and Transceiver) chip. Following Intel, he went to Zilog, where he followed up with the very successful SIO chip, a two-port serial asynchronous/synchronous interface chip, an extension of his previous work. He remembers his search: "I talked to a lot of people... What struck me was that every computer company was working on networking technology and every one told me the same thing: 'Boy, just think, if we can control the wire, we're going to control the business.' It was clear to me that that's not what the customer wanted and that there was an opportunity there."[37] Ungermann began talking to others in networking including Metcalfe, wanting to be sure of the market and clear in his vision.

Meanwhile, for those Ungermann had hired at Zilog and left behind, it became a waiting game to see what Exxon, the parent company, would do next. Charlie Bass would be one of the first to join Ungermann, as Ungermann recalls: "Charlie decided, as everybody did, that his career wasn't going to be at Zilog, so we decided to get together. We started kicking things around about what we'd do."[38]

In July 1979, Bass resigned from Zilog and Ungermann and Bass incorporated their new company—Ungermann-Bass (UB). Ungermann later remarked in an interview with *Data Communications* magazine in 1980: "I think people do what they know. My roots go back to engineering and local area networks, and I've felt for a long time that local networks were someday going to make it big."[39]

Once they had decided to focus on local area networking, Bass led an engineering team strengthened over the coming months with the additions of Davidson,

37. Ungermann interview, Computer History Museum.

38. Ungermann interview, Computer History Museum.

39. "Jogging entrepreneur is now running more for his local-networking firm," *Data Communications*, September 1980.

Kennedy, and five others from Zilog.[40] After investigating and rejecting the use of broadband, Bass orchestrated consensus for Ethernet, influenced by rumors of talks between Xerox and DEC.[41]

With the question of access method settled, the next question was which networking protocol software to use, TCP or XNS? Their decision to use the Z80 microprocessor, a legacy from their Zilog days, dictated their choice. Davidson remembers his reasoning: "I looked very hard at whether to implement TCP in the original Z80 product or XNS. But we were stuck with a very limited capability in our 64K (of memory) based Zilog Z80 systems. I decided against the complexity of TCP, and that served us very well for several years, especially when Xerox came out with their office systems."[42]

Ungermann, meanwhile, began what would be an exasperating search for the venture capital needed to finance UB's growth. Ungermann recalls: "During that time, we talked to everybody in the financial community, and there were few Venturers in the venture capital community."[43] Venture capitalists hesitated to invest because UB lacked a seasoned marketing/sales executive, a "third partner." Once understood, Ungermann contacted management recruiters and soon learned of James (Jim) Jordan, vice president of sales at Four-Phase Systems Inc. Jordan, a veteran of 10 years with Four-Phase and with 700 people reporting to him, regularly received calls from headhunters eager to pitch him on their once-in-a-lifetime job opportunity. Routinely dismissing such calls, this time Jordan listened. On hearing UB intended to sell networking products he readily agreed to a meeting. At Four-Phase, Jordan had been losing business to Datapoint's early ARCNET networking system. He recalls his frustration at trying to get Four-Phase to take networking seriously: "I spent a lot of time in product planning meetings at Four-Phase and said: 'Look, this is a problem. We need to be looking at it. This is the way of the

40. Bill Carrico: "They basically took a concept that nobody wanted to pursue internally, and went and did something with it." Bill Carrico and Judith Estrin, oral history interview with James L. Pelkey, June 23, 1988, Los Altos, CA. Computer History Museum, Mountain View, CA. Available from https://archive.computerhistory.org/resources/access/text/2018/03/102740285-05-01-acc.pdf.

41. Dalal: "I remember the days that Charlie Bass and Ralph Ungermann left Zilog and hung around Xerox trying to figure out what they were going to do next." Yogen Dalal, oral history interview by James L. Pelkey, August 2, 1988, Santa Clara, CA. Computer History Museum, Mountain View, CA. Available from https://archive.computerhistory.org/resources/access/text/2018/02/102738752-05-01-acc.pdf.

42. John M. Davidson, oral history interview by James L. Pelkey, August 18, 1992. Computer History Museum, Mountain View, CA. Available from https://archive.computerhistory.org/resources/access/text/2013/05/102746647-05-01-acc.pdf.

43. Ungermann interview, Computer History Museum.

future.' But I just couldn't convince the senior management that that was the way it was going to go. So I really believed in the whole concept of LANs."[44]

Even though UB had little cash and a staff of only 14 engineers and no marketing people, Jordan's experience competing against Datapoint had informed him of the opportunity and he made the "huge decision"[45] to join UB in January 1980. In his words: "I was bored to death. I thought it was a good idea. I liked the idea. I just believed in it. And I liked Ralph." With Jordan's help, UB management completed the business plan and in February closed their initial round of financing, raising $1.5 million with a company valuation of $2.2 million. Bessemer Venture Partners, Oak Investment Partners, and Venad Associates divided the investment.[46]

That same month, UB announced their first product: the Network Interface Unit-1, or NIU-1. The NIU-1, an Ethernet terminal switch that could be configured to support from 8 to 32 asynchronous terminals, would ship in July; making UB the first company to ship unbundled Ethernet products. (Xerox had shipped Ethernet but only as part of a system.) In addition, UB publicized its vision of "vendor independent networking," a vision very different than Metcalfe's and 3Com's "personal computer networking." Jordan reflects:

> You honestly have to give Ralph a lot of credit. He was really the strategist on it. The marketplace was really viewed as all this large installed base by multiple vendors, so you've got all this DEC, IBM, Data General, and HP gear, so where's the market? Well, the market is trying to get some communication capability between this heterogeneous installed base, so that's why, if you go back in the early days, and look at all the Ungermann-Bass stuff, it talks about vendor independent networking.[47]

In late spring of 1980, UB received inquiries from both Bolt Beranek and Newman (BBN) and Sytek. Each intended to bid the NIU-1 on a major RFPQ (Request for Price Quotation) being let by MIT Lincoln Labs. Bass relates the optimism at that moment: "We're cooperating with both BBN and Sytek, giving them everything we could to allow them to bid our product and win this contract. And we were

44. James (Jim) Jordan, oral history interview by James L. Pelkey, July 19, 1988, Hillsdale, CA. Computer History Museum, Mountain View, CA. Available from https://archive.computerhistory.org/resources/access/text/2018/04/102740315-05-01-acc.pdf.

45. Jordan interview, Computer History Museum.

46. Joining the Board of Directors would be Stewart Greenfield of Oak Investment Partners who was also a member of the Board of Micom. So would Neil Brownstein, who had invested in Telenet, the company Larry Roberts had headed.

47. Jordan interview, Computer History Museum.

feeling like we were in the catbird seat, that we had both of these guys bidding our product."[48]

Management's optimism turned to frustration and disappointment in September when they got a call from BBN, as Bass explains: "They said: 'Well, bad news. We lost to Sytek.' And we said: 'Oh, too bad,' and we hung up the phone and cheered—Only to learn that Sytek had bid their own product." The result was a shock and contempt for their rival: "Well, from that day forward they were the enemy, and they were the company to hate. Now, I think we overdid it, and all this got blown out of proportion, but it probably helped motivationally."[49]

Pliner, president of Sytek, also remembers the Lincoln Labs project. Lincoln Labs had described it as a high-speed, host-to-host interconnectivity product, which Sytek did not have at the time: "And we said 'Why don't you go buy Ungermann-Bass,' and they said, 'No, we want a broadband network.' We bid two options: Ungermann-Bass and our high-speed broadband network that we never had, it was going to have to be developed. We won the bid on our second option. To this day, I believe Ralph still thinks that I used him."[50]

Every sale was a struggle and invariably faced competition from the data PBX. Jordan explains: "The LAN companies lost business to the data PBX guys for a while, because you couldn't really do much more for the user than a data PBX could."[51] Trying to pitch features that would become advantageous in the future was a hard sell, especially with the price difference: "And big data PBXs, in large configurations, were $300 a port, maybe $200 a port whereas our initial pricing was something like $650 to $700 per port. For us there was a real push to get to $500 per port—it seemed to be the magic number at that point in time." Solving the cost problem would take time. Until then, Jordan had to find customers who would buy into the bigger vision of networking; customers willing to buy into the promise of a future now, as Jordan explains: "It was totally a technology pitch, because you couldn't really provide an application solution, so you'd tell them how great the technology was: 'This thing runs at ten megabits,' and 'Wow, gee whiz.'"[52]

The fledgling LAN start-ups also lacked the substantial financial and organizational resources and enviable market presence of the data communication

48. Charles (Charlie) Bass, oral history interview by James L. Pelkey, August 16, 1994, Palo Alto, CA. Computer History Museum, Mountain View, CA. Available from https://archive.computerhistory.org/resources/access/text/2018/03/102738753-05-01-acc.pdf.

49. Bass interview, Computer History Museum.

50. Pliner interview, Computer History Museum.

51. Jordan interview, Computer History Museum.

52. Jordan interview, Computer History Museum.

companies. What they did have was vision and entrepreneurial drive and those differences would prove substantial.

6.5 Data Communications Companies Respond with the Data PBX

6.5.1 Micom: The Data PBX and IPO

Norred's search for his replacement as vice president of development concluded quickly. Stephen W. Frankel knew as soon as he met Norred that he wanted to work for Micom. Frankel had spent the last 7 years at another small data communication start-up, Tran Telecommunications Inc. (Tran)—one of the earliest innovators of the data PBX—where he had risen from software engineer to both vice president of engineering and vice president of marketing. When Tran agreed to be acquired by Amdahl, Frankel decided he had no interest remaining simply an employee and began looking for an entrepreneurial opportunity. When he met Norred, they had an instant meeting of minds and he joined Micom in January 1980.

Frankel faced two immediate challenges: staffing an organization and finishing the development of a number of products. Frankel remembers inheriting an organization consisting of: "Bill Norred and one very capable programmer and a couple of helpers and that was it."[53] Norred had little time for engineering, so adding personnel became Frankel's top priority. Without badly needed staff, there was no chance of completing the unprecedented number of projects in progress. These projects included the development of new variations of the Data Concentrator, such as adding modems for the first time.[54] The Micro600 Port Selector, on the other hand, qualified as a truly challenging new development.[55]

In combination with his prior experience engineering data PBXs, Frankel's personal energy and disciplined management were sorely needed by Micom. He remembers the state of the Micro600 when he assumed responsibility for the

53. Stephen (Steve) Frankel, oral history interview by James L. Pelkey, April 26, 1988, Rancho Palos Verdes, CA. Computer History Museum, Mountain View, CA. Available from https://archive.computerhistory.org/resources/access/text/2018/07/102738828-05-01-acc.pdf.

54. Norred: "I always swore, after having gone through ADS, that I never really wanted to be in the modem business." William (Bill) Norred, oral history interview by James L. Pelkey, April 27, 1988, Simi Valley, CA. Computer History Museum, Mountain View, CA. Available from https://archive.computerhistory.org/resources/access/text/2018/07/102738827-05-01-acc.pdf. Evans persisted, however, and they agreed to test the waters by first selling modems integrated with other products. So, just as they had OEM'd their product to Codex, GDC, and Paradyne, they now elected to OEM modems from UDS, the firm specializing in OEM'ing modems to others. The Micro8000 Concentrator Modem was introduced in early 1981.

55. The other new project was the Micro400 Local Dataset, a substitute for a modem over short distances.

project: "The data PBX didn't work particularly well. It was in development and, not too much after I got there, it was going out in beta testing."[56] That the Micro600 had problems is small wonder given its architectural history. Norred had first proposed building a data PBX for Case, one to replace the one they were OEM'ing from Gandalf in 1973.[57] Case had declined. Three years later, another customer, International Telephone and Telegraph (ITT), needed a telex switch to selectively monitor different ports and lines for problems. Norred developed a product that "in effect, was the architecture of the data PBX. But to be perfectly honest, I don't even remember how we got from A to B. . . I know that we developed it by taking our 5040 controller and developing the switching module. . . I remember, it was a product that was built for ITT, almost by pointing, not by drawings."[58]

In 1977, another customer, Computer Science Corporation (CSC), needed a product to connect lots of terminals with multiple computers. Norred recalls: "CSC was instrumental in the data PBX as well, from a market standpoint, because they also were getting ready to buy a lot of these Infotron switches. Seems like we used to stay very close with CSC, in terms of what was going on. They were our customer that was providing a lot of input to us and the direction we went."[59]

Micom began shipping their Micro600 Port Selector in 1980. Although not called a data PBX, it was one: interconnecting many terminals and peripherals to multiple computers. Fueled in part by the instant success of the Micro600, sales soared to $32.8 million for 1981, up 112% over 1980; straining Micom's ability to finance growth from profits and its small capital base. With only $67,000 in cash and over $2 million in debt, Norred and Evans welcomed the news from investment bankers that the dormant IPO market for technology companies was showing stirrings of life. Their shareholders concurred, and needing capital to satisfy the impressive demand for their products, raising equity at the prices public investors were willing to pay, well, it seemed like a no-brainer.

In May 1981, Micom issued its Preliminary Prospectus, and the investment bankers began coaching Norred and Evans for the road show: when management makes presentations to potential institutional investors in hopes of selling them on becoming buyers of stock on the offering. Before the road show began, Norred and Evans attended the important Interface trade show. Catching them by surprise, Codex announced new multiplexers meant to replace the ones it

56. Frankel interview, Computer History Museum. Frankel's experience with Data PBXs came from his time at Tran.

57. Gandalf had introduced the first Data PBX.

58. Norred interview, Computer History Museum.

59. Norred interview, Computer History Museum.

was purchasing through its OEM deal with Micom. Since Codex was a significant OEM customer, and OEM sales constituted 18% of Micom's sales, the investment bankers expressed alarm at the implications for Micom's revenues, and suggested the IPO might have to be postponed, if not canceled. A financial disaster loomed. Norred and Evans tracked down the president of Codex, Art Carr, and asked for a meeting. After nervous pleasantries, Carr remembers Evans asking him:

> "So you won't buy any more of these?" And I said: "First off, nothing stops like a curtain coming down. We'll have some number of these we'll buy from you on probably a declining basis as ours comes up. . ." So he said: "You're telling me you're still going to keep buying from me?" And I said: "That's what I'm telling you and that's what you want to hear, Roger."[60]

With the IPO back on track, Norred and Evans began the exciting and nerve-racking rite of passage for successful entrepreneurs: the road show. Through 19 presentations, and meetings with prized investors, Norred and Evans excelled as they told Micom's story: Micom sells low-cost, easy-to-use data communication products to minicomputer users. The market for connecting terminals to remote minicomputers is growing faster than 23% per annum; the market is only 14% penetrated; and Micom holds a commanding 85% market share. As for competitors Timeplex and Infotron, they targeted their statistical multiplexers to customers interested in networking, and therefore innovated their products to be feature rich. Micom emphasized low cost and ease-of-use: the "box business," not networking. It was a story that sounded like music to investors' ears. On June 19, 1981, Micom Systems Inc. went public at $30.00 per share, raising in excess of $25 million with a market capitalization of nearly $190 million.[61]

Norred and Evans were committed to the strategy of selling boxes and of not getting into the much more complex networking business. What they did not realize, however, was their new Micro600 Port Selector, the data PBX, would soon take them in directions challenging not only to their business strategy but Micom's very existence.

6.5.2 Codex: The Data PBX, 1977–1981

When Codex began shipping their 6000 Series statistical multiplexers in 1977, they had to ship engineers to customer sites to troubleshoot the product. During these

60. Art Carr, oral history interview by James L. Pelkey, April 6, 1988, Newton, MA. Computer History Museum, Mountain View, CA, https://archive.computerhistory.org/resources/access/text/2015/10/102737982-05-01-acc.pdf.

61. Both Norred and Evans sold some stock on the offering, their remaining shares, valued at $30.00 per share, totaled $3.7 million and $2.1 million, respectively.

site visits, engineers identified customers' unmet needs. Displaying initiative in response to one such customer, one motivated engineer created a prototype of a new switching product, then approached management hoping to start a new product line. Pugh, now in strategic marketing after the merger with Motorola in 1978, recalls: "It was a development program that was not spec'd by marketing. It was something that one of the engineers did for a couple of customers. And apparently our controls weren't tight enough, because we let him do it. And then he came to marketing, and he said, 'Gee. I got this thing here that will do all these things.'"[62]

In 1980, Codex introduced the product as the IMS 7700, a switch that managed incoming telecommunication links to multiple computers and could be configured as either a data PBX or a matrix switch. Pugh remembers: "The data PBX was really more of a premise-type product as opposed to wide-area network product which the matrix switch was."

The management of Codex meanwhile had defined a new vision of "integrated communications." It was a vision that left little room for dial-up products. Carr summarized the vision to the press in April 1981: "Codex products will tackle problems of *exchange*, getting information into the network; *transport*, getting information through the network to its destination; and *command*, controlling the network from a central site."[63]

Codex's definition of a network was a wide area network, from the building out into the telephone network as it were, not an intra-building or premises-type network. As a definition, it would lead Codex into new product growth directions, as well as keep them from investing in products that were seen as intra-building or departmental, such as data PBXs or LANs. Nevertheless, because of a growing demand for data PBXs, before the end of 1981 Codex introduced their new IMS 7800 data PBX and matrix switch.[64]

Both Micom and Codex introduced data PBXs not from having a grand vision of emerging market dynamics but in response to specific customers' needs to interconnect their growing base of terminals to their growing numbers of computers. Creating a data PBX proved to be a small step after mastering statistical multiplexing. No big decisions committing to large development programs or extensive market research were required. Not having done so, however, would have unexpected consequences.

62. John Pugh, oral history interview by James L. Pelkey, February 25, 1988, Canton, MA. Computer History Museum, Mountain View, CA. Available from https://archive.computerhistory.org/resources/access/text/2016/03/102738098-05-01-acc.pdf.

63. Quote from *Computerworld*, April 20, 1981, 81.

64. Datapro Feb. 1986 C12-010-302.

6.6 Early LAN Start-ups Struggle, 1980–1981

6.6.1 Sytek: A Broadband Network and a Need for Cash

In February 1981, Sytek began shipping their comparatively inexpensive two-port broadband terminal server: LocalNet 20. A direct consequence of its Lincoln Labs development contract, two LocalNet 20s, costing a total of $2,500, made a network. Although both Sytek and UB, with its NUI-1, positioned their products as terminal servers, Sytek's customers tended to be those building campus-wide networks, whereas UB's wanted to create departmental networks. Having diverted resources to LocalNet 20, consulting revenues shrunk, and Sytek management had little choice but to raise capital. They began talking to venture capitalists.

6.6.2 Ungermann-Bass: Xerox, Broadband, and Chips

With each passing month of 1980, UB management tried desperately to find customers. Charlie Bass discovered the first significant opportunity when, over a dinner with David Liddle in San Francisco, he learned Xerox needed a product to interconnect their Star workstations to asynchronous terminals and peripherals of other vendors. Bass pitched Liddle on using UB's NIU-1s. Intrigued, Liddle asked if UB would be willing to conform their version of XNS to Xerox's and upgrade to the 10-megabit per second Ethernet. Without hesitation Bass committed to doing so, knowing that being able to claim interoperability with Xerox's products gave UB valuable credibility. Before the end of the year a handshake sealed the agreement with specifics and timetables to be negotiated.

Aside from the handshake with Xerox for a product that would not be available until well into 1981, they were still in need of cash. Not having the new product didn't seem to bother investors, however. The enthusiasm for networking investments enabled UB to close their second round of financing in November, raising $5 million on a nearly eight times step-up in company value to $19 million. For fiscal, and calendar, year 1980, UB had sales of $436,000 with a loss of $1.2 million.

To convert the Xerox handshake into formal contracts and then manage the ongoing OEM relationship, management courted Judy Estrin of Zilog. Following the exodus of engineers to UB in 1979, Estrin had been promoted to engineering manager for networking, and Carrico had become business unit manager. At the June 1980 National Computer Conference trade show, Zilog introduced their Z-Net LAN, a scaled-down Ethernet made possible in part by the informal flow of information between employees of PARC and Zilog. Zilog's future, however, turned increasingly on decisions made by Exxon Office Systems and networking seemed to interest no one. Estrin remembers: "We spent an infinite amount of time trying to deal with Exxon Office Systems—trying to get them to use the Z-Net technology. It was just, politically, very difficult."[65]

By late 1980, Estrin had had enough and, assured by Ungermann that he had learned the importance of focus from his Zilog experience, she joined UB on February 1, reporting to Jordan and responsible for the Xerox account. Estrin remembers:

> One of the things I felt at Zilog is they were doing too many things, trying to be too much, and I even remember sitting with Ralph before I accepted the offer and saying: "You did this at Zilog. Are you going to do this again?" "Absolutely, positively, not. We're going to focus, we're going to do this," and I got to UB, and they had their first product out, and they were going in a million directions.[66]

Exploration of directions even included a conversation with Evans of Micom, their data PBX nemesis. Bass remembers: "the wonderful thing about this business is you can sit down with your arch enemy and explore common interests, and I think we were trying to see how these technologies might converge, how we might do something together. It didn't get anywhere, but we certainly had the conversations."[67]

After Sytek introduced the broadband LocalNet 20 in February 1981, UB management learned they had more than data PBXs to contend with. Broadband had appeal in its low cost and its futuristic ability to handle voice and video in addition to data. Perhaps the animosity UB harbored for Sytek was motivation as well, but it did not take long for UB management to justify the development of a broadband product. To jump-start development, Bass suggested they recruit Gregory Hopkins of MITRE, an acknowledged expert in broadband and holder of patents regarding CSMA/CD over broadband. In June, Hopkins joined UB, opening an office in Burlington, MA.[68] Jordan remembers: "We started this broadband engineering operation in Burlington. It worked for me. I don't remember why. Looking back on it, it's probably a great way to start a rift."[69]

Engineering then began development of new, lower-cost Ethernet products, to be finalized once Ethernet chips were available from Intel. Ungermann knew the risks of waiting but there seemed little choice given the expense of doing their own

65. Carrico and Estrin interview, Computer History Museum.

66. Carrico and Estrin interview, Computer History Museum.

67. Bass interview, Computer History Museum.

68. Dataletter, *Data Communications*, July 1981, 15.

69. Jordan interview, Computer History Museum.

silicon. Then luck knocked on their door and an alternative appeared. One of their investors, Kleiner Perkins, introduced them to Silicon Compilers, a new start-up, as Bass remembers: "They came, and they wanted to test their technology on something hard. So we said: 'Well, we've got something hard for you. We'd like to have an Ethernet chip.' So they come in and they started running equations and talking to Alan Goodrich, who was our hardware designer."[70]

With everything going UB's way, in July 1981 they announced their fully compliant 10-megabit Ethernet NUI executing fully compliant XNS. Success seemed assured.

6.6.3 3Com: Product Strategy in Anticipation of a PC

In the spring of 1981, with the fiscal year about to end, management met to adopt the annual operating plan for the coming year. Krause argued the need to aggressively reduce product costs using semiconductor technology to reduce chip count and printed circuit board space, known as "real estate." Krause remembers:

> There are very few things that I blew Bob [Metcalfe] away with, but this was one of them (see Figure 6.2). I said: "OK, this is 1981 and this is 1986 and we've got to go from here to here." And Bob said: "What do you mean? How are we going to do that?" So I said: "Well, Bob, first of all, that's your job, figuring out how we're going to do it, but if we're going to make a mass market out of this, and we're going to connect PCs together, we've got to go from here to here, because taking a $2,000 Apple and spending $4,000 to connect it isn't going to compute. So we've got to figure out how to do that. And a way to do that is through semiconductor VLSI integration over time, so let's start with our Unibus.[71]

Metcalfe agreed. However, when two other new product ideas were suggested, an Ethernet controller for Apple or other existing personal computers, or a terminal server, he remained unyielding, quickly ending any discussion. His vision of networking was personal computers networked with Ethernet. Metcalfe considered the existing personal computers as little more than toys. He was certain that sufficiently powerful personal computers would become available and preferred simply to wait. Even the compelling argument that UB was growing rapidly by selling terminal servers would not change Metcalfe's thinking, as he recalls:

> I stubbornly stuck with the idea that, "No, no, no. Connecting terminals to CPUs is a relatively low-grade application of my technology." It was intended to connect PCs together. Our problem was that there weren't any PCs, or

70. Bass interview, Computer History Museum.

71. Krause interview, Computer History Museum.

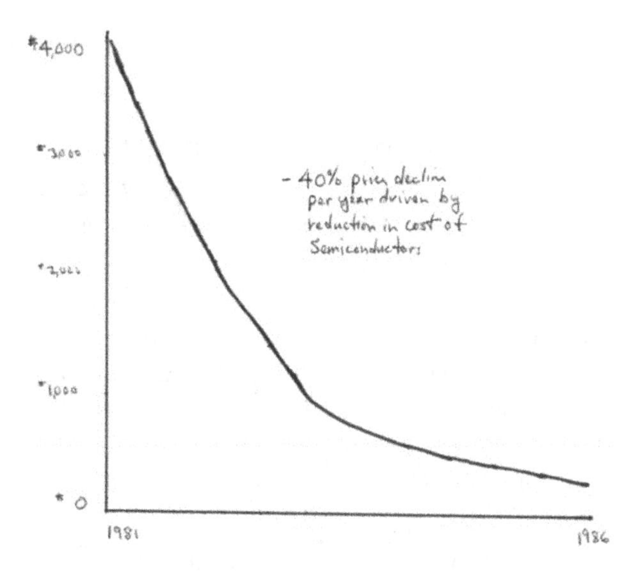

Figure 6.2 3Com Ethernet pricing objective. Source: Bill Krause, personal communication, June 13, 2021. Used with permission.

> rather the PCs that existed were Apple IIs, which cost $1500 and Ethernet in those days cost $4300.[72]

Metcalfe and Krause recognized their existing products were unlikely to generate enough sales to attain profitability and that they needed to develop products that had significant sales potential with large enough volumes to justify the cost and effort of manufacturing a VLSI[73] chip. To stimulate their thinking, Metcalfe arranged for the two of them to visit both PARC and Stanford. Krause remembers: "Bob was trying to educate me about the Ethernet Gestalt, so he took me over to PARC and wandered me around there, and he took me over to Stanford, and he introduced me to this guy who was working on something called the Stanford University Network."[74]

Strategizing afterwards, Metcalfe and Krause agreed that the next product 3Com should build was an Ethernet adaptor for Multibus, the bus being employed in the Stanford University Network and favored by those using the new Motorola microprocessors. While not necessarily the homerun they wanted, it leveraged their existing competencies and seemed like a solid product to add to their product line and

72. Metcalfe interview, Computer History Museum.

73. VLSI (Very Large Scale Integration) was the next generation semiconductor technology after LSI (Large Scale Integration).

74. Krause interview, Computer History Museum.

would use the chips they intended to design and develop while they waited for a real PC to be introduced.

6.7 The Emergence of the Networking Market-Structure

The period from 1976 to 1981 saw the networking industry evolve from a gestation phase characterized by early research and testing to an emergent phase where actual products were creating profits for early entrepreneurial start-ups. It is notable that many of the individuals involved in the development of early networking products cite the same sources of information as key to their understanding of this new technology. Research on networks from the ALOHAnet, ARPANET, Bell Labs, and Xerox PARC served as the basis for most of the technologies used in the development of local area networking products. This research grew out of the government-sponsored projects that investigated new types of computing networks as they related to large scale government and university computing environments. With the advent of the minicomputer and the growth of business computing, corporations and small businesses also faced similar challenges of connectivity. The NBS and MITRE workshops and LACN Symposium shed light on both public and private sector demand for networking solutions and served to validate the market.

Following the symposium, entrepreneurs with an understanding of this unique opportunity took action, launching the early LAN start-ups. Each company adopted its own unique strategy for success in an uncertain market. Metcalfe kept 3Com focused on interconnecting minicomputers as they waited for a high-performance desktop computer to be introduced. Ungermann and Bass were much more pragmatic: they knew customers wanted to interconnect their growing legions of terminals to computers from different vendors. They also proved early on that they were not even wedded to Ethernet, as was 3Com. Sytek introduced a low-cost broadband terminal server, envisioning a future product that could transmit voice, data, and video. The success of these three firms would inspire others and contributed to a rapid increase in competition in the coming years.

Yet even as these networking firms jostled amongst themselves, they had more serious competition from data communication firms selling data PBXs. These firms were responding to real needs of real customers, not anticipating future needs. Micom had been incrementally innovating a data PBX product ever since it sought to get its main customer, Case, to replace the OEM data PBX from Gandalf with one of their own. Codex responded in a similar manner, addressing specific client needs with a data switch for both local and wide area switching. But the data communications firms had no vision of the coming disruption of personal computing, or if they did, it was hard for them to justify pursuing it when their research budgets had already been earmarked for innovations to traditional circuit-switched communications products.

By 1981, the LAN market-structure had clearly emerged and was evolving into the competitive phase, with start-ups introducing additional products and seeking to capture additional markets. Many firms like 3Com and UB realized the importance of developing networking chips in order to bring the price of LAN connections down to a level competitive with that of the data PBX. The strength of the industry as a whole was evident in the community relationships that had evolved. The establishment of the 802 committee was essential to the evolution of badly needed standards that could help propel the industry to a much larger market. To this end, the players themselves sought to strengthen their own positions through arrangements like the DIX consortium.

6.8 In Perspective

To achieve success, the early entrepreneurs of the LAN industry needed a unique combination of skills in their teams. Engineering talent in the many fundamentals of network communications, as well as an ability to find and negotiate development contracts, was also essential to the creation of a start-up's first products. The ability to attract and secure the investment capital necessary to bankroll further product development and growth was also essential. Finally, they needed to be able to effectively sell their technology. Unlike the early market for data communications products, where start-ups could capture market share by incrementally innovating existing products from the incumbent AT&T, the early entrepreneurs of local area networking had a much tougher sell. In this case, the producers had to go out and push their solutions to create the market, especially since the existing data communications solution, the data PBX, did what most customers wanted for a lower price.

This combination of skills rarely existed in one person, but in the case of Robert Metcalfe his abilities in all these areas were essential to the early success of 3Com. Metcalfe was not only a co-inventor of Ethernet; he was its most effective salesman. As a negotiator, getting Exxon to fund the development of 3Com's first products was essential to 3Com's early success. Metcalfe was also instrumental in forging the relationship of the DIX consortium, placing the weight of industry leaders behind Ethernet. The same skillset was a requisite for UB and Sytek. Engineering talent and arrangements with large companies were key to early growth. In UB's case, their initial contract with Xerox gave them needed software protocols to support their products. For Sytek, the contract with Lincoln Labs was instrumental in the development of their network interface unit.

The paradigm shift that these early LAN companies were advancing was not immediately appreciated by consumers. The advantages of packet switched networks over circuit switched data communications would become much clearer with further advances and cost reductions in computing. With the advent of the desktop computer, the real value of networking would become apparent.

The Chaos of Competition: Networking, 1981–1982

7.1 Overview

By the early 1980s, large corporations were clearly serious about buying products to enable their computers to communicate with other computers and peripheral devices. For networking entrepreneurs, it was a time to act, knowing that if they failed to launch their companies soon they risked being left behind. But the surge in products from these entrepreneurial start-ups and existing companies left many potential customers confused with choice overload. The available networking technologies included Ethernet, token ring, token bus, and scores of proprietary local area networks. In addition, corporate customers were being pinched by the government's economic policy of the early 1980s when interest rates soared to nearly 20% as the Fed attempted to fight rising inflation. For the moment, growth remained sluggish for the new networking market-structure.

While entrepreneurs struggled to define their strategies, market experts offered a much grander vision of computers transforming the office and the corporate enterprise. Labeled "The Office of the Future," it was an economic prize worthy of any strategic plan. Many analysts predicted that the entrenched private branch exchange (PBX) vendors, already interconnecting and switching voice communications, would be the logical vendors to deliver these new data services. This $2 billion plus product category was itself undergoing a revolutionary change brought on by the entrepreneurial firm ROLM, which had introduced a computerized PBX, or CBX. The leading company in the PBX market, AT&T, however, was prohibited from introducing a CBX by the FCC. It was rapidly losing market share, challenged by the data communications firms as they innovated their own solutions to data switching in the form of the data PBX. When the tide of market deregulation that began with Carterfone in 1968 came to a dramatic conclusion in 1982, and AT&T agreed to be dismembered, it was at last granted permission to compete in computer markets, including data transmission.

The introduction of the IBM personal computer in August 1981 set the stage for a paradigm shift from centrally located mainframe computing to one of distributed desktop computing. While some networking companies welcomed the introduction of the PC, to others it made little difference as they chose to remain focused on their existing mainframe and minicomputer customers. Both start-ups and incumbents saw the rapid pace of technological, regulatory, and economic changes as potential opportunities, but in this stage of the new market-structure of networking, confusion and uncertainty made the path forward treacherous.

7.2 The Office of the Future, the PBX to CBX, and AT&T

The grandiloquent, yet vague, vision of "The Office of the Future" cast a presentable spin on what was largely white-collar automation. As a vision it served exactly the same purpose as J.C.R. Licklider's "Intergalactic Network:" to guide the creators and users of technology into a shared future. There was little doubt about the need for information automation. Lewis Branscomb, Chief Scientist of IBM, would write as late as 1983 that the information explosion was "proceeding at the rate of two file drawers per office worker per year."[1] In 1981, the Office of the Future vision did not need to be precise for many of the technologies remained undefined. What seemed assured, however, was that all the voice, data, and even video information of the office would somehow be brought together to create a new source of productivity that would justify the massive investment needed to build out these new products and services. Central to making the vision a reality was the question of what technology would switch data flowing between the information appliances such as computers, terminals, peripherals, telephones, and the yet-to-be-invented. The two key candidates were shaping up to be the traditional voice PBX or the emerging LAN technologies.

The PBX, first introduced in 1879, seemed the most obvious choice.[2] A PBX is an on-premises telephone exchange, or switch, that connects to an outside telephone service provider such as AT&T, while enabling a large number of on-premise telephones to interconnect to each other without involving the service provider. Cabling, generally "twisted-pair" wires, runs from the PBX to every desktop telephone on the premise. This wiring, already in place to handle voice transmission, would presumably provide data transmission as well, or at least that was what the PBX manufacturers wanted themselves and the world to believe.

1. Lewis M. Branscomb. 1983. Networks for the nineties. *IEEE Communications Magazine*, October 1983, 38–43.

2. M. D. Fagen, ed. 1975. *A History of Engineering and Science in the Bell System: The Early Years (1875–1925)*. Bell Telephone Laboratories Inc., 659–693.

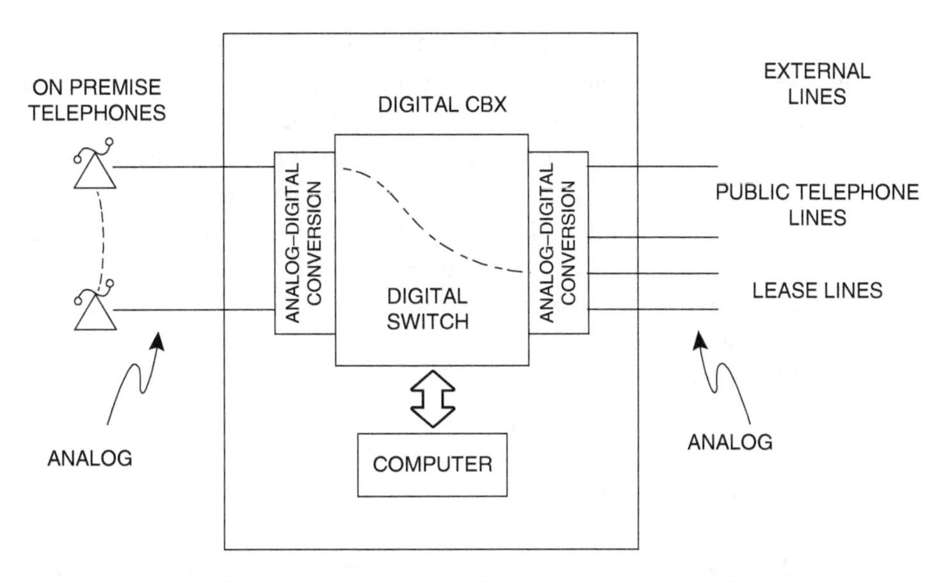

Figure 7.1 The ROLM CBX. Illustration by Jan Helsel from a drawing by Robert Maxfield. Used with permission.

In 1980, the annual sales of PBXs totaled $2.65 billion. AT&T dominated the market with a 45% market share, down drastically from its 100% share in 1968. (The same Carterfone decision that had freed foreign attachments from the monopolistic control of AT&T made market competition possible in PBXs.) While other firms entered the market, at first they did little but incrementally improve on AT&T's well-known PBX architecture.

A major transition occurred in January 1975 at the International Communication Association trade show when a new entrant, ROLM, upended the PBX business by introducing a computer-based PBX, or CBX.[3] The heart of the ROLM CBX was a Data General computer that performed both functions of digital switch and computer-based control. Digital switching made it possible to integrate voice and data into a single system and computer control made possible a wide range of applications as never before (see Figure 7.1). The competition would eventually follow ROLM's lead. In 1978, Northern Telecom introduced a CBX, the SL-1. The significant advantages of the CBX began taking their toll, and in 1980 22% of all PBX's sold were CBXs.

3. ROLM was founded on June 1, 1969, by four graduates of Rice University who had migrated to Silicon Valley. At first, they created and sold a military ruggedized Data General Nova computer. While successful, their CEO, Ken Oshman, had larger visions than a $10-million military contract business. In 1973, management made plans to enter the PBX business.

Yet AT&T could not sell a CBX. In 1977, the FCC thwarted their efforts to introduce computer-like features in their Dimension PBX, believing it was enforcing Computer Inquiry I. In 1980, Computer Inquiry II made it clear AT&T could not sell products with imbedded information technology unless they did so through a separate subsidiary. AT&T began creating a subsidiary while simultaneously fighting for their right to maintain their monopoly in telecommunications as well as compete in unregulated (e.g., computer) markets. Lawyers argued that a separate subsidiary denied them the use of their significant economic resources, which was not in the public interest.

While AT&T was watching from the sidelines, others entered the seemingly lucrative CBX market, believing that all new sales of PBXs would be CBXs, the entire installed base of over $10 billion would convert to CBXs, and the coming need to interconnect computer equipment would be best met with CBXs. In 1981, AT&T's market share had dropped to 40% (see Table 7.1).

In 1981, Datapoint announced an advanced CBX, the Information Switching Exchange (ISX). The ISX was not only a CBX but could interconnect to Datapoint's proprietary ARCnet LAN. It foreshadowed a new fourth generation of PBXs, ones merging the features of CBXs and LANs. In the early 1980s, venture capitalists funded seven fourth-generation companies, to become known as the Start-up Seven: CXC, Ztel, Cyber Digital, Telenova, Prolink, LanTel, and David Systems.

Table 7.1 **PBX market shares 1980–1983 ($ millions)**

Company	1980	Market Share	1981	Market Share	1982	Market Share	1983	Market Share
AT&T	1,200	47.5	1,150	39.7	950	30.9	850	25.9
GTE Corp	135	5.3	150	5.2	130	4.2	135	4.1
Northern Telecom	200	7.9	250	8.6	450	14.6	590	18.0
ROLM	160	6.3	244	8.4	326	10.6	432	13.2
Mitel Corp	225	8.9	325	11.2	370	12.0	405	12.3
Intecom					30	1.0	70	2.1
Other	605	24.0	775	26.8	820	26.7	800	24.4
Total	2,525	100.0	2,894	100.0	3,076	100.0	3,282	100.0
Market Growth			14.6%		6.3%		6.7%	

Source: Based on Smith Barney Research: Telecommunications October 10, 1985. Maxfield, Katherine. *Starting Up Silicon Valley: How ROLM Became a Cultural Icon and Fortune 500 Company* (Austin, Texas: Greenleaf Book Group, 2014), 126–228.

In 1981–1982, the trade press ran numerous articles weighing the advantages of the CBX versus the LAN for interconnecting voice and data communication needs.[4] Experts could be found on both sides of the argument. And then there was the growing chorus of voices extolling the benefits of integrating CBXs and LANs. The vast confusion of what technology was best bordered on the unbelievable with few fully comprehending the coming impact of personal computers, a category of products validated when IBM introduced its personal computer: the IBM PC.

7.2.1 The IBM PC, 1981–1982

In April of 1977, thousands of hobbyists, PC developers, and curious onlookers crowded into the Civic Auditorium in San Francisco for the West Coast Computer Faire to see the latest offerings of what was then the beginnings of the personal computer revolution. Of all the new products, the Apple II and the Commodore PET attracted the most attention, not just to hobbyists but to the larger market of consumers and "technology"-interested individuals. Then in December 1979, Dan Bricklin, a Harvard MBA student, conceived a software product that ran on an Apple II and mimicked the possibilities of doing calculations on a blackboard. It was called VisiCalc, short for Visible Calculator, and it quickly penetrated the corporate workplace. For example, in the first 9 months after introduction, 25,000 Apple IIs, out of a total of 130,000 Apple IIs sold, used VisiCalc.

The usefulness of the program on an Apple II was so transparent that sales personnel and management of IBM began to hear customers asking when IBM was going to follow suit and introduce a personal computer of its own. The requests quickly began filtering up to the executive branch and the subject was discussed in weekly management committee meetings. Most executives didn't understand the relevance of the topic; they believed these strange little computers had no place in their organizations, viewing them as nothing but toys. CEO Frank Cary remained ambivalent but his instincts informed him that if IBM were going to act, it needed to be quickly, something that was not in the DNA of IBM. So he identified William "Bill" Lowe, whom he believed was not so jaded, and they agreed on a few givens: the operation would be run as a "skunk" works, completely outside any part of IBM, the computer would be introduced in a year, everything was to remain a complete secret and Cary would run interference. The schedule called for Lowe to have a

4. "The office's future: CBX or local net?" *Data Communications*, February 1981, 30–32; "Controlling the electronic office: PBXs make their move," *Electronics*, April 7, 1981, 139–148; "CBX unveilings continue at a fast pace," *Data Communications*, July 1981, 44–45; "Which technology will rule the automated office?" *Data Communications*, November 1981, 66–79; "The Integrated CBX revolution," *Data Communications*, Dec. 1981, 156; "Comparing the CBX to the local network—and the winner is?" *Data Communications*, July 1982, 103–113.

plan ready to present at an August 1980 management committee meeting. Before the meeting Lowe told Cary: "The only way we can get into the personal computer business is to go out and buy part of a computer company or buy both the CPU and software from people like Apple or Atari—because we can't do this within the culture of IBM."[5] Before the meeting ended, a disgruntled team of executives nonetheless approved the plan, including that the subject remain a secret.

Lowe would make an inspired choice in recruiting Donald "Don" Estridge, with a reputation as being a "renegade," to run the operations. They negotiated deals with Intel for the microprocessor, the 8088 "computer on a chip," for the brains of their PC and with Microsoft for the operating system, known as DOS, for disk operating system.[6] Another problem was sourcing software.[7] IBM entered the personal computer business leveraging external economies rather than attempting everything internally as they had with the successful System/360. Those decisions contributed to achieving the goal of introducing the IBM PC in just a year.

On August 12, 1981, IBM introduced their IBM PC. "This is the computer for just about everyone who has ever wanted a personal system at the office, on the university campus or at home," stated its press release. No expletives sounding a new day. No grand vision of the future; simply another routine press release. It was an understated introduction and was kept a secret up to the last moment. According to historian James Cortada, IBM set the de facto standards for PCs: "When Estridge introduced the PC to the world, IBM's competitors would have to respond quickly, so they, too, increasingly would have to use DOS and Intel chips."[8]

The IBM PC may have been a technological "de facto standard," but most importantly it bore the imprint and endorsement of IBM. Before its introduction, businesses purchased personal computers of different makes with little or no coordination within the business, thus creating potential problems for networking, maintenance, and training, causing concern to data processing managers. For those corporations that had taken action and organized all their data processing

5. James Chposky and Ted Leonsis. 1988. *Blue Magic: The People, Power, and Politics Behind the IBM Personal Computer*. Facts on File, 9.

6. When Microsoft committed to provide IBM with an operating system, they actually did not have one, but knew where they could buy one for $75,000. It was called QDOS, which stood for Quick and Dirty Operating System.

7. They also had the start-up Lotus Development Corporation provide an upgraded version of VisiCalc, software program titled Lotus 1-2-3, released in January 1983, that became the killer application.

8. James W. Cortada. 2019. *IBM: The Rise and Fall and Reinvention of a Global Icon*. MIT Press, Cambridge, MA, 390 and 396.

activities under vice-presidents of MIS Departments, the IBM PC represented a safe choice and could be made a standard without much disagreement.

So despite the early doubts and resistance of IBM executives, the initial sales of the PC surpassed the official projections of selling 1 million PCs in the first three years; actual sales were $1 billion in the first year, and by the second year they were selling 200,000 units/month.[9] Without knowing it, IBM had ushered in the change from host-centric to distributed data processing.

7.2.2 IBM's Token Ring LAN, 1981–1982

In the fall of 1980, IBM executives watched Xerox television ads on Monday Night Football announcing the benefits of its new computer system, the Star System 8000, interconnected with an Ethernet LAN. When discussing what IBM's response would be, they initially drew a blank. So another task force was organized just as had been done to strategize for the personal computer.

Daniel Warmenhoven, a task force member, recalls a key meeting to discuss the company's strategy:

> I remember the meeting well. One of the recommendations was we just adopt Ethernet. And the answer came back 'We can't do that, because you can't be an industry leader by following somebody else's implementation.' And at the time it was already pretty clear that DEC was getting very closely aligned—it wouldn't be so bad if it was Xerox only, but having DEC in the fray, that was like a declaration of war. I mean, the Axis Powers had formed, and IBM had to have a different solution, so the alternative was to pick the token ring.[10]

The IBM task force learned that its Zurich laboratory had been working with token ring technology ever since 1977.[11] MIT Professor Jerry Saltzer spent 1977 and 1978 working with IBM on their token ring network in White Plains and visited the Zurich lab where Saltzer and the lab staff compared notes. He recalls, "I basically supplied them with every piece of input that we had learned." As to why IBM selected token ring versus getting involved with Ethernet, Saltzer suggests the likely scenario that when the Zurich lab decided to study local area networking, they would have quickly come in contact with the Cambridge ring due to frequent

9. Cortada, *IBM*, 390 and 392.

10. Daniel J. Warmenhoven, oral history interview by James L. Pelkey, March 9, 1988, Atherton, CA. Computer History Museum, Mountain View, CA. Available from https://archive.computerhistory.org/resources/access/text/2020/02/102792020-05-01-acc.pdf.

11. 1976—Phillipe Janson goes to work at IBM Zurich after graduating from MIT.

visitors to the lab from Cambridge. While there was talk of the development of Ethernet at Xerox PARC, nothing had been published on it yet so it was still relatively unknown at that time. Saltzer also points out that there were significant differences between token ring and Ethernet, and he felt "that if you were to start off with a completely free slate, no history behind you of any kind, and ask yourself which is intrinsically better... I believe the answer is the token ring. And I think that they (Zurich) quickly came to that same conclusion themselves, that its got some fundamentally superior properties."[12]

Warmenhoven remembers the months from October to the end of the year when the token ring plan, a "resource definition" in the IBM terminology of the day, had to be completed so funding of the project could begin in 1981. Warmenhoven, who reported to Murray Bolt, remembers:

> Murray and I were probably the key architects of what I would consider to be three fundamental elements in this thing. The first one is that it had to be a structured system, so even though it was a ring, it was going to be a star wired system. It was going to model the phone systems. It started off with passive concentrators, but the whole cabling system and everything was kind of a star. The second one was that it would not be single ring, it would be a full mesh, and it would be strictly peer-to-peer across the mesh. Now, at the time, SNA was mainframe polled, and so here's your first anathema at IBM, that it's not mainframe centered. It is totally distributed. The third element, and this is really an interesting wrinkle, it had to be available for non-IBM device attachment, and this was another anathema at IBM. This leads to the conclusion you want the chip set available in the semiconductor merchant market. Murray, basically, I think, more than anybody else, made the decision that he was going to get the chip set designed by one of the major semiconductor manufacturers. The three big candidates were Intel, Motorola, and TI.[13]

The task force members were aware of the PC skunk works being managed by Don Estridge. Even though Warmenhoven and Bolt were aware of the PC under development, they felt the main application of their efforts to develop token ring would be to network smart workstations and minicomputers.

The token ring that would be the LAN to compete with Ethernet was not as easy to accomplish as was selling the PC; it required coordinating and working with many different divisions within IBM to secure their agreement to make token

12. Jerome Howard Saltzer, oral history interview by James L. Pelkey, March 7, 1988, Cambridge, MA. Computer History Museum, Mountain View, CA. Available from https://archive.computerhistory.org/resources/access/text/2016/10/102717242-05-01-acc.pdf.

13. Warmenhoven interview, Computer History Museum.

ring available. As for the efforts to select a merchant chip manufacturer, by year-end 1981, after nearly a year of investigation, IBM decided to work with Texas Instruments (TI). Nearly another year was then spent negotiating the design of the chip(s). On September 16, 1982, IBM and TI made known their intentions to develop integrated-circuit chips for an IBM "local area network."[14] The article further confirmed that IBM was using the "token-passing" technique.

Warmenhoven remembers the meeting with TI managers shortly after the public announcement: "TI came in probably 10 days after the contract was signed, and said they were off the schedule by a year. I mean, they may have started the discussion 'We're off by up to 6 months,' but by the time you get into it, it's off by a year."[15] Token ring was suddenly looking like a 1984 product, not a 1983 product.

7.3 Early LAN Start-ups, 1981

7.3.1 3Com

Bob Metcalfe fully grasped the importance of the IBM PC. Although he and the company were committed to completing the Unibus and Multibus adapters, he couldn't resist defocusing their efforts for a few days to investigate the IBM PC. Krause remembers:

> The credit Bob should get here is that he went out and bought an IBM PC and he set it up in the middle of the design lab... and Ron Crane started poring all over this thing and, before you knew, we understood everything we needed to know: we knew what the power slot budget was, we knew the physical size, we knew the chip count that we had to get to meet the power budget. So we began learning a lot of things.[16]

As tempting as the IBM PC was, Krause kept the company focused on building the Multibus board and reducing the costs so that a PC Ethernet controller might be possible. At the time, the cost of an Ethernet controller was almost as much as a PC itself.

Eyeing the future, Metcalfe and Krause saw they needed more money. So they began talking to venture capitalists. In one of their conversations another fortuitous connection was made, not an uncommon event when talking to venture capitalists eager to demonstrate the value they could bring as an investor. When

14. "IBM and Texas Instruments Inc. Plan Joint Work," *Wall Street Journal*, Sept. 16, 1982, 13.

15. Warmenhoven interview, Computer History Museum.

16. Bill Krause, oral history interview by James L. Pelkey, August 15, 1994. Computer History Museum, Mountain View, CA. Available from https://archive.computerhistory.org/resources/access/text/2020/01/102740543-05-01-acc.pdf.

Pierre Lamond of Sequoia Capital met with Krause and Metcalfe to investigate doing a second round, he said he had heard that a new chip manufacturer was looking for a partner to develop an Ethernet chip. So, through Sequoia, Metcalfe and Krause met Gordy Campbell, the founder of Seeq Technology Inc. Before the end of the year, 3Com and Seeq began joint development of an Ethernet chip—reason for optimism and a need for money. In January 1982, 3Com closed a second round of financing totaling just over $2 million. That same month Interlan would introduce their products in direct competition with 3Com's controllers.

In April 1982, management began holding a series of planning meetings that would culminate in a new product direction for the company. Two former Hewlett-Packard employees brought in by Krause, Lazar (Larry) Birenbaum and Larry Hardke, conceived the EtherSeries strategy—clearly derived from the guiding vision of Metcalfe. EtherSeries was to be introduced in October 1982 and would consist of two elements: Etherlink and EtherShare. Etherlink was a board-level Ethernet controller that would fit into an IBM PC and made possible file sharing between hard disks and printer sharing. EtherShare was a file server supporting up to 20 IBM PCs and offering 10 megabytes of storage (see Figure 7.2).

Not having the cash to finance continued development of its existing Multibus and Unibus controllers as well as EtherSeries, the choice was made to divert all funds to EtherSeries. The controllers would be sold for as long as there were profitable customers. Management fully understood they were making a bet-the-ranch decision.

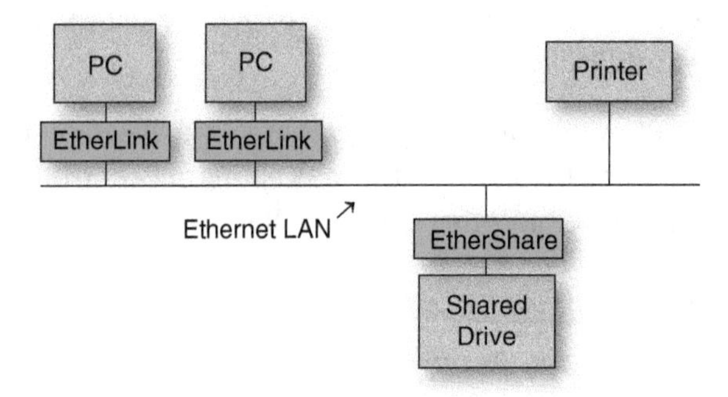

Figure 7.2 3Com EtherSeries. Illustration by James L. Pelkey and Loring G. Robbins. Source: Based on Bill Krause, oral history interview by James L. Pelkey, August 15, 1994. Computer History Museum, Mountain View, CA. Available from https://archive.computerhistory.org/resources/access/text/2020/01/102740543-05-01-acc.pdf; Robert Metcalfe, oral history interview by James L. Pelkey, February 16, 1988, Portola Valley, CA. Computer History Museum, Mountain View, CA. Available from https://archive.computerhistory.org/resources/access/text/2013/05/102746650-05-01-acc.pdf.

For fiscal year ending May 1982, 3Com's revenues soared 250% to $1.8 million with a loss of $690 thousand. But their burn rate—expenses needed to execute the EtherSeries plan—would consume their roughly $2 million of cash in less than a year. The impact of Interlan's entry had made it clear that their current products were rapidly being driven obsolete; meaning cash from sales would be harder and harder to come by. If EtherSeries was either late to market or didn't sell, 3Com faced a bleak future. So ran the pending obituaries in the press.

In June 1982, 3Com's Board of Directors, concerned with how to grow sales even faster, approved a plan to promote Krause to CEO and put Metcalfe in charge of sales and marketing. It proved to be a brilliant move. Metcalfe remembers the turnaround: "We really started heading into the tank. So we made *me* head of sales and marketing, which is my major accomplishment at 3Com. I mean, I did a lot of other things, but *that* was the thing that I really did, was get us to a million a month."[17]

To get sales to $1 million a month took competence aided by the aura of an industry leader, the man who had invented Ethernet. In Metcalfe's words:

> I could get an appointment with anybody that I wanted to, because I was the inventor of Ethernet, and they would talk to me. So unlike a lot of other salespeople, I had an entrée anywhere I went. And I'm good at personal selling. I mean I can talk to people and I listen to them, and then I have intelligent things to say and then they want to buy my products later.[18]

In October 1982, 3Com introduced the EtherSeries: IBM PC-compatible EtherLink controllers and the EtherShare file server. The price of an EtherLink interconnecting two PCs and a shared disk drive was $950 per computer: a price breaking the mythical $1,000 per computer price point and down sharply from $3,000 per connection just a few years earlier. The efficient single chip design of the Seeq Ethernet chip made the lower price possible (see Figure 7.3).

The XNS-based EtherSeries took advantage of the knowledge gained from working with XNS and TCP/IP networking protocols. The product offered some of the higher-level services inherent in these networking systems such as file sharing, print sharing, and a platform on which to build other user applications. These services and features reflected a computer user's point-of-view, one very different than those of the data communications community that thought in terms of physical

17. Robert Metcalfe, oral history interview by James L. Pelkey, February 16, 1988, Portola Valley, CA. Computer History Museum, Mountain View, CA. Available from https://archive.computerhistory.org/resources/access/text/2013/05/102746650-05-01-acc.pdf.

18. Metcalfe interview, Computer History Museum.

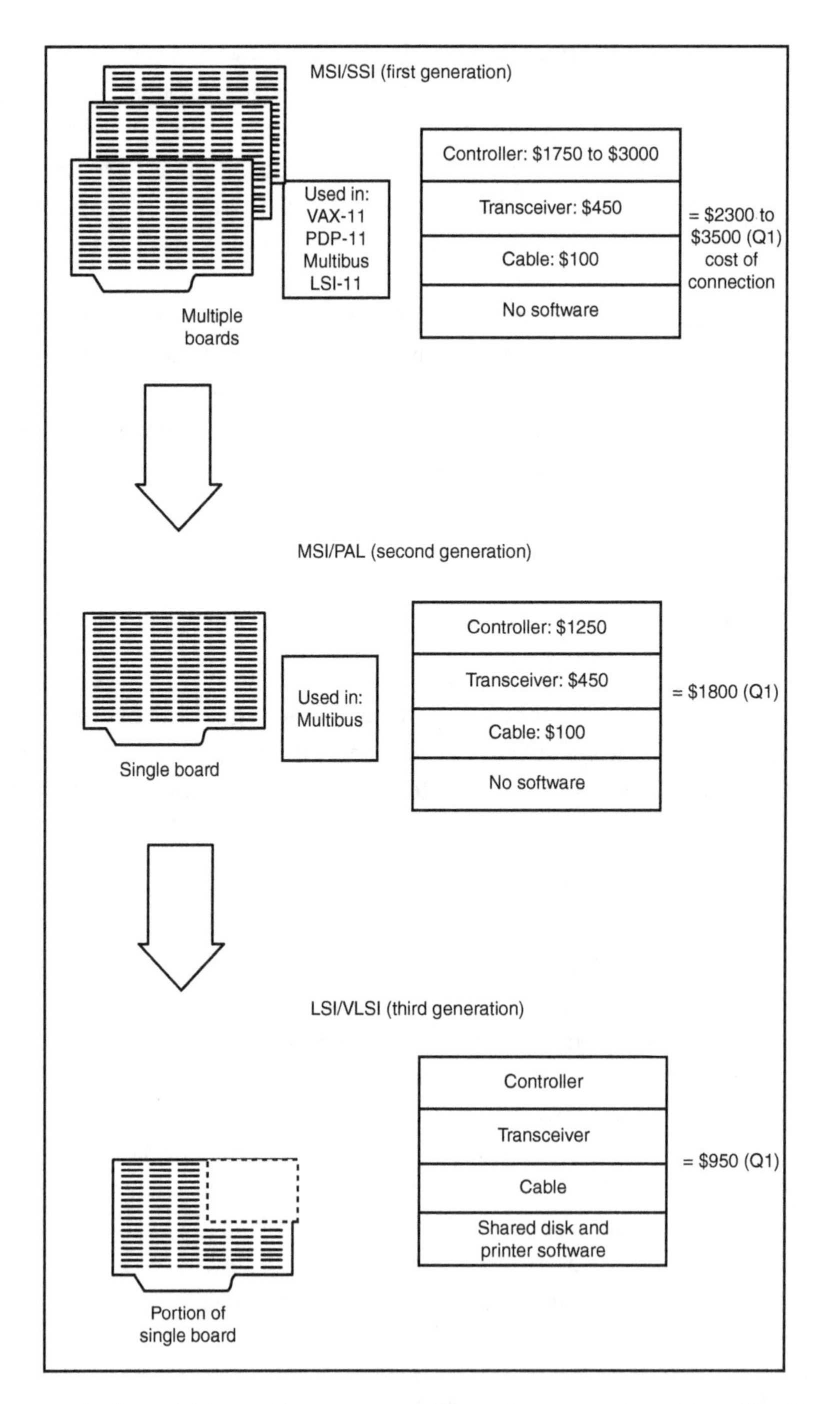

Figure 7.3 Evolution of 3Com Ethernet controllers. Source: Robert Metcalfe, "Controller/transceiver board drives Ethernet into PC Field" Mini-Micro Systems, January 1983, 179–190. Used with permission.

connections and moving bits reliably over those connections. EtherSeries would be a success. 3Com had skirted disaster.

7.3.2 Ungermann-Bass

Even though they had just introduced their 10 megabits per second Ethernet with fully compliant XNS in July 1981, management still felt at risk: they did not have a confirmed semiconductor chip strategy in place. They were certain they did not want to use the announced Intel chip. Conversations with management of the start-up Silicon Compilers had been encouraging, but they had not heard back from them in weeks. After UB rejected initial designs for the chip due to a lack of desired features, they sent the Silicon Compilers personnel back to their semiconductor foundry, Seeq, with a list of requirements.

They thought the issue had been settled, but soon after rumors surfaced that Silicon Compilers and Seeq were working on a chip with 3Com. When the press release announced the collaboration between Seeq, Silicon Compilers, and 3Com for an Ethernet chip, as Bass states: "Well, we hit the roof. We called Kleiner Perkins and said: 'Wait a minute. You can't do that. We gave you everything we know, and now we're hearing that one of our chief competitors is getting the PR and the advantage of working on this deal.' So we had this summit meeting."[19]

Kleiner Perkins resolved the matter by giving UB $500,000 with UB relinquishing any intellectual property claims. The experience left management even more certain they needed a chip solution. Bass remembers the realization: "We had spent so much energy in this, we're thinking: 'There's an opportunity here, building chips.' So I said: 'Look, I'm going to call Ken Katashiba at Fujitsu. Those guys, they know how to build chips. They don't know anything about what this culture is all about or what this market opportunity is about.'"

Bass brought Katashiba to the National Computer Conference in Chicago. At the conference, Bass, "dragging Ken around by the buttonhole," showed him what Xerox was doing with Ethernet and what Zilog was doing with Z-Net. Bass presented his case to Katashiba that the LAN business was about to take off and with it would come a big demand for networking chips. He proposed a partnership between Fujitsu and UB to build such a chip. "Well, Ken bought it... So we cut a sweet deal with Fujitsu, where they, in effect, paid all of the up-front engineering costs to build that part, and we had the part before Intel finally released their part."[20]

Technological progress came easier than sales. Jim Jordan remembers:

19. Charles (Charlie) Bass, oral history interview by James L. Pelkey, August 16, 1994, Palo Alto, CA. Computer History Museum, Mountain View, CA. Available from https://archive.computerhistory.org/resources/access/text/2018/03/102738753-05-01-acc.pdf.

20. Bass interview, Computer History Museum.

> The first customers you were getting were typical of almost any new technology. The ones you were getting were the universities, the guys that always try the first new thing in technology. In any kind of commercial account, it was always the engineering department that bought them. In the early days of LAN you didn't sell anything to the blue (IBM) side of the shop—nothing. It all went in the engineering side. It was always going on DEC equipment. That was one of the reasons the market didn't take off sooner than it could have, because IBM has the major influence in the big accounts. IBM, in the early '80s, was resisting because they didn't have anything, so they were telling the MIS guy: "You're going to lose your control."[21]

As tough a sell as it was, UB reported sales for 1981 of $3.8 million and a loss of just over $300 thousand. They clearly had seized early market leadership and built a head of steam. And they had cash of over $8 million to finance their aggressive vision. (They issued another round of Preferred Stock during the year for nearly $6.5 million.)

In February 1982, UB introduced a 5-megabit broadband Ethernet, a product leveraging the skills and knowledge of Gregory Hopkins and his team. But problems completing the product delayed shipments until September.

In great demand as a speaker, Ralph Ungermann remembers wanting to raise the awareness of UB within the investor community—knowing there would always be a need for more money: "Our real competitors in those days were the PBX guys, right? I was on 50 conferences with ROLM: Ungermann-Bass versus ROLM. ROLM was going to be the hub of the office, right?"[22]

While Ungermann talked to the financial community, Bass gave talks to customer forums. Bass recalls: "I spent half my life, in those days, giving seminars and tutorials all over the place on the planet to anyone who would listen, because this was the early stage of evangelical kind of business. You had to go out and convince people the stuff worked, that it made sense that it was going to be around."[23] At one of the conferences, Bass was approached by someone from IBM in Raleigh

21. James (Jim) Jordan, oral history interview by James L. Pelkey, July 19, 1988, Hillsdale, CA. Computer History Museum, Mountain View, CA. Available from https://archive.computerhistory.org/resources/access/text/2018/04/102740315-05-01-acc.pdf.

22. Ralph Ungermann, oral history interview by James L. Pelkey, July 20, 1988, Mountain View, CA. Computer History Museum, Mountain View, CA. Available from https://archive.computerhistory.org/resources/access/text/2018/03/102738765-05-01-acc.pdf.

23. Bass interview, Computer History Museum.

wanting to learn more about the industry. Familiar with IBM's efforts with token ring in the US and in Zurich, Bass decided to pay a cold call to IBM in Raleigh. He learned that IBM was going to let a contract to build a token ring to broadband bridge. What an unbelievable opportunity to expand the reach of UB's products. There was also a human component as Bass remembers: "I'm having problems with Ralph and Jordan and beginning to feel a bit disenfranchised in the company." Bass took the project on as a mission, putting his "heart and soul into [it]."[24] He enlisted the help of UB engineer John Davidson to put together the bid. After submitting the bid, Bass and Davidson flew to Raleigh to talk with Murray Bolt, Dan Warmenhoven, and others at IBM. The meeting went well, as Davidson remembers: "Probably what they felt was: 'Well, here's a good, small, fast-moving company that knows something about broadband. We like Charlie. These technical guys seem to know what they're talking about. We'll pick them,' My perception is that we were competing against others for this opportunity, including Sytek."[25]

In the course of discussions of how they would deliver the token ring technology, Bass contacted Amdax, another small start-up with plenty of token ring expertise and a 50-megabit token ring network in development. After meeting with Amdax, as Bass remembers: "[we] realized this was one smart bunch of engineers and no way in hell did we want to do what they're doing."[26] Once UB won the IBM contract, they began negotiating the acquisition of Amdax. UB's offer was accepted with a close scheduled for January of 1983.

The year 1982 was a great year for UB: sales totaled $11.3 million, up nearly 200%, with profits of $300 thousand. The team of Ungermann, Bass, and Jordan was working, even if there were some signs of stress. With the number of projects adding up, they chose not to respond to the IBM PC at the time, reasoning that there were not enough installed to drive new product planning. Ungermann explains the challenge of expanding into new products as a now established company with a solid base of customers: "What happens to most pioneers? You get a customer base, they're demanding things, you've got commitments, you've got contracts, you're doing well, you're meeting your business plan. All of a sudden, a new opportunity comes up, it's hard to get the company focused on that."[27]

---

24. Bass interview, Computer History Museum.

25. John M. Davidson, oral history interview by James L. Pelkey, August 18, 1992. Computer History Museum, Mountain View, CA. Available from https://archive.computerhistory.org/resources/access/text/2013/05/102746647-05-01-acc.pdf.

26. Bass interview, Computer History Museum.

27. Ungermann interview, Computer History Museum.

7.3.3 Sytek

No one was happier than the management team of Sytek when Wang announced its broadband local area network, WangNet in June 1981.[28] Michael Pliner recalls the effect it had on Sytek: "Wang was great for us by the way. Wang was going out telling everybody that broadband is great and couldn't deliver it, ok, and we let them fight Ethernet. I mean, we just said, 'If you want broadband, we can deliver, here it is,' and it worked."[29] While competitors like UB were specializing in department networks, Sytek found their niche in large, campus-wide networks where broadband systems performed well and were cost effective.

Sytek's growth required more capital. So Pliner began the search for investors. His quest took Sytek down a different path than Ungermann-Bass and 3Com. During his search, he was unexpectedly approached by Lou Solomon from the cable television equipment manufacturer General Instrument Corporation (GI). Solomon was interested in Sytek's broadband network technology for its potential application in metropolitan area cable TV service. Pliner was impressed and saw an opportunity to expand his company's reach in the broadband market: "Now, remember, GI was the IBM of the cable industry, ok. So, with Lou Solomon's vision and the kinds of things that we were looking at, I said, 'Take some money from these guys and let's go even further ahead than just local networking, let's get into metropolitan networks.'"[30] Before year-end 1982, GI invested $6 million with the right to invest more in the future to bring their ownership to 51% of Sytek.

7.4 Emerging LAN Competition, 1981

7.4.1 Interlan

With each passing month of 1980, Paul Severino's entrepreneurial yearnings grew harder to ignore. He knew he could no longer repress what he longed to do most: start a company. Uncertain as to what the company's focus might be, he searched for a compelling idea, a vision of economic potential around which to organize a company. First, he drew upon his own experiences and his hard-earned lessons: computer design and networking at Prime, bus level products at Data Translation, and the OEM strategy so key to DEC. He then scanned the technical and

28. "Broadband at base of Wang's far-reaching local network," *Data Communications*, July 1981, 30–31.

29. Michael Pliner, oral history interview by James L. Pelkey, April 8, 1992. Computer History Museum, Mountain View, CA. Available from https://archive.computerhistory.org/resources/access/text/2018/04/102740326-05-01-acc.pdf.

30. Pliner interview, Computer History Museum.

trade literature, imagining numerous fits between promising technologies and his competencies. And then he saw Xerox's Ethernet Blue Book.

> I was looking for something else, and the only other thing I had done was this computer interconnect stuff... but I couldn't see it until I saw the first Blue Book... You know, the biggest problem you have with doing something that's proprietary from a small company is that nobody wants to buy it. So, if this thing really looks like it could be a standard, this is the place to do it. And it turns out, by the time that I looked at this, there was only really one company that was visible in LANs and that was Ungermann-Bass. 3Com hadn't really announced any products yet, and it was really a consulting house.[31]

As a sanity check, Severino sought the counsel of a few trusted friends, such as Russell Planitzer, a vice president at Prime. Over a few dinner conversations they brainstormed ideas until early October when Severino laid out the case for local area networking. Planitzer listened more intently than usual because he had decided to leave Prime to join the venture capital partnership J.H. Whitney and knew he needed to find investment opportunities. Planitzer offered to work on a plan together if he could have a right of first refusal. Severino, knowing he needed financial backing and knowing no one he would rather have as an investor, readily agreed. "So that's what we did, and we built this business plan about a LAN company that was going to be board level oriented, which was a different approach from what was going on then. The first computers we would connect to were Unibus, Multibus, and Q-bus machines."[32]

They thought their plan was sound, but others were decidedly less eager to invest. Severino and Planitzer listened as the J.H. Whitney partners told them that they needed an Ethernet expert. The obvious place to look was DEC, where they soon identified Dave Potter as the best candidate. As Severino recalls, "One Saturday morning, I just gave him a call, told him who I was, what I was doing, and told him I wanted to talk to him about starting an Ethernet company."[33] Potter agreed to join Severino and in May 1981, the partners of J.H. Whitney agreed to invest. On June 1, 1981, Severino founded Interlan Inc. Work began immediately with the objective to develop products and have them available for sale by the end of the year.

---

31. Paul Severino, oral history interview by James L. Pelkey, March 16, 1988, Cambridge, MA. Computer History Museum, Mountain View, CA. Available from https://archive.computerhistory.org/resources/access/text/2017/11/102738590-05-01-acc.pdf.

32. Severino interview, Computer History Museum.

33. Severino interview, Computer History Museum.

Interlan exemplified the quick-to-market advantages of a start-up. They introduced their first Ethernet boards in January 1982, just six months after incorporation. 3Com had introduced their first boards several months earlier. They soon discovered that their products were slower than the 3Com boards as a result of using the Zilog Z-80 microprocessor. Paul Severino remembers, "We didn't have a lot of time to figure that out because we were so fast getting to market that there was a little hiatus there where 3Com gained some ground. Our board was slower until we changed it to a bit slice (microprocessor) in July. Then we really had them sort of on the run."[34]

Interlan didn't initially offer any networking protocols. But in 1982 they decided to incorporate XNS, for reasons very similar to those argued within Ungermann-Bass and others. Severino recalls the internal debate over XNS versus TCP/IP:

> We were looking for protocols that had certain characteristics that were efficient, that could be made to go fast. So we picked XNS, along with Ungermann-Bass and Bridge and 3Com and everybody else in the field, because if you looked at the two protocols from a technical point of view, XNS was designed for Ethernet, and TCP was designed for big wide area communications systems and had lots of overhead to it.[35]

Interlan had a great first year. Sales in 1982 were $2.4 million with a loss of $1.1 million.

7.4.2 Bridge Communications

In February 1981, when Judith Estrin left Zilog for Ungermann-Bass, Bill Carrico wondered whether it might not be time for him to jump ship as well. When Carrico told Estrin that he intended to leave Zilog, Estrin confided that she was not happy at UB: "Within 2 weeks, I sensed that I had made a mistake in that I was in a role that just wasn't fulfilling to me. I had come into a role without enough responsibility."[36]

Having worked very closely and successfully together at Zilog, Carrico and Estrin began to discuss starting a company together. However, Estrin first wanted to complete the UB OEM agreement with Xerox for XNS, which she finished in May. She then resigned from UB, evoking both surprise and shock—no one left a high-profile start-up, and certainly not after just 5 months. Once it became clear that she was

34. Severino interview, Computer History Museum.

35. Severino interview, Computer History Museum.

36. Bill Carrico and Judith Estrin, oral history interview with James L. Pelkey, June 23, 198, Los Altos, CA. Computer History Museum, Mountain View, CA. Available from https://archive.computerhistory.org/resources/access/text/2018/03/102740285-05-01-acc.pdf.

founding a competitive company, the feelings of many at UB turned to resentment and even anger.

In June 1981, Carrico and Estrin incorporated Bridge Communications. They first looked to carve out a new strategy rather than simply imitate others. As they identified the existing companies and their strategies, they envisioned a world populated with incompatible networks and a need to interconnect them: For example: How would computers and devices on a Zilog network connect to those on an Ethernet network? And what about the problems of interconnecting XNS networks to TCP networks? What was going to happen when IBM introduced their rumored token ring network? Estrin describes their initial business strategy: "Now, when we started Bridge, we didn't have the intention to compete against Ungermann-Bass. Our first business plan was very focused on bridges and gateways, but as internetworking, connecting networks, as opposed to the networks themselves."[37] But as they began product design, they saw that network controllers were a logical extension of designing bridges and routers. At the time few networks were being interconnected, so logic prevailed and they broadened their vision to include Ethernet controllers and terminal servers.

The business plan came quickly after the vision, but they lacked personal funds to bankroll a company and had little choice but to run the venture capital gauntlet, which fell to Carrico. Estrin began consulting to pay their living expenses, including a contract for Xerox, where she helped document their XNS protocols before they were put in the public domain.

Just like Severino had concluded, Carrico remembers a similar thought process concerning which networking technology to offer: "We did Ethernet and XNS because those were the things that were closest to being a standard, and from day one, we felt that standards were going to be the key to our business."[38]

On September 25, 1981, four founders, Carrico, Estrin, Eric Benhamou, and Jean-Pierre Boespflug, incorporated Bridge Communications. Between a first closing in December and a second closing in February 1982, they sold $1.8 million of Series A Preferred Stock to venture capitalists with a post-money valuation of $2.8 million. With $2 million in the bank, Bridge Communications management had to commit to a product architecture. For a microprocessor, they had a better choice than the Zilog Z-80—the newly available 16/32 bit 68000 from Motorola. For a networking operating system, they too decided on XNS. Carrico felt there were too many issues with TCP/IP at the time: "We did XNS, and we did not do TCP/IP, because we knew

37. Carrico and Estrin interview, Computer History Museum.

38. Carrico and Estrin interview, Computer History Museum.

that it had a lot of warts in a local area network situation. It was reasonably easy to sell XNS early on because at least it was in the public domain."[39]

In December, Bridge Communications began shipping its first product: a terminal communications server. Having started its product development cycle almost 2 years after Ungermann-Bass, Bridge was able to incorporate the latest technologies into its products, gaining a needed edge on the more established and larger Ungermann-Bass.

7.4.3 Proteon

In early 1979, MIT's Laboratory for Computer Science gave the consulting firm Proteon a $100,000 contract to develop Version 2 of their token ring Local Network Interface, ostensibly because they would get a product faster than doing it themselves. But it took Proteon until June 1981 to deliver working boards. In the same month, Proteon made its first commercial shipment, to UCLA, and in August its first international sale, to the Norwegian Defense Research Establishment.

Salwen's decision to take Proteon in a new direction, away from his lucrative consulting business and into the fledgling market for network products, was difficult, but it was an opportunity he could not resist:

> I was on a TWA flight, and before the movie they had these little shorts, you know, and they had a short subject on the office of the future, and there was the goddamn yellow cable. And I said, this is ridiculous... I'm just frustrated as hell. I know I've got this really good product, and I'm not going to get anywhere myself, and I got to decide either I'm going to take in venture capital, stop the research business, and throw all of my energies into this token passing ring communication explosion, or I'm just going to forget about it, because the frustration isn't worth it, because I see the other guys... during '82 it looked like Metcalfe was going to fail... but they fixed a lot of the problems, and it took off. It was a massive successful marketing coup. Massive! And that was beginning to show in January of '83. In November of '82, they were on the ropes.[40]

Despite quick and encouraging sales, the availability of token-ring controllers barely caused a ripple in the gathering tide of Ethernet.

39. Carrico and Estrin interview, Computer History Museum.

40. Howard Salwen, oral history interview by James L. Pelkey, January 28, 1988, Westborough, MA. Computer History Museum, Mountain View, CA. Available from https://archive.computerhistory.org/resources/access/text/2020/01/102792007-05-01-acc.pdf.

7.4.4 Concord Data Systems

In 1979, Ken Miller, Director of Modem Development for Codex—the largest modem company in the world—wondered if this was all he was meant to be, an employee tied to the safety net of a large company. Somehow in the process of becoming large, Codex's burgeoning bureaucracy had stifled the boldness, and yes fun, of the cash-strapped, "let's go for it" company Miller joined in 1972. He recalls: "I got frustrated. A lot of people at Codex got frustrated then because they were used to the early days, the early go-go years when you could get things done easily."[41] He was inspired by those who had already left Codex and successfully started their own companies: Jerry Holsinger, founder of Intertel, and Jim Vander Mey, founder of Integral Data Systems.

Miller's frustrations stemmed from his inability to convince his superiors to enter a new product market. When promoted to Director of Modem Development, Miller became Codex's representative to the CCITT modem standards committee. There he learned of a new 1,200bps dial-up modem standard—V.22—just then being formulated. Since no firm then sold a V.22 modem, Codex had as good a chance as any other firm to dominate. For over a year he had been returning from CCITT meetings filled with entrepreneurial enthusiasm, committed to selling Codex management on the opportunity to expand beyond their exclusively leased line modem focus. But every time his efforts were thwarted. To Miller it made no sense and begged the question of why he remained at Codex.

The proximate cause for leaving Codex, however, was the company's relocation from Newton to Mansfield, MA. A tolerable commute had become downright ugly. "I didn't want to move, especially if I was uncertain about Codex. But then, I mean, I always liked small companies. . . I had always had a little bit of a dream of starting a company, but never really had the guts to do it!"[42]

Then, as if a prayer had been answered, he received a phone call from a former Codex engineer, Mike Kryskow, now working at Gould-Modicon. Miller remembers the catalytic question: "Hey, we're working on some future networking stuff, and it's really communications, and we got all these consultants in here and they don't know what they're doing, and we need some help. Could you consult?" In the past he wouldn't have given such a proposal a moment's thought, but then he had never

41. Ken Miller, oral history interview by James L. Pelkey, February 23, 1988. Computer History Museum, Mountain View, CA. Available from https://archive.computerhistory.org/resources/access/text/2015/10/102737985-05-01-acc.pdf.

42. Miller interview, Computer History Museum.

considered leaving Codex before. Surprising even himself, he said: "O.K., I'll come up and look."[43]

Miller consulted over the 1979 year-end holidays and discovered he had not been misled. After the first of the year, he made calls to friends in other companies and heard of numerous consulting opportunities. He soon gave notice at Codex, leaving in the middle of March. Miller remembers the conflict he experienced: "That was the most gut-wrenching thing for me to do, because I'm leaving a salary. I had a wife and kids and a mortgage and everything else. . . and I didn't have a job. I had to go scrounge it up. But the opportunities that came by were just amazing."[44]

In March 1980, Miller formed Miller Associates. He continued consulting to Gould-Modicon on their efforts to create a communication network capable of meeting the rigorous real-time needs of manufacturing: a network interconnecting factory floor equipment with the computers controlling and directing manufacturing. Miller also learned that Gould/Modicon was not the only company thinking about networking computers and peripherals. Kryskow, however, had devised a new scheme, to become known as token bus, and Miller, convinced of the unique needs of factory automation, became thoroughly "enamored with token bus." Token bus differed from token ring in topology: the token is broadcast over a linear or tree-shaped bus or backbone instead of passed in a closed loop or ring. The broadcast token contained only one address, that of the next station authorized to communicate, the token address then would be updated at that next station, similar to the mechanism of token ring. Miller believed the deterministic behavior of token passing crucial to factory automation.

Within months, Miller came into contact with a whole new community of local area networking believers who reinforced his sense that something special was happening. As he saw it, "local networks were really in their infancy. So I looked around and said: 'There's an opportunity here. All these people participating are computer people. This isn't a computer problem, this is a data communication problem."[45]

The computer people he met kept talking about Ethernet. But for Miller, Ethernet had a serious problem: it could not guarantee an access response time because it was based on probabilistic access. Furthermore, the longer the medium the greater the propagation delay, which increased the indeterminate response times. An uncertain response time might be acceptable for office automation, but Miller knew it had no chance of satisfying the real time needs of factory automation.

43. Miller interview, Computer History Museum.

44. Miller interview, Computer History Museum.

45. Miller interview, Computer History Museum.

Token bus, on the other hand, could guarantee response times. Assuming this insight was one the "computer-types" had glossed over, Miller saw a golden opportunity to transform Miller Associates into a product company selling token bus products.

However, Miller had so much consulting work he had no time to devote to token bus. Uncertain as to what to do, Miller convened a small group of friends whom he thought might be interested in joining a start-up for a planning session between Christmas and New Year, 1980, at the Colonial Inn in Concord, MA. Not attending the meeting, but critical to being seen as a credible token bus company, was Kryskow of Gould-Modicon who had committed to join Miller's new company. Miller recalls the meeting:

> We said: "Hey, look. We want to do token bus LANs, but that's a long-range thing, I mean, we're committed to standards, and a standard doesn't exist, so one of the things we have to do is get it through the standards committee. There's a lot of work. It's a system-oriented product. But we also have identified this other thing that we know a hell of a lot about. It's a market that's here and now. It's dial modems. And so let's do both." There's a short-range strategy, get the company going, and the longer range one which we thought, at the time, would be a higher growth field.[46]

They encouraged Miller to write a business plan, a prerequisite before meeting with venture capitalists. After months of drafts and redrafts, Miller began meeting with anyone who would see him. In one surprising presentation with Tom Stevenson, president of Fidelity Ventures, Miller was "preaching the gospel of token passing," while at each step, Stevenson responded with detailed technical arguments supporting Ethernet. Miller was stumped: "I said: 'How the hell does this guy know this?' It turns out he had just gotten aced out from investing in 3Com and he had been filled with all of Metcalfe's propaganda."[47]

Realizing he needed help, Miller recruited a financial consultant, John Plakans, to help him polish his plan. Plakans introduced Miller to Kevin Landry of TA Associates. Miller also connected with Analog Devices Enterprises through a neighbor. Both companies made offers to invest in Miller's company. Analog Devices' offer involved delayed payments based on progress milestones. Miller was put off by the constraints. As he put it bluntly: "I said: 'Ah, screw that shit. Who knows, this is a volatile business. You could end up changing direction. I don't want to get too constrained.' And also, it was a clear direction. If you were with Analog,

46. Miller interview, Computer History Museum.

47. Miller interview, Computer History Museum.

you were going to get acquired. So we went with TA and closed $1.4 million in May 1981."[48]

A potentially devastating confrontation at a company meeting happened soon afterwards. Miller recalls the drama: "I got a bit panicked because Mike Kryskow was going bananas!... He said: 'You're not flamboyant enough to be president. You'd be a good VP of engineering. We need to go get another president.' I said: 'God damn it, NO!' And the guy finally didn't join."[49] Knowing he needed a token passing expert, Miller then recruited Tom Phinney of Honeywell to replace Kryskow. Phinney, however, would not leave Phoenix, AZ. Miller, feeling he had little choice, agreed to locate Concord Data Systems' LAN expert nearly a continent away.

Miller's decision to focus first on the emerging V.22 dial-up modem opportunity scored an early win. Their distributor in the UK started taking product in December 1981. Then in May 1982, they won a major order from the Swedish PTT for $2.7 million. In winning, they beat out L.M. Ericsson, Vadic,[50] Siemens, and Nokia. Miller recalls: "It was a big win. We beat out Vadic. There was shock at Vadic from that. Total shock! 'Who the hell are they?'"[51] In winning the Swedish contract, Concord Data Systems was able to extend their reach throughout Europe through the same distributors that Codex was using, by offering them a category of products Codex was not selling—dialup modems.

The success in modems immediately impacted their LAN plans. Miller, wanting someone else to manage engineering, brought Ross Seider aboard as vice president of engineering. But his two modem engineers rebelled, refusing to work for Seider. Feeling trapped by his commitments to Seider and the venture capitalists, Miller compromised and split engineering into two groups. While not the solution he preferred, his prior experience with a departmentalized structure at Codex gave him comfort the structure could work. He recalls the rift: "Ross Seider, the guy from Codex, became VP of engineering for LANs. Maybe they were a little bit prima donnas, but the two modem engineers, Northam and Kameya, didn't want to work for Seider. So there was from the beginning a split in engineering."[52] Seider worked in Boston, while Phinney, the expert in token bus LANs, worked in Phoenix.

48. Miller interview, Computer History Museum.

49. Miller interview, Computer History Museum.

50. Technically, Vadic is Racal-Vadic, having been acquired by Racal in 1978.

51. Miller interview, Computer History Museum.

52. Miller interview, Computer History Museum.

7.5 The Data Communication Competitors, 1981–1982

7.5.1 Micom

The success of Micom's IPO in June 1981 gave management the resources they needed to invest in their new hot product, their Micro600 Port Selector. It would be renamed a data PBX within a year and be positioned against LANs, the direct and most-serious competition. Initially Micom would prosper with its data PBX. There were moments of concern at the beginning, however. Norred recalls:

> There were discussions on more than one occasion, two that I can recall, where we came very close, and it was almost my recommendation, to get out of the business, to literally kill the product line, because the concentrator product line was doing so well, it had so many things going for it, being a product rather than a system-oriented product, and I think that every time we got to the point where we were going to kill the product, we got another order for 50 or something. It was that kind of situation. We were getting so many orders for it that it was very tough to cut it off.[53]

Steve Frankel, head of engineering and soon to be head of marketing, remembers managing the data PBX development and its evolution into a much more complex product: "We had enough channel strength and enough resources to find another layer of sales and supporting people to start making some real headway in that market, and then we really started evolving the data PBX into a much more... capable product." Added features included distributing the access to the switch, increasing the capacity of the switch, adding data over voice facilities, and integrating statistical multiplexers and protocol converters. "The end product of all of that integration of technology was that Micom ended up becoming the leading supplier of that product."[54]

Roger Evans, vice president of marketing at the time, and soon to become co-president with Norred, remembers being concerned about LANs, but never having the money to do anything about them. Understanding how they planned their

53. William (Bill) Norred, oral history interview by James L. Pelkey, April 27, 1988, Simi Valley, CA. Computer History Museum, Mountain View, CA. Available from https://archive.computerhistory.org/resources/access/text/2018/07/102738827-05-01-acc.pdf.

54. Stephen (Steve) Frankel, oral history interview by James L. Pelkey, April 26, 1988, Rancho Palos Verdes, CA. Computer History Museum, Mountain View, CA. Available from https://archive.computerhistory.org/resources/access/text/2018/07/102738828-05-01-acc.pdf.

annual budget gives insight into the importance they placed on operating results versus strategic management:

> I know exactly why we didn't develop a LAN. We had a very simple, extremely simple-minded approach to running this business, which is why we were so consistent from a profit standpoint for so many years. We had a purely top-down budgeting approach in this company. What I mean by that is that for each year we put the annual operating plan together, we looked at what our sales projections were for the year. We knew that we were going to make 20% pre-tax, so that was a given. What was left was, after we applied out what we knew would be the manufacturing costs for the revenues we were planning, and we were pretty good at being able to project that—we ran a pretty tight ship from that standpoint. What was left was operating expenses, and we divided that up against a formula that I don't think we changed from one year to the next, in terms of the percent of operating expenses that went to marketing and development and G&A. . . It's one of the things that Wall Street loved. The way we got there, however, had some side effects. One of the side effects was that the development pot was, if you will, fixed. It was fixed in the sense that there was never any attempt to decide that strategically, we had to do certain things and, therefore, we might need more bucks in development to accomplish them, and something else might have to give, maybe even pre-tax profit. We never went through that cycle at all. It was totally pre-ordained what the development dollars were.
>
> Secondly, Bill and I were both extremely conservative. We both felt the same way, that when it came to figuring out priorities from the product development standpoint, the number one priority was protecting our position. We had seen far too many companies lose a market position that they developed by getting so enamored with other areas that they allowed somebody to come up behind and take away what was rightfully theirs. We focused on protecting the high ground that we had already achieved; that was our number one priority. Our number two priority was adding enhancements to increase our revenue potential on the high ground. Number three was developing new products that were closely allied to the areas that we were already in, and if there were any bucks left, and there never were, going into significantly new product areas. We identified LAN as something we should really be in. Unfortunately, given the way that we ran this business, it never got funded.[55]

55. Roger Evans, oral history interview by James L. Pelkey, January 15, 1988, Simi Valley, CA. Computer History Museum, Mountain View, CA. Available from https://archive.computerhistory.org/resources/access/text/2015/09/102737975-05-01-acc.pdf.

The success of the data PBX may have created operational problems, but it would soon represent over one-third of Micom's revenues. Who could argue with success? Micom's budgeting process resulted in the success of the data PBX, but it also made it less likely that they would ever have the money to fund the development of LANs, or any other strategic product opportunities.

7.5.2 Codex

Once Codex was integrated within Motorola, Motorola executives encouraged Codex management to begin strategic planning without concern for resources, but to focus on how to grow into a much larger company. John Pugh, who was head of strategic planning for Codex during this period, remembers the mandate to define a strategy: "Motorola kept pushing you on what you're going to be when you grow up. 'You can do anything you want except acquire IBM.'"[56] Codex initiated studies that revealed potential growth in PBX and teleconferencing as well as local area networking.

In 1982, Art Carr was promoted to head of the newly formed Information Systems Group comprised of Codex, UDS, ESE, a Canadian electronics start-up, and the recently acquired Four Phase, a computer company in California. Carr recalls his attitude towards LANs: "We got a late start on LANs. That was during my time, and we got basically a no start." Carr remembers his response to the hype around LANs: "I think that we were all very skeptical about the LAN business. We started hearing about LANs from the Chief Executive Office of Motorola within a year of being acquired. There were a lot of magazine articles about LANs but there weren't any LANs... I was digging my heels in, saying: 'I know what I'm doing. Get off of my ass.'"[57]

But the pressure to get into the LAN business did not back off. Motorola's management knew IBM was going to introduce a token ring LAN, having competed for the semiconductor contract and lost to TI. After repeated prodding from management, Pugh initiated a study to determine what Codex's response should be to the emerging LAN business. The report came out in November 1982. Pugh remembers: "We convinced the company that that was a good business. It was a necessary business because we were not going to be in the PBX business. We had decided

56. John Pugh, oral history interview by James L. Pelkey, February 25, 1988, Canton, MA. Computer History Museum, Mountain View, CA. Available from https://archive.computerhistory.org/resources/access/text/2016/03/102738098-05-01-acc.pdf.

57. Art Carr, oral history interview by James L. Pelkey, April 6, 1988, Newton, MA. Computer History Museum, Mountain View, CA, https://archive.computerhistory.org/resources/access/text/2015/10/102737982-05-01-acc.pdf.

that... capturing the data at its source was going to be important to maintaining our strategic thrust outside the walls."[58]

Not having anyone on staff with the expertise to lead their efforts, they hired an executive search firm who turned up a name too good to be true: Murray Bolt. Who better than the manager heading up IBM's token ring project? Bolt, knowing he was in the penalty box for the delays in the token ring project, jumped ship and joined Codex in December 1982.

7.5.3 Other Data Communication Competitors

Few other data communication companies made a serious investment in LANs, and none became market factors. Racal-Milgo announced a LAN based on the Cambridge Ring, a token passing network IBM had studied and passed on. It came to nothing. When Paradyne hired Jerry McDowell for networking product planning, he brought in Bob Metcalfe to consult, but after failing to convince management to pursue a LAN product, McDowell left for Wang to assume responsibilities for WangNet. Paradyne management had enough to do to stay competitive in modems and multiplexers supporting its customers with their modem-based PIX network management system.

7.6 A Second Wave of LAN Competition, 1982

7.6.1 Digital Equipment Corporation (DEC)

DEC management, led by Gordon Bell, favored Ethernet ever since making it a core element of their 1978 VAX strategy. They, along with their two other DIX partners, Intel and Xerox, had participated intensely in finalizing their proposed Ethernet standard published on September 30, 1980. Before they could bring any products to market, however, they too had to wait for Ethernet semiconductor chips that were not expected before the end of 1982. In June 1982, as part of their DECnet Phase IV announcement, DEC announced Ethernet controller boards for delivery in 1983, with parts of the system, the transceivers, available later in 1982. No longer would they let the early Ethernet LAN companies prey on their customers without defending themselves.

7.6.2 Excelan

Kanwal Rekhi was hired by Zilog to plug the gaps in management left by those defecting to start Bridge Communications. By the end of 1981, he had seen enough of the chaos at Zilog. By the time they had working products in the middle of 1981,

58. Pugh interview, Computer History Museum.

as Rekhi remembers, "Zilog was falling apart as a company." Rekhi watched as several individuals from upper management, including CEO Manny Fernandez, left to start their own companies. He was left "with a couple of people doing all these machines with all the problems of management above us missing. So there was nobody there above us."[59]

And there was nobody to sell the Zilog products: a Z-80 personal computer, the Z-Net LAN, and a file server. By the end of 1981, Rekhi too had had enough. In January 1982, Rekhi, Navindra Jain, and Inder Sing founded Excelan to develop an Ethernet controller board much faster than the ones being sold by 3Com and Interlan. Their strategy was to design boards for all bus types: Unibus, Q-bus, VMEbus, Multibus, as well as IBM PC bus and Macintosh. "Our idea was a bunch of protocols on board that could go into any of those environments without having to redo the protocols, and so we were the first ones to do the intelligent Ethernet boards."[60]

Intelligent boards were so called because they had a microprocessor fast enough to process the Ethernet protocol on the board itself, meaning network processing did not have to be handed off to the computer. It made the board much more expensive than those of 3Com and Interlan, but for those OEMs that wanted speed and performance, Excelan carved out a new niche.

7.6.3 Communication Machinery Corporation

Excelan's exclusivity of the intelligent Ethernet controller market niche would be brief. A new start-up, Communication Machinery Corporation (CMC), announced similar products in early 1983. Larry Green, Dave Oster, and Dale Taylor founded CMC on February 5, 1981, providing design engineering services to firms marketing communication systems. In 1982, they received a contract from Associated Computer Consultants (ACC) to design and build an emulator for the LANCE Ethernet chip. ACC held the contract with AMD. CMC would work closely with AMD and DEC, the originator of the project. Here, DEC was creating an Ethernet chip in competition with Intel, their partner in DIX. By year-end 1982, CMC had raised $2.5 million of venture capital.

7.6.4 General Electric

General Electric (GE) had been involved in networking ever since Metcalfe had convinced them to pursue the HomeNET project in 1979. Rumors frequently circulated about GE's networking strategy. Then in April 1982 GE announced a baseband

59. Kanwal Rekhi, oral history interview by James L. Pelkey, August 17, 1994, Palo Alto, CA. Computer History Museum, Mountain View, CA. Available from https://archive.computerhistory.org/resources/access/text/2018/04/102738774-05-01-acc.pdf.

60. Rekhi interview, Computer History Museum.

networking scheme designed to tie industrial electronic equipment together in manufacturing facilities. Quoting from *Electronic News*, April 4, 1982:

> GE enters the local network market competing for installations in the factory against Gould's Factory Automation division. Future entrants in that market niche are expected to include Texas Instruments, Siemens and Schlumberger. In the OEM market, GEnet will compete against such vendors as Xerox, Sytek, Amdax and Ungermann-Bass.[61]

GEnet was to be a 5-megabit per second network based on a proprietary version of Ethernet.

7.7 The Settlement of the AT&T and IBM Antitrust Lawsuits

7.7.1 The AT&T Settlement, January 1982

In February 1981, William F. Baxter became the new Assistant Attorney General for Antitrust for the newly elected president, Ronald Reagan. He was a Stanford law professor with strong ideals and a deep understanding of economics and competition. On taking office his two superiors recused themselves from involvement in the AT&T antitrust case due to conflicts of interest. Baxter thus became the chief Justice Department official on the case—reporting to the White House. Baxter decided to handle the case personally and not be burdened with what had happened before him and the implied constraints. He saw the case as one of extending what the FCC had started—to separate from AT&T that best regulated by the government, from that better controlled by the forces of market competition.[62] On his first meeting with the chief counsel and negotiator for AT&T, Howard Trienans—who had come not from within AT&T but from an outside law firm, and was thus similarly unencumbered by past practices—Baxter terminated past negotiations and stated his position: AT&T should divest the Operating Companies and go about its business competing with the Long Lines, Bell Labs, and WE. Period.

On September 3, 1981, Judge Vincent Biunno of the New Jersey District Court ruled that the FCC's Computer Inquiry II Final Decision preventing AT&T from competing in unregulated markets, unless as separate subsidiaries, was a legal modification of the 1956 Consent Decree. AT&T immediately filed an appeal.

By December, AT&T, anticipating a decision by Congress to pass communication legislation—legislation that might be much worse than Baxter's offer—relented.

61. *Electronic News*, April 4, 1982.

62. Peter Temin and Louis Galambos. 1987. *The Fall of the Bell System: A Study in Prices and Politics*. Cambridge University Press, New York, 219.

A joint press statement was released on December 31, 1981, announcing talks that might lead to the "settlement of pending litigation."[63] Baxter then went to work securing Administration support for the agreement; support not to be presumed. On January 8, the Justice Department and AT&T, Baxter and Brown, signed a decree ending the antitrust suit.[64] Then in an intricate series of legal maneuvers, the case was to be moved from the New Jersey District Court to Judge Greene's court. Or it was supposed to be moved, only Judge Biunno accepted the agreement instead of referring it to Judge Greene, which meant it could be appealed and thus not final.

In both Houses of Congress legislation began emerging seeking to change the terms of the agreement to better assure that local telephone rates remained low and the principle of universal service remained intact. Concerned elected officials still saw long distance telephone service as a monopoly, a monopoly needing to be regulated, in part, so that subsidies could continue to flow from interstate to intrastate revenues, and thus help sustain low local rates. The Justice Department, AT&T, and now an angry Judge Greene, who saw his authority abused by the New Jersey court, all wanted their agreement to be made final and not complicated by legislative action. AT&T began a publicity campaign inciting public protest over legislation, which proved successful, and the three parties succeeded in having court authority transferred to Judge Greene's court. Judge Greene then inserted ten modifications, all of which were accepted, and the settlement was finalized on August 24, 1982. One of the ten amendments to the agreement was that the Bell Operating Companies could provide customer premises equipment (CPE); they just couldn't become manufacturers. They would have to buy CPE from competitive firms, which would include AT&T.

The dismembered AT&T had two parts. First, a succeeding corporation having the same name: AT&T—composed of Western Electric, Bell Laboratories, and Long Lines. It had all of the manufacturing, most of the research and development, and the long-distance telephone network. The other part of the dismembered AT&T was all the local telephone companies: to be organized into seven Regional Bell Operating Companies see Figure 7.4).

Indicative of the business judgment of the day, Arthur D. Little executive Frederic G. Withington, remarked: "On the surface, AT&T appeared to give away the

63. Fred W. Henck and Bernard Strassburg. 1988. *A Slippery Slope: The Long Road to the Breakup of AT&T*. Greenwood Press, 228.

64. On the same day, the Justice Department withdrew its case against IBM. Baxter saw one way to introduce competition for IBM was to let AT&T compete in the computer market.

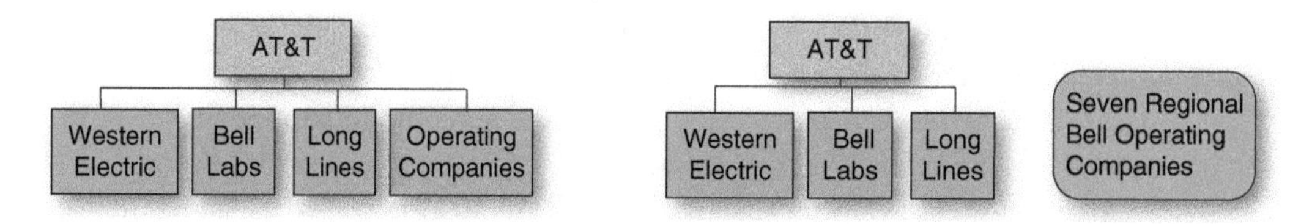

Figure 7.4 AT&T reorganization, January 1982. Illustration by James L. Pelkey and Loring G. Robbins. Source: Based on Temin, P., & Galambos, L. (1987). The Fall of the Bell System: A Study in Prices and Politics. Cambridge: Cambridge University Press. doi: 10.1017/CBO9780511572388, p. 13 and Schlesinger, Leonard A., Davis Dyer, Thomas Clough, and Dianne Landau. Chronicles of Corporate Change: Management Lessons from AT&T and Its Offspring. Lexington Books, 1987. pp. 153–155.

store. But a second, more studied look indicates that they really gained the store. In fact, you might ask if AT&T lost any power at all."[65]

7.8 IBM Antitrust Suit

AT&T was not the only company ending long-standing litigation with the government; on January 8, 1982, the same day that the Justice Department announced the settlement of the AT&T antitrust lawsuit, the government also announced the dismissal of the 1969 antitrust lawsuit against IBM. After 6 years of discovery and over 6 more years in trial, the suit that had cost IBM an estimated $1 billion, and had required them to produce over 760 million documents, was suddenly dropped.[66] We assume that after the long and expensive case against AT&T, the government was not willing to continue spending on the case with IBM, and simply threw in the towel. IBM avoided being broken up as the lawsuit sought, but the effect on the company's business strategy was unmistakable. Their decision to unbundle their software products from their hardware systems had encouraged competition and jump-started the software industry. The strategy of incorporating outside technology into their personal computers was a dramatic shift away from the proprietary technology of earlier computer products. Also, in the development of their token ring LAN product, managers decided that the technology be compatible with hardware from other vendors. Even after the suit had been dropped, IBM management continued to weigh their decisions against any appearance of monopolistic control of the industry—a burden, needless to say, that would impact IBM for many

65. Datamation, September, 1982. https://www.computerhistory.org/collections/catalog/102661165.

66. John E. Lopatka. 2000. United States v. IBM: A monument to arrogance. *Antitrust Law Journal* 68, 145–62.

years. As an example, in 1986, IBM turned down an offer from Bill Gates to make a 10% equity investment in Microsoft, not wanting to be perceived as influencing the market for PC operating systems.[67]

7.9 Ethernet Chips, Boundless Hope and Market Confusion

By October 1982, the progress of Ethernet chip development had become generally known. At first there would be four Ethernet chips (see Table 7.2).

The availability of Ethernet chips had already driven the size of a controller from two printed circuit boards to one and from $3,000 to less than $1,000. The data PBX was still cheaper (roughly $650 per connection) but it did not enjoy the steeply declining cost curve of Ethernet. This advantage, when combined with the communication speed of 10Mbps, not a paltry 19, 200bps, gave Ethernet a growing advantage. The data PBX speed per connection seemed like enough in the paradigm of terminals connecting to computers, but not when the paradigm became computers-to-computers after the introduction of the IBM PC.

The Ethernet chip would also create substantial early mover advantages since token ring chips from TI would not be available for an estimated 2 years—2 years that in reality would become 4 years. Token bus, a broadband design, required the use of RF modems, not the simple transceiver of Ethernet, and modems would preclude token bus from ever becoming a chip in time. So Ethernet vendors were about to seize a huge market advantage.

The market for LANs was projected to soar to $1 billion somewhere between 1986 and 1990; depending upon whose forecast you believed; this up from a market ranging between $50 and $100 million in 1982.[68] The more optimistic forecast would prove correct, implying a growth rate between 70–110% per year. For the firms selling local area networks, especially Ethernet products, the lofty market estimates

Table 7.2 **Ethernet chip delivery dates**

Vendor	Semiconductor Foundry	Delivery Date	Details
Ungermann-Bass	Fujitsu	1982	(3 chips)
3Com	Seeq (Silicon Compilers)	January 1983	$135 (1 chip)
Xerox (DIX)	Intel	Q2 1983	$90 (2 chips)
DEC (CMC)	AMD and Mostek	Late 1983	$65 (2 chips)

Source: Based on John Markoff. 1983. VLSI chips accelerate local-area network race. *InfoWorld,* Oct 10, 1983, 15. Larry Green. 1983. LANCE widens DEC's networking future. *Hardcopy,* April 1983.

67. That investment would have been worth $3 billion in 1993.

68. Local Area Networks—Networks and Architectures, Datapro, November, 1982, c11-010-103.

might have made raising money easier, but in the short-term it invited unmitigated competition. In 1982, estimates of the number of firms with announced LAN products ranged as high as 200. There would be over 60 vendors selling Ethernet products by 1984.[69] In addition to the sheer number of competitors, there were the complications of competing against the lumbering CBX and PBX vendors, the promises of the integrated CBX-LAN vendors, the data PBX firms, and dozens of proprietary local area networks extolling their special advantages. The endless debates of what were better—baseband (i.e., Ethernet) or broadband (i.e., token bus)—added yet another layer of confusion.[70] In sum: chaos.

7.10 LAN Market-Structure, 1981–1982

By the end of 1982, the number of choices available to customers looking to invest in LAN technology was "staggering," according to a Datapro report on the status of LAN offerings (see Table 7.3). The report went on to read:

> Depending on whose study you read, somewhere between 40 and 200 companies now claim they manufacture equipment they term "local area networks." You must choose among a wide range of technologies, capabilities, capacities, degrees of software support, building wiring schemes, and prices. No two vendors offer identical solutions, and comparison is difficult.[71]

No longer an unknown technology, LAN products and services were highly visible at conferences, trade shows, and in industry publications. While anxious customers were now more educated as to what LANs could offer, companies selling LANs still faced challenges on many fronts when pitching their products. By the end of 1982 the price advantage of data PBXs and the promise of CBXs were still hard to ignore, and the lack of a dominant LAN product meant companies were hesitant to commit to networking solutions that might become obsolete.

The LAN market-structure, now in the competitive phase, would remain there into the mid-1980s until the establishment of standards and the adoption of a dominant LAN design. To survive meant companies had to differentiate from the competition. Specializing was risky as over committing to a single LAN technology could end up steering a company down a dead end; however, many companies experienced early success in this stage of market uncertainty by creating their own

69. 3Com Form S-1 Registration Agreement for their 1984 financing, p 13.

70. The confusion of this debate already had UB introduce an Ethernet over broadband (UB) and token ring was seen as working with either.

71. Local Area Networks—Networks and Architectures, Datapro, November, 1982, page 101.

Table 7.3 **LAN products, 1982**

Type of Medium	Company/Product	# of Commercial Networks Installed
Baseband coax	Datapoint ARCnet	5,000
	Destek Desnet	210
	Prime Ringnet	200
	Network Systems Corp. Hyperchannel	170
	Ungermann-Bass Net/One	160
	Xerox 8000 System Ethernet	130
	3Com Corp. Ethernet	100
	Three Rivers Ethernet	20
	DEC, DECnet/Ethernet	6,000+ nodes
Broadband coax	Interactive Systems/3M Videodata	300
	Sytek LocalNet	150
	Amdax CableNet	100
Twisted-pair wire	Convergent Technologies Convergent Cluster	5,000
	Digital Microsystems HiNet	2,000
	Corvus Omninet	1,500
	M/A-Com Keyring	100
16-wire flat cable	Nestar Model A/Cluster One	500

Source: Based on Datapro report on Local Area Networking, November 1982.

niche. Sytek was first to market in broadband networking. Interlan focused on their minicomputer background with their OEM Ethernet adapter boards. Excelan, and later CMC, focused on workstation manufacturers, selling high-end controllers with onboard processors that supported a wide range of LAN protocols. Concord Data Systems chose to differentiate from the Ethernet firms with its token bus technology for factory automation networks. If these submarkets experienced real growth, then these strategies rewarded companies with significant growth in market share.

A prime example of successful niche market focus was 3Com and their aggressive strategy to pursue the PC LAN market. The decision to divert all resources to the development of the EtherSeries products for the PC and to discontinue development of their minicomputer products was a risky bet. Had the PC market not materialized or had the development of the products been delayed, 3Com's future may have been very different. Interlan had been very successful in capturing market share from 3Com in the minicomputer market, and the decision to stop development of its Unibus and Multibus Ethernet controllers meant 3Com would have had a difficult time competing with Interlan had they needed to refocus on this market.

The driving force in LAN development at this time was the need for affordable Ethernet chips. As the three main LAN competitors raced to market with their respective chip manufacturers, they set the stage for the first wave of competitively priced LANs.

In the interim, early adopters for LANs were found in universities, government agencies, and engineering departments of corporations using data intensive CAD and CAE applications on minicomputers and workstations. With the spread of the PC, the new paradigm of desktop computing began to disrupt traditional corporate computing architectures. MIS departments in large corporations, traditionally the realm of 'Big Blue' mainframes, faced pressure to provide their companies with networking solutions before their main suppliers, AT&T and IBM, had solutions of their own to offer. Instead, MIS managers turned to the independents, like Proteon, for networking products in order to keep up with the trend towards enterprise networks. As a result, MIS took on greater roles in the financial accounting structure of the companies, absorbing the management of communications budgets as well as maintaining computing across the enterprise.

While the economic potential of the LAN market had been validated, the market-structure in the early throes of competition saw most vendors struggling to find the right fit for a breakout product and strategy that would ensure rapid growth. Returning to the words of the Datapro LAN report from December 1982: "The marketplace itself has not yet jelled. No vendor involved in data processing, office automation, or communications wants to be left out, and every vendor seems to have a different solution to the LAN 'problem.'"[72]

7.11 In Perspective

The years 1981–1982 witnessed the early uncertainties and confusion of a forming market. In this short period, entrepreneurs set the course and strategy for their start-ups. Each was attempting to position their companies to take advantage of opportunities emerging from the rapid spread of computing throughout the corporate world. Without the benefit of hindsight, it is interesting to hear in the words of the entrepreneurs the logic or intuition behind their decisions. Each had a vision of the future and was trying to make it happen. The great benefit of this effort

72. Datapro LAN report, 1982.

to future technologists was that by pursuing these individual strategies and innovating the many different technologies available at the time, they were constantly improving their products, educating consumers on the benefits of connectivity, and changing the way we do business.

Networked computing was indeed a paradigm shift, and as such it took time for the entrepreneurs to make its case. LAN start-ups needed to break into the mainstream market. In the words of Geoffrey Moore, they needed to "cross the chasm" between the early adopters who shared the vision of networking and the larger population of pragmatic consumers. Many potential LAN customers were reluctant to do more than experiment until a dominant design had emerged. Given the wide assortment of alternatives, it was not clear that the best design would emerge from market competition or be forced by institutional agreement. As the different invested parties began to acknowledge this roadblock to widespread growth of the industry, government agencies, universities, and the networking companies themselves motivated the creation of standards making bodies to come to impartial recommendations.[73] There was too much investment involved and too much capital needed to grow the market; the market was stalled until the issue of dominant design had been resolved. The making of standards is common to communications, whether it is languages or protocols, and the same would be true for networking.

73. We have published an article that focuses on standards development across the three market-structures examined in this book. See Russell, A., Pelkey, J., & Robbins, L. (2022). The Business of Internetworking: Standards, Start-Ups, and Network Effects. *Business History Review*, 1–36. doi:https://doi.org/10.1017/S000768052100074X.

The Need for Standards: Networking, 1975–1984

8.1 Overview

By the early 1980s, innovation in local area networking had given rise to an overwhelming number of networking alternatives. The resulting state of confusion discouraged potential buyers and left the market in a state of flux. Given low levels of demand, networking companies and their customers faced an uncertain future. As early as December 1980, a respected market research firm issued a report forecasting LAN sales to grow from essentially zero to $3.2 billion by 1990.[1] A year later, the *Economist* magazine summarized the state of affairs in local area networking as "a technological jungle in which experts violently disagree and potential buyers stand aghast."[2] Could technological order emerge from this chaos?

While the focus of our book has been on the emergence of new markets pioneered by new firms, market order does not always coalesce when many competitive technologies exist to meet similar user needs. Technological outcomes don't always follow from market competition alone; in many cases, the creation of technical standards helps to reduce diversity and stimulate market growth. However, establishing the social structures needed to create and administer standards can be every bit as challenging as the founding of new companies. As is the case with other markets, in the networking market the adoption of standards helped to create market order and usher in a period of explosive growth. The institutional entrepreneurs who led these new standards-making institutions faced both political and economic challenges. They were successful when they were able both to secure the backing of existing authority structures and to steer rivals toward collective decisions and actions.

1. "Local net market explosion predicted for '80s, '90s" *Computerworld*, December 15, 1980, 62.

2. "Local networks—A matter of choice," *The Economist*, December 12, 1981, 99–100.

In this chapter, the stories of three important standards-making efforts in the field of networking will be presented from their beginnings in the late 1970s to technological order in 1984. They are

- the establishment of LAN standards by the Institute of Electrical and Electronics Engineers (IEEE) committee 802;
- the adoption of the seven-layer Open Systems Interconnection (OSI) model of networking by the International Standards Organization Technical Committee (ISO/TC) 97 Subcommittee 16 (SC 16);
- and the development of networking protocols in a variety of venues, such as DARPA's TCP/IP, Xerox's XNS, and international protocols by ISO/TC 97 Subcommittee 6 (SC 6).

It is important to note that these three threads of the history of networking standards took place at the same time and many individuals and interested parties participated in multiple organizations around these efforts. Institutional entrepreneurs, such as Maris Graube and Charles Bachman, played key roles that drove progress in standards-setting. The examples that we discuss illustrate the ways that individuals applied lessons learned from their own experiences, and newer institutions applied—or in some cases ignored—lessons from related standards development projects. Entrepreneurs needed to be aware of actions in other standards committees because standards for networking and internetworking arose from a loosely coupled, interdependent system for standards-setting that had equal parts cooperation and competition. The irony of standardization is that there is no overarching (or standard) authority for approving standards. Rather, the ecosystem of global standards for computer communications has competition and confusion built into its very fabric.

To help readers navigate these institutional and technical complexities, Figure 8.1 details the various standards that will be addressed in this chapter in relation to the OSI Reference Model, approved as a Working Draft (WD) by the ISO in late 1979. Based on layers and stacks, it represents a cumulative effort dating to the design of operating systems and the experiences with ARPANET (see Figure 8.1). The main specifications relating to networking presented in this chapter are

- Xerox's Pup Protocol to XNS
- DARPA's TCP Protocol to TCP/IP
- IEEE Committee 802 standardizing Ethernet (CSMA/CD) and token protocols (influenced by DIX [DEC, Intel, and Xerox], IBM, and others)

OSI Reference Model		TCP/IP	XNS	IEEE 802 / DIX	CCITT
7	Application				
6	Presentation				
5	Session				
4	Transport	TCP	XNS		X.28/X.29
3	Network	IP			X.25
2	Data Link		MAC Layer	MAC Layer	LAP B
1	Physical			CSMA/CD or TOKEN	V.22

Figure 8.1 Networking layers and stacks. Source: Illustration by James L. Pelkey and Loring G. Robbins.

- ISO creating Transport and Network Protocols influenced by the CCITT, ECMA (European Computer Manufacturers Association), DIX, and XNS and TCP/IP
- ISO creating Data Physical Protocols influenced by the CCITT and IEEE

8.2 IEEE Committee 802: The Battle for LAN Standards

At the end of Chapter 5, we described a series of meetings in 1979, hosted by MITRE and the National Bureau of Standards (NBS), designed to identify problems and potential solutions related to the diversity of protocols for local area networking. After co-chairing the Local Area Communications Network Symposium in May 1979 with Norman Meisner of MITRE, an energized Robert Rosenthal returned to the NBS and began organizing an effort to develop Federal Information Processing Standards for local area networking. NBS pursued a novel approach to formulating standards. Rosenthal recalled, "We were trying to position ourselves to develop standards in the voluntary community that we could adopt for use in the government. This is an important concept. We said: 'This is our approach. We want to work with industry in a voluntary arena to get industry backing for products so that we can buy those products.'" Understanding the power of industry to create robust, viable solutions and even de facto standards, his approach contrasted with that of his counterparts at DARPA: "The Department of Defense, at the time, would throw money at a problem until it got solved. Vint Cerf and company went off to invent TCP at the time because they got lots of DOD money to make networks work.

We said: 'Fine, you do whatever you need to do, but our approach is to work with industry.'"[3]

Soon thereafter, Rosenthal, in his role as Chairman of the Institute of Electrical and Electronic Engineers (IEEE) Technical Committee of Computer Communications (TCCC), learned of an effort underway to form a group under its microprocessor technical committee to study data highways. (Data highway was another expression for LANs; an expression used in process control for the electrical connections between process control sensors and monitoring equipment.)

Problems of interconnecting computer equipment were not unique to the office. Similar needs existed on the factory floor or in the interconnection of instrumentation equipment. Maris Graube, who would become a key figure in the evolution of LAN standards, started out oblivious to LAN developments, either for the office or factory. Graube remembers, "I had never read anything about LAN's. I knew nothing about data communications, zero, zip, I mean absolutely nothing."

In 1976, Graube, an engineer, joined Tektronix Inc. in Portland, OR, not for professional reasons but because he wanted to live in Oregon. After having been turned down twice for jobs by Tektronix, a friend told him of their need for someone to look into what they should be doing with the new IEEE 488 instrumentation interface standard. Hewlett Packard (HP), their major competitor, had introduced equipment using the standard and Tektronix management feared losing market share without adopting the standard in their own products. Although it was a job "no one else wanted," Graube leaped at the opportunity and moved to Oregon.

Converting to the 488 standard proved imperative and Graube led its introduction and diffusion throughout Tektronix's products. His professional interest and motivations captured, he began attending meetings to formulate "codes and formats," another expression for standards. Focus centered on higher-layer formats, or protocols, that would impose information onto the data transmitted. He remembers:

> It occurred to me that there were some severe limitations to the 488 interface specification. The distance can only be 20 meters between instruments. If you needed to automate the larger laboratory, this was not appropriate. And various techniques for extending the distance of that particular technology were inadequate. So I was thinking: 'Gee, there must be something that has a little bit longer length to it that operates in the megabit per second kind of

3. Robert Rosenthal, oral history interview by James L. Pelkey, May 4, 1988, Washington, DC. Computer History Museum, Mountain View, CA. Available from https://archive.computerhistory.org/resources/access/text/2020/04/102792038-05-01-acc.pdf.

data rate.' You don't need to go extremely fast. I didn't know exactly what it was.[4]

In a casual conversation with a magazine writer, Graube learned Professor Ted Williams at Purdue University led an Industrial Process Control Workshop. Again, Graube got involved, even chairing the group for a couple of years, before concluding their "PROWAY" (Process Control Data Highway) inadequate for a laboratory setting. Again, his curiosity and willingness to make a job of what no one else wanted to do led him to investigate the possibility of standards for computer instrumentation. After researching the standards bodies in existence at the time, he concluded that such a standard was not being discussed. A chance meeting with Bob Stuart, who had been instrumental in establishing standards efforts for microprocessors within IEEE, prompted Stuart to suggest: "Well, why don't you just form a little standards group under the microprocessor standards umbrella." Stuart guided Graube in the process of establishing a standards committee for networking. As Graube remembers: "I still didn't know what a local area network was."[5]

Graube submitted a proposal to the IEEE Standards Board to create a local area network standard for laboratory and office settings. After confirming no other such standard effort was underway, the IEEE Standards Board authorized Standards Project 802 in October 1979, under the sponsoring organization of Rosenthal's TCCC, not the microprocessor group.[6] Graube, the appointed chairman, needed next to form a technical committee to formulate the standard. Members of Committee 802, as it would come to be known, had to be members of the IEEE and could not represent the interests of any organization—even their employers—and had to volunteer their efforts. The goal: a draft standard with the support of three quarters of those participating in its creation. Rosenthal remembers that moment: "Everything was in place."

Graube scheduled the first Committee 802 meeting for February 28, 1980, concurrent with the spring meeting of COMPCON. (Since members participated voluntarily, meetings were generally held in conjunction with trade shows or other technical meetings.) Uncertain of how many people might attend the mandated open meeting, Graube arranged for a small meeting room at the Jack Tar Hotel

4. Maris Graube, oral history interview by James L. Pelkey, July 12, 1988, Portland, OR. Computer History Museum, Mountain View, CA. Available from https://archive.computerhistory.org/resources/access/text/2020/04/102792042-05-01-acc.pdf.

5. Graube interview, Computer History Museum.

6. M. Graube. 1982. Communications: Local area nets: A pair of standards: Confronted by marketplace needs, the IEEE 802 Committee is proposing standards for two kinds of networks: Contention access and token passing. *IEEE Spectrum* 19 (June 1982), 60–64.

in San Francisco. To his, and everyone else's, surprise, the crowd, estimated at as many as 150, overflowed into the hallway and delayed the start of the meeting. Many were simply curious engineers preferring to join their own rather than a night out sightseeing. Others, like Robert Metcalfe and John Shoch, had vested interests, and still others, like the "droves" of Bell Labs engineers, came out of habit. When the meeting finally began, Rosenthal recalls with awe: "All we had was Maris to stand up and organize it."[7]

With help from others more experienced, Graube weathered the melee and established the goal of one standard: "roughly a megabit per second and a kilometer long and connect some 100 devices or so and be made for the commercial environment." Before adjourning, Rosenthal proposed their work conform to the recently published OSI Reference Model. After affirming the proposal, the next meeting was set for May 27–31, 1980, at NBS.

As chairman, Graube wielded significant influence and authority both to transform his vision into the standard as well as to structure the needed subcommittees. In both regards he relied heavily on his PROWAY experiences. For example, he wanted to follow the PROWAY approach of first establishing the functional requirements for the standard and avoid the parade of companies lobbying for their products to be declared the standard. Once the functional requirements had been agreed to, however, Graube wanted to proceed differently from PROWAY, which had become mired in the process of evaluating whether a given company's product best fit the standard. He recalls: "At the end they thought that there would be one product that was more outstanding than the others, and that would be selected as the standard."[8]

Graube recognized that no vendor would vote for a competitor's product and so a standard was unlikely to emerge. Instead, Graube wanted to create the standard and then let companies build products to conform to it—non-proprietary products that would benefit from open competition.

Despite Graube's clear view of how to proceed, he underestimated the number of technological alternatives that existed, the economic stakes at risk and the efforts corporations would make to influence Committee 802. Rosenthal sensed the inherent friction of interests represented by those attending that first meeting: "You could feel fire in the air!"[9]

As much as Graube wanted to preclude corporations from unduly influencing the dynamics of standards making, he was not to have his way.

7. Rosenthal interview, Computer History Museum.

8. Graube interview, Computer History Museum.

9. Rosenthal interview, Computer History Museum.

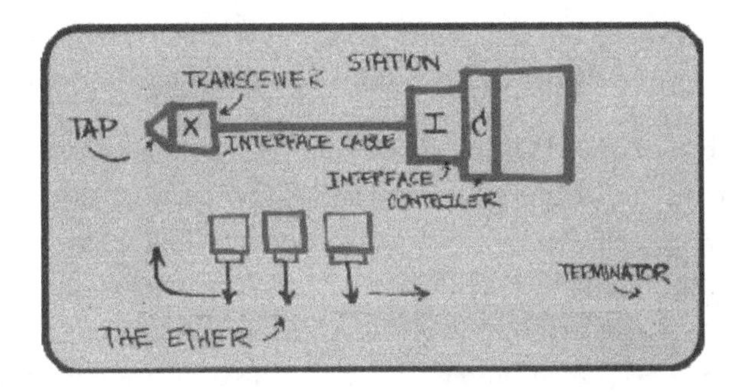

Figure 8.2 Ethernet model. Source: Dr. Robert M. Metcalfe, 1976. Reprinted with permission.

8.3 DIX

Over the summer of 1979, Metcalfe continued to shepherd the possibility of three-way cooperation among Xerox, DEC, and Intel to commercialize Ethernet. Finally, that fall, the three firms met at the Boxborough Sheraton in Boxborough, MA. Acknowledging Metcalfe's essential role, they invited him to the pre-meeting dinner. The following day the technical teams of the three companies met without marketing people or Metcalfe. Slighted not in the least, Metcalfe turned his attention to how his fledgling 3Com could fund products that would conform to the technical specifications he expected DIX to negotiate and then publish.

To avoid antitrust legal complications, the DIX members had to agree to place the results of their collaboration in the public domain for the purpose of creating a standard. On the surface, the formation of IEEE Committee 802 would have seemed an ideal means to make Ethernet a standard, if not *the* standard. However, Graube's bias against any corporation usurping the authority of Committee 802 set the two efforts on a collision course.

Furthermore, it quickly became obvious that the DIX members did not share a common view of what the Ethernet standard should be. In fact, their differences often gave rise to tensions straining the collaboration to the breaking point. But each time, the strength of their collective commitment to the commercial opportunities of local area networking prevailed and they resolved their differences. (The description and lexicon of Ethernet at the time is shown in Figure 8.2)

Contributing to the problems was each company's technical team came with their own prejudices, competencies, and requirements. Kaufman of Intel remembers:

> The issues really were cabling and controller chips... I think what pushed up the cost most, in the early years, was Xerox and DEC's insistence of having coax, because they were interested in all the very real problems of installing

> this stuff and making it work and making it reliable. Whereas the rest of us were much more hackers, we were willing to pull anything if it would work.[10]

The transceiver needed to convert the signal from digital to analog was another stumbling block. Kaufman remembers how limited knowledge of this element was at the time: "There were debates about could anybody build a transceiver that would really work at any speed reliably despite the existence proof of what had been running at PARC. This was a black art by one guy in a closet, and a lot of theoretical work was spent by people on 'What should a transceiver do and could it work?'"[11]

In contrast, Liddle of Xerox remembers his team's perspective: "We thought that the Xerox design was conservative and then those guys jacked it further up, but that was all right, because they wanted it to be reliable. So it was a very tight piece of engineering that was done!"[12]

While work progressed, the central issue of transferring proprietary, patented, technology from Xerox to DEC and Intel remained unsolved. Xerox had flourished controlling its technology. From the beginning, Xerox's desires to keep PARC's innovations secret suggested Xerox might not agree to license Ethernet. Nevertheless, work progressed under the leadership of Liddle, Kaufman, and Dave Rodgers of DEC.

After intense negotiations, the three companies decided to execute two agreements: one between Xerox and DEC and the other between Xerox and Intel. There would be no three-way agreement, although the two agreements were linked by conditions. Liddle recalls:

> All three parties had to agree to implement this product as a standard for their future products. It didn't have to be their only network they used, but they all had to agree to implement it and support it. Xerox proposed to license, for one thousand dollars each, the Ethernet technology and to reserve for them a block of addresses and so forth. Intel had to agree to manufacture an integrated circuit chip set to implement the protocols and control. Digital had to agree to design and manufacture a low-cost transceiver.[13]

10. Phil Kaufman, oral history interview by James L. Pelkey, June 17, 1988, Campbell, CA. Computer History Museum, Mountain View, CA. Available from https://archive.computerhistory.org/resources/access/text/2013/05/102746652-05-01-acc.pdf.

11. Kaufman interview, Computer History Museum.

12. David Liddle, oral history interview by James L. Pelkey, October 11, 1988, Mountain View, CA. Computer History Museum, Mountain View, CA. Available from https://archive.computerhistory.org/resources/access/text/2013/05/102746649-05-01-acc.pdf.

13. Liddle interview, Computer History Museum.

Liddle then faced the challenge of securing the agreement of Xerox. The strength of his argument rested in his belief that it was in the best interests of Xerox to license the technology and that DEC and Intel were ideal organizations to partner with. Fortunately, Peter McCullough, the President of Xerox, believed Xerox should creatively use its technology to acquire technology and commitments from others. When Liddle made his presentation to McCullough, he remembers McCullough quickly saying: "What a great idea. Trading the rights to this patent for improvements and all that, and their commitment to make parts, and then use it as a standard. What a great idea."[14]

By now, word of DIX had spread. Other companies wanted to participate. Gordon Bell of DEC remembers getting calls from Olivetti, saying: "We want to be part of that." Bell knew that more participants would add complications to the collaboration: "I said: 'No way. We've got eight of the best people I know designing it now. Any more people will hurt it. We've got plenty of people inside of DEC that would like to be part of it. I'm sure Intel's got a lot of people. Xerox could probably drum up people. This thing is going so well. Let's not mess it up. You can comment once its available.'"[15]

Kaufman, on the other hand, sought to stimulate as much support as possible since Intel wanted ready customers for its new chip: "We worked, trying to influence a lot of other companies, because for us, the whole goal was, besides some altruistic one about making communications work and advancing the state of the art, to generate customers who were ready for the chips we were going to build."

One of the prized potential customers for Intel was HP. Every couple of months Kaufman would have lunch with Dave Crocket, head of strategy and planning for HP. In addition to bemoaning the difficulties of trying to effect strategies in their organizations, they discussed technological developments including networking. HP had multiple networking technologies being developed and Crocket believed that the groups would be more likely to support an external standard than to trade their own solution for another group's. He pushed Ethernet as the best solution.

Intel's strategy for establishing early leadership in the market for Ethernet chips was to make the chip as complex as possible. Kaufman remembers their reasoning: "because that was Intel's advantage: If we could set the high-water mark that

---

14. Liddle interview, Computer History Museum.

15. C. Gordon Bell, oral history interview by James L. Pelkey, June 17, 1988, Cupertino, CA. Computer History Museum, Mountain View, CA. Available from https://archive.computerhistory.org/resources/access/text/2013/05/102746646-05-01-acc.pdf.

everybody else had to come up to have a viable controller, there would be something that we did best, we'd take advantage of our ability. So, that first chip really was a whole computer."[16]

As development dragged on, the DIX collaborators faced the risk of being left at the altar by Committee 802. With the three companies still months away from defining their own standard for Ethernet, their concern turned to the upcoming Committee 802 meeting and fears that momentum might build for an alternative technology. To forestall irreversible action by the committee, they decided to announce just prior to the May meeting that they would publish their standard in September. It was not an easy task. Liddle remembers that hammering out the press release was "harder to accomplish than the original contract."

8.4 IEEE Committee 802 and DIX

At the May IEEE Committee 802 meeting, DIX supplemented their press release with a two-page description of Ethernet with the message: "This is a reasonable approach to creating a local area network and if the committee wants to consider it, we'd be willing to work with them. If they don't want to consider it, we're going to do it anyway, but we'd still be willing to participate."[17]

Opposition immediately decried DIX's heavy-handed tactics as undermining the goal of standards-making independent of corporate influence. DIX also received public support, such as from Greg Hopkins, chairman of the International Federation of Information Processing (IFIP) standards-making body, which like the IEEE had created a working group or committee to develop a LAN standard. Quoted in *Data Communications* in June 1980, Hopkins opined: "This is a significant announcement because of the sheer size of the companies involved and is a step toward the integrated office of the future."[18]

Graube did not welcome DIX's actions. If Ethernet became a de facto standard outside the IEEE 802 process, it might undermine the authority and legitimacy of Committee 802 to create a successful standard. As much as he frowned on DIX-type efforts, neither did he want DIX to act independently of Committee 802. From that same *Data Communications* article of June 1980, Graube urged cooperation: "Other companies may have other opinions, and Xerox may not be able to satisfy everyone's needs... The US is no longer alone as the technological leader, so we will

16. Kaufman interview, Computer History Museum.

17. Marvin Sirbu and K. Hughes. 1986. Standardization of local area networks. Presented at the Fourteenth Annual Telecommunications Policy Research Conference, Airlie, VA, April 1986, 11.

18. *Data Communications*, June 1980, 26.

have to comply with international standards—just because the U.S. has a de facto standard does not mean that it will be accepted overseas."[19]

Against this swirling background of intrigue, the agenda of the May meeting to organize a committee structure to begin standardization efforts led to three subcommittees: the Physical Level, Link Level, and High-Level Interface subcommittees.

The Physical Level subcommittee chaired by Jerry Clancy (of Honeywell) intended to create the functional specifications for the physical media and how to signal over it. The Link Level subcommittee chaired by Nathan Tobol (Codex) would define the protocol imposed on the Physical Level signals—whether polled or token passing, for example. More open-ended was the High-Level Interface subcommittee chaired by Allen Rochkind (Spectra Physics).

Graube would soon learn that the definition of these hardware interfaces were not the only areas of confusion challenging the committee: "At that time, interface to me meant a hardware interface—how does a chip, a semiconductor part, interact with a microprocessor. That's the interface I thought about. As it turned out, it's more of a logical interface than a hardware one, and we have very little to say about how the microprocessors work."[20]

But the committee was energized and ready to get to work. Graube recalls the hectic pace to become a hallmark of Committee 802: "We basically started out with great enthusiasm. There were many meetings held. I think we held a meeting every two months or so, and they grew very quickly from three-day meetings to full-week meetings, and a lot of times we'd start on Sunday and work all through the week."[21]

After the June Physical Level subcommittee meeting, held in tandem with a PROWAY meeting, many PROWAY members switched the focus of their efforts to IEEE 802. In another effort to speed committee work, a further subcommittee, the Media Access Group, was formed and scheduled a meeting for September.

At the September meeting of the Media Access Group, held at Gould-Modicon in North Andover, MA, the discussions turned decidedly more technical. So far, those attending Committee 802 meetings had been shadow boxing with four camps of technological interest. The first camp was DIX and its Ethernet, or CSMA/CD, technology. The second camp consisted of the much more loosely organized PROWAY advocates who favored a token technology of some kind. The computer giant IBM constituted the third camp, rumored to favor token ring, but unwilling to make their intentions clear. Their dominant market position seemingly gave them the

19. *Data Communications*, June 1980, 26.

20. Graube interview, Computer History Museum.

21. Graube interview, Computer History Museum.

opportunity to set a de facto standard. IBM's indecision hovered over every conversation like a black cloud. Could Committee 802 act without IBM revealing its LAN? The fourth, the chaotic camp, grew weekly as firms announced proprietary LAN solutions of every kind. Graube's goal of one standard seemed to recede in the distance.

Adding pith to the September meeting, Mike Kryskow of Gould-Modicon presented a paper on a token bus protocol he had created. The contrast between a deterministic token network and the probabilistic CSMA/CD caused many to question whether CSMA/CD could be the standard. A token standard gained momentum.

On September 30, DIX released their Ethernet specification as promised. Known as the "Blue Book" by the color of its cover, Kaufman remembers: "Some 25,000 copies were printed on my Intel budget and passed out to the world." The combined influence of the three companies, plus many others willing to support the establishment of Ethernet as a standard around which to build new products, gave DIX and Ethernet a momentum that far outweighed any other solution at the time. But the repercussions were significant, as Kaufman continues:

> What we tried to say was: 'Here it is. We've signed up for it. We're going to make this work, and if you want to put a standards stamp on it, that's fine.' Of course, we didn't really take into account the fact that there were lots of other people in the world with other axes to grind that would try to perturb the standard, and in hindsight, maybe we should have just held it quiet for another couple of years until we were delivering, but we took it to the IEEE and a lot of people spent a lot of money fighting Ethernet.[22]

Liddle characterizes the waiting committee of skeptical engineers as: "The howling mob at the IEEE."[23]

In an October announcement meant to stem the token tide, HP endorsed, and pledged active support, for a CSMA/CD standard. (An action seeded in the monthly meetings between Kaufman and Crockett.) Don Loughry of HP reflects on the tension:

> In the May meeting... DEC, Intel and Xerox presented their Ethernet solution. They made a strategic blunder. They basically said: 'We have THE answer.' But it backfired. They didn't understand what they had to do to sell something, that you just don't present a solution and expect one hundred

22. Kaufman interview, Computer History Museum.

23. Liddle interview, Computer History Museum.

> other companies to say: 'Rah,' especially the likes of the large companies involved.[24]

The next meeting in Phoenix in December loomed like a championship prize-fight. If there was to be one standard, a choice between CSMA/CD and token passing seemed imperative. Ever aware of the growing conflict, Graube saw the writing on the wall:[25] "It was becoming clear to me that things were not going to converge into anything."

Loughry of HP, who would play an important role during and after the meeting, remembers:

> So, at this December meeting, this was known and kind of forecast by those that were on the inside, to be a real shoot-out, because this was the time that they were going to sink CSMA/CD and it was going to be buried, and some rather large companies were determined to make that happen. I was sort of elected, or promoted, or whatever—nominated—by the likes of Metcalfe and John Shoch, to be the cheerleader and the spokesperson for CSMA/CD.[26]

Kaufman of Intel remembers the attitude of the DIX members, especially Intel: "Our strategy fundamentally was 'they're not going to kill Ethernet, and if IEEE kills Ethernet, we don't care because there's nothing else at this point.'" While the collaborative effort of DIX to present their solution as a de facto standard was their primary goal, they were also aware that approval of Ethernet by the committee would greatly improve its marketability. Opposition from the token supporters was their main obstacle, however, as Kaufman remembers:

> IBM was talking about token ring, but had no spec, and if they did have a spec, they wouldn't release it, and the people they sent clearly didn't speak for IBM and kept saying they wouldn't speak for IBM. So what the IEEE was talking about in terms of token was a non sequitur to us. We were going to ship CSMA/CD no matter what, and we were going to follow the IEEE, and if they settled on something, we'd ship it that way. If they didn't settle on something by the time the chip was ready, we'd ship the chip, and that's why we were calling it the 'Eithernet' chip, because of all the variations that were

24. Donald C. Loughry, oral history interview by James L. Pelkey, July 6, 1988, Palo Alto, CA. Computer History Museum, Mountain View, CA. Available from https://archive.computerhistory.org/resources/access/text/2020/04/102792044-05-01-acc.pdf.

25. *Data Communications*, December 1980.

26. Loughry interview, Computer History Museum.

> coming along in CSMA/CD, not because we were going to make a token ring part of it. Nobody knew how to make one of those.[27]

At the meeting a combination of the PROWAY and IBM proponents aligned in favor of token technology as the basis of the future Committee 802 LAN standard. In the vote to endorse tokenism, the ayes failed to achieve the required three-quarters majority.[28] It was equally apparent, however, that neither could CSMA/CD—Ethernet—attract a three-quarters majority. Seemingly at an impasse, Committee 802 crafted a compromise: two standards would be created. The choice avoided failure, even disbanding. Two new subcommittees, CSMA/CD and token passing, appended the existing three subcommittee structure. Loughery became chairman of the CSMA/CD subcommittee[29] (see Figure 8.3). To maintain some semblance of one standard, the Committee required all specifications other than the access algorithms to be identical and all members continued to vote on both standards. The unintended outcome of these rules was to seed future conflict.[30]

Rosenthal, an informed user, felt betrayed: "My view was that this was a real disaster. Here I was trying to make standards for use in the government, and now I've got to choose between two technologies. I was furious, but I had to live with that."[31]

In January 1981, the editorial headline in *Data Communications* magazine's Viewpoint read: "IEEE decision places a roadblock in local networking's path." The scathing editorial ended with: "The IEEE should reconvene its local network standards committee as soon as possible and should face up to the challenge of the industry by deciding on a meaningful standard for local-network access."[32]

Graube in an article in the same issue of *Data Communications* labeled the Committee 802 decision as: "sort of a cop out." LAN technologies and politics had complicated the plans of Committee 802.

27. Kaufman interview, Computer History Museum.

28. Rosenthal: "The meeting was packed full of IBM'ers, it was packed full of everybody who had a stake. Then the PROWAY people were there, the old-time process control community that didn't want anything to do with token ring. They loved the bus technology, but they couldn't deal with the probabilistic nature of CSMA/CD. They had to be deterministic, so they had a token mindset, but it wasn't token ring, it was token bus. So you had two important camps, the token camp versus the CSMA/CD camp. The vote was taken." Rosenthal interview, Computer History Museum.

29. Loughery had prior standards experience with X3-T9 (488 instrumentation standard).

30. Sirbu and Hughes, "Standardization of local area networks," 3.

31. Rosenthal interview, Computer History Museum.

32. *Data Communications*, January 1981.

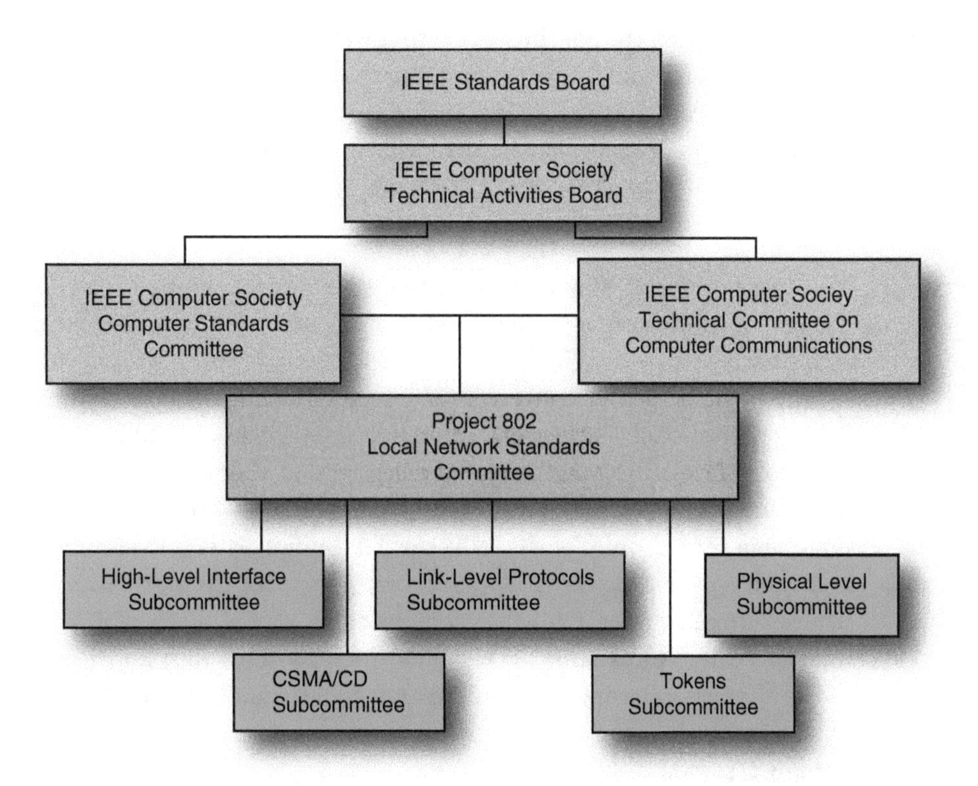

Figure 8.3 IEEE Committee 802 subcommittee structure. Based on Ware Myers. 1982. Toward a local network standard. *IEEE Micro*, Aug. 1982, 29.

The life-saving reorganization of IEEE Committee 802 in December 1980 to create two standards—token passing and CSMA/CD—eased immediate tensions without solving fundamental problems. The token-bus and token-ring factions had aligned solely to fight adoption of CSMA/CD, papering over substantive differences. Since the token and CSMA/CD standards had to advance in unison—according to IEEE 802 rules—the token coalition erected numerous hurdles to the better-prepared CSMA/CD community. The reorganization also spawned an unintended consequence: Committee 802's struggles to define LAN standards became newsworthy. The larger technical and commercial communities would scrutinize future actions of Committee 802 as never before by. LAN standards had become important.

A disappointed Graube witnessed his goal of one standard compromised away and knew if he didn't assert the authority of his office the slippery slope of fractious debate might preclude any standards. Seeking to understand the progress of the subcommittees in an effort to focus future meeting agendas, he remembers:

> I simply asked each of the people that were working on documents to give me what they had. I took them all back to Tektronix and I put together a composite document, our first Draft A, and it was a total mess. You could see that there just wasn't any standard whatsoever. All we were doing was listing a catalog of the way you could do things, rather than the way you should do things.[33]

A mess or not, in May 1981, Draft A represented Committee 802's stake in the ground, or more aptly, a mirage on shifting sands. Work on a next version began immediately.

The obvious lack of convergence induced growing concern within NBS and Xerox whether Committee 802 could create standard(s). NBS, having already decided in favor of CSMA/CD, feared delays and further compromises might lead to a standard not to their liking. To rally support for CSMA/CD, and prove it was more than the stepchild of DIX, NBS turned again to ECMA, the organization that had been so constructive in working towards an OSI Class IV protocol.[34] Meanwhile, Xerox had been lobbying Siemens to become a reseller of its soon-to-be introduced Star workstation. As Siemens' interests in reselling Xerox's Star grew, so did its interests in having ECMA adopt a CSMA/CD standard equivalent to Ethernet, the LAN built into the Star workstation. Siemens consequently began promoting a CSMA/CD standard within ECMA.

As for Committee 802, if its internal contortions did not cloud the future of LAN standards enough, a steady stream of new LAN technology announcements, all claiming superiority over those being debated within IEEE 802, were reported by the press.[35] No announcement caused more problems than that of Wang Laboratories' WangNet in June 1981.[36] A leader in word processing and office automation, Wang had enough market power to cause a stir with every new product announcement and WangNet was no exception. By reshuffling the very technologies considered by Committee 802, WangNet seized instant credibility and disrupted the existing standards debates. Like the token bus proposed by the PROWAY supporters, WangNet was a broadband network. Carved out of its enormous bandwidth was a 12 megabits per second CSMA/CD channel, rather than

33. Graube interview, Computer History Museum.

34. ECMA members were AEG-Telefunken, Burroughs, Cii Honeywell Bull, DEC, Ericsson Information Systems, Ferranti Computer Systems, IBM, ICL, Olivetti, NCR, Nixdorf, Phillips, SEMS, Siemens, Sperry Univac, and Xerox.

35. *Electronics*, January 27, 1982, 90–95.

36. "Broadband at base of Wang's far-reaching local network," *Data Communications*, July 1981, 30–31.

the 10 megabits per second of Ethernet. In addition, WangNet promised channels carrying voice, video, and even traditional point-to-point data communications. In short, WangNet promised something for everyone.[37] Wang promised delivery ranging from February to October 1982.

The WangNet announcement highlighted why Committee 802 needed to publish LAN standards as soon as possible. In mid-1981 that meant transforming the Draft A mess into a Draft B that could be submitted for membership voting. Seeking help from others, Graube remembers his frustrations with ISO: "I don't think the ISO people knew what they were doing, because at times, we would ask for their guidance, in terms of how we described these standards, the Reference Model. It was a mess, trying to track what they were doing, using them as guidance."[38]

Wang's announcement created problems for IBM as well, and that in turn created additional problems for Committee 802. The superficially aligned token factions now found the competitors IBM and Wang under the same roof. Robert Donnan, who had been recruited out of retirement by IBM in early 1981 to organize its LAN standards-making efforts, held the title of "Standards Project Authority." Donnan's career included leading the team that announced SDLC in 1969 and years of experience beginning with the SDLC/HDLC standardization process and interfacing with ECMA, CCITT, and ISO.[39] He knew a priority was to create an insurmountable distinction between token ring and token bus. He remembers the impossible bedfellows in the fall of 1981:

> It turned out that, just constantly, the needs of token ring and token bus were divergent. The token ring people saw a very fancy priority scheme, for instance, which is in token ring today, with which you can do all sorts of weird and wonderful things that aren't even possible in token bus. This has to do with the nature of everything going by every station, which is true for token ring and not for token bus. If you say; 'Make ring and bus look alike,' what you do is reduce it to one common denominator, and you get the worst of both worlds.[40]

37. Broadband used radio frequencies to carve out channels and, hence, could easily carry voice and video. A broadband system such as CSMA/CD could not carry voice or video until they were digital signals, not analog ones.

38. Graube interview, Computer History Museum.

39. IBM created the role of Standards Project Authority to replace the confusion that resulted from "15 IBMers" attending standards meetings. Robert Donnan, oral history interview by James L. Pelkey, July 12, 1988, Atlanta, GA. Computer History Museum, Mountain View, CA. Available from https://archive.computerhistory.org/resources/access/text/2016/04/102738111-05-01-acc.pdf.

40. Donnan interview, Computer History Museum.

The illusion of one token standard, created as a means to defeat CSMA/CD, was destined to collapse, hastened by the market entry of Wang.

Finally, in October 1981 Committee 802 published a 400-page Draft B to a waiting and critical audience. Doubters argued its certain failure: too many details and too many options. The supporters of Ethernet again felt frustrated that the passage of their standard was being held up by the need to also create a token passing standard. How could they put pressure on Committee 802 to pass a CSMA/CD standard equivalent to the Blue Book? For help they once again appealed to ECMA members. In November 1981, their efforts paid off when ECMA created technical group TG LN under Technical Committee 24 to develop LAN standards.

At the December 802 Committee meeting, the incompatibilities between token bus and token ring (accentuated by animosities between IBM and Wang) led to a reordering of the standards-making efforts from CSMA/CD and tokenism to bus and ring.[41] Token bus was argued to be more aligned with CSMA/CD, itself a bus-based technology proven to work over a broadband cable, such as MITRE's own broadband CSMA network. What better logic than grouping bus-based LANs that could be baseband-CSMA/CD or broadband-token bus, and token ring-based LANs?[42]

The orthogonal leap in LAN argument created both confusion and an ensuing war of words of baseband versus broadband. It now pitted DIX against Wang instead of IBM against Wang. Jerry McDowell, who had attended IEEE 802 meetings from the very beginning, joined Wang in late 1981 to assume responsibility for all communications technologies, including WangNet. He remembers the war of words that entangled LANs for years:

> What tended to happen was that every time that there was a trade show, I'd get invited to speak about broadband and Liddle or Bell would be talking about the baseband technology and the press wars were: "baseband vs. broadband—which is better?" And we'd cast spears at each other, and I'd say, "Look, on broadband I can do video and I can do voice and I can do data," and they'd turn around and say, "Yeah, but who needs it?"[43]

With Draft B assumed all but dead, and ECMA rumored to be closing in on LAN standards, and the Committee 802 again reorganizing, standards-creating by Committee 802 appeared to be unraveling once again. Loughry, of HP and leader of the

41. Maris Graube. 1982. Local area nets: A pair of standards. IEEE Spectrum, June 1982, 60–64.

42. *Data Communications*, March 1982.

43. Jerry McDowell, oral history interview by James L. Pelkey, April 10, 1992, San Jose, CA. Computer History Museum, Mountain View, CA. Available from https://archive.computerhistory.org/resources/access/text/2020/01/102740544-05-01-acc.pdf.

CSMA/CD camp, opines: "Dissension was appearing in the ranks. There was bad press at that time that IEEE 802 was going nowhere, nobody could agree, etc. Well, this was because we were not abiding by our own rules. We were just really not doing things in a healthy technical way, or a healthy political way." Graube recalls the chaos: "I'd toss and turn at night and go to those meetings like going off to wars."[44]

In February 1982, Committee 802 met under intense pressure to hammer out a passable Draft C. Drafts A and B had been works-in-process circulated to solicit feedback that could be incorporated into the eventual standards. Such an iterative approach now seemed slow and indecisive, however. The time had come to specify standards: period. To do so seemed impossible if they had to hold to their original and lofty goal of having all access methods—CSMA/CD, token bus, and token ring—operate over all media, for example, baseband and broadband cable, twisted pair wiring, and fiber optics. An expedient solution coming out of December's reorganization, and confirmed by market behavior, was to associate each access method with a primary medium. While compromising the initial goal, it did look like a way to streamline the standards-making process. Hence, the baseband cable access method became CSMA/CD, broadband cable became token bus, and twisted-pair wiring became token ring. A path to standards seemed to have been cleared.

In that same February meeting, the CSMA/CD standard moved further away from the DIX proposal. In the March 1982 *Data Communications* magazine, Graube judged the two CSMA/CD proposals: "Total incompatibility."

Then, later in February 1982, the tug-of-war to define a CSMA/CD standard intensified. ECMA's TG LN committee, which had worked in close cooperation with Xerox, DEC, Siemens, and Olivetti, completed a draft CSMA/CD standard closer to DIX's Blue Book than the Committee 802 proposal that was diverging from the Blue Book. Adding even more pith to DIX's call for an Ethernet standard, 24 companies made public their intention to introduce Ethernet products.[45]

If Committee 802 members felt they had finally resolved the impasse to standards, it must have been a shock to read the headline of a *Data Communications* March Viewpoint editorial: "The grim tale of a standards committee that has lost sight of its role and its importance." Disparaging the proposal of associating each access method with a primary medium, the editorial ended with:

44. Loughry interview, Computer History Museum; Graube interview, Computer History Museum.

45. *Data Communications*, March 1982, 44. Also in February, Xerox announced Siemens would market the Star product line in Europe.

> Before the IEEE 802 committee is guilty of trying to engineer a giant leap backwards, it ought to think through the consequences of its proposal. If approved, it will shine as the brightest example ever of a non-standard standard. If rejected—as well it should be—the committee will move even further away from its once universally held posture of seriousness.[46]

An article in that same issue of *Data Communications* was titled: "Local network standards: No utopia." It warned of the need for market acceptance:

> The buyer well knows that many major high-technology innovations have been made commercial successes not by established giants, but by start-up ventures. Therefore buyers who have to select a local network product will not have their prayers answered by standards-making bodies. Those who are not early adopters will wait for marketplace standards no matter when the 802 or any other committee formulates standards.[47]

With the institutional legitimacy of Committee 802 at risk, 22 members, including all committee chairmen but not Graube or Rosenthal, drafted a response published in the April *Data Communications* Viewpoint. In it, they argued of the enabling role of standards to encourage VLSI semiconductor manufacturing to achieve lower-cost LAN chips: "The solution to the volume problem is, of course, the development of appropriate standards that not only enable equipment of varying manufactures to intercommunicate but provide the volume by narrowing the alternatives—and thus the raison d'être for IEEE Project 802."[48]

The critical press and undeniable confusion belaboring LAN standards caused problems for more than Graube and Committee 802. Bell of DEC remembers many testy meetings justifying DEC's involvement in the fight for a CSMA/CD standard: "The Operations Committee kept saying: 'Why are we giving this to the world?' I said: 'Wait a minute. We're not giving anything to the world. We don't have a protocol, we don't happen to have the patent on either CSMA/CD or the ring."[49]

In March 1982, Committee 802 met again to resolve impasses to completing Draft C.[50] Four technical presentations by IBM personnel clarified its view of token ring technology and provided the data needed to specify a standard: one logjam broken. Equally, the actions of ECMA gave impetus to create a CSMA/CD standard

46. *Data Communications*, March 1983.

47. *Data Communications*, March 1983, 173–180.

48. *Data Communications*, April 1982, 13–14.

49. Bell interview, Computer History Museum.

50. "In a sudden reversal IEEE embraces Ethernet," *Data Communications*, April 1982, 35–38.

close to the Blue Book, the opposite of what had been decided in February. Many, including Donnan, viewed the actions of ECMA as an "end run"[51] around Committee 802 with the intent to force conformance to its, and essentially the Blue Book's, Ethernet. Their efforts proved successful. Committee 802 once again acted to preserve its institutional legitimacy and changed its standard to conform to the proposal of ECMA.

Graube recalled that the committee "simply bit the bullet and said: 'OK, let's move over to the ECMA position,' and that's the kind of technology that was incorporated in the IEEE 802.3 standard. It's basically as a result of this process of accommodating these different views."[52]

Even as Committee 802 labored towards a Draft C, Graube and Rosenthal huddled, anxious to end the committee's meanderings. Influencing them were the suggestions accompanying many of the votes to approve three or even four standards.[53] Rosenthal remembers their conversation after they accepted the inevitability of three standards: CSMA/CD, token bus, and token ring: "Maris and I had long conversations about how to get rid of the personality problems and focus more on an organization and structure that would support outputs that we would be proud of, rather than the in-fighting. So we had to get rid of that old structure. We had to put in place an infrastructure that would be conducive to making real things happen."[54]

They then turned to a division chief at NBS, John Riganetti, who helped them put in place the structure they wanted. Graube remembers the challenges of restructuring IEEE 802 to reflect three standards: "I can remember having heart-to-heart talks with some of the opponents of this particular scheme of doing things, because they were losing their jobs as chairmen of these groups, which was not something they liked to do, nor was it easy for me to disenfranchise them, but it was something that needed to be done."[55]

Bolstering his resolve and logic was the likelihood of IBM and DIX creating standards. In June, for example, ECMA ratified a LAN standard very close to the DIX proposal by a vote of 13–2, including the affirmative vote of IBM.[56] (IBM voted for a DIX-like CSMA/CD with the tacit agreement that it would receive similar support

51. Bob Donnan, quoted in *Data Communications*, April 1982, 38.

52. Graube interview, Computer History Museum.

53. Announcement of new LAN technologies continued, such as Burroughs timed-token access method, a variation on IBM's token proposals. *Data Communications*, June 1982.

54. Rosenthal interview, Computer History Museum.

55. Graube interview, Computer History Museum.

56. *Data Communications*, June 1982, 80–82.

for its LAN standard when announced—a date not yet set.)[57] That same month, DEC publicly announced its plans to deliver Ethernet products compatible with the Blue Book.[58] In July 1982, 19 companies announced public support for the ECMA CSMA/CD standard.[59] The press also reported Ethernet semiconductor chip announcements, or rumored announcements, by Intel, Seeq, Fujitsu, Advanced Micro Devices, and Mostek.[60]

The behind-the-scenes effort to reorganize Committee 802 proved timely as de facto Ethernet standardization again challenged Committee 802's role and authority. At the August meeting, the results of the voting on Draft C were reported. CSMA/CD received more than the needed three-fourths majority, as did token bus.[61] Token ring came close, 73%, but needed another vote to pass. A proposal was then made by DIX to reorganize into three standards-making efforts: CSMA/CD, token bus, and token ring.[62] Each of the three standards would share a common link layer protocol, although the definition would differ from that being created within OSI. Furthermore, the three standards subcommittees would act independently. Loughry recalls their key decision: "We said: 'The plenary is no longer a decision-making body. . . just dissemination of information, status reporting,' and each of the individual committees really did the voting, and the executive committee would either affirm or deny what the working groups brought forward. We built in what you'd expect of normal, reasonable democratic process."

The new subcommittees became link layer (802.2), CSMA/CD (802.3), token bus (802.4), and token ring (802.5). Loughry became chairman of 802.3, Donnan of 802.5, and Dave Carlson of AT&T 802.2. A succession of chairmen headed 802.4. Along with the reorganization, the decision was made to resubmit all three standards to another vote in hopes of improving the acceptance level of all. (The vote would only be on the proposed changes, however.)

57. Sirbu and Hughes, "Standardization of local area networks."

58. *Data Communications*, June 1982, 38–40. See also "Inside DEC's newest networking phase," *Data Communications*, September 1983, 215–223.

59. *Mini-Micro Systems*, August 1982, 29. The 19 companies were Honeywell, Computer Technology Ltd., DEC, Fujitsu Ltd. (UK), HP, Intel, Information Technology Ltd., International Computers Ltd., Logica VTS, L.M. Ericsson, Mitel Corp., Network Technology Ltd., Nixdorf Computer Corp., Office Technology Ltd., Olteco Olivetti Telecom, Siemens, 3Com, Three Rivers Computer Corp., and Ungermann-Bass.

60. "Dual-chip sets forge vital link for Ethernet local-network scheme," *Electronics*, Oct. 6, 1982, 89–91.

61. "IEEE okays CSMA/CD and token bus, while token ring nears completion," *Data Communications*, September 1982, 48–53.

62. Sirbu and Hughes, "Standardization of local area networks."

Then out of left field, Olof Soderblom, a Swedish citizen, pronounced he held a US patent issued in 1980 for a token-passing networking scheme covering the token ring under consideration. IBM, in fact, had already paid him $5 million for an unlimited license for future use.[63] If uncertainty had clouded past token ring discussions, Soderblom's assertion cast darkness over its future.

In November 1982, DIX released version 2.0 of its "Blue Book" Ethernet to reflect changes from the many months of negotiations with Committee 802 and ECMA. It then essentially conformed to Committee 802's Draft D. In December, at the meeting held at DEC, Committee 802 forwarded its CSMA/CD recommendation, standard 802.3, to the IEEE TCCC for approval. However, both token bus and token ring required more work. In the meantime, several projects to integrate networking protocols and applications matured, including some important efforts at Xerox.

8.5 Networking Strategy at Xerox: 1979–1981

The efforts of Xerox's Systems Development Division (SDD) to upgrade the Pup protocol to XNS progressed nearly in parallel with TCP/IP during these same years. Yogen Dalal, who had assumed management of most of SDD's networking group after Metcalfe's departure in late 1978, stayed abreast of changes to TCP and OSI. Dalal remembers:

> We were aware of the concept of the [OSI] Reference Model... We considered it somewhat academic, that it was a reference model that attempted to formalize what all of us knew, and the Reference Model, as most models did, attempted to concentrate on the bottom layers because people had experience with the bottom layers, and the higher layers became sort of fuzzy because you hadn't got to that yet.[64]

In 1979, when Dalal learned from his boss, David Liddle, that Xerox, DEC, and Intel were cooperating to standardize Ethernet, Dalal argued that Xerox should also commercialize XNS or try to make it a standard. Dalal remembers asking Liddle:

> 'Why can't we get Xerox to sell or to standardize its network architecture product in addition to its commercial product?' We had something, we knew it was the cat's meow, an important revolution, and we were going to make it succeed. Other parts of the company had similar visions of grandeur, but

63. "Patent snafu hits 802," *Data Communications*, August 1982, 38–39.

64. Yogen Dalal, oral history interview by James L. Pelkey, August 2, 1988, Santa Clara, CA. Computer History Museum, Mountain View, CA. Available from https://archive.computerhistory.org/resources/access/text/2018/02/102738752-05-01-acc.pdf.

> were afraid that if they gave the standard out, they would lose control. That was the biggest mistake Xerox ever made.[65]

Xerox management feared making XNS public even more than Ethernet, for the proprietary technology that made possible sophisticated printers, print servers, and file servers resided in XNS, not Ethernet. The first commercial product built around the new capabilities of XNS and Ethernet was the Xerox 8000 Network System (X 8000) announced in November 1980, just 2 months after DIX made public the Blue Book and 1 month before the public unveiling of TCP/IP.[66] The X 8000 consisted of a graphics-based user computer (the 860 workstation), laser printers, and various other peripherals, all connected using Ethernet and XNS. Metcalfe, now with 3Com, opines in the December issue of *Data Communications* that the architecture of the X 8000: "points the way for future design of shared-resource networks."[67]

Xerox's strategy for XNS contrasted starkly with the wide distribution policy the DOD had for TCP/IP. Xerox wanted to keep XNS proprietary and under its control. Xerox had created XNS so that all of its office products might work together seamlessly, hoping to seize a competitive advantage over more entrenched companies like IBM in the battle for the "Office of the Future." But customers had become leery of one-vendor solutions and wanted all vendors' equipment to interoperate. That realization had prompted Xerox to license Ungermann-Bass to port XNS to its NIU terminal switch in the fall of 1980, as described in Chapter 5. Permitting customers to connect other vendors' computer terminals to Xerox XNS networks was a trivial decision compared to the one of making XNS public and giving away what many inside Xerox thought to be a real competitive advantage. Those arguing otherwise, to make XNS public, wanted to make Ethernet the LAN of choice, and there was no doubt that XNS made Ethernet sing.[68] Metcalfe remembers:

> We were working on LANs, and he [Cerf at DARPA] was working on 50 kilobit per second telephone circuits and that's a substantial difference. And that's why TCP is so slow and XNS is so fast. So, XNS was built to be carried over multi-megabit per second transport facilities, and TCP was designed with an

65. Dalal interview, Computer History Museum.

66. *Data Communications*, December 1980, 26.

67. *Data Communications*, December 1980, 26.

68. "The missing link to full Ethernet compatibility is high-level software," *Data Communications*, October 1981, 50.

intuition about modems and slow stuff. So you run TCP on a LAN and it is slow, in fact, it's twice as slow, half the speed of XNS.[69]

In October 1981, the market pressure on Xerox to make XNS public grew substantially when Xerox announced its 8010 Star Information System; a workstation designed to be an "electronic desktop" and pioneered the icon-based user interface.[70] (Its price, $15,000, proved way too expensive and the product was destined to fail.)

Unable to justify keeping XNS completely under wraps, Xerox made some, but not all, of XNS public in December 1981.[71] Dalal recalls:

> What happened was, with Ethernet being out there, they felt that you had to give the next levels out, so they got XNS, in terms of the datagram and the session protocol and Jim White's Courier, which is a way to exchange procedure calls back and forth, but they were hesitant to send out the filing protocol, the printing protocol, the name look-up protocol, the electronic mail protocol; all the protocols that you really needed to do something. Again, I think they felt the lower level protocols, it was OK to send out so that the Ungermann-Basses and the Bridges could build connectivity hardware, but nobody could really build servers that would compete with Star or the filing systems that Xerox was producing.[72]

The fact that Xerox published only the lower layers of XNS mattered little to the start-up LAN companies whose first-generation products were largely terminal switches, known derisively as "milking machines." LAN vendors had the choice to either wait patiently or invent their own network protocols, for as of year-end 1981 neither TCP/IP nor OSI were available. So even with its minimal functionality, XNS use spread: making it the early market leader of LAN protocols.

8.6 ISO/OSI (Open Systems Interconnection): 1979–1982

The tensions between competition and standardization that raged in the local area networking community between 1979 and 1982 had direct parallels, at the exact same time, in the world of internetworking. As we saw in Chapter 5, experts working

69. Robert Metcalfe, oral history interview by James L. Pelkey, February 16, 1988, Portola Valley, CA. Computer History Museum, Mountain View, CA. Available from https://archive.computerhistory.org/resources/access/text/2013/05/102746650-05-01-acc.pdf.

70. Datapro 1982, Xerox 8000 Network (Ethernet), pp. C11-931-101—107.

71. "Xerox high-level protocols debut," *Data Communications*, January 1982, 38–40.

72. Dalal interview, Computer History Museum.

in ISO/TC 97 SC 16, led by Charles Bachman, chose to begin their work by specifying a Reference Model. ISO approved the Reference Model as a Working Draft in 1979, and had authorized SC 16 to make the requested changes and resubmit it as a Draft Proposal (DP).[73]

The Reference Model provided the flexibility to accommodate different protocols at various layers. This was a wise decision, since, as we have seen, there was no clarity around important topics, such as LAN protocols. Nevertheless, protocol development at other levels could proceed because of the OSI Reference Model's modular design, where technical details within one layer should not, in theory, impact other layers. One consequence of this decision was that OSI, at first, had a lot of empty boxes.

Therefore, the leaders of standards committees had strong incentives to finish their work, secure consensus, and promote their protocols as sufficient solutions to plug into one of the many empty boxes in the OSI Reference Model. Indeed, the availability of TCP/IP and XNS exerted new pressures on OSI to adopt LAN protocol standards promptly. But competing ideas about what should go into standards made prompt action rather difficult.

Embedded in the Reference Model WD was the fundamental assumption of communications by making connections, *not* launching datagrams, despite the fact that the leading LAN technologies used datagrams, not connections, to communicate between devices.[74] Since the Reference Model WD failed to embrace datagram protocols, it could not satisfy the rapidly growing LAN community. In OSI terminology, physical or virtual circuit architectures create connections before transmitting data whereas datagram architectures simply transmit data without establishing connections, hence, connectionless. The predominant LAN technologies, such as CSMA/CD and token passing, were connectionless and therefore were unaddressed by the Reference Model WD.

The connection-based Reference Model satisfied the PTTs, but for those wanting reliable end-to-end communications over the public data networks or LANs changes would have to be made, including a change to the Reference Model to allow connectionless communication; creating a transport layer protocol to provide reliable end-to-end service; and creating a connectionless network layer protocol.

The omission of connectionless communications from the Reference Model WD concerned many European computer scientists as well as Rosenthal and others

73. ISO's process for standardization consisted of several steps, each indicating increasing levels of acceptance: Working Draft, Draft Proposal, Draft International Standard, and International Standard.

74. Datagrams threatened the paradigms of both circuit-switching and virtual-circuits networks.

at the NBS committed to having the US Government adopt the eventual OSI standards. But since NBS's pioneering network, NBSNET, used a CSMA/CD, or connectionless, protocol, if OSI did not include connectionless protocols resembling those evolving in the US, NBS would have to abandon its goal of adopting OSI standards. In response, NBS pursued a multi-prong strategy. First, NBS sought help from the American National Standards Institute (ANSI), the US representative to ISO. However, ANSI's members, comprised of companies that favored proprietary technologies, raised questions about the economic value of international standards.

NBS next approached the ECMA. Although not a formal member of ISO, ECMA attended SC 16 meetings by invitation. ECMA shared NBS's concern regarding the lack of OSI connectionless protocols for LANs. For years, ECMA had monitored or participated in discussions regarding the need for datagram protocols. So ECMA welcomed NBS as an ally and invited NBS representatives to ECMA meetings.[75]

John Heafner, head of NBS's Systems and Network Architecture Division starting in January 1979 and responsible for all NBS networking activities, including OSI protocols, remembers wanting OSI to adopt transport protocols similar to the DOD TCP protocol:[76] "So through ECMA and other sources, we pushed the definitions written in ISO-ese of the DOD protocols, in particular Class IV Transport, which is the match with TCP. Our thrust from the beginning was to work in ISO, and to some extent CCITT, to make sure that government needs were covered when those protocols were being developed."[77]

In early 1980, knowing time was of the essence, ECMA submitted a draft proposal to both ISO and CCITT recommending four classes of transport protocols, ranging from a minimal protocol for connection networks to a TCP-like protocol for connectionless networks. (All classes would function over a connection-oriented network layer.)[78] ECMA, however, needed an inside champion to argue their cause.

75. Bachman: "ECMA was very, very important, because ECMA was working on their own drafts between our meetings, and ECMA tried to provide a power equivalent to IBM." Charles Bachman, oral history interview by James L. Pelkey, October 26, 1988, Cambridge, MA. Computer History Museum, Mountain View, CA. Available from https://archive.computerhistory.org/resources/access/text/2018/02/102738717-05-01-acc.pdf.

76. Heafner had been responsible for connecting RAND to the Arpanet.

77. John F. Heafner, oral history interview by James L. Pelkey, May 5, 1988, Birmingham, MA. Computer History Museum, Mountain View, CA. Available from https://archive.computerhistory.org/resources/access/text/2020/04/102792040-05-01-acc.pdf.

78. *Data Communications*, August 1980, 31–32.

In the spring of 1980, ECMA's champion emerged. The French PTT, influenced by the changing regulatory environment in the U.S.—that is, deregulation and the Computer Inquiries—and their growing awareness of the merging of computers and telecommunications, recruited Hubert Zimmermann from INRIA, a data processing research institute, to join Centre National d'Etudes des Telecommunications (CNET), the research institute for the French PTT—its Bell Labs. Zimmermann's new role ideally positioned him to bridge the differences separating ISO and CCITT. He reflects:

> One of the reasons for moving was the will of the French PTT to put together, or to get more, of the data processing culture. It was agreed that I would keep participating in standards, as I had done before, and from that time was in a much better position to act as a go-between ISO and CCITT. So I was, within ISO, still in charge of the OSI reference model group, and people knew that I had moved to the PTT's. They could see that it did not change my way of managing and pushing things, and it was clear that it was supported by the French PTT.[79]

In August 1980, facilitated by Zimmermann as well as the more receptive attitude within CCITT to data processing-oriented standards, CCITT and ISO jointly announced tentative support for ECMA's transport protocol proposal.

Zimmermann's next challenge was managing the approval of the Reference Model at the November SC 16 meeting in Berlin. Amid the air of excitement, success could not be assumed. Zimmermann knew the current version of the Reference Model had problems. How could it not? Designed as it was by an international committee in record time. Some problems were merely cosmetic, such as the correct use of the English language. Other problems were more serious. The US delegation, for example, repeatedly questioned the fundamental objective of a Reference Model. They lobbied that the Reference Model be circulated as a simple technical report rather than passed as a standard with permanent consequences. Zimmermann thought the Americans undervalued the benefit of making the Reference Model hard to change. (He also recognized the ambivalence among the Americans; many whom would prefer the market decide technological issues, not a public body.)

The problem that concerned Zimmermann most was whether the right balance between "time to market" and technological elegance had been achieved. Many people, including Zimmermann, recognized that a collaborative standards process

79. Hubert Zimmermann, oral history interview by James L. Pelkey, May 25, 1988, Paris, France. Computer History Museum, Mountain View, CA. Available from https://archive.computerhistory.org/resources/access/text/2018/01/102738698-05-01-acc.pdf.

did not result in a perfect technical answer. However, for a standard to work in the real world required widespread acceptance despite technical weaknesses and conflicting requirements. Zimmermann recalls: "I was convinced pretty early that we shouldn't have something which was far from being perfect from a technical point of view, but had to be accepted and endorsed by the major players. We put a fair amount of pressure for, at some point in time, just freezing things, and saying: 'Unless there's a very good reason to change something, we won't change it.'"[80]

At the SC 16 meeting in Berlin in November 1980, an air of excitement fueled by nearly 3 years of hard work energized every crowded meeting room. As the estimated 200 attendees eagerly awaited the vote to approve the Reference Model as a DP, each country delegation formally presented their review of the Reference Model and recommended, or not, its passage. John Aschenbrenner of IBM led the US delegation that again argued that the Reference Model should be approved as a technical report, not as a standard. The dull thud that followed hardly had time to reach the back of the room when Mike Purton of the British Standards Institute gave, as Bachman would recall, "his infamous speech," condemning the Reference Model for its misuse of the English language.

Zimmermann remembers the backlash to Purton's speech reporting that the UK delegation:

> Had given this document to their experts, and they had said unanimously that this document should be put in the basket. That was the end of it, because telling this to a bunch of people who had been working hard as hell to produce something, who know that it's not really perfect but it has some value, telling them that it's just good for the paper basket, that was the end of it. Everybody agreed. The US said: 'We'll just abstain. We'll not oppose,' and that is the way the OSI Reference Model moved to the DP stage.[81]

Making the OSI Reference Model a DP effectively ordered the layering of computer communication protocols even though OSI had yet to create an actual protocol standard.

In November 1980, the sigh of collective relief that the OSI Reference Model had advanced to the DP stage reinvigorated those seeking to influence the various protocol designs. For the members of ISO TC 97/SC 16, the definition of the transport layer protocols, especially the need for an end-to-end datagram protocol, became

80. Zimmermann interview, Computer History Museum.

81. Zimmermann interview, Computer History Museum.

a priority. CCITT already had made its demands known when it approved its transport layer standard for teletext several months earlier.[82] In January 1981, ECMA standardized on the five classes of transport protocols it had earlier recommended to both ISO and CCITT: TP2 being equivalent to CCITT's S.70 and TP4 being equivalent to TCP.[83] Predictably, these actions influenced the proceedings of SC 16 that prized agreement with both CCITT and ECMA and joint meetings ensued.

With the Reference Model advancing to the DP stage, its near certain standardization induced a flurry of commercial activity. At the National Computer Conference (NCC) in May, data communications took center stage for the first time; with seminars such as "Transport and Session Protocols in the Context of the ISO Reference Model" and "Local Networks and the Ethernet in Particular." Luminaries such as Vint Cerf, Greg Hopkins, David Potter, and John Day gave talks.[84] Articles on OSI ("Coming of age: A long-awaited standard for heterogeneous nets,"[85] and "Reality and the proposed OSI standard"[86]) began appearing in technical and industry publications. And the undeniable importance of the connection protocol X.25 gained support, first with AT&T announcing products in January, and then IBM announcing in June. No wonder Zimmermann had felt the pressure to complete work on the Reference Model so protocol standards work could begin: market forces were already at work.

In January 1982, less than a year after circulating the Reference Model DP to its members for passage, TC 97 approved the Reference Model as a Draft International Standard (DIS) and forwarded it to ISO for vote by its full membership. With virtually all of the uncertainty about the Reference Model becoming a standard eliminated (notwithstanding the continuing criticism from the US delegation that the Reference Model should be a technical document and not a standard), both committees, SC 6 and SC 16, felt pressured to begin producing the protocols needed to actually build products. To do so meant creating two standards—services and protocols—for each layer.[87]

---

82. *Data Communications*, January 1981, 68.

83. "Standard ECMA-72: Transport Protocol" ECMA, January 1981.

84. J. Peter Schmader. 1981. Computer conference sharpens focus on data communications. *Data Communications*, April 1981, 129–132.

85. Harold C. Folts. 1981. Coming of age: A long-awaited standard for heterogeneous nets. *Data Communications*, Jan. 1981, 63–73.

86. Bert D. Moldow. 1981. Reality and the proposed OSI standard. *Data Communications*, June 1981, 77–80.

87. Peter F. Linington. 1983. Fundamentals of the layer service definitions and protocol specifications. *Proceedings of the IEEE* 71, December 1983, 1341–1345, doi: 10.1109/PROC.1983.12776. The Service standard sets forth the capabilities delivered to the user of the layer, the next higher layer,

In June 1982, SC 16 at its Tokyo meeting acted first when it approved as DPs both transport layer service and protocol standards (ISO/DP 8072 and 8073). The US, represented by ANSI, once again voted no—citing incompatibility among the five classes of protocol standards as well as the claim that the DP could not be implemented.[88] Efforts to resolve the US objections, as well as objections of others, prior to forwarding the DPs to TC 97 took on a new level of seriousness. Modifying TP4, the virtual circuit protocol over connectionless networks, was assigned to the NBS, virtually guaranteeing a protocol similar to TCP. Despite the differences, the quick action on DP 8072/73 reflected real cooperation with both CCITT and ECMA. (After all, both CCITT and ECMA got what they wanted and more: TP0 providing minimal functionality, consistent with a connection network layer such as X.25, and TP4, providing functionality comparable to TCP, sought by the computer community.)

On the other hand, progress within SC 6 to create a connectionless protocol at the network layer stalled while the committee completed its connection-based Service and Protocol standards. In part, progress lagged because the Reference Model did not yet call for connectionless communications.

By the fall of 1982, votes began coming in on the Reference Model Draft International Standard (DIS 7498) and the US once again voted no.[89] While the three objections that accompanied the no vote were the same ones the US had attached to prior yes votes, the fact that the US—the secretariat—voted no seemed divisive.[90] In a December 1982 *Data Communications* article titled: "Network users group shocked as ANSI votes against OSI model," Sheldon Blauman, founder of the Network Users Association (NUA) was quoted:[91] "It is both a surprise and a shock to me. A vote against Open Systems Interconnection is like a vote against apple pie and motherhood. I see the situation as rather frightening."

Even though the final vote on DIS 7498 tallied 22 yes, 2 no, and 1 abstention, declaring 7498 an International Standard remained on hold while an effort was made to resolve the US objections. (Voting no with the US was Germany.)

---

and the constraints on the layer immediately below. (Hence, the Service standards for the transport layer specify the constraints on the network layer and include capabilities for users of both the transport and session layers.) Protocol standards specify how products worked to deliver the Service capabilities.

88. A. Lyman Chapin. 1983. Computer communication standards. *Computer Communication Review*, Jan. 1983, 40–43.

89. This is after the US had abstained at the DP stage vote.

90. Chapin, "Computer communication standards."

91. *Data Communications*, December 1982, 50. NUA members included Ford, Bechtel, Grumman, TRW, and McDonnell Douglas.

At year-end 1982, the promise of OSI to bring order to the conflicting technologies within computer communications remained just that, a promise. The overarching OSI architecture of the Reference Model seemed close to becoming an international standard. But since DIS 7498 assumed a connection paradigm, accommodating the connectionless world of LANs meant a Reference Model addendum—a document modifying an existing standard—although being worked on, had to be voted through the same DP, DIS, ISO process.

In one encouraging note, SC 16 passed a TP4 version of DP 8073: a virtual circuit protocol over a connection-based network. Yet until SC 6 passed a connectionless network layer, LAN products using ISO OSI standards remained only a distant possibility. What were LAN manufacturers to do in the meantime?

At year-end 1982, two connectionless, or datagram, communication protocols for LANs did exist: TCP/IP and XNS. Their success would impact the eventual outcome of OSI.

8.7 The LAN and OSI Standards Efforts Meet

In the summer of 1982, Graube and Rosenthal began focusing on what they saw as the next challenge in local area networking: the higher layer protocols. The two shared concerns over the timeliness of higher-layer software, especially the transport layer, the layer required for reliable end-to-end communications over a network. Graube remembers their motivation after it had become clear that at least one LAN standard, CSMA/CD, would be passed:

> "What do we do for these higher-layer protocols?" Obviously, it was just like with the 488 standard business, where we had the transport mechanism, but the instruments still couldn't communicate because there was no data format specified. So I wanted to see what we could do in terms of getting some agreements, what have you, for these higher-layer protocols; what was really needed.[92]

Rosenthal also recognized the need for testing of the protocols that each vendor would create. An OSI standard, while necessary, was not sufficient condition to assure commercial LAN products. Standards specifications could be implemented in an unlimited number of ways, hence the near certainty of incompatible implementations. To solve that problem, Rosenthal saw the use of agreements—contracts—among organizations to implement compatible versions of transport protocol standards. But how would he get organizations to agree? Rosenthal remembers:

92. Graube interview, Computer History Museum.

> In order to pull this off, we had to get some agreements. That's the key word, "agreements." We had to get the people highest up in these organizations to commit resources. We had to get a commitment of the CEOs, somebody with signature authority, had to be able to say: "Here's the check, you make it happen. Pull out all the stops. OSI is important. Make it happen." We had to get the technical people to ask the question: "Make what happen?" We had to say: "Make this happen," and we had to lay it out for them.[93]

One CEO who responded to the invitation of NBS to attend a meeting was Roger Smith of General Motors (GM). GM had formed a task group in 1980 to look at the possibility of using computer-based automation to combat growing competition from companies producing in lower labor cost economies.[94] In 1981, GM held exploratory conversations with IBM, DEC, and HP. From these efforts came the release of GM's Manufacturing Automation Protocol (MAP) version 1.0 in 1982.[95] Since MAP operated over the LANs that interconnected automation equipment, GM was eager to hear what NBS had to say.

An ideal opportunity to discuss these issues with a wider community was after the IEEE 802 meeting held at DEC in December 1982. Graube convened a handful of concerned insiders to discuss how to create OSI transport layer software. Representatives of roughly six companies, Rosenthal, and Graube attended. While all expressed concern, no one knew precisely what to do and little came of the meeting until shortly after Graube submitted his trip report at Tektronix. Graube remembers the response: "The lightning bolt came down from the lawyers, through my boss, to me, and Zap! 'Though shalt not do things like that anymore!'" Tektronix lawyers had recently dealt with the Department of Commerce on another standards matter and issues of antitrust had surfaced. Questions of standards preventing trade and of monopolistic practices had cooled Tektronix lawyers to the idea of companies meeting, clandestine or not, to discuss and create standards.

Graube remembers telling Rosenthal: "'Gee, I got my fingers slapped here for our little meeting in Tewksbury,' and Robbie says: 'Well, no problem. We hold these workshops at NBS all the time on various topics. Why don't we hold an NBS workshop on implementers of local area networks?'" As Graube points out, there was an additional level of propriety to the location of the meetings: "It works

93. Rosenthal interview, Computer History Museum.

94. "MAP: A user revolt for standards," *Data Communications*, December 1985, 147–156.

95. Michael A. Kaminski, Jr. 1986. Protocols for communicating in the factory. *IEEE Spectrum*, April 1986, 56–62.

nicely because the National Bureau of Standards works under the Department of Commerce, where the antitrust division is also located."[96]

In February 1983, the first NBS International Workshop for Implementers of OSI met. Graube, viewed as the protagonist, was elected Chairman. Conversation quickly turned to the difficulties of ensuring compatible implementations and the desirability of motivating cooperation. Then similar to Roberts' and Kahn's motivation in 1972 to stage a public demonstration of ARPANET at the ICCC trade show, those attending the NBS OSI workshops came to the same conclusion: a public demonstration to coalesce cooperative behavior. They knew it would take time to organize, and settled on the largest computer tradeshow, the NCC to be held in July 1984.

The collision of LAN interests and antitrust concerns could be read elsewhere when in February IBM offered to buy 12% of Intel for $250 million and the Justice Department and Federal Trade Commission made known their reservations.[97] IBM publicly stated its investment was to assure that Intel, a leading US semiconductor manufacturer and supplier of the microprocessor used in the IBM PC, had the capital to stay competitive with the aggressive Japanese semiconductor manufacturers (IBM accounted for 13% of Intel's sales).

In May 1983, ISO formally approved the Reference Model standard: ISO 7498. Already in process was an Addendum to the Reference Model to cover connectionless transmission. SC 6, which had focused on creating a connection-oriented network layer protocol (8348) to submit as a DP, began work on a connectionless Addendum to 8348.

As of the summer of 1983, ISO had standardized the Reference Model and approved a connectionless transport protocol. They had yet to decide on what to do about the LAN protocols being developed within IEEE, and supported by ECMA, or a connectionless network layer protocol. Nevertheless, the promise of standards bringing an end to LAN confusion seemed almost within reach.

8.8 The Emergence of a Dominant Design: 1983–1984

The years 1983–1984 represented a turning point in the history of the LAN market, as, finally, the technological–political dance of chaos and uncertainty gave way to standards resolution and economic growth. The first to benefit were Ethernet vendors. In 1983, Ethernet became an IEEE, ECMA, and effectively an ISO/OSI standard. In addition, the conversion of ARPANET to TCP/IP on January 1, 1983,

96. Graube interview, Computer History Museum.

97. *Data Communications*, February 1983, 25. This action also highlights the interconnecting of market-structures.

represented a milestone for DARPA in that TCP/IP had been successfully ported to all the leading computers of the day. By mid-year it would be available for the IBM PC. In contrast, Xerox refused to release more of XNS and, as a consequence, nearly all the LAN start-ups would engineer their next generation products using TCP/IP, not XNS. As for IBM, the lumbering giant, it would not be until 1984 before it made its LAN intentions clear. That same year, the NCC public demonstration of OSI software was an important first step in proving the concept of vendor-independent OSI LAN software; albeit commercial products were still years away. As the finalization of standards became apparent, sales of LAN products soared 141% in 1983. Two years later they reached nearly $1 billion. Here then is a summary of those two critical years.

On June 23, 1983, a day many had fought long and hard for, the IEEE ended years of debate and misdirection and approved Ethernet as standard 802.3. DIX and the corporate support Ethernet had garnered prevailed. It was the news supporters within ECMA had sought. With renewed energy they pressed their arguments that ISO adopt the CSMA/CD standard. The fact was that Ethernet worked despite years of arguments to the contrary.

In July 1983, IEEE 802 forwarded its token bus recommendation to the TCCC for approval. Miller of Concord Data Systems remembers his role in the process: "We succeeded in getting token bus passed, so great, holy shit, a little company pushed that through. We pretty much wrote the standard. The other company that participated was Amdax, another token bus start-up."[98]

Token ring, on the other hand, remained in limbo due to IBM's vacillating leadership. In September 1983, they staged a technology demonstration of token ring in Zurich. Even so, no one expected a token ring standard recommendation to be out of committee until the spring of 1984.[99]

In September 1983, ISO SC 6 met. As expected, the membership passed the recommendation that the IEEE 802 LAN standards be adopted. Little doubt remained that the recommendations would be approved by ISO at its next meeting in January 1984. The need for SC 6 to create a connectionless network layer protocol was all that stood in the way for ISO/OSI to have a comparable LAN protocol stack to TCP/IP over Ethernet.[100]

98. Ken Miller, oral history interview by James L. Pelkey, February 23, 1988. Computer History Museum, Mountain View, CA. Available from https://archive.computerhistory.org/resources/access/text/2015/10/102737985-05-01-acc.pdf.

99. *Data Communications*, December 1983, 15.

100. Around this time SC 6 took over responsibility for the transport layer as well. SC 16 was disbanded and a new committee, SC 21, became responsible for the top three layers of the Reference Model.

One big question hovered over the emerging standards, however: What was IBM going to do? (A decision referred to by some as: "the most speculated upon product of the decade."[101]) The world's dominant computer company had played its cards so close to its vest that it now seemed confused and oddly incompetent. Even without IBM's stamp of approval, LANs had successfully run the gauntlet of international standards making. If IBM did not act soon, they might be left with the role of runner-up. Perhaps that motivated a cloaked presentation by Texas Instruments in February at the International Solid State Circuits Conference of a token ring chip set it had under development.[102] If intended to quell rumors, it did little but fan them: chip problems held up IBM's plans.[103]

On May 8, 1984, IBM made one of the most vilified product announcements of all time when it recommended the IBM Cabling System and pronounced its Statement of Direction.[104] According to the Statement of Direction, IBM intended to implement a "star-wired token ring local area network using the IBM Cabling System within the next two to three years." Implied was compatibility with the IEEE 802 standard. Far from a product announcement, IBM, the most dominant computer company, long thought unassailable technologically, could only recommend how to wire ones' facilities, and to trust that its LAN solution would be available in 2 to 3 years. If ever an action had been meant to forestall market development, IBM delivered it that ignominious day.

While IBM shadow danced, the NBS-led efforts to stage OSI-compliant LAN demonstrations at NCC progressed. In March 1984, GM and McDonnell Douglas held the first MAP users group meeting with 36 companies attending. Boeing, not to be left behind, announced that with the help of NBS it would lead the creation of an OSI protocol stack for technical and office environments, later to be named Technical and Office Protocols (TOP).[105] That same month, March, NBS released information on the OSI Class 4 Transport (TP4) compatibility testing programs under development. It identified 421 scenarios to test the 5,700 lines of C code needed to implement TP4.[106] (Another metric of the complexity of TP4: an

101. *Datamation*, January 1984, 13.

102. *Electronics Weekly* Sept. 17, 1984, 17.

103. *Data Communications*, April 1984, 16.

104. *Data Communications*, August 1985.

105. TOP, as was MAP, would be organized under the Society of Manufacturing Engineers (SME) for reasons similar to why other multi-company standard-making efforts were organized under the IEEE or NBS. Steven A. Farowich. 1986. Communicating in the technical office. *IEEE Spectrum*, April 1986, 63–67.

106. *Data Communications*, March 1984, 277–285.

Intel spokesperson claimed it took 50 man-months to develop.[107]) The considerable commitment needed to prepare for NCC had narrowed the list of potential participants to 15 companies.[108]

While general reviews of the NCC show held in Las Vegas, Nevada, on July 9–12, 1984, were mixed, all praised the NBS-led demonstrations. One review called NCC "by and large a ho-hum affair" with the exception of "two eye-opening demonstrations of Open Systems Interconnection for local area networks."[109] The GM-coordinated MAP over token bus (802.4) demonstration interconnected seven devices from Allen-Bradley, Concord Data Systems, DEC, Gould, HP, IBM, and Motorola. The more limited Boeing demonstration had files being swapped using TP4 over Ethernet (802.3) between eight vendors: Advanced Computer Communications, Charles River Data Systems, DEC, Honeywell Information Systems, HP, ICL, Intel, and NCR. The often-critical *Data Communications* editorial column, Viewpoint, ran the headline in August 1984: "Vendor–user partnership gives new meaning to standards." The article ends: "We anxiously await such products from all the participating vendors and congratulate them for what we hope becomes a role model for continued vendor–user cooperation."[110]

The workings of IEEE Committee 802, ISO, NBS, GM, and now Boeing may have grabbed the headlines and the steering wheel chartering the future course of LANs, but the immediate driving force of LANs rested firmly with the IBM PC. In 1983, the growth rate of PC connections exceeded the overall market growth rate by 50%.[111] The market for PC LANs was predicted to grow from $49 million in 1983 to $232 million in 1988.[112] So when IBM introduced its second-generation PC, the IBM PC AT on August 1, 1984, it is little wonder that they felt the need to also introduce a LAN.

On August 14, 1984, after years of waiting, rumors, predictions, obfuscation and stonewalling, IBM finally introduced its first LAN: the IBM PC Network.[113] Was it the feared token ring that leveraged the customers' investment in the IBM Cabling System? No and no again. It was a 2-megabit per second CSMA/CD broadband network OEM'ed from the start-up Sytek. Promising to carry video, it smacked of a

107. *Computerworld*, July 23, 1984, 52.

108. *Electronic News*, July 9, 1984.

109. *Electronics Week*, July 23, 1984, 45.

110. *Data Communications*, August 1984, 13.

111. Local Area Network Equipment, Dataquest 1987, 77 and 80.

112. *Electronics Week*, Dec. 10, 1984, 20. Total LAN sales exceeded $1 billion.

113. Technically, the PC Network was IBM's second LAN. The first was the PC Cluster introduced in 1983 which had bombed. *Data Communications*, October 1984, 77.

poor man's WangNet. Even so, experts welcomed IBM's market entry with pronouncements such as: "IBM's announcement will change attitudes in the end-user community, which has hesitated to adopt local area networks."[114] In August, AT&T introduced its first LAN, a slow version of CSMA/CD known as StarLAN.

IBM was not alone in publicly aligning itself with one LAN technology and then switching its choice.[115] In the fall of 1984, the DOD, which had funded LAN development from the beginning, announced that it would adopt the ISO standards, implying that ISO protocols would supplant the existing DOD standard TCP/IP protocols.[116] This decision was further supported in a National Academy of Sciences study commissioned by the DOD.

Several other important decisions were announced in the fall of 1984. In September, the IEEE approved the token bus standard (802.4). It was automatically adopted by ISO as an OSI standard. On October 31, the momentum for OSI standards received another boost when the NBS issued its first Federal Information Processing Standard 107 titled: Local Area Networks: Baseband Carrier Sense Multiple Access with Collision Detection Access Method and Physical Layer Specifications and Link Layer Protocol. It would become part of the government stack of protocols being developed by NBS known as Government OSI Information Protocols, or GOSIP. ISO's OSI appeared the clear winner among computer communication protocols.

In October, IEEE 802 forwarded the token ring (802.5) standard recommendation to IEEE TCCC. On December 31, 1984, all four IEEE 802 LAN standards were approved by ANSI. ISO approved all four standards as well.

8.9 In Perspective

The long trek of LAN standards making began in March of 1978 with the first meeting of ISO/TC 97/SC 16. It reached successful completion nearly 6 years later, by the end of 1984. Along the way, engineers, business leaders, and government officials from around the world logged countless hours and miles, devoted to meetings where seemingly every word of every technical proposal was debated, revised, and debated again. In the process, networking experts such as Maris Graube, Robert Rosenthal, and Hubert Zimmermann found themselves cast as protagonist of political battles—with big profits and international prestige on the line.

114. "IBM's first net well received; analysts call for more," *Computerworld*, August 20, 1984, 5. The quote is from Everett Meserve of Arthur D. Little.

115. Jean Bartik. 1984. IBM's token ring: Have the pieces finally come together? *Data Communications*, August 1984, 125–139.

116. *Data Communications*, November 1984, 15.

By the end of 1984, with the rules of the game settled, it was time to see what firms could best compete. No longer would compromises, agreements, and votes decide the future of LANs; it would be product offerings, prices, and availability.

Embraced within the new rules were connectionless, or datagram, protocols that had been dismissed by the powerful CCITT. Individual initiatives, backed by technical arguments about the best ways to deliver on the promise of packet-switched networking—had prevailed and overcome the power of the entrenched. Our next chapter delves back into the companies jostling for control in the networking market-structure. These companies included established firms trying to navigate the technical and market transition from data communications to networking, as well as start-ups that came to networking with talent and fresh ideas about computer communications.

Market Order: Networking, 1983–1986

9.1 Overview

By the end of 1982, the networking market-structure had transitioned into the competitive phase. As one industry analyst put it, "Local area networking has emerged from its infancy into a healthy, brawling adolescence."[1] It seemed everywhere they looked corporate executives saw announcements of trade shows featuring a wide array of networking products. Press reports routinely compared various solutions in an effort to make sense of the confusion. A key factor in the growing buzz around networking was the unexpected tsunami created by the introduction of the IBM PC in 1981, which continued to inundate the landscape of business computing. Corporate managers had seen the value in desktop computing with the popularity of spreadsheet applications like VisiCalc for the Apple II, SuperCalc for the Osborne 1 portable computer, and Lotus 1-2-3 for the IBM PC. The success of the IBM PC rapidly accelerated computer purchasing by corporate America. As the budgets for data processing assumed a larger percentage of total corporate spending, Management Information Systems (MIS) departments became ripe targets for networking products and services—once every corporate desktop became the home of a computer, a flood of new software applications created a demand for shared information at higher communication speeds.

By 1983, the stock market was showing signs of strength after nearly two decades of lackluster performance. The government's economic policies of the late 1970s and early 1980s were starting to have a positive effect on the economy and the venture capital industry. New commitments to venture funds soared to $500 million in 1980 and by 1983 they reached nearly $3.5 billion. In that year alone, venture capital investments exceeded $2.5 billion. 3Com president Bill Krause smiled when he

1. "Local Area Networks" Datapro, November 1983, 101.

recalled the early 1980s, a time "when money was falling like apples off a tree."[2]. Any promising company or idea could find capital, adding to the competition and to confusion in the market. To encourage the belief in a new economic frontier, investment banks such as Morgan Stanley and Alex. Brown & Sons held investment conferences to identify the leading firms of networking. While their products were in demand, uncertainty remained as to what products and firms would prevail.

Where did this promising new communication technology leave AT&T and IBM, the two giants that observers had been expecting to dominate communications and computers for decades? In 1982, with its agreement to divest itself of its regional Bell Operating companies, AT&T had finally won the freedom to compete in the computer market, but it would take until 1984 for it to offer competitive products. IBM had avoided serious antitrust problems and continued to dominate the computer industry. Its hold on the market even tightened with the introduction of the IBM PC, yet, like AT&T, as of 1983 they did not yet have a networking product to sell.

Of utmost importance to the growth of the networking market was the effort to adopt networking standards. As told in the previous chapter, this effort culminated in the adoption of two of the three main networking technologies available, Ethernet and token bus. This would have a major impact on the sales of networking products, especially Ethernet, even as many corporate customers still awaited IBM's product.

9.2 The Established Powers

9.2.1 Alex. Brown & Sons Conference, March 1983

In March 1983, Alex. Brown & Sons, a leading investment bank specializing in raising capital for high technology companies, held a three-day conference at the Hyatt Hotel in Baltimore, MD. Prominent data communication firms and firms focusing on the emerging networking market made presentations (see Table 9.1). An opening presentation by an Alex. Brown partner encouraged investors to view the time as "unique" to buy computer communications stocks.

The executives of some of the companies had the following to say[3]:

William Norred, President and CEO of Micom Systems Inc.: Micom's story would remain the same: marketing-oriented, profit-driven. Their strategy: product versus

2. Bill Krause, oral history interview by James L. Pelkey, August 15, 1994, Mountain View, CA. Computer History Museum, Mountain View, CA. Available from https://archive.computerhistory.org/resources/access/text/2020/01/102740543-05-01-acc.pdf

3. Remarks are paraphrased from the Pelkey's notes taken at the meeting.

Table 9.1 **Selected presenters at the Alex. Brown & Sons Telecommunication Seminar**

Data Communication Firms	CBX Firms	Networking Firms
Micom Systems Inc.	ROLM Corp.	Ungermann-Bass
Digital Communications Associates	Intecom	Sytek
Gandalf Technologies Inc.	CXC Corp.	Network Systems Corp.
Infotron Inc.	Mitel	
Paradyne Corporation	Ztel	
Timeplex Inc.		

Source: James L. Pelkey's notes from the conference. Alex. Brown & Sons Telecommunications Seminar, March, 1983 - Selected Presenters.

market oriented; product, not network oriented; and while they wanted to remain the leader in concentrators (multiplexers), they were now focusing on local connections, that is, port selectors, or data PBXs, which constituted 16% of their sales and would grow at 30–50% over the next few years. The data PBX was the LAN of the day.

Robert Wiggins, Chairman, President and CEO of Paradyne Corp.: Paradyne's mission was changing from data communications to networking. The driving force for networking was the need for information. Communication of data would become as popular as voice. Local networking was coming into promise. In response to a question, Wiggins said he did not worry about competition: product development cycles precluded that concern. (Interestingly, Wiggins did not mention the risks of the large Social Security Administration contract they had recently won—a contract soon to turn into a nightmare.)

Edward Botwinick, President and CEO of Timeplex Inc.: Timeplex's market was private, distributed data networks. The three laws of data communications were: networks never get smaller, slower, nor remain the same. Timeplex's most important product was the Evolution II, a switching multiplexer, also known as a port selector or data PBX. He outlined how it was leading Timeplex into large system orders.

Ken Oshmann, President of ROLM Corp.: ROLM was the largest supplier of digital PBXs (CBXs) in the world. AT&T and IBM were their competitors. ROLM delivered products that integrated voice data switching. Data could be switched at 19,200bps: today's need!

Ralph Ungermann, President and CEO of Ungermann-Bass Inc.: Ungermann-Bass was in the communications system market selling LAN products. The market in 1984 would be $386 million. The three technological issues for LANs were: baseband versus broadband, CSMA/CD versus token passing, and rings versus buses versus stars.

Mike Pliner, President of Sytek Inc.: Sytek's competition was UB. Their LocalNet LAN was a broadband LAN as was their MetroNet, introduced in 1982. Their strategy: provide turnkey network/data communication solutions. (They used Paradyne modems and multiplexers when needed.) Pliner believed that once they reached $25 million in revenue, Sytek intended to go public.

As hopeful as the future seemed, networking remained mired in confusion between what technology best served the needs of computer communications: LANs or data PBXs. The year ahead would see a steady flow of articles extolling which technology was better. Few saw the profound effect the personal computer revolution would have on the needs of the communication system of the future. PBX companies would continue to introduce CBXs[4]; all kinds of products would be introduced to enable CBXs to support data devices; new start-ups like CXC and Ztel, along with computer company Datapoint, would announce CBXs with integrated LANs[5]; PBX companies would announce technologies to interface to minicomputers[6]; and workstations integrating voice and data would be announced.[7] In all, no consensus was clear as vendors tried to stake out market leadership with press releases and product announcements.

9.2.2 AT&T: Computers and LANs

Even after the breakup, AT&T remained dominant in customer premises equipment (CPE), one of their core businesses, with approximately $4 billion of CPE assets transferred to the new AT&T on January 1, 1984.[8] CBXs had begun gobbling gigantic bites out of its market share beginning in the late 1970s. AT&T, free to begin competing after January 2, 1982, would take until 1983 before introducing its first CBX, the System 85 designed for large installations: it could support up to 32,000 lines. A year later they introduced a smaller CBX, the System 75 that supported a maximum of 800 lines.[9] They would continue to lose market share as shipping

4. "Handicapping the heavies in the great PBX derby," *Data Communications*, April 1983, 58–59.

5. "Fourth gGeneration CBX for 1984," *Data Communications*, April 1983, 15.

6. "ROLM CBX now has IBM 3270 gateway," *Data Communications*, May 1983, 254; "Minis fighting way into office market," Electronics, May 5, 1983, 101–102; "I, Computer, take thee, PBX," *Datamation* March 1984, 134–149; "Comparing the two PBX-to-computer specifications," *Data Communications* May 1984, 215–222.

7. "Workstation supports voice at 64kbit/s; data and graphics too," *Data Communications*, May 1983, 234.

8. "Intecom," *Harvard Business School*, 386–053, 1985, p. 9.

9. *Bell Labs Technical Journal*, January–March 2000, 6.

problems compounded already being late to market. Not until 1984 was AT&T again truly competitive.[10]

Finally free to sell computer products, AT&T realized that to compete effectively with the likes of IBM, DEC, and Siemens, it needed a partner with experience in computer manufacturing. In December 1983, AT&T confirmed rumors that it was going to purchase part ownership of the Italian office equipment company Ing C. Olivetti & Co. In March 1984, AT&T announced its entry into the computer field by introducing a computer product line of six machines ranging in price from $9,950 to $340,000. In June, AT&T announced the first four models of its first personal computer made by Olivetti, the PC 6300. Since it used the Intel 8086, it was faster than the IBM PC, but not more than the recent IBM PC XT or AT computers. Elserino Piol, Olivetti's executive vice president for corporate strategy and development, traveled weekly from Ivrea, Italy to Paris to board the Concorde flight from Paris to NYC, negotiated the deal between Olivetti and AT&T, returning each Friday to Ivrea. The grueling schedule lasted a month before the two sides shook hands. Their agreement was for AT&T's personal computer to be the foundation for an office automation system. In Piol's words: "The future battle in the market is no longer for the mainframe computer. It is in wiring a company and office together, linking all its machines into a system. This is the fundamental trump card that AT&T has, and we are going to help them use it."[11]

In mid-1984, AT&T finally introduced its 1Mbps Ethernet-like network that ran over telephone wire, known as StarLAN. While it became the IEEE 802.3e 1BASE 5 standard and experienced early success due to its use of existing phone cabling, it ultimately failed to become a market factor due to its slow speed and incompatibility with Ethernet. AT&T did not give up on competing in the LAN market, however, continuing to upgrade its StarLAN, which, along with the SynOptics' LattisNet, would serve as the basis for the IEEE standard for Ethernet over UTP, 10Base-T.

9.2.3 IBM: CBXs and LANs—Does It Need Both?

IBM introduced its first PBX in Europe in the late 1970s. To help develop a PBX for the increasingly competitive market, in 1982, IBM signed a development agreement with the Canadian telecommunications company Mitel for a CBX. Dissatisfied with Mitel's progress, in the summer of 1983 IBM abandoned its relationship and by then a $370 million investment.

The rising star of the CBX market was ROLM, which commanded a 16% market share in the PBX market. Even though ROLM had a very successful CBX business,

10. Smith Barney Research, AT&T, Oct. 10, 1985, p. 20.

11. Smith Barney Research, AT&T, Oct. 10, 1985, p. 5; *Business Week*, July 16, 1984, 41.

management knew they needed a strong data partner if they wanted to continue to take market share from AT&T. In the fall of 1982, top management began quietly discussing the idea of partnering with a computer company; the list of candidates included the leading minicomputer companies. They soon began negotiations with Hewlett-Packard (HP), but eventually talks stalled. Rumors that IBM was dissatisfied with the Mitel relationship gave ROLM executives hope that their entrepreneurial company might strike a deal with Big Blue. Ken Oshman, the CEO of ROLM, made contact with IBM, and a deal was struck. In June 1983, IBM purchased 15% of ROLM for $228 million. IBM appeared as intent on getting into the PBX business as AT&T was on getting into the computer business.

IBM's intention to enter the LAN business had become equally complicated. Its token ring LAN was not expected to be ready until 1984 and, in fact, would slide to late 1985. The Entry Systems Division, responsible for the PC, and planning to introduce an upgraded PC in 1984, argued that they needed to have a LAN earlier to compete in the marketplace.

With all the confusion between PBXs and LANs, in December 1983, IBM convened yet another task force to explore whether they needed both. The conclusion must have been yes, for in 1984, IBM bought the balance of ROLM stock they did not own for $70.00 per share for a total of $1.25 billion, valuing ROLM at $1.8 billion. In total, IBM had paid $1.55 billion for ROLM.[12]

9.2.4 The Computer Companies

Networking for mainframe computers was a relatively small market, served by one start-up in particular, Network Systems, but for the growing number of minicomputer companies, responding to customer needs for communication solutions was essential to maintaining an edge on the competition. Of the main minicomputer companies, 5 elected to choose Ethernet and roughly 15 elected other technologies. Four entrepreneurial start-ups chose Ethernet while one chose a broadband LAN. In 1983, a trade press article listed 25 LAN vendors either manufacturing or developing Ethernet products: 4 start-ups (3Com. UB, Bridge Communications, and Interlan), 8 computer companies (DEC, HP, Data General, Siemens, Tektronix, Xerox, ICL, and NCR), and 7 chip manufacturers (Intel, AMD, Mostek, Fujitsu, National Semiconductor, Rockwell, and Seeq). Not all computer companies selected Ethernet, for example: Prime Computers (token ring: Ringnet), Datapoint (proprietary:

12. Maxfield, Katherine. 2014. *Starting Up Silicon Valley: How ROLM Became a Cultural Icon and Fortune 500 Company*. Greenleaf Book Group 248. IBM's acquisition of ROLM would eventually fail to give IBM significant market share in the PBX market. In 1988, IBM was forced to sell ROLM.

ARCnet), Sytek, Network Systems, and Wang Laboratories (broadband: proprietary; and token bus) and Corvus, Convergent Technologies and Nestar (baseband: proprietary).

9.2.5 Digital Equipment Corporation

DEC management understood the importance of LANs early on. Their participation in DIX, active involvement in IEEE 802, and pioneering the sale of minicomputers into the engineering workstation market, all convinced DEC of the importance of local area networking. In May 1982, DEC announced Phase IV of its evolving network architecture (Digital Network Architecture) that would support Ethernet. In April 1983, DEC announced its Ethernet controller for their Unibus-based computers called the Deuna, (DEC Ethernet-to-Unibus communications controller) and began selling it in July for $3,500.[13] A steady release of more Ethernet controllers and terminal servers, especially the DEC Server 100 in 1984, made DEC a formidable competitor. No longer could Ethernet start-ups feast on the DEC customer base.

9.3 The Leading LAN start-ups, 1983–1986

9.3.1 3Com

The year 1983 began hopefully for 3Com. In 1982, management changed their focus of distribution from OEMing to minicomputer companies and their customers to selling their new personal computer LAN, EtherSeries, through retail computer stores. They knew their success depended on the rapid growth in the number of retail stores and chains selling computers. In January 1983, a new venture capital–backed start-up, Businessland, announced plans to launch a chain of computer retail stores. Fortuitously, Robert Metcalfe knew one of the board members, Enzo Turesi, from his days of consulting to Olivetti. Turesi arranged a meeting between Metcalfe and Dave Norman, president of Businessland. Businessland quickly became an important reseller of 3Com's EtherSeries.

Sales for fiscal year ending May 1983 soared 162% to $4.7 million. 3Com earned a small profit of $15,000. In June, management strengthened its balance sheet by raising $3.6 million of venture capital, with a post-money valuation of $41 million.

In the summer of 1983, two important events in the history of LAN protocols occurred with barely any public notice. The first was the Xerox announcement that it was not going to release any more of the higher-level XNS protocols. Yogen Dalal, who had brought XNS into existence when he worked for Xerox PARC, and had left Xerox with David Liddle and Don Massaro to form a new company, Metaphor,

13. *Computerworld*, April 11, 1983.

remembers that Xerox was ambivalent about releasing their higher-level protocols: "I think they felt the lower-level protocols were ok to send out so that the Bridges and the Ungermann-Basses could build connectivity hardware, but nobody could really build servers that would compete with Star [Xerox's 8010 Information System] or the filing systems that Xerox was producing."[14] 3Com had embedded XNS in EtherSeries and undoubtedly had hoped the higher-level protocols would become available.

A second LAN protocol announcement, in August, would prove even more far reaching. The University of California, Berkeley, released version 4.2BSD of the UNIX operating system. This version incorporated the TCP/IP code optimized by Bill Joy with Ethernet in mind. Within 18 months, over 1,000 licenses had been sold. No longer did firms need to start from scratch to create TCP/IP for their products: companies that licensed 4.2BSD received the source code for TCP/IP. Again, 3Com had an advantage. They had been shipping TCP products from inception and, although they had decided to stop innovating their TCP bus-based products in favor of EtherSeries, they retained considerable TCP/IP competence in house. Confirming demand for this expertise, in the fall of 1983 a joint development agreement was executed with Bridge Communications under which 3Com would OEM its Multibus/TCP product to Bridge for use in a terminal server.

In the fall of 1983, 3Com signed an OEM agreement with Texas Instruments. While it was called an OEM agreement, it was really a sale of 3Com's EtherSeries for Texas Instrument's internal use. Soon, agreements were signed with Businessland, Entre Computer Centers, Computercraft, and even a service agreement with Xerox.[15]

In October 1983, Businessweek ran a cover story: "Personal computers: And the winner is IBM."[16] The article quoted a respected market analyst, Michele Preston of L.F. Rothschild, Unterberg, Tobin: "The biggest surprise is how quickly, and to what extent, IBM has become so dominant." Over 150 companies had entered the fast-growing market where sales for personal computers doubled in 1982 to $2.6 billion and were expected to rise to $4.3 billion in 1983. The article claimed IBM was buying enough parts to build 2 million personal computers for the following year.

14. Dalal remembers that Xerox was "hesitant to send out the filing protocol, the printing protocol, the name look-up protocol, the electronic mail protocol; all the protocols that you really needed to do something." Yogen Dalal, oral history interview by James L. Pelkey, August 2, 1988, Santa Clara, CA. Computer History Museum, Mountain View, CA. Available from https://archive.computerhistory.org/resources/access/text/2018/02/102738752-05-01-acc.pdf.

15. "3Com expands LAN retail channels," *Electronic News*, December 19, 1983, 36.

16. "Personal computers: And the winner is IBM," *Businessweek*, October 3, 1983, 76–90.

Clearly the decision by 3Com's management to focus on Ethernet for personal computers, specifically those for the IBM PC, had been a success. Yet the growth in the PC market also brought competition, not only for network adaptors, such as dozens of Ethernet competitors, but also for new ideas as to how to make LAN-connected PCs more functional. The firm that would cause the most trouble for 3Com would be Novell, a company that focused on selling not LAN adapters or servers but a LAN operating system that made LANs more functional and easier to use. Soon the value of LANs would be more than the cost-savings of sharing printers and disks but for applications like email, database, and word processing.

By November 1983, the success of 3Com's EtherSeries product family could be read in their financials. Sales for the 6 months ending November 1983 were $6.2 million, a 234% increase over 1982. Net income leaped to $910,000, up from $72,000. Sales of EtherSeries network adaptors and software accounted for 44% of 3Com's sales. OEM sales to Sun Microsystems remained a meaningful 12% of sales.

On March 21, 1984, the financial success of 3Com led to their initial public offering. While not the first of the LAN companies to go public, that honor would go to UB, 3Com would raise $12.8 million of needed capital with a post-money valuation of $80 million. Rapid sales growth continued, with sales for the 6 months ending November 1984 totaling $22.1 million, a 251% increase over 1983.

3Com invested part of the money raised from its IPO into developing new network adaptors, a new EtherShare network server based on an IBM PC, and software giving their networks advantages over those supplied by competitors like Novell. Their evolving strategy had roots not only in Metcalfe's original vision and his experiences at Xerox PARC, but also the success of Sun Microsystems, a customer that proved the need for high-performance network servers, especially for engineering applications. 3Com took their lead but focused on personal computer LANs, especially for the IBM-compatible PC.

On March 30, 3Com unveiled its Intel-based dedicated network servers. The 3Servers, named to reflect their three functions—peripheral sharing, information exchange, and gateway access to other 3Com networks—were meant to provide minicomputer capabilities to personal computer networks. Bill Krause remembers studying the success of Sun Microsystems and the advantages they had created for their 68000-based Unix clients: "We were taking the next step to getting more value out of what we were selling than just LAN adaptor cards and software. We wanted to sell servers. We were going to become the Sun of the DOS PC world."

Any sense of overconfidence management may have had should have been shattered when Novell's next-generation network operating system, Advanced NetWare/86, began shipping in June. Nevertheless, Krause remembers: "We ignored it. We didn't think it mattered. We thought they were dead wrong, because without the applications, how could they succeed?" 3Com's financial success continued unabated with sales of $46.3 million for fiscal year ended May 1985, up 177%. The decision to increase development of servers and other computer products marked a significant shift in the company strategy. Krause and many of the engineers formerly from HP were "computer guys" who outnumbered the networking engineers, and their experience in hardware design was now put to use in the development of additional hardware for their PC DOS products.

The focus on computers soon led to the pursuit of a merger with computer manufacturer Convergent Technologies. In the summer of 1985, a personal relationship between Krause and Paul C. Ely, Jr., that had ended abruptly when Krause left HP for 3Com—Ely had been Krause's superior—now just as suddenly resumed. Ely had left HP and was in the midst of turning around the minicomputer and desktop computer company Convergent Technologies Inc. as president. Ely was keen on making acquisitions to grow Convergent. In a fitting match, Krause and the management of 3Com had evolved a vision of workgroup computing and believed that if they could also sell the computers that populated their LAN installations they could grow a significantly larger company, just as Sun Microsystems was doing. Krause remembers:

> So we're sailing that summer again, the summer of '85, and I was telling him about the workgroup computing vision, and he says: "You know, at Convergent, we have exactly the same vision, only we use CTOS [their proprietary operating system]. Why don't we merge the companies? We'll cash cow CTOS and we'll use our OEM relationships with Burroughs and AT&T to fund really becoming the Sun of DOS."[17]

While conversations continued in earnest, 3Com still had a company to run. In November 1985, 3Com introduced the first products of its software division: 3+software. In addition to a suite of software, 3Com introduced the concept of workgroup computing: users on 3Com LANs, sharing information and becoming more productive as a group.

On November 26, 1985, 3Com and Convergent announced they would merge in a transaction valuing 3Com at $133.6 million. The vision of workgroup computing, the long-standing desire to sell computers, the "HP" culture within 3Com, and the intense competition from other LAN companies all combined to motivate 3Com management to buy into a larger vision made possible by the merger. It seemed to make sense and the shareholders of 3Com began giving their formal support.

17. Krause interview, Computer History Museum.

Then on March 20, 1986, a week before the merger, they encountered an unexpected problem. Convergent announced disappointing financial results: sales were down and profits had dropped to 5 cents a share from 14 cents the previous quarter. Much of the decline was blamed on slowing sales of computers to AT&T. As part of the process to complete the merger, 3Com had retained its investment bankers, Robertson Colman & Stephens, to render a fairness opinion on the proposed valuation for 3Com. Given the drop in the profitability of Convergent, Robertson Colman & Stephens refused to give the needed opinion.[18] In announcing the stunning decision to cancel the merger, Krause said: "It's one of those unfortunate circumstances where you have an obligation to receive a fairness opinion, and if that can't be rendered you can't proceed."[19]

The post-merger collapse period proved to be challenging. Krause remembers:

> It was a very difficult thing, because we really had sort of emotionally consummated the merger, and it was a very hard time for me personally, because here I had patched up things with my old mentor and was really looking forward to working with him again. If that merger would have gone through, I think both companies would have been extremely successful. I was able to regroup my own emotional energy, to gather up our own internal efforts and refocus them and getting us moving down the path, sort of what I call the period of oscillation, going back and forth with: "Should we be a workgroup computing company, or should we go back to our roots in networking?"[20]

From the outside, 3Com appeared not to skip a beat, reporting sales of $48 million for the 6 months ended November 1986, up 73%. The robust personal computer LAN market swept them upward despite the distraction of the failed Convergent merger. So, while sales of their PC LANs were thriving, the company's workgroup strategy required more market research. Krause quickly learned that their customers were happy with their PC servers and were not keen to buy another expensive computer to use as a server.

Krause recalls thinking through this new strategy and its implications:

> So we went off to go be a computing company. Only this wasn't solving any problems that our customers had. So this was the first clue that I got that the computer and communication industries were changing from being the emerging growth phase to where you could just take any technology and throw it up in the air and the vacuum for product would just suck it up, to

18. "What went wrong between 3Com and Convergent?" *Data Communications*, May 1986, p. 97.

19. "Convergent, 3Com call off merger at last minute," *Wall Street Journal*, March 27, 1986.

20. Krause interview, Computer History Museum.

> being a more mature market where you actually had to do market research, market analysis, go out and talk to your customers and understand what they wanted and needed.[21]

Krause had seen the potential challenge that lay ahead for 3Com, given the mismatch between their chosen strategy and the needs of their customers. Convincing Metcalfe to re-examine his vision for the company would be an even greater challenge.

9.3.2 Ungermann-Bass

The management of Ungermann-Bass faced challenges similar to those of 3Com going into 1983. And significantly more. UB had adopted a vendor-independent strategy that required selling more than Ethernet products. Even so, Ethernet competition, the announcements of Xerox and Berkeley, and how to react to the personal computer phenomenon added to management's opportunities and woes.

The year 1983 began with the formal acquisition of Amdax, the source of the token ring technology needed to satisfy their IBM contract. Charlie Bass remembers: "I took over the engineering group, fired the head of that group, and handed them the proposal we had given IBM, and said: 'OK guys, this is the job. This is what we have to do.'"[22]

As the year unfolded, UB felt the competitive pressure from the new entrant, Bridge Communications. UB had based the architecture of their LAN adapters on the Zilog Z80 processor, drawing on their prior experience with the Z80. The Z80 microprocessor had performance issues, however, and UB management had little choice but to move to an Intel chip for their second-generation products. Recognizing that UB had a big transition between product generations, Bridge jumped on the opportunity to beat them to market, introducing their Motorola-based products.

UB not only faced the growing head-to-head competition with Bridge but the growing problem of not having a LAN solution for the PC. Jim Jordan, vice president of sales and marketing, remembers the impasse around this problem: "The PC started to be a big deal and it [was] evident to everybody that if you're going to be in networking, you really had to get into PC networking... I was going crazy, because we were starting to get hurt in the sales area, because we really didn't

21. Krause interview, Computer History Museum.

22. Charles (Charlie) Bass, oral history interview by James L. Pelkey, August 16, 1994, Palo Alto, CA. Computer History Museum, Mountain View, CA. Available from https://archive.computerhistory.org/resources/access/text/2018/03/102738753-05-01-acc.pdf.

have any PC installations, and it was becoming obvious that they were becoming ubiquitous."[23]

Jordan desperately wanted to have a low-cost PC interface card like 3Com's with minimal functionality. Bass also wanted to get into PC networking, but with an adapter that had sufficient processing power and memory to off-load the networking overhead from the PC onto the adapter board—a solution that surely would require the use of expensive Intel 186-microprocessors. Jordan referred to Bass's solution as "a typical goddamned engineer approach to the problem." Ungermann, on the other hand, didn't want to be in the PC networking business at all. The three executives met to discuss strategy before Ungermann went on the road with the investment bankers preparing to take UB public. The most important issue was whether or not they were going to get into the PC networking business. Ungermann would not be dissuaded and remained unyielding. But Jordan and Bass would not relent, as Jordan recalls:

> So Ralph went to Europe, and Charlie and I got us in the business while he was gone. We absolutely did. We started designing one of these [PC adapter] things, and made a commitment with TI. They had, I think, signed a letter of intent with 3Com, and we gave them a technical pitch and said: "We're going to get into the business. Here's why our solution is better than 3Com's, because we're going to put some memory in and blah, blah, blah..." and that was when TI was really getting into the PC business. So they called up 3Com and cancelled and signed a deal with us. We took it away from 3Com. We had an OEM deal with TI, and Ralph comes back from Europe and went crazy. It's the best thing that ever happened to the goddamned company.[24]

Committing to a solution for the PC was one thing, but they still needed to source the processors and, as Bass soon found out, they were not the only ones pressuring Intel for product, as he recalls:

> In the midst of this, I'm trying to figure out: "Can you even get an Intel 186 microprocessor? What's it going to cost?" This was at a time when they were on allocation. So I go to Bill Davidow [Intel VP of marketing], got down on my hands and knees, and said: "Please sell us 186's." Bill just played me like a flute. "Well, you don't know, how many do you really think you can sell?"

---

23. James (Jim) Jordan, oral history interview by James L. Pelkey, July 19, 1988, Hillsdale, CA. Computer History Museum, Mountain View, CA. Available from https://archive.computerhistory.org/resources/access/text/2018/04/102740315-05-01-acc.pdf.

24. Jordan interview, Computer History Museum.

> And this was coincident with 20 companies in the personal computer business all claiming 20 percent market share and forecasting to Intel how many they needed to maintain their 20 percent market share. "I need 1,000, and I'll pay anything, Bill, as long as I can meet TI's cost," which I couldn't.[25]

Their investment bankers did not see these internal dramas. They saw the leading company in networking, a market of unlimited potential driven by a steady growth in computing. On June 23, 1983, UB became a public company, raising $28.5 million of cash with a post-money valuation of $288 million—roughly half the value of Micom! A far cry from the start-up begging for investors 3 years earlier.

While investors were eager to pour money into the red-hot networking market, there was no sign of consensus around a dominant technology; on the contrary, major players were eager to assert their own market dominance. UB learned of yet another technology rising to prominence when Bass, on one of his frequent trips to Raleigh to manage the IBM token ring-to-broadband product, learned that General Motors (GM) had been pressuring IBM to implement a LAN protocol being developed by GM called MAP (Manufacturing Automation Protocol):

> Here I am going to Raleigh regularly, talking to Dan and he starts telling me these stories about [GM president] Roger Smith calling [IBM president] Akers and telling him: "You're going to do MAP, or we're tossing you out, because DEC's going to do MAP, and if you guys don't do MAP, you're not going to do business with General Motors." And I'm sitting there saying: "Holy shit! This is important. I should pay attention. This is going to happen." So I start telling Ralph we've got to do MAP, that IBM is going to do it, and General Motors is serious about this, Boeing is serious about this—this is really going to happen.[26]

Bass began to analyze the potential for a MAP business unit and proposed growing it slowly until it was able to generate enough revenues to grow on its own. The response from Ungermann and Jordan was skeptical at first, but neither could deny the potential.

UB finished their fiscal year with sales of $25.4 million and profits of $1.9 million. Yet neither Ungermann nor Jordan were satisfied, having vastly more ambitious visions in mind and wanting to grow much faster. Undoubtedly, the conversations they had been having with Bass influenced their thinking. As they began investigating this potential market, the only competitor seemed to be Concord Data Systems (CDS), and its only product was a 5Mbps token bus box, not a board,

25. Bass interview, Computer History Museum.

26. Bass interview, Computer History Museum.

and without a connection to a 10Mbps token bus network. Jordan remembers their conclusion: "Ralph and I thought the token bus, or MAP, market was going to be large. I think everybody did at the time. This was early 1984. We decided we wanted to get into it."[27]

But to get into yet another LAN technology meant more R&D expenditures, which were already consuming a large part of their profits. The solution they favored was finding a partner for a joint venture. UB would provide the technology while the partner would provide the funding and the credibility of a major corporation standing behind the new technology. With a list of potential companies including GE, the company they intended to approach first, they brought their proposal to the board. Jordan recalls the board's reaction: "We said: 'We're going to propose to [GE] that we start this company. We want $6 million, we'll give them 40% of the company, we'll take 60%. We'll put in the technology, we'll manage it, we'll come out with MAP products.' The board said: 'Good luck. I'm sure GE's going to give you $6 million for 40% of this make-believe company.'"[28]

Not discouraged in the least, Ungermann, Bass, and Jordan quickly called on GE. The conversations soon accelerated, and in a matter of weeks they were negotiating a contract essentially the same as they had presented to the board. On October 10, 1984, in a joint press announcement, UB and GE announced their joint venture: Industrial Networking Inc. (INI). UB contributed technology and management for 60% of the voting stock and GE contributed $2 million in cash and $4 million in notes for 40% of the voting stock. Losses in the joint venture were to be absorbed by GE.

More major sales opportunities in 1984 kept revenues on the rise. They signed a $15 million OEM contract with Codex. The terms of the contract gave Codex a warrant to purchase 654,000 shares of UB common stock at an average exercise price of $15.30. In the third quarter, UB began shipping Network Interface Units (NIUs) using the Intel 80186 and Motorola 68000 microprocessors. With the new 16/32 bit microprocessors, UB now had the second-generation networking products they needed to stay competitive with the upstarts, especially Bridge Communications.

The decision of Xerox not to release the higher layers of the XNS protocol had a delayed impact on UB. However, by mid-1984 a decision to convert from XNS to TCP/IP or the emerging OSI standard could no longer be delayed. Bass, as vice president of engineering, had the responsibility of making the final decision. Although very familiar with TCP/IP, he had been giving tutorials on the coming importance of OSI, and, maybe most importantly, had heard that GM was putting pressure on

27. Jordan interview, Computer History Museum.

28. Jordan interview, Computer History Museum.

IBM to support the MAP/OSI protocol stack. Bass opines: "Well, the confusing factor was OSI. I mean—and here's where I made a huge judgment mistake in gauging the potential importance of OSI—it was one of the biggest flaws in my crystal ball ever."[29] Ungermann, who was intimately involved in pitching the MAP project to GE, also recalls the importance of the decision: "We made a huge bet on OSI." The new 16-bit NIUs conformed to the bottom five layers of the OSI protocol.[30]

Meanwhile the efforts to develop a personal computer product ran into problems: problems both technical and political. The clash between Bass and Jordan over how to design a PC product dragged on. Jordan's sales staff would outline features their customers wanted and Bass's engineers would respond with the lengthy schedule needed to implement the requested features. Eventually the designs for two PC products were finalized and the Net/One Personal Connection family was introduced in late 1984, 1 year after signing their contract with TI.

In the midst of these technical struggles, IBM decided to cancel its contract with UB. Bass explains the decision as being the result of management turnover: "In 18 months, we went through three generations of management in Raleigh, and each time they would come in, they would re-evaluate, they would re-spec, and affect the project dramatically... The third generation shut it down... This was really my swan song with Ungermann-Bass."[31]

Before the end of the year, Ungermann elevated both Jordan and Bass to the positions of executive vice president. But, as Bass remembers, Jordan ended up with all the responsibilities: "We both became EVP... Ralph made me one too to make me feel good, but, in fact, I was without portfolio, and I just told Ralph, 'I'm done.'"[32] Bass soon resigned, although he remained vice chairman of the board.

UB booked another record for fiscal year 1984. Sales grew 106% to $52 million and profits rose to $6.8 million up from only $.5 million. Codex accounted for 12% of sales and INI 6%. UB seemed to be clicking in all gears As Ungermann would say in the Annual Report dated February 27, 1985: "1985 promises to be most rewarding for Ungermann-Bass."

But the fiscal year 1985 turned abruptly ugly. In March revenues came in at $12.0 million, a skimpy 11% increase over 1984; compared to the accustomed triple digit growth of the past and what management had projected for the year. UB lost

29. Bass interview, Computer History Museum.

30. Ralph Ungermann, oral history interview by James L. Pelkey, July 20, 1988, Mountain View, CA. Computer History Museum, Mountain View, CA. Available from https://archive.computerhistory.org/resources/access/text/2018/03/102738765-05-01-acc.pdf. See also "Ungermann-Bass Net/One," Datapro Research May 1985, C11-882-101.

31. Bass interview, Computer History Museum.

32. Bass interview, Computer History Museum.

$2.1 million of operating income—losses before tax consequences. In an investor research report published by Montgomery Securities dated May 13, 1985, Ronald E. Elijah identifies the reasons as production problems with broadband modems, a slowing down in the growth rate of minicomputer sales, and the lack of OEM sales. OEM sales had historically been as high as 20%. The reason: no sales of product to Codex for the last two fiscal quarters. Codex had disappeared as a UB customer.

There was good news as well. INI had won the first major MAP contract, the one let by GM, making for a great start for UB. A president was hired: Joe Schoendorf. Schoendorf and his new team quickly put together a sales budget of $20 million for the year and an expense plan aimed at dominating the emerging industrial LAN market of MAP and token bus. An additional expense was their commitment to developing a VLSI token bus chip.

The first quarter loss jolted Ungermann into making still more management changes. Jordan soon resigned, joining the board. Bass soon returned to do strategic marketing. Since his departure the prior fall, Bass had been consulting with IBM, working with Warmenhoven on IBM's telecommunication strategy.

By mid-year, the misstep from XNS to OSI had been corrected with an implementation of TCP/IP for both the PCs and terminal servers. But management changes and even more new products could not overcome the financial hole of the first quarter. Even though sales for 1985 rose to $72.2 million, up 38%, a shocking operating loss of $1.9 million could not be avoided. The $20 million of revenue budgeted by INI came in at $8 million with only $3.6 million of UB sales made to GE.[33] Most significant was their expense running rate, which had been calculated based on the $20 million projected revenue.

UB management clearly had problems reigning in their R&D expenses, which soared to 19.2% of revenues. The cost of maintaining the breadth of products and technologies necessitated by their vendor-independent strategy was becoming prohibitive. (In contrast, for the same year, 3Com's R&D expenses totaled only 8.2% of revenues.)

In March 1986, UB management, now concerned with their dwindling cash, sold $34.5 million of Convertible Subordinated Debentures in a public underwriting. But the financial burden of supporting so many technologies persisted into 1986, as Jordan remembers:

> One of the financial knocks against the company in the financial community was that Ungermann-Bass did too many different things, too many different technologies. You heard it a lot in the financial arena. They say: "You guys are biting off too much. You've got too many different technologies going on

33. UB 1985 Annual Report.

> here," and the standard answer to that was: "Look, they're all basic networking, very similar. They're just a little bit different architectures, and protocols are all the same, blah, blah, blah," which is bullshit. They really are different technologies and we *were* biting off too much. That was a valid criticism, especially looking back on it.[34]

In December 1986, the cash problems of INI required a solution. Too little revenue and too many expenses forced UB and GE to invest another $10 million into INI. UB's share was $6.4 million: from then on UB would record 57% of future earnings and losses—losses UB could hardly bear.

The year 1986 proved to be an even more difficult year than 1985. While sales grew 54% to $110.9 million, an operating loss of nearly $2 million was reported. Net income totaled just $18,000. R&D costs remained high: 17.5% of revenue before accounting adjustments. A market research organization had INI sales in 1986 as only $16 million.[35]

9.3.3 Sytek

Michael Pliner, president of Sytek, had every reason to feel confident that his company's strategy of selling broadband networks into large university campuses was unique and destined for success. With engineering focused on demonstrating a metropolitan-wide network for his corporate investor, General Instruments (GI), Sytek's direction seemed set—that was, until he gave a talk at Brown University in the spring of 1983. Pliner remembers a crowd twice as large as they had expected:

> We were all crammed in this room and about twelve IBM representatives were there, including Jim Turner from Entry Systems Division. . . He looked at this technology and he said, "This is fantastic, we can put IBM PCs on campus-wide networks, Metropolitan-Networks." They bought into the same thing that GI [had]: carry video; multi-media; put it all in the same network.[36]

When IBM executives approached Pliner to express their interest in developing Sytek's LocalNet 40 product for application as a PC networking product, Pliner was sure that the technical solution would be too expensive to meet IBM's price point. So Pliner declined: "I said: 'Why don't you go talk to Ungermann-Bass, they can do

34. Jordan interview, Computer History Museum.

35. "Pinpointing MAP's future," *Computerworld*, Feb. 15, 1988, pp. 47 and 54.

36. Michael Pliner, oral history interview by James L. Pelkey, April 8, 1992. Computer History Museum, Mountain View, CA. Available from https://archive.computerhistory.org/resources/access/text/2018/04/102740326-05-01-acc.pdf

that with Ethernet.' And they did but they kept coming back and said, 'No, we want broadband. We gotta be able to go on campus networks.'"[37]

After IBM agreed to an increase in price, Sytek management decided that it was worth the risk, even though, in Pliner's words: "we knew that there was only a 60–40 shot we would ever make it."[38] So Pliner and Sytek agreed, and they quickly redirected most of Sytek's engineering resources to developing a broadband product for IBM. Most of the effort required to demonstrate the metropolitan network for management and GI had been completed. Pliner had already demonstrated interactive cable TV on a metropolitan network in Sacramento, but the price had been too high: "I mean you're talking about a thousand or fifteen hundred dollars for a box that was going to sit in front of your TV that would allow you to interact with a terminal. People weren't going to pay the money necessary for cable companies to make a profit. We were too early and it just wasn't going to happen."[39]

The investment from GI may have failed to materialize a viable metropolitan network, but the GI manufacturing plant in Mexico looked like the solution to achieve the aggressive cost target for the IBM product. However, a four-month development overrun before prototypes were ready complicated the handoff of a difficult-to-manufacture high-technology product to the GI facility.[40] With a product introduction scheduled for August, IBM expressed concern about whether they would have enough initial inventories to meet demand.

On May 8, 1984, IBM announced its IBM Cabling System and a "star-wired token ring local area network using the IBM Cabling System within the next two to three years." Sytek management did not react with concern since IBM management seemed so fully committed to the Sytek PC LAN.

On August 14, 1984, IBM announced its first LAN: the PC LAN, a re-engineered Sytek LocalNet. What was telling in the specifications was that it limited the number of stations to 72, when the compelling advantage for broadband came into play with a large number of stations. Pliner remembers the enormity of getting ready for the PC LAN introduction: "So when IBM came out with the PC LAN, it was three boards shrunk down to one and we were able to manufacture it, and before we even announced the product, we had manufactured 14,000 of them, and we filled up the IBM distribution channel. So it was a good relationship at that time."[41]

---

37. Pliner interview, Computer History Museum.

38. Pliner interview, Computer History Museum.

39. Pliner interview, Computer History Museum.

40. "Out from the shadow: Sytek emerges," *Dataquest Research Newsletter*, February 1986.

41. Pliner interview, Computer History Museum.

In September, IBM invested $6 million for 4.9% of Sytek, valuing Sytek at over $120 million. Even the difficulties of manufacturing product in Mexico did not seem to dampen their relationship. Pliner recalls the challenges: "We *tried* to manufacture in Mexico. We never successfully did that. We said: 'This is too high tech of a product. It cannot be manufactured in Mexico,' and moved it back and we set it up here, and we had an excellent, high quality manufacturing plant."[42]

Good news continued. In December 1984, Sytek signed an agreement with DEC under which the two companies would market each other's products. Then as Pliner had promised at the Alex. Brown conference, he started discussing going public with investment bankers. However, 1985 started with those hopes dashed: investment bankers informed the company they were unable to take Sytek public.[43] Reasons cited were production problems with the product they were shipping to IBM, low gross margins, and the uncertainty about IBM's token ring plans. Knowing they need more capital, Pliner approached Metcalfe and Krause at 3Com with the idea of merging. The talks lasted only a few meetings. In March 1985, IBM announced a new $50 million contingent commitment to buy Sytek's broadband product sold as the PC LAN. Sales, however, remained sluggish.

Then, on October 15, 1985, IBM finally announced its IBM Token Ring Network. Before the announcement, Pliner and his team had been meeting with IBM representatives to discuss the storm brewing around IBM selling both the PC LAN and the token ring LAN. Pliner remembers being told by the IBM representative: "Yeah, you know, we're going to have to go back to look at the numbers and I don't have them here, but maybe you can get that from talking to. . ."[44]

After returning from their meeting with IBM, Pliner and his team concluded: "We better come up with a new strategic plan." When IBM made their token ring announcement, consultants were baffled. Their reaction was: "You're crazy. This makes no sense at all. How can you take this expensive product and constrain it to a PC on a workgroup LAN?"

For Pliner and Sytek, the writing was on the wall: "So, nobody bought it, and IBM couldn't sell it very well, and that was the end. Then we scaled down and eventually stopped manufacturing altogether. Because of our terminal-to-host connectivity, and terminal-to-host was still a stable market, we were able to keep the company

42. Pliner interview, Computer History Museum.

43. "Industry watch," *Data Communications*, November 1985, 94.

44. Pliner interview, Computer History Museum.

relatively profitable, but not great."[45] Sytek finished 1985 fifth in sales among LAN vendors.[46] The loss of IBM sales, however, portended a bleak future for Sytek.

9.4 Other LAN start-ups

9.4.1 Bridge Communications

In January 1983, Bridge Communications raised $3 million from venture capitalists with a post-money valuation of $11 million, up 200% from the valuation of February 1981. Now shipping their terminal server, they faced two primary sources of competition: data PBXs and UB. Judith Estrin remembers selling against data PBXs:

> In the first two years, we had like a five-to-one price differential, so there you sold to the people who were not bottom line conscious, but who were productivity conscious, making decisions based on productivity. We had features and sex appeal galore in the product: modularity of growth; the software features; the distribution; we had a whole list of things that you could do with this product that you couldn't do with a data PBX, even though the function, the black box function, was the same. It wasn't until 3 years into the company, as costs came down, that we were really able to go in and not only compete on a productivity, but on a price.[47]

Competing against UB was different, as Bill Carrico recalls: "It's funny because one of the ways that Bridge got beat up in the early years was Ungermann-Bass had broadband. . . Our product, overall, was superior, but we didn't have broadband, so they emphasized broadband, which is pretty typical."[48] With the cash raised from the financing, management began engineering a broadband product. They also had to solve the problem created by Xerox withholding the higher layers of XNS. Acting quickly, they did a TCP/IP and Multibus technology transfer and license agreement with 3Com. Though their XNS implementation had superior performance to TCP/IP, demand for the widespread standard increased into 1984. For 1983, revenue was $3.2 million, with a loss of $1.5 million.

In June 1984, Bridge announced an OEM agreement with Contel Information Systems under which Contel would OEM $10 million of product over 3 years. Then

45. Pliner interview, Computer History Museum.

46. Dataquest report on Sytek also had them in first place.

47. Bill Carrico and Judith Estrin, oral history interview with James L. Pelkey, June 23, 1988, Los Altos, CA. Computer History Museum, Mountain View, CA. Available from https://archive.computerhistory.org/resources/access/text/2018/03/102740285-05-01-acc.pdf.

48. Carrico and Estrin interview, Computer History Museum.

in late 1984, UB finally introduced their 16/32 bit products. Estrin remembers being underappreciated by their competition:

> Ungermann-Bass refused to acknowledge that we were going to be a serious competitor. For two and a half years after we started they didn't come out with a new software release. We had all these more advanced features. They thought: "We don't need to worry about Bridge." They kind of went about their own way, and by the time they stopped and said: "Uh, oh," it was too late. That's what happened with the data PBX guys too.[49]

For 1984, revenues soared to $13.4 million, up 319%. A small operating loss resulted but net income totaled $.5 million.

The management of Bridge had positioned themselves in direct competition with UB, defining their market as general purpose LANs, not PC LANs. To compete successfully meant staying technologically ahead of UB in terminal servers, adding broadband products, finding a way to offer PC products, offering both token ring and factory automation, that is, MAP, products, and distinguishing their approach with better internetwork functionality. They had already leaped ahead of UB with their first-to-market terminal servers employing 16/32-bit microprocessors. Broadband products were under development. As for PC Ethernet controllers, they turned to their relationship with 3Com with which they already had a joint development contract. Estrin recalls: "I knew Bob Metcalfe, and we were located very close. Then we had a reference sell arrangement with them, and then we OEM'ed their product."

Development of a broadband product was relatively straightforward, but manufacturing RF modems was not so easily mastered. Knowing they needed help, they acquired Coherent Systems in March 1985, the same month they announced their broadband controllers. Bill Carrico recalls eliminating UB's advantages: "All that kind of went away when we introduced broadband, and the main thing broadband's good for, the main place we've always sold broadband, is where people just wanted the long distance."

In 1985, sales soared 128% to $30.5 million with net income of $4.2 million. In April 1986, Bridge Communications went public, raising $22.3 million with a company valuation of $96 million. The year 1986 proved to be another successful year with sales increasing 51% to $46.2 million, albeit net income grew more slowly to $5.1 million. The costs of pursuing a general-purpose LAN strategy showed signs of catching up with Bridge just as it had with UB.

49. Carrico and Estrin interview, Computer History Museum.

9.4.2 Interlan

Paul Severino, President of Interlan, knew that to grow revenues would require more than selling Ethernet controllers for host-to-host connections. With attention to producing a low-cost terminal-to-host product, Interlan introduced a very competitive asynchronous terminal server in August 1983. Once Interlan began selling their terminal server, three issues arose that involved considerable effort and expense: offering other LAN protocols, creating a personal computer product, and building a direct sales organization.

Severino remembers their strategy regarding LAN protocols: "We wanted TCP/IP. We just kept putting it off. Then we tried to get XNS. What we did was, we went to Xerox and Xerox finally let us have the filing protocols. And my feeling was that if we can get the filing protocols, then we can start to provide this multivendor file transfer capability." Severino felt that Interlan should offer solutions for all layers of the OSI model: "So what we did was, instead of going back and implementing TCP, which is a transport layer thing, we went up to the filing protocols on XNS. And it was just difficult because we said: 'Gee, we got to add value here. Let's get the file transfer stuff put together between UNIX, VMS and MS-DOS; those three.' So you had a system."[50]

In 1983, Interlan had revenue of $6.7 million, up 180%, with a small profit of $154,000. In early 1984, management turned their attention to creating a personal computer Ethernet controller. Creating a PC product, however, proved as challenging as creating host controllers. Announced in mid-1984, the Net/Plus did not ship until November 1984.[51]

With a PC product to sell, it was time to begin building a direct sales organization and to phase down their use of manufacturers' representatives. But creating the direct sales force required cash, something Interlan had little of. Compared to the capital raised by some of the other LAN start-ups, Interlan had received a relatively modest amount, $5 million since its founding, and the cash required to fund the development of a direct sales force took a toll on their bottom line. In the fall of 1984, the board of directors considered the option of going public to raise the needed cash, but as Severino remembers:

> By the fall of '84, we had no cash and we actually had a little debt... and we just didn't feel that the market and the company was really ready to go out to the public markets. My feeling is that if I were to take the company public, I'd

50. Paul Severino, oral history interview by James L. Pelkey, March 16, 1988, Cambridge, MA. Computer History Museum, Mountain View, CA. Available from https://archive.computerhistory.org/resources/access/text/2017/11/102738590-05-01-acc.pdf.

51. Datapro, PC Communications, June 1985, p. 15.

> have to feel very, very strongly that I'm going to make all the numbers I'm talking about. I just don't want to get into a situation where you're selling stock and not getting there. It's not the kind of way I like to do business.[52]

The next obvious solution was to sell the company, so Interlan retained the investment bank, Alex. Brown & Sons, to find a buyer and subsequently met with a number of companies to discuss the possibility of an acquisition or merger. Ralph Ungermann remembers: "I had looked at Interlan very, very closely... They were an OEM company. We're an end-user company. I looked hard at it. We decided that we needed to focus, and so we chose not to get involved with an OEM company, but it would have filled out our product line some."[53]

When Micom came knocking at the door, negotiations proceeded rapidly. Micom had sufficient market capitalization to be able to afford the price Interlan was looking for. And Micom was in dire need of a LAN solution due to soft sales in the data PBX market. Both parties proceeded aggressively to complete the deal and in March of 1985 Micom acquired Interlan for $65 million.

9.4.3 Concord Data Systems

Ken Miller knew he had a serious competitor when UB acquired Amdax Corporation on January 1, 1983. Miller had worked closely with Amdax management to bring into being a token bus LAN standard. Miller remembers when the token bus technical specification was finalized for voting by the 802.4 committee in 1983: "We succeeded in getting token bus passed, so great, holy shit, a little company pushed that through. We pretty much wrote the standard. The other company that participated was Amdax, another token bus start-up."[54].

Token bus was now inevitable. CDS no longer had to wait for a standard to be voted on before starting product development, confident that the standard would not be changed before final approval.[55] Soon, the problem became missed engineering schedules and commitments. Creating a token bus controller proved more difficult than projected and, by mid-year, CDS still had no saleable product. Miller recalls key components of the problem: "The RF modem was a problem because we couldn't get people. Then to do even a terminal server... we had to do the upper layer, so we thought: 'Hey, it's going OSI.' You couldn't buy OSI layers, so we ended

52. Severino interview, Computer History Museum.

53. Ungermann interview, Computer History Museum.

54. Ken Miller, oral history interview by James L. Pelkey, February 23, 1988. Computer History Museum, Mountain View, CA. Available from https://archive.computerhistory.org/resources/access/text/2015/10/102737985-05-01-acc.pdf.

55. It was approved September 1983 by IEEE.

up doing our own transport layer, which was a whole shitload of code!... We were kind of naïve, but we were cocky." Miller's earlier opinion that local area networking was a data communication problem, not a computer problem, seemed open to question. In any case, CDS found token bus to be much more challenging than dial-up modems, the other set of products they were innovating and selling.

As 1983 progressed, it became obvious that they had to improve the performance and reduce the costs of their token bus implementation. The solution required VLSI semiconductor technology to reduce the functionality embodied in dozens of chips, covering significant printed circuit board space, into one or two chips. CDS began interviewing semiconductor foundries to both design and fabricate the chips. Management visited Intel, Advanced Micro Devices, Signetics, Western Digital, and AMI, a division of Gould. Not surprisingly, given Miller's long association with Gould, they selected AMI. CDS management believed that once their custom chips became available, hopefully in a year, their products would be superior to those of their competitors. They assigned Phinney the responsibility of managing the project out of Phoenix.

The more immediate need, however, was generating revenues and cash. CDS had adopted an OEM sales strategy using manufacturers' representatives. An important advantage of this strategy was that only a few large customers would have to be supported, not many small ones. A disadvantage, however, was that CDS had little, if any, contact with the ultimate buyers. Competing for the limited number of known OEM customers were: UB (with Amdax), Interactive Systems (a start-up now part of 3M), and even Sytek. When Phillips became their first OEM, confidence surged, and an intensified effort was made to convince GE to switch from Ethernet to token bus. Then in mid-1983, they received a call from GM. Miller recalls:

> They said they had this MAP [Manufacturing Automation Protocol] project. They had been talking to Interactive Systems. They had been talking to Allen Bradley about this. They said: "Hey, you guys are furthest along. We want token bus. We've already selected 802.4 to be the lower two layers of MAP. We want to tie this thing together in the factory. So we want this multi-vendor demonstration to happen at the NCC [National Computer Conference] show in the summer of 1984." Well, we couldn't pass that up. Here's the big corporate presence.[56]

CDC hadn't finished the terminal server product, but to satisfy GM it diverted resources away from the terminal server development. But they rationalized: GM

56. Miller interview, Computer History Museum.

was worth it. If they could just pull this off, they would be uncontested market leaders.

Fortunately, Miller did not have to wonder about their modem business, for it basically kept getting better and better. When they introduced their new V.22bis 2,400bps modem, it proved to be all Miller had promised: "In 1983, we came out with an auto-dial version, and it's really the auto-dial version that's like a Classic Coke product."[57]

As a consequence of their increasing market presence, Roger Evans of Micom visited Miller expressing interest in an OEM deal for dial-up modems from CDS. Miller remembers Evans wondering "Why are you trying to build a LAN business?"[58] Miller turned down Evans' query to buy modems, just as he had earlier declined Bass's overture to OEM RF modems.

In late 1983, CDS finally completed development of its token bus controller, the TIM, or Token Interface Module. It connected factory floor devices to token bus through the V.35 interface. CDS also implemented the lower layers of the MAP protocols in the TIM as specified in the first draft of the proposed MAP standards. Unfortunately, it did not support the RS-232 interface, and, therefore, could not be used as a terminal server. Not having a token bus terminal server proved a serious problem. Customers wanted to buy terminal servers, not the V.35 interface controller CDS was selling. The terminal server was still languishing in development due to limited engineering resources—most of them had been diverted to supporting GM for NCC.

With their token bus TIM generating minimal revenues, Miller had little choice but to raise more capital. Some argued CDS should go public, after all LAN companies were hot and CDS had a convincing story to tell: they were the token bus market leaders. Miller remembers: "I said: ' Geez, you know, LAN really isn't launched. I think we really ought to get our act together and have both sides of the business humming.' I mean, you go to do a public offering and that can be very diverting. So, I went on a road show. I went to Europe. To a whole bunch of cities."[59] Miller traveled most of June selling a $5 million private placement. Investors, however, were unwilling to commit until the NCC show proved successful.

At NCC, CDS provided the token bus controllers that show participants needed to connect to the shared token bus LAN. It seemed to matter little that the connections were via an external box, not an internal bus-based controller—token bus worked. CDS was a hit of the show. Miller easily remembers: "Oh, that show was

57. Miller interview, Computer History Museum.

58. Miller interview, Computer History Museum.

59. Miller interview, Computer History Museum.

euphoric. Unbelievable show. There was us, little us, you know, with only—I mean they were all billion dollar plus companies and there was a big press conference and all this shit. The first hoopla about MAP... We were on top of the world."[60]

In June 1984, CDS raised $7 million in financing, $2 million more than they were asking. They were valued at $34 million. Not bad considering only 2 years earlier the company's value was $8 million. But why shouldn't the value of their shares increase? They were working with GM, easily the largest potential token bus customer. DEC and Allen Bradley would soon be OEM customers. There were clouds forming on the horizon, however. Phone calls to GE were not being returned. Even requests for meetings with GE personnel were being deferred. GE had to be converted to a token bus vendor. By delaying, they were missing sales, and the opportunity to be a significant token bus player.

For the fiscal year ending September 1984, budgeted revenues of $12 million had been surpassed. Revenues totaled $15.5 million with marginal profitability. CDS entered its 1985 fiscal year an organization filled with confidence, focused on winning the GM contract in the spring. But problems soon arose when plans for a second-generation V.22bis modem had to be postponed. Miller remembers: "There weren't enough resources in modem engineering. It was sort of getting sucked up in LAN."[61] As important as the modem issues were, CDS management soon encountered a bigger problem. On October 10, a thunderclap echoed through the halls and offices of CDS, stunning management with the news that UB and GE had formed a joint venture, Industrial Networks Inc. (INI), to compete in the MAP-token bus market.

Notwithstanding the existence of INI, CDS management still felt they were in the driver's seat to win the GM business. After all, they were the ones who helped GM pull off NCC. These views were held in spite of the fact that ever since NCC GM had been telling CDS that they wanted the standard to be 10 megabits. Unfortunately, CDS had decided to base their first products on 5Mbps RF modems. To now innovate a 10Mbps RF modem and then re-engineer their existing products would be a difficult and costly, not to mention time consuming process.

CDS had little choice but to continue selling the advantages of 5Mbps products. Miller remembers his logic: "Look you're better off with six channels... than you are with three 10 megabit per second channels not using standard TV cabling." But GM was insistent. "It was a little tougher sell. They were beating us up that the next revision of MAP was going to specify 10 megabits. I probably didn't do

60. Miller interview, Computer History Museum.

61. Miller interview, Computer History Museum.

enough selling."[62] As the spring approached, Miller spent less and less time calling on GM; partly because he didn't enjoy the best of relationships with the GM buyer, and partly because he didn't have the solution GM wanted. Nonetheless, CDS management remained optimistic. No one was willing to think the unspeakable.

The spring of 1985 brought ruthless competition in the dial-up modem business spurred by new modem chips from Rockwell. The GM contract took on even more significance. And then the decision came. GM had selected INI over CDS. A stunned Miller recalls: "I didn't believe it. Couldn't believe it! Just couldn't believe it. It was terrible gloom."

Losing the GM business was a severe blow. INI aggressively pressed their advantage. Miller remembers the onslaught: "INI had so much money. They were throwing money around like crazy. They were—Schoendorf was in all these articles, you know: 'This is my LSI chip.' They were putting salesmen in the field like it was going out of style." Adding to their woes, CDS was also experiencing internal problems, as Miller confessed: "We were losing money. I had been beat up. We didn't have enough marketing. . . We hired a marketing guy and he turned out to be a disaster. There were some management problems at the same time."[63]

CDS did not become uncompetitive instantly—they would sign Honeywell as an OEM customer—but CDS was no longer the perceived technology leader. Miller remembers the ongoing challenges: "That's when it was unraveling a bit. And at the same time, the modem business was less profitable. It was more competitive. At the time, we also had all our financial statements combined together, so it was hard to determine what the hell was going on. So I was under real pressure."[64]

In the December 1985 issue of *Data Communications*, an article titled: "MAP: A user revolt for standards," prominently mentioned CDS. It stated that CDS's "Board-level prototype implementations of the MAP chip set will be available in March 1986, and general deliveries are slated to begin in the second or third quarter of 1986." The same article reported: "So far, INI has spent $25 million in organizing and developing its MAP board products, and it expects to spend another $25 million expanding its sales and service force and continuing development of MAP-compatible products."[65]

Despite continuing optimistic forecasts for the MAP-token bus market, Andy McLane, Board member and the company's original venture capitalist, was

62. Miller interview, Computer History Museum.

63. Miller interview, Computer History Museum.

64. Miller interview, Computer History Museum.

65. "MAP: A user revolt for standards," *Data Communications*, December 1985.

concerned. Could CDS compete successfully against a strongly motivated, well-funded competitor; especially given CDS's weak financials? He argued the company needed to find a corporate partner, a partner with money, a strategic partner like the one UB had found. Miller remembers the negotiations with Gould, the parent of AMI, the semiconductor foundry developing CDS's token bus chips: "We decided we wanted a corporate partner. That was the thing to do. So Gould had been after us. We had some very strong discussions with Gould. In fact, we got an offer on the table for a minority investment. But the problem is, it was taking you over without taking you over. Betwixt and between is no good."[66]

CDS had faced this choice years earlier with Analog Devices. Just as then, they declined. Discussions with their OEM customer, Allen Bradley, developed, but at the last minute they backed out due to the deteriorating modem business. The CDS Board of Directors scrambled. Straining for ways to put a positive spin on a deteriorating situation, they considered splitting in two: a LAN company and a modem company. After all, wasn't that what potential corporate partners had been saying? Miller remembers the problem with the modem business: "Both Gould and Allen Bradley said: 'We're not interested in this modem business!' You know, the financials were going to shit, so they got scared off. And so we talked with a bunch of others too. We knew that MAP was being talked about as this fantastic market, it's going crazy, so we had a lot of people courting us."[67]

The idea quickly became a decision. Given the growth and excitement of the LAN business, it was concluded money would be easier to raise for their token bus company. So, they formed Concord Communications Inc. with the mission to become the leader in token bus local area networking. Shortly thereafter, management finally acknowledged that the project to develop VLSI token bus chips with AMI had been a disastrous failure. Not only did it leave CDS without the chips it had been counting on for success, it had also cost the company $12 million with nothing to show for it.

Miller remembers the disastrous consequences: "So we waited—and actually it bled the modem side. It was awful. So we couldn't hire people and, oh it was awful. And there was also a big rivalry in the company. Big jealousy in the modem people: 'Oh, those fucking guys have been a bunch of prima donnas.'"[68]

With the board's recommendation to hire a new manager, they went out to raise money for the new LAN company. The LAN market, especially the MAP segment,

66. Miller interview, Computer History Museum.

67. Miller interview, Computer History Museum.

68. Miller interview, Computer History Museum.

had not lost its luster. Concord Communications raised $7 million with a company valuation of $22 million in June 1986.[69]

9.4.4 Proteon

In 1983, Proteon was struggling to generate the cash it needed through operations. While raising money from venture capitalists seemed possible, Salwen was unwilling to cede management control to those he viewed as more interested in "flipping" his company—preferring a quick return rather than building a "real" company—that was until he met Jon Bayless, a partner of the venture capital firm Sevin Rosen Bayless Borovoy. Bayless had begun calling on the company in early 1983. Even then, Salwen politely shunned Bayless's overtures; but a project undertaken in August threatened the company's existence. Salwen remembers: "A fellow from National Advanced Systems, Larry Corey, insisted that we do a PC card and do it now. I had no money; I mean I was strangulating for lack of funds. You have to understand this, and yet we committed to him to do a PC card, which led to P-1300."[70] They started the project in August and by November, they delivered the product.

Then the serendipitous: Novell, the company with the leading LAN operating system, contacted Proteon. After testing their software on Proteon's PC adapter card, they had been very impressed with the performance and offered to give Proteon a part of their booth at the November 1983 Comdex tradeshow. Salwen recalls Ray Noorda, president of Novell, plugging Proteon to his customers at the tradeshow: "I can remember John Doerr, of the preeminent venture capital firm, Kleiner Perkins Caufield & Byers, standing there talking to me, and Ray Noorda, again and again, with his arm around somebody, saying: 'Now, I'd like to show you something really special.'"[71]

By December 1983, amid the stress of juggling insufficient cash between payroll and accounts payable, and never having enough to invest in market opportunities, Salwen accepted the inevitable. He agreed to terms and raised $2.4 million of Convertible Preferred Series A Stock. In doing so, he ceded management to the investors and agreed to increase the burn rate by hiring a management team. (Investors were led by two of the most coveted partnerships: Sevin Rosen Bayless

69. Concord Data Systems, the modem company, had an opportunity to merge with Microcom, another modem company, but rejected the offer as being too unfair.

70. Howard Salwen, oral history interview by James L. Pelkey, January 28, 1988, Westborough, MA. Computer History Museum, Mountain View, CA. Available from https://archive.computerhistory.org/resources/access/text/2020/01/102792007-05-01-acc.pdf.

71. Salwen interview, Computer History Museum.

Borovoy and Kleiner Perkins Caufield & Byers.) Salwen afterwards devoted himself to engineering, LAN standards activities, and Board responsibilities.

A search for a new president and vice president of finance began immediately and a temporary president was installed. While the investors had confidence in token ring, they needed an immediate strategy while they waited until IBM made its intentions known. Their best guess for when that would happen was 1985 at the earliest. Given that the token ring market was not going to take off before IBM's endorsement, then either the market would continue to lumber until 1986 or other technologies would be adopted by customers—a sobering outlook.

Management and the board agreed to pursue three product development strategies: continue to improve the ProNET-10 product line, which included the PC adapter; introduce a high-speed token ring backbone LAN, a product essential to their university and campus customers; and develop products that made interconnection with other LAN technologies more effective and efficient. During 1984, Proteon's product announcements reflected primarily incremental innovations to the ProNET-10.

In March 1985, Proteon announced its backbone LAN: the ProNET-80, "the first commercially available local area network to operate at speeds up to 80Mbps."[72] With this product, Proteon distanced itself from the other would-be token ring competitors.

On October 15, 1985, IBM announced its Token Ring Network.[73] As expected, the Token Ring Network conformed to the IEEE 802.5 LAN standards. What was slightly surprising was its maximum 4Mbps speed, given the 10Mbps speed of existing Ethernet LANs and of competitor token ring LANs. While other vendors took weeks to respond, Proteon announced its ProNET-4 the same day as IBM made its announcement. The ProNET-4 came with not only the IBM PC interface but also Q-bus, Multibus, VMEbus, and IBM-compatible microcomputer interfaces. No matter what one thought of the IBM announcement, all agreed a giant dark cloud had lifted and there should be no more question that the token ring LAN market would take off. And it would!

9.4.5 Excelan

Entering 1983, Excelan viewed its product advantage to be a single-board Ethernet controller design with a powerful microprocessor to off-load the LAN protocol

72. Proteon ProNET Local Area Networks, pgs C11-695-101:106, Networks and Architectures, DataPro, Sept. 1986.

73. IBM Token-Ring8 Network, pgs. C11-491-501:509, Networks and Architectures, DataPro Jan. 1986.

processing from the host computer.[74] Excelan would focus on high-performance, not low-cost, applications, especially the engineering workstation market. In early 1983, Excelan introduced their first products. Kanwal Rekhi remembers: "We saw the opportunity of being suppliers of networking to all these people who didn't have TCP/IP. So we focused on TCP/IP with an Ethernet board. We signed up just about everybody, everybody except Apollo and Sun. We had about 35, 40 OEMs."[75]

Success forced the need for more capital. In December, they raised $2 million from venture capitalists. Management then got overly ambitious. Rekhi recalls the different views he and co-founder Inder Singh had on their mission:

> He wanted to do the servers, he wanted to do the OSI. He was real sure that, if you don't do it now, this market is going to be taken, and I kept saying that we don't have the resources... Even in the networking, he wanted to do the Ethernet, token ring, token bus, OSI, XNS, TCP/IP, and it ended up you were doing lots of stuff and lots of under-funded, half-manned projects, and you know what happens when you are spending money and you have nothing to show for it.[76]

The financial results for 1984 reflected both their sales success and high R&D expenses. Revenues were $5.2 million with a loss of $2.4 million. R&D costs totaled $2.1 million, 40% of sales. Taking advantage of investors eager to invest in LAN companies, in November 1984 they sold a fourth round of preferred stock, raising $3.2 million, with a post-money valuation of $17 million.

Excelan's efforts to engineer too many products for too many emerging LAN markets caught up with them in 1985. In August 1985, the Board felt the need to make changes, firing CEO Inder Singh and appointing Rekhi interim president. Rekhi immediately retrenched, focusing on the engineering workstation market, not the office market, and only on Ethernet and TCP/IP. Rekhi turned to consultants for instant help, including Dan Lynch, a TCP/IP expert from his ARPANET experiences. Excelan narrowed their focus to high-speed computer-to-computer connections.

The financial results for 1985 reflected the new focus on their core business: sales increased 90% to $9.9 million with net income of $100,000. In a presentation prepared for investment bankers dated December 1985, management highlighted

74. "The front-end approach to local area networking," Prepared by the Marketing staff of Excelan Inc., Dec. 15, 1982.

75. Kanwal Rekhi, oral history interview by James L. Pelkey, August 17, 1994, Palo Alto, CA. Computer History Museum, Mountain View, CA. Available from https://archive.computerhistory.org/resources/access/text/2018/04/102738774-05-01-acc.pdf.

76. Rekhi interview, Computer History Museum.

their sales growth, the introduction of a personal computer controller, more DEC-compatible products, and the addition of three more sales offices. In the same presentation, they outlined future products for the second half of 1986, including MAP protocols, token ring, token bus, and a terminal server. The lure of building a bigger company was hard to resist.

In April 1986, the search for a president ended with the hiring of C. Richard Moore. Moore had been president of an engineering workstation company and previously had held a number of positions within HP. Sales in 1986 increased 120% to $22 million with net income of $2.4 million. Excelan had averted disaster.

9.4.6 Communications Machinery Corporation, 1985–1986

Larry Green, President and co-founder of Communications Machinery Corporation (CMC), along with Dave Oster and Dale Taylor, had a vision mirroring that of Excelan: design an Ethernet controller with sufficient intelligence to off-load LAN protocol processing from the host computer and focus on the engineering workstation market. By virtue of having built an emulator for the LANCE Ethernet controller chip designed by DEC and fabricated by Advanced Micro Devices and Mostek, CMC created a line of Ethernet controllers around the LANCE chip. In June 1984, they raised $4 million in venture capital.

Then a series of missed sales and engineering projections, caused in part by delayed shipments of LANCE chips, prompted investors to make management changes. In 1985, a new president was recruited to replace Green, who resigned. Sales grew slightly in 1985, to $1.8 million, putting more strains on cash and forcing a firm-saving financing of $600,000 in December 1985. Sales grew to $3.5 million in 1986, but a loss of $200,000 still resulted. A combination of Excelan signing up key OEMs and the LANCE chip being late to market left CMC struggling for survival.

9.4.7 SynOptics Communications Inc.

Ronald V. Schmidt and Andrew K. Ludwick founded Astra Communications, later renamed SynOptics, in June 1985 in Mountain View, CA. Schmidt was originally hired by Xerox PARC in 1980 as a research scientist to develop a high-bandwidth version of Ethernet over fiber optic cable. Schmidt solved the nagging issues of reliability and network management arising from Ethernet's bus topology by adapting Ethernet to a hub-based star topology. Initially running on fiber optic cable, Schmidt saw similarities between his design and the topology of IBM's new cabling system. Recognizing the opportunity, he further adapted his version of Ethernet to run on the shielded twisted pair wire of IBM's installations. The idea was to offer one product that could run both Ethernet and token ring. Xerox agreed to license the technology to Schmidt and Ludwick for equity in their new company. First shipped in late 1985, SynOptics' "LattisNet" was an immediate success. In early 1986, SynOptics began talking to venture capitalist to raise sorely needed capital. Despite the early success of LattisNet, they met with more doubters than venture capitalists willing to invest. Finally, in August 1986, they closed their offering, and raised the needed cash.

9.5 The Data Communication Competitors, 1983–1984

9.5.1 Codex

In early 1983, Murray Bolt joined Codex, assuming responsibility for three new product directions for Codex: a PBX, teleconferencing, and LANs. Bolt began staffing his organization and learning his way around Codex. The PBX opportunity seemed a sure bet and was being encouraged by Motorola. Pugh remembers the decision of Art Carr, the former Codex president, now Motorola VP responsible for Codex, about the question of pursuing the PBX market: "After we'd gone through all of these massive studies on it and even lined up potential deals with Nixdorf and a couple of other companies, Carr said: 'No way. We will not do that. I will not bring Codex into that business.' . . . Motorola said: 'Okay. Then we won't do it.' Which was one of our better decisions, obviously."[77]

The emphasis shifted to entering the LAN business. But to do so required hiring the right people. Bolt quickly set out to hire engineers with experience in LANs, but they were hard to come by and many of his new staff had to be pulled from other departments. The growing organizational costs soon became a concern. Carr remembers his meetings with Jim Storey, Codex's president:

> I used to have Storey give me rundowns, a quarterly thing, and I was looking at his budget one day and I said: "Geez, Jim, if you look at all of these lines and you look at the operating cost as a percent of revenue, then you look at the LAN business," and the LAN business was called an independent business unit, which was supposed to be a technique to have a lean, entrepreneurial type shop inside of a bureaucracy, his budget was bigger, and his organization chart was more elaborate, and Jim said: "Well, these are my Codex organizations, and this is my IBM organization." I said: "What

77. John Pugh, oral history interview by James L. Pelkey, February 25, 1988, Canton, MA. Computer History Museum, Mountain View, CA. Available from https://archive.computerhistory.org/resources/access/text/2016/03/102738098-05-01-acc.pdf.

are you doing about that?" He said: "Well, I got to give him time. I got to give him a chance."[78]

Under pressure to generate revenues, and having no internally developed products on the horizon, Bolt pursued an OEM deal to resell LAN products from the firm he knew best: UB. Charlie Bass remembers: "Murray really liked us. We had done a great job for him, and he wanted to deliver Codex into the 20th century. And he came up with this great strategy of being an OEM of pretty much everything we made."[79]

In mid-1984, Codex began selling LANs repackaged from UB. Selling LANs proved to be much more difficult than Codex management had imagined. In 1985, the lure of heading a high-profile start-up was too tempting and Murray Bolt left Codex for the fourth generation CBX firm, Ztel Corporation. James Storey, president of Codex, turned to John Pugh to replace Bolt. Pugh's first action was to get rid of the head of marketing because he had no background in networking. A replacement with a limited background in networking was hired, but eventually Pugh had to fire him for the same reasons. Pugh remembers: "We were foundering from a marketing standpoint. I think we had good engineers. But we couldn't define the programs well enough so that they would stick. And at the same time, I was suffering from funding."[80]

The challenge of reselling products from UB eventually proved impractical, especially considering the two companies were competing for the same customers. UB was selling the same products and were able to market them ahead of Codex. Codex then tried engineering their own products using software they had licensed from UB. But the lack of revenue did not justify the expense of development. When Jim Storey left and Motorola replaced him with John Locket, the focus on the LAN business began to wane. By 1987, Codex had attempted and failed to enter the LAN business.

9.5.2 Micom

By 1983, Micom's revenue growth no longer rested entirely on the sales of its statistical multiplexer products. Revenues from its data PBX products had grown to equal nearly one-third of sales and forced management to make significant changes to

78. Art Carr, oral history interview by James L. Pelkey, April 6, 1988, Newton, MA. Computer History Museum, Mountain View, CA, https://archive.computerhistory.org/resources/access/text/2015/10/102737982-05-01-acc.pdf.

79. Bass interview, Computer History Museum.

80. Pugh interview, Computer History Museum.

how they both innovated and sold products. When Steve Frankel took over marketing, he created mini-business units called Marketing and Development teams: "I put marketing and engineering people together, and those teams would focus on a particular marketplace, segment of the communications market. It was that strategic decision that allowed the company to create this very expensive data PBX business."[81]

But selling the more complicated and longer sales-cycle data PBX required Micom to evolve their very successful sales rep organization, as Frankel explains: "We had enough channel strength and enough resources to find another layer of sales and supporting people to start making some real headway in that market, and then we really started evolving the data PBX into a much more capable product."[82] In 1983, Micom's sales grew only 50% over 1982. Management rationalized the results to the continuing recessionary economy and, more importantly, to the slowdown in minicomputer sales. Fortunately, the data PBX had grown to nearly a $20 million product line.

By the spring of 1984, however, when the sales of data PBXs slowed unexpectedly, management had to face the fact that competition for data PBXs was heating up. Frankel recalls: "The PC, and as a result of the PC, in my view, the local area network, was really starting to come up, and right in parallel with that was a tremendous push being exerted by the voice/data PBX manufacturers. So you had this tremendous collision of evolving technology." From Micom management's perspective it was unclear which one would come to dominate. The necessity of having a voice switch on site gave the voice/data PBX manufacturers a logical advantage to serving customers' needs, but could their technology serve the evolving needs of business computer users? Frankel began to see the writing on the wall: "As we went around and talked to customers and potential customers, it became clear that their desire was, as a result of the advent of the PC, more file transfer, and a lot more desktop processing and that kind of thing."[83]

Roger Evans, executive vice-president, remembers the shift happening with customers:

> It was the data PBX customer who was increasingly putting PCs on the desk where terminals had been. He was increasingly saying: "If you're going to stick around, you're going to have to provide high speed communications in

81. Stephen (Steve) Frankel, oral history interview by James L. Pelkey, April 26, 1988, Rancho Palos Verdes, CA. Computer History Museum, Mountain View, CA. Available from https://archive.computerhistory.org/resources/access/text/2018/07/102738828-05-01-acc.pdf.

82. Frankel interview, Computer History Museum.

83. Frankel interview, Computer History Museum.

> your local network product. The data PBX is fine for our terminals, but not fine for PCs." And then, in parallel with that, we have DEC essentially making their very open statement that it was going to murder the data PBX because its whole strategy was going to be based on convincing its customers that if you didn't have a capability of taking 10 megabits to the desk, you were living in yesteryear. And all of a sudden to sell a data PBX you almost had to wear a grubby raincoat, because if a customer was going to buy a data PBX, *he* wore a grubby raincoat because he didn't want anybody to recognize him doing it.[84]

Evans and Frankel began discussing what to do. They came to different conclusions. Evans thought they should develop a voice/data PBX product, whereas Frankel thought LANs were going to eclipse the data PBX market. Bill Norred, president, joined in on the long discussions, trying to decide what their strategy should be. Ultimately, they saw that the PBX business was slowing down and that, according to Norred: "we just felt we were not likely to be in a position to be a significant factor in that marketplace."[85]

The conclusion was to see if there was a LAN company they could acquire. While many of the opportunities in LAN sales were coming in the PC market, Micom wanted to maintain and grow its minicomputer business and grow LAN revenues from its existing core customers, following later with PC products. Potential acquisitions included Bridge Communications, which made sense since they used many of the same sales reps. But conversations with Bridge failed to stimulate any interest. Bill Carrico, president of Bridge Communications remembers:

> We talked to the Micom guys. They came to us and said: "Maybe we should buy you," and we said: "No thank you." They have a box mentality and a hardware mentality, and the LAN business, the general-purpose LAN business, was a system business, software system-sell. At Bridge, we outnumbered software engineers to hardware engineers like ten to one. It was a software business, and these guys—it was probably the inverse.[86]

84. Roger Evans, oral history interview by James L. Pelkey, January 15, 1988, Simi Valley, CA. Computer History Museum, Mountain View, CA. Available from https://archive.computerhistory.org/resources/access/text/2015/09/102737975-05-01-acc.pdf.

85. William (Bill) Norred, oral history interview by James L. Pelkey, April 27, 1988, Simi Valley, CA. Computer History Museum, Mountain View, CA. Available from https://archive.computerhistory.org/resources/access/text/2018/07/102738827-05-01-acc.pdf.

86. Carrico and Estrin interview, Computer History Museum.

The opportunities seemed limited until they received a call from Alex. Brown & Sons on a retainer to sell Interlan. Conversations progressed rapidly. In December 1984, Frankel left Micom for another entrepreneurial opportunity. Evans began negotiating the acquisition of Interlan.

9.5.3 Micom—Interlan

Micom management became convinced that Interlan represented the best opportunity to jump-start their entry into the LAN business. Bill Norred, president, describes his reasoning: "The convincing factor that caused me to decide that we should do Interlan was the fact that we felt that the window of opportunity may be very narrow—whether we could develop our own products in sufficient time to be a factor in the marketplace."[87]

On March 1, 1985, Micom acquired Interlan for 1.7 million shares of stock, valued at $65 million the day of the transaction, and merged Interlan into a newly formed subsidiary named MICOM-Interlan Inc. Micom management began integrating Interlan's operations into those of its own. Paul Severino, formerly President of Interlan, became Corporate Vice President, Product Planning and Technology, Micom, and Chairman of the Board of MICOM-Interlan Inc. He remembers: "We did the deal. I can tell you that every investor at Interlan made a lot of money. Most of the founders did pretty well at that price, and the problems came literally the day after the merger when, you know, just everything changed." Evans let go Interlan's distributors and sales reps and hired a new manager to oversee operations of both companies. As Severino tells it, "he was the wrong guy" and many of the Interlan officers soon left.[88] Without a sales staff to sell Interlan's products, development slowed to a near halt and business was flat.

At the time of the acquisition, Evans was transitioning the company from using sales reps to selling direct, since many of their existing data PBX customers preferred dealing direct. Evans recalls the problem: "because we still had the rep arrangement in place, we were still paying the commissions, so... we made the commitment that, as part of the Interlan acquisition, we would transition to a direct sales organization, and we would restructure our relationship with our reps and essentially phase them out."[89]

Micom's Annual Report for Fiscal Year March 1985 reported the mix of Interlan's LAN sales and their own local area networking, mostly data PBX, sales (see Table 9.2).

87. Norred interview, Computer History Museum.

88. Severino interview, Computer History Museum.

89. Evans interview, Computer History Museum.

Table 9.2 **Micom networking sales, 1983–1985 ($ millions)**

Fiscal Years Ending in March	1983	1984	1985
Micom LAN (data PBX)	20.7	40.1	54.3
Interlan LAN	2.4	6.7	18.0
Total Networking	23.1	46.8	82.3

Based on the Micom Annual Report, 1985.

The report also indicated that although Interlan had net income of $1.2 million for the 12 months ending March 1985, for the 3 months of January–March 1985 they lost $1.8 million. Interlan dearly needed the cash infusion from Micom.

In September 1985, Severino, frustrated in his new role of planning combined with his minimal influence in the affairs of MICOM-Interlan, resigned.[90] He remembers the impasse: "I knew that Micom had to make some leaps in order to really compete again, and I wanted to take off a group and just go build the next generation of product, and Roger and I just couldn't come to an agreement that that was the right thing to do."[91]

In February 1986, MICOM-Interlan finally announced the TCP/IP products that had been too expensive to develop before the acquisition. For the 12 months ending March 1986, data PBX sales dropped 25%.[92] Total LAN sales would equal $58.4 million, 30.8% of sales. Firm sales dropped 2% from 1985 and net income dropped 58%. The changes brought on by the personal computer were taking their toll. Norred recalls:

> One of the issues that we did not do an adequate job of dealing with is recognizing that the microcomputer was a revolution, not an evolution, and we didn't deal with it in a revolutionary kind of way. There are very few things in the history of data communications that don't evolve relatively slowly, but the impact that the PC had on the computing/data communications industry as a whole I think far exceeded anybody's expectations.[93]

On September 9, 1986, Norred turned over the reins of Micom to Evans who became President and Chief Executive Officer. Norred's role became limited to Chairman of the Board. MICOM-Interlan sales grew only slightly in 1986.

90. Severino began investigating starting a MAP company.
91. Severino interview, Computer History Museum.
92. MICOM-Interlan 1987 Annual Report.
93. Norred interview, Computer History Museum.

9.6 New Data PBX Competitors

Those with entrepreneurial ambitions had many reasons to start firms in the early 1980s: the sudden availability of venture capital and hot IPO markets; a brilliant idea that compelled them to act; or the pervasive buzz of opportunity around the personal computer, VLSI semiconductor technology, new programming languages, operating systems or applications software; or simply the fact that their neighbors or friends or work mates had acted and they did not want to be left with nothing but envy. The need to interconnect computers and peripherals motivated all kinds of solutions, and for many the cost advantage held by data PBXs over LANs seemed insurmountable. Two examples of data PBX start-ups were Metapath and Equinox.

9.6.1 Metapath

In 1979, Bruce Hunt, who had introduced LAN thinking to Zilog with his Ariel network, left Zilog and entered Stanford University to pursue his master's degree with Fouad Tobaji as his advisor. At the start of 1980, he needed to find work. Tobaji suggested Stanford Research Institute and Hunt soon had a job that enabled him to keep exploring extensions of CSMA/CD. Before long he conceived an idea around which to start a company. Having no savings, Hunt talked to his brother, who loaned him $20,000 to reduce his concepts to a VLSI chip. By August 1982, Hunt had built twenty prototypes using his custom chips, prototypes that made possible inexpensive interconnections among computing devices. Hunt called the product a desktop data switch. Then came the challenge of finding capital to finance his company. Hunt remembers:

> We started visiting venture firms and my brother had a friend who was working for one of Norm Dion's start-ups, and they were interested in data communications. So we gave a presentation to Bill Harry, who was Vice President of Development. He concludes by saying: "Well, I'd like you to meet Norm Dion." So that night I called Craig Johnson [Hunt's lawyer], and he said: "Bruce, you're in the big time. Don't blow it." He explained Norm Dion was the founder of Dysan, the leading floppy disk drive company. Literally, I think we slept 2 hours until that Monday.[94]

On Monday, Hunt and his team met with Dion and Harry. After Dion introduced himself, Hunt made his presentation, after which Dion said "that was very

94. Bruce Hunt, oral history interview by James L. Pelkey, July 21, 1988, Foster City, CA. Computer History Museum, Mountain View, CA. Available from https://archive.computerhistory.org/resources/access/text/2013/05/102746651-05-01-acc.pdf.

interesting and we'll talk to you later" but with no time set. Two weeks passed without any word from Harry. Hunt remembers being nearly ready to conclude Dion was not interested when:

> They finally asked us back, and we came in on Monday; but this time all my papers were open and on the desk. Norm started to really probe me, and boy, probably the toughest interview I ever went through in my life. I was in such a state of excitement that my brain was racing like absolutely crazy. Finally, he stopped the meeting, and says: "Well, thank you, I think I've had enough," and then he sat there, and literally, he put his head down and he started to think, and I'm sitting there and I'm saying to myself: "My God, should I say anything?" But you think I'm going to say anything now? No way! At 45 minutes he looks up and says: "I think I'm going to do the deal," and that was it. . . He says: "I want you to estimate what it will take to get you to this stage, and that's what we'll do." So we said: "$640,000" and that's the way he started the company."[95]

By December 1983, Hunt's data switch, named the Robin, had proven successful and Metapath was incorporated. In January 1984, $4 million of venture capital was raised with Dion's venture capital arm and Oak Investment Partners leading the round. (Oak had been an early investor in UB, Micom, and many other computer communication companies.) That same month, Metapath introduced Robin. Sales proved difficult, and a down financing of $570,000 to save the company was raised in January 1985 at one-fifth the price of the 1984 financing. For 1985, sales totaled only $700,000.[96]

9.6.2 Equinox

Bill Dambrackas knew firsthand of the ripe opportunities in the field of computer communications. From his experiences at Racal-Milgo and Infotron, he was aware of both the sales and engineering success of Micom and reckoned it was time to start his own company. So, in February 1983, Dambrackas founded Equinox. His idea was to create a low-cost data PBX to be sold through the same distribution channels Micom was abandoning as they converted to a direct sales organization. In December 1983, Equinox introduced their DSS-1, a data switching system capable of interconnecting 1,320 terminals and computer ports. Success came rapidly. In 1985, a financing led by Oak Investment Partners and DEC secured $3 million

95. Hunt interview, Computer History Museum.

96. In 1987, Metapath was acquired by Prentice, another firm struggling to cope with the market changes.

with a company valuation of $30 million. Equinox would be buffeted by market conditions and competition but would eventually become a public company in 1993.

9.7 LAN and Data Communications Market-Structures, 1985–1986

What was it like being an executive in a data communication or networking firm on the eve of 1985? Each executive had to make sense of market researchers' estimates and projections.[97] Assuming an average 3 years to plan and complete a product development cycle, near the end of 1984 a data communications executive might have felt optimistic about data PBXs but cautions about launching a new product development program in this category; further investments in statistical multiplexers and modems looked promising. LANs also looked like a solid bet but given the complexity of the technology would require considerable capital investment or acquisition. As the results of 1985 and 1986 were booked, however, these projections proved grossly optimistic. While there was some growth in the modem category, the explosive growth in local area networking was evidence of a massive shift in the future of data transmission away from circuits to packet switched networks. For the data communications executives it was soon clear that if they had not invested in LANs, it was likely too late. Table 9.3 gives a brief glimpse of what these executives saw when they looked into their crystal balls.

Table 9.3 **1984 product category sales: actual & projected ($ millions)**

Product Category	1983 Actual	1984 Actual	1984 Projections For 1988	1985 Actual	1986 Actual	1988 Actual
Modems	918	1,047	1,592	1,167	1,243	1,262
Statistical Multiplexers	245	289	919	303	319	194
Data PBXs	77	119	422	143	86	80
LANs	152	326	1,030	593	913	2,820

Based on "Modems" Dataquest Inc, TCIS, October 1989, 16; "Statistical Multiplexers" Dataquest Inc, TCIS, September 1989, A1; "Data PBX" Dataquest Inc, TCIS, November 1989, 6; "Data PBX" Dataquest Inc, TCIS, October 1987, 14; "Local Area Network Equipment" Dataquest Inc, TCIS, October 1989, 40.

97. Estimates came from companies including Dataquest and Datapro.

Given these projections, it is no wonder Codex and Micom executives were so interested in minding their existing markets. In addition, both Codex and Micom were participating in the equally attractive networking market with data PBXs. Making investment bets on either or both categories, however, would turn out to be a big mistake.

LAN executives, on the other hand, could expect their category sales to grow from $326 million to over $1 billion. Yet, by 1988 these forecasts proved overly cautious. LAN sales grew nearly nine times to $2.8 billion, while data PBXs, their once mighty competition, essentially collapsed as a category.

The LAN market, of over 200 hundred firms and many hundreds of announced products just a few years earlier, began consolidating to an oligopoly, with 11 firms controlling 68% of the market in 1985 (see Table 9.4). The difference of $16 million in the total size of the LAN market in 1985—between $593 million and $577 million—in the two tables were MAP sales. In 1985, INI ($8 million) and CDS ($3.5 million) controlled the MAP market.

The 1985 LAN market of $577 million was subdivided into four major segments (see Table 9.5): terminal servers, personal computers, computer-to-computer, and engineering workstations. Given that the personal computer segment hardly existed in 1981, it was by far the fastest growing. From the same Dataquest report, 66% of all networks were baseband: the only reason broadband accounted for 34%

Table 9.4 **Top 11 LAN vendors, 1985**

Company	Dollar Value ($ millions)	Market Share (%)
Digital Equipment Corporation	84.1	14.6
3COM	48.3	8.4
Ungermann-Bass	39.9	6.9
IBM	36.3	6.3
Sytek	34.5	6.0
Network Systems Corporation	34.4	6.0
Excelan	27.3	4.7
Bridge Communications	25.2	4.4
Apollo Computer	24.3	4.2
Wang	19.8	3.4
Interlan	18.0	3.1
Others	184.6	32.0
TOTAL	576.7	100.0

Based on Dataquest, Telecommunications Industry Services, December 1986, 101. (Eleventh firm, Interlan, added by the authors.)

Table 9.5 **LAN market share by market segment, 1985**

Market	Dollar Value ($ millions)	Market Share (%)
Terminal Servers	190.2	33.0
Personal Computer	181.7	31.5
Computer-to-computer	98.6	17.1
Engineering Workstations	67.3	11.6
Office Workstations	25.1	4.4
Other	13.8	2.4
TOTAL	576.7	100.0

Based on Dataquest, Telecommunications Industry Services, December 1986, 23.

of the market was the shipment of the PC LAN by IBM. Ethernet, a baseband network, equaled roughly 40% of all networks sold. It was estimated that less than 7% of all terminals and 5% of all personal computers were connected to networks.

The sales of data PBXs peaked in 1985 when sales reached $143 million. Market share data for 1986, after the unexpected drop to $85.6 million, speaks to the dominance of Micom and the rapid growth of Equinox (Table 9.6).

Given this overview, how prepared were the firms of focus in this history on the eve of 1985? Micom faced severe tests given the coming collapse of both the statistical multiplexer and data PBX markets. Codex tried to get into the LAN market but was extremely ineffective. UB had made a huge bet on MAP, which was consuming resources and earning no return. 3Com was riding the success of the IBM personal computer. Sytek, hoping to go public, depended on IBM selling the PC LAN over its token ring product, a questionable assumption. Interlan was seeking a merger partner. Bridge Communications had jumped technologically ahead of UB. CDS suffered from the slowness of MAP sales as well as the burden of riding a wave of unproven technology. Excelan and CMC chased the high bandwidth workstation

Table 9.6 **Top five data PBX vendors, 1986**

Company	Dollar Value ($ millions)	Market Share (%)
Micom	31.6	37.0
Gandalf	15.0	17.5
Equinox	10.0	11.7
Develcon	9.0	10.5
Infotron	6.0	7.0
Others	14.0	16.3
Total	85.6	100.0

Based on Dataquest, Telecommunications Industry Services, October 1987, 23.

segment, which comprised only 12% of the market in 1985. And the big firms, DEC and IBM, were beginning to make their presences known.

9.8 In Perspective

Driving the dynamic in the networking market-structure was the phenomenal growth in the demand for computer networks. By the end of 1986, there were an estimated 100,000 computer networks. Yet even as the growth in the creation of computer networks drove sales upward at 80% per annum, one sector flailed in comparison. MAP, or factory automation, sales totaled a disheartening $30 million in 1986, a far cry from the billion-dollar market projected in 1982–1983. Those firms that had made big bets on MAP, such as UB and CDS, suffered the effects. On the other hand, 3Com, which had focused on the robust personal computer market, prospered, notwithstanding a strategic diversion. Not that betting on personal computers was a certain recipe for success—witness the results of Sytek. The firms dominating data communications, Codex and Micom, struggled to understand the importance of LANs and the impact of the personal computer, and had to either OEM product from a LAN vendor or acquire such a firm.

The phenomenon of the growth in computer networks was not the only compelling dynamic in corporate communications during 1983–1986. Corporations were also beginning to privatize their data and voice networks. Responding to competition in the market for carrier services, in early 1984, AT&T and the RBOCs began pricing digital T1 circuits to corporations so attractively that significant cost savings could now be gained by building private telephone networks. As we shall see in the following chapter, existing data communication firms and a new breed of start-ups jumped on the opportunity to sell products that added value to these T1 services.

10 Adaptation of Wide Area Networks: Data Communications, 1979–1986

10.1 Overview

In 1982, AT&T, facing the relentless advance of digital technologies and the press of market competition, filed for, and received, tariffs to lease high-speed digital circuits. To become known simply as T1, it would allow corporate customers to replace 24 of the highest speed analog circuits then available with one 1.544 million bits per second (Mbps) T1 digital circuit. The cost savings were irresistible. In 1983, the sales of the multiplexers needed to interconnect slower speed data circuits to a T1 circuit totaled a surprising $30 million. In 1984, sales of these T1 multiplexers doubled to $60 million. What began as an opportunity to save costs quickly became a strategic rationale for corporations to begin building their own wide area communication networks, or WANs, in a phenomenon known as "Be Your Own Bell."

The first data communication firms to introduce T1 multiplexers did so not out of grand strategic visions but because customers wanted T1 circuits to consolidate their data lines and save costs. Only later did the data communication firms offer the add-on cards needed to support digitized voice channels, again being pulled into the larger market of voice communications rather than recognizing it as an opportunity. As more data communication firms entered the market, their products reflected incremental innovations, not the radically new architectures required by corporate executives to manage their increasingly complex voice and data WANs and LANs.

Others, however, read the future differently. In 1981–1982, Tymnet, a value-added network provider, initiated a project with Satellite Business Systems (SBS) to provide a cross-country high-speed digital service completely bypassing AT&T.

A number of the people involved with the project quickly recognized the need for a sophisticated T1 multiplexer that did not then exist. They proposed that Tymnet build and sell such a product, but management did not envision themselves as sellers of equipment and turned the business proposal down. Convinced of the value of their insight, four people soon resigned from Tymnet to become entrepreneurs. Within a year, former Tymnet employees would be responsible for the founding of three new T1 multiplexer companies.

The T1 multiplexer market emerged from the convergence of the three distinct markets of data communications, telecommunications, and networking. For the companies that could master the technical demands of all three, the future was bright. By 1988, sales of T1 multiplexers soared to nearly $400 million, far exceeding those of statistical multiplexers. Yet only two of the high profile T1 multiplexer start-ups avoided failure or acquisition. This chapter explores the emergence and rapid growth of the early T1 multiplexer market and the effect it had on existing data communications and networking companies.

10.2 The Revolution of Digital Transmission, 1982–1984

10.2.1 AT&T and the T1 Tariffs, 1982–1984

In 1982, AT&T received tariffs to lease digital data transport services through the High Capacity Terrestrial Digital Facility or Tariff No. 270. AT&T had finally decided to make available to its corporate customers a technology that it had been using internally since 1962 and had been making available to the Defense Department since 1957.[1] To many this decision came as a surprise. But for those in the know, it was inevitable, both because of the overwhelming economics of digital transmission as well as the pressures of market competition.

The basic digital transmission carrier or circuit, known as T1, transmits 1.544Mbps. Channel banks, also called channel service units, interleaved twenty-four 64 thousand bit per second (Kbps) sub-channels onto the T1 circuit. The 64Kbps sub-channel, or DS-0 channel, was the standard voice grade channel, equivalent to the 56Kbps data circuit with its additional 8Kbps of signaling overhead per channel[2] (see Figure 10.1). In time, improvements in voice compression would reduce the number of bits required to transmit voice to 8Kbps, thus making it possible to transmit 192 traditional analog voice circuits over one T1

1. "All about T1 multiplexers," DataPro Research, C35-010-751, July 1986. This publication began DataPro's coverage of T1 multiplexers.

2. "The anatomy and application of the T1 multiplexer," *Data Communications*, March 1984, 186. The first voice digitization was known as Pulse Code Modulation (PCM). The next generation was Adaptive Differential Pulse Code Modulation (ADPCM) that required only 32Kbps.

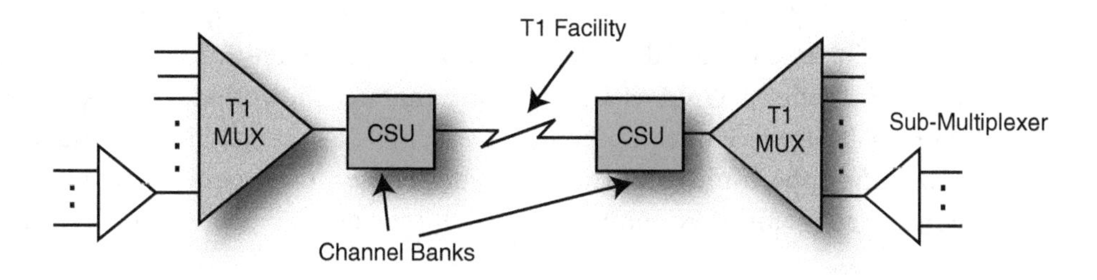

Figure 10.1 T1 circuit with channel banks. Illustration by James L. Pelkey and Loring G. Robbins. Source: Datapro Research, "All About T1 Multiplexers" July 1986, C35-010-755.

circuit.[3] The effect was to dramatically increase the bandwidth of the existing telephone network—after making the investment transforming the analog circuits into digital—and to dramatically reduce the costs of telecommunications.

In 1982, when AT&T received Tariff No. 270, digital transmission was a proven technology and available from a growing number of competitors. There were, of course, the Other Common Carriers, such as MCI and Sprint, who were aggressively marketing the advantages of T1 to corporate customers in hopes of taking market share from AT&T. Since they were still building out their networks, they could employ digital technologies immediately, giving them the attacker's advantage. Second, microwave technologies were making it easy to build communication networks without burying wire, cable, or optical fiber in the ground. There were over 40 new Digital Transport Service (DTS) microwave licenses submitted to the FCC by firms wanting to qualify as new common carriers. Third, cable companies, particularly the metropolitan cable operators, were claiming they could provide data and digital voice communication bypass services; bypass as in eliminating much of the intra-LATA telephone services from the local Bell Operating Companies. (Intra-LATA services are telephone calls made within one area code—within one central office (CO) switch—and are considered local calls. Inter-LATA calls are long distance calls.) Finally, corporate customers were learning that other new technologies were making it possible to extend communication networks to reduce costs and increase functionality, such as the claims of the vendors of broadband LANs that their communication networks could carry data, voice, and video, encompassing entire campus facilities and bypassing the telephone network. In January 1984, immediately post-divestiture, AT&T began actively marketing T1 services under the product name Accunet T1.5.[4]

3. Eight voice channels per each 24 DS-0 sub-channel.

4. "The anatomy and application of the T1 multiplexer," *Data Communications*, March 1984, 183–195.

To obtain the advantages of T1, corporations required equipment to multiplex their various slow-speed data circuits onto the T1 circuits—for AT&T customers that meant into the DS-O sub-channels of the channel banks that connected to the T1 circuits. That piece of equipment, a T1 multiplexer, created both wonderful new economic opportunities for the existing multiplexer companies and, in time, dire consequences for those companies that did not act or respond appropriately.

10.3 The T1 Multiplexer

T1 multiplexers interconnect by multiplexing and de-multiplexing many slow-speed data and digitized voice circuits through a T1 circuit. The first-generation T1 multiplexers were designed for data circuits only. Known as point-to-point T1 multiplexers, they differed radically from the existing paradigm of statistical multiplexers because they could accommodate vastly larger number of input circuits. The digital output circuits fed into channel banks, not modems. First-generation T1 multiplexers gave users very little managerial control. But second-generation "networking" T1 multiplexers first gave users manual, and later automatic, rerouting of circuits; adaptive bandwidth management; flexible configuration of network topologies; and reliable system architectures. The outcome of the T1 market competition was determined by the firms that quickly embraced networking capabilities in their T1 products.

The size and growth rate of the T1 multiplexer market was directly correlated with the number of T1 circuits. Each end of a T1 circuit, or termination, represents the potential need for a T1 multiplexer. The first installations of T1 circuits were local circuits connecting a corporation's circuits through the CO or bypassing the CO and directly interconnecting a corporation's locations or facilities. Up until around 1985, the demand for T1 circuits exceeded the ability of the Regional Bell Operating Companies (RBOCs) to install them, and that, in turn, drove the demand for private bypass networks. By 1988, the importance of private bypass networks declined as either AT&T/IXCs (Interexchange carriers) or the RBOCs were able to supply the needed T1 circuits.

10.4 The Beginnings of "Be Your Own Bell"

The revolution from analog to digital transmission led corporations to install their own private communication networks, or wide area networks, in a phenomenon then known as "Be your own Bell." From the perspective of 1988, Audrey MacLean, the Western Region vice-president of Tymnet, a leading supplier of value-added networks, remembers the reasons for the emergence of wide-area networks and the motivation to "Be your own Bell":

> Suddenly, in the wake of the break-up of the Bell Systems and the confusion that that caused, major corporations decided: communications is no longer simply an operating expense, it's so integral to the communication flow and the information flow in your company that it behooves you, strategically, to take control of that resource. So, for the first time, companies decided: "Hey, this network is critical to our business operation," and they hadn't thought about it like that before.[5]

MacLean saw that many large corporations were introducing the role of senior information officer, revealing the decision these firms were making to manage communications internally and take over operations that had traditionally been left to the phone company. "The bottom line was that, through a relatively small increase in capital expenditures, usually to the tune of maybe one to two percent of one year's communications budget, you could reduce your on-going facilities charges in the network by as much as six or more percent, which typically came right off your bottom line."[6] When combined with the strategic advantages of enterprise communication networks, these cost savings were very attractive to companies.

The explosive growth in the use of computers following the introduction of personal computers, especially the IBM PC in 1981, combined with the increasing use of local area networks, drove the need for higher data transmission speeds over the traditional voice telephone networks. At first the needs were met using modems and statistical multiplexers, but these networks proved too slow, and in retrospect were invariably designed to fit the needs of specific application(s). As high-speed digital transmission became available, the cost savings made possible by consolidating numerous data networks over one "utility" network were compelling. Corporations, by investing in capital equipment, such as purchasing T1 multiplexers and leasing digital T1 circuits, could in effect replace all the switching and transmission costs they had always looked to AT&T for, but without also absorbing all the overhead and settlement costs imbedded in AT&T pricing. It was possible for corporations to recover all their investment in capital equipment in less than a year through the savings obtained by eliminating the cost of analog leased-lines. When corporations also consolidated their voice circuits over these early digital networks, they were creating their own wide area networks (WANs). As the Chief Information Officers (CIOs), or their equivalents, began demanding more

5. Audrey MacLean, oral history interview by James L. Pelkey, April 29, 1988, Redwood City, CA. Computer History Museum, Mountain View, CA. Available from https://archive.computerhistory.org/resources/access/text/2020/03/102792033-05-01-acc.pdf.

6. MacLean interview, Computer History Museum.

sophisticated management tools and product capabilities, the traditional suppliers of data communication products frequently struggled to respond. Corporations suddenly wanted more than first-generation products, they wanted to buy integrated systems and one-stop shopping with single vendor accountability, service, and support. Corporate buyers were quickly driving industry consolidation.

10.5 Data Communications: First Signs of Digital Networks, 1982–1985

Beginning around 1982, the data communications industry was coalescing into an oligopoly dominated by those firms selling leased-line modems and statistical multiplexers. New market opportunities had to be balanced against the ever-present need to improve existing products to gain or protect market share. One opportunity already observed was the need corporations had to interconnect terminals and multiple computers. Those data communication firms electing to respond to the emergence of networking did so by introducing data PBXs. Data PBXs appeared competitive until PCs made obvious the need for higher communication speeds—and data PBXs all too quickly withered into obscurity. The PC equally impacted the modem business, with new entrants, such as Hayes, U.S. Robotics, Telebit, and Microcom, not the existing firms, recognizing the opportunities and established early market leadership. Digital T1 transmission and the T1 multiplexer start-ups, such as Network Equipment Technologies and Cohesive Networks, would prove even more threatening to the success and survival of the existing data communications firms.

10.5.1 General DataComm

From its founding in 1969, General DataComm Industries Inc. (GDC) had a history of responding to customer needs rather than anticipating them. Such was the case with T1 multiplexers, a product they first introduced in 1977, years ahead of any competitor. In this case, the need came from Texaco, one of GDC's existing customers, with headquarters in Houston, TX. Already using GDC's 1251 multiplexers on analog leased-lines, they saw an opportunity to save money with a new T1 tariff: In reading the Digital Data Service (DDS) ruling covering the AT&T circuits between Texaco's two data centers, management learned that there was a special DAL-3 tariff covering T1 that was only for the local metropolitan area. Robert Smith, GDC's vice-president, remembers their proposal: "They said to us: 'Look, we can buy lots of your 1251s to give us the low-speed channels, but we'll only do it if you give us something that will allows us to put it into a T1 pipe.'" Smith explains what they did in response:

> So we had a 12-channel multiplexer, and we kind of reengineered the back plane and the high-speed common card and cranked it up, and we came up with a 6-channel multiplexer that would run at 1.5 megabits per second. We plugged that in front of our 1251s and ran them at 256 into the channels and Texaco went with their T1 and that, as far as I know, was the first commercial T1 data application ever in the country.[7]

There were other customers interested in the cost savings achieved by multiplexing a T1 line, as Smith recalls: "We thought, well maybe we could sell a few more of these, so we built 20. Well, low and behold they sold, and we said: 'Gee, we ought to crank up our build plan to about 80 units." And we did, and they went out pretty quick too. So we said: "Hey, maybe there's a market here."'[8]

In 1981, GDC introduced their Megamux T1 multiplexer, a design evolved from their early "kludge-like" products. The Megamux was a simple point-to-point multiplexer that relied on hardware switching that made frequent and dynamic reconfigurations of the data lines difficult.[9] The Megamux also had minimal network management capabilities. In brief, it was a product that consolidated a number of expensive low-speed circuits into one T1 circuit and thus saved customers money. But it lacked the software features that would be needed by customers who wanted to build networks, a growing need of corporations. When first introduced, the Megamux supported only data, not digitized voice, a deficiency corrected a year later when they introduced a CVSD voice channel card.

The two years of 1981 and 1982, however, were traumatic for GDC. Accustomed to greater than 20% annual sales growth, management struggled to understand a sudden drop in sales growth to only 8% in 1981. The problems persisted into 1982 when sales growth remained a stagnant 6%. GDC would lose $1.2 million on revenue of over $60 million—the first of the major multiplexer companies to lose money. The principal reason: sales of equipment to telephone companies, especially to General Telephone & Telegraph, a key customer, plummeted. GDC management had little choice but to cut expenses. They slashed engineering costs by 10% rather than increasing them by the normal 10% or more. New projects were delayed or abandoned as monies were diverted to projects promising immediate sales. One product essentially abandoned was the Megamux. Smith remembers: "We were OEMing a statistical multiplexer from Micom for several years, and we decided

7. Thomas Thompson and Robert Smith, oral history interview by James L. Pelkey, March 11, 1988, Middlebury, CT. Computer History Museum, Mountain View, CA. Available from https://archive.computerhistory.org/resources/access/text/2017/11/102738591-05-01-acc.pdf.

8. Thompson and Smith interview, Computer History Museum.

9. Yankee Group, *Building Blocks*, July 1984, p. 132

we should do our own. When we got done with Megamux, we threw engineering resources to that, and didn't focus on the T1."[10]

In 1983, the market for T1 multiplexers continued to grow to an unexpected $ 30 million. GDC's Megamux, still one of the few T1 multiplexers available, contributed to a resurgence of sales. With sales growth of 43% in 1983, GDC returned to profitability.

At the time, only two firms posed viable competition: Avanti and Datatel. Essentially start-ups, they like GDC had innovated point-to-point T1 multiplexers in response to customer demand or because they had related technologies that were easily reconfigured into a T1 multiplexer. However, unlike GDC, they did not have established customer bases or distribution systems.

The success of GDC's Megamux continued into 1984, garnering a 35% market share in a market that doubled to $60 million. GDC also captured a 10% market share in statistical multiplexers. However, not investing in the Megamux left them with a vulnerable product, a vulnerability about to be exploited by their long-standing nemesis: Timeplex.

10.5.2 Timeplex

In December 1983, Timeplex entered the T1 multiplexer market with the announcement of its Link/1. Making three-node networks possible, not just point-to-point connections, the Link/1 represented a first step towards a networking T1 multiplexer. In addition, each Link/1 could support five T1 circuits compared to just one per each Megamux, a significant competitive advantage. Smith of GDC remembers: "Timeplex could build a triangle network: three-point network, interconnect with three muxes, and we had to take six because we had two per link to do it. So they got the real jump based on the networking marketplace."[11]

Like GDC, Timeplex sold a full line of data communication products, albeit OEMing its modems from Universal Data Systems (dial-up modems) and Paradyne (leased-line modems). Technology was never considered Timeplex's strength: Timeplex was known for its aggressive marketing and sales organization. The Link/1, for example, did not even offer networking reconfiguration capabilities equal to those of the GDC Megamux.[12] Nevertheless, in 1984, Timeplex seized a sizeable 16% market share for T1 multiplexers on the strength of its distribution network and strong ties with the RBOCs (see Table 10.1). Timeplex, like the other early data communication companies, conceived T1 multiplexers as products to

10. Thompson and Smith interview, Computer History Museum.

11. Thompson and Smith interview, Computer History Museum.

12. "Data Com Building Blocks," Yankee Group, July 1984, 129.

Table 10.1 **Statistical and T1 multiplexer sales, 1984 ($ millions)**

	Statistical Multiplexer Revenue	Percent Market Share	T1 Multiplexer Revenue	Percent Market Share	Total Multiplexer Revenue
Timeplex	40	16.7	11.3	16.6	51.3
Codex	50	20.9			50
GDC	25	10.5	24.0	35.4	49
Micom	47	19.7			47
Infotron	40	16.7			40
Combined Total	202	84.5	35.3	55.8	40
Market Total	239	100.0	63.3	100.0	302.3

Based on "Data Com Building Blocks," Yankee Group, July 1984, 107, 118.

save customers money by consolidating their data circuits and, only later, would they add voice support to their systems. Ed Botwinick, president of Timeplex, remembers: "Everybody said T1s are very expensive... I said: "I don't care how expensive they are, if you fill them up, they may represent a major saving in terms of getting rid of lower speed lines. Communications needs are going up and we're going to put voice on these things."[13]

In 1985, Timeplex displaced GDC as the leading T1 multiplexer vendor, capturing nearly one-third of the $158 million market with sales of $48 million. In doing so, the Link/1 comprised an astonishing 40% of Timeplex's sales.

10.5.3 Codex

As of 1983, Codex, the largest data communication firm and the leading supplier of data communication networks, had yet to enter the T1 market. Clearly, Codex had lost its entrepreneurial drive, in part because of the loss of three talented entrepreneurial engineers: Dr. Jerry Holsinger (1970), Dr. James Vander Mey (1977), and Ken Miller (1980) who all went on to found successful companies. Codex would increasingly depend on other firms for innovation through OEM or distribution agreements. The inability of Codex management to manage innovation development would be acknowledged years later by John Pugh, then vice president of

13. Ed Botwinick, oral history interview by James L. Pelkey, March 10, 1988, Woodcliff Lake, NJ. Computer History Museum, Mountain View, CA. Available from https://archive.computerhistory.org/resources/access/text/2018/02/102738718-05-01-acc.pdf.

marketing. Both he and James Storey, Codex's President, believed in the importance T1 multiplexers: "T1 was in the multiplexer product line. We knew they were falling behind, and Jim Storey was extremely frustrated because he could not get the programs moving."[14]

In 1983, management had no choice but to conclude that their internal development efforts were a failure and began negotiations to OEM a T1 multiplexer from Avanti. In 1984, Codex introduced its 6240 T1 multiplexer, a repackaged Avanti point-to-point multiplexer. Codex represented 40% of Avanti's sales that first year, but a few million dollars represented an insignificant market presence.

10.5.4 Micom

Micom, the highly profitable leader in statistical multiplexers, was unwilling to allocate the financial resources to develop a T1 multiplexer, just as they had not funded the internal development of a LAN. Bill Norred, President, remembers they had the basis of a T1 multiplexer in their TDM but still could not overcome constraints: "We had the basis of a T1 product for years and years. In fact, when I designed it, I always knew some day we'd probably take it to T1 rates, yet it never got evolved into a T1 product because we could never really figure out a way to find the resources to do it." As of yearend 1985, Micom had not yet entered the T1 multiplexer market.

10.5.5 Digital Communications Associates

In 1980, investors in Digital Communications Associates (DCA), frustrated with the leadership of the founder John Alderman, began the search for a new president to lead the company that laid claim to be the first to introduce a statistical multiplexer. On February 1, 1981, they hired Bertil Nordin, who would, with an infusion of $3.5 million of venture capital, quickly transform the sleepy little company in Norcross, GA, into a market presence.[15] Nordin remembers: "So, our feeling was at the time that if you're going to be one of the longer term players, you better put together a pretty broad spectrum of data communications products and become pretty large or you're not going to be one of the survivors."

In February 1983, buoyed by the prospects of their new statistical multiplexer, DCA went public and raised $24 million.[16] A few months later they acquired Technical Analysis Corporation that had a hot product named IRMA that enabled IBM PCs

14. John Pugh, oral history interview by James L. Pelkey, February 25, 1988, Canton, MA. Computer History Museum, Mountain View, CA. Available from https://archive.computerhistory.org/resources/access/text/2016/03/102738098-05-01-acc.pdf.

15. "Merger signs sprouting DCA quadruples revenues," *Data Communications*, April 1984, 90–92.

16. Alex. Brown & Sons was the lead manager.

to connect to IBM mainframe computers. DCA management then set their eyes on the modem manufacturer Rixon, a subsidiary of the French conglomerate, Schlumberger Ltd. They soon reached a deal that for $27 million would transform DCA into a leading data communications firm with realistic prospects of reaching $100 million of revenue in 1985.

However, CASE, the British data communication firm that had played such an important a role in the early years of Micom, had a distribution deal with Rixon. Rixon resold the CASE multiplexers and CASE was not about to lose its key reseller. After complicated negotiations, DCA backed out of the deal, saving $27 million, but not gaining the sales force and product line it so dearly desired.[17] DCA needed a sales force to sell the T1 multiplexer it had negotiated the rights to manufacture and sell from Scitec, an Australian company. In 1985, DCA had yet to establish a presence in the T1 market.

10.5.6 Other Data Communications Firms

By 1985, the T1 multiplexer market was no secret. Dataquest projected that sales would exceed $300 million in 1988, nearly a third of the sales that were projected for the once fast-growing statistical multiplexer market. All the leading statistical multiplexer companies would be forced to offer T1 multiplexers, although most, like Codex, would turn to OEM arrangements. Infotron and Paradyne began by reselling the Datatel product.

What many of the data communications firms missed, however, was that the T1 multiplexer was not just a way to save costs and, maybe, even tiptoe into the voice market, but into a market much larger than their smaller modem and multiplexer markets. T1 reflected the important transition from analog to digital communication networks, networks essential to the rapidly escalating needs of corporations to interconnect their computers and peripherals and, in the near future, to interconnect their islands of LANs. But not everyone was blind to the sea change underway.

10.5.7 Tymnet and the Caravan Project, 1982

In early 1982, Sarah Schlinger, director of business planning of Tymnet, decided she had learned enough. It was time to prepare a business plan and present it to her superiors. If her responsibility was to articulate how Tymnet might more aggressively pursue the coming opportunities in wideband communication services, she had potentially found a jewel. Her only hesitation: the opportunity was to build a product for resale, not a service to sell more time on Tymnet's packet-switching

17. "Follow-up: DCA fumbles the Rixon acquisition," *Data Communications*, May 1984, 96.

network or private networks to corporate customers. But the fact that the idea had emerged from an on-going project Tymnet had with SBS gave her confidence that the idea to build a T1 multiplexer would not be dismissed out of hand.

Tymnet was founded in the late 1970s to administrate and develop the packet-switching network Tymshare had spent a decade building to serve their time-sharing customers. Tymshare recognized that corporate customers needed to interconnect their growing base of geographically dispersed computers and peripherals—a need independent of the need for time-sharing services—and through Tymnet they could provide such networks either as a service or by creating private networks to then sell. The project that had led to the idea of building a T1 multiplexer came from an experiment Tymnet was conducting with SBS that would interconnect a customer's computers and peripherals in New York City and San Francisco using Manhattan Cable in New York City, SBS's long-haul satellite connection, and microwave radio services in the Bay Area. Audrey MacLean, Western regional manager of Tymnet, was responsible for getting customers for the experiment. Tymnet's first customer for the private packet-switched network was TRW, followed by Bank of America. MacLean was keenly interested in the larger opportunity that these early private networks represented:

> I looked at what the Bank of America's overall communications need was, and saw that the X.25 network that I had sold them really only covered a small cross-section of their application needs, and that if I looked at their whole global data network plan, and if I also concurrently looked at their voice network that they were rolling out at the time—I think they bought $15 million of PBXs at about the same time they bought the $6 million worth of packet switches—it began to occur to me that it would make logical sense for them to, in some fashion, at least in terms of the transmission, integrate these two networks.[18]

The experiment provided for T1 connection all the way to the end user's location, which, given the high bandwidth, presented an ideal opportunity to service both voice and data traffic on the same link. The challenge was how to interconnect and switch the multiple T1 satellite circuits and the multiple data and voice circuits (or DS-0 circuits) at customer's locations. MacLean remembers:

> There were multiplexers, such as the type made by General DataComm, that could take N inputs and one T1 output. There were channel banks that could take 24 or 48 voice inputs and one T1 output, but they were all the traditional multiplexer triangles, if you will, in terms of their architecture. They were not

18. MacLean interview, Computer History Museum.

switches. So in order to put together a switching core in these main hub locations in the network, you literally had to back-to-back cross wire multiplexers to begin to have switching.[19]

Roger Chrisman, who had joined Tymnet to head up the engineering for the SBS project and reported to Art Caisse, had the responsibility of creating the hardware to interconnect and switch the T1 or DS-1 circuits. MacLean remembers:

> Roger used to walk around disgruntled, bitching about the fact that this was one step up from carrier pigeon. So, it was as his thinking began to grow about the kind of switch that he needed to solve the problem that he came up with the thinking of building a switch that handled multiple DS-1s and was able to move traffic from one DS-1 onto another within the same switching mechanism.[20]

This was the product idea Schlinger had studied and reduced to a business proposal and submitted to her Tymnet superiors. They in turn took it to the management of Tymshare. Again, MacLean remembers:

> A proposal was taken forward to the board of Tymshare, and the board turned it down, primarily because they didn't envision themselves as a hardware company. They saw themselves more as a user of other people's hardware, and provider of X.25 software technology.[21]

MacLean, Chrisman, Caisse, and Schlinger were all disappointed and yet partly relieved. If Tymnet did not want to act, then their consciences were clean if they did.

10.6 Entrepreneurs: The T1 Start-ups, 1982–1985

10.6.1 Network Equipment Technologies

In July 1982, MacLean, Chrisman, and Caisse resigned from Tymnet to pursue the business opportunity their superiors had turned down. They knew no product existed to interconnect and switch the growing number of alternatives in wideband transmission services with customers' lower speed data and even voice lines. They also did not believe the opportunity would go unnoticed for long. So they began meeting to plot their product and firm strategy. But after a month of intense

19. MacLean interview, Computer History Museum.

20. MacLean interview, Computer History Museum.

21. MacLean interview, Computer History Museum.

conversations and debate, they found they could neither agree on a product specification nor who should play what management roles. In August, MacLean and Chrisman parted company with Caisse. MacLean recalls: "Art Caisse was contemplating building DTS microwave systems and Roger and I were dead set against that."[22]

In October, Chrisman's wife, Sarah Schlinger, joined them. MacLean, more certain than ever of her views, remembers:

> If you took those same networking concepts that we had employed in the X.25 packet switch arena, and brought them over to a physical layer only T1 network, and offered that same level of management control and reliability to the end user, that, combined with the economic and strategic motivations, would be a sure-fire way to successfully win over a large number of the potential private network customers in the country.[23]

They knew they needed others with complementary skills and knowledge, specifically a software expert with network management experience. One person they all could agree on was Robbie Forkish. Forkish had worked with them at Tymnet and was now with Bell Northern Research, or BNR. So they called him up and invited him to lunch without signaling their true purpose. Surprised, Forkish told them he was happy where he was and that he was working on BNR's next generation product in their office automation area. Furthermore, he was learning about voice applications, an area that had always been a problem when he was with Tymshare. Forkish remembers his thinking at the time: "I felt, perhaps not so correctly, as it turns out, that the PBX was going to play a role competitive to the LANs."[24] But Forkish also sensed the opportunity that was discussed, and, after a group Thanksgiving dinner, he made the big commitment, although he would not formally begin until February of 1983.

After polishing their business plan, MacLean began calling on venture capitalists to raise the money needed to launch their company. She was making some progress but not with the first-tier funds that she so desperately wanted. At the same time, the small team knew they needed to fill two noticeable holes in the founding team: a head of engineering and a president. Chrisman remembered someone who had impressed him while working on the Caravan project at Tymnet: Walt Gill, the chief engineer of the Telecommunications Equipment Division,

22. MacLean interview, Computer History Museum.

23. MacLean interview, Computer History Museum.

24. Robbie Forkish, oral history interview with James L. Pelkey, July 7, 1994, Redwood City, CA. Computer History Museum, Mountain View, CA. Available from https://archive.computerhistory.org/resources/access/text/2020/03/102792034-05-01-acc.pdf.

Avantek Inc. Chrisman contacted Gill who independently had recognized the need for some kind of switching product. Gill was intrigued with the ideas Chrisman shared but was unwilling to commit until he knew who was going to be president.

The venture capitalists asked MacLean the same question during her investment presentations. As difficult as that conversation can often be, a conversation frequently ending friendships or standing in the way of a firm's founding, MacLean knew they needed to fill the role of president: "We all sat around a coffee table and said: 'We're not ever going to go to second-tier venture firms.' We could have had the deal funded, quite frankly. I knew that I was going to be selling to Blue Chip companies, and I couldn't do it without first-tier venture funding and the right kind of management structure for the company." She also knew that person would have to be someone else: "None of us had ever seen ourselves as the president of the company."

Fortunately, the partners of one of the first-tier funds was sufficiently interested that when the curriculum vitae of an executive looking for a start-up arrived unexpectedly in the mail, with a cover letter describing the opportunities he saw in telecommunications, opportunities sounding very similar to those in the business plan of MacLean's team, James Anderson, general partner with Merrill, Pickard, Anderson & Eyre, quickly put MacLean in touch with Bruce Smith.

Smith was currently president of Communication Satellite Corporation's (ComSat) Technology Products Group and had been on the board of SBS. As such, he had shared many of the ideas of Maclean and her team. She recalls the synchronicity of Smith's letters to the VC community: "He decided that he was not a big corporate guy and really wanted to go grow something on his own."[25]

A first meeting, a lunch, was scheduled for April 1, 1983, even though MacLean would not be able to attend. Smith remembers the conversation with Chrisman, Forkish and Gill:

> They described to me a product that they had come to in different ways: Walt out of installing a lot of datacom product in the microwave business and believing that there was an opportunity for products that interconnected in complex ways, topologies that weren't point-to-point. At this point in time, nobody had a non-point-to-point product. So he came to it from an applications standpoint, where I came to it from a more broad environmental standpoint. Roger and Robbie had come to the idea that a box could be made which would largely be a data engine, and that perception was driven primarily out of the Tymnet perception that a network can be built around nodal engines. The rest of the world thought that, by the time you get smart, you

25. MacLean interview, Computer History Museum.

> had central office switches, or you had point products like PBXs that functioned independently—same thing with multiplexers that basically functioned independently of all the other ones that might be someplace else. So the Tymnet people had this concept of interconnectivity which is not at all different than the perception I had because of the time division multiple access way you manage satellite communications.[26]

Smith and MacLean met soon afterwards in Washington, DC, and had a similar meeting of the minds. Numerous phone calls followed until Smith and Gill mutually committed to joining the now credible enterprise in May. Three venture capital funds advanced $150,000 so space could be leased and minimal offices assembled. Smith remembers:

> We created a strategic statement of what it was the business was about, which was that the thousand largest companies worldwide, 600 in the US, were going, over time, as the world deregulated, to need a product which would allow them to interconnect this new, increasingly cheap, sets of bandwidth; that, at the beginning, bandwidth wouldn't be cheap so the ability to interconnect it and use it efficiently was important, and using it efficiently meant voice and voice compression; that as bandwidth prices fell, efficiency of use would be less of an issue, but the ability to handle very complex topologies would become the issue—all of this in the concept of what this thing was as a manager of a fixed plant.[27]

The concept of a manager of a fixed plant emerged out of the deregulation of telecommunications, changing technological alternatives, and the growing importance of information to corporate management. Again, Smith: "The conceptual framework for NET was what had happened, or what would happen, would be a move from call/minute type economic thought to a fixed plant utilization type of thought to where the economic advantage, if you will, was in managing that fixed plant more effectively."[28]

To know that they were not just talking to themselves, MacLean called on friends and former business associates and arranged for a trip back East in July to talk to decision makers of potential customers. Appreciatively and with awe, Smith remembers the round robin trip that included meetings MacLean had set up with

---

26. Bruce Smith, oral history interview by James L. Pelkey, October 20, 1988, Menlo Park, CA. Computer History Museum, Mountain View, CA. Available from https://archive.computerhistory.org/resources/access/text/2020/03/102792032-05-01-acc.pdf.

27. Smith interview, Computer History Museum.

28. Smith interview, Computer History Museum.

telecom and information executives from some of the major US companies. Smith summarizes some of what they learned:

> We heard every single one of them say: "I don't believe you can do it, but if you can do it I'll buy a truckload." We also began to comprehend the speed with which the applications environment was changing on these people. We got a real clear sense of fear—fear of the break-up, fear of costs rising, and fear of this enormous growth in demand without any ability to predict it.[29]

They had a vision, they had the facts, and they quickly finalized an operating plan. In August 1983, Oak Management Corporation; Merrill, Pickard, Anderson & Eyre; and J.H. Whitney & Company invested $4.4 million with a pre-money valuation of $2.1 million.[30] Technically, they incorporated as MetroLink, a name that MacLean insisted sounded like a sausage vendor. Smith, in typical let's-get-this-decided-and-move-on, told the pregnant MacLean that she could not sit or excuse herself until the name question was settled. So, a question that had nagged the group from the beginning took minutes to solve and Network Equipment Technologies (NET) was born. In September, Gill and Forkish started hiring engineers and the real work of clarifying and specifying the product began. Smith remembers: "In the early year or so it was all the engineering founders and then Walt, with me in the other direction having some conversations around and about, but there was a lot of architectural 'what problem are we trying to solve?' 'How will that problem change over time?' kinds of things at the front end. Out of that came a much stronger idea."[31]

MacLean recalls the diversity of the talent they soon had sitting around the table: "NET was the only place where, really, you had X.25, data networking, voice telephony, speech processing, and transmission backgrounds, all assembled from the early stage of the design effort."[32]

The NET fixed plant manager, metaphorically thought of as the new railroad switch, switched circuits not packets. The design strongly reflected Smith's knowledge of satellite TDMA architectures learned at Comsat and Gill's familiarity with large TELCO switches, a design that would permit NET to build much larger nodes and handle much more complex network topologies than the competition. Forkish remembers: "We never got stuck in the mode of debating the 'connection versus

29. Smith interview, Computer History Museum.

30. Stewart Greenfield of Oak Management would join the Board of Directors. He had also served on the boards of Micom and Ungermann-Bass.

31. Smith interview, Computer History Museum.

32. MacLean interview, Computer History Museum.

connectionless' issue because in a circuit switch it seemed pretty obvious that we would build connection-oriented sessions. We wanted to be innovative, but we wanted to use proven technology in being innovative."[33]

As the engineers teased every implication out of their concepts before building hardware or writing software, Smith fleshed out the plans for the organization, including the major, but seemingly obvious to him, decision to create direct sales and field service organizations. MacLean remembers with admiration:

> Bruce built the kind of financial structure for the company that enabled him to build the sort of direct sales and service capability that I think was as critical to the success of NET as was the technology base. In order for us to really take a walk between the giants' toes, the giants being IBM and AT&T, we would need to run faster, and furthermore we would need to have our own ability to deliver solutions to the end users who were all Blue Chip companies and expected us to have first-tier funding, deep pockets, and the kind of documentation, training, and service support that they knew needed to accompany a product that was going to sit strategically in the backbone of their network.[34]

As confident as they were all becoming, there always existed the nagging concern that one of the leading data communication firms might introduce a product to better than the one they were developing. In early 1984, they received an invitation to hear about the new T1 multiplexer being introduced by Timeplex. They almost did not want to attend the presentation, fearing that their hopes to be first to market had been seriously dashed. Forkish remembers: "Timeplex had just announced their Link/1 product. There were people who thought that we should simply pack up our bags: Timeplex was going to walk away with this market and we shouldn't even try."[35]

The NET team was concerned about Timeplex until they attended a Timeplex Link/1 briefing held in Santa Clara. As they answered questions, the Timeplex presenters revealed their lack of knowledge about key issues that the NET development was addressing. As Forkish remembers: "it was after that meeting, that Timeplex briefing, that we sort of became very encouraged again. We had a new resolve. We didn't think of them as a threat, so we charged right off."

33. Forkish interview, Computer History Museum.

34. MacLean interview, Computer History Museum.

35. Forkish interview, Computer History Museum.

The will to restrain themselves from announcing a product until the product had been fully thought through soon paid big dividends. Forkish proudly remembers:

> We actually coded the entire system in about 6 months. It was one of the most satisfying efforts I've been involved in. It was highly focused and well directed, but we had a charter and a goal, and we had developed precisely, or at least reasonably close, to where we thought we'd end up. In the first year, I was not at all a manager. I was very much a leader, if you can draw a distinction between those two. I was as much leading the "charge of the light brigade" as anything, and that simply set up circumstances that can never be duplicated except in the environment of a start-up and creating something out of nothing.[36]

MacLean may have been pregnant, but she was not going to let any overlooked detail derail the success they were all beginning to anticipate:

> I talked to a couple of presidents of large PBX companies at the time, and I saw that they were really perceptually frozen in this view of the PBX being the office controller, and I don't think they could see the fact that there was an opportunity for someone to focus on the transmission management problem and offer value to all the PBXs in a way that left the user an autonomy of selection of PBXs. So, I think that there's the perceptual frozenness that keeps the mainframe from inventing the mini, from inventing the micro, and the same thing happened here, where the PBX guys thought they were going to control the world and the data guys thought that they were better than the PBX guys, and nobody was really thinking about the integrated problem, I think, in a way that was able to come in and not displace the installed bases that everybody had, but add value to it. Most of them were too intent on protecting their own product strategies, and that sort of myopic focus can really get you locked in to where you miss seeing an opportunity.[37]

September 1984, the time had come to beta test their Integrated Digital Network Exchange (IDNX) on a customer's premises. NET had a choice of a number of beta test sites, but Smith thought it essential that they be located in New York City and have a history of being an experienced beta test site customer. So they selected Bankers Trust, a choice that was prescient. NET had two design choices that

36. Forkish interview, Computer History Museum.

37. MacLean interview, Computer History Museum.

remained undecided and had long-lasting competitive implications: voice compression and dynamic routing. Forkish remembers their successful implementation of the yet to-be-standardized ADPCM voice compression and the advantages of working with a company wise to beta testing a product. Forkish remembers:

> So the folks at Bankers Trust did what they called their Pepsi test. They sent a note through all their user organizations that said: "Starting in two weeks, on a Tuesday, we're going to convert from PCM to ADPCM. Please let us know what you think," and then they did it the next day. Sure enough, two weeks later they got complaints about "the quality is worse today than it was yesterday," and they said: "Oh, by the way, we did it two weeks ago. We'll see what happened last night." So they solved the problem of managing their own users in a very clever and creative way, and it's interesting that the end user and the vendor had to be creative working together to make the installation a success.[38]

To NET designers, dynamic routing meant much more than not forcing a customer to reconfigure hardware in the case of a circuit failure. They wanted the IDNX to reroute so quickly that the customer did not even know it had happened. To prove their claims, they organized a demonstration in which two New York brokers were talking on the phone and while talking, NET broke the T1 connection and the IDNX rerouted the call so fast the brokers we unaware that the T1 connection had failed. Similarly, if the T1 connection failed during a Host-to-Host session, the IDNX rerouted so quickly the computers did not have to go through any restart procedures. Forkish remembers: "I think it's that concept and what we ultimately dubbed 'Applications Availability' that became the key differentiator for NET."[39]

Meanwhile, Smith and his financial officer, Thomas Rota, had begun the arduous process of raising more money. Exactly how much depended on their corporate strategy. Some investors balked on hearing how much would have to be raised to build a direct sales and a field service organization, money that would undoubtedly result in dilution and a feared lower return on their investment. Smith recalls the loggerhead:

> The board of directors thought I was absolutely out of my mind, that the amount of money and dilution we'd have to tolerate was such that it was a whacko thing to do. My view was that "I'll settle for a smaller piece of a larger pie, thank you very much, but I don't know how to do this any other way," and we got down to the point where I basically said: "If you want to run the

38. Forkish interview, Computer History Museum.

39. Forkish interview, Computer History Museum.

> business, you can do that. This is the only way I know how to make it successful, and I'm prepared to step aside if you don't like that," and that solved that. It was a necessary step on this particular issue.[40]

In September 1984, NET raised a second round of venture capital totaling $7.5 million. The pre-money valuation was $15.0 million. NET had become a hot investment in no small measure due to Smith's fervor, which was broadly shared in the company. The basis of their confidence was, as Smith recalls: "We thought we understood the business better than anybody else on earth, and probably we did."[41]

With money in the bank, a satisfied beta customer, and a product ready for introduction, Smith staged another of his larger than life events, one meant to raise fear in their competitors and to inspire confidence in their potential customers. Smith staged their IDNX introduction in New York City, in Morgan Stanley's corporate auditorium with such well-known and respected figures as Howard Anderson of the Yankee Group and Dixon Doll and Dick Wiley.

NET began shipping IDNXs in January 1985. The IDNX qualifies as the first truly networking T1 multiplexer (The Timeplex Link/1 could create only minimally complex networks). A networking multiplexer differed from the point-to-point multiplexers in the complexity of networks that could be created and the embedded management control required (see Figure 10.2). Some of the key features that would distinguish the IDNX are:

- Demand assigned bandwidth allocation—calls could be set up on demand and bandwidth was used only for the duration of call.
- Dynamic alternate routing—no operator intervention was necessary
- Flexible network topologies
- Reliable system architecture
- Sophisticated voice compression—32Kbits ADPCM available

In their first full fiscal year ending March 1986, NET's sales totaled an astonishing $8.7 million. An impressive accomplishment given that Timeplex sold $11 million of its Link/1 in its first year and Timeplex had the advantage of an existing sales force and distribution network. Nevertheless, NET still lost $6.2 million, indicative of the considerable expense of building sales and support organizations.

40. Smith interview, Computer History Museum.

41. Smith interview, Computer History Museum.

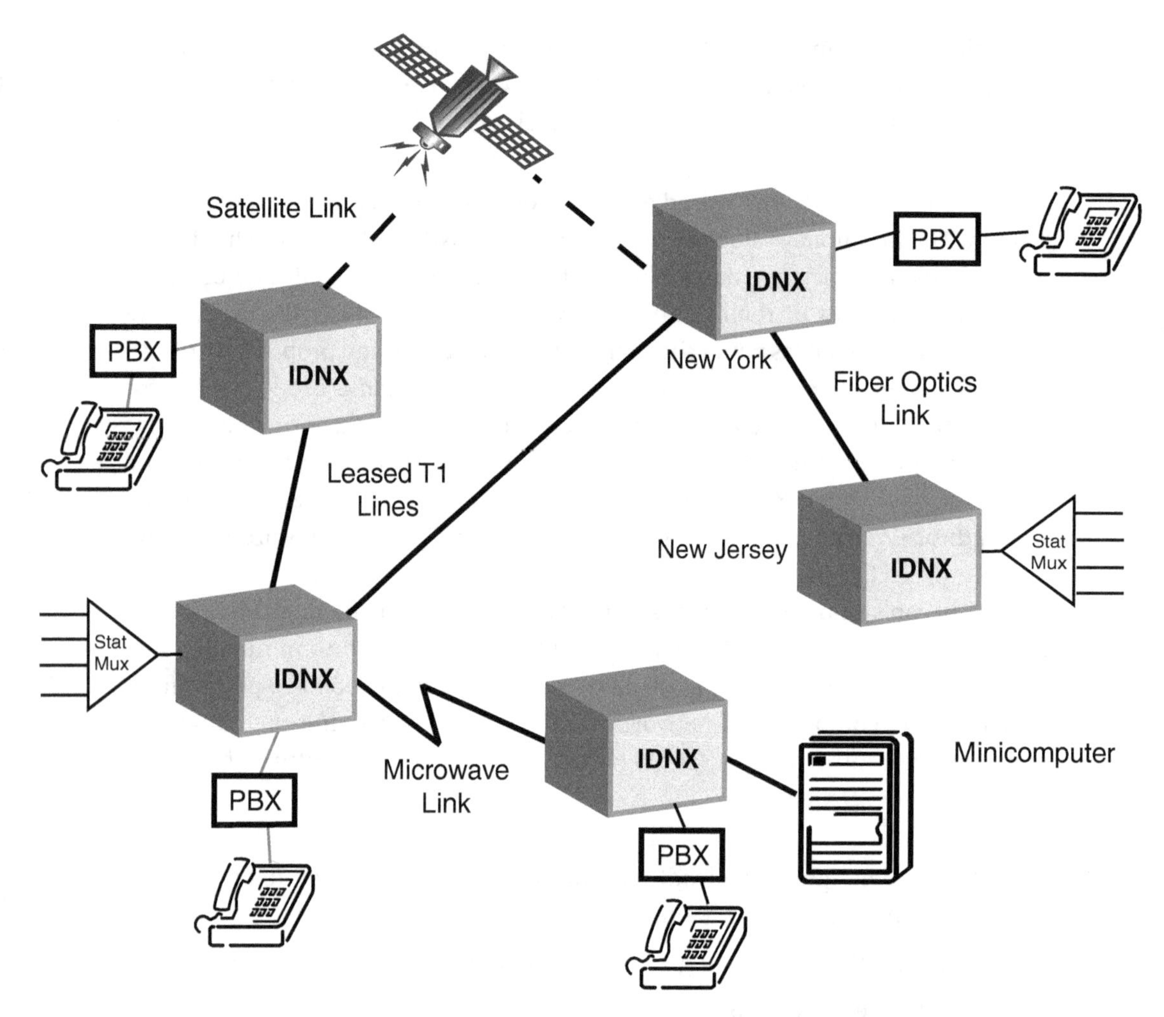

Figure 10.2 NET IDNX T1 multiplexer network. Illustration by James L. Pelkey and Loring G. Robbins. Source: Based On: NET marketing brochure and "Industry Research Report on Network Switching," The Yankee Group, December, 1985.

10.6.2 Cohesive Networks

After Art Caisse, Audrey MacLean, and Roger Chrisman parted company in July 1982, Caisse wasted little time before incorporating his new company, Cohesive Networks, in September. After further deliberation, and strongly influenced by those he recruited to join him as well as the feedback he had received from potential investors, Caisse changed the product/market opportunity of Cohesive Networks from a DTS microwave system to a high-end T1 multiplexer similar to that of NET.

After closing a $2.8 million first round of venture capital, Cohesive rented office space a short drive from NET. Reflecting on the competitive spirit that motivated each company, a spirit reminiscent of that between Ungermann-Bass and Bridge, Forkish of NET remembers: "We had, I think, respect, fear, and dislike all at the same time for Cohesive, because we knew we were going to compete with them... and I think both companies probably made it into more of an enemy type perception than they had to, but it was also part of our feel for motivation. We simply were not going to be beaten by those guys."[42]

By early 1985, Cohesive Networks had closed a $7.5 million second round of financing and began selling its CN-1; a T1 multiplexer positioned essentially head-on against NET's IDNX. But NET held a key advantage, it was already shipping product. The management of Cohesive, feeling the need to generate credibility and to ramp sales faster than they were projecting, began discussing the idea of OEMing their product to a number of leading data communication companies. Meetings were held with Codex, by then dissatisfied with its Avanti product, Amdahl, and GDC. By the spring of 1985, a lucrative deal was signed with GDC, one calling for GDC to buy $40 million of CN-1s. GDC began selling the CN-1 in September 1985 as the MegaSwitch. Sales of the MegaSwitch for calendar year 1985, however, were a disappointing $1.5 million with a loss of roughly $5 million.[43]

10.6.3 Network Switching Systems

In November 1983, Alan Zucchino resigned as manager of private networks for Tymnet and founded Network Switching Systems (NSS), the third T1 multiplexer spinout founded by former Tymnet employees. NSS also targeted the product opportunity for a high-end networking multiplexer and although NSS held the advantage of better market data, it also bore the huge disadvantage of being later to initiate product development. NSS management believed they held an ace up their sleeve, however, for their product would combine the benefits of both circuit and packet switching. Zucchino remembers the gap in Tymnet's product line: "I realized that we [Tymnet] needed circuit switched capability as well as the packet switch—to handle [IBM's Systems Network Architecture] SNA, for example. There wasn't a product to switch a complex network."[44]

42. Forkish interview, Computer History Museum.

43. Author estimates from the DCA 1987 Annual Report, p. 22.

44. "Napkins and needs: How the super T1-mux makers took off," *Data Communications*, March 1985, 89.

In February 1984, NSS closed a $2.8 million first round of venture capital and then in April 1985 closed a second round of $9.3 million, with a post-money valuation of $15 million.[45] In addition to venture capitalists, Infotron invested $3 million for 20% of NSS. Infotron also intended to become an OEM and to integrate NSS's advanced technology into its own Infostream 1500/2000 T1 multiplexer that it had announced in December 1984. NSS projected it would begin shipping beta units of their N16 high-capacity digital switch in the third quarter of 1985.[46]

10.6.4 Spectrum Digital

In March 1984, a team led by former MCI employees founded Spectrum Digital. Although not technically a spinout of Tymnet, there was an important connection. Audrey Maclean remembers the meeting that she, Bruce Smith, and Walt Gill had had with MCI during their July 1983 tour to collect market data and meet with potential customers: "We went to MCI, because we wanted to also understand their perspective, in terms of what their users were asking for. We had a series of conversations under non-disclosure with MCI, and then two or three people that had been included in those discussions left MCI, and they went out and formed Spectrum Digital."[47]

Reflecting the red-hot excitement being generated by the prospects for the T1 market within the investment community, Spectrum Digital went public in May 1985, even though Spectrum Digital was not expected to ship its NET1.5 T1 multiplexer until the second quarter of 1986. The NET1.5 was targeted at the low end of the high-end of the market and could be configured as an inexpensive point-to-point T1 multiplexer. In the fall of 1985, following the lead of Cohesive Networks and NSS, Spectrum Digital embarked on an OEM strategy signing Paradyne as its domestic partner and Marconi for overseas distribution. Eyeing the opportunities before them, Spectrum Digital management realized they needed $6 million to complete the NET1.5. To raise the funding, they had to go back to private investors and, in so doing, ran afoul of the Securities and Exchange Commission. After resolving the legal difficulties, Spectrum brought in new management, including a new president, Joseph Pisula, formerly a vice president of Timeplex, and closed a private round of $15 million in 1986. Unfortunately, their problems caused two other OEMs, Racal Milgo and Infinet (formerly Intertel) to end their agreements and, to keep from losing Paradyne they had to give Paradyne exclusive manufacturing rights.

45. "Network Switching," The Yankee Group, Dec. 1985, 91.

46. Network switching systems, *Venture Capital Journal*, July 1985, 38.

47. MacLean interview, Computer History Museum.

10.7 Market Analysis: Samples of Expert Opinions, 1984–1987

In 1984, experts eagerly wrote about a rapidly emerging T1 multiplexer market. By early 1987, they seemingly had pronounced the winners and declared the market foreclosed to new entrants. The following excerpts from a sampling of reports from two of the most respected market research firms—the Yankee Group and Datapro Research—and two leading investment banks covering communication technologies—Alex. Brown & Sons and Salomon Brothers—document this change in the T1 multiplexer market. The executives of all the firms in this history not only had access to this information, they were often readily providing interviews and data. Even so, the uncertainty of whether one was reading fact or fiction, hopeful dreams or futures already decided, made building a company's strategy on the views of experts very risky.

10.7.1 The Yankee Group

In July 1984, a report on modems and multiplexers titled "Building Blocks" read:

> The multiplexer was first introduced as a network product in order to better utilize and consolidate modem resources. As digital facilities have become more prevalent (private microwave, satellite, and TDS [Terrestrial Digital Services] services from AT&T) the multiplexer's role has shifted to become a gateway to the wideband digital world. The Yankee Group believes that the multiplexer market will grow to $305 million in 1984. The most significant growth will come in the T1 multiplexer market segment, which will grow 75% to $68 million in 1984.[48]

In December 1985, a report based on actual case histories titled "Private Network Strategies" identified some of the reasons corporations were beginning to build their own wide area communication networks:

The Yankee Group observed specific trends in the area of communications management:

- Many users are just beginning to use communications strategically;
- Planned growth of data communications needs far exceeds that for voice communications;
- The integration of voice and data, on both a facilities and managerial level, is a top priority among many users;
- Vendor dissatisfaction is growing.[49]

48. Yankee Group, *Building Blocks*, July 1984, 87.

49. Yankee Group, "Private Network Strategies," p. i.

As for the vendor dissatisfaction, the report further writes:

- Vendors should interact, not react;
- Vendors should provide a single point of contact for the user;
- Vendor contacts should be accessible.

That same month, from another report titled "Network Switching:"

> The Yankee Group believes network switches are the key to network communications and control and, hence, are the key to network equipment vendor dominance. In short, whoever controls the network switches, controls the network. . . the T1 multiplexer market will be the fastest growing segment of the network switch market. . . . . . Factors contributing to this growth are:
>
> - The divestiture of AT&T;
> - The emergence of information as a strategic and operational resource;
> - The growth of electronic data interchange;
> - The PC explosion, and
> - Improved microprocessor technology.[50]

10.7.2 Datapro Research

In July 1986, Datapro began coverage of T1 multiplexers with its report "All About T1 Multiplexers."

> We began to see a flurry of activity in the T1 multiplexer market in 1983, soon after the tariffing of High Capacity Terrestrial Digital Facility in 1982. The subsequent availability, in 1984, of T1 facilities for commercial use turned the "flurry of activity" into a boom. Now, in 1986, we can define a distinctly separate and rapidly expanding market segment for T1 multiplexers that are used in data communications.[51]

10.7.3 Alex. Brown & Sons

In December 1986, Alex. Brown & Sons issued a report titled: "T1 Multiplexing Reaches a New Dimension." They wrote enthusiastically about the market:

> We believe the major long-term beneficiaries of the T1 marketplace have emerged. It is unlikely that a company without sufficient market share among the Fortune 1000 by 1988 will be able to gain sufficient installations in

50. Yankee Group, "Network Switching."

51. Datapro Research, "All About T1 Multiplexers." July 1986, p. C35-010-751.

the future... This means that, in the long, T1 vendors must gain sufficient revenues and installations prior to growing these installations by selling a variety of additional communications gear... The opportunity presented by the need to sell more than just wide-area networking products (T1 multiplexers), but the need to become a "complete product offering" by selling additional local-area networking products.[52]

10.7.4 Salomon Brothers Inc.

In February 1987, Salomon Brothers issued a comprehensive report titled: "Telecommunications Equipment—The United States Market." The section on T1 Multiplexers reads in part:

> The T1 Multiplexer market is booming. We project annual revenue growth of 25% in 1987 and 1988... The T1 multiplexer market is highly competitive. For typical T1 network users, the need to minimize risk of network failure takes precedence; consequently, product selection is based on reliability first, functionality next, and then price. Market leader Timeplex is being challenged at the fastest-growing high end of the market by more innovative products that are richer in features such as four-to-one voice compression, voice/data integration, complex network management, and intelligent switching.[53]

10.7.5 T1 Multiplexer OEM Relationships, 1985

Table 10.2 identifies the leading data communications multiplexer firms and the OEM relationships they had made with the leading T1 multiplexer start-ups as of 1985. These relationships indicate how difficult it was for the start-ups to develop market distribution on their own and equally how difficult it was for the existing firms to master these new technologies internally. Fortunately for those firms that had acted quickly, they had opportunities that most of the nearly 40 firms offering T1 multiplexers in 1986 did not have.[54] This form of market consolidation, where the firms of an emerging niche are being absorbed by the firms of an existing market, differs from what happened in the LAN market, where the existing data communication firms acted too late or were disinterested, and most minicomputer firms tried and failed to enter the networking market.

52. Alex. Brown & Sons Inc, "T1 Multiplexing Reaches a New Dimension," December 1986, 6.

53. Salomon Brothers, "Telecommunications Equipment—The United States Market," 35–36.

54. "T1mux market heats up at high and low ends. Mergers ahead?" *Data Communications*, June 1986, 87.

Table 10.2 **T1 multiplexer OEM relationships, 1985**

Data Communication Firm	T1 Multiplexer Start-Up
Timeplex	None
None	Network Equipment Technologies
General DataComm	Cohesive Networks
Infotron	Network Switching Systems
Paradyne, Milgo, Infinet	Spectrum Digital
Codex	Avanti, StrataCom

Created by James L. Pelkey and Loring G. Robbins.

10.8 Data Communications: Wide Area Networks, 1985–1988

The combination of market forces channeling firm actions and firm actions giving rise to market dynamics is clearly read in the above excerpts from reports by market experts. For those data communications firms that did not respond to the needs of large corporate customers for both more sophisticated network switches and "one stop shopping," their futures seemed bleak, as if they would not be one of those to pass through the "narrowing neck of the funnel." But mostly, the years ahead would be the tale of those who could execute and those who could not.

10.8.1 Digital Communications Associates

In early 1986, flush with cash from the failure to acquire Rixon, Nordin had tasted the vision of becoming a force within data communications. He knew DCA had to participate in the networking sector of the T1 multiplexer market and sell more than a point-to-point multiplexer. Nordin remembers the problems of developing a networking switch: "We had a product called the Netlink, which was a point-to-point product, a very good product. But, frankly, we didn't have the engineering resources and perhaps to an extent the vision."[55]

So never one to put off to tomorrow what needs to be done today, Nordin made contact with the two leading T1 start-ups, NET and Cohesive. In his meetings with them, he urged them to weigh the advantages of joining forces with a public company, one with a significant market presence. Craig Huffaker, vice president of finance of DCA, remembers that NET had begun thinking about going public and investment bankers, including Alex. Brown & Sons, had convinced them they would be a hot deal: "Bert [Nordin] actually talked with both firms about acquisition and

55. Bertil (Bert) Nordin, oral history interview by James L. Pelkey, October 29, 1988, Norcross, CA. Computer History Museum, Mountain View, CA. Available from https://archive.computerhistory.org/resources/access/text/2020/03/102792036-05-01-acc.pdf.

we could have done either one. But Bert was averse to paying the kind of price tag NET thought they were worth, so we went to Cohesive."[56]

The management of NET was not interested in the rumored $100 million being offered by DCA, especially when access to the public markets was being dangled before them. Nordin's conversations with Cohesive, on the other hand, quickly found traction. The OEM deal with GDC had proven a failure and Cohesive management knew they were falling behind their archrival NET and, more pressingly, were running out of cash. Rumors abounded about a potential deal. Huffaker remembers the reaction from NET: "Now, NET got real upset that we were doing a deal with Cohesive. They thought it was going to be a major blow to them for us to acquire Cohesive because we already had a sales force, we were out there selling and we were already publicly trading which gave us more credibility and all. And so they were very concerned about that."[57] Before the deal was set to close, NET filed a lawsuit against Cohesive for $10 million, claiming, in Huffaker's words, "a bunch of garbage in hopes that we would walk away from the deal."[58] After examining the lawsuit and determining that it had little merit, DCA told its investors that they would assume the lawsuit and closed the deal. In September 1986, DCA bought Cohesive for 1.6 million shares of stock valued at $28 million. Instantly, DCA was seen as a market leader able to challenge Timeplex and NET.

10.8.2 Network Equipment Technologies

The head of steam that NET management had been promising for the last 2 years became obvious during the first half of 1986. In March, NET announced its second product the IDNX/40. It sold for $45,000–$70,000 depending on the configuration, roughly half the sales price of the IDNX/70. In early April, management told the board that revenues topped $8.7 million for its first full fiscal year. The good news would continue. Their sales ramp rate was so fast, NET became profitable in April 1986 with revenues of $6.7 million for the quarter ending June 1986 with profits of $400,000.

Bruce Smith, the President and CEO, remembers not only why NET was successful but why the competition was not:

> You take my product and you compare my box with the Cohesive box, I have some advantages. Take the networks that I can build and the certainty I can

56. Craig Huffaker, oral history interview by James L. Pelkey, April 9, 1992, Palo Alto, CA. Computer History Museum, Mountain View, CA. Available from https://archive.computerhistory.org/resources/access/text/2020/03/102792035-05-01-acc.pdf.

57. Huffaker interview, Computer History Museum.

58. Huffaker interview, Computer History Museum.

> provide for critical applications, and get a customer to think about his whole problem, I win hands down almost all the time. The company was designed that way, and the product was designed to fit into that sort of an architectural concept, and I think that credit needs to be shared among all of the early people, in terms of reaching up into that next level. You talked about the second generation; "what is this thing really, what's the layer beyond the layer I would think about?" Culturally, I think that's the thing that differentiated us from our competitors. I think it's the cultural limitation that meant that the General Datacomm's didn't make it. We defined the problem differently. That's the issue. It is the attacker's advantage.[59]

Attacking meant leaving no sales on the table. Management was learning that when customers created their new networks using IDNX's, they almost always had to buy more statistical multiplexers and other slower speed data communication equipment. But since NET did not manufacture such equipment, the customers had to buy product from other data communication firms that not only meant giving competitors business, but also leaving the door open for them to convince the customer to buy their T1 multiplexers, not NET's. This was a problem that had to be solved if NET was going to be seen as a full-service network provider.

In August 1986, wasting no time, NET acquired ComDesign Inc. of Santa Barbara, CA, for $6.2 million.[60] Bob Dolan had founded ComDesign in 1977 to build LAN products, that was, until he heard about Micom. Dolan remembers: "I saw this little company, Micom, that was making a killing of $5 million and then $15 million fiscal years selling statmuxes, I thought 'That's kind of great, but it doesn't do that much. It's kind of a trivial thing.'"[61] Based on the success of Micom's data concentrator, and Dolan's skill at designing efficient, low-cost products, ComDesign introduced a number of low-end statistical multiplexers.

By 1986, ComDesign had revenues of $12 million but had not attained a scale that gave management or investors confidence that they would ever become a public company. So when NET came courting, the conversations progressed quickly, particularly when they learned that NET intended to go public as soon as possible.

During this period, NET filed a lawsuit against Cohesive, as discussed above, to cease use of NET proprietary information that had been edited and used against

59. Smith interview, Computer History Museum.

60. NET 1987 Annual Report, p. 35.

61. Robert (Bob) Dolan, oral history interview by James L. Pelkey, January 6, 1988, Menlo Park, CA. Computer History Museum, Mountain View, CA. Available from https://archive.computerhistory.org/resources/access/text/2015/09/102737968-05-01-acc.pdf.

them in selling situations. After DCA investigated the lawsuit and had their lawyer discuss the matter with Smith, Nordin of DCA agreed to stop the practices and NET withdrew the lawsuit.

NET's sales growth continued to impress investment bankers and conversations about going public led bankers, lawyers, and NET management to gather around a conference table for several days to write a prospectus. In January 1987, NET became a public company, raising $26 million with a post-money valuation of nearly $200 million. Investor demand soon drove the stock price to $27.00 per share, valuing NET at more than $300 million. (Venture investors who originally bought shares at $.0166 realized a 96,285% return and those who bought shares at $.75 in June 1986 realized a 2,033% return.)[62] For fiscal year ending March 1987, NET's sales were $47.4 million, representing a growth rate of 450%. Profits totaled $5.1 million.

To the winners go the spoils and, on June 16, 1987, NET and IBM announced terms of an agreement between their two companies. IBM would begin selling the NET products under a non-exclusive worldwide marketing, installation, and service agreement. IBM would also contribute funding to future NET product development and incorporate NET technology into its networking products.[63]

As Richard Kimball, the research analyst covering NET for Montgomery Securities wrote in June of 1987: "We believe the stock will continue to command a significant premium based on robust market growth, the company's product and management abilities to fully exploit these strong markets, and the fact that earnings are expected to almost quadruple in fiscal 1988, expand over 60% in fiscal 1989 and more than 40% long term."[64]

10.8.3 Codex

By the summer of 1986, executives of Codex knew their T1 multiplexer strategy had serious problems. The rapidly growing T1 market was approaching $200 million, and they were stuck participating in the marginalized point-to-point segment with their OEM product from Avanti. Codex needed a networking multiplexer if they were going to be a credible factor in supplying large corporations—their target market—with the network switches they needed to build out their WANs. Any doubts they may have had were instantly swept away in September when they learned that DCA had acquired Cohesive Networks. Fortunately, an investment

62. Economic Newsletter, *Data Communications*, February 1987, 35.

63. Network Equipment Technologies Inc., Montgomery Securities, June 24, 1987, 10.

64. Network Equipment Technologies Inc., Montgomery Securities, June 24, 1987.

banker with Montgomery Securities presented another option, StrataCom, that looked like a good fit.[65]

StrataCom was founded in January 1986 as part of the legal reorganization of Packet Technologies. (AMOCO, the oil company and sole financial backer of Packet Technologies, resisted the company's efforts to raise more money. AMOCO eventually relented, giving a spinout the right to sell a T1 multiplexer, a technology it considered unimportant.) Packet Technologies, founded in 1983 by a team including Paul Baran, had initially planned to build products to enable two-way communications over cable networks. Then from conversations with Michigan Bell came the idea of building a more efficient product for intra-central office T1 communications. Not surprisingly, given the founders, the T1 multiplexer that StrataCom introduced was based on packet switching, a very different architecture than the circuit switching of all the existing T1 multiplexers sold at that time.

Codex had two things StrataCom was in short supply of: capital and distribution. So in the early spring of 1987, Codex invested $2.5 million in StrataCom and agreed to cap their ownership of StrataCom to no more than 20%. Codex, in turn, gained worldwide rights to market, install, and service StrataCom's Integrated Packet Exchange (IPX) T1 multiplexer. In 1987, StrataCom had revenues of $5.3 million. Sales of $3.2 million to Codex represented 60% of their sales. Reflecting the ever higher costs of market entry, StrataCom lost $6.0 million. Codex had secured the rights to a networking multiplexer, but sales of $3.2 million of an OEM product hardly made them a market force.

10.8.4 Micom

In 1986, Micom management was not oblivious of the T1 market. They read the same reports as everyone else. They simply thought that their customers did not require the bandwidth of T1 and, in any case, they had more than enough on their plate to consider pursuing a new major product direction. The acquisition of Interlan in 1985 and its integration was proving all-consuming. Then in the spring of 1987, Bill Norred decided it was time to step down and give management control to Roger Evans, who became President and CEO. In the Annual Report for 1987, dated May 28, 1987, Evans and his new management team wrote: "We plan to enter the T1 market and widen our product line during fiscal 1988 to address this market, the most rapidly growing segment of the data communications market today."[66]

Then, just as they had with LANs, Micom entered the T1 market by acquisition, taking on the struggling Spectrum Digital for $19.4 million. As Evans commented

65. The investment banker from Montgomery Securities was co-author James L. Pelkey.

66. Micom 1987 Annual Report.

in their 1987 Annual Report: "The Spectrum product is ideal for our requirements, because our customers have smaller networking applications, but they are technically astute buyers in a way that the typical IBM customer isn't so much. So what we spec'd, and then found Spectrum met, was an NET level of functionality in a smaller package, and I couldn't be more delighted with the technology we found as a fit for that."[67]

Their problems would be more than a product, however, as noted in *Data Communications* in August 1987: "Micom must overcome a lack of experience in T1 networking and a shortage of qualified sales personnel to be successful in the very competitive market."[68]

10.8.5 Timeplex

In 1986, the sales of T1 multiplexers continued to be a bonanza for Timeplex. After sales of $48 million in 1985, sales soared 66% to $80 million in 1986. Timeplex continued to command about one-third of the total market. In the spring of 1986, they also announced their next flagship T1 multiplexer—the Link/2. Two improved features in the Link/2 were support for digitized voice and CBXs. Surprisingly, the Link/2 did not increase the number of T1 circuits that could be switched—6 circuits—even as the new high-end switches of NET, the IDNX, could switch 32 circuits and Cohesive Networks, the CN-1, could switch 15 circuits. Market data in mid-1986 reported that the average-sized network was 26 nodes and many companies were expanding their networks to 50 to 100 nodes.[69] Had Timeplex misread the market or had they chosen to focus on their traditional mid-sized accounts? Edward Botwinick, Chairman and CEO, when interviewed in June 1986, admitted that the T1 market "is a lot bigger than I would have told you a year ago."[70] He further implied that Timeplex might announce a larger switch in 1987, yet it would take a couple of years for it to reach the market.

In early 1987, rumors of a potentially industry altering alignment began circulating in that Timeplex was nearing an agreement with IBM. Imagine then the shock when in June NET and IBM announced their joint marketing and development agreement. Botwinick and Timeplex reacted quickly. First came the introduction of its Unified Network Management System. Then came the Link/100 networking switch, able to switch 144 T1 circuits and 15,000 input/output ports. Timeplex

67. Micom 1987 Annual Report.

68. Economic Newsletter, *Data Communications*, August 1987, 33.

69. "T1mux market heats up at high and low ends. Mergers ahead?" *Data Communications*, June 1986, 90.

70. "T1mux market heats up at high and low ends. Mergers ahead?" *Data Communications*, June 1986, 90.

showed no signs of falling behind and knew they needed to create credibility quickly. Soon rumors began appearing, for example in *Data Communications* in July:

> Usually reliable rumormongers say that T1 industry leader Timeplex Inc., still rattling from IBM's tapping of arch-competitor Network Equipment Technologies as its vanguard into the T1 arena, is itself looking to team up with a leading computer power. And the target reportedly is Digital Equipment Corp. If such a technological and marketing marriage does make it to the altar, there could end up being three major players in T1 data networking and network management: IBM/NET/SNA/Netview, et al.; AT&T; and DEC and Timeplex/Timeview.[71]

The need to secure a partner made sense, but DEC proved yet another rumor without substance. On November 19, 1987, Unisys, the mainframe computer conglomerate, announced it was acquiring Timeplex in a stock swap valued at $307 million. Computer and communications, communications and computers, emerging and merging in order to both survive and grow.

10.8.6 Other Data Communication Firms

GDC, first to market a T1 multiplexer in 1977, dominated the market in 1983. Then they acted aggressively in signing an OEM contract with Cohesive in 1985. However, poor execution and then the loss of the Cohesive contract, due to its acquisition by DCA, suddenly dropped GDC into a weak fourth place. Infotron meandered as well with first its own limited product, then the hopeful investment in NSS, and then more feeble attempts on its own. NSS never could get product to market. In the spring of 1987, Bolt Beranek and Newman bought NSS for $18 million. Paradyne and Milgo released press announcements and sold product OEMed from others, or their own limited-functionality products, but never became market forces.

10.8.7 T1 Market-Structure

In the short span of 4 years, from the beginning of 1984 to the end of 1987, the sales of T1 multiplexers skyrocketed by a factor of ten: $30 million to $300 million (see Table 10.3). During these same years, sales of data communications firms' former engine of growth, statistical multiplexers, had peaked and were rapidly shrinking. In 1988, sales of statistical multiplexers would total less than $200 million, a far cry from the $900 million predicted in 1985. Initial growth in the T1 multiplexer market was driven by the cost savings of replacing multiple analog communication lines with multiplexed digital lines. The existing data communications companies were well positioned to capture this early demand. Companies like GDC responded to

71. Dataletter, *Data Communications*, July 1987, 16.

Table 10.3 **T1 multiplexer market, 1983–1989 ($ millions)**

	1983	1984	1985	1986	1987	1988	1989
Point-to-Point	30.0	45.9	85.0	96.3	100.0	100.8	85.0
Networking		15.0	72.9	144.5	208.8	283.2	324.4
Total	30.0	60.9	157.9	240.8	308.8	383.2	409.4

Source: Based On: 1984: "Data Com Building Blocks" Yankee Group July 1984; Dataquest, June 1986; Dataquest, August 1989; Dataquest, May 1991.

customer needs by innovating early T1 multiplexers with designs based on their point-to-point statistical multiplexers.

The widespread availability of digital communication circuits in the wake of the AT&T breakup created opportunity for cost savings, but it also created uncertainty for major corporations around data and voice communications. With corporations expanded their budgets for communications infrastructure, communications was no longer just an 'expense,' it was a complex resource that needed to be managed internally. The startups in the T1 industry that understood these complexities were best positioned to take advantage of the upheaval. NET's advantage was in the broad experience of its founding team in the fields of telecommunications, networking, satellite communications, and voice compression. It also realized these customers would pay for a robust, reliable network and the ability to evolve more complex networks. Incumbents in the data communications with early T1 products used their standing to stay competitive after innovating early products but were burdened by previous commitments of capital resources and engineering talent. As a result, they eventually lost ground to the startups that could master the complexities of networking multiplexers and were left to distribute "end user" multiplexer products through OEM partnerships with incumbents in existing markets (see Table 10.2).

10.9 In Perspective

The transition from analog to digital transmission, and the consequent demand for T1 multiplexers, represented a much more profound shift than many of the firms of data communications were able to master. Once corporations had invested in T1 multiplexers and tasted the cost savings and their many strategic advantages, they began demanding products with capabilities that they once looked to AT&T to provide. Products that provided adaptive routing, dynamic bandwidth management, and automatic backup, for example. These new capabilities far exceeded the concepts of network management that had evolved for the point-to-point data networks constructed using modems and statistical multiplexers.

Yet as much of an advance as the new networking T1 multiplexers were, with one sole exception (StrataCom), they were based on circuit switching. Accordingly, they encountered problems that were, by this point, all too familiar to experts who had embraced packet switching. Computer and LAN traffic was burst-like in nature and did not fit ideally within the confines of fixed circuits, no matter how fast they could be switched. As of mid-1987, these problems were beginning to be recognized, and the T1 multiplexer firms started reacting. But they would not be fast enough to command the new market, a story that fills the last chapter of this history: Internetworking. Again, entrepreneurs, without the baggage of existing customers, innovated the products that at first seemed to co-exist with T1 multiplexers—and then began absorbing T1 as simply the physical layer solution it had always been.

Market Consolidation: Data Communications and Networking, 1986–1988

11.1 Overview

For a company to transform from a start-up with a successful run of products into an industry leader dominating multiple product categories, it must successfully expand into new markets. All too often, the attempt at this transformation ends the company's independence or causes it to fail altogether. The mid to late 1980s was a challenging time for companies in data communications and networking. Executives were faced with critical decisions about how to execute the company's business plan: what markets to be in, what technologies to pursue, what products to develop, who to hire or let go, and how to ensure sufficient capital. In both data communications and networking, companies experienced intense competition, a sign of maturing markets. To be successful long term, they needed to increase profit margins beyond the slim margins of products in highly competitive categories. This could be achieved either by innovating new products in a company's current markets or expanding into new markets with higher growth. The challenges were significant, often requiring adaptations in all aspects of operations. This is where many companies become also-rans.

In maturing markets, many factors can constrain the performance of even the most successful companies. These factors include errors in strategy, ineffective management, operational inefficiencies, and poorly executed acquisitions and mergers. For the companies followed in *Circuits, Packets, and Protocols*, such failures often led to loss of market share, acquisition, or break-up. In this time period, the data communications companies struggled to respond to the new paradigm in computing—the evolution from data transmission via fixed circuit connections, a relic of analogue voice communications, to networks of computers communicating messages broken into small packets of data, then transmitted through multiple routes and reassembled at the final destination. Even for the companies that effectively innovated in the categories of modems and multiplexers, the expansion into the networking market was fraught with technical and marketing challenges few could navigate successfully. The networking start-ups themselves faced numerous challenges in their own markets, especially how to effectively develop and market the networking technologies they chose to support.

In the mid to late 1980s, the adoption of several de facto and de jure standards made evident the growing need to interconnect disparate networks, opening up a new market for computer communications: internetworking. As this new market was emerging, many of the networking companies responded to this need with products designed to connect networks at the physical layer and, later, at the level of networking protocols. However, possessing the engineering talent and the ability to produce products in this new category were not enough to ensure success in this new market.

11.2 Data Communications: Firms Adapting or Dying? 1987–1988

11.2.1 Codex

At the start of 1986, Codex was in the final stages of constructing its new headquarters, known as "The Farm." It was a grand, upscale New England red brick, 250,000 square foot headquarters on a 44-acre site in Canton, MA. Though Codex remained the largest data communications company, profits were taking a hit and Motorola executives had concluded that Codex president Jim Storey was not forthcoming in disclosing all the costs of developing "The Farm." In the spring, Motorola president John Mitchel suddenly let Storey go.

Shortly thereafter, John Lockitt was promoted from within to be president and chief executive officer of Codex, ending the run of founder presidents. Under other circumstances, Lockitt might have seemed a perfect choice for president: an engineer who had risen to vice-president of engineering, though his failure to develop a T1 multiplexer should have been cause for concern. The many other tasks he was responsible for included producing a Five-Year Plan outlining the future of the company and completing construction of The Farm. Reporting to him directly were 12 senior reports, more than the number of engineers he had formerly managed. Reflecting the bureaucratic disarray that had become Codex, only three of his new reports were accountable for product development and marketing, that is, sales and future products.

Art Carr, president before Storey, and now leading a venture capital start-up, expressed concerns: "It seems to me, from a distance, that Codex has got an excellent strategy, financially, but the engineering organization, which in the dawning of my experience there in 1968 was the biggest engine in the world, is now the weakest link in implementing the strategy."[1]

Carr's views were especially valid for the product categories not included in the company's original core focus, but Codex remained strong in the leased line modem business, owing much to the work of Dave Forney. Despite the fact that after the acquisition by Motorola Forney had been promoted to management, he continued to influence Codex's leased line modem innovation. Such was the case when he helped recruit Lee-Fang Wei from Bell Labs in 1983. Wei worked out some "very implementable multi-dimensional schemes"[2] that superseded V.32's two-dimensional trellis coded modulations. These new schemes resulted in the 2680, the first practical 19,200bps leased line modem, introduced in 1985.[3] Codex sold 100,000 of its 2600 modem series in 3 years, controlling some 44% of the American leased line modem market.[4] The revenues from leased line modems constituted more than half of Codex's domestic sales and just under half of its international sales in 1986–1987.[5]

In the summer of 1986, Forney returned to Codex as a Motorola vice president, responsible for managing modem product development. The market for modems was clearly changing due to the personal computer. Forney describes the state of the dial-up modem market in 1988:

> The world moved very much more rapidly in the dial business, and we are dug in at the 9600 end of the dial business, where it's a high-technology game, where the technology is very closely related to the high end of the leased line business. There I think we're doing much better, but still, we've

1. Art Carr, oral history interview by James L. Pelkey, April 6, 1988, Newton, MA. Computer History Museum, Mountain View, CA, https://archive.computerhistory.org/resources/access/text/2015/10/102737982-05-01-acc.pdf.

2. G. David Forney, Jr., oral history interview with James L. Pelkey, July 28, 1988, Boston, MA. Computer History Museum, Mountain View, CA. Available from https://archive.computerhistory.org/resources/access/text/2016/04/102738110-05-01-acc.pdf.

3. Lee-Fang Wei. 1985. Multidimensional, convolutionally coded communication systems. US Patent 4,713,817, filed April 25, 1985; Lee-Fang Wei. 1987. Trellis-coded modulation with multidimensional constellations. *IEEE Trans. on Inform.* Theory, Vol. IT-33, 4, July 1987, 483–501; "Codex Modem Adds Error-Correcting Data," *Micro Marketworld* 8, 22 (November 1985), 92.

4. Forney interview, Computer History Museum.

5. Based on Pelkey, Chapter 14, Exhibit 14.12.1—Codex Forecasted Revenue 1987. Retrieved September 13, 2018 from https://historyofcomputercommunications.info/section/14.12/codex/.

> found it's an almost completely separate culture. The people who participate in the dial business are almost orthogonal to the people who are in the leased line business. The methods of distribution are certainly different. The pace of change, the emphasis on features, the types of the features are different. You don't have multiplexing in a dial market. You hardly have network management, but you have very strong features for interacting with a PC, which we've been slow on. Hayes set the standard for the command set.[6]

As Forney states, the new market for dial-up modems for the PC differed drastically from the markets Codex was familiar with. Just as some networking companies failed to appreciate the massive disruption caused by the PC, it would seem Codex had missed an opportunity to advance their expertise in modem technology to this new high-growth market.

Modem technology exists in the physical layer, or bottom layer, of the OSI Model. However, the leading edge of computer communications in 1987 was the domain of computer scientists and network theorists who were pushing the frontier of the network layer, the layer in the OSI Model for interconnecting networks—hence, the looming challenge for Codex.

For 1986, Codex had revenue of $389 million. Profits, however, were flat with 1985 as Codex continued to bury the costs of its new headquarters and the losses incurred by failed attempts to OEM other vendor's LAN and T1 products. Nevertheless, Codex remained the largest computer communication company, and for the years 1982–1986, Codex reported an impressive compounded annual growth rate of 18.8%, including the minimal 8% of 1986.[7]

By 1987 Codex was still predominantly a leased line modem company and conclusively a data communications company. Having innovated the 9,600bps lease-line modem in 1968 endowed Codex with a lasting market advantage. Although only recently having entered the dial-up market where it already had a 13% market share, some benefit of dominating the leased line market can be assumed. However, that advantage did not help Codex enter either the LAN or T1 multiplexer markets.

In early 1987, Lockitt oversaw and approved the Five-Year Financial Plan. The plan is the blueprint of how Codex management was going to build a $1.1 billion company by 1992. But the strategy for competing in the areas of T1, LANs, and internetworking are vague and belie the difficulties Codex had already experienced in

6. Forney interview, Computer History Museum.

7. Codex 1988–1992 Worldwide Strategic Business Unit Plan, April 15, 1987, and The Five-Year Financial Forecast.

developing products for these markets. Forney points to the budgetary process that had failed Codex, much like its executive leadership had:

> Since at least 1974, we have spent more of our development money outside the modem area than in the modem area, because our five-year plans always looked the same. Small growth for next year, less growth for the second year, maturing and, depending on our particular mood, one percent up or one percent down, and every year we just moved it out, changed the axes, both axes.[8]

John Pugh, Codex vice president of marketing at the time of the emerging T1 market, remembers the challenges Codex experienced trying to develop a T1 product. As early as 1980 they saw the presence of high-speed digital T1 lines as a threat to their analog multiplexer products. Initially, they were able to convince their customers of the price advantages of staying with their analog products, but eventually they made the decision to develop their own T1 product:

> We were not very successful in terms of getting a program going. We actually screwed around with it for about 2 years, and never came up with a product. I think it was [lack of] management commitment. The company was getting a whole lot bigger. It was getting more difficult to manage. There was much more competition for funding of the various programs, and nobody put together a good program. At that point in time, we also decided we wanted to get into the LAN business. So we started spending money in the LAN area, and the T1 area, we just got behind. So we solved that by OEMing products from Avanti and Stratacom.[9]

Carr offers his perspective on the challenges facing Codex management: "What's happening... seeing from the outside, and I don't know the details, Codex is depending entirely too much on buy-out product, as opposed to what it's doing inside, and they've got a monumental organization down here in Canton that isn't turning out the product."[10]

---

8. Forney interview, Computer History Museum.

9. John Pugh, oral history interview by James L. Pelkey, February 25, 1988, Canton, MA. Computer History Museum, Mountain View, CA. Available from https://archive.computerhistory.org/resources/access/text/2016/03/102738098-05-01-acc.pdf.

10. Carr interview, Computer History Museum.

Before the end of 1988, two announcements would seem to undermine Codex's Five-Year Plan. On July 25, 1988, *Network World* ran a front-page article titled: "Struggling Codex trims work force."[11] Not the banner of a prosperous business behemoth. It reads that 250 employees out of a work force of 4,500 were laid off—a 6% reduction. It also states that Codex probably "overestimated" sales of T1 multiplexers. Their deal with Stratacom for a T1 networking multiplexer had not produced significant market presence, just as the earlier LAN agreement with Ungermann-Bass (UB) had failed. Then in December, Codex announced a 30% price reduction for its modems, forced to do so by IBM's pricing.[12]

That same December 1988, Codex announced that it was putting its headquarters up for sale.[13] While still an industry leader, the future for Codex was uncertain; their immediate concern was trimming back lavish expenses and focusing on their core strategy.

11.2.2 Micom

Although posting a slightly better year than 1986 (sales were up 4% and earnings up 13%), there was no doubt that 1987 had been a very difficult year for Micom. The data PBX business was drying up with no prospect for recovery. The market for statistical multiplexers was also showing every sign of having had its day in the sun. In fact, the concept of selling products, a marketing distinction maintained by Micom, kept them from pursuing the high risks and major organizational changes required to sell networking systems. The systems business was one that Bill Norred, founder and past president, major shareholder, and now chairman of the board, had avoided like the plague.

In early 1988, Norred and two other major shareholders became concerned for the value of their shares and pressured the board to either buy their shares in a friendly transaction or threatened to sell their shares to other buyers. (As major shareholders it was not possible to sell their shares without adversely affecting the share price of the company.) Roger Evans, president and CEO, aware of the precarious nature of the business, worked hard to find a solution for his long-standing friend's wishes and to preserve the stability of the company's share price. By early April, Evans had secured the necessary financing and Micom announced a tender offer for 4.8 million shares of stock at $16 per share. (Norred and Mr. and Mrs. Thornton, would be selling a total of 4.194 million shares, nearly all of the 4.8 million shares.) Then on April 13, Micom announced a delay in the commencement

11. "Struggling Codex trims work force," *Network World*, July 25, 1988, 1, 4.

12. "Codex marks down its modems by 30%," *Network World*, December 12, 1988, 810.

13. *Boston Globe*, January 1, 1989.

of the offer until after April 26, with the offer subsequently having to remain open for 20 business days.

In offering to buy back shares, Micom had opened itself up to being acquired. Soon after the tender offer had been made public, the Board announced that it had received offers from an undisclosed number of unidentified suitors. (Since the prices being proposed were above the prevailing market price of $13.50, the Board had the fiduciary responsibility on behalf of all shareholders to explore the offers.) The Board announced it had taken three steps: a committee of the Board had been established to study the offers, the services of the investment banks Goldman Sachs & Co. and Volpe & Covington had been retained, and the tender offer had been cancelled.[14] In early August, Micom announced it had entered a definitive agreement to be acquired by a company formed by Odyssey Partners, a major leveraged buyout firm. The all-cash offer translated into the purchase of each outstanding share of Micom for $16.00 per share.

Including fees, expenses, and refinancing of existing debt, the total purchase price to Odyssey Partners was $334 million. Immediately prior and connected with the acquisition, Micom sold its "MICOM Digital" subsidiary for $9.5 million; effectively the Spectrum Digital acquisition made in 1987 for $19.4 million. The $9 million became part of the $51 million of cash of the company. To finance the $334 million, the surviving private company's balance sheet read:

- Assumed $248 million of Debt
- Issued $34 million of Preferred Stock
- Issued $1 million of Common Stock
- Retained $51 million of Micom's cash.

In comparison, Micom only had $5.8 million of long-term debt on March 31, 1987, the day before the deal. Essentially, the value of the company the founders had created was roughly $242 million. To reduce the debt, Odyssey's strategy was to sell all operations other than the Black Box subsidiary.

11.2.3 Network Equipment Technologies

Many management teams might have rested on their laurels after the accomplishments that Network Equipment Technologies (NET) management achieved in 1987: becoming a public company in January, signing a major agreement with IBM in June, and growing sales from $47.4 million for fiscal year ending March 1987 to $90.6 million for 1988. But not the team Bruce Smith and the other founders had

14. "Micom eyes $250M-plus suitor," *Electronic News*, May 2, 1988, 31.

assembled. They dreamed of NET as one day being a Fortune 500 corporation now in the very early stages of its history. One way to get there was to listen to customers and anticipate their needs. The acquisition of ComDesign helped NET expand its product line to include statistical multiplexers. This helped their customers build out their data communication networks. When Smith, Maclean, and Tony Russo, vice president of marketing, routinely traveled to meet with their customers, they began to sense their customers' need to interconnect their LANs and WANs. Having little LAN expertise in-house, and little time to master it, the logical conclusion was to acquire a LAN company. Fortunately, a prime candidate was conveniently headquartered a few miles down the road in San Jose, CA: Excelan.

Excelan, a public company since February 1987 and growing rapidly, had yet to create the organizational depth needed to tackle the larger opportunity of selling directly to large corporations—organizational resources NET had already put in place. Excelan also had the high-performance Ethernet products and TCP/IP protocols that NET's customers needed. So when NET management came calling, the conversations proceeded quickly. From Excelan's perspective, and unknown to NET management at the time, the sudden arrival of NET held the prospect of solving a problem of company leadership the Board was facing. The CEO the Board had hired to facilitate the February IPO, Dick Moore, had lost their confidence and replacing him seemed fraught with risks. So NET arrived like a "white knight."

On April 13, 1987, the companies announced Excelan would merge into NET. When the transaction was completed in July, NET would be giving stock valued at an estimated $119.4 million to the shareholders of Excelan, or about 30% of the value of the combined companies.[15] It was a blockbuster of a merger and left little doubt about what corporations wanted: seamless interconnectivity of their LANs and WANs.

After the merger was announced, however, the Excelan Board was faced with the crisis they had hoped to avoid. Kanwal Rekhi, then Executive Vice President and Director remembers:

> After the merger was announced, Moore left, anyhow. And so I became the CEO again, the second time. The first thing I told the board, if they do that merger, I'm done the day after the merger, because I don't think this merger made sense. I said every time I looked at them, their way of doing business, it just doesn't smell right to me. And one of the board members came up to

15. *Wall Street Journal*, April 15, 1988, 10.

me, and said: "If you don't want the merger, we won't do it." So we didn't do the merger. And the board members were very happy in the end.[16]

On May 16, NET claimed Excelan was in breach of its obligations under their merger agreement. On June 28, the companies announced the merger was "terminated by mutual consent." The public documents left unclear what the breach was, only that efforts to renegotiate had failed.[17]

After abandoning their deal, both companies turned in great years for 1988. NET's sales rose to $136 million, up an impressive 50%. Excelan's sales rose even more impressively to $65.9 million, up 69%. Clearly the markets for communications products remained robust even as the pressure for market consolidation continued.

Towards the end of 1988, NET and Cisco Systems began negotiating an OEM agreement in which NET would resell Cisco products on a nonexclusive basis under the NET label. The deal would also allow NET to incorporate Cisco's router technology in NET's products according to a license agreement with Cisco.[18]

11.3 Other Data Communications Companies

11.3.1 Digital Communications Associates

Management of Digital Communications Associates (DCA) quickly concluded that the acquisition of Cohesive Networks in September 1986 would not lead to the dominant company they wanted to build. Other leading firms in data communications, like Codex, Micom, and NET either had entered or were rumored to be interested in entering the local area networking market. To DCA CEO Bert Nordin, it was only logical that DCA should follow suit. In August 1987, DCA acquired the assets of Fox Research, the developer of 10NET, for $10 million.[19] Subsequent to the acquisition, DCA renamed Fox Research to 10NET Communications, Division of DCA. 10NET was a simplistic, resource-sharing network. When it was upgraded to StarLAN in

16. Kanwal Rekhi, oral history interview by James L. Pelkey, August 17, 1994, Palo Alto, CA. Computer History Museum, Mountain View, CA. Available from https://archive.computerhistory.org/resources/access/text/2018/04/102738774-05-01-acc.pdf. The interview with Kanwal Rekhi was conducted in 1994 after the events being described whereas the interviews with NET personnel were conducted before the proposed merger with Excelan. Hence, the absence of quotes from NET executives.

17. *Wall Street Journal*, June 28, 1988.

18. Cisco internetworking products, June 1990, C11-154-103.

19. "Acquisition and merger plans proceed," *Network World* August 31, 1987, 7.

February 1987, it made little difference. Eager to sell more than just an entry level LAN, when UB's stock price tumbled during the October 1987 market crash, DCA quickly made an offer to merge the two firms. UB's Board of Directors had no interest in the hostile takeover and rejected DCA's efforts. Still, as of the end of 1988, DCA had transformed itself through the acquisition of Cohesive Networks and Fox Research and now offered a wide range of communications products that included T1 multiplexers and a low-end LAN product.

11.3.2 Racal/Milgo

Racal Data Communications Group (RDCG) had been mostly content remaining a modem company after its acquisitions of Milgo and Vadic in 1977. By the mid-1980s, however, RDCG began broadening its product offerings by distributing other companies' products. Although Racal/Milgo had been selling statistical multiplexers ever since 1980, it was not until 1984 when they introduced their first T1 multiplexer, the Omnimux T1, with great fanfare, though ultimately it was not competitive with either the NET or Timeplex offerings. By then the T1 multiplexer market had become intensely competitive with eight new entrants in addition to the existing competitors: NET, Timeplex, DCA, and Paradyne.[20]

11.3.3 Timeplex

Timeplex had been either the leading or the second performing firm in the T1 market along with NET ever since both firms introduced their first T1 products in 1983. In 1987, Timeplex introduced its Link 2 family with interfaces to CBX's to keep pace with NET's IDNX family of multiplexers.

After NET's deal with IBM (see Chapter 10), experts opined that it would not be long before Timeplex would be forced to align with a major computer company. The best guess was with Digital Equipment Corporation (DEC). In 1986, the last year Timeplex financial data was available, sales were $119 million. As expected, in November 1987, Timeplex was acquired by a larger computer company, however, the surprise was that it was Unisys and not DEC that made the acquisition for $307 million.

11.3.4 Paradyne

Paradyne had long challenged Codex and Milgo for leadership in the market for high-speed modems. As the market evolved, management began seeing modems as an important sub-system of larger systems that could help them become a much

20. According to Datapro in April 1985, new T1 multiplexer companies included: Amdahl, Avanti, Canoga Data System, Datatel, Gandalf, Infotron, ITT Telecom, Tau-tron, and Tellabs. Datapro, April 1985, C35-708-104.

larger, and more valuable company. They gallantly bid on a new "intelligent terminal system" for the Social Security Administration and won the contract. The project turned into a nightmare for Paradyne after lawsuits were brought against them by the Administration for misrepresenting the availability of its product.[21] In December 1988, AT&T, playing the "White Knight," acquired Paradyne for $237 million.

11.4 Networking: Firms Responding to Market Consolidation, 1987–1988

11.4.1 3Com

Sales and profits of 3Com grew substantially in 1986. The last-minute break-up of the proposed merger with Convergent Technologies in March 1986, however, left 3Com management uncertain as to the future direction of the company. As Bill Krause, Bob Metcalfe, and other key managers met, they examined their long-term goals. Krause remembers wanting to ensure that 3Com "became an icon in Silicon Valley." He also thought that many of his colleagues at other start-ups overstayed their time. "So I made a commitment that, at the end of ten years, 'I'm out of here, and I encourage you guys to do the same thing.'" This goal begged another question: "So this all sort of fit in with the fact that there were 3 or 4 more years to go before 10 years was up for me and we needed to get somebody in place to be our potential successor."[22]

Management then turned to the question of their core strategy: should they be a workgroup or communications company? The board of directors also wanted a resolution to this issue. When the board met in January 1987, a decision was reached: to become the second largest communication company, conceding leadership only to DEC.

Soon afterwards, Krause remembers a call from Bert Nordin of DCA: "Bert Nordin was chasing everybody. He badly, badly wanted to merge with 3Com. He flew me down to Atlanta and gave a big pitch and argued the merits of merging, and then he took me out to dinner."[23] The board realized market consolidation was inevitable and encouraged Krause and Metcalfe to analyze the best options for 3Com. They were also decidedly against any combination with DCA.

21. Pat Leisner. 1987. Paradyne fined $1.2 million after guilty plea in fraud case. *Associated Press*, March 6, 1987. Retrieved January 25, 2021, from https://apnews.com/article/0a65402356aed4290c9b2531aa6bd514.

22. Bill Krause, oral history interview by James L. Pelkey, August 15, 1994. Computer History Museum, Mountain View, CA. Available from https://archive.computerhistory.org/resources/access/text/2020/01/102740543-05-01-acc.pdf.

23. Krause interview, Computer History Museum.

By this time, Krause and Metcalfe had been meeting frequently with Bill Carrico and Judith Estrin of Bridge Communications. Estrin explains the relationship of the two companies:

> We had been talking off and on for years, because first, we did joint development with them, and I knew Bob Metcalfe, and we were located nearby. Then we had a reference sell arrangement with them, and then we OEMed their product. Metcalfe, Krause, Bill, and I used to get together for lunch every couple of months, just to talk about the relationship. You know, how was the OEM relationship? How can we do these things? Every once in a while it [the idea of a merger] came up, and it was never the right time and no one wanted to talk about it. This time, it was kind of the right time for both companies, and I think Krause called Bill.[24]

Concurrently, Carrico and Estrin had also been assessing how to create an enduring strategy. Carrico remembers:

> We were convinced that we had covered the one segment of the marketplace very well, what we call "the general-purpose LAN segment." There was another segment of the LAN market, which we called "the system vendor segment," which is DEC with its networking equipment. The third piece was "PC networking," which was really very distinct because the PC networking was focused on application sharing over the network, where the general purpose was focused much more on communications and connectivity. So the customer said: "Wait a minute. I've got these PC networks and I've got these general-purpose multi-vendor networks. I don't want to have to buy this from two vendors."[25]

As effective entrepreneurs, they needed to act quickly in response to the real need their customers had identified. To that end, Carrico and Estrin had begun serious conversations with Novell, 3Com's principal competitor. In early 1987, however, the parties terminated conversations. So when Krause called Carrico after 3Com's January board meeting, both parties were now willing to discuss a merger. Carrico remembers their position at the time: "I don't think there was any issue in our minds about the strategic benefit. From that perspective, we'd do it again."[26]

---

24. Bill Carrico and Judith Estrin, oral history interview with James L. Pelkey, June 23, 198, Los Altos, CA. Computer History Museum, Mountain View, CA. Available from https://archive.computerhistory.org/resources/access/text/2018/03/102740285-05-01-acc.pdf.

25. Carrico and Estrin interview, Computer History Museum.

26. Carrico and Estrin interview, Computer History Museum.

Wasting little time, on July 27, 1987, 3Com and Bridge announced a merger valued at $193 million.[27] When the merger was finalized on September 29, the value of $151 million was significantly lower due to the decline in the market price of 3Com's stock. Nonetheless, for the 4 months ending September 30, 1987, 3Com's sales were $42.3 million and Bridge's $25.8 million giving, after accounting eliminations, combined sales of $67.9 million and net income of $4.1 million. The financial markets were valuing the "new" 3Com at a little more than two times sales, a far cry from the venture capital multiples enjoyed just a few years earlier.

In a report on Bridge Communications by Datapro, dated June 1987, the significant investment required to participate in the general-purpose LAN market is mirrored in pages of products.[28] In contrast, a similarly composed list of 3Com's products would barely fill a single page. A noteworthy inclusion in the list of Bridge's products were four Data Link level bridges, both local and remote. The merging of these two companies had clearly created a leading communications company with an early footprint in the internetworking market.

Krause, who retained overall management responsibility as the CEO of 3Com, had seemingly found his successor when Carrico was named president and COO of the combined companies. On a personal level, Krause could easily entertain thoughts of soon leaving 3Com—just as he had imagined. Estrin became one of six general managers reporting to Carrico.

Metcalfe assumed the title of general manager of the Distributed Systems Division—euphemistic for workgroup computing. Uncertainty remained around their core strategy: how was communications to become the focus of the company while significant investments were still being made in workgroup computing? Krause laments the challenge of focusing on communications while Metcalfe, the founder of the company, remained fixated on computing:

> Then we had this moment of uncertainty about whether or not we should be a computer company or a communication company. And I bet on the wrong idea, but the right guy, who was one and the same. Carrico had the right idea, which was become a communication company. Metcalfe wanted to continue being a computing company and continue with the 3Station project. He thought we were on the right track. So I bet on Metcalfe's strategy, which was the wrong thing to do, but Metcalfe was the right guy, because it turned

27. "3Com, Bridge Communications to merge in stock swap valued at $193 million," *Wall Street Journal*, July 27, 1987.

28. "Bridge Communications Local Area Network Product Line" Datapro, June 1987, 103–107.

out that Carrico recognized, and to Bill's credit he recognized it, that he was an entrepreneur and that he should bail out and go start another company.[29]

As is often the case after a merger, the two companies faced the challenge of reconciling their two cultures. Carrico explains: "What was the big surprise was the culture clash was much more than I ever imagined it would be. I certainly knew that there were culture differences. I knew what I was getting into, but it was just real hard."[30] Harder still was the change in responsibilities both Estrin and Carrico had assumed. Now working as a manager disconnected from the engineering team by the six general managers who reported to him, Carrico missed interacting directly on day-to-day issues. Estrin, on the other hand, had moved from being second in command at Bridge to being a general manager at 3Com. Neither felt called to remain in these positions. In May 1988, Carrico and Estrin resigned, to briefly rest, and then to research another fertile market into which to launch another start-up. Krause, on the other hand, again assumed the mantle of president and once again the ponderous and tiring responsibility of resolving the unresolved decision of company focus. He remembers: "So Bill left... I took Bill's presidency back... and Eric [Benhamou] moved over to head up the software division, and Bob was heading up the distributed systems division. I had chosen Bob, and Bill had opted out. So we were off to go do our workgroup computing strategy."[31]

The superb financial results of 3Com continued with sales for fiscal year ending May 1988 of $252 million, up from $156 million, or up 62%, and net income of $22.5 million, up from $16.2 million, or up 39%. But not all was a walk in the park. The challenges of merging two different sales forces, and the disappointing results of the LAN Manager network operating system were forcing Krause to reconsider the choices that had been made. He reflects: "I had concluded that I had made a serious strategic error in trying to become a workgroup computing company, because we really didn't have the horses to compete with people like IBM and Compaq and Dell and AST and all these other guys. We just didn't have it."[32]

3Com had inherited strong engineering talent in communications and internetworking from their merger with Bridge, but the decision to focus on workgroup computing led to much of this talent leaving after the departure of Carrico and Estrin. Many of these engineers found work with the internetworking start-up, Cisco, where their experience in routing and bridging was better suited. Still, by 1988, 3Com had established a presence in the internetworking market, with a market share of 19% of the installed base of bridges and routers, thanks largely

29. Krause interview, Computer History Museum.

30. Carrico and Estrin interview, Computer History Museum.

31. Krause interview, Computer History Museum.

32. Krause interview, Computer History Museum.

to the products inherited from Bridge Communications. However, the indecisiveness around the company strategy, more specifically, the unwillingness to focus on computer communications, did not bode well for its internetworking future.

11.4.2 Ungermann-Bass

The understanding that IP routing represented a new and potentially significant market was not lost on engineers and managers within existing networking firms. Both DEC and Proteon were selling successful hubs and routers. But successful engineering and development did not always result in management approval of a product. Such was the case with UB, where the initiative of engineer John Davidson and others led to an early implementation of a router. This effort was undermined in part by UB's efforts to reduce the high cost of its product development and marketing: in 1986, UB's net income totaled only $18,000 on sales of $110.9 million.

Davidson explains the origins of UB's potential entrance into the router market:

> In 1986, it became apparent that we could do something with our 68K-based bridging product and software to turn it into a router. And I had my group of people create an IP router in 1986, and not just for purposes of show. I decided "We're going to go get some business with this router, and then we're going to bring it to one of these crazy planning meetings we have and I'm going to say: "By the way, we've already done it."[33]

Working with a customer out of the Philadelphia sales office, Davidson and his team deployed six prototypes placed at the ends of T1 lines. The routers connected the customer's six networks together. They also included PC-based management software providing specific functionality outlined by the customer. Based on the prototypes, Davidson and his team won the business, beating out Proteon and Cisco. Davidson continues the story: "I brought that product and that result to a planning meeting in 1986, and maybe representative of our problems at that point, it was rejected flat out as not what the customers wanted. "Customers want bridges, not routers," and they asked us to stop working on it."[34]

Weighing on the minds of UB management was what to do about the INI division and the financial relationship with General Electric (GE). Making the issue even more difficult was the fact that INI was Ralph Ungermann's idea. Ungermann recalls the criticism he took for the company's strategy and reveals an understandable bitterness regarding the failed MAP/GE decision:

---

33. John M. Davidson, oral history interview by James L. Pelkey, August 18, 1992, Mountain View, CA. Computer History Museum, Mountain View, CA. Available from https://archive.computerhistory.org/resources/access/text/2013/05/102746647-05-01-acc.pdf.

34. Davidson interview, Computer History Museum.

> It's actually a very simple strategy, and it was highly criticized, but every single company that's not a computer company has adopted it behind us. So, it was highly criticized, but widely accepted. The idea was that if you want to buy a system from IBM, it's going to be token ring. If you want to buy a system from DEC, it's going to be Ethernet. If you want to buy a system from both of them, it's going to be Ethernet and token ring, ergo, a business opportunity, a niche. A broad product offering is required to support that niche, so you're not in business unless you've got a product line. So everybody said: "Ungermann-Bass is unfocused. They're doing too many things," but today, Bridge does token ring and broadband and Ethernet, and in fact, mastering those technologies is not very tough. Well, that's not true. Token ring investment was an enormous investment, and broadband technology was a big investment, but they're do-able. They're engineering feats that, if you've got good engineering organizations, you can really do.
>
> The thing that got Ungermann-Bass in trouble was we poured all of our money into that factory networking business unit, and all of our resources into that, and all of a sudden somebody decided that the technology that we were delivering—and we had 70% market share—was going to be made obsolete by a new standard, and that maybe it is our fault for not driving that standard more, but we didn't, and it happened, and all of a sudden we had an obsolete business unit with a huge portion of our resources going into it, and we had to shift from that. We had to shut that down, meld it back into the organization, and change a lot of people's careers and direction, and everything else.
>
> So it was an enormous dislocation for this company, but we take risks and we missed one. So what? You keep going. We took a gamble on broadband, made a go. We made a gamble on being able to provide an IBM compatible token ring, and we're doing that, and we picked MAP, and we missed. So we picked three out of four, and that hurts, but so what? We're going to keep going. We're the only company that can come in today and provide you with a very broad connectivity of IBM and DEC, all based on open standards, and today I think everybody recognizes that's the only winning strategy for an independent LAN company. So everybody has adopted that strategy.[35]

The need to cut losses and curtail the painful drain on capital forced a restructuring of the relationship with GE. After protracted discussions, in October 1987,

35. Ralph Ungermann, oral history interview by James L. Pelkey, July 20, 1988, Mountain View, CA. Computer History Museum, Mountain View, CA. Available from https://archive.computerhistory.org/resources/access/text/2018/03/102738765-05-01-acc.pdf.

UB announced that GE would exchange its 36% interest in INI for a 3.6% interest in UB with a 4-year option to buy another 3.6% of UB's stock. INI was soon shut down and reabsorbed, ending the days of big spending on MAP.

Even though 1987 was shaping up to be a good year, certainly much better than it could havc been given 1986, there was no way management could have anticipated the market crash of October 1987. With its share price driven down from nearly $12.00 per share to just over $7.00 per share, investors jumped to the conclusion that the company was struggling to remain independent. The ever-opportunistic DCA approached the Board in November with an offer to merge the two companies. The merger bid by DCA was $9.75 per share for a total of $175.5 million. When the UB Board displayed little interest, DCA threatened to begin a tender offer to take hostile control of the company.[36] UB responded aggressively saying the transaction was not "in the best interest of the company and its shareholders, suppliers and customers." On November 16, DCA announced that it was dropping its hostile takeover but would hold its roughly one million shares of UB stock. As word leaked out, the price of UB's shares dropped $.75 to close at $7.50.[37]

While UB had defeated the merger bid of DCA, it left Ungermann shaken. He soon hired Goldman Sachs to seek out a buyer and began talks with several potential companies, including Intel and HP. Bass shared his perspective on the decision to put the company he co-founded up for sale: "Now, I maintain there didn't have to be a deal. I mean, this being in play is partly a state of mind, and I think the company did not need to be sold. It was not in trouble. It was simply being hounded. Ralph was tired. Ralph was taking a beating on Wall Street, and he didn't like it."[38]

In December 1987, conversations began in earnest with Tandem Computers. For Tandem, the decision would be a strategic risk in order to make them more competitive with DEC and IBM. For UB, the merger was more like finding a safe harbor. Ungermann viewed Bridge Communications as his main competition for UB's multivendor LAN strategy. Speaking of the future of Bridge after the merger with 3Com, he states: "I am absolutely 100% convinced that there will be no Bridge division as an effective competitor against us in another two years... They're losing focus and direction in our market, and that's great." Now viewing DEC and IBM as the main competition for LAN customers, Ungermann rationalized the need to align with a larger company:

---

36. "Offer for Ungermann-Bass is considered by company," *Wall Street Journal*, Nov. 13, 1987.

37. "Unsolicited bid to acquire Ungermann-Bass is dropped," *Wall Street Journal*, Nov. 16, 1987.

38. Charles (Charlie) Bass, oral history interview by James L. Pelkey, August 16, 1994, Palo Alto, CA. Computer History Museum, Mountain View, CA. Available from https://archive.computerhistory.org/resources/access/text/2018/03/102738753-05-01-acc.pdf.

> At the same time, we've got IBM with more and more capability every day, and so therefore we say: "Oh, geez, we better get to be part of a bigger company, because all these guys are sitting up here saying: 'Geez, this is a strategic decision, and we only have three strategic vendors, and who's Ungermann?'"[39]

On February 22, 1988, Tandem announced its proposal to acquire UB for $260 million, $85.5 million more than the DCA offer.[40] Each UB shareholder would receive $12.50 in cash per share and the convertible subordinated debenture holders would receive $833.34 per $1,000 of face principal.[41]

Davidson shared the views of Bass; while he understood that the financial stability that merging with a larger company would afford, allowing them better standing in future bids for multi-million dollar projects, he was skeptical: "When the proposal for a merger came, I voted against it, thinking we're independent, we're still making money and we can do some great new products if we would just do 'em. So it took some convincing before I voted for it."[42]

As expected, on March 18, Tandem Computers announced the successful conclusion of its tender offer with 95% of the outstanding shares tendered. The acquisition was formally completed on June 30, 1988. Jim Jordan, no longer with the company but still knowledgeable about the market, explains: "It probably makes an awful lot of sense for Tandem. Their main competitor has got to be DEC, and DEC's more of a networking company than anybody else around right now. DEC is the biggest competitor Ungermann-Bass has."[43]

In July 1988, Ungermann, now a vice-president and director of Tandem, reflects: "Already it's impacted our business very substantially and significantly, in terms of our opportunity to go in and deal with companies we'd never even think of getting into as a strategic communications supplier." Now that UB had chosen a partner, Ungermann set his strategy to gaining large corporate clients in competition with DEC and IBM. "So are we big enough? Two billion. Well, we've got to grow fast, but Tandem has the reputation and the ability to deliver complex, strategic on-line

39. Ungermann interview, Computer History Museum.

40. "Merger with Tandem will give Ungermann-Bass financial edge," *PC Week*, Feb. 23, 1988, 129.

41. "Tandem woos UB to merger," *Communications Week*, Feb. 22, 1988, 1.

42. Davidson interview, Computer History Museum.

43. James (Jim) Jordan, oral history interview by James L. Pelkey, July 19, 1988, Hillsdale, CA. Computer History Museum, Mountain View, CA. Available from https://archive.computerhistory.org/resources/access/text/2018/04/102740315-05-01-acc.pdf.

systems, and therefore, we've been able to bid on and win some deals that we just would have not been able to do."[44]

Their future now tied to the fortunes of Tandem, the history of UB demonstrates how one strategic investment in a technology with a high cost of development and without a validated market can end a company's independence. The acquisition ended the run of one of the most successful independent networking companies in the early evolution of the networking market. It is interesting to note that the value UB had created by the time it was acquired by Tandem was almost the same as the company value Micom had created from the introduction of their statistical multiplexer to the sale of the company to Odyssey. Even as networking was experiencing remarkable success and growth, the value of one of the forerunners and leaders in the industry would be quickly dwarfed by the industry leaders of internetworking.

11.4.3 Concord Communications

In August 1986, Concord Data Systems executives and investors came to the difficult conclusion that there was only one option left to save the company and divided CDS into two companies; one to focus on dial-up modems and one on MAP/token bus. The profits from dial-up modems, the fortunes of which had suddenly declined, could no longer fund the unremitting investment required by MAP/token bus. The simple fact was that continuing to fund MAP/token bus seemed certain to bankrupt CDS. The charter of the new company, Concord Communications Inc. (CCI), was the capital draining MAP/token bus business. Simultaneous with the reorganization, CCI closed a $9 million financing, $7 million of which was new money, with a post-money valuation of $22 million. Investors chose to ignore sluggish MAP revenues, focusing instead on the aggressive promotion of MAP by General Motors (GM) and the success of the Autofact '85 Show that had painted a promising future for MAP and factory automation. The management of CCI was now free to weave an exciting story beginning with the pioneering innovation of token bus, leading to its adoption as the LAN technology of manufacturing giants like GM, and selected as the LAN for MAP/OSI.

In 1988, Ken Miller, the founder of CDS, remembered the fortunate timing of the 1986 reorganization: "I mean, CCI got the money at the right time, boy. It was right after that, that MAP stalled."[45] The softening sales of MAP/token bus quickly tested the optimism of the new CCI management team. Exhibiting a sense of survival unpracticed by prior management, Tony Helies, the new CEO of CCI, launched an

44. Ungermann interview, Computer History Museum.

45. Ken Miller, oral history interview by James L. Pelkey, February 23, 1988. Computer History Museum, Mountain View, CA. Available from https://archive.computerhistory.org/resources/access/text/2015/10/102737985-05-01-acc.pdf.

immediate effort to cut costs. Since costs for a start-up are principally personnel costs, Helies had little choice but to reduce headcount. By early 1987, CCI was down to 55 employees, a staff reduction of roughly 30% in 6 months. Now the challenge was to reclaim the perception of market leader from INI, the joint venture of UB and GE, that itself was reorganizing. The ideal opportunity was to stage a high-profile presentation at the highly publicized Enterprise Networking Event (ENE) scheduled for June 1988. To do so meant mastering the MAP communication protocols of the Network and Transport Layers, something that had eluded them in the past. Being late had its advantages, however, for the communications standards for MAP were final; they would not be coding software to changing specifications.

CCI could hardly have envisioned a more successful ENE. In addition to hosting an exhibitor's booth, they played prominent roles in three of the eight sponsor booths, those of GM, Deere & Co., and Process Industries. Prominent in use was their Series 4200 broadband to carrierband bridge that allowed transparent connections between the 802.4/10Mbps broadband and the 802.4/5Mbps carrierband—all token bus. The Series 4200 extended the useful life of CCI's slower 5Mbps technology and demonstrated its mastery of both the higher speed 10Mbps technology and the OSI communication software. The success made all the pressure they had endured from GM for the past year somehow bearable. They had reclaimed the mantle of technology leader through their own hard work as well as the unexpected disappearance of INI/UB.

For a joyous management team returning from ENE, the prospect of achieving the coming year's ambitious financial goal of $10 million in revenues, and profitability, seemed much more realistic than before ENE. Their new expertise with the MAP communication protocols was generating new sales opportunities as well, especially with DEC. Eventually, the reality of the market forced management to examine their guiding vision: Did they really believe the MAP/token bus market was going to take off? Helies responded by forming task groups to explore what were their best strategic choices leading to a reliable and prosperous future. In the fall of 1988, a team ventured to the West Coast and the TCP/IP Interop conference. So, even as they were committed to achieving a revenue plan of $10 million in MAP/-token bus, they had concluded internally that their future might have to include a change in strategy.

11.5 Other LAN Companies

11.5.1 Excelan

When the announced merger between Excelan and NET collapsed on June 28, 1987, other companies interested in Excelan probably saw Excelan as a company "in play." But not Kanwal Rekhi, who became president after the failed merger. He preferred to focus on building a significant company than making money through "financial engineering." The revenue results for the 2 years ending December 1987 and 1988—$39 million and $66 million—certainly justified his assessment and leadership.

11.5.2 Sytek

The token ring announcement by IBM on October 15, 1985, left Sytek struggling for survival. It was not until the second quarter of 1988 that they again attained profitability.

Sytek and 3Com discussed a merger, but the merger did not make sense financially due to the structure of the deal, so it was called off. The question still remained—could they survive as an independent company?

11.5.3 Communication Machinery Corporation

In July 1988, Rockwell International bought Communication Machinery Corporation for an estimated $40 million and renamed it Rockwell Network Systems.

11.5.4 SynOptics

In August of 1987, SynOptics was the first vendor to ship 10Mbps Ethernet over unshielded twisted pair (telephone) cable. Success of the 10Mbps LattisNet led to SynOptics' IPO in August 1988, raising $12.6 million at a share price of $13.50.[46] SynOptics' advantage was short lived, however, and by 1988 other vendors, including HP, UB, AT&T, and Cabletron, would ship 10Mbps Ethernet products, also for UTP cable. The advantages of the hub-based star topology of these Ethernet products fueled high growth in the hub market. The two leaders were Cabeltron and SynOptics, soon joined by a crowded market with a dozen or more competitors including Racal-Interlan.

11.5.5 Proteon

Proteon's history was closely connected with MIT's Laboratory for Computer Science (LCS). Proteon had developed the ProNET-10 token ring network under contract from the LCS and funded by DARPA (see Chapter 6). The bond between Proteon and LCS was further reinforced that year when LCS professor David Clark joined Proteon's Board of Directors.

Another significant development for Proteon had evolved from the personal relationship between Salwen and LCS head Mike Dertouzos. In 1984, LCS researcher Noel Chiappa shared an insight for a multi-protocol gateway he had

46. By 1990, SynOptics shares were trading as high as $34.

been developing with Dertouzos. Dertouzos authorized Chiappa to begin work on the code for what would become known as the "MIT C gateway" and introduced Chiappa to Salwen—for the charter of the LCS did not include building, much less marketing, products.[47] Chiappa was soon working at both MIT and Proteon. At MIT, before the end of the year, Chiappa's vision led to internetworking router software running in all of the DEC MicroVAX IIs linking Ethernet to the token ring backbone.[48]

On October 15, 1985, the same day that IBM had announced its token ring LAN, Proteon established early leadership in the emerging internetworking market with the introduction of the p4200 LAN gateway, the commercial version of Chiappa's MIT C gateway. The p4200 could interconnect its new ProNET-4, and its ProNET-10 and ProNET-80 networks as well as Ethernet LANs and public WANs.[49] The ProNET-Linkway software for the p4200 was derived from Chiappa's vision and the working MIT C code. The p4200 is considered the first commercially available multi-protocol router. (The use of the term router came only over time; finally taking hold in 1987. The p4200 was known first as a LAN gateway, then a gateway router, and finally router.) Proteon further broadened its product line with new passive ProNET Wire Centers that supported a wide range of media connections including shielded twisted pair, coaxial cable, and optical fiber.

In December 1985, the lengthy search for a new President came to a close. Francis Sciricco, a young, fast-track GE executive, then managing a consumer appliance division in Kentucky, made the leap to the promising, but struggling technology company. The desperate need for a president had outweighed his lack of technology experience. He faced the daunting tasks of bringing executive order to the systems and structure of a company no longer a start-up but too often acting as such, as well as the urgent need to refine the development and marketing strategies in a rapidly shifting technology market. The chaos within the "corner office" hardly had time to settle when a disastrous fourth quarter precipitated change throughout the management ranks, including the resignation of Sciricco in early 1987.

L.J. Sevin, lead investor and Board Member, assumed the thankless role of Acting President. No one knew better than he that the company's future rested on the completion of a timely search, and this time, on successfully finding a fully qualified technology executive. Within days of settling into the flow of operations,

47. John Dix. 2006. Router man. *Network World*, March 27, 2006. Retrieved from http://www.networkworld.com/supp/2006/anniversary/032706-routerman.html.

48. "Token ring ties MIT Ethernet local nets," *Network World*, May 1, 1989, 27–30.

49. "Token ring ties MIT Ethernet local nets," *Network World*, May 1, 1989, 27–30.

the highly regarded Sevin concluded the same as had management: the networking market was highly competitive. Now that IBM had announced what could be disparagingly described as unimpressive products, the competition unleashed a barrage of products, trying to gain market share before IBM had time to exercise its market power. Customers too, no longer fearing that IBM might introduce a radically superior technology, began to flock to vendors with Ethernet solutions. The Ethernet companies, with the compelling advantage of multiple chip suppliers and strong sales, were able to offer aggressive price cuts. In the increasingly hostile market, acting as president was a role Sevin wanted to shed as soon as possible.

Remaining competitive required product upgrades and new products. In February 1987, Proteon announced its p4210 gateway interface.[50] Specifically designed to work with the p4200, the p4210 enabled its various token ring networks as well as those of IBM, including those of competitors like 3Com and UB—any products conforming to the 802.5 standard—to communicate with, and route over, Ethernet networks.

In March 1987, Proteon announced a series of new enhancements for its ProNET-4 network to make the network compatible with a wide variety of IBM's communications interfaces. Then in July, they announced more enhancements necessitated by competing with IBM, this time for its ProNET-10 networks.[51] To match the price reductions by Ethernet competitors, Proteon also announced a 30% price reduction for its ProNET-10 adapters. Lower sales prices brought on by competition combined with higher operating costs were depressing earnings. It was obvious to Sevin that more cash was needed both to protect the balance sheet as well as attract a candidate for president. At the August board meeting, Sevin reported the search had uncovered no qualified candidates, and that the company's distribution strategy needed to include many more value-added resellers (VARs). At the October meeting, the board dealt largely with the yet-to-close financing. After a lengthy discussion of pricing, it seemed fair to price the round down by 30% from the last round—but not nearly as deep a "haircut" as some new investors wanted. Proteon had clearly lost its patina and was now seen more as a turnaround.

In November came the good news (the "financeable event") the board and existing investors had been waiting for: Patrick Courtin was named president, chief executive, and member of the board. He had the technology knowhow long sought, including 10 years of experience with DEC. While his coming aboard had little impact on the financial results for 1987, he did facilitate closing the financing

50. "Interface links Ethernet, token ring networks," *Network World*, Feb. 2, 1987, 22–23.

51. "Proteon net to support IBM PS/2." *Network World*, July 20, 1987, 3.

of $2.4 million, raising the total venture capital investment to $17.4 million.[52] In December, he announced the projections for 1988: sales of $37 million and net income of $1.2 million, projections that helped in the closing of the Preferred D round financing. A month later, the results for 1987 were made known: sales of $22.3 million, up 15% over 1986, with a loss of $5.7 million (a loss equal to one-third of the venture capitalists' total investment). Hopefully the yearend actions and decisions would contribute to a successful 1988.

At the Interface Trade Show in March 1988, Proteon introduced its second-generation p4200 gateway. Faster and more reliable, the new p4200 supported TCP/IP, DECnet, and XNS, no longer was it just hardware interfaces but communication protocols as well. In an interview in May, Courtin said sales for 1988 were doing great, helped by the recently announced p4200. In fact, the sales of gateways and high-speed products, that is, ProNET-80, accounted for 40% of Proteon's sales.[53] At the Board meeting in June, Courtin indicated sales for 1988 might total $40 million and then soar to $75 million in 1989. The sales breakdown for 1989 was estimated to be $50 million of adapters, $20 million of routers, that is, gateways, and $5 million of high-speed products.

In November 1988, Proteon introduced a new router for smaller networks: it didn't have a T1 connection but rather slower 64Kbps connections. Reflecting the demand for solutions, and a more complete product for its corporate friend Novell, the p4100 employed a TCP/IP backbone that connected to IPX(N), the Novell interface and communication protocol.

Proteon had a successful 1988. Sales of $40.6 million, up 82%, and income from operations of $1.1 million. Cash totaled $1.6 million. Proteon was second only to IBM in the market for token ring adapters and a perceived leader in the fast-growing internetworking market. If Proteon qualified as a turnaround, it might be said "so far so good."

11.5.6 Digital Equipment Corporation

By 1986, as the internetworking market was just emerging, DEC was the leading LAN vendor controlling 20% of the market for LAN adapters and 35% of Ethernet adapter shipments. No corporation had more incentive to innovate products to interconnect LANs than did DEC. In 1984, DEC had launched the first successful Ethernet bridge, the LAN Bridge 100. To provide a remote bridge, DEC partnered with Vitalink, resulting in the TransLAN products. In July 1985, DEC entered

52. Proteon IPO documents.

53. "Proteon chief pulls firm back on track," *Network World* May 16, 1988, 25–26.

the gateway market with its External Document Exchange gateway providing services between DEC's All-In-1 environments and IBM's DISOSS nodes. Finally, DEC entered the router market partnered with Vitalink for its TransPath series of products. Just as DEC had pioneered in the early LAN market, management had been convinced early of the importance of internetworking.

11.6 Summary of the Data Communications Market-Structure

From its origins in the technologies of early military and government communications systems, the data communications market-structure was emerging by the mid-1960s. Early companies like Codex and Milgo established themselves in the market for leased line modems, where independents could offer products far superior to the technology available from AT&T. With the boom in corporate computing, including terminal systems like the IBM System/360 and the advent of time-sharing, a significant demand existed for communications products. Initially, the demand was met solely by the supplier to AT&T's monopoly, Western Electric. With the FCC's Carterfone decision, the floodgates were opened to entrepreneurs eager to serve this market with products that improved on existing designs. Companies like Vadic and General DataComm achieved early success through innovations of existing Bell modems. The development of time division multiplexing, first from the start-up ADS, then Codex and others, continued the evolution of technologies designed to transmit digital information efficiently over analogue phone lines.

Within a few years after the Carterfone decision, the data communications industry was well established. Trade organizations like the IDCMA used their collective strength to challenge AT&T's remaining restrictions on access to its network, just as the Computer Industry Association challenged IBM's control of the market for computer peripherals.

By the mid-1970s, the rush of data communications start-ups had flooded the market and the competition for customers had driven down prices. After an initial period of growth, the market began to flatten out. A downturn in the economy and lack of venture capital spending caused additional drag on the market. With the advent of the microprocessor, however, companies saw new opportunities to enhance their existing products. Innovations in statistical multiplexing led by Codex and Infotron in 1976 breathed life into this product category. This in turn increased demand for high-speed modems as customers took advantage of cost savings gained by multiplexing data communications onto fewer high-speed lines. The use of microprocessors led to improvements in modems, with products supporting diagnostic and multi-point features from Intertel, DCA, and GDC appealing to customers connecting larger networks of modems. Codex's innovation of QAM technology, first introduced in their highly successful 4800, and, later, the 9,600bps LSI modem, kept them at the forefront of the high-speed modem market.

Within 2 years, other data communications companies had followed suit with their own microprocessor-based modems and multiplexers. Paradyne trimmed costs to innovate a lower priced 9,600bps LSI modem in 1975, and other companies, as well as AT&T, added products to a soon crowded high-speed modem market. In the market for multiplexers, it didn't take long for the bottom to fill in, with Micom's introduction of their low-priced, user-friendly "data concentrator" in 1978 breaking ground for scores of imitators.

By the late 1970s, many of the leading data communications firms were acquired, reflecting the challenge these companies faced maintaining their growth in a highly competitive market in which price erosion was a constant reality. Codex and Milgo were acquired in 1977 and Vadic and UDS in 1978.

The mid-1980s saw a few of the data communications firms making entries into the market for networking products and services, but for most companies the technical and organizational challenges were too great. Some companies, like Codex, attempted to resell products from LAN vendors, while others, like Micom and DCA, acquired LAN companies. Still others, like Paradyne with its PIX system of networked modems and Micom with its popular data PBX, attempted to offer alternative solutions to the new architecture of LANs. These products were initially successful, offering significant price advantage over LANs. However, the advent of the personal computer and desktop computing exposed the Achilles' heel of the modem and data PBX networks—their limited data transmission speeds. Soon, these solutions were eclipsed by local area networks. Exemplifying the rise and fall of the data PBX market, of the eight high profile hybrid data PBX/LAN companies founded in the mid-1980s, all but one, David Systems, were out of business by 1988.[54] Mastery of packet-switching was the key difference between the datacom companies that failed to make the transition to the networking market-structure and the networking companies that succeeded in the LAN business.

When AT&T introduced commercial T1 service, several existing datacom firms, as well as new start-ups, responded by innovating multiplexers for T1 lines, offering customers attractive cost reductions. GDC and Timeplex were early leaders in this market. After the breakup of AT&T, and the uncertain future of the telecom market, companies scrambled to find their own alternatives to the uncertainty in the unregulated carrier market. New start-ups NET and Cohesive were the first

54. Jeff Matros. 1988. The start-up seven and where they failed" *Network World*, November 1988, 25.

to offer T1 multiplexing for both data and voice, in a popular shift to privatized communication networks known as "be your own Bell."

By 1988, the market-structure for data communications was organized around the key product categories of modems and multiplexers. The T1 multiplexer had introduced a new product category that was a hybrid of both data communications and networking categories. Firms that were able to make significant innovations in their core products succeeded in riding the market the longest, achieving the necessary profit margins from new products to outlast the pressure of competitive pricing. This was evident in modems (Codex and Milgo), multiplexers (ADS, Codex, and Micom), data PBX (Micom and Gandalf), and T1 multiplexers (General DataComm and NET). Other companies were quick to follow these leaders, able to carve out new submarkets with lower priced streamlined products, advances in semiconductors, and innovative marketing and distribution. Micom, with its low-end statistical multiplexer, and Paradyne, with its lower priced high-speed 9600 LSI modem, were examples of companies exploiting a new customer base, such as the less tech-savvy office manager, and targeted through new, lower cost distribution channels.

The cycle of market-structure dynamics in data communication was closely related to the common carrier services. From its gestation period in the early days of modems and the slow, incremental innovation of the AT&T products, to the rise of NET in the wake of the uncertainty following the breakup of that monopoly, datacom companies' fortunes depended on the success of products that could send bits faster and more efficiently on the physical lines of the common carrier networks. Codex is the enduring example of the datacom company that had pioneered technology in the early market, rescued itself from near failure, and made repeated innovations that secured dominance in its core product category. While it failed to gain traction in markets outside its core business, it continued to innovate the high-speed leased line modem category into the late 1980s.

11.7 Summary of the Networking Market-Structure

The networking market-structure emerged from numerous entrepreneurial efforts that built on the research of packet-switching from government-sponsored projects such as ALOHAnet and ARPANET. With the development of the minicomputer, computers became more commonplace throughout many businesses and institutions, as did the need to connect these computers to terminals, peripheral devices, and other computers. Initially expressed by customers of the minicomputer companies, this need was largely left unmet, leaving the opportunity open for smaller companies and start-ups.

Early movers, like Datapoint with its proprietary networked computer systems, and Nestar with its focus on networking for the Apple II, saw their products gain early acceptance in small segments of the general computer market. While limited to computers from single vendors, the success of these early networking products provided proof that the market was real. But even before these early products, examples of networking technology were developed in disparate places, such as the manufacturing network that Ralph Ungermann managed at Collins Radio in the late 1960s; Jerry McDowell's work developing a network for the New Zealand banking system in the early 1970s; or the early in-house ring network co-designed in 1977 by Bill Farr at Prime Computers.

The engineers responsible for early implementations of networking often found inspiration in the same sources—pioneers mentioned in earlier chapters such as Donald Davies, Paul Baran, Louis Pouzin, Robert Metcalfe, and the engineers of the ARPANET. As important as published research was in the dissemination of knowledge about networking technology, the flow of ideas in the pools of engineering talent around universities and companies was even more fertile. Dave Farber's ring network at UCI drew inspiration from his association with Wayne Farmer and Ed Newhall at Bell Labs and would lead to the development of ring networks at MIT and later IBM and Proteon. Of seminal importance in the early networking industry was the community of engineers in two key organizations: former engineers from Zilog and Xerox PARC were responsible for the founding of four of the most successful networking companies of the 1980s: 3Com, UB, Bridge Communications, and Excelan.

The founding of three iconic networking start-ups, 3Com, UB, and Sytek in 1979, marked the end of the emergent stage of the networking market-structure. In their ability to raise capital and successfully market networking products, these companies demonstrated that the market was now viable. As these early start-ups began to compete for similar customers and distribution channels, the formation of a networking industry was taking shape. Early success tempted others to enter the market. Some established themselves in unique segments of the market, for example, Sytek, servicing campus area broadband networks, and Excelan, offering networking for high-end workstations. Other companies, like Bridge, tried to beat the early start-ups at their own game by acting quickly to introduce faster and cheaper products. Arguably the most significant decision to capitalize on a new segment of the LAN market was 3Com's move to go after the new PC market and abandon its initial market of minicomputers. Conceding their market leadership in the minicomputer business to the new start-up, Interlan, 3Com's early jump on the PC market eventually paid huge rewards. The ability to reduce the price of a network connection through skilled engineering and partnerships with chip manufacturers, and an innovative distribution strategy of selling through retailers, gave 3Com a significant early lead and dominant market share.

As the number of new independents grew, the industry was further altered by the entrance of the major computer companies such as DEC, Wang, and HP. DEC succeeded in capturing significant market share due in part to their alliance with Intel and Xerox. Wang, HP, and other minicomputer companies were also successful. The effect of the largest incumbent in the computer industry, IBM, was to stall the progression towards a dominant design and an ordered market, as it delayed release of its product to the large installed base of "Big Blue" firms. In the interim, it succeeded in putting its weight behind technical alternatives to the widespread adoption of Ethernet.

The eventual adoption of LAN standards established the long-awaited answer to the question customers had been asking since the beginning: "which technology should I buy?" With the rules defined, the industry could ensure a value proposition to the consumer. The result was a dramatic increase in the market. By 1984, the number of networking vendors had grown to over 100.[55] This was the height of the competitive stage of the market-structure. Differentiation in the market was driven both by customer demand and by the industry in the form of competing technologies, creating submarkets around manufacturing (token bus/MAP), the major incumbent (IBM's future token ring product), and the largest and fastest growing market segment (Ethernet).

As competition in the industry drove profit margins down, and the cost of staying competitive remained high, especially given the high cost of R&D spending, consolidation began to play a significant role in the early evolution of the market-structure. By 1988, UB, Bridge, and Interlan had been acquired. Sytek had struggled to recover from the loss of their IBM business, and CCI, after their spinoff from CDS, had begun to seek alternatives to its MAP strategy. Proteon was well placed to take advantage of IBM's work in securing a token ring standard and to service the broad market of Big Blue's installed user base. Like DEC, Proteon was also poised to become an early player in the internetworking market.

11.8 In Perspective

At the end of 1988 many of the companies observed throughout this history had been acquired, or were in decline, symptoms of the challenges faced by firms in maturing markets. What might have seemed a logical source of growth for these companies, expanding into new markets, in fact were not. With few exceptions, data communications companies were unable to succeed selling products in the

55. Datapro report on local area networks, November 1983, 114.

networking market, just as many of the networking companies were unable or chose not to expand into the internetworking market.

Executive decisions concerning company strategy were fundamental to the fates of these companies. Even companies with an abundance of talent could not survive with a troubled business plan. Leadership with a strong vision and an ability to provide company focus is essential for long term success. The difficulty of trying to balance differences of opinion on strategy is told repeatedly by executives of many of these companies, especially UB, 3Com, CDS, Excelan, and Codex.

Strategic partnerships were also key to company survival. In data communications, this often meant merging with a larger company or finding a customer willing to fund and license product development, as Paradyne did with Datran. In networking, it meant aligning with universities and other centers of cutting-edge research, as Proteon was connected to MIT, 3Com to Xerox PARC, and UB and Excelan to Zilog. Development and manufacturing partnerships were also important. In the case of Ethernet, these partnerships helped companies to establish early gains in adoption, thereby overcoming early technical shortcomings. In the case of token bus, promising arrangements with industry leading companies helped fuel the optimism around the technology but could not overcome technical challenges (especially RF modems) and an untested market. While aligning with IBM helped the customers and vendors that had chosen to adopt token ring, market gains would be hampered by IBM's lateness to market and the new paradigm of desktop computing in which customers were no longer loyal to one vendor but instead valued interconnectivity.

In the late 1980s, the demand for computer networks continued its fast-paced growth. As the markets of data communications and networking became highly competitive, a new market for internetworking products ushered in the next phase of rapid growth in computer communications. The technological challenges were significant, as was the lack of consensus on which strategies would prove to be the most effective. Both Proteon and DEC were examples of successful companies that were able to transition from building networking products to developing products to address the needs of the internetworking market. These companies and a new breed of start-ups presented in Chapter 13 will build the new industry of internetworking, connecting a growing number of disparate LANs. But first we need to revisit the theme of government-market boundaries, specifically the varieties of government support for internetworking.

Government Support for Internetworking, 1983–1988

12.1 Overview

As we have seen in Chapters 10 and 11, the networking market-structure reached a phase of stability in the early to mid 1980s. But as the emergence of Ethernet as an industry standard and quickly emerging dominant design, it also raised a bigger question: how could users combine networks into internetworks?

This question vexed administrators in multiple agencies in the United States federal government who used many different tools at their disposal to hasten the emergence of the internetworking market-structure. In this chapter we focus on two agencies that proved especially influential: DARPA, within the Department of Defense (DOD), and the National Bureau of Standards, within the Department of Commerce.[1] In previous chapters we saw these agencies flex their muscle to invest in research and development, recruit and train students and full-time staff, arrange for purchasing and procurement of computer communications products, and sponsor workshops and demonstrations. Despite the era's prevailing rhetoric of "free markets," these government agencies took deliberate steps to nudge internetworking markets towards maturity—with some impressive results.

By the early 1980s, internetworking had become a two-horse race between the TCP/IP protocols championed by DARPA and the OSI architecture and protocols

1. After 1988, NBS became NIST, National Institute for Standards and Technology. There were, of course, many other government and NGO organizations that contributed, notably the National Science Foundation with its NSFNET that began operations in 1986. See Janet Abbate. 2010. Privatizing the Internet: Competing visions and chaotic events, 1987–1995. *IEEE Annals of the History of Computing* 32, 10–22; Shane Greenstein. 2015. *How the Internet Became Commercial*. Princeton University Press; Karen D. Frazer. 1996. *NSFNET: A Partnership for High-Speed Networking Final Report, 1987–1995*. Merit Network Inc., Ann Arbor, MI.

developed through international collaboration. Once again, as we saw with networking, a few motivated entrepreneurs played essential roles in advocating for their own respective visions of the future. Vinton Cerf and Robert Kahn had been catalysts for DARPA—but by the early 1980s they were looking to pass the baton to other members of the community. To accomplish this, they needed to build new institutions and governance mechanisms, which we describe in this chapter.

At the same time, leaders in other agencies in the US federal government voiced their clear preference for networks using OSI protocols, not TCP/IP. Two especially active advocates, John Heafner and Robert Rosenthal, worked for the Bureau of Standards. They participated in standards committees, organized gatherings of vendors and users lobbied officials in other federal agencies, and stimulated collective action amongst private actors. Likewise, in Europe computer scientists and bureaucrats were active in a variety of settings, trying to influence the technical and economic outcomes of internetworking through national governments, Europe-wide collaborations, and industrial policy at the volatile intersections of "national champion" computer firms and national telecom monopolies.

The energetic work of Cerf, Kahn, Heafner, and Rosenthal exemplifies some of the complexities of advocacy that stretched across *government–market boundaries*. A close look at their work illustrates the shallowness of caricatures of the private sector as the sole engine of innovation and the public sector as an antagonist at best, or clueless, bumbling bureaucrats at worst. At his inaugural address in 1981, President Ronald Reagan famously said, "Government is not the solution to our problem; government is the problem."[2] He may not have known that, deep in the bureaucracy that he oversaw, civil servants worked feverishly to sponsor research, negotiate standards, set rules for procurement, and coax private companies to work together. Their goal: to make internetworking happen.

12.2 TCP/IP Internet

12.2.1 DARPA Continues Its Commitment, 1980–1983

The DOD funded networking research as early as the mid-1960s, primarily through ARPA. The anecdote from 1966 (see Chapter 3), where ARPA-IPTO Director Robert Taylor had three different terminals on his desk to access three different incompatible computers, was only the tip of the non-interoperable iceberg in networking. ARPA's subsequent sponsorship of the ARPANET and other computer research aimed to solve this problem that market forces alone were not solving. Between the

2. Ronald Reagan, "Inaugural Address," January 20, 1981.

1960s and the 1980s, IPTO funding nurtured a community of expert users and network designers who, over time, spread knowledge of packet switching in universities, private companies, and start-ups. Nevertheless, the plague of incompatibility was unrelenting as ARPA and many other organizations designed and built new networks. The cumulative effect of this patronage was to leapfrog market forces and push TCP/IP into operational use. Such a strategy proved far more efficient than battling with the likes of IBM, Xerox, Honeywell, and foreign governments and computer companies in national and international standards bodies.

There were many people who made profound contributions to the growth of the ARPANET and the emergence of TCP/IP as viable protocols for internetworking. In the 1970s and 1980s, the contributions of two researchers—Vint Cerf and Robert Kahn—stood out over the others, for two reasons. The first is technical: Cerf and Kahn were the two authors of the initial TCP paper and specification in 1973 and 1974, and they played leading roles in discussions about how to adapt and update TCP to be useful beyond its native environment of the ARPANET. The second reason is organizational: Cerf and Kahn both had leadership roles within DARPA, and they used the authority of these roles to shape the future of their internetworking protocols as well as the broader community.

To recap some highlights described in detail in Chapters 5 and 8, Cerf and Kahn led the development of the TCP/IP protocols starting in 1973. Cerf and Kahn advocated for international adoption of TCP, for example, through the meetings of the International Network Working Group (INWG). Despite their lack of success with INWG, Cerf and Kahn understood that their mandate was to produce useful internetworking solutions for their patron. As a result, they continued to work on TCP and IP, and lobbied the US DOD to make TCP/IP an official communication protocol standard. In January 1980, after a year of code testing, their colleague and friend Jon Postel published the two new protocols, TCP and IP, as Request for Comments and simultaneously as DOD standards.[3]

Once published as standards, the hard work of converting all networks, including ARPANET, to TCP/IP began. The date of January 1, 1983, was set for the cutover of ARPANET to TCP/IP. There were encouraging early signs of progress. By August 1980, DARPA-funded researchers had implemented the new TCP/IP protocol in 12 gateways interconnecting 10 networks.[4]

3. Jon Postel, ed. 1980. DOD Standard Internet Protocol. RFC 760, http://tools.ietf.org/rfc/rfc760; Jon Postel, ed. 1980. DOD Standard Transmission Control Protocol. RFC 761, http://tools.ietf.org/rfc/rfc761.

4. Jonathan B. Postel, Carl A. Sunshine, and Danny Cohen. 1981. The ARPA Internet protocol. *Computer Networks* 5 (July 1981), 261–271.

The intended cutover date for ARPANET, January 1, 1983, remained several years in the future. But the project timeline was not without perils. First, Bolt Beranek & Newman (BBN) had to make ARPANET's Subnet TCP/IP-compatible. Then came the complicated issue of creating host TCP/IP code for all the essential computers connected to ARPANET. There was no desire to let each host site create its own version of TCP/IP, a painful lesson learned in creating the original host software now to be replaced. In 1981, DARPA awarded seven contracts to create computer host code (see Table 12.1).

Bill Joy, a computer science graduate student at Berkeley working on one of the DARPA contracts, was given the TCP/IP code from BBN to integrate into the upgraded version of UNIX that Joy was developing for the VAX computer.[5] In mid-1982, Berkeley released a new version of UNIX that included a version of TCP/IP. But it was not the version of TCP/IP that BBN had written for DARPA. Bill Joy, who had been given the task of incorporating the TCP/IP code from BBN, found it lacking and decided to rewrite it. Kahn remembers: "Bill Joy just didn't feel like this [the BBN code] was as efficient as he could do if he did it himself. And so Joy just rewrote it. Here the stuff was delivered to him, he said, 'That's a bunch of junk,' and he redid it. There was no debate at all. He just unilaterally redid it."[6] A company, university, or other user could now purchase a UNIX source code license from Berkeley for $32,000 and receive TCP/IP code essentially free. As noted in Chapter 9, Berkeley sold over 1,000 licenses within 18 months.

Others began porting the code to other computers and, overnight, XNS had a real competitor: a competitive product not constrained by the release of higher layer functionality. The diffusion of TCP/IP was also aided by the agreement Kahn

Table 12.1 **TCP/IP implementations**

Contract With	Implementation
BBN (Bolt Beranek & Newman)	BBN C-Series Systems; TOPS-20
MIT	IBM PC
University of California, Berkeley	BSD Unix 4.2
University of California, Los Angeles	IBM Mainframes running MVS O/S
University of Wisconsin	IBM Mainframes running VM O/S

Source: *Data Communications*, November 1987, 221.

5. *Data Communications*, November 1987, 221; Jon Postel, ed. 1981. Internet Protocol. RFC 791, https://tools.ietf.org/html/rfc791; Jon Postel, ed. 1981. Transmission Control Protocol. RFC 793, https://tools.ietf.org/html/rfc793.

6. Robert Kahn, oral history interview with James L. Pelkey, February 22, 1988, Reston, VA. Computer History Museum, Mountain View, CA. Available from https://archive.computerhistory.org/resources/access/text/2016/10/102717241-05-01-acc.pdf.

had made with Gordon Bell and Sam Fuller of DEC for DEC to sell bundled VAXs at low prices to universities. Kahn remembers: "I convinced Gordon Bell and Sam Fuller that if they made these VAXs available, people would explore interesting ways to do distributed computing on them, and that was going to be the wave of the future, and they might as well understand it."[7]

With the sudden widespread availability of TCP/IP for VAX, and the subsequent porting of Joy's TCP/IP code to other computers, momentum swept TCP/IP forward in a way no one could have planned. Once again, DARPA played a critical role in determining the future of local area networking as a consequence of its primary objective of upgrading ARPANET protocols (just as IMPs and TIPs had been used to create an early version of LANs). It is notable that DARPA's role here resembles some dynamics of path dependencies that have been richly described by the economist Paul David.[8] In this case, DARPA's objectives did not necessarily align with that of leaders outside of DARPA, particularly those in Europe and active in OSI, who had a different vision of internetworking. Rather, DARPA officials—including Cerf and Kahn, at the center of the action—remained committed to making TCP/IP operational and widely available.

To accomplish this, DARPA remained focused on its rapidly approaching January 1983 deadline to convert ARPANET to TCP/IP. Converting ARPANET to TCP/IP required leaders and plans. That job fell to Dan Lynch, who in 1980 left Stanford Research Institute to become responsible for the computer facilities at the University of Southern California's Information Science Institute (ISI), the biggest node on the ARPANET. Just as Roberts before him, Lynch would have to resort to strong-armed tactics to force the users of ARPANET to convert to TCP/IP. Cerf remembers one attention-getting tactic: "Somewhere in the middle of 1982, we turned off the NCP capability for one entire day on the ARPANET, [so that] the only people able to communicate [were] the ones who had implemented TCP. There was a lot of noise as a result, but it got attention."[9]

Complaints and problems intensified as summer became September. Lynch recalls their strategy to increase reliance on the new protocols: "I remember when we really started getting serious in September and had TCP-only half days and then

7. Kahn interview, Computer History Museum.

8. David, P. A. (1985). Clio and the Economics of QWERTY. *The American Economic Review*, *75*(2), 332–337; David, P. A. Path dependence: a foundational concept for historical social science. *Cliometrica* **1**, 91–114 (2007).

9. Vinton Cerf, oral history interview with James L. Pelkey, February 8, 1988, Reston, VA. Computer History Museum, Mountain View, CA. Available from https://archive.computerhistory.org/resources/access/text/2015/11/102738017-05-01-acc.pdf.

whole days and then there was sort of a monthly event and then I think we did a three day one around Thanksgiving."[10]

With the conversion date of January 1, 1983, looming ever larger, the white light of attention fell first on Lynch and then onto Clark, whom Cerf had appointed Chairman of the Internet Working Group in September 1981. Cerf was increasingly moving to the periphery of the action and felt the time had come for him to leave DARPA. When he announced his resignation from DARPA to join MCI and manage their email efforts in December 1982, the news seemed hardly noteworthy to those in the trenches scrambling to prepare for New Year's Eve. Lynch, to commemorate the toil of the occasion, used his own money to make 500 white pins with a message in red: "I survived the TCP transition, 1/1/83." And they did survive for the transition happened on schedule—at least for some of the aRPANET sites. Several sites missed the deadline, illustrating the difficulty of switching from "locked-in" host protocols. So notwithstanding crashes and lingering problems, one could no longer doubt TCP/IP worked, for it now could run over networks ranging from Ethernet to ARPANET.

To this point, the growth of TCP/IP had not been a function of market forces but rather of the continued sponsorship of the US government. Such sponsorship had served TCP/IP's promoters well for the purposes of research and implementation. But as OSI gained support amongst vendors, standards committees, and large customers—including the very US government agencies that sponsored TCP/IP—leaders in the TCP/IP community saw the need to improve and promote their protocols more aggressively if they were to succeed.

To accomplish the twin goals of improvement and promotion, TCP/IP advocates gradually improvised new governance structures. This effort had been underway since the late 1970s with the 1979 creation of the Internet Configuration Control Board (ICCB), which Cerf created as an advisory group. Kahn later referred to this group as a "kitchen cabinet" of knowledgeable people in the field.[11] Kahn told an interviewer in 1990:

> When we started the Internet program in the mid-1970s, originally it was just me in the office running the program. And after Vint was hired, then it was just Vint running the program with me to kibitz. And he was so good at what he did that he basically had everything in his head. What I worried about

10. Daniel Lynch, oral history interview with James L. Pelkey, February 16, 1988, Cupertino, CA. Computer History Museum, Mountain View, CA. Available from https://archive.computerhistory.org/resources/access/text/2016/02/102717120-05-01-acc.pdf.

11. Robert Kahn, oral history interview by Judy E. O'Neill, April 24, 1990, Reston, VA. Charles Babbage Institute, University of Minnesota, Minneapolis.

> was what would happen if he got hit by a truck? Number two, what would happen if he would ever have to leave? And number three, how was anybody else in the community ever going to be part of the thinking process. So he set up, after some discussions, a kind of kitchen cabinet, if you will, of knowledgeable people that he would convene periodically. These were mostly the workers in the field, the key people who were implementing protocols.... When [Cerf] left, that group stayed intact.[12]

Kahn understood the importance of a stable leadership structure that could persist after the founding figures—he and Cerf—had departed. If progress was to continue, and community cohesion was to persist, the efforts of this next generation of leaders would be crucial.

When Cerf stepped down as the head of the ARPA Internet program in December 1982, he was replaced by Barry Leiner. Leiner continued along the path of increasing formalization in governance and decision-making about the Internet. In 1984, he disbanded the ICCB and created the Internet Advisory Board (IAB). One notable feature of the IAB was the creation of task forces to facilitate specialized discussions on technical issues such as gateway algorithms, privacy, and security. Leiner believed this structure could accommodate the increasing numbers of engineers and computer experts who were using the ARPANET or TCP/IP and wanted a seat at the table in discussions about future developments.[13]

The IAB's strategy was to create two distinct groups. The first, called the Internet Architecture Task Force, would focus on the long-term architectural direction of TCP/IP. The second, the Internet Engineering Task Force (IETF), would focus on the Internet protocols for operations and engineering in the near-term. The IETF immediately became the center of gravity for Internet standards, growing from 21 people at its first meeting in 1986 to over 100 attendees at each of its three meetings in 1988.[14] The rising interest in these technical meetings mirrored the enthusiastic adoption of TCP/IP protocols. One measure of this enthusiasm was the sharp increase in host computers on the TCP/IP Internet, which increased by more than two orders of magnitude in the mid-1980s: from 235 hosts in May 1982, to 1,961 hosts in October 1985, to 56,000 hosts in October 1988. In an era of strong enthusiasm for nurturing commercial "spin-off" applications of DOD research, the IAB

12. Kahn interview, Charles Babbage Institute.

13. For a detailed analysis of the shifting institutional landscape in the IAB, see Andrew L. Russell. 2014. *Open Standards and the Digital Age: History, Ideology & Networks*. Cambridge University Press, New York, 234–241.

14. Internet Engineering Task Force, "Past Meetings," https://www.ietf.org/meeting/past.html.

and IETF could be considered as organizational spin-offs from DARPA's extended investments in packet-switched networking.

IAB members also took steps to champion TCP/IP in the private sector by teaching equipment vendors about the features and advantages of TCP/IP. Once again, Dan Lynch provided a spark. Lynch, who was instrumental in managing the ARPANET's transition to TCP in 1983, was now a consultant. He worked with the IAB to plan a workshop in Monterrey, CA, and invited equipment vendors to learn about TCP/IP. Lynch saw the event as an attempt to get "the apostles of TCP to come out of their ivory towers" and provide some guidance for vendors implementing their protocols.[15] Lynch recalls:

> The dozen or two dozen who actually built this stuff, I went to them and said: "You guys have failed. You built this beautiful thing, and the world is starting to use it, and they're abusing it, and you have failed to communicate to them what its real potency is, where it's really headed, what problems it's really headed to solve. They're just using it for these little small things, and you've got to go awaken them." And they did. They loved that. They said, "sure." [. . .] So I put together a conference [in Monterey in August of '86], invitation only. . . That was an outrageously successful conference.[16]

This conference, the first "TCP/IP Vendors Workshop," featured a mix of leaders from the TCP/IP research community and representatives from 65 vendors, such as Ungermann-Bass and Excelan. But there was a sticking point: how would anyone ensure that all TCP/IP-based products would implement the protocols in a consistent manner? Vendor representatives were disappointed that no certification and conformance testing process existed. Others, such as Judith Estrin at Bridge Communications, worried that neither Lynch nor the IAB had any authority to declare industry standards.[17] A marketing manager at Ungermann-Bass, Barton Burstein, summarized the problem in 1987:

> At the OSI side there's no product. At MAP, GM has funded a very large technical staff. COS [Corporation for Open Systems] has a tremendous budget. Then look at TCP/IP with its number of customers and vendors. It's five to

15. Lynch interview, Computer History Museum.

16. Lynch interview, Computer History Museum.

17. Susan Kerr. 1987. Stuck in square one. *Datamation*, March 1, 1987. And Paulina Borsook. 1987. TCP/IP and interoperability: Separating myth from reality. *Data Communications*, August 1987, 60–61.

six times more dense or populous than OSI, and you've got Dan Lynch and his answering machine.[18]

Lynch's belief in TCP/IP, experience as a consultant to Excelan, and entrepreneurial spirit pushed him along. He continued organizing vendor conferences to promote TCP, including the "TCP/IP Interoperability Conference" in Monterrey on March 16–19, 1987; the "2nd TCP/IP Interoperability Conference" in Arlington, VA, on December 1–4, 1987; and the "TCP/IP Interoperability Exhibition and Solutions Showcase" in Santa Clara on September 28–30, 1988. It was at this latter conference, in 1988, where Lynch debuted a slick new title: Interop. We'll take a closer look at Interop—and the companies and products that populated it—at the end of our next chapter, Chapter 13.

In between conferences, Lynch founded a newsletter, *Connexions: The Interoperability Report*, which he described as an "attempt to satisfy the need for information exchange between users, vendors, and the R&D community." His editorial advisory board included TCP/IP leaders such as Vint Cerf, David Clark, and Jon Postel. The newsletter itself explained the various technical concepts and listed over 140 vendors that were offering or developing TCP/IP products.[19]

12.2.2 US Federal Agencies Lend Support to TCP/IP

The National Science Foundation (NSF) also provided some support for TCP/IP when it launched the NSFnet in 1985. At first, the goal was to link together five supercomputer centers with custom-built routers designed by David Mills at the University of Delaware. His "fuzzball" routers used TCP/IP since the purpose of the NSFnet was to connect the NSF-funded supercomputers with campus and regional networks through the ARPANET. By July 1988, 217 networks were connected with NSFnet.[20] Subsequent phases of NSFnet expansion provided access to researchers more generally—but there was no intention, at least during the 1980s, for it to meet the needs of businesses, private users, or anyone outside the computer-related research community.[21]

18. Kerr, "Stuck in square one." Lynch also included a not-so-subtle jab at the slow pace of OSI standards and product development: in contrast to the Corporation for Open Systems (COS) that NBS formed to promote OSI, Lynch dubbed his vendor alliance the Coalition for *Working* Systems (CWS) [emphasis added]. In the quote, the author changed ISO to OSI for clarity's sake.

19. Lynch interview, Computer History Museum; *Connexions*, Premiere Issue Spring 1987.

20. Dennis Jennings et al. 1986. 'Computer networking for scientists. Science 231, 474, 943–950; David L. Mills. 1988. The fuzzball. *Proc. ACM Special Interest Group on Data Comm. Symp.* ACM Press, 115–122; Frazer, *NSFNET*, 5.

21. The privatization of the NSFnet backbone eventually would become a key turning point for the widespread adoption of the TCP/IP Internet. See NSF report; "Project Solicitation for Management

A complementary report was published in November 1987 by the Federal Coordinating Council for Science, Engineering and Technology (FCCSET). This report was requested by the White House Office of Science and Technology Policy, in response to a charge from the US Congress in 1986. The FCCSET group, chaired by Gordon Bell, recommended the use of DARPA's protocols in the construction of an advanced computer network to interconnect academic, industrial, and government research facilities in the US. Membership included representatives from the Departments of Commerce, Defense, Energy, as well as NASA, NSF, National Institutes of Health, and the intelligence community. In 1988, a National Research Council committee chaired by Leonard Kleinrock published a study, Toward a National Research Network, that stressed the importance of interoperable, high-speed networks. These findings were supported enthusiastically by Senator Al Gore, who would go on to sponsor the highly influential High Performance Computing Act of 1991, commonly referred to as the "Gore Bill."[22]

Clearly, TCP/IP had some signs of accomplishment by the 1980s, as well as some indications of continued momentum and support. But would it be enough? Demand for internetworking solutions was rising, and OSI had long been the favorite to be the global standard for internetworking. The best illustration of the uphill struggle for TCP/IP came in discussions within the DOD—the agency that sponsored TCP/IP. In 1983, DOD and National Bureau of standards wanted to compare two competing transport protocols, TCP and its counterpart in OSI called TP-4, to inform their purchasing decisions.[23] They asked the National Research Council to study the issue, which ended with the NRC's 1985 report. The report recommended the immediate adoption of TP-4 and TCP as co-standards—and to

---

and Operation of the NSFnet Backbone Network," NSF 87-37, National Science Foundation, 15 Jun. 1987; Janet Abbate. 2010. Privatizing the Internet: Competing visions and chaotic events, 1987–1995. *IEEE Annals of the History of Computing* 32, 10–22; Shane Greenstein. 2015. *How the Internet Became Commercial: Innovation, Privatization, and the Birth of a New Network*. Princeton University Press. As Abbate, Greenstein, and others have documented, the eventual expansion of the TCP/IP Internet allowed interconnection among users in a variety of networks, such as Bulletin Board Systems, regional networks, private networks, and the Arpanet and NSFNET.

22. National Research Council (U.S.)., Kleinrock, L., & National Science Foundation (U.S.). (1988). *Toward a national research network*. Washington, D.C: National Academy Press.

23. John F. Heafner, oral history interview by James L. Pelkey, May 5, 1988, Birmingham, MA. Computer History Museum, Mountain View, CA. Available from https://archive.computerhistory.org/resources/access/text/2020/04/102792040-05-01-acc.pdf; National Research Council. 1985. *Transport Protocols for Department of Defense Data Networks*. National Academy Press, Washington, DC.

"move ultimately toward exclusive use" of OSI protocols.[24] The conclusion from DOD was clear: the international OSI standards, wherever they could be used to "support military requirements," should be "implemented as rapidly as possible to obtain maximum economic and interoperability benefits."[25]

These discussions within DOD, and the tenor and conclusions of the 1985 NRC report more generally, were among many indications that TCP/IP would be replaced or absorbed by OSI. OSI had strong support from industry, and, in November 1985, *Data Communications* had declared that OSI was "heading for full bloom."[26] But there was a catch: the OSI protocols remained unavailable as a "commercial offering." This raised the stakes for companies, as well as for agents of coordination—standards bodies and sympathetic government agencies—to help OSI reach its commercial potential.

12.3 OSI's Champions in US Federal Agencies

In the early 1980s, there was no notable opposition from DoJ or FCC for internetworking. Indeed, their vigilance over IBM and AT&T—such as Bernard Strassburg at the FCC and Bill Baxter at Department of Justice—cleared the way for entrepreneurs to bring new technologies to market. This permissive environment was nurtured even further by research support from DARPA (as explained above), and strong interest from NBS to nurture and support networking and internetworking.

12.3.1 National Bureau of Standards

In January 1979, the NBS hired John Heafner to manage a newly created Systems and Network Architecture Division (SNAD) of the Institute for Computer Sciences and Technology of NBS. All Federal Government local area networking and OSI standards responsibility would thereafter reside in SNAD. Heafner explains the action of the US Congress:

> NBS has a mandate from Congress to provide standards for ADP [automated data processing], communications and so forth. It's part of their role. The program was reviewed here at NBS in the mid-to-late '70s, as to why they hadn't done anything significant, and the answer coming out of that was:

24. Donald C. Latham, quoted in Jon Postel. 1985. A DOD Statement on the NRC Report. May 1985, RFC 945. See also "No ISO protocol yet for Defense," *Data Communications*, April 1985, 15.

25. "No ISO protocol yet for Defense," *Data Communications*, April 1985, 15.

26. "OSI heading for full bloom," *Data Communications*, November 1985, 16.

> "Yes, they haven't done anything significant, and the reason is they don't have enough funding." In 1978, the budget was trebled.[27]

Heafner was well prepared for his new assignment. In 1969, he was responsible for connecting RAND to the ARPANET. When the ARPA-sponsored research group at RAND, led by the visionary Keith Uncapher, spun out in 1972 to become the Information Sciences Institute (ISI) affiliated with the University of Southern California, Heafner joined ISI. He then worked at ISI until he moved to the NBS in 1979. Thus, he was well aware of many of the dynamics impacting the strategy he would need to fashion.

The tremendous changes re-shaping local and wide area networking technologies had three dimensions: First was the obvious fact that the Federal Government was going to buy a lot of computers and increasingly want those computers to share information. Second, IBM, which was the largest vendor of computers to the Federal Government, had zealously protected its proprietary software. And third, there were uncertain outcomes from the considerable investment and knowledge the DOD had in the TCP/IP protocols.

Heafner remembers:

> Sort of the way I put it when I came here is that we will have won when DOD buys OSI from IBM. We will have covered all the bases, getting the largest supplier to supply to the largest consumer, and do it in a standardized way. Our thrust from the beginning was to work in ISO, and to some extent in CCITT [International Telegraph and Telephone Consultative Committee], to make sure that government needs were covered when those protocols were being developed.[28]

During 1982, NBS held meetings with companies to learn how to move OSI forward. In Chapters 5 and 8 we met Robert Rosenthal, who had been active in networking standards since the early 1970s. Rosenthal viewed his role as providing support for collaboration and growth. Rosenthal remembers:

> In order to pull this off, we had to get some agreements. That's the key word, "agreements." We had to get the people highest up in these organizations to commit resources. We had to get a commitment of the CEOs, somebody with signature authority, had to be able to say: "Here's the check, you make it happen. Pull out all the stops. OSI is important. Make it happen." We had to get the technical people to ask the question: "Make what happen?" We had to say: "Make this happen," and we had to lay it out for them. They came

27. Heafner interview, Computer History Museum.

28. Heafner interview, Computer History Museum.

> back to us immediately and said: "There's too many options here." A DEC guy says: "I'm going to implement it this way, and the IBM guy's going to implement it that way, and we're at different altitudes. Why don't we go to the National Bureau of Standards, where we can all be peaceful, sit around the table, our techie guys can sit around and talk to each other without all the fears that you might have," non-disclosure and all that stuff, we can deal with that here at NBS, "let's ask the Bureau of Standards, good solid government agency with a good, strong reputation, if they'll do that for us." So industry came to the Bureau of Standards and said: "Please help us. Put together a workshop that looks like a big umbrella where out techies can get together, roll up their sleeves, and agree on what it is we'll implement." And we said: "That's a good idea."[29]

Rosenthal further reflected on how his mandate—and therefore the tactics he used—differed substantially from advocates of TCP/IP, such as Vint Cerf. Rosenthal told Pelkey in 1988, "The Department of Defense, at the time, would throw money at a problem until it got solved. Vint Cerf and company went off to invent TCP at the time because they got lots of DOD money to make networks work. We said: "Fine, you do whatever you need to do, but our approach is to work with industry."[30]

The NBS commitment to work with industry was evident in the events that they organized and sponsored. One example was the first Implementors Workshop at NBS in February 1983, where participants agreed that a proof-of-concept network and public demonstration could encourage companies to commit to OSI, produce OSI products, and assure their products all worked together, somehow.

12.3.2 OSINET, a Sandbox for Interoperability

Heafner aired a proposal one evening at the National Computer Conference (NCC) in Las Vegas in June 1984, aiming to solve a problem vexing vendors: products that would not interoperate. (See Figure 12.1 for the trajectory of OSI in the United States.) He recalled in a 1988 interview:

> I presented a white paper proposing the OSINET to the vendors participating in the NCC '84 in Las Vegas. At that time, it was called the NBS-CatNet, or concatenated network. It was just several pages of notes, proposing: "Do you want to continue this work?" Vendors do not want to key up for a demo every year or two or whatever. What we needed was some sandbox where we

29. Robert Rosenthal, interview by James L. Pelkey, May 4, 1988, Washington, DC. Computer History Museum, Mountain View, CA. Available from https://archive.computerhistory.org/resources/access/text/2020/04/102792038-05-01-acc.pdf.

30. Rosenthal interview, Computer History Museum.

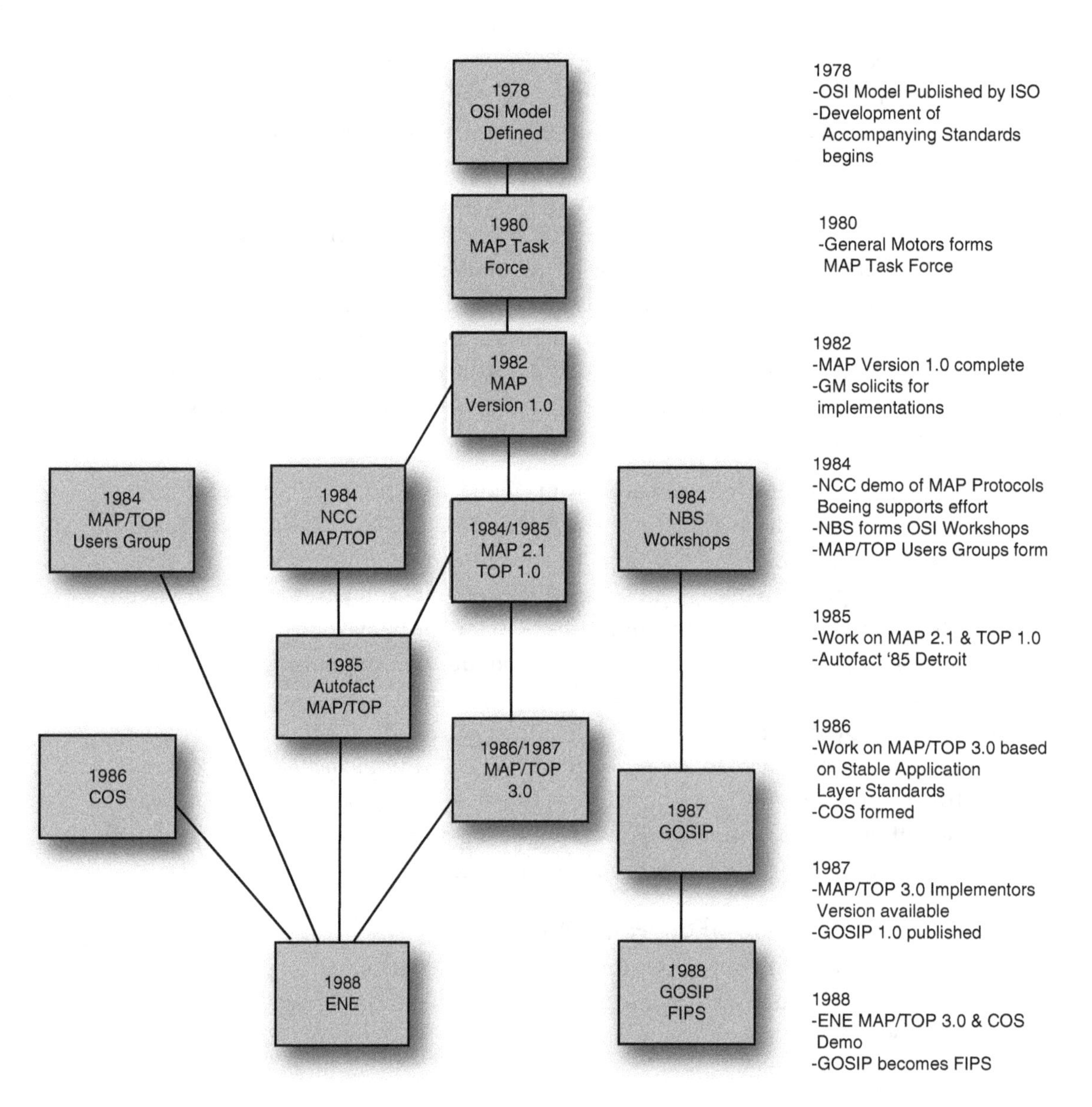

Figure 12.1 OSI history in the US. Illustration by James L. Pelkey and Loring G. Robbins. Source: RETIX Business Plan, February 1989.

could really play and do inter-operation testing and develop the test technology and methodology behind all of this. What was envisioned was a sandbox to play in, and that's what the OSINET is today. I credit Maris Graube with that idea.[31]

31. Heafner interview, Computer History Museum.

By the end of year 1984, the NBS finalized its first Federal Information Processing Standard (FIPS 107) titled: Local Area Networks: Baseband Carrier Sense Multiple Access with Collision Detection Access Method and Physical Layer Specifications and Link Layer Protocol.[32] The standard was expected to lead to considerable savings in government expenses and reduced network integration problems. As Rosenthal explained, "I get calls all the time from GSA, The Government Services Administration, saying: 'What is this FIPS 107?' And I say: 'It's this Technology,' and people say: 'Great.' Anyone in the government can buy products without all the paperwork and shenanigans. They say: 'Buy something that FIPS 107,' and it makes life very easy for ADP managers all over the government. Rosenthal, who had participated in the process from the very first IEEE 802 meeting in February 1980, remembers with pride in 1988:

> This is what I make: a Federal Information Processing Standard. It's the only one that we have in networking in the government right now, dated 1984, October 31st, and titled, "Local Area Networks: Baseband Carrier Sense Multiple Access with Collision Detection Access Method and Physical Layer Specifications and Link Layer Protocol." It's a mandatory procurement and standard. I told IEEE to let the world know, and put the fact on their cover for 802.3 and portions of 802.2. That's what this does. So I won at the game. I made the rules, played the game, and I won.[33]

The challenge for the 21 companies that had committed to demonstrating OSI protocols at Autofact '85 was to create products that could pass the conformance tests of OSI standards. As it would turn out, conformance testing was a very tall order. Even at that, conformance did not mean interoperability. And there might not have been any tests at all if not for the cooperation between NBS and the participating companies. Jerry Mulvenna, one of the NBS staff responsible for preparing for Autofact explains:

> This is an area of government/industry cooperation. When we developed the "internet" protocol for the test system for the Autofact, we couldn't do it. We didn't have all the in-house resources to do it. Three companies, Intel,

32. Federal Information Processing Standard 107. "Local Area Networks: Baseband Carrier Sense Multiple Access with Collision Detection Access Method and Physical Layer Specifications and Link Layer Protocol." National Bureau of Standards, Gaithersburg, MD, 1984.

33. Rosenthal continued, "Industry can go fight your ring and bus battles until you're blue in the face. We do not care anymore. We got what we wanted out of it. Let us move on to a richer set of problems: What's happening at the upper layers of OSI?" Rosenthal interview, Computer History Museum.

> Honeywell, and NCR, sent us people to work here full time at NBS for 4 or 5 months, to develop the test system that we needed to test out the "internet" protocol at Autofact.[34]

The organizers of the OSI demonstration knew they needed to prove to the world that OSI worked; that customers could now buy products to implement Manufacturing Automation Protocol (MAP), Technical and Office Protocols (TOP), and OSI-based internetworking solutions. Such solutions were directed at large manufacturers wanting to achieve productivity gains comparable to those attained in their office systems. General Motors, for example, bought equipment from over 100 vendors but lacked standards: hence its substantial support of MAP.[35] Customers (such as General Motors) that used a variety of information systems and networks would buy the next generation of internetworking products as long as it was clear that the ultimate goal of interoperability would be met. The OSI demonstration organizers felt both the pressure to make OSI launched and the weight of so much to do. There remained all the work left unfinished from NCC, the added complexity of integrating numerous interconnected networks, as well as the goal of substantially scaling up the sophistication of the demonstration. The good news was they would have their audience: the show drew a record 30,000 people with approximately 200 vendors exhibiting MAP-compatible and automation products.[36]

The OSI demonstration interconnected two locations: Detroit, MI, and London, England. In Cobb Hall, Detroit, there were three LANs: two token bus LANs, one from Concord Data Systems and one from INI, and a CSMA/CD LAN. These three LANs supported MAP and TOP applications as if one integrated LAN. They, in turn, were connected to a X.25 public data network that connected them "seamlessly" to another 5Mbps Concord Data Systems token bus LAN in London (see Figure 12.2). In addition to data processing equipment such as computers and terminals, a variety of factory automation devices, including robots, vision systems, and engineering workstations, let customers play three different applications: a custom-designed version of the ancient game Towers of Hanoi, or Hot Potato, or

34. Jerry Mulvenna, oral history interview by James L. Pelkey, May 5, 1988, Washington, DC. Computer History Museum, Mountain View, CA. Available from https://archive.computerhistory.org/resources/access/text/2020/04/102792039-05-01-acc.pdf.

35. Paulina Borsook. 1986 Kaminski of GM: A mission for a swift factory standard. *Data Communications*, March 1986, 109.

36. Pau Korzenlowski. 1985. GM's MAP steals show at Autofact. *Computerworld*, November 11, 1985, 1.

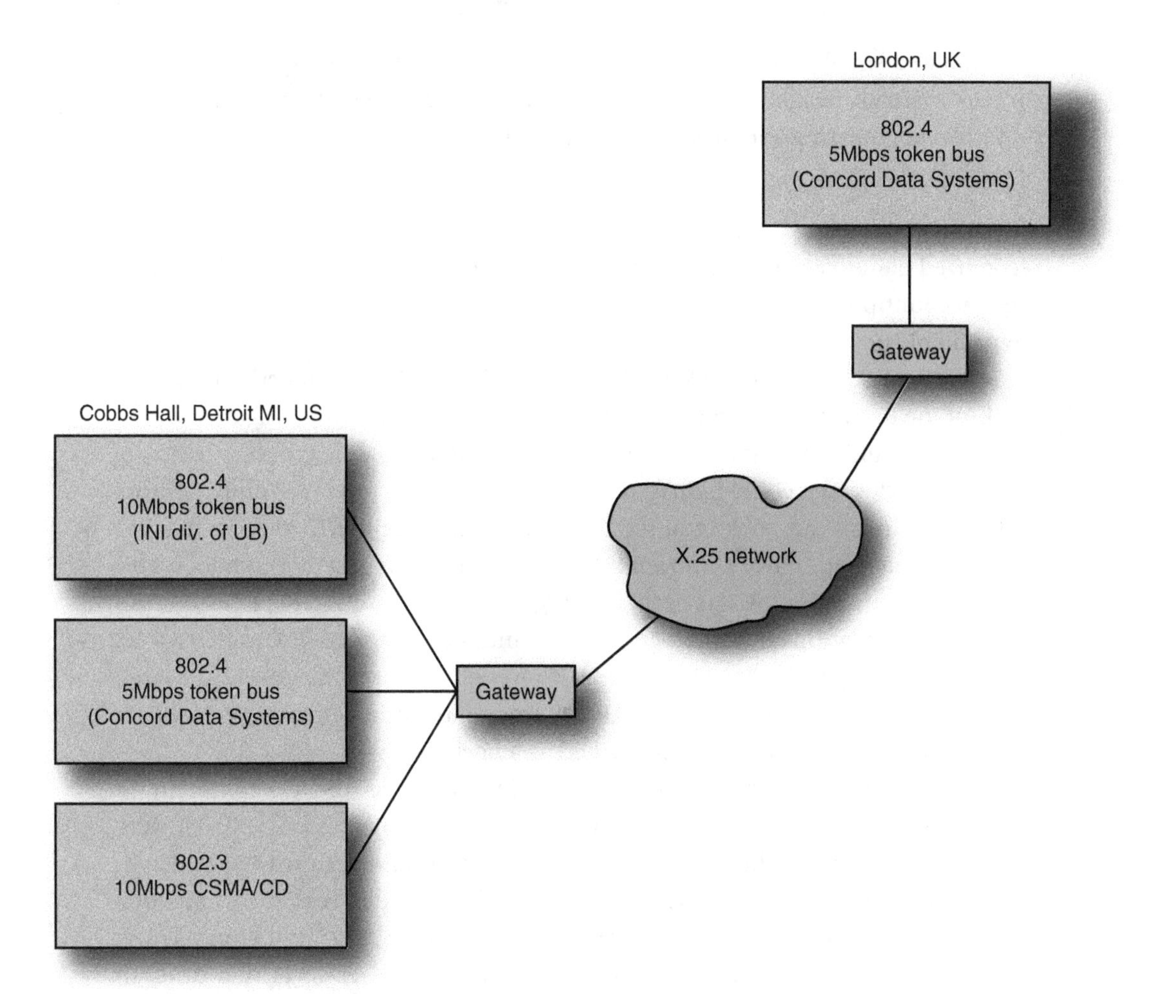

Figure 12.2 Autofact '85 OSI demonstration. Illustration by James L. Pelkey and Loring G. Robbins.

an interactive FTAM application.[37] The 21 companies demonstrating equipment were able to communicate across all five interconnected networks.[38] A later NBS publication would describe the demonstration:

> Using OSI protocols, Manufacturing Automation Protocol (MAP) and Technical and Office Protocol (TOP), the participating companies integrated a

37. Michael A. Kaminski. 1986. Autofact '85: Preview of new protocols in action. *IEEE Spectrum*, April 1986, 58–59.

38. Lee Mantelman. 1985. MAP: GM and Boeing promise a real four-bus circus. *Data Communications*, October 1985, 78–79.

> simulated small-scale factory operation, supported by office systems. The MAP systems, designed for the plant floor, and the TOP systems, designed for the engineering and office applications, were connected for information exchange.[39]

While well attended and hailed in the trade press as a success, even outsiders recognized demonstrations were different than working products for sale. As one press account put it, "On the show floor, there are plenty of demonstrations but few available products."[40]

So far, the NBS had played a key role in converting the OSI "connectionless" protocols of the Network and Transport Layers to Intermediate Systems against which the vendors could test their implementations. But there was much more work to do. The NBS concluded it could help in four ways: continue to host the Implementors Workshops, finish the work required for a functioning OSINET, continue testing gateways/routers on OSINET, and spin the NBS testing tools and methodologies off into a new organization(s). The corporate organizers also had their "plates full," so if everyone's attention and time were to be maintained, they had no time to waste. The first meeting of the TOP user group convened in December 1985. In March 1986, the MAP user group released MAP 2.1. Among its improvements was support for the 10Mbps token bus of INI, described as a backbone network.

Perhaps the most difficult challenge facing NBS was the development of OSINET from a promising idea to a useful platform. The objectives of OSINET were to verify tests results, facilitate vendor-to-vendor testing, and perform OSI research. But OSINET development was behind schedule since needed resources had been reassigned to Autofact. Mulvenna remembers that OSINET "Came along slowly because General Motors and others were promoting Autofact '85 at that time. In fact, all of our technical people were working on the IP Test System and refining the transport test system pre-Autofact '85." With the demonstration at Autofact now over, NBS shifted funds towards OSINET and solicited resources from outside. Vendors could connect to the NBS test gateways using the Accunet X.25 network, the same network recently created to interconnect the London and Detroit-based demonstrations of Autofact '85. One gateway enabled participating vendors to test if their products conformed to X.25, token bus, and CSMA/CD compliant implementations, as well as supportive applications. A second gateway was essential for

39. "Implementing Open Systems Interconnection," NBS Workshop for Implementors of Open Systems Interconnection, Institute for Computer Sciences and Technology.

40. Pau Korzenlowski. 1985. GM's MAP steals show at Autofact. *Computerworld*, November 11, 1985, 1.

the support, and hopefully the cooperation, of the DOD. It translated TCP/IP and OSI protocols, at least as far as the constraints of both protocols allowed. Any Government agency and organization supporting OSINET could use these gateways. Mulvenna, then responsible for OSINET, later described the organizations:

> OSINET is an organization of vendors and users that use an X.25 network as the backbone to test and demonstrate OSI protocols. It arose out of the need, in 1984 and 1985, when the vendors were getting together in one place and saying: "There's got to be a better way of at least running the interoperability testing of our products." Vendors are supporting and using OSINET because they want to be able to simulate the real live environment in which their products are going to be marketed... Vendors who will be selling competing products in the marketplace [are] cooperating with each other because they realize it is in their own best interest to do so.[41]

OSINET consisted of three elements: the network, a steering committee to manage the network and all the OSINET projects, and a technical committee to carry out the technical work assigned by the steering committee. Into 1988, NBS chaired the steering committee, operated an information center, administered the testing, and provided assistance to Federal Government agencies wishing to join OSINET.

The NBS served as the certifying organization for OSINET members for the first four layers of the ISO Model. OSINET could also meet the need for vendor-to-vendor interoperability testing. Vendors, once they interconnected their products over OSINET, could each run tests against the others' implementations. Customers might also require all of their vendors to pass NBS tests of interoperability. These tests reduced, even minimized, much of the risks of buying OSI implementations that might not interoperate with those from other vendors.

OSINET members also had access to a gateway the NBS had created for the DOD to convert TCP/IP protocols to those of OSI. Mulvenna explained in 1988: "We also have developed our application layer gateway here at NBS, which will transform the OSI protocols to the DOD protocols. It is to help the TCP/IP world move toward, and work with, the OSI world, to push them, gently, in the direction of OSI. The gateway will be available to both the DOD users and the OSI users on OSINET."[42]

Testing for conformance, interoperability, and TCP/IP-to-OSI conversion was important, but it was far from sufficient. An obvious barrier to market success was the growing installed base of TCP/IP implementations—since customers already

41. Mulvenna interview, Computer History Museum.

42. Mulvenna interview, Computer History Museum.

successfully using TCP/IP products would be less likely to replace working software.[43] Another problem could come from those customers wanting seven-layer interoperability tests, not just the four-layer tests developed and supported by the NBS. The NBS, however, had been clear that it was not going to perform similar roles for layers five through seven. Between the work it was doing to facilitate cooperation amongst private companies, and its efforts to persuade the DOD to adopt OSI, NBS staff had their hands full.

12.3.3 Government Support for OSI Implementations

To be responsible to the needs of vendors, the NBS created a non-profit organization, the Corporation for Open Systems (COS), to which it transferred non-exclusive rights of all its testing and gateway intellectual property and some of the related assets. COS would satisfy user needs for layers five to seven services. In 1985, the political climate was for government to shrink, not grow. Rosenthal recalls: "The fundamental concept was NBS had all this test technology, and Reagan had a privatization mindset, and still does, so what better thing than to try to get COS out of it?"[44]

COS would be the first of two initial recipients of the NBS testing tools and methodologies. Announced in the first quarter of 1986, the trade press warmly received the news.[45] There were still questions, such as IBM's participation, but the prevailing reaction was positive. It would now be up to COS "to develop a consistent set of specifications, test methods and services for all OSI layers and application protocols."[46]

All too quickly the initial optimism and hope turned to criticism. Some criticism was justified, such as over COS turning down the tools already developed by Europeans, or frequently changing the rules of membership. Then there was the appearance of the NBS not living up to its own standards. For example, in June 1987, *Data Communications* magazine reported that COS had selected TCP/IP for an internal network, not the equivalent OSI protocols. The reason: the computer vendor, SUN Microsystems, did not yet support OSI protocols. A COS researcher, Steve

43. William Stallings. 1988. TCP/IP: Should you feel guilty? A communications conundrum. *Data Communications*, May 1988, 294.

44. Rosenthal interview, Computer History Museum.

45. Viewpoint, "Standards group's strength must still be tested," *Data Communications*, February 1986, 13.

46. Implementing Open Systems Interconnection, NBS Workshop for Implementors of Open Systems Interconnection, 1986, p. 7.

Smith told a reporter, "I realize it may look bad, but we do plan to migrate [to the OSI protocols.]"[47]

Meanwhile, procurement of computer and networking equipment by the agencies of the Federal Government had continued. The lack of OSI products, as well as the bewildering choices of OSI protocols, encouraged the purchase of proven TCP/IP products. The same factors that inspired the creation of the MAP and TOP profiles in the private sector now plagued government procurement. Customers (in this case the Federal Government) wanted to reduce complexity, increase compatibility, and buy dependable and useful products. After all, the purpose of internetworking products was to make organizations more efficient and productive. Critical to user adoption, then, was overcoming the confusion that the development of networking and internetworking standards had left.

To solve many of these problems, in September 1986, NBS held the initial meeting of government agencies wanting to create a Government OSI Profile, or GOSIP. Representatives from 19 government organizations participated in the effort to "coordinate the acquisition and operation of OSI products by the Federal government."[48]

Once GOSIP was specified, the plan was for it to become a FIPS. Heafner remembers:

> When I first got here, the notion was: "Let's write down all of these specifications and go publish them as soon as we can as FIPS." Really, I stayed here until I felt my job was done, which was to write the initial GOSIP. That was all that was needed. We don't need to write, and to republish and re-track and maintain the same standards that ANSI, ISO, CCITT, and IEEE are doing. We simply need to write a procurement specification that references that work, and that's what has been done with GOSIP.[49]

47. Dataletter, "For own in-house network, COS selects TCP/IP," *Data Communications*, June 1987, 15.

48. Departments of Agriculture, Commerce, Defense, Energy, Education, Health and Human Services, Housing and Urban Development, Interior, Justice, Labor, Transportation, Treasury; the Environmental Protection Agency, General Services Administration, Library of Congress, NASA, National Communications System, National Science Foundation, and Office of Management and Budget. US Government OSI User's Committee, *US Government Open Systems Interconnection Profile (GOSIP) Version 1.0*, October 27, 1987.

49. Heafner interview, Computer History Museum.

The collaborations between federal agencies to produce GOSIP proceeded more harmoniously than Mulvenna anticipated, as he told Pelkey in 1988: "It's interesting that DOD was a major contributor to GOSIP. You would think that, of all the government agencies, they would have the most at stake in the status quo. That may be true for some of the people at the lower levels, but there has been a recognition by some of the higher people in DOD that OSI is the way to go."[50]

Mulvenna also noticed that the DOD agencies were "major contributors to the writing of the GOSIP document, major because they were more informed on the issues than perhaps some of the other government agencies, and they realized the services that the OSI protocols would provide them, because of their work with TCP/IP."[51] In other words, DOD officials did not take a combative approach to the choice between TCP/IP and OSI. Like many people experienced with internetworking, they believed that researchers and standards bodies would find ways to make TCP/IP compatible with the more comprehensive capabilities that OSI promised.

More encouraging signs were to come in 1988, including the formation of the International Public Sector Information Technology Group to coordinate GOSIPs published by Australia, Canada, Japan, Sweden, the United States, the United Kingdom, and West Germany.[52] Their focus on standards for public procurement complemented the detailed discussions within OSI committees, where the details of specifications emerged slowly and at times irrationally. The inclusive process was messy, as all high-stakes bureaucratic negotiations are. But despite the sniping of critics, and some occasional displeasure from insiders about OSI's slow pace, it seemed only a matter of time before global markets for internetworking would grow sharply.[53]

In August, the American government published GOSIP as Federal Information Processing Standards 146, Version 1, with the expectation that it would become a federal procurement requirement in August 1990. While FIPS 146 did not mandate that all federal systems migrate immediately or exclusively to OSI, Heafner, Mulvenna, and Rosenthal could at last congratulate themselves for a job well done. They had done their part. The future of internetworking now was in the hands of equipment vendors and their customers.

50. Mulvenna interview, Computer History Museum.

51. Mulvenna interview, Computer History Museum.

52. "The tales they tell when GOSIPs get together," *Data Communications*, December 1988, 16.

53. Dozens of research articles in 1988 document the nuances of OSI growth and adoption. See for example Volume 7, Issues 1–2 of the journal *Computer Networks & Interfaces*, featuring articles about OSI adoption and implementation in the US, Germany, the Netherlands, France, and Japan.

12.4 In Perspective

One irony of internetworking in the early 1980s was the divided support of the US federal government. To anyone unaccustomed with American political institutions, it must have looked schizophrenic. On the one hand, DARPA's sponsorship of packet-switched networking, first in the ARPANET and subsequently in the support of TCP/IP and its proponents, was envied around the world. No single company or government body had provided a comparable level of financial support that resulted in such widespread technical development. But, on the other hand, officials in US federal agencies who were keeping tabs on OSI's development were reaching a consensus that TCP/IP would amount to little more than an interesting experiment, or perhaps, at best, a transitional set of internetworking protocols that would be used until OSI matured.

With two sets of competing standards specified, the race was on to ensure interoperability and to help industry build useful products—and soon. Both camps had people thinking and acting like entrepreneurs. Dan Lynch, advocating for TCP/IP, organized vendors' workshops and published the *Connexions* newsletter. John Heafner and Robert Rosenthal, advocating for OSI, organized vendor workshops and lobbied federal agencies to commit to OSI—even though there was a lack of products that could deliver on OSI's promise.[54]

Now we turn to our final chapter—the vendors charged with making standards-compliant products for internetworking. The next chapter turns to consider these vendors, their leaders, their constraints, and their products.

The first internetworking products to reach $100 million market were hubs, led by SynOptics and Cabletron. The next products were bridges. But to connect networks together, new devices emerged that could address network protocols. These latter products—routers—became the dominant design.

As we will see in Chapter 13, during the mid-1980s, public events for both OSI and TCP/IP attracted thousands of attendees and proved the viability of internetworking. These events illustrate a line of continuity that we have seen across the three market-structures of computer communications: data communications, networking, and internetworking. For it was at these events—conferences, trade shows, and public demonstrations—that experts could mingle, potential customers could discover new applications and possibilities, and companies were forced to move beyond hype and put actual working technologies on display.

54. Advocates for the Internet and TCP/IP were increasingly well organized and funded, as well. See G.M. Vaudreuil. 1988. The Federal Research Internet Committee and the National Research Network. *SIGCOMM Comput. Commun. Rev.* 18, 3 (May/June 1988), 6–9. DOI: https://doi.org/10.1145/62075.62076.

Competition in computer communications was as relentless as it was unpredictable. Not only were established companies struggling to keep up with new technologies and more nimble start-ups, the start-ups were competing against one another, and everyone involved had to cast their lot with technologies that were not yet standardized or that had "anticipatory" standards that had not yet demonstrated market viability. Our final chapter begins with accounts of the two biggest internetworking events of 1988—ENE and Interop—where the competition between OSI and TCP/IP was evident. We then conclude *Circuits, Packets and Protocols* with some reflections on the internetworking market-structure that stabilized after 1988, and thoughts about the consequences of internetworking for the global economy.

The Emergence of Internetworking, 1985–1988

13.1 Overview

By 1985, the growth of local area network installations had increased corporate budgets for information technology (IT), transforming the role of IT from a small operation to a major department with functions across the entire enterprise. Corporations needed to take two steps to leverage the full capability of LANs: first, connect all their computers to LANs, and second, interconnect their LANs into enterprise-wide networks. At the start of 1987, these enterprise networks remained more of a promise than a required capital investment. But it didn't take long for the new start-ups of internetworking—SynOptics, Retix, Vitalink, Cisco, and Wellfleet—to ship products, and for dozens of other companies to enter the market. By the end of 1988, the third wave of computer communications—internetworking—was under way.

As we have seen many times in this history of computer communications, public demonstrations helped to consolidate and publicize existing capabilities while helping to identify the work that remained to be done. Three demonstrations featured the networking and internetworking capabilities of OSI: the National Computer Conference in 1984, the Autofact trade show in 1985, and the Enterprise Networking Event (ENE) in 1988. The alternative to the OSI protocols were those that had been birthed and shepherded by DARPA: TCP/IP. The US federal government had made clear their preference for networks using OSI protocols, not TCP/IP. Nevertheless, a growing band of diehards and vendors eager to market new products continued to offer solutions that leveraged the popularity of TCP/IP. They too staged a series of annual demonstrations culminating in the Interop trade show of 1988. In these demonstrations, TCP/IP proved robust and viable, even if many observers saw it simply as an interim solution before the full commercial deployment of OSI.

This chapter observes the formative economic history of the organizations and products of internetworking. The important products were local and remote bridges, hubs, gateways, and routers. Of particular interest will be the contrast between political institutions that prioritized the creation of consensus around international standards for future product development (as we saw in Chapter 12), while economic organizations—again primarily venture capital-backed start-ups—focused on developing products to meet existing market needs. We then give accounts of the two biggest internetworking events of 1988—ENE and Interop—highlighting the developers and proponents of the two competing models of internetworking: OSI and TCP/IP. The chapter ends with a brief look at the market-structure of internetworking as it was poised to enter a stage of phenomenal growth.

13.2 Interconnecting Local Area Networks

By 1986, corporate IT managers no longer needed to be convinced of the benefits of interconnecting their computers into networks. Data published by two leading research firms provided ample support. The preeminent market research firm Dataquest estimated that there were 560,000 installed Ethernet LAN connections.[1] Assuming five computer connections per network gives an estimated 100,000 Ethernet networks. In 1986, 650,000 Ethernet LAN connections were shipped. That number nearly doubled to 1,260,000 in just one year. The market research firm International Data Corporation (IDC) reported similar numbers in 1987 when they estimated a domestic installed base of 27 million personal computers in business environments in 1987 with only 11% connected to LANs.[2] They projected the number of personal computers in business environments to swell to 38 million by 1989 with 28% attached to LANs—a 65% growth rate over the 6.6 million personal computers attached to LANs in 1988. It didn't take much imagination to see the potential increase in demand for internetworking products given the potential value of shared data, peripherals, and access to email.

Interconnecting LANs throughout large corporations with distant facilities created more complicated problems than simply interconnecting local LANs. Decisions had to be made as to whether to force all LANs to conform to the same standards (e.g. Ethernet, token ring) as well as conform to the same communication protocols (e.g. TCP/IP, DECnet, XNS, NetWare, etc.) which in themselves could

1. Dataquest Incorporated, June 1988, 82–84.

2. "Basic connectivity high on users' lists," *Network World*, April 11, 1988, 16.

vary dramatically from one vendor's implementation to another. Another major problem was that the communication speeds of LANs were greater than those of modems, the dominant devices used to interconnect to distant facilities. A solution could force major installation costs, such as upgrading to T1 facilities, upgrading to sophisticated protocol software such as TCP/IP, or waiting for the future release of OSI protocols.

LAN vendors had labored for years over how to create the best computer communication networks. The nearly universal agreement as to the lower four layers of the OSI Reference Model had helped to make sense of the wide range of networking components and technologies. These were the layers that dealt with creating reliable communications between computing devices. Nevertheless, it had taken years to sort out first the specific standards of the Data Link Layer and then the Transport Layer, and then to create successful products. At first, the primary problem had been how to optimize the function of one LAN network. But by 1983–1984, corporations wanted to interconnect their growing number of LANs with WANs, necessitating the importance of the Network Layer standards—standards that had not yet been incorporated into products.

The different types of products described here—repeaters, hubs, bridges, gateways, and routers—were not developed sequentially. (These products, and their place within the seven-layer OSI reference model, are summarized in Table 13.1.) Products appeared on the market as soon as companies could master the elements of engineering necessary to make them functional. With a functional product developed, companies then had the challenge of finding new customers—to say nothing of keeping up with the latest products from competitors and shifting winds of technical standards.

13.2.1 Repeaters and Hubs: Physical Layer Solutions for Extending a Network

If a customer only had Ethernet LANs, and not too many devices connected to them, then the most straightforward solution was repeaters. Neither complicated nor expensive, repeaters function entirely on the Physical Layer of the OSI Reference Model. Their simplicity also gives rise to a fundamental limitation: they boost every signal as if locked in broadcast mode. Thus, all the traffic on one LAN continues onto the next, cumulatively, quickly degrading the performance of the interconnected LANs.

A more functional cousin to the repeater, a hub performs the role of re-transmitting network traffic to multiple ports. Hubs became essential for connecting components of local networks. As the evolution of Ethernet expanded to

Table 13.1 **Network models and products**

<table>
<tr><th>Layer</th><th>OSI</th><th>DOD</th><th colspan="4">Products</th></tr>
<tr><td>7</td><td>Application</td><td rowspan="3">Application</td><td></td><td></td><td></td><td rowspan="7">Gateways</td></tr>
<tr><td>6</td><td>Presentation</td><td></td><td></td><td></td></tr>
<tr><td>5</td><td>Session</td><td></td><td></td><td></td></tr>
<tr><td>4</td><td>Transport</td><td>Host-to-Host</td><td></td><td></td><td></td></tr>
<tr><td>3</td><td>Network</td><td>Internet</td><td></td><td></td><td rowspan="3">Routers</td></tr>
<tr><td>2</td><td>Datalink</td><td rowspan="2">Network Access</td><td></td><td rowspan="2">Bridges, Switches</td></tr>
<tr><td>1</td><td>Physical</td><td>Repeaters, Hubs</td></tr>
</table>

Created by James L. Pelkey and Loring G. Robbins.

include star topology in the late 1980s, hubs would take on the role of the network control point as the hub sat in the wire closet and connected to the network nodes.

In the early stages of internetworking, incremental innovation yielded modest improvements in repeaters and hubs, such as the ability to detect faults in a connected LAN and to isolate the offending LAN. Repeaters, however, could never overcome the limitations inherent in not knowing the source and destination addresses of connected devices. Nor could repeaters or basic hubs ever interconnect different types of LANs, such as Ethernet and token ring. These limitations, combined with the compelling economic advantages of interconnecting networks, motivated vendors to take on the more complex and costly task of innovating more advanced products for internetworking. The first of those products were bridges.

13.2.2 Bridges: Connecting the Data Link Layer

By making use of the information contained in the Data Link Layer, bridges offered major advantages over repeaters or hubs. The price to be paid, however, was a much more expensive and complex product that contained logic and memory. Bridges, also known as Medium Access Control (MAC) bridges, use the source and destination addresses in packets to build tables of what addresses have come on what interfaces, or links. Afterwards, if it receives a packet with destination addresses that are in the table, the bridge only sends the packets using the interfaces it has seen the source addresses come from. It will not send the packets down all interfaces (see Figure 13.1).

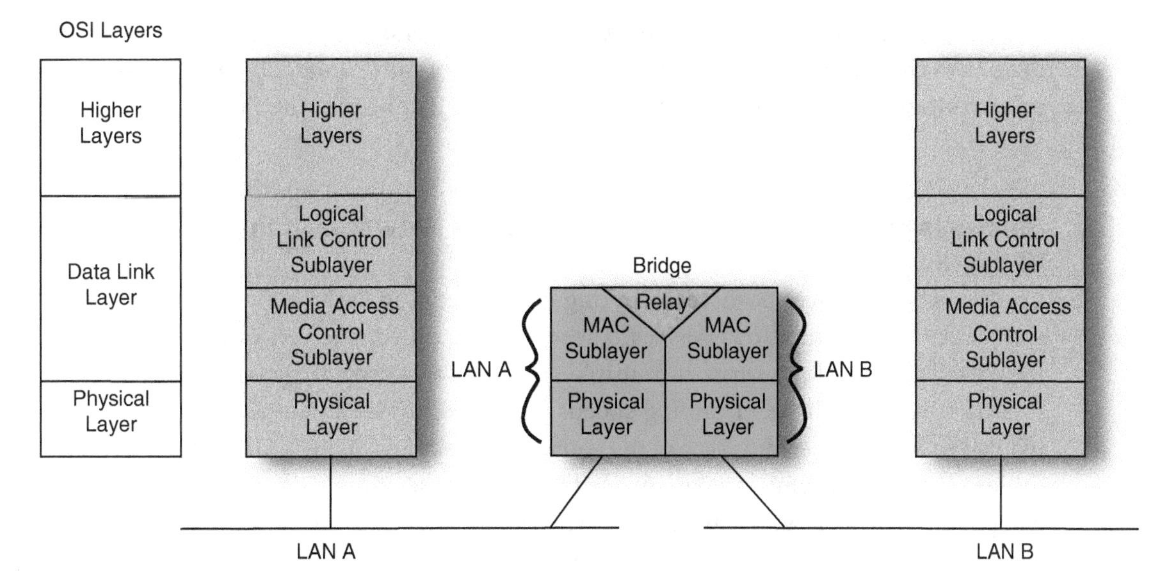

Figure 13.1 A network bridge. Illustration by James L. Pelkey and Loring G. Robbins. Based on Datapro Reports on PC & LAN Communications: LAN Internetworking Overview, 52–107.

The ability to read and use the address information in packets (or datagrams) give bridges even more advantages. If the destination address is on the network originating the packet, then the packet need not be forwarded to other networks, thereby further reducing network traffic. This ability also enables users to subdivide an existing network to improve the performance of both new networks. For example, if a network includes both engineering workstations and office PCs, a bridge can be used to isolate these different types of computers onto two new networks, likely improving the performance of both new networks. Despite these advantages, bridges have some limitations—such as the inability to route dynamically and to bridge incompatible networks, such as DECnet and IBM token ring. This meant that they could not meet the needs of corporations and institutions wanting to create geographically dispersed, large enterprise networks containing different standard local area networks.[3]

3. While bridges filtered packets via software and connected two to four ports, the need to connect larger networks and interconnect more networks would eventually, once network speeds increased, lead to the invention of the networking switch, a hardware-based routing device supporting multiple ports.

These first products of internetworking—repeaters, hubs, and bridges—operate in the physical and link layers at the bottom of the OSI model. Truly transparent interoperability between networks required connection at the Network Layer.

13.2.3 Gateways and Routers: Integrating Countless Networks at the Network Layer

Engineers and product designers working at the Network Layer built even more sophisticated and ambitious devices. These devices, called gateways and routers, ideally would be able to support multiple protocols and provide dynamic packet routing to adapt to links of varying speeds and conditions. In addition, addressing had to include the addresses of the source and destination network and of the devices. There are useful comparisons between this type of multi-level addressing and postal addresses, which include the street addresses of senders and recipients, as well as their corresponding cities, states, and countries.

Both gateways and routers alike fulfilled the functions that OSI defined for Intermediate Systems. The OSI Reference Model described "Intermediate Systems," which were internetworking devices that could implement the Network Layer.[4] Intermediate Systems use all the information contained in the headers of packets and can create new protocols between systems that allow sophisticated forms of control and security beyond the basic relay and routing functions (see Figure 13.2). The subnetworks connecting Intermediate Systems and End Systems could be as numerous and as diverse as needed to construct a cost-effective and reliable enterprise network. Subnetworks ranged in complexity from a serial line to unlimited combinations of LANs and WANs.

Vendors struggled to develop products that could interconnect existing LAN and WAN networks while also anticipating future needs. Initially, the products of choice were gateways, which required extensive hardware and software to translate between the multiple LAN technologies available at the time, and between many of the existing higher-level protocols. With time, companies realized that building and selling gateways was no simple task.

An alternative to gateways, routers were first sold by Proteon in 1985 and Cisco Systems in 1986. As the internetworking market grew in 1987 and 1988, the terms "gateway" and "router" gained greater clarity. Routers functioned with protocols at the Network Layer, whereas the more sophisticated gateways integrated the higher-level layers of once-incompatible computing environments such as DECnet and

4. Christine Ware. 1983. The OSI network layer: Standards to cope with the real world. *Proceedings of the IEEE* 71 (December 1983), 1384–1387.

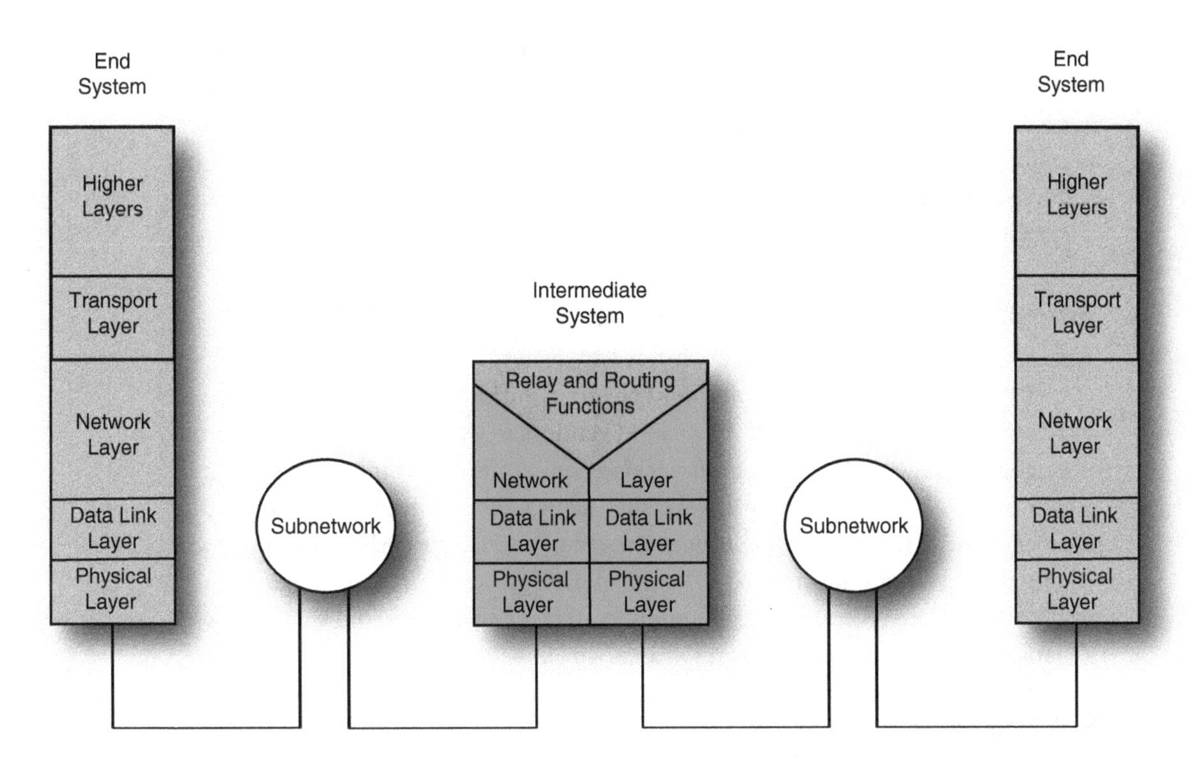

Figure 13.2 Network layer subnetwork interconnection. Illustration by James L. Pelkey and Loring G. Robbins. Based on *Data Communications*, May 1986, 122.

Table 13.2 **Internetworking revenues, 1987–1988 ($ million)**

Product Category	1987	1988
Local Bridges	25	47
Remote Bridges	34	58
Gateways/Routers	23	60
TOTAL	82	165

Source: Datapro.

IBM's SNA.[5] Not until 1987 did market research firms begin reporting on the new market sector of internetworking (see Table 13.2).

In 1988, industry observers brimmed with excitement over the quickening pace of internetworking evolution and the promising markets for hubs, bridges, routers, and gateways. The driving forces were customer demand and global competition, especially among young companies and entrepreneurs who recognized these new

5. Bob Bradley. 1985. "Interconnection draws DEC, IBM networks closer," *Data Communications*, May 1985, 241–248.

opportunities.[6] The facilitating framework was ISO's OSI model and the standards that OSI committees were producing at all levels of the seven-layer OSI Reference Model. As the internetworking market became reality, only a few questions remained: What companies would capture market leadership? Would IBM commit fully to the momentum of OSI? And, most crucially for customers, how soon would they be able to buy OSI-compliant products?

13.3 Internetworking: Entrepreneurs and Start-ups, 1985–1988

The early products that served to interconnect local networks were developed out of the specific needs for internetworking solutions. Often, it was the need expressed by the customer that motivated vendors to expand into this new product category. As a result, existing networking companies responded first with their own products in their own submarkets, such as Proteon's early gateway connecting it's three token ring LAN products with Ethernet, and DEC's early bridge products for interconnecting Ethernet LANs. As the market grew, internetworking products began to generate revenues large enough to attract entrepreneurial start-ups with a focus on internetworking product categories alone.

13.3.1 Hub Companies

The popularity of star-configured Ethernet, developed initially by AT&T for its StarLAN in 1984 and then by SynOptics in its LattisNet in 1985, brought about a rapid growth in the market for networking hubs. Many existing computer and networking companies were successful in developing hubs, including Ungermann-Bass, 3Com, AT&T, Racal-Interlan, and DCA. The rapid growth in the hub market was led by SynOptics and start-up Cabletron, founded in 1983, which found early success selling equipment for the original StarLAN networks. Both SynOptics and Cabletron led the evolution of hubs from basic lower-level devices to "intelligent" hubs, which contained router modules and hardware and software for networking management. Other start-ups included: David Systems, Gateway Communications, NetWorth, Fibermux, Laniet, BICC, Data Networks, and Nevada Western.

13.3.2 Vitalink Communications Corporation

The story of Vitalink is one of management willing to face the failure of their founding strategy and steer their company into the strong currents of a growth market before it was too late. When the founders incorporated Vitalink in 1980, they had an initial strategy to build private, corporate satellite data communications systems. By 1984, what was once a promising opportunity had turned into

6. "From systems to standards, the pace quickens in networking," *Electronics*, April 14, 1988.

a capital-intensive, fiercely competitive market. Seeking out a new niche to leverage their competences and past investments, Vitalink teamed up with DEC to solve mutual, yet distinctly different, problems. At the time, DEC sought a solution for interconnecting multiple Ethernet-based LANs primarily within a building. Given their experience interconnecting different kinds of networks, it was natural for Vitalink to bring to the collaboration ideas for interconnecting multiple, disparate Ethernets. A result of their cooperation was the creation of the first remote bridge, a bridge connecting networks via a telecommunications service. Introduced in 1985, Vitalink's TransLAN interconnected one Ethernet LAN to as many as eight long-haul networks, via terrestrial or satellite links. Vitalink and DEC next signed expanded co-development and co-marketing agreements. Vitalink would benefit by selling its TransLAN to potential customers generated from DEC's marketing systems. (Surprisingly, however, the Ethernet hardware Vitalink used in its TransLAN product was sourced from Bridge Communications, not DEC.)[7]

By mid-1986, financial constraints forced Vitalink management into uncharted strategic territory. Intense competition in the private satellite business had made it difficult to grow revenue or attain profitability. Challenged, management took two actions. First, they decided to narrow their satellite strategy to the new VSAT technologies and cease building private networks requiring special programing and development. Informing their decision was the fact that 80% to 90% of TransLAN products ran over terrestrial lines, and since it was TransLAN that was growing revenues, they refocused the satellite business to support TransLAN.[8] The more modest VSAT strategy still leveraged past satellite investments while serving the same users who were purchasing their remote bridges. Secondly, the sales success of remote bridges demanded more investment and management attention. In October 1986, the management of Vitalink announced a strategic repositioning: to create products filling out their 802 WAN architecture, and cease installing and servicing wide-area networks.[9] Vitalink would focus on interconnecting local area networks using the 802.3 Ethernet standard. TransLAN would support DECnet, XNS, TCP/IP, and similar higher-level protocols. Increased bridge investment led to two new communication software packages, TransSDLC and the new TransLINK, a frame level multiplexer. Despite these painful choices, the company was still losing money. Pressed for cash, they refinanced their capital equipment and raised $5.5 million, funds needed for product development and working capital.[10] The

7. Bridges and Gateways, the Yankee Group, 1985, 22–24.

8. Bridges and Gateways, the Yankee Group, 1985, 10.

9. "Vitalink targets wide net market," *Network World*, Nov. 24, 1986, 9–10.

10. "Vitalink expands realm," *Network World*, October 13, 1986, 11.

good news was that company revenues for 1986 were about to double to $10 million on the strength of remote bridge sales. The TransLAN represented more than 50% of Vitalink's revenues.

Continuing the drive for innovation and competitive advantage, in early 1987 Vitalink and DEC announced a second important result of their co-development agreement: the Spanning Tree Protocol (STP). The STP addressed the need to create loop-free transmission within a topology of Ethernet LANs interconnected with bridges.[11] Before STP, users had to manually interconnect all nodes within a bridge network in order to know that there were no loops (loops could overload the network and cause network failure). Spanning tree networks permit multiple connections between bridges, but only connections that do not create loops. There is no calculation of an optimum path.

The continued double-digit growth of remote bridge revenues, and the success of the DEC relationship, prompted Vitalink management to make a bold decision. In mid-1987, they decided to stop making any investments in the satellite business and to put it on the market for sale, and, absent a buyer within a year, to completely close the business down. By the fall, finding little interest among potential buyers, one of the company's founders, Al Horley, then responsible for the satellite business, resigned in order to negotiate its purchase. Although having minimized the cash drain on Vitalink, the growth of the bridge business required cash. Fortunately, the bridge market, and the internetworking market in general, had become recognized as a "hot" market. After the satellite business had been in principle terminated, investment bankers began calling on Vitalink management to pitch the idea of an IPO.

With revenues of $17.5 million for the fiscal year 1987, and growth of the bridge business exceeding 100%, Vitalink decided in favor of access to the public market and the capital they needed to properly finance their growth. On March 3, 1988, Vitalink went public at a price of $8.25/share, selling 2.3 million shares and raising nearly $19 million with a company valuation of $44 million.

Nearing the deadline they had set for the sale or closure of the satellite business, in September 1988 Horley organized a new company, Vitacom, and negotiated the final sale of the business for an undisclosed sum.[12] Then in November 1988, Vitalink and DEC signed a new agreement giving DEC the right to resell Vitalink's TransLAN product line directly to its customers. It was likely that this agreement expanded the number of people selling the TransLAN by a factor of ten. The year

11. Lixia Zhang. 1988. Comparison of two bridge routing approaches. *IEEE Network* 2 (January 1988), 44–48.

12. "Vitalink sells off satellite division to small start-up," *Network World*, Nov. 21, 1989, 12.

1988 was another great year for Vitalink with profitable revenues of $37.4 million.[13] Vitalink was thought to control 70% of the remote bridge market.

13.3.3 Retix

In the spring of 1984, Andrew (Andi) De Mari learned that Ing. C. Olivetti SpA of Italy (Olivetti), his former employer, had signed a mega-contract with AT&T, one calling for AT&T to purchase 22% of the ownership of Olivetti, and, among other terms, for Olivetti to supply AT&T with a personal computer AT&T would resell as its own.[14] De Mari's entrepreneurial instincts quickly envisioned an opportunity. Logically, if Olivetti intended to supply a competitive personal computer to AT&T, they would want a source of StarLAN adapter cards. (The "StarLAN" version of Ethernet was a standard AT&T had championed in standards committees as an Ethernet standard for twisted pair wiring, a compelling advantage for the phone company.) Di Mari knew, after contacting former associates within Olivetti, that Olivetti management had no plans to engineer and manufacture a StarLAN card and would be open to a proposal from Di Mari. Furthermore, De Mari had received unmistakable signals that Olivetti's venture capital team would be interested in investing in a start-up he headed.

StarLAN might have been a source of sales and venture capital to launch a company, but De Mari doubted it would serve as the basis of an eventual IPO company. In discussions with those he hoped would join him, the idea of focusing on OSI software seemed a wiser strategy.[15] De Mari remembers a meeting of engineers in late 1984: "We looked at the networking market and decided that if we developed products like network bridges and routers that connect networks that didn't exist at that time, we would surely go out of business. We sensed a growing interest in OSI (Open Systems Interconnection), so we decided to gamble our entire company on the future of OSI."[16]

In March 1985, De Mari and the founding team incorporated Retix with an initial investment of $700,000. De Mari knew that he would need to raise significantly more money if Retix was to become a public company, possibly $10 million or more over the next few years. The first step had to be to close Olivetti as a corporate partner, for Olivetti was known as a venture capital investor and, if they decided not

13. "Vitalink Communications· · ·.," Datapro C11-966-101, LANs, Sept. 1989.

14. See Chapter 9 for further details.

15. The logic mirrors that of Concord Data Systems: one technology to launch a company—dial-up modems or StarLAN adapter cards—and another technology to build an IPO company—token bus LANs or OSI software.

16. "Retix cashing in on OSI," *Network World*, Sept. 22, 1986, 25.

to invest in Retix, it signaled the wrong assessment of both Retix's future business prospects and Olivetti's confidence in the management of Retix. Meanwhile, thanks to sales of StarLAN adapter cards to Olivetti, sales for 1985 totaled nearly $722,000. If AT&T was successful in selling personal computers, the future of Retix seemed promising.

The years 1985 and 1986 were consumed with meeting the needs of Olivetti, that is, AT&T; developing an OSI business; and building out the company's infrastructure. While selling StarLAN adapter cards hopefully meant more than selling to AT&T, it was clear that success would be tied to the success of AT&T. The challenge would be to form strong relationships with AT&T personnel without upsetting Olivetti or creating new problems. Developing an OSI business required a continued presence in standards-making bodies; selecting, coding, and productizing those standards judged to be the best market opportunities; and creating profitable relationships with the leading companies staking a claim in the emerging OSI market. Most importantly, Retix had to prove it was the OSI leader by providing as much OSI software as possible to the vendors participating in the ENE trade show scheduled for June 1988. Building out the infrastructure included hiring the right people as quickly as possible, growing sales and profits, making sure financial resources were always available when needed, and initiating efforts to enter the internetworking market.

In August 1986, Retix closed a $1 million round of Preferred Stock with Olivetti. All was going as planned. Then in November 1986, AT&T announced a major shake-up in its flagging computer operations. An untenable loss estimated to be as much as $800 million for 1986 precipitated management and strategy changes.[17] The news for Retix could be interpreted positively—since ties between AT&T and Olivetti were strengthened when Vittorio Cassoni, an Olivetti senior executive, was named President of the newly formed Data Systems Division, consisting of AT&T's computer businesses.

Retix's sales soared to $5.2 million ($3.7 million) in 1986.[18] While sales of $1 million to Olivetti reflected AT&T's problems selling computers, sales of licenses of OSI software more than made up any weakness in StarLAN sales. (Furthermore, sales of MAP licenses represented approximately half of OSI sales.) On the other hand, by the end of 1986 the project to develop an Ethernet and StarLAN bridge had fallen an estimated 6 months behind plan. The reasons for the delay, difficulties

17. "AT&T computer shake-up rattles out a warning," *Chicago Tribune*, Nov. 9, 1986, 1–2.

18. In a company acquisition, accounting conventions could require a restatement of prior year financials to reflect the results of both companies. In this case we report the restated revenue and include Retix's sales in parenthesis.

hiring experienced talent in the United States, prompted De Mari to accelerate discussions of international product development and even the possibility of making an acquisition. Conversations ranged from securing a grant from the Irish Development Authority to assessing companies as acquisitions. The focus quickly settled on the UK company TSL Communications. The crush of activities also elevated the priority of raising new investment capital from venture capitalists. As warned, venture capitalists quickly voiced a closing condition that a new president with IPO experience be hired.

In June 1987, Retix finally entered the internetworking market with its RetixGate Model 2244: a two-port local bridge interconnecting Ethernet and StarLAN LANs. Even so, Retix was late to market and faced intense competition. In August, Retix closed a $5.5 million financing based on a $16 million pre-money valuation. While a new president had not yet been hired, encouraging interviews had turned up promising candidates. Before the end of the year, terms would be finalized with Steve Frankel, formerly with Micom and recently president of Emulex. For mutual reasons, Frankel would consult with Retix for up to a year before becoming an employee. (He formally joined Retix in September 1988.) A key factor in closing the financing was the prominent role Retix had secured in the upcoming ENE trade show.

Fiscal year 1987 was another impressive year with revenue growth of 126% to $13.6 million ($10.0 million) and with net income of $560,000. The budget for 1988 positioned the company to become a public company. Retix was now recognized as the market leader in the fast-growing OSI software market with a 50% market share. The OSI market was forecasted to grow from $15 million in 1987 to $164 million in 1991.[19] So far, competitors were other small start-ups: notably Touch Communications, founded by angel investor Charlie Bass, founder of Ungermann-Bass, and The Wollongong Group of Palo Alto, a leader in the TCP/IP software market and of comparable size to Retix. International competitors played a more prominent role than usual. Sydney Development Corporation of Vancouver, BC, Marben of Paris, and Logica of London were start-ups financed with private capital.

The year 1988 would be an important year for Retix, as it was for most computer communication companies. In January, Retix announced its second local bridge: the RetixGate Model 2255, a two-port bridge adding support for Thin Ethernet (the 10BASE2 standard).

In April 1988, the trade press made much of the fact that AT&T had declined to increase its stake in Olivetti.[20] Days later, another press release confirmed Cassoni

19. James L. Pelkey, Personal Communication, June 26, 1987.

20. "Trouble in AT& T–Olivetti paradise," *Computer Business Review*, April 17, 1988.

was leaving AT&T and returning to Olivetti as managing director. As for their 10-year agreement, nothing was said. Soon Retix management learned that AT&T had cut its purchase orders by 75%. No longer could Retix assume a close and favorable relationship with AT&T, which in turn cast new importance on mounting an aggressive internetworking strategy.

In June came ENE, considered the preeminent event for the Computer Communication industry for 1988. If the OSI standards and especially the MAP/TOP and GOSIP Profiles were to gain the needed economic momentum to displace the existing communication standards, such as TCP/IP, SNA, and DECnet, companies had to leave ENE convinced to convert to OSI immediately. For Retix, it was the opportunity to demonstrate their OSI leadership, in particular with X.400 and Directory Services, and to introduce key new products (X.400 and FTAM end user products, and a MAP 3.0 compliant MAC Level bridge) to bolster OSI sales.[21] Retix would fare better than did the show itself, for the Corporation of Open Standards (COS) failed to have their conformance testing software ready, leaving critics to conclude that user acceptance of OSI was still a season away. That assessment notwithstanding, Retix's sales of OSI technology and products received a big boost.

In December, in an aggressive step to boost its position in the internetworking market, Retix acquired all the outstanding common stock of TSL Communications Ltd. In a transaction accounted for as a pooling of interests, Retix now had a source of its remote bridge products, engineering personnel, and the European market presence that would have taken years to accomplish otherwise.

Revenues for 1988 grew 99% to $27.0 million ($21.3 million) with net income of $822,000. While management had successfully grown two new product lines in exciting emerging markets—OSI technology and products as well as local and remote bridges—Retix's future remained tied to the outcome of the Olivetti and AT&T relationship and of AT&T's ability to sell personal computers (see Table 13.3).

Table 13.3 **Retix revenue mix, 1988**

Product Line	Revenues ($ thousands)	Percent of Total
LAN Controllers and Hubs	11,659	43.2
OSI Technology and Products	6,187	22.9
Internetworking (Bridges)	6,672	24.7
Support and Custom Engineering	2,475	9.2
Total Revenue	26,993	100.0

Based on Retix Consolidated Profit & Loss, 1988–1990.

21. Enterprise '88 Show Directory.

The uncertainty and challenge in establishing the 1989 financial plan was forecasting a high revenue growth rate and profitability consistent with the last 3 years in order to qualify for an IPO, and to do so without knowing what AT&T and Olivetti were going to do, or if OSI was really going to take off.

13.3.4 Wellfleet Communications

After Micom acquired Interlan on March 1, 1985, Paul Severino, Interlan president and key founder, became vice-president of product planning and technology for Micom. Moving to a staff position made sense but was not without its own risks. Severino remembers:

> I had been trying for a few years to get out of day-to-day operations and become more of a strategy/technology-oriented person, but still with my eye on getting the next generation of products out the door. So the deal that was cut with Micom was that I would become a Micom VP and I would be looking at this whole corporate strategy thing, which I did for the first four or five months. But the problem was that the Interlan side was just being kept closed, even to me, and I wanted—I knew that Micom had to make some leaps in order to really compete again, and I wanted to take off a group and just go build the next generation of product, and Roger and I just couldn't come to an agreement that that was the right thing to do.[22]

Unable to reach an agreement with Roger Evans, the CEO of Micom, and tired of the cross-country travel from his home outside Boston to and from Micom's headquarters just north of Los Angeles, Severino resigned in September 1985. He harbored no fear of being unemployed, only excitement about starting another company. His entrepreneurial nature had free reign once again to shape his future. He fondly recalls:

> When I left, in September of 1985, I actually started working on a project to build a company that was going to be doing factory automation systems. I was going to go back to my data acquisition days, but I was going to do it with MAP. But I wasn't going to be a networking company. I wanted to be a computing company. I wanted to provide the workstation of the factory that was networked like an Apollo system. I wanted to do this real-time

22. Paul Severino, oral history interview by James L. Pelkey, March 16, 1988, Cambridge, MA. Computer History Museum, Mountain View, CA. Available from https://archive.computerhistory.org/resources/access/text/2017/11/102738590-05-01-acc.pdf.

> cell controller, UNIX real-time, with integrated MAP networking, and literally using the MAP network as a mechanism by which you could have real-time networked operation over the network.[23]

In November at the Autofact Trade Show, Severino saw Ralph Ungermann, CEO of Ungermann-Bass. He remembers a snippet of their conversation: "Ralph says: 'What are you doing here.' I said: 'Well, I'm looking at factories.' He said: 'You're not going to go be an industrial networking company are you?' I said: 'No, no I'm looking at the computer side of the business,' which I was."[24]

Severino and his team continued their investigation until they realized:

> We looked at that for 6 months, there was about four of us. The problem we found: first of all, factory users don't buy from new companies; secondly, there isn't an application in the factory that drives a network like there is in CAD, like there is in the engineering environment, like there is in just a distributed data processing environment. There isn't an application. The only application that we found that drove a network into GM was literally downloading programmable logic into numerical controllers with programs instead of ROMs. That was the only application that we found, and clearly that's not a fancy application, so we just made the decision, even though we had a plan and we had figured out what the products should be, we just said: "This is crazy. This is not going to be where you grow in the networking business."[25]

On seeing Ungermann at an Alex. Brown & Sons conference in March 1986, Severino shared his conclusion to an unconvinced Ungermann:

> He said: "Did you start that company?" I said: "No, I didn't." He said: "Why not?" I said: "I can't find an application that's going to drive networks in a factory." He said: "No, it's there. We got it. We got all the OEMs lined up. It's all happening." I said: "Ralph, I'm telling you, I just can't put my finger on what's going to drive users to install networks in a factory. It isn't flexible manufacturing. It isn't this concept of timecards all over the factory. I don't see it."[26]

23. Severino interview, Computer History Museum.
24. Severino interview, Computer History Museum.
25. Severino interview, Computer History Museum.
26. Severino interview, Computer History Museum.

Not discouraged in the least, he and his team began looking elsewhere. Severino then recalled learning about T1 at Micom:

> I became aware of T1 when I was poking around for Micom looking at different kinds of companies. In fact, the first time I actually became aware of T1 was when I actually went down to visit Avanti. Now it became clear to me that T1 was important and that, if you believe the way I do, that LAN traffic is going to dominate what happens in computing and computers, then computer systems are going to be connected with LANs from now on until I can see. As soon as you understand that, then the next step is the world still needs to be interconnected. Companies still have remote sites and they still want to get at the classical datacom problem; therefore, you need different kinds of devices than modems and multiplexers. You need routers and bridges. You need things that work differently, and if you mate those up with the technology of T1, you ought to be able to access a group of customers and have that problem and make a business out of it.[27]

In May 1986, Severino and three former employees of Interlan, William Seifert, Steve Willis, and David Rowe, incorporated Wellfleet Communications Inc. The mission: to develop, manufacture, market, and support a family of high-performance, multi-protocol internetworking products. Next came the task of raising the money needed to adequately finance the more encompassing vision to create a systems supplier not just a product-oriented company, as had been the case with Interlan. Severino naturally turned to his friend and business partner, Russell Planitzer of J.H. Whitney, his lead investor at Interlan, to play that role again. Planitzer agreed. They immediately approached Ed Anderson, a former investor in Interlan and associated with Alex. Brown & Sons. On the strength of his experiences with Severino, having made money on the Interlan investment, he agreed to participate. They both joined the Board of Directors, and before the end of fiscal year ending June 1987, Interlan had raised nearly $6 million with J.H. Whitney investing $3 million. In July 1987, Art Carr, now President and CEO of Bytex and formerly CEO of Codex, also joined the Board of Directors. Severino remembers the distinction between Interlan and Wellfleet:

> In the Interlan approach I had my eyes focused on a particular segment and I didn't care whether I was the number one company or number two company. All I wanted to make was a profitable business. But now we raised a lot more money, and our product is going after a segment which we think is

27. Severino interview, Computer History Museum.

> going to be a very important segment, and we're going after it with a product that's very fully functional as we come out the door.[28]

To build an internetworking company also required recruiting an engineering team with a diverse set of experiences, just as Bruce Smith had done at Network Equipment Technologies. In Severino's words: "If you look at the people that are in Wellfleet today, the engineering people, we have people that are out of BBN, we have people that are out of AT&T, we have people that are out of the computer companies that are doing LANs: a wide spectrum of people with different kinds of expertise."[29]

The challenge now became getting product to market as soon as possible. In deciding which elements of their product were most important to introduce first, they had to assess who they thought their competition would be. Severino remembers: "I believed that Vitalink would probably be the biggest threat."[30] Severino would be surprised to encounter another start-up: Cisco Systems.

Product development began in earnest in mid-1987. Indicative of the productivity that is so often evident in start-ups, Wellfleet Communications shipped the first of what would be three major products able to bridge or route LANs and WANs in April 1988. The Link Node, or LN, could support an aggregate of 16 connections (8 of which could be LANs). In June 1988, the Concentrator Node, or CN, was released and able to support an aggregate of 52 connections. Then in May 1989, the Feeder Node, or FN, was released and supported an aggregate of 4 connections. These three products, plus a UNIX-based software package that provided network management tools, could be configured in systems to support thousands of connections.

Soon after the CN was released, Wellfleet Communications encountered performance problems with both its LN and CN products that delayed shipment schedules until late 1988. Brad Baldwin, an analyst with the market research firm Dataquest, reported "the delays caused Wellfleet to virtually concede the T1 side of its business to Vitalink and Cisco Systems."[31] Fortunately the company had raised nearly $4 million in a third round of private financing that had been intended to finance the company's growth and would now be largely consumed by the delays in revenues. For the fiscal year ending June 30, 1988, Wellfleet Communications reported revenue of $320,000 with a net loss of $4.1 million. Ending cash was $3.8 million.

28. Severino interview, Computer History Museum.

29. Severino interview, Computer History Museum.

30. Eric Nee, "Cisco and Wellfleet in a Rout," *Upside Magazine*, Feb/March 1991, 46.

31. Industry Watch, *Data Communications*, July 1989, 63.

13.3.5 Cisco Systems

Leonard Bosack and his wife, Sandy Lerner, started Cisco Systems for very different reasons than those motivating Paul Severino and his team. They didn't have to spend years finding the seed of a great idea, one around which to create a fast-growing company to take public, and holding the potential to support a large, successful enterprise. They had little calling to become entrepreneurs or to chase corporate profits. In fact, if anything, they were happy academics willing to give what they had or knew away, resistant to even marking-up their production costs to make a profit. But when Stanford University said they could not build product on university property and sell it to commercial companies, they felt they had little choice but to leave Stanford. In doing so, they started a journey that most entrepreneurs can only dream of and few ever have the opportunity to realize: a company worth hundreds of billions of dollars.

Bosack and Lerner met in 1977 while sharing time on Stanford University's minicomputers.[32] Lerner was a graduate student and Bosack fit the description of a "computer nerd." They fell in love, married, and took jobs with the computer departments of the Business School (Lerner) and Computer Science Department (Bosack). As such, they became involved in a number of efforts by Stanford to create a unified campus network. Stanford had thousands of different computers and users wanted to share information across the computers as if there was really only one integrated system. To do so, the computers, with their different operating systems and communication protocols, had to be able to easily exchange information. After a number of failed efforts, by June 1980, Bill Yeager, an engineer with the Medical School, had created a working router. Even so, it still did not connect to the Ethernet network that was integral to the Stanford University Network (SUN).

Frustrated, in 1982, Bosack, Lerner, and other engineers worked without authorization to create both an interface between Yeager's router and Ethernet and then to pull the coaxial cable needed to connect the computers throughout the campus. Yeager joined their efforts as did other engineers and before long their "skunk works" project was a success. To build additional routers, Bosack and Lerner converted their living room into an assembly room. Routers were then tested on the SUN network and the IMP's that connected to the ARPANET. Word of the routers spread both within Stanford and through the crude email of the day to other research centers and universities. Swamped with orders and needing a way to satisfy demand, other than by using their living room and credit cards, they approached Stanford and the Office of Technology Licensing (OTL). OTL could not

32. This early history of Cisco is based on Richard Brandt, David Bunnell, and Adam Brate. 2000. *Making the Cisco Connection: The Story Behind the Real Internet Superpower*, John Wiley & Sons.

offer a solution that would take less than years. Again frustrated, they left Stanford to start a business that would become Cisco Systems.

On December 10, 1984, Bosack and Lerner incorporated Cisco Systems.[33] Little changed other than that they could now take orders from any organization. As the order flow increased, the living room got more and more crowded and the need for cash more pressing. In the roughly 8 months to July 31, 1985, sales totaled $109,000. The lack of cash and, therefore, the need for investment capital to grow an organization and develop the market, forced Bosack and Lerner to mortgage their home and borrow as much as they could on their credit cards and from friends. Strapped for cash to pay their bills, Lerner took a daytime job managing the research computing systems for Schlumberger Computer Aided Systems Laboratory.

The constraint of cash had two other effects on the early history of Cisco Systems. First, unable to invest in a direct sales organization, the company had to resort to using manufacturer's representatives who were only paid when sales were made. This limited sales to customers that did not need a lot of technical support, organizations such as universities, research laboratories, and government agencies. These early adopters were also the easiest to reach through their Stanford connections and email networks. The second effect was the liberal use of part-time and contract engineers to develop products, primarily software products that executed on a small number of generic hardware platforms.

Revenues for the 12 months ending July 31, 1986, were essentially flat year over year: $129,000. Bosack and Lerner realized that if they wanted to be successful, they needed capital and professional help. So, they, like so many entrepreneurs before them, began the search for venture capital. Finding venture capital proved a lot more challenging than Bosack and Lerner had imagined. Bosack recalled, "We must have talked to 80 to 90 different venture firms. We got turned down by just about everyone."[34]

It quickly became apparent that without serious management, the probability of raising capital at an acceptable valuation was remote. So, in January 1987, they hired a President and Chief Executive Officer, William Graves, and then a vice-president, finance in March.

One of the venture capital firms they approached was Sequoia Capital, one of the most successful and largest venture capital firms in Silicon Valley. Sequoia Capital had the resources not just to evaluate investment projects they received or discovered, but to do the research and thinking required to become strategic

33. Initially, the company name was written with a lower case "c," the name originating from the name of nearby city San Francisco. Eventually, the name was changed to Cisco with a capital "C."

34. Eric Nee. 1991. cisco and Wellfleet in a rout., *Upside Magazine*, Feb./Mar. 1991, 43.

investor—to look for investments they wanted to make. When they listened to Bosack and Lerner, the partners of Sequoia heard not a company needing capital but a raw start-up needing everything—everything, that is, other than an intriguing jump on a product idea they had identified in their partners' meetings as compelling. Bosack and Lerner felt mentally stripped but not rejected: they realized the partners, and especially the managing partner, Don Valentine, weren't questioning the product viability, only their ability to build a company fast enough to compete with much larger, entrenched competition. They left agreeing to provide the information, and time, so that Sequoia Capital's partners could do their due diligence. They also knew that if they got an offer from Sequoia Capital, they would take it.

The fact that sales for fiscal year ending July 31, 1987, were $1.5 million, with nearly a 10% net income before taxes, kept cash usage to a minimum and enabled the company to continue to grow modestly while they sought venture capital.

Valentine soon proposed that Sequoia Capital invest $2.5 million for 32 percent of the company. Bosack and Lerner would retain 30 percent of the company, ownership that would vest over 4 years. Valentine would become a member of the Board of Directors and, much to the relief of the founders who recognized that they had no interest in the management aspects of the company, would assume responsibility for finance, and help Graves build a management team, sales organization, and "operations process."[35] Bosack became chief technology officer and Lerner vice president of customer services. The financing closed in December 1987.

In early 1988, during an interview for an article to be published in *Electronics* magazine, Graves made a number of telling comments.[36] First, he referred to Cisco Systems' products as gateways—not routers—and terminal servers. Second, he stated that their gateway technology could handle networks as large as 100,000 subnets in an integrated WAN comprised of multi-media, multi-protocol, and multi-vendor subsystems. At this time his claims were largely marketing hyperbole, but in the future Cisco and others would make the products to prove his claims prophetic.

Don Valentine, and a fellow senior partner, Pierre Lamond, began devoting the kind of time to Cisco Systems that few companies receive. It became obvious to them that a stronger management team was needed and, in May 1988, Graves was replaced with an interim president until an executive search could identify a candidate acceptable to Sequoia Capital.

Fortunately, the $2.5 million investment Cisco Systems raised proved to be sufficient as eager customers placed orders on attractive terms and the lack of competition allowed the company to essentially build product once orders were received.

35. Brandt, Bunnell, and Brate, *Making the Cisco Connection*, 10–12.

36. "Inside technology," *Electronics*, April 14, 1988, 74.

The combination kept the growth in working capital (accounts receivable plus inventory less accounts payable) to a minimum. Thus, Cisco grew by more than a factor of three for the fiscal year ending July 1988 without having to sell more stock. The sales for fiscal year 1988 totaled $5.5 million with net income before taxes and interest of $555,000.

In October 1988, John Morgridge became the new President and CEO. He would prove to be a superb hire as was the management team he soon recruited. In December 1988, Valentine became Chairman of the Board of Directors. All was going as hoped and planned—other than growing contention with the founders.

Although Cisco was a small organization compared to those Morgridge had managed, his due diligence had accurately revealed to him that the company's products were superb, maybe the best currently available, and, given the market prospects, he had potentially joined a large company disguised as a small one. Even so, he could not have hoped for the outcomes awaiting him.

13.4 Internetworking: Public Demonstrations in 1988

The 1980s marked the beginning of the computer industry's massive trade shows, epitomized by COMDEX. The power of such events did not escape the notice of the promoters of internetworking standards and products. The chief promoters of the era's two internetworking approaches—OSI and TCP/IP—held significant public demonstrations in 1988 (see Table 13.4), on a larger scale than previous gatherings such as the NBS Implementors workshops and Dan Lynch's TCP/IP Vendors Workshop. Both events shared the same purpose: to convince customers that their quests for network interoperability were over.

13.4.1 Enterprise Networking Event

By the fall of 1986, the NBS might have reviewed its actions since 1982 and concluded that it had largely achieved the vision set out by Heafner in 1979: that the DOD buys OSI from IBM. With IBM having blessed MAP earlier in the year, and the DOD having made OSI a co-equal standard to TCP/IP in 1985, the unanswered issue remained the availability of competitive OSI products. To incentivize vendors to build OSI products that interoperated, what better a way than to give contracts for them to do exactly that! Planning for the next big public exhibition began soon after Autofact '85. Only this time the effort would result not in an OSI demonstration but an exposition of products interconnected, working seamlessly, and, most importantly, available for sale. The ENE scheduled for June 5–9, 1988, in Baltimore, MD, was to be the final coming out party for OSI networking (see Figure 13.3).

Three groups sponsored ENE: Corporation for Open Systems (COS), the MAP/-TOP Users Group, and the Society of Manufacturing Engineers. A total of 50

Table 13.4 **ENE and Interop**

	Enterprise Networking Event (ENE)	Interop
Date	June 5–9, 1988	September 26–30, 1988
Vendors	50	54
Attendees	10,000–11,000	5,000
Profiles/Software	MAP/TOP	NSMP/OSPF
Communication Protocols	OSI	TCP/IP
Government Sponsors	Department of Commerce The Institute for Computer Sciences and Technology (ICST) National Bureau of Standards (NBS)	Department of Defense Defense Advanced Research Projects Agency (DARPA)
Sponsors	Corporation for Open Systems (COS) The MAP/TOP Users Group The Society of Manufacturing Engineers (SME)	Interop Internet Activities Board (IAB)

Based on "Open OSI Product & Equipment News" Vol. 1, No. 3, June 6, 1988; "Connexions—The Interoperability Report" Vol 2, No. 11, November 1988.

vendors participated in nine booths, whose sponsors highlighted the event's focus on large-scale manufacturing: GM, Boeing, TRW, John Deere, the Air Force/ Industry Coalition, and Process Industries. COS itself sponsored a booth, as did Britain's Communication Networking for Manufacturing Applications and the British Department of Trade and Industry (in conjunction with British Telecom).

The build-up to ENE contained a mix of hype, promises, and skepticism that was, by this point, a familiar feature of OSI promotions. ENE's organizers could boast that the event's 50 vendors marked a significant jump from 16 vendors at NCC in 1984 and 21 vendors at Autofact '85. All the American computing giants—including IBM, HP, AT&T, Xerox, Data General, Wang, and Honeywell—would be there, as well as leading European manufacturers and a number of smaller and younger internetworking companies such as 3Com, Apple, SUN Microsystems, Micom, Retix, and Touch Communications.[37] Keynote speakers from the upper levels of the Department of Defense, Arthur Andersen, and the Commission of

37. "Giant MAP/TOP demo slated for '88," *ComputerWorld*, December 14, 1987, 55.

Figure 13.3 ENE Proceedings. Source: James L. Pelkey's Conference Proceedings (photo by Loring G. Robbins).

European Communities would reinforce the message that all major stakeholders were behind the global adoption of OSI.[38]

The conference and exposition spotlighted MAP/TOP Version 3.0. An April article in *Data Communications* touted the new capabilities in TOP 3.0, which had thus far been cast as the "weaker sibling of the more acclaimed MAP. . . With Version 3.0, however the tables may be turned. TOP has a strong chance of outdistancing MAP as well as many single-vendor offerings."[39] TOP's new capabilities

38. *ENTERPRISE Conference Proceedings, June 5–9, 1988, Baltimore, Maryland*. Society of Manufacturing Engineers, Dearborn, MI, 1988.

39. *Data Communications*, April 1988.

included standardized, multi-vendor applications such as graphical data interchange, electronic mail, remote file access, remote terminal access, network directories, and—significantly for beleaguered system administrators—network management.[40] Conveniently for NBS officials like Jerry Mulvenna, most of the software on display also fit within GOSIP, which would be published as FIPS 146 during the same decisive month of June 1988.

Not everyone was convinced that the stars were aligning for the big coming out party of MAP, TOP, and GOSIP. Members of COS grumbled that their annual dues of $200,000 were being wasted, the group was being poorly managed, and plans for COS to offer comprehensive conformance testing at ENE would be delayed.[41] The lurking fear was that the OSI's history was repeating itself, and that certified interoperable OSI products would remain unavailable. Critics noted the gulf between "COS promises" and "COS deliveries," and likened COS to a "sprinter who suffers a hamstring pull out of the starting gate."[42] COS became a convenient scapegoat for problems that were endemic throughout 10 years of OSI development: the lack of products, erosion in customer confidence, and annoying tendency for OSI to promise more than it delivered.

ENE confirmed both the hopes of OSI's supporters and the fears of its critics. Vendors were able to demonstrate OSI standards for network management and electronic mail, but the absence of certified conformance testing confirmed that customers would still need to wait for certified OSI products. Instead of products for sale, the estimated 10,000–11,000 attendees saw mostly prototype demonstrations—a marginal improvement on Autofact '85.[43] Even MAP 3.0, presumably the most proven of the OSI profiles, was a disappointment. Experts noted that MAP installations were few and far between, and that MAP performance testing would not exist for another 2 or 3 years.[44] Worse still, a conflict over intellectual property between General Motors and the North American MAP/TOP Users Group threatened to destabilize the market further.[45] Even "Mini-MAP," a three-layer version of MAP intended to be simpler, faster, and cheaper than the original, was

40. Thomas J. Routt. 1988. Under the big TOP at Enterprise '88: TOP 3.0's debut. *Data Communications*, April 1988, 155.

41. John Bush. 1988. COS fiddles with testers while OSI vendors burn. *Data Communications*, February 1988, 51.

42. "COS must act now to reaffirm its OSI role," *Data Communications*, February 1988, 13.

43. John Bush. 1988. COS bats.500 in Baltimore. *Data Communications*, July 1988, 55.

44. Joseph Braue and Lee Mantelman, "European testers make MAP conformance an ENE success," TK citation.

45. Paul R. Strauss. 1988. Flexibility or heresy? The struggle to redraw MAP. *Data Communications*, November 1988, 49–56.

"discredited" by the end of 1988 because it had yet to be deployed. A MAP consultant, Paul Nelson of Venture Development Corp., admitted "I'm not bullish on the market."[46]

Despite some lingering disappointment in the wake of ENE, OSI supporters remained steadfast. They insisted that OSI was maturing, its capabilities were robust, products were appearing, and its support was growing amongst vendors and customers in corporations and governments around the world.[47]

13.4.2 Interop

Despite the transition plans laid out by DOD and NBS to migrate to OSI, the growth of the TCP/IP installed base, the release of more products by more vendors, and the accolades from the technical community, all continued. The ARPANET veteran David Retz summarized the state of affairs in November 1987:

> By the end of 1986, there were more than 100 vendor offerings of TCP/IP and its associated DARPA protocols. Moreover, major vendors, including IBM and Digital Equipment Corp. have recently begun to offer TCP/IP as part of their product lines··· While the long-term strategic direction taken by most companies is in the implementation of the OSI model and its protocols, TCP/IP appears to be solving the short-term problems of connections between networks and has been addressing many of the issues that relate to the implementation of ISO protocols on existing networks. Given the inherently long life cycle of communications software, the TCP/IP protocols are expected to continue as a major influence for years to come.[48]

Six months later, a report from the market research firm Infonetics confirmed that the TCP/IP market was changing rapidly, and that a "dramatic increase in the commercialization of TCP/IP has occurred," and that increasing numbers of users were seeking solutions to integrate diverse computer equipment and networks. "Every sector of the market is planning to purchase TCP/IP products in the next year," the report continued. "There is no indication that OSI is affecting purchase intent." Further, customers still were confused about the functions of bridges and routers, which opened up opportunities for "vendors to enter this market." Many

46. "The incredible shrinking Mini-MAP," *Data Communications*, November 1988, 50.

47. Paul R. Strauss. 1988. The standards deluge: A sound foundation or a Tower of Babel? *Data Communication*, September 1988, 150–164.

48. David Retz. 1987. TCP/IP: DOD suite marches into the business world. *Data Communications*, November 1987, 225.

users had indicated plans to transition from TCP/IP to OSI, but Infonetics concluded, "By the time OSI products are available and proven, considerable investment in TCP/IP will have been made." Given this investment and the imminent improvements to TCP/IP products, the "compatibility, performance and reliability of OSI products must first be proved through field testing before users will be willing to commit to a substantial investment in OSI."[49]

Skeptics also wondered about migration paths between installed TCP/IP networks and OSI-compliant protocols. The response of the TCP/IP community came in the form of an Internet RFC specifying a Simple Network Management Protocol, or SNMP.[50] In a "show of support for multi-vendor network management," vendors such as Proteon, Cisco Systems, and Wellfleet planned to introduce SNMP-based products at Interop. These products, such as Proteon's Overview, provided a graphical interface for tools to manage the status of Internetworks and network devices—precisely the type of product that network managers longed for. They also provided simple migration paths for users who would eventually adopt OSI's Common Management Information Protocol once it was standardized.[51]

Interop's "show network" featured lots of products: "every medium, every bridge box, every router you can imagine," according to Peter de Vries of the Wollongong Group, which was responsible for the Interop network (see Figure 13.4). The network provided connections between all of the vendors on display, as well as links to NSFNET, the regional BARRNET in San Francisco, and a variety of other networks. Vendors could participate in TCP/IP "bake-offs," where they could check to see if their equipment interoperated with other vendors' products. Self-appointed "net police" went so far as to hand out "tickets" to implementations that did not comply with the TCP/IP specifications.[52]

In many respects, Interop '88 was far more successful than ENE. It featured working products from more vendors than ENE. Also, in contrast to ENE, the target audiences differed in important ways. Where ENE carried the burden of MAP, TOP, and GOSIP expectations to provide comprehensive solutions for large-scale manufacturing, office, and government procurement, Interop stayed focused on the immediate and narrower problems of network interconnection. In the "age of standards," as *Data Communications* declared, this focus on internetworking product

49. Infonetics, "TCP/IP: The User Perspective 1988," May 1988, 1.

50. J. Case, M. Fedor, M. Schoffstall, and J. Davin, August 1988, "A Simple Network Management Protocol," RFC 1067, http://www.ietf.org/rfc/rfc1067.txt.

51. Mary Petrosky. 1988. Vendors to unveil bevy of SNMP wares. *Network World*, September 19, 1988, 19–20.

52. "Show network joins 54 vendors, remote links," *InfoWorld*, October 10, 1988, 18.

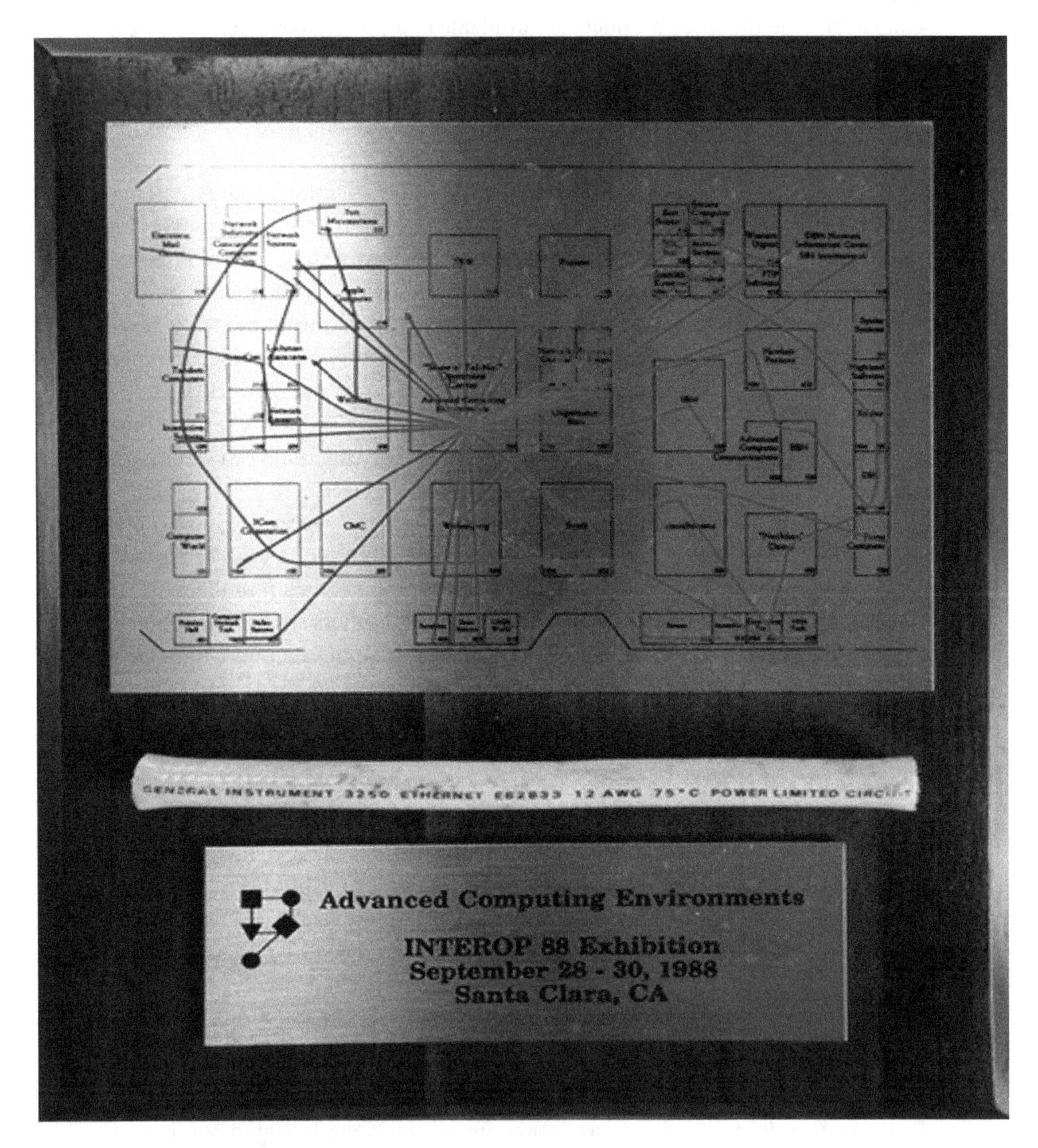

Figure 13.4 Interop '88 commemorative plaque. Source: Plaque given out by Dan Lynch to vendors and engineers (photo by Loring G. Robbins).

Figure 13.5 Interop '88. Photo courtesy of Margot Simmons.

compatibility, interoperability, and connectivity energized the ~5,000 attendees (see Figure 13.5) as well as the market for TCP/IP products.[53]

13.5 Internetworking Market-Structure

By the end of 1988, the internetworking market-structure was well established and was beginning to show signs of higher growth and competition. The short term seemed to belong to entrepreneurs and venture capital-backed start-ups with working TCP/IP products. And while OSI's proponents in government and industry struggled to bring OSI products to the market, their strategy to garner a widespread global consensus around the future of internetworking was still on track.

A limited number of existing companies and a few well-funded start-ups, both with strong engineering background in networking hardware and protocols, were

53. "The age of standards: Promises, products, and problems," *Data Communications*, September, 1988, 13.

responsible for launching this emergent stage of the market-structure. The technology of the network level products—gateways and routers—was complex, which kept the number of early entrants in the market to a minimum. Successful products were often the result of combined efforts with universities, like Proteon's connection with MIT and Cisco's roots in the Stanford University computing community. Start-ups like Wellfleet, even with ample financial backing and a strong, diverse engineering team, struggled to release competitive products in this early stage. Table 13.5 shows the importance of key networking companies in the early internetworking market.

The data in Table 13.6 reveals an important point: in 1988, these products needed to interface multiple networking standards and protocols. Clearly for this market-structure to take off into the high growth competitive phase, a consensus around dominant design would have to evolve.

The overlaps and confusion between OSI and TCP/IP contributed to the unsettled nature typical of market-structures that are still in a phase of emergence. Despite speculation in the press and sniping between respective advocates of TCP/IP and OSI, leaders of the Internet community had recognized at its first meeting in January 1986 that they would need to convert TCP/IP to OSI-compatible packets.[54] To that end, the IAB and IETF had established Working Groups in 1987 to integrate Internet and OSI technologies for electronic mail, directory services, and fundamental network protocols. And vendors such as 3Com claimed to be motivated by the challenge—and market opportunities—of mapping TCP/IP systems to their OSI equivalents.[55] Optimists believed the standards wars were in the past

Table 13.5 **1988 Bridge and router installed base**

Company	Installed Base Market Share (%)
DEC	28
3Com	17
Vitalink	12
Ungermann-Bass	5
Proteon	4
Cisco Systems	4
Other	28
TOTAL	100

Based on *Data Communications*, July 1989, 63.

54. Proceedings of the first IETF meeting.

55. H. Kim Lew and Cyndi Jung. 1988. Getting there from here: Mapping from TCP/IP to OSI. *Data Communications*, August 1988, 161–175.

and a harmonious era of internetworking was just around the corner, as the NBS's Rosenthal summarized in 1988:

> There's a clear message to industry, to the TCP developers of the world, to begin tooling up for OSI. A very pleasant migration strategy, if you will; very supportive of US industry, just like a new horizon, another goal for industry to reach, very well specified.[56]

Rosenthal and others were reasonable to expect that it was only a matter of time before the new horizon of OSI would approach—even if many were unsure that the migration would be "pleasant." The final plot twist of the drama of internetworking standards—the triumph of TCP/IP and the collapse of OSI—wouldn't become fully evident until the mid-1990s.

13.6 In Perspective

The evolution of internetworking in the mid to late 1980s was built on technologies that were a culmination of over two decades of research, product development, and market validation. Born out of the unique set of circumstances that combined large government and institutional sponsored research and development efforts, widespread proliferation of computing technologies, and a new culture of venture-backed entrepreneurship, the internetworking industry cemented the dominance of computing in the workplace.

While the pioneers of local area networking had to wait for the arrival of the computer on each desktop before the market began to demand their products, once the value of these products had been established a process was set in motion for the growth of connected computing. As businesses, governments, and educational institutions adopted networking, the demand for interconnectivity was a logical outcome based on network effects. In this regard, the challenges of producer-driven economics of the early networking market gave way to the dominance of demand-driven growth in the internetworking market. As the building blocks of the networking industry were standardized and commoditized and the spread of networks began to take off, demand for interconnection followed without the previous barriers to adoption experienced by the early LAN companies.

By the end of 1988, the demand for internetworking was outpacing the ability of governing and standards-making bodies to foster consensus on a path forward.

56. Robert Rosenthal, interview by James L. Pelkey, May 4, 1988, Washington, DC. Computer History Museum, Mountain View, CA. Available from https://archive.computerhistory.org/resources/access/text/2020/04/102792038-05-01-acc.pdf.

Table 13.6 **1989 router vendors**

Vendor	Product Type	Product	Local Nets Connected	Protocols Supported	Price
NET	Router	Lan Exchange 50	802.3 to 802.5	TCP/IP, DECnet, XNS, X.25, AppleTalk	$21,000 (for one link)
3Com	Local Routing Bridge	IB/2000	802.3 to same	Not appl.	$5,250
Ungermann-Bass	Routing Bridge	Net/One Ethernet to Ethernet	802.3 to same	Not appl.	$9,450
Ungermann-Bass	Routing Bridge	Net/One Token Ring to Ethernet	802.3 to 802.5	Not appl.	$9,450
Proteon	Router	p4100 Series Router	Ethernet Versions 1 and 2 to 802.3; 802.5 to Proteon Pro-net-4 and ProNet-50	TCP/IP, XNS, IPX	$3,795

Table 13.6 *(continued)*

Vendor	Product Type	Product	Local Nets Connected	Protocols Supported	Price
Proteon	Router	p4200 Series Router	Ethernet Versions 1 and 2 to 802.3; 802.5 to Proteon Pro-net-4 and ProNet-50	TCP/IP, XNS, IPX	$7,900 (base)
Communication Machinery Corp. (CMC)	Router	DRN-3200 DDN Gateway	802.3 to X. 25	TCP/IP, DDN, X.25	$11,990
Cisco	Router	AGS	802.3 to 802.5	TCP/IP, DDN, X.25, DECnet, AppleTalk, IPX	$15,000
Vitalink	Router/ Bridge	TransPATH	802.3 or 802.5	Not appl.	$12,500 to $20,000
Wellfleet	Router	Link Node/ Concentrator Node	Ethernet Versions 1 and 2; 802.3 to same	TCP/IP, XNS, IPX, OSI, AppleTalk	$10,000 (Link Node) $18,000 (Concentra-tor Node)

Based on *Network World*, August 7, 1989, 34–38.

The result was a market that validated multiple technologies and product solutions. Even as the dominant designs of Ethernet and TCP/IP were emerging, for internetworking solutions to offer true interoperability, support for the many LAN technologies and protocols would be a requirement well into the next decade.

Conclusions

Our story ends in 1988, with optimism and enthusiasm about the as-yet-unrealized potential of computer-communication networks. The promise of these new technologies was driven by relentless efforts of entrepreneurs from private companies, government agencies, and academic institutions, doing their utmost to learn about digital technologies in the midst of uncertainty and rapid change. The most eager users of these digital networks were not individual consumers; rather, they were the companies and organizations that sent representatives to standards committee meetings and trade shows like Interop and the Enterprise Networking Event. Experts who participated in these collaborative venues were on the forefront of design and production decisions about how digital internetworking would work.

So much had changed in the two decades between 1968 and 1988. The incumbent giants AT&T and IBM had been diminished by the combination of antitrust suits, changes in regulatory policy (such as the Carterfone decision and *Computer* inquiries), and market competition. Together, these changes cleared a path for hundreds of start-up companies to compete in market-structures for data communications, networking, and internetworking. Government officials in the United States had to recalibrate their strategies to fit within new frameworks of deregulation and global competition. As a result, their approach to the convergence of computer and communication technologies was inescapably experimental since the underlying regulatory approaches were new. Underlying this rapid growth in technologies, universities all over the world graduated students at all levels who were expert in computer communications, producing a huge influx of talent into the workforce.

In this final chapter we'll review some data about the three market-structures featured in the book. We'll reflect briefly on the internetworking market-structure after our close analysis ends in 1988. And we'll reflect more generally on the enduring consequences of computer communications for the global economy and society.

14.1 Summary of Market-Structures, 1968–1988

In the chapters of this book, we have shown how these events all contributed to the emergence of three distinct market-structures. In each case, we have seen how the market-structure proceeded through three stages: The early stage of *emergence*, then rapid growth of revenue through *competition*, then *order*, evident in the flattening of revenues and constriction of the number of firms. These stages map to the slopes of the S curve that is so familiar to business students, managers, and executives.

The first market-structure, data communications, emerged between 1967–1971 in response to regulatory changes, the need for remote peripheral connections to mainframe computers, growth in the number of time-sharing and service bureau firms, advances in semiconductor technology, availability of venture capital, and a hot IPO market. The *competitive* phase in this market-structure was in the 1970s, and *order* was established in the late 1970s.

The second market-structure that we examined, networking, started to emerge in the late 1970s, fueled by the boom in minicomputer sales. In 1979, eager entrepreneurs launched three important LAN start-ups: 3Com, Ungermann-Bass, and Sytek. The competitive phase of networking, in the early 1980s, was particularly intense as over 100 firms announced products (both the datacom and networking market-structures grew to over 100 firms). The networking market exploded with the introduction of personal computers, and battles over standards and network topologies raged in committees and boardrooms. Order was established in the mid to late 1980s with the growing popularity of Ethernet and token ring networks—and the control of the market by a handful of vendors.

The third market-structure, internetworking, emerged out of the conditions of networking. Corporations soon found themselves managing a proliferation of isolated networks, often from different vendors and of different technologies. Interconnecting these disparate networks into larger enterprise-wide networks became the next phase of growth for computer communications. Some data communications and networking companies, such as NET, Proteon, and DEC, understood the technology of internetworking and were successful in selling products for this new market. But none were able to establish themselves as market leaders. They were largely consumed with their own market opportunities, or problems, and lost out on what would in time be the largest computer communication market. A new breed of internetworking firms emerged, including SynOptics, Retix, Cabletron, Chipcom, StrataCom, Wellfleet, and Cisco Systems. The products these and a score of existing companies developed introduced a variety of hardware and software solutions designed to integrate the popular networking technologies of the day.

Table 14.1 **Computer communications market revenues, 1982–1988 ($ millions)**

	1982	1983	1984	1985	1986	1987	1988
Data Communications							
Data Modems	675	791	866	934	962	993	873
PC Modems	96	127	182	233	281	307	389
Multiplexors	180	245	289	303	319	256	194
Data PBX	45	77	119	143	86	82	80
T-1 Multiplexors		30	61	158	241	309	388
Total	996	1,270	1,517	1,771	1,889	1,947	1,924
Networking							
Local Area Networks	64	153	327	594	914	1,676	2,821
Internetworking							
Bridges and Routers			20	30	45	90	175
Total Computer Communications	$1,060	$1,423	$1,864	$2,395	$2,848	$3,713	$4,920

Based on "Local Area Network Equipment," "Modems," "Statistical Multiplexers," "Data PBX," Dataquest Inc., September, October, November 1989.

The internetworking market-structure rapidly exhibited signs of dramatic and highly profitable growth—from $81.4 million in revenues in 1987 to $165 million in 1988.

The overall picture that emerges across these three market-structures is very clear: immense growth and profitability (see Table 14.1). In the short span of four years, 1985–1988, the revenue of the Computer Communications market doubled, its growth rate leaping to 32% in 1988 on the back of the 68% growth in LANs. Obviously, not all products were doing as well as others, such as the stagnating category of Data Modems compared to LANs. It is easy to see why Codex was under pressure to find another product to fuel sales growth like LANs; sales of Data Modems having been flat since 1984. Or, if a company selling primarily multiplexers didn't also sell T1 Multiplexers, they were likely having problems, or were seeking to merge.

Figure 14.1 represents the same data but in simplified, graphical form, which emphasizes that in the late 1980s the total *computer communications* market was growing rapidly, based predominantly on the high growth of networking, while growth in data communications was minimal. The exception in the data communications market was the T1 Multiplexer category, which experienced a market growing at 25% in 1988. Even so, the leading firm in T1 multiplexers, NET, grew at the impressive rate of 50% in 1988—faster than many networking companies.

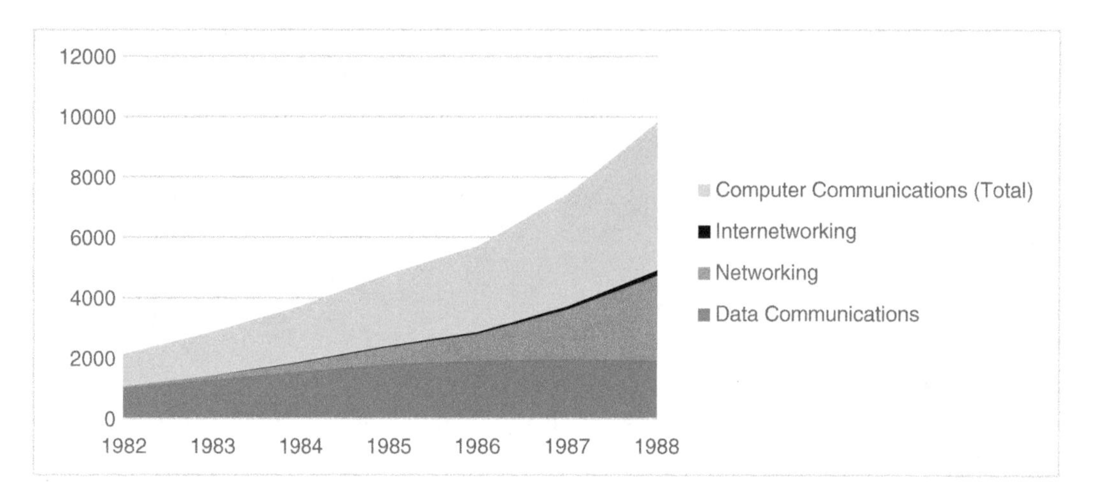

Figure 14.1 Computer communications market revenues ($ millions) 1982–1988. Based on "Local Area Network Equipment," "Modems," "Statistical Multiplexers," "Data PBX," Dataquest Inc., September, October, November 1989.

14.2 Internetworking, 1988–2020

It would be strange for us to end this book without remarking on some significant changes in internetworking that occurred *after* 1988. We do not have the same depth of source material to analyze the subsequent decades, but we can place some of the more significant developments into our analytical framework.

By the 1990s, dominant designs were established in both networking and internetworking. The first was the establishment of Ethernet as the dominant design for networking. By the mid-1990s, Ethernet had become the choice of IT professionals with regards to price, performance, and, most importantly, interoperability. As the industry coalesced around Ethernet, the requirements of internetworking devices to interconnect rival technologies eventually became unnecessary.[1]

The second dominant design came with the victory of the TCP/IP Internet in its "standards war" against OSI. In many organizations, TCP/IP networks were envisioned as an interim solution but became permanent when OSI products failed to materialize in the market. OSI's fundamental problem—its inability to reconcile too many distinct stakeholder perspectives—arose, ironically, from its democratic

1. This evolution of Ethernet, which was adopted by IEEE as the 10Base-T standard in 1990, was based in part on AT&T's StarLAN, and SynOptics' LattisNet. The switch to a star configuration organized around a central hub and the use of telephone wire removed the remaining technical advantages of token ring networks and cleared the way for mass adoption of Ethernet. Continued upgrades to Ethernet standards followed, including 100Mbps "Fast Ethernet" (1995); Gigabit per second (1999); and 10Gbps (2006). For an in-depth history of Ethernet, see Urs von Burg. 2001. *The Triumph of Ethernet: Technological Communities and the Battle for the LAN Standard*. Stanford University Press.

commitment to an inclusive design and standardization process. As OSI staggered under its own weight, TCP/IP's momentum came from many sources. In the United States, the National Science Foundation's NSFNET supported TCP/IP connections first for university researchers and, after 1991, for commercial traffic. That same year, Internet users around the world could download Tim Berners-Lee's inventions, the software and browser that connected them to the World Wide Web.[2] By the late 1990s, the Web and Internet—no longer referred to as the DOD Internet or TCP/IP Internet—fueled the dot-com era, the birth of thousands of new start-ups, and, in many ways, profound transformations throughout the global economy.[3]

Again, our fundamental point is this: behind every connection to the Internet, there was a TCP/IP router built by one of the companies in the internetworking market-structure. The global expansion of the Internet drove—and was enabled by—the expansion of this market-structure.

One company in particular emerged as the victor: Cisco Systems, founded in December 1984.[4] Cisco was a product of its environment. Founded by two Stanford employees, Cisco benefitted from government-subsidized research, sources of talent at nearby universities, labor markets with experienced executives, engineers, and managers, and ready sources of venture capital. Cisco's early successes were the results of good products and good timing. It got a head start with multi-protocol routers and established a strong reputation there. A chief competitor, Wellfleet, stumbled early with delays in getting products to market. Cisco was able to take advantage, thanks to their robust marketing and sales efforts.

Simply put, Cisco was better at telling a great marketing story to large companies and making key inroads in a variety of industries. They did exceptionally well to meet the needs of large enterprise customers. In 1990, Cisco was the leader for single and multi-protocol routers, with 35% of the market

2. Berners-Lee worked at the European research organization CERN, which had authorized the use of TCP/IP internally in 1988, and a year later in external connections to the Internet—another indication that Europe's hardline support of OSI had started to wither with the lack of commercial OSI products. Ben Segal. A Short History of Internet Protocols at CERN. Retrieved January 1, 2021, from http://ben.web.cern.ch/ben/TCPHIST.html.

3. To appreciate the broad outlines and nuances of the Internet's successful privatization and global adoption, readers should start with Janet Abbate. 1999. *Inventing the Internet*. MIT Press; and Shane Greenstein. 2015. *How the Internet Became Commercial: Innovation, Privatization, and the Birth of a New Network*. Princeton University Press.

4. Insider accounts of Cisco's success include David Bunnell and Adam Brate. 2000. *Making the Cisco Connection: The Story Behind the Real Internet Superpower*. John Wiley & Sons; Ed Paulson. 2001. *Inside Cisco: The Real Story of Sustained M&A Growth*. John Wiley & Sons. See also Computer History Museum, "Center for Cisco Heritage," https://computerhistory.org/center-for-cisco-heritage/.

(compared to DEC with 20.3%, 3Com with 13.2%, and Wellfleet with 8.7%.)[5] And when Cisco went public on February 16, 1990, its IPO document cited over 4,000 systems that had already been installed "by over 400 customers in the industrial, financial, government and university markets, including Aetna Life and Casualty Co., AT&T, Ford Motor Company, General Electric Company, Harvard University, The Hewlett-Packard Company, [and] Morgan Stanley & Co. Inc."[6]

Cisco's mastery of the technical aspects of multi-protocol routing, before the dominant design of the TCP/IP router emerged, fueled its early rise to market dominance. Cisco also responded well to the rapid expansion of TCP/IP-based networks in the late 1980s and early 1990s, which drove unprecedented demand for routing products. It nurtured strong connections with the TCP/IP community early in its history and continued to build those connections in the 1990s and 2000s. Moreover, Cisco built effective strategic partnerships, and became widely admired in Silicon Valley for its track record of acquiring start-ups with key innovations in internetworking technology and telecommunications switching.[7] This outward-facing approach helped Cisco build a strong reputation for high quality engineering and an ability to bring important innovations to its customers—vital factors for maintaining its strong position in the lucrative market segments for routers and switches.

By 1999, Cisco had established a commanding 77% market share in the router market. Its closest competitor, Nortel (which had acquired Bay Networks, the company that was formed by the merger of Wellfleet and SynOptics), trailed with only 6.9%, followed by Fujitsu (2.5%) and 3Com (2.4%).[8] And on March 27, 2000—near the peak of the dot-com bubble—Cisco's market capitalization exploded to $569 billion, making it the *most valuable company on earth.*[9] As we noted earlier, we're not in a position to analyze this era of internetworking history in any detail; but we're sure that historians who study this period will need to reckon with Cisco's continued success, as well as the rise of competitors such as Juniper Networks and Huawei.

---

5. International Data Corp, Framingham, MA. "Analysis of Internetwork Market."

6. Cisco, Company Prospectus and Registration Statement for Initial Public Offering, 1990.

7. One example of a profitable partnership was Cisco's agreements with hub companies, like Cabeltron and SynOptics, to sell its routers as components of "intelligent" hubs.

8. Mark Doms. 2003. Prices for Local Area Network Equipment. Federal Reserve Bank of San Francisco, June 2003.

9. Brad Reese. 2010. Cisco's storied past as the most valuable company on earth. *Network World*, February 18, 2010, https://www.networkworld.com/article/2229885/cisco-s-storied-past-as-the-most-valuable-company-on-earth.html; "Cisco ascends to most valuable company," *CNET.com*, January 2, 2002, available from https://www.cnet.com/news/cisco-ascends-to-most-valuable-company/.

Finally, it's also important to note that Cisco's continued success depends, to a significant degree, on the fact that the dominant design for internetworking has remained consistent since the late 1980s. This long phase of stability—three decades and counting, as of this writing—stands in sharp contrast to the rapid technological and market changes that we have seen in the period between 1968 and 1988. To be sure, there have been incremental innovations, particularly in wireless standards and equipment. But the Internet backbone remains dependent on version 4 of the Internet Protocol, despite numerous (unsuccessful) attempts to transition to IP version 6 (specified in 1998), as well as various "clean slate" exercises to design a new set of Internet protocols that escape the "lock-in" factor of IP version 4.

14.3 Three Themes

The three central themes that we developed to analyze the period from 1968–1988 also provide a useful framework for understanding the post-1988 period. We'd like to take a little time to illustrate how these themes can help to inform an analysis of internetworking after 1988, and to raise some questions that researchers should address.

Our first theme, *entrepreneurship*, has been an intense focus of researchers, investors, and ambitious individuals all over the world. In many ways, Joseph Schumpeter is widely regarded as the patron saint of the digital economy. The phenomenon of "creative destruction" has been felt in almost every conceivable industry, with "disruptions" occurring in markets such as traditional "landline" telephone service, local bookstores, and even the mundane tasks of hailing a taxi or booking a hotel room. The impact of entrepreneurial start-ups on the evolution of the digital economy is hard to overstate, and companies founded during the Internet era—such as Amazon, Google, and Facebook—are now among the most highly-valued companies in the world.

A new business model, embodied by Cisco, features a start-up firm that uses venture capital and acquisitions to build market share rapidly. The growth in venture capital investment played an important role in our story from 1968–1988, and only grew in importance afterwards, during the "Get Big Fast" era of dot-com growth in the 1990s.[10]

The emergence of cable modems provides one example of entrepreneurship in internetworking in the 1990s. One early cable modem start-up was LanCity,

10. William Lazonick. 2009. *Sustainable Prosperity in the New Economy? Business Organization and High-Tech Unemployment in the United States*. W.E. Upjohn Institute for Employment Research, Kalamazoo, MI; Brent Goldfarb and David A. Kirsch. 2019. *Bubbles and Crashes: The Boom and Bust of Technological Innovation*. Stanford University Press.

founded by the Iranian American engineer Rouzbeh Yassini—who is sometimes celebrated as the "father of the cable modem." LanCity was the first company to successfully innovate a low-cost cable modem at a time when the dominant providers of high-speed Internet service were all telecommunications companies offering T1, T3, and DSL. Other companies—some start-ups, some established—followed, and standards for cable modems ultimately were set within IEEE and CableLabs, a consortium funded by the cable television industry. The publication of the CableLabs DOCSIS standard in 1997 was an important step in validating the work of start-ups like LanCity and accelerating the adoption of a standard device in many people's homes today.

We would hope to see histories of internetworking after 1988 address several questions about entrepreneurship: who were the most effective entrepreneurs in the arenas of standards-setting, public support for R&D, and national and international policies to facilitate innovation and competition? And, within established companies, what were the consequences of the "intrapreneurship" trend—was it effective in driving the internal transformation of companies such as GE or IBM? What were the most successful new companies producing routers and switches, both for fixed and wireless access to the Internet? And how did regional planners fare with their attempts to build "innovation districts" that could replicate the successful features of Silicon Valley?[11] In contrast to popular accounts of Silicon Valley that feature entrepreneurs in the heroic mold—Jobs, Zuckerberg, and so forth—we hope *Circuits, Packets, and Protocols* has demonstrated that teams and collectives are essential for building successful companies. All of the successful companies in these three industries, including Codex, 3Com, and Cisco, relied on multiple individuals with expertise in key areas such as establishing a company mission and vision, management, engineering, marketing, and sales, among others.

The prospect of lasting success has remained elusive for many start-ups. Despite the confident predictions of futurists and management consultants, very few (if any) individuals had a vision and clear understanding of where these technologies were going and how to get there.[12] With the exception of Cisco, not

11. The entrepreneurial culture of Silicon Valley has served as a model for regional innovation districts in the United States and around the world. AnnaLee Saxenian. 1996. *Regional Advantage: Culture and Competition in Silicon Valley and Route 128*. Harvard University Press; Martin Kenney, ed. 2000. *Understanding Silicon Valley: The Anatomy of an Entrepreneurial Region*. Stanford University Press; Margaret Pugh O'Mara. 2005. *Cities of Knowledge: Cold War Science and the Search for the Next Silicon Valley*. Princeton University Press.

12. Incumbents missed opportunities with striking regularity. Common examples include Microsoft's late entry to the web, Blockbuster's demise in the face of streaming video, and taxi companies ignoring the potential for app-based ride-hailing.

a single company that we feature in this book was able to create lasting success on the basis of computer communications. Rather, they were all crowded out, one way or another, by upstarts and newcomers.[13] Perhaps in anticipation of this likely scenario, business school courses in entrepreneurship often emphasize strategies for selling out and moving on, rather than creating a stable and sustainable business model. Indeed, successful entrepreneurs have a relentless streak in them, which means they rarely give up after one failed attempt. One of the most enduring lessons from the dynamic, Schumpeterian worldview is this: since technologies and markets are always changing, it is imperative that historians pay attention to entrepreneurs and new companies that are on the forefront of change.

Our second theme of *government–market boundaries* also continued to be vitally important after 1988. The US federal government shaped computer communications in a variety of ways, including through immigration and tax policies, support for higher education, a continued reliance on the private sector to develop technical standards, subsidies for research, and attempts to use regulation to limit social or economic harms arising from private actors. Increasingly, issues of government involvement in industry, including battles over intellectual property rights, have taken on international and global dimensions, evident in regulations around security and encryption as well as diplomatic standoffs over state-backed vendors such as the Chinese company Huawei. The effect of tariffs and other trade policies on global supply chains highlights another intersection of governments and markets. Many technological developments are negotiated across these boundaries, including the development of new standards such as IP version 6 and cellular standards (3G, 4G, 5G). These standards were increasingly negotiated on a global scale, under the watchful eye of government officials in the European Union and China.

Federal investments in R&D and infrastructure continued after 1988. It's worth pausing to note the deep significance of SAGE and the ARPANET—projects that required the funding and organization of many levels of oversight and implementation, and that no other government agency, and certainly no private company, could afford to attempt. Once the success of ARPA's investment in TCP/IP became

13. Here we would also like to note the failures of the incumbents in our story, namely AT&T and IBM, in their dogged pursuit of opportunities available in each other's markets as the technologies of computing and communications converged. Even with their sizable R&D budgets and high-profile acquisitions, IBM's efforts to sell communications products and AT&T's efforts to sell computers resulted in the loss of billions for both companies. See John Markoff, "I.B.M. to Sell Rolm to Siemens," The New York Times (December 14, 1988), Section D, p. 1; and John J. Keller, "Disconnected Line: Why AT&T Takeover Of NCR Hasn't Been A Real Bell Ringer," Wall Street Journal, September 19, 1995, p. A1.

more widely understood in the 1990s, policymakers sought to replicate the model to develop technologies in clean energy and security—efforts whose success may be best evaluated after decades, not months or years.[14] In early 2020, journalists and officials pointed out that DARPA itself had invested in DNA and RNA vaccines in 2011, at a time when no company or government agency would take the risk—efforts that paid off handsomely a decade later with the development of vaccines for COVID-19.[15] But other ambitious programs, such as NSF's "Clean Slate" initiative for networking, did not seem to generate industry-changing results. A closer look at internetworking since 1988 surely would need to consider the relative benefits of different kinds of government investments.

Many applications have been made possible by internetworking, including social media, voice over IP, gaming, and telehealth. Entrepreneurship and innovation in these areas is possible thanks to the low boundaries to entry for software applications, and the relatively frictionless and unregulated environment that new companies exploit to "move fast and break things" (to steal a phrase from Facebook's early motto). However, companies that push limits in this environment also have attracted the scrutiny of government regulators who were torn between nourishing their growth and limiting their negative effects on citizens. After the Justice Department's 1999 high profile antitrust case against Microsoft, there was a notable turn toward restraint in federal antitrust enforcement in the first two decades of the 21st century. Policymakers tended to have little faith in their own abilities to predict and steer fast-moving digital markets, preferring an approach where "platform competition" in the market would work out most problems. Regulators in Europe were less enamored by companies such as Facebook and Google, and in 2021 there seemed to be a growing appetite on both sides of the Atlantic to hold these companies accountable for anticompetitive behaviors.

Our third theme, *learning*, likewise remained prominent in the post-1988 period. As the internetworking market-structure grew, companies struggled to hire educated engineers. Around the world, universities responded by creating new graduate programs and churning out more qualified engineers—aided by heavy investments from national governments. A study from 2019 noted that 65,000 students graduate from US bachelor degree programs in computer science, compared

14. Erica R. H. Fuchs. 2009. Cloning DARPA successfully. *Issues in Science and Technology* 26, 1, 65–70; "DARPA 'lookalikes' must ground their dreams in reality," *Nature* 579 (March 11, 2020), 173–174.

15. Steve Usdin. 2020. DARPA's gambles might have created the best hopes for stopping COVID-19. *Biocentury*, March 19, 2020, https://www.biocentury.com/article/304691/darpa-s-gambles-might-have-created-the-best-hopes-for-stopping-covid-19.

to 185,000 in China and 215,000 in India.[16] Companies needing more specific skills experimented with in-house training (such as Motorola University), and developed programs to train and certify professionals, such as the dozens of certifications offered by Cisco and Microsoft. The vast amounts of information available on the World Wide Web created new opportunities for learning in every demographic, from infants to senior citizens. Some educational institutions shifted to on-line learning faster than others—and many who waited were suddenly forced on-line in 2020 due to the COVID-19 pandemic. The Internet and Web facilitated informal learning around subjects of all kinds, from people who wanted to learn to code, to those seeking information about home repairs or hobbies, to those who looked for inspiration in TED talks, podcasts, and more.

As with our two other key concepts, we can imagine several questions related to learning that we recommend to scholars who research the period after 1988. A retrospective look at business school cases would be fascinating: which companies were first held up as exemplars but were later removed from the annals of success stories? There also has been a notable interest amongst scholars and executives alike to learn from failure: what approaches to innovation worked, what didn't, and why? Finally, we have noticed some reluctance, again amongst both scholars and industry professionals, to scrutinize the origin myths of the Internet itself, or to revisit aspects of the Internet where the veneer of novelty has worn off. For example: the openness of the Internet was a key of its rapid adoption; but it also has made security and privacy much more difficult to enforce. And, despite the many flaws of IP version 4 that are widely known, why has it been so difficult to learn from these flaws and build and deploy superior protocols?

14.4 Final Thoughts

Given the spread of internetworking into every conceivable aspect of life in the 21st century, it can be challenging to address the reasonable question that every history book should answer: So what? Why should readers care? We would like to conclude *Circuits, Packets, and Protocols* by highlighting a few ideas that stand out to us as especially important for readers to take away.

The first idea is the *foundational importance of packet-switching*, which we view as a world-historical innovation. The story of computer communications is, by and large, a series of stories about incremental innovations that were patched together by technical standards, dozens of companies, and hundreds of brilliant minds. But the single most important innovation was packet-switching, invented

16. Prashant Loyalka, et al. 2019. Computer science skills across China, India, Russia, and the United States. *Proceedings of the National Academy of Sciences* 116 (April 2019), 6732–6736.

independently by Paul Baran at RAND and Donald Davies at the National Physical Lab. Both men, working in strikingly different contexts, saw the potential for computers to help create more robust systems of communication that could overcome the vulnerabilities in more centralized networks. A third visionary, Louis Pouzin, had the most advanced grasp of how to implement these ideas in a new paradigm of networking, the datagram-based Cyclades project he led in France in the 1970s.

Thanks to packet-switched networks and internetworking, specifically the advent of Voice over IP, a person on one part of the globe can talk or share video with someone on another continent for the same cost as connecting to the local Internet service provider. Packet switching has made possible more robust and efficient transfer of information at a fraction of the cost. The result is the global boom in connectivity that many of us take for granted, evident in real-time tracking of parcels and improved logistics in manufacturing, shipping, and transportation. When combined with the ever-increasing power of computation, Internet-enabled connectivity also feeds the growth of industries such as data analysis, machine learning, and artificial intelligence.

The second idea that we'd like to emphasize here is one that we chose not to emphasize throughout the book—the *mixed societal implications of computer communications*. Indeed, most readers will have been familiar with networking and internetworking not because they knew much about the companies or technical standards we have discussed, but rather because they have experienced and witnessed changes in the world around them. As we finish this manuscript, there is a notable increase in pessimistic views about whether or not global interconnection has been a blessing or a curse. Internet users endure waves of misinformation, spam, malware, and services designed to addict us and steal our attention. Citizens and regulators are taking aggressive actions to curb the harmful actions of dominant internetworking corporations such as Amazon, Facebook, and Google. The extent to which these platforms have permeated the global population raise concerns over their largely unregulated behavior in managing, and selling, user data. The issues range from the threat of individual data privacy to the potential destabilization of governments. At the same time, regulators and activists worry that the benefits of internetworking are not equitably distributed. Although citizens on the other side of the "digital divide" are untroubled by the caustic effects of social media, they do not have access to the benefits provided by digital networks—we are thinking in particular of formal and informal opportunities for education and learning, access to financial services, telehealth, and the possibility of remote work.

While the risks of unregulated commercial activity at the massive scale of today's digital platforms is becoming real, the benefits of the global reach of the

Internet are real as well. The original vision of the early pioneers of computing, like Paul Baran, J.C.R. Licklider, Robert Taylor, and Louis Pouzin was to facilitate collaboration among communities of like-minded researchers in distant locations and to reduce dependency on centralized authorities. To these ends, the Internet has been an undeniable source of power. It has also been a source of comfort and an ally for those who are confronting major global challenges, such as threats to public health, extreme weather-related disasters, and the growing demand for food production and delivery. We are certain that internetworking will continue to aid those whose goal is to ease the suffering of others or to address the many injustices of global society.

The final idea we would like our readers to consider is that our account in *Circuits, Packets, and Protocols* is only one of many possible reconstructions of the era between 1968 and 1988. We have drawn on close to 2,000 pages of interview transcripts, company and industry financial data, and the personal experiences of James L. Pelkey from his career as an executive and investor in these industries. We have done our best to present the material in a way that illustrates the character and decision-making process of each of the individuals involved in this history from their perspective at the time of these events. As a technological history, we tried to strike a balance between including enough detail to demonstrate the rapid changes of the inner workings of computer communication technology—without overwhelming readers. As a business history, it was our goal to bring attention to some of the key events and patterns in the evolution of these businesses and the market-structures in which they existed. We also tried to render a realistic picture of the uncertainty that was an ever-present reality in these companies and organizations. And, as we stated in the Introduction, we did our best to insulate our analysis from our knowledge of who would emerge as the winners and losers of the events we described. We are fortunate that Pelkey had the interest and foresight to conduct and record so many interviews. These were indeed the key elements that allowed us to take a comprehensive approach that uses a horizontal scan across entire market-structures, as opposed to the customary vertical approaches focused on specific firms or products. We believe that scholars who seek to illuminate the dynamics of emerging technologies would do well to replicate Pelkey's large-scale, real-time interviewing strategy. We close by repeating our invitation for readers to explore the transcripts of the interviews and additional market research in the James L. Pelkey Collection at the Computer History Museum, to draw their own conclusions, and to share their ideas, too.

APPENDIX

List of Interviews

Name	Affiliation	Date	Bio	Transcript	Pages
Abramson, Norm	University of Hawaii	10/13/1988	bio	transcript	13
Bachman, Charles	ISO Open Systems Interconnect (OSI)	10/26/1988	bio	transcript	11
Baran, Paul	RAND Corporation	01/12/1988	bio	transcript	24
Bass, Charlie	Ungermann-Bass	08/16/1994	bio	transcript	28
Bell, Gordon	Digital Equipment Corporation (DEC)	06/17/1988	bio	transcript	35
Bingham, John	Vadic	03/23/1988	bio	transcript	18
Botwinick, Edward	Timeplex	03/10/1988	bio	transcript	12
Carr, Art	Codex	04/06/1988	bio	transcript	34
Carrico, Bill	Zilog, Bridge Communications	06/23/1988	bio	transcript	29
Cerf, Vint	UCLA, Stanford, ARPA IPTO	02/08/1988	bio	transcript	15
Chu, Wesley	UCLA	02/18/1988	bio	transcript	15
Clark, David	MIT, Proteon	03/07/1988	bio	transcript	20
Clark, Wesley	MIT Lincoln Labs, Washington Univ.	03/07/1988	bio	transcript	15
Crocker, Steve	Network Working Group (NWG)	01/12/1988	bio	transcript	35
Dalal, Yogen	Xerox PARC	08/02/1988	bio	transcript	14
Dambrackas, Bill	Infotron, Milgo, Equinox	03/09/1988	bio	transcript	22

Name	Affiliation	Date	Bio	Transcript	Pages
Davidson, John	BBN, Zilog, Ungermann-Bass	08/18/1992	bio	transcript	26
Davies, Donald	National Physics Laboratory	05/27/1988	bio	transcript	21
Day, John	ISO Open Systems Interconnect (OSI)	07/11/1988	bio	transcript	25
Dolan, Robert	ComDesign	01/06/1988	bio	transcript	12
Donnan, Robert	IBM	07/12/1988	bio	transcript	9
Dow, James	Data General, Microcom	02/25/1988	bio	transcript	9
Estrin, Judy	Zilog, Bridge Communications	06/23/1988	bio	transcript	29
Evans, Roger	CASE, Micom	01/15/1988	bio	transcript	21
Farber, Dave	Bell Labs, UC Irvine, NSF	03/08/1988	bio	transcript	17
Farr, Bill	DEC, Prime Computer	04/07/1988	bio	transcript	16
Fernandez, Manny	Zilog, Dataquest	01/06/1988	bio	transcript	10
Forkish, Robbie	Tymnet, Network Equipment Technologies	07/07/1994	bio	transcript	17
Forney, David	Codex	07/28/1988	bio	transcript	30
Frank, Howard	Network Analysis Corporation	05/02/1988	bio	transcript	24
Frankel, Steve	Micom, Retix	04/26/1988	bio	transcript	18
Graube, Maris	Tektronix, IEEE 802 committee	07/12/1988	bio	transcript	20
Grumbles, George	Universal Data Systems	11/28/1988	bio	transcript	17
Heafner, John	National Bureau of Standards	01/12/1988	bio	transcript	19
Heart, Frank	MIT Lincoln Labs, BBN	07/11/1988	bio	transcript	13
Hill, Jay	IBM, Paradyne	07/27/1988 10/26/1988	bio	transcript	18

Name	Affiliation	Date	Bio	Transcript	Pages
Holsinger, Jerry	Teldata, Codex, Intertel	04/06/1988	bio	transcript	30
Huffaker, Craig	Digital Communications Associates	04/09/1992	bio	transcript	11
Hunt, Bruce	Zilog, Metapath	07/21/1988	bio	transcript	15
Johnson, Johnny	AFCS, Vitalink, Telebit	05/03/1988	bio	transcript	13
Jordan, Jim	Ungermann-Bass, Telebit	07/19/1988	bio	transcript	26
Kahn, Robert	BBN, ARPA IPTO	02/22/1988	bio	transcript	59
Kaufman, Phil	Intel, Silicon Compilers	06/17/1988	bio	transcript	14
Kinney, Matt	Milgo	03/09/1988	bio	transcript	27
Kleinrock, Leonard	UCLA	04/27/1988	bio	transcript	18
Krause, Bill	Hewlett-Packard, 3Com	08/15/1994	bio	transcript	24
Krechmer, Ken	Vadic	01/06/1988	bio	transcript	23
LaBarre, Lee and Paul Brusil	MITRE Corporation	04/06/1988	bio	transcript	16
Licklider, J.C.R.	MIT Lincoln Labs, BBN, ARPA IPTO	06/28/1988	bio	transcript	12
Liddle, David	Xerox	10/10/1988	bio	transcript	24
Loughry, Don	Hewlett-Packard	07/06/1988	bio	transcript	28
Lynch, Dan	ARPA, SRI, Interop	02/16/1988	bio	transcript	15
MacLean, Audrey	Tymnet, Network Equipment Technologies	04/29/1988	bio	transcript	27
Maxwell, Kim	Vadic	07/19/1988	bio	transcript	38
McDowell, Jerry	Paradyne, Wang Labs	04/10/1992	bio	transcript	24
Metcalfe, Bob	Xerox PARC, 3Com	01/12/1988	bio	transcript	63
Miller, Ken	Codex, Concord Data Systems	02/23/1988	bio	transcript	42

Name	Affiliation	Date	Bio	Transcript	Pages
Mulvenna, Jerry	National Bureau of Standards	05/05/1988	bio	transcript	20
Nordin, Bert	DCA	10/29/1988	bio	transcript	11
Norred, Bill	American Data Systems, Micom	04/27/1988	bio	transcript	36
Nyborg, Phil	Computer & Communication Industry Association	01/25/1988	bio	transcript	8
Pliner, Mike	Ford Aerospace, Sytek	04/08/1992	bio	transcript	12
Pogran, Ken	MIT, BBN	10/27/1988	bio	transcript	10
Postel, Jon	NWG, SRI, ISI	02/18/1988	bio	transcript	28
Pouzin, Louis	INRIA	11/28/1988	bio	transcript	19
Pugh, John	Codex	02/23/1988	bio	transcript	57
Rekhi, Kanwal	Zilog, Excelan	08/17/1994	bio	transcript	15
Roberts, Larry	MIT Lincoln Labs, ARPA IPTO, Telenet	04/21/1988 06/17/1988	bio	transcript	33
Rosenthal, Robert	National Bureau of Standards	05/04/1988	bio	transcript	24
Saltzer, Jerry	MIT Laboratory of Computer Science	03/07/1988	bio	transcript	39
Salwen, Howard	Proteon	01/28/1988	bio	transcript	17
Severino, Paul	DEC, Prime, Interlan, Wellfleet	03/16/1988	bio	transcript	24
Slomin, Mike	FCC Common Carrier Bureau	03/10/1988	bio	transcript	36
Smith, Bruce	Network Equipment Technologies	10/20/1988	bio	transcript	18
Smith, Mark	Universal Data Systems	11/28/1988	bio	transcript	16
Smith, Robert and Thomas L. Thompson	General DataComm	03/11/1988	bio	transcript	29
Strassburg, Bernard	FCC Common Carrier Bureau	05/03/1988	bio	transcript	17

Name	Affiliation	Date	Bio	Transcript	Pages
Taylor, Robert	IPTO, Xerox PARC, DEC	06/16/1988	bio	transcript	8
Ungermann, Ralph	Zilog, Ungermann-Bass	07/19/1988	bio	transcript	22
Warmenhoven, Dan	IBM	03/09/1988	bio	transcript	14
Wecker, Stuart	DEC	10/25/1988	bio	transcript	22
White, James	NWG, SRI, Xerox PARC, IFIP, CCITT, 3Com	05/05/1988	bio	transcript	38
Wiggins, Robert	Paradyne	11/29/1988	bio	transcript	17
Wilkes, Art	American Data Systems	05/09/1988	bio	transcript	26
Zimmerman, Hubert	INRIA, CNET, INWG, ISO OSI	05/25/1988	bio	transcript	11

APPENDIX

Bibliography

Selected Data and Source Material

The sales and valuation data used throughout *Circuits, Packets, and Protocols* comes from a variety of sources. These sources include Dataquest, Datapro, Yankee Group, Frost & Sullivan, Alex. Brown & Sons, Montgomery Securities, financials, corporate annual, and research reports, trade publications (such as *Business Week*, *Communications Week*, *Computerworld*, *Datamation*, *Data Communications*, *Electronic News*, *IEEE Spectrum*, and many others), ephemera from trade shows and conferences, and scientific and scholarly publications. Much of the data is publicly available at James L. Pelkey's website. See "How To Explore This Site" at: https://historyofcomputercommunications.info/explore.html.

Selected References

Janet Abbate. 2000. *Inventing the Internet.* MIT Press.

Janet Abbate. 2001. Government, business, and the making of the Internet. *Bus. Hist. Rev.* 75, 147–176. DOI: https://doi.org/10.2307/3116559.

Janet Abbate. 2010. Privatizing the Internet: Competing visions and chaotic events, 1987—1995. *IEEE Ann. Hist. Comput.* 32, 10–22. DOI: https://doi.org/10.1109/MAHC.2010.24.

Atsushi Akera. 2001. Voluntarism and the fruits of collaboration: The IBM user group, Share. *Technol. Cult.* 42, 710–736. DOI: https://doi.org/10.1353/tech.2001.0146.

Philip Anderson and Michael L. Tushman. 1990. Technological discontinuities and dominant designs: A cyclical model of technological change. *Adm. Sci. Q.* 35, 4 (Dec. 1990), 604–633. DOI: https://doi.org/10.2307/2393511.

W. Brian Arthur. 1994. *Increasing Returns and Path Dependence in the Economy*. University of Michigan Press.

W. Brian Arthur. 2009. *The Nature of Technology: What It Is and How It Evolves*. Simon & Schuster.

W. Brian Arthur. 2013. Complexity Economics: A Different Framework for Economic Thought |Santa Fe Institute. Retrieved January 24, 2021 from https://www.santafe.edu/research/results/working-papers/complexity-economics-a-different-framework-for-eco.

C. Gordon Bell and John E. McNamara. 1991. *High-Tech Ventures: The Guide for Entrepreneurial Success*. Basic Books.

Wiebe E. Bijker. 1997. *Of Bicycles, Bakelites, and Bulbs: Toward a Theory of Sociotechnical Change*. MIT Press.

John A.C. Bingham. 1988. *The Theory and Practice of Modem Design*. Wiley.

Mark Blaug. 1992. *The Methodology of Economics: Or How Economists Explain*. Cambridge University Press.

Timothy Bresnahan and Manuel Trachtenberg. 1995. General purpose technologies: 'Engines of growth'? *J. Econom.* Special Issue, 65 (January), 83–108.

David C. Brock (Ed.). 2006. *Understanding Moore's Law: Four Decades of Innovation*. Chemical Heritage Foundation.

Gerald W. Brock. 1981. *The Telecommunications Industry: The Dynamics of Market Structure*. Harvard University Press.

John Brooks. 1976. *Telephone: The First Hundred Years*. Harper & Row.

David Bunnell and Adam Brate. 2000. *Making the Cisco Connection: The Story Behind the Real Internet Superpower*. John Wiley & Sons.

William D. Bygrave and Jeffry A. Timmons. 1992. *Venture Capital at the Crossroads*. Harvard Business School Press.

Martin Campbell-Kelly. 1987. Data communications at the National Physical Laboratory (1965–1975). *IEEE Ann. Hist. Comput.* 9, 3–4 (July–Sept 1987), 221–247. DOI: https://doi.org/10.1109/MAHC.1987.10023.

Martin Campbell-Kelly. 2003. *From Airline Reservations to Sonic the Hedgehog: A History of the Software Industry*. MIT Press, London.

Martin Campbell-Kelly and Daniel D. Garcia-Swartz. 2013. The history of the Internet: The missing narratives. *J. Inf. Technol.* 28, 18–33. DOI: https://doi.org/10.1057/jit.2013.4.

Alfred Dupont Chandler. 1962. *Strategy and Structure: Chapters in the History of the Industrial Enterprise*. Doubleday.

Alfred Dupont Chandler. 1977. *The Visible Hand: The Managerial Revolution in American Business*. Harvard University Press.

Alfred Dupont Chandler and Takashi Hikino. 1990. *Scale and Scope: The Dynamics of Industrial Capitalism*. Belknap Press.

Alfred D. Chandler, Jr. and James W. Cortada (Eds.). 2000. *A Nation Transformed by Information: How Information Has Shaped the United States from Colonial Times to the Present*. Oxford University Press, New York.

Jeff Chase and Jon Zilber. 2019. *3Com: The Unsung Saga of the Silicon Valley Startup that Helped Give Birth to the Internet—and Then Fumbled the Ball*. BookBaby.

Clayton M. Christensen. 1997. *The Innovator's Dilemma: When New Technologies Cause Great Firms to Fail*. Harvard Business School Press.

R.H. Coase. 1990. *The Firm, the Market, and the Law*. University of Chicago Press.

Horace Coon. 1976. *American Tel & Tel: The Story of the Great Monopoly*. Books for Libraries Press.

James W. Cortada. 2019. *IBM: The Rise and Fall and Reinvention of a Global Icon*. MIT Press.

Paul A. David and Shane Greenstein. 1990. The economics of compatibility standards: An introduction to recent research. *Econ. Innov. New Technol.* 1, 3–41. DOI: https://doi.org/10.1080/10438599000000002.

Paul A. David and W. Edward Steinmueller. 1994. Economics of compatibility standards and competition in telecommunication networks. *Inf. Econ. Policy* 6, 217–241.

Paul A. David and Mark Shurmer. 1996. Formal standards-setting for global telecommunications and information services. *Telecomm. Policy* 20, 789–815. DOI: https://doi.org/10.1016/S0308-5961(96)00060-2.

John Day. 2007. *Patterns in Network Architecture: A Return to Fundamentals*. Prentice Hall PTR.

John Day. 2016. The clamor outside as INWG debated: Economic war comes to networking. *IEEE Ann. Hist. Comput.* 38 (July–September 2016), 58–77.

Laura DeNardis. 2014. *Protocol Politics: The Globalization of Internet Governance.* MIT Press.

Rémi Déspres. 2010. X.25 virtual circuits—Transpac in France—pre-Internet data networking. *IEEE Commun. Mag.* (November 2010), 40–46. DOI: https://doi.org/10.1109/MCOM.2010.5621965.

Digital Equipment Corporation. 1982. *Introduction to Local Area Networks*. Digital Equipment Corporation.

Dixon R. Doll. 1978. *Data Communications: Facilities, Networks, and Systems Design*. Wiley.

Mark Doms and Chris Forman. 2003. Prices for local area network equipment. *Inf. Econ. Policy* 17, 365–388. DOI: https://doi.org/10.1016/j.infoecopol.2004.12.002.

Giovanni Dosi. 1984. *Technical Change and Industrial Transformation: The Theory and an Application to the Semiconductor Industry*. Springer.

Mary Douglas. 1986. *How Institutions Think*. Syracuse University Press, New York.

Nathan Ensmenger. 2010. *The Computer Boys Take Over: Computers, Programmers, and the Politics of Expertise*. The MIT Press, Cambridge, MA.

M.D. Fagen (Ed.). 1975. *A History of Engineering and Science in the Bell System: The Early Years (1875–1925)*. Bell Telephone Laboratories.

Bradley Fider and Morgan Currie. 2016. Infrastructure, representation, and historiography in BBN's Arpanet maps. *IEEE Ann. Hist. Comput.* 38, 3, 44–57. DOI: http://dx.doi.org/10.1109/MAHC.2015.69.

Bradley Fidler and Andrew L. Russell. October 2018. Financial and administrative infrastructure for the early Internet: Network maintenance at the Defense Information Systems Agency. *Technol. Cult.* 59, 899–924. DOI: http://dx.doi.org/10.1353/tech.2018.0090.

Franklin M. Fisher, John J. McGowan, and Joen E. Greenwood. 1985. *Folded, Spindled, and Mutilated: Economic Analysis and U.S. V. IBM*. MIT Press.

Richard N. Foster. 1986. *Innovation—The Attacker's Advantage*. McKinsey & Company, New York, NY.

Richard N. Foster and Sarah Kaplan. 2001. *Creative Destruction: Why Companies That Are Built to Last Underperform the Market—And How to Successfully Transform Them*. Crown/ Archetype.

Paul Freiberger and Michael Swaine. 1984. *Fire in the Valley: The Making of the Personal Computer*. Osborne/McGraw-Hill.

Louis Galambos. 1983. Technology, political economy, and professionalization: Central themes of the organizational synthesis. *Bus. Hist. Rev.* 57, 471–493. DOI: https://doi.org/10.2307/3114810.

Louis Galambos. 1992. Theodore N. Vail and the role of innovation in the modern Bell System. *Bus. Hist. Rev.* 66, 95–126. DOI: http://dx.doi.org/10.2307/3117054.

Louis Galambos. 2005. Recasting the organizational synthesis: Structure and process in the twentieth and twenty-first centuries. *Bus. Hist. Rev.* 79, 1–37. DOI: https://doi.org/10.2307/25096990.

Louis Galambos. 2018. The entrepreneurial culture and the mysteries of economic development. *Essays Econ. Bus. Hist.* 36, 290–320. DOI: https://doi.org/10.3917/rfhe.011.0060.

Louis Galambos. 2020a. The entrepreneurial culture: Mythologies, realities, and networks in nineteenth-century America. *Acad. Manage. Perspect.* (7 February 2020). DOI: https://doi.org/10.5465/amp.2019.0132.

Louis Galambos. 2020b. The entrepreneurial culture and bureaucracy in twentieth-century America. *Enterp. Soc.* 22, 3, 635–662. September 2021. DOI: https://doi.org/10.1017/eso.2020.15.

Louis Galambos and Franco Amatori. 2016. The entrepreneurial multiplier effect. *Enterp. Soc.* 17, 763–808. DOI: https://doi.org/10.1017/eso.2016.41.

Robert W. Garnet. 1985. *The Telephone Enterprise: The Evolution of the Bell System's Horizontal Structure, 1876–1909*. Johns Hopkins University Press, Baltimore.

Annabelle Gawer and Michael A. Cusumano. 2014. Industry platforms and ecosystem innovation. *J. Prod. Innov. Manage.* 31, 3, 417–433. DOI https://doi.org/10.1111/jpim.12105.

Paul Alan Gompers and Joshua Lerner. 1999. *The Venture Capital Cycle*. MIT Press.

Shane Greenstein. 2008. Innovation and the evolution of market structure for Internet access in the United States. In William Aspray and Paul E. Ceruzzi (Eds.), *The Internet and American Business.* MIT Press.

Shane Greenstein. 2015. *How the Internet Became Commercial: Innovation, Privatization, and the Birth of a New Network*. Princeton University Press.

Katie Hafner and Matthew Lyon. 1996. *Where Wizards Stay Up Late: The Origins of the Internet*. Simon & Schuster.

Thomas Haigh, Andrew L. Russell, and William Dutton. 2015. Histories of the Internet: Introducing a special issue of information & culture. *Inf. Cult.* 50, 2. DOI: http://dx.doi.org/10.1353/lac.2015.0006.

David M. Hart. 2001. Antitrust and technological innovation in the U.S.: Ideas, institutions, decisions, and outcomes, 1890–2000. *Res. Policy* 30, 923–936. DOI: http://dx.doi.org/10.1016/S0048-7333(00)00165-7.

Hans Dieter Hellige. 1994. From SAGE via Arpanet to Ethernet: Stages in computer communications concepts between 1950 and 1980. *Hist. Technol.* 11, 1, 49–76. DOI: http://dx.doi.org/10.1080/07341519408581854.

Fred W. Henck and Bernard Strassburg. 1988. *A Slippery Slope: The Long Road to the Breakup of AT&T*. Greenwood Press.

Rebecca M. Henderson and Kim B. Clark. 1990. Architectural innovation: The reconfiguration of existing product technologies and the failure of established firms. *Adm. Sci. Q.* 35, 1, 9–30. DOI: http://dx.doi.org/10.2307/2393549.

Jack High. 2009. Entrepreneurship and economic growth: The theory of emergent institutions. *Q. J. Austrian Econ.* 12, 3, 3–36.

Micheal A. Hiltzik. 2000. *Dealers of Lightning: Xerox PARC and the Dawn of the Computer Age.* Harper Business, New York.

Thomas Parke Hughes. 1988. *Rescuing Prometheus: Four Monumental Projects that Changed the Modern World.* Pantheon, New York.

Thomas P. Hughes. 1989. The evolution of large technological systems. In Wiebe E. Bijker, Thomas P. Hughes, and Trevor Pinch (Eds.), *The Social Construction of Technological Systems: New Directions in the Sociology and History of Technology*. MIT Press, Cambridge, MA.

Thomas Parke Hughes. 1993. *Networks of Power: Electrification in Western Society, 1880–1930*. JHU Press.

Manley R. Irwin. 1967. The computer utility: Competition or regulation. *Yale Law J.* 76, 1299. DOI: https://doi.org/10.2307/794825.

Manley R. Irwin. 1997. Confessions of a telephone regulator: The FCC's AT&T investigation of 1972–1977. *Rev. Ind. Organ.* 12, 303–315. DOI: http://dx.doi.org/10.1023/A:1007799726490.

Richard R. John. 2010. *Network Nation: Inventing American Telecommunications*. Harvard University Press, Boston.

Steven Johnson. 2001. *Emergence: The Connected Lives of Ants, Brains, Cities, and Software*. Scribner.

Robert E. Kahn. 1994. The role of the government in the evolution of the Internet. *Commun. ACM* 37, 15–19. DOI: https://doi.org/10.1145/179606.179729.

Martin Kenney (Ed.). 2000. *Understanding Silicon Valley: The Anatomy of an Entrepreneurial Region.* Stanford University Press.

Steven Klepper. 2015. *Experimental Capitalism: The Nanoeconomics of American High-Tech Industries*. Princeton University Press.

Ronald R. Kline. 2019. The modem that still connects us. In William Aspray (Ed.), *Historical Studies in Computing, Information, and Society*. Springer.

Richard N. Langlois. 1992. External economies and economic progress: The case of the microcomputer industry. *Bus. Hist. Rev.* 66, 1–50. DOI: http://dx.doi.org/10.2307/3117052.

Richard N. Langlois. 2002. Modularity in technology and organization. *J. Econ. Behav. Organ.* 49, 19–37. DOI: https://doi.org/10.1016/S0167-2681(02)00056-2.

Bruno Latour. 1987. *Science in Action: How to Follow Scientists and Engineers through Society*. Harvard University Press.

Steven Levy. 1984. *Hackers: Heroes of the Computer Revolution*. Anchor Press/Doubleday.

Kenneth Lipartito. 1997. 'Cutthroat' competition, corporate strategy, and the growth of network industries. *Res. Technol. Innov. Manag. Policy* 6, 1–53.

Kenneth Lipartito. 1989. *The Bell System and Regional Business: The Telephone in the South, 1877–1920*. Johns Hopkins University Press, Baltimore.

John E. Lopatka. 2000. United States v. IBM: A monument to arrogance. *Antitrust Law J.* 68, 145–162.

Stephen J. Lukasik. 2011. Why the Arpanet was built. *IEEE Ann. Hist. Comput.* 33, 4–21. DOI: http://dx.doi.org/10.1109/MAHC.2010.11.

Daniel C. Lynch and Marshall T. Rose. 1993. *Internet System Handbook*. Addison-Wesley.

Robert MacDougall. 2006. Long lines: AT&T's long-distance network as an organizational and political strategy. *Bus. Hist. Rev*. 80, 297–327. DOI: https://doi.org/10.1017/S0007680500035509.

Carl Malamud. 1992. *Exploring the Internet: A Technical Travelogue*. Prentice Hall PTR, Englewood Cliffs, NJ.

Franco Malerba, Richard R. Nelson, Luigi Orsenigo, and Sidney G. Winter. 2016. *Innovation and the Evolution of Industries: History-Friendly Models*. Cambridge University Press. DOI: https://doi.org/10.1017/CBO9781107280120.

Bruce Allan Mann. 1988. *Venture Capital Financing*. Practising Law Institute.

C. Mantzavinos, Douglass C. North, and Syed Shariq. 2004. Learning, institutions, and economic performance. *Perspect. Politics* 2, 75–84. DOI: https://doi.org/10.1017/S1537592704000635.

Katherine Maxfield. 2014. *Starting Up Silicon Valley: How ROLM Became a Cultural Icon and Fortune 500 Company*. Greenleaf Book Group.

Mariana Mazzucato. 2013. *The Entrepreneurial State: Debunking Public vs. Private Sector Myths.* Anthem Press, London.

Thomas K. McCraw. 2009. *Prophet of Innovation: Joseph Schumpeter and Creative Destruction*. Harvard University Press.

Alexander McKenzie. 2011. INWG and the conception of the Internet: An eyewitness account. *IEEE Ann. Hist. Comput.* 33, 66–71. DOI: https://doi.org/10.1109/MAHC.2011.9.

John E. McNamara. 1977. *Technical Aspects of Data Communication*. Digital Equipment Corporation.

J.S. Metcalfe and Ian Miles. 1994. Standards, selection and variety: An evolutionary approach. *Inf. Econ. Policy* 6, 243–268. DOI: https://doi.org/10.1016/0167-6245(94)90004-3.

David C. Mowery and Nathan Rosenberg. 1989. *Technology and the Pursuit of Economic Growth*. Cambridge University Press. DOI: https://doi.org/10.1017/CBO9780511664441.

Paul Miranti. 2008. Chandler's paths of learning. *Bus. Hist. Rev.* 82, 2, 293–300. DOI: https://doi.org/10.1017/S0007680500062784.

Richard Robinson Nelson. 1982. *Government and Technical Progress: A Cross-Industry Analysis*. Pergamon Press.

Eli Noam. 1992. *Telecommunications in Europe*. Oxford University Press, New York. DOI: https://doi.org/10.1177/027046769401400335.

Simon Nora and Alain Minc. 1981. *The Computerization of Society: A Report to the President of France*. MIT Press, Cambridge, MA.

Arthur L. Norberg and Judy E. O'Neill. 1996. Transforming Computer Technology: Information Processing for the Pentagon, 1962–1986. Johns Hopkins University Press, Baltimore.

Douglass Cecil North. 1981. *Structure and Change in Economic History*. Norton.

Douglass C. North. 1990. *Institutions, Institutional Change and Economic Performance*. Cambridge University Press. DOI: https://doi.org/10.1017/CBO9780511808678.

Douglass C. North. 2010. *Understanding the Process of Economic Change*. Princeton University Press.

Douglass C. North and Robert Paul Thomas. 1973. *The Rise of the Western World: A New Economic History*. Cambridge University Press. DOI: https://doi.org/10.1017/CBO9780511819438.

Margaret Pugh O'Mara. 2019. *The Code: Silicon Valley and the Remaking of America*. Penguin Press, New York.

Jason Oxman. 1999. *The FCC and the Unregulation of the Internet*. Federal Communications Commission Office of Plans and Policy Working Paper No. 31. July.

C. Partridge. 2008. The technical development of Internet email. *IEEE Ann. Hist. Comput.* 30 (April), 3–29. DOI: https://doi.org/10.1109/MAHC.2008.32.

C. Perez. 2003. *Technological Revolutions and Financial Capital*. Edward Elgar Publishing.

Michael E. Porter. 1980. *Competitive Strategy: Techniques for Analyzing Industries and Competitors*. Free Press.

Emerson W. Pugh. 1995. *Building IBM: Shaping an Industry and Its Technology*. MIT Press.

Leonard S. Reich. 1985. *The Making of Industrial Research: Science and Business at GE and Bell, 1876–1926*. Cambridge University Press, New York.

T.R. Reid. 1984. *The Chip: How Two Americans Invented the Microchip and Launched a Revolution*. Simon & Schuster.

Jeffrey Rohlfs. 1974. A theory of interdependent demand for a communications service. *Bell J. Econ. Manage. Sci.* 5, 16–37. DOI: https://doi.org/10.2307/3003090.

Nathan Rosenberg. 1982. *Inside the Black Box: Technology and Economics*. Cambridge University Press.

Nathan Rosenberg and L.E. Birdzell. 1986. *How the West Grew Rich: The Economic Transformation of the Industrial World*. Basic Books.

Roy Rosenzweig. 1998. Wizards, bureaucrats, warriors & hackers: Writing the history of the Internet. *Am. Hist. Rev.* 103, 5 (December).

Andrew L. Russell. 2006. 'Rough consensus and running code' and the Internet–OSI standards war. *IEEE Ann. Hist. Comput.* 28, 48–61.

Andrew L. Russell. 2014. *Open Standards and the Digital Age*. Cambridge University Press. DOI: https://doi.org/10.1017/CBO9781139856553.

Andrew L. Russell. 2017. Hagiography, revisionism & blasphemy in Internet histories. *Internet Hist.* 1, 1–2, 15–25. DOI: https://doi.org/10.1080/24701475.2017.1298229.

Andrew L. Russell and Valérie Schafer. 2014. In the shadow of ARPANET and Internet: Louis Pouzin and the Cyclades network in the 1970s. *Technol. Cult.* 55, 4, 880–907. DOI: https://doi.org/10.1353/tech.2014.0096.

Andrew L. Russell, James L. Pelkey, and Loring G. Robbins. 2022. The business of internetworking: Standards, start-ups, and network effects. *Bus. Hist. Rev.* 1–36. DOI: https://doi.org/10.1017/S000768052100074X.

Tony Rybczynski. 2009. Commercialization of packet switching (1975–1985): A Canadian perspective. *IEEE Commun. Mag.* 47, 12 (December 2009), 26–32. DOI: https://doi.org/10.1109/MCOM.2009.5350364.

Garth Saloner. 1989. Economic issues in computer interface standardization: The case of UNIX. *Econ. Innov. New Technol.* 1, 1–2, 135–156. DOI: https://doi.org/10.1080/10438599000000008.

Peter H. Salus. 1995. *Casting the Net: From ARPANET to INTERNET and Beyond.* Addison-Wesley, New York.

AnnaLee Saxenian and American Council of Learned Societies. 1996. *Regional Advantage: Culture and Competition in Silicon Valley and Route 128, with a New Preface by the Author*. Harvard University Press.

Valérie Schafer. 2012. *La France en Reseaux*. Nuvis, Paris.

Leonard A. Schlesinger, Davis Dyer, Thomas N. Clough, and Diane Landau. 1987. *Chronicles of Corporate Change: Management Lessons from AT&T and Its Offspring*. Lexington Books.

Susanne K. Schmidt and Raymund Werle. 1998. *Coordinating Technology: Studies in the International Standardization of Telecommunications*. MIT Press, Cambridge, MA.

Joseph A. Schumpeter. 1954. *History of Economic Analysis*. Oxford University Press, New York. DOI: https://doi.org/10.1086/ahr/60.1.62-a.

Joseph A. Schumpeter. 1976. *Capitalism, Socialism and Democracy*. Routledge.

Joseph A. Schumpeter. 1983. *The Theory of Economic Development: An Inquiry into Profits, Capital, Credit, Interest, and the Business Cycle*. Transaction Publishers.

Joseph A. Schumpeter. 1991. *The Economics and Sociology of Capitalism*. Princeton University Press.

Marvin A. Sirbu and Laurence E. Zwimpfer. 1985. Standards setting for computer communication: The case of X.25. *IEEE Commun. Mag.* 23, 3, 35–44. DOI: https://doi.org/10.1109/MCOM.1985.1092535.

Marvin A. Sirbu and Steven Stewart. October 1986. *Market Structure and the Emergence of Standards*. Department of Engineering and Public Policy, Carnegie Mellon University.

Douglas K. Smith and Robert C. Alexander. 1988. *Fumbling the Future: How Xerox Invented, then Ignored, the First Personal Computer*. William Morrow & Co.

David Stauffer. 2000. *Big Shots, Business the Cisco Way: Secrets of the Company That Makes the Internet*. Wiley.

Jonas Warren Stehman. 1925. *The Financial History of the American Telephone and Telegraph Company*. Houghton Mifflin.

Alan Stone and William L. Stone. 1989. *Wrong Number—The Breakup of AT&T*. Basic Books.

Andrew S. Tanenbaum. 1996. *Computer Networks*. Prentice Hall.

Peter Temin and Louis Galambos. 1987. *The Fall of the Bell System: A Study in Prices and Politics*. Cambridge University Press.

Jasper L. Tran. 2019. The myth of Hush-A-Phone v. United States. *IEEE Ann. Hist. Comput.* 41, 4, 6–19. DOI: https://doi.org/10.1109/MAHC.2019.2910008.

Steven W. Usselman. 1993. IBM and its imitators: Organizational capabilities and the emergence of the international computer industry. *Bus. Econ. Hist.* 22, 2, 1–35.

Steven W. Usselman. 1996. Fostering a capacity for compromise: Business, government, and the stages of innovation in American computing. *IEEE Ann. Hist. Comput.* 18, 2, 30–39. DOI: https://doi.org/10.1109/85.489748.

Steven W. Usselman. 2004. Public policies, private platforms: Antitrust and American computing. In R. Coopey (Ed.), *Information Technology Policy*. Oxford University Press, New York. DOI: https://doi.org/10.1093/acprof:oso/9780199241057.001.0001.

Steven W. Usselman. 2009. Unbundling IBM: Antitrust and incentives to innovation in American computing. In S.H. Clarke, N.R. Lamoreaux, and Steven W. Usselman (Eds.), *The Challenge of Remaining Innovative: Insights from Twentieth-Century American Business*. Stanford University Press, Stanford. 249–280.

Andrew H. Van de Ven. 1999. *The Innovation Journey*. Oxford University Press.

Richard H.K. Vietor. 1994. *Contrived Competition: Regulation and Deregulation in America*. Harvard University Press, Cambridge, MA.

Lee Vinsel. 2019. *Moving Violations: Automobiles, Experts, and Regulations in the United States*. Johns Hopkins University Press.

Urs von Burg. 2001. *The Triumph of Ethernet: Technological Communities and the Battle for the LAN Standard*. Stanford University Press.

Urs von Burg and Martin Kenney. 2000. Venture capital and the birth of the local area networking industry. *Res. Policy* 29, 1135–1155.

M. Mitchell Waldrop. 2001. *The Dream Machine: J.C.R. Licklider and the Revolution That Made Computing Personal*. Viking.

Neil H. Wasserman and Earl. R. Wasserman. 1985. *From Invention to Innovation: Long-Distance Telephone Transmission at the Turn of the Century*. Johns Hopkins University Press.

Oliver E. Williamson. 1975. *Markets and Hierarchies, Analysis and Antitrust Implications: A Study in the Economics of Internal Organization*. Free Press.

Oliver E. Williamson. 1985. *The Economic Institutions of Capitalism*. Simon & Schuster.

John W. Wilson. 1985. *The New Venturers: Inside the High-Stakes World of Venture Capital*. Addison-Wesley.

JoAnne Yates. 1989. *Control through Communication: The Rise of System in American Management*. Johns Hopkins University Press, Baltimore.

JoAnne Yates and Craig. N. Murphy. 2019. *Engineering Rules: Global Standard Setting since 1880*. Johns Hopkins University Press.

Jeffrey R. Yost. 2011. *The IBM Century: Creating the IT Revolution*. IEEE Computer Society Press.

APPENDIX C

Timeline

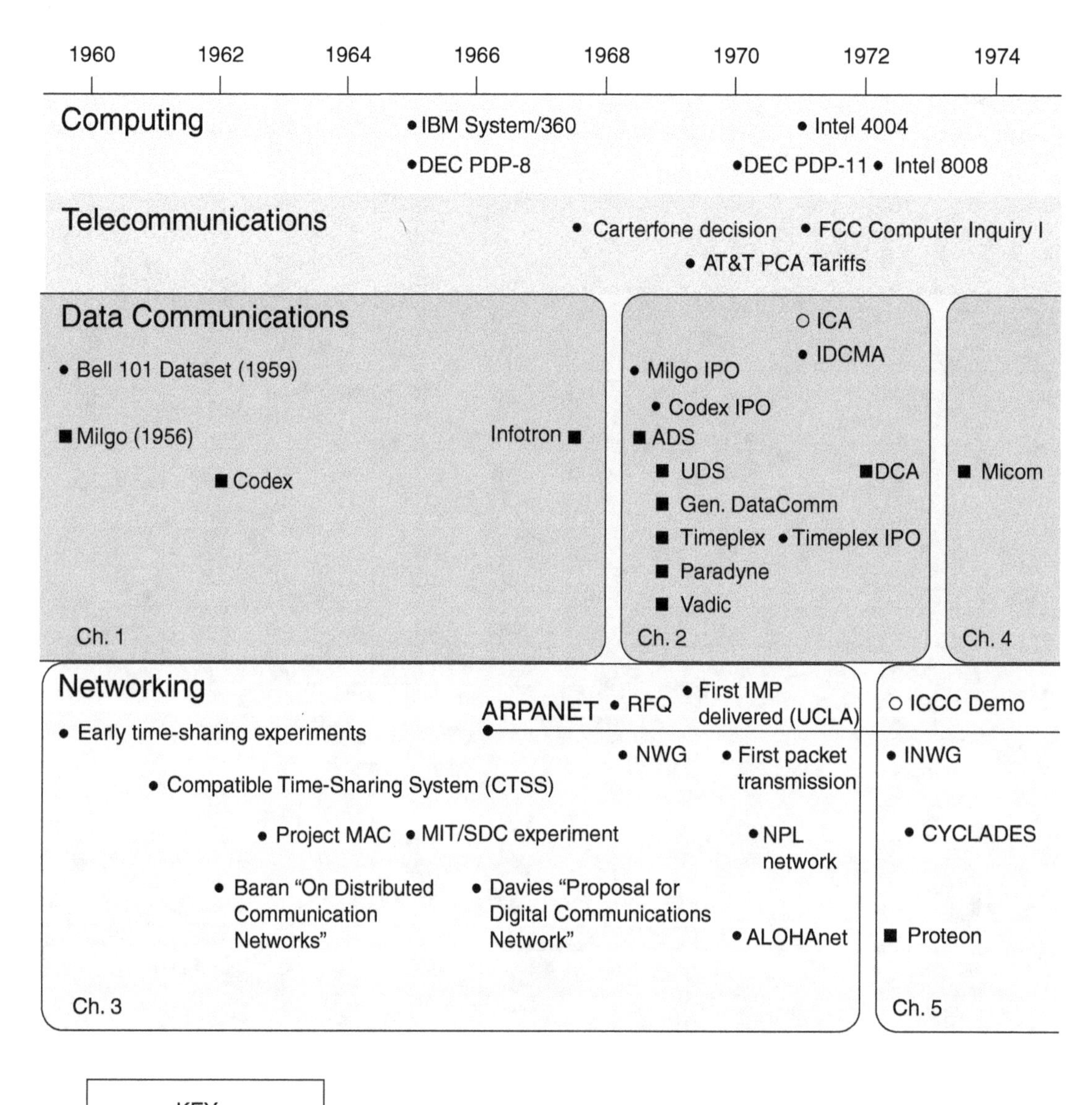
1960
1962
1964
1966
1968
1970
1972
1974
Computing
• IBM System/360
• DEC PDP-8
• Intel 4004
• DEC PDP-11
• Intel 8008
Telecommunications
• Carterfone decision
• FCC Computer Inquiry I
• AT&T PCA Tariffs
Data Communications
• Bell 101 Dataset (1959)
■ Milgo (1956)
■ Codex
Infotron ■
Ch. 1
○ ICA
• IDCMA
• Milgo IPO
• Codex IPO
■ ADS
■ UDS
■ DCA
■ Gen. DataComm
■ Timeplex
• Timeplex IPO
■ Paradyne
■ Vadic
Ch. 2
■ Micom
Ch. 4
Networking
• Early time-sharing experiments
• Compatible Time-Sharing System (CTSS)
• Project MAC
• MIT/SDC experiment
• Baran "On Distributed Communication Networks"
• Davies "Proposal for Digital Communications Network"
ARPANET
• RFQ
• First IMP delivered (UCLA)
• NWG
• First packet transmission
• NPL network
• ALOHAnet
Ch. 3
○ ICCC Demo
• INWG
• CYCLADES
■ Proteon
Ch. 5
KEY
■ Company founded
□ Merger/Acquisition
▲ Standard
○ Trade show

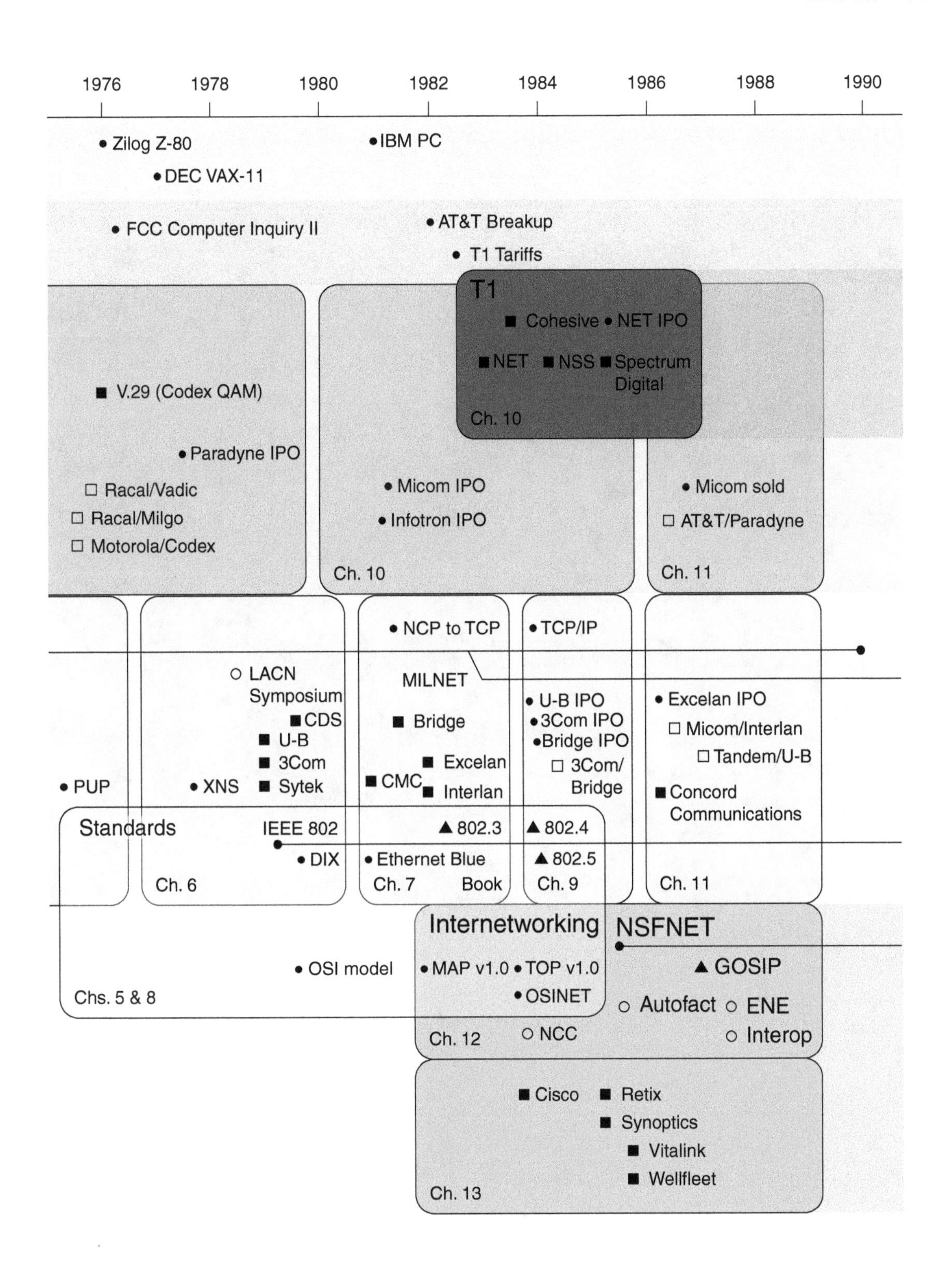
1976
1978
1980
1982
1984
1986
1988
1990
Zilog Z-80
DEC VAX-11
IBM PC
FCC Computer Inquiry II
AT&T Breakup
T1 Tariffs
T1
Cohesive
NET IPO
NET
NSS
Spectrum Digital
Ch. 10
V.29 (Codex QAM)
Paradyne IPO
Racal/Vadic
Racal/Milgo
Motorola/Codex
Micom IPO
Infotron IPO
Ch. 10
Micom sold
AT&T/Paradyne
Ch. 11
NCP to TCP
TCP/IP
LACN Symposium
MILNET
CDS
U-B
3Com
Sytek
Bridge
Excelan
CMC
Interlan
U-B IPO
3Com IPO
Bridge IPO
3Com/ Bridge
Excelan IPO
Micom/Interlan
Tandem/U-B
Concord Communications
PUP
XNS
Standards
IEEE 802
802.3
802.4
DIX
Ethernet Blue Book
802.5
Ch. 6
Ch. 7
Ch. 9
Ch. 11
Internetworking
NSFNET
OSI model
MAP v1.0
TOP v1.0
OSINET
GOSIP
Autofact
ENE
Interop
Chs. 5 & 8
Ch. 12
NCC
Cisco
Retix
Synoptics
Vitalink
Wellfleet
Ch. 13

Author Biographies

James L. Pelkey

James L. Pelkey spent his career as an investor and executive, including terms as a general partner at Montgomery Securities, President of Sorcim Corporation and Digital Sound Corporation, and, after his retirement, Trustee and Chairman of the Santa Fe Institute. He is a graduate of Rensselaer Polytechnic Institute (1968) and Harvard Business School (1970). He now lives in Maui, Hawai'i.

ORCID: https://orcid.org/0000-0002-4862-925X

Andrew L. Russell

Andrew L. Russell is Professor of History and Dean of the College of Arts & Sciences at SUNY Polytechnic Institute in Utica, New York. He is the author of numerous books and articles on the history of technology, standardization, and innovation, including *Open Standards and the Digital Age: History, Ideology, and Networks* (Cambridge University Press, 2014), and co-author with Lee Vinsel of *The Innovation Delusion: How Our Obsession with the New Disrupts the Work That Matters Most* (Currency, 2020).

ORCID: https://orcid.org/0000-0002-4279-0958

Loring G. Robbins

Loring G. Robbins is a freelance writer based in Maui, Hawai'i. Previously, he worked as an animator and animation director for several media startups in the San Francisco Bay Area.

ORCID: https://orcid.org/0000-0002-5506-9801

Index

CPSIA information can be obtained
at www.ICGtesting.com
Printed in the USA
LVHW060319071222
733478LV00004BA/63